Advances in *Chinese* Spoken Language Processing

Advances in Chinese Spoken Language Processing

Chin-Hui Lee
Georgia Institute of Technology, USA

Haizhou Li
Institute for Infocomm Research, Singapore

Lin-shan Lee
National Taiwan University

Ren-Hua Wang
University of Science and Technology of China

Qiang Huo
The University of Hong Kong

World Scientific

NEW JERSEY • LONDON • SINGAPORE • BEIJING • SHANGHAI • HONG KONG • TAIPEI • CHENNAI

Published by

World Scientific Publishing Co. Pte. Ltd.
5 Toh Tuck Link, Singapore 596224
USA office: 27 Warren Street, Suite 401-402, Hackensack, NJ 07601
UK office: 57 Shelton Street, Covent Garden, London WC2H 9HE

British Library Cataloguing-in-Publication Data
A catalogue record for this book is available from the British Library.

ADVANCES IN CHINESE SPOKEN LANGUAGE PROCESSING

ISBN-13 978-981-256-904-2
ISBN-10 981-256-904-9

Printed in Singapore by B & JO Enterprise

PREFACE

It is generally agreed that speech will play a major role in defining next-generation human-machine interfaces because it is the most natural means of communication among humans. To push forward this vision, speech research has enjoyed a long and glorious history spanning the entire twentieth century. As a result in the last three decades we have witnessed an intensive technology progress spurred on by recent advances in speech modeling, coordinated efforts between government funding agencies and speech communities for data collection and benchmark performance evaluation, and easy accesses to fast and affordable computing machineries. In the context of spoken language processing, we consider a collection of technical topics ranging over all aspects of speech communication, including production, perception, recognition, verification, synthesis, coding, analysis, and modeling. We have also seen quite a few spoken language system concepts moving out of research laboratories, and being deployed into real-life services and applications.

To benefit the entire world population, such natural voice user interfaces have to be developed for a large number of languages. For example successful spoken language translation systems are expected to facilitate global communication among people from different corners of the world to converse with each other by simple speaking and listening to their own native languages. In this sense, the particular group of languages that are not extensively studied will not be ready to get incorporated into the future global village of interactive communications. Realizing this desperate ,urgency, the speech and language researchers in the US and Europe have promoted and benefited tremendously from a series of large-scale research projects sponsored by government agencies and industry in the last three decades. Most of these efforts focused on developing research infrastructures for Indo-European languages, such as English, French, and German. On the other hand the family of spoken Chinese is mostly tonal and analytic in nature. It consists of a wide variety of languages and dialects that are currently being used by a large population spreading over a wide geographical area. Many languages in the Sino-Tibetan family have a strong historic tie with spoken Chinese as well. Studies of Chinese spoken language processing (CSLP) will therefore not only enhance our understanding in Chinese, but also trigger advances in other similar languages, such as Japanese, Korean and Thai. To support CSLP, the individual government in the four major Chinese-speaking regions, China, Hong Kong, Singapore and Taiwan, has sponsored many related projects to establish language-specific research activities. However coordinated efforts among researchers from and shared research infrastructures across different regions have been rather limited until the later 90's.

Some spotty ideas have been raised by concerned researchers in the mid 90's to resolve the above situation. A real breakthrough came in the summer of 1997 when an ad hoc group was formed with the goal of creating an international forum for exchanging ideas and tools, sharing knowledge and experiences, promoting cross-region collaborations, and establishing a broad Chinese spoken language processing community. This core group included nine members, Profs. Taiyi Huang and Ren-Hua Wang from China, Profs. Chorkin Chan and Pak-Chung Ching from Hong Kong, Prof. Kim-Teng Lua and Dr. Haizhou Li from Singapore, Profs. Lin-shan Lee and Hsiao-Chuan Wang from Taiwan, and Dr. Chin-Hui Lee from USA. After a few months of intensive e-mail discussions, the group members finally met at the National University of Singapore in December, 1997. The result of this gathering was truly ground-breaking. A few special interest groups were formed to address some of the critical issues identified above. Some progress reports were prepared and key events were planned. Nonetheless the most significant outcome was the organization of a biennial meeting, called the International Symposium on Chinese Spoken Language Processing (ISCSLP), specifically devoted to CSLP-related issues. It was designed so that this forum will be hosted, in turns, by one organizing team from the four major Chinese-speaking regions. An ISCSLP Steering Committee, consisting of the above-mentioned nine members, was also established to oversee the related activities. With the enthusiastic support that the Committee received from Prof. Lua and Dr. Li, it was decided that the inaugural meeting, ISCSLP-98, be held in Singapore as a satellite event of the 1998 International Conference on Spoken Language Processing (ICSLP-98) in Sydney, Australia. Since then three follow-up meetings had taken place in Beijing, Taipei and Hong Kong in the years of 2000, 2002 and 2004, respectively. The number of accepted papers has also seen a steady increase from 55 in 1998 to over 100 in 2004, with symposium participants growing to over 200. The amount of support from the CSLP community has been tremendous, and this support also translates into a fast accumulation of knowledge and shared resources in the field of Chinese spoken language processing. To extend the group's impact on the general speech community a special interest group on CSLP (SIG-CSLP) was established within the International Speech Communication Association (ISCA) in 2002 at the

Taipei ISCSLP meeting. Very quickly, this SIG has become one of the most active groups in ISCA.

This year we are coming back to the Lion City after a full cycle of four successful ISCSLP gatherings. At this significant point in history to commemorate the tenth anniversary of the formation of the broad international CSLP community, Prof. Chin-Hui Lee thought it is timely fitting that the community collectively documents recent advances in CSLP. Although there are many general speech processing books available in the market, we have not seen a single volume dedicated solely to CSLP issues. Most of the materials are scattered in different literatures with some of them written in Chinese and not easily accessed by other scholars. With a great endorsement from Dr. Haizhou Li and generous grants from industrial sponsors in Singapore, Prof. Lee contacted one distinguished leader in the field from each Chinese-speaking region, and an international editorial team was then assembled in December 2005. An outline was drafted and a list of potential authoring teams was proposed. Instead of having another general speech book, the team decided to have a quality publication focusing on truly CSLP-related topics with illustrations of key concepts using mainly CSLP examples. Emphases were particularly devoted to highlighting differences between CSLP and general speech processing. Because of this requirement the team has to pass by many top colleagues in the CSLP community because they have not been actively involved in speech research using Chinese spoken language materials. After two months of back-and-forth discussions and revisions, a publication plan was finalized. In late February 2006 invitations were extended to distinguished colleagues who have demonstrated expertise in selected areas with specific guidelines in line with the intended scope of the book which is tutorial and overview in nature. To effectively utilize the limited page allowance, technical details were intentionally omitted and referred to already published references. Special challenges were also issued to encourage cross-region authoring cooperation when addressing common technical issues. The community's responses were overwhelming. We have collected 23 chapters covering a wide range of topics in three broad CSLP subject areas: principles, system integration, and applications. A roadmap to explore the book is outlined as follows.

Part I of the book concentrates on CSLP principles. There are 11 chapters: (1) Chapter 1 is a general production-perception perspective of speech analysis which is intended for all speech researchers and is equally applicable to any spoken language; (2) Chapter 2 presents some background materials on phonetic and phonological aspects of Chinese spoken languages; (3) Chapters 3-5 forms a group of topics addressing the prosodic and tonal aspects of Chinese spoken languages. Chapter 3 provides an in-depth discussion on prosody analysis. The concept of prosodic phrase grouping which is a key property of Chinese spoken languages is illustrated. Another unique problem for tonal languages is tone modeling. Chapter 4 addresses issues related to tone modeling for speech synthesis. The important subject of Mandarin text-to-speech synthesis is then presented in Chapter 5; (4) Chapters 6-10 contain the group of subjects related to automatic speech recognition. Chapter 6 gives a review on large vocabulary continuous speech recognition of Mandarin Chinese highlighting technology components required to put together Mandarin recognition systems. Details are given in the next four chapters. Chapter 7 concerns with acoustic modeling of fundamental speech units. The syllabic nature of Mandarin, which is another unique property for syllabic languages, can be taken into account to effectively model continuous Mandarin speech. Tone modeling for Mandarin speech recognition, which is usually not considered in recognition of non-tonal languages, is discussed in Chapter 8. Because of the analytic nature of Chinese many single-character syllables are considered as words. Some special considerations are needed in language modeling for continuous Mandarin speech recognition. This is discussed in Chapter 9. Modeling of pronunciation variations in spontaneous Mandarin speech is key for improving performance of spoken language systems. This topic is presented in Chapter 10; and (5) Chapter 11 addresses the critical issue of corpus design and annotation which is becoming a key concern for designing spoken language systems. The tonal and syllabic nature of Mandarin makes corpus design a challenging research problem.

Part II of the book is devoted to technology integration and spoken language system design. There are seven chapters: (1) Chapter 12 is about speech-to-speech translation which is one of the grand challenges for the speech community. A domain-specific system is presented and some current capabilities and limitations are illustrated; (2) Chapter 13 is concerned with spoken document retrieval. Data mining and information retrieval are two technical topics that are impacting our daily lives. Spoken document retrieval encompasses these two areas. It is a good illustration of speech technology integration; (3) Chapter 14 presents an in-depth study on speech act modeling and its application in spoken dialogue systems; (4) Chapter 15 deals with a unique problem of transliteration that translates out-of-vocabulary words from one letter-based language like English into another character-based language like Chinese for many emerging speech and language applications; (5) Chapters 16 and 17 are devoted to two major languages in spoken Chinese, namely Cantonese and Min-nan. Issues in modeling for speech recognition and synthesis are highlighted. Tone modeling with these two languages is of special interest because there are more tones to deal with and some of the tone differences are subtle and pose challenging technical problems to researchers; (6) An increasingly important subject that has attracted attention among speech researchers is the use of speech technologies to assist in language learning and evaluation. For example, the Putonghua Proficiency Test is currently conducted almost entirely in a manual mode. Chapter 18 deals with some issues about automating such processes.

Part III of the book concerns with applications, tools and CSLP resources. There are five chapters: (1) Chapter 19 discusses an audio-based digital content management and retrieval system for data mining of audiovisual documents; (2) Chapter 20 presents a dialog system with multilingual speech recognition and synthesis for Cantonese, Putonghua and English; (3) Chapter 21 presents a large-scale directory inquiry field trial system. Due to the potential of having an unlimited vocabulary, many technical and practical considerations need to be addressed. Pronunciation variation is also a major problem here. It is a good example of illustrating technical concerns in designing real-life Chinese spoken language systems; (4) Chapter 22 describes a car navigation application in which robustness is a main concern because of the adverse speaking conditions in moving vehicles. Interactions between speech and acoustics are of utmost importance in this hand-free and eye-free application; (5) Finally Chapter 23 provides a valuable collection of language resources for supporting Chinese spoken language processing.

In summary, putting together such an extensive volume in such a short time is a daunting task. The editors would like to express their sincere gratitude to all the distinguished contributors. Without their timely endeavor, it would not be possible to have such a quality book. A special thank is extended to two industry sponsors in Singapore for their generous financial support. A dedicated team at World Scientific Publishing has also assisted the editors continuously from the time of inception to final production of the book. Finally the editors are greatly indebted to Ms. Mahani Aljunied for her painstaking effort to make all chapters consistent in style, uniform in quality, and conforming to a single standard in presentation. Her education training in linguistics and her interest in spoken language processing made a big difference in finishing this historic volume in time.

Chin-Hui Lee, Atlanta
Haizhou Li, Singapore
Lin-shan Lee, Taipei
Ren-Hua Wang, Hefei
Qiang Huo, Hong Kong

LIST OF CONTRIBUTORS

Shuanhu Bai
Institute for Infocomm Research,
Heng Mui Keng Terrace, Singapore

Berlin Chen
National Taiwan Normal University,
Taipei

Jung-Kuei Chen
Chunghwa Telecommunication
Laboratories, Taoyuan

Sin-Horng Chen
Department of Communication
Engineering,
National Chiao Tung University,
Hsinchu

Yuan-chin Chiang
Institute of Statistics,
National Tsing-hua University,
Hsinchu

Jen-Tzung Chien
Department of Computer Science and
Information Engineering,
National Cheng Kung University,
Tainan

Pak-Chung Ching
Department of Electronic Engineering,
The Chinese University of Hong Kong,
Hong Kong

Min Chu
Speech Group,
Microsoft Research Asia, Beijing

Chuang-Hua Chueh
Department of Computer Science and
Information Engineering,
National Cheng Kung University,
Tainan

Jianwu Dang
School of Information Science,
Japan Advanced Institute of Science
and Technology, Ishikawa

Li Deng
Microsoft Research,
One Microsoft Way, Redmond

Pascale Fung
Human Language Technology Center,
Department of Electronic & Computer
Engineering, Hong Kong University of
Science & Technology, Hong Kong

Yuqing Gao
IBM T. J. Watson Research Center,
Yorktown Heights

Liang Gu
IBM T. J. Watson Research Center,
Yorktown Heights

Taiyi Huang
Institute of Automation,
Chinese Academy of Sciences, Beijing

Qiang Huo
Department of Computer Science,
The University of Hong Kong,
Hong Kong

Mei-Yuh Hwang
Department of Electrical Engineering, University of Washington, Seattle

Chih-Chung Kuo
Industrial Technology Research Institute, Hsinchu

Jin-Shea Kuo
Chunghwa Telecommunication Laboratories, Taoyuan

Chin-Hui Lee
School of Electrical & Computer Engineering, Georgia Institute of Technology, Atlanta

Lin-shan Lee
Department of Electrical Engineering, National Taiwan University, Taipei

Tan Lee
Department of Electronic Engineering, The Chinese University of Hong Kong, Hong Kong

Aijun Li
Institute of Linguistics, Chinese Academy of Social Sciences, Beijing

Haizhou Li
Institute for Infocomm Research, Heng Mui Keng Terrace, Singapore

Min-siong Liang
Department of Electrical Engineering, Chang Gung University, Taoyuan

Qingfeng Liu
USTC iFlytek Speech Laboratory, University of Science and Technology of China, Hefei

Yi Liu
Human Language Technology Center, Department of Electronic & Computer Engineering, Hong Kong University of Science & Technology, Hong Kong

Wai Kit Lo
Department of Systems Engineering and Engineering Management, The Chinese University of Hong Kong, Hong Kong

Dau-cheng Lyu
Department of Electrical Engineering, Chang Gung University, Taoyuan

Ren-yuan Lyu
Department of Computer Science & Information Engineering, Chang Gung University, Taoyuan

Helen M. Meng
Department of Systems Engineering & Engineering Management, The Chinese University of Hong Kong, Hong Kong

Yao Qian
Microsoft Research Asia, Haidian, Beijing

Jianhua Tao
NLPR, Institute of Automation, Chinese Academy of Sciences, Beijing

Chiu-yu Tseng
Institute of Linguistics, Academia Sinica, Taipei

Hsiao-Chuan Wang
National Tsing Hua University, Hsinchu

Hsien-Chang Wang
Department of Information Management, Chang Jung University, Tainan County

Hsin-min Wang
Institute of Information Science, Academia Sinica, Taipei

Jhing-Fa Wang
Department of Electrical Engineering, National Cheng Kung University, Tainan City

Jia-Ching Wang
Department of Electrical Engineering, National Cheng Kung University, Tainan City

Ren-Hua Wang
USTC iFlytek Speech Lab, University of Science & Technology of China, Hefei

Si Wei
USTC iFlytek Speech Laboratory, University of Science and Technology of China, Hefei

Chung-Hsien Wu
Department of Computer Science and Information Engineering, National Cheng Kung University, Tainan

Meng-Sung Wu
Department of Computer Science and Information Engineering, National Cheng Kung University, Tainan

Bo Xu
Institute of Automation, Chinese Academy of Sciences, Beijing

Gwo-Lang Yan
Department of Computer Science and Information Engineering, National Cheng Kung University, Tainan

Chung-Chieh Yang
Chunghwa Telecommunication Laboratories, Taoyuan

Jui-Feng Yeh
Department of Computer Science and Information Engineering, National Cheng Kung University, Tainan

Shuwu Zhang
Institute of Automation, Chinese Academy of Sciences, Beijing

Thomas Fang Zheng
Department of Physics, Tsinghua University, Beijing

Bowen Zhou
IBM T. J. Watson Research Center, Yorktown Heights

Yiqing Zu
Motorola China Research Center, Shanghai

CONTENTS

Part I

Principles of CSLP

CHAPTER 1

SPEECH ANALYSIS: THE PRODUCTION-PERCEPTION PERSPECTIVE

Li Deng[†] and Jianwu Dang[‡]

[†]*Microsoft Research*
One Microsoft Way, Redmond, WA 98052
[‡]*School of Information Science*
Japan Advanced Institute of Science and Technology
1-1 Asahidai, Nomi, Ishikawa, 923-1292
Email: {deng@microsoft.com, jdang@jaist.ac.jp}

This chapter introduces the basic concepts and techniques of speech analysis from the perspectives of the underlying mechanisms of human speech production and perception. Spoken Chinese language has special characteristics in its signal properties that can be well understood in terms of both the production and perception mechanisms. In this chapter, we will first outline the general linguistic, phonetic, and signal properties of spoken Chinese. We then introduce human production and perception mechanisms, and in particular, those relevant to spoken Chinese. We also present some recent brain research on the relationship between human speech production and perception. From the perspectives of human speech production and perception, we then describe popular speech analysis techniques and classify them based on the underlying scientific principles either from the speech production or perception mechanism or from both.

1. Introduction

Chinese is the language of over one billion speakers. Several dialect families of Chinese exist, each in turn consisting of many dialects. Although different dialect families are often mutually unintelligible, systematic correspondences (e.g., in lexicon and syntax) exist among them, making it easy for speakers of one dialect to pick up another relatively quickly. The largest dialect family is the Northern family, which consists of over 70% of all Chinese speakers. Standard or Mandarin Chinese is a member of the Northern family and is based on the pronunciation of the Beijing dialect. Interestingly, most speakers of Standard

Chinese have another dialect as their first tongues and only less than one percent of them speak without some degree of accent.

According to a rough classification, Mandarin Chinese has five vowels, three high /i, y, u/ (one of them, /y/, is rounded), one mid /ə/, and one low /a/. When the high vowels occur before another vowel, they behave as glides. The context dependency of the vowels has simpler rules than that for English.

There are 22 consonants in Mandarin Chinese. Compared with English, the distribution of consonants in Mandarin Chinese is more closely dependent on the syllable position, and the syllable structure is much simpler.

There are two types of syllables – full and weak ones – in Mandarin Chinese. The former has intrinsic, underlying tone and is long, while the latter has no intrinsic tone and is short. A full syllable may change to a weak one, losing its intrinsic tone and undergoing syllable rime reduction and shortening (similar to syllable reduction in English).

In contrast to English which has over 10,000 (mono) syllables, Mandarin Chinese has only about 400 syllables excluding tones (and 1300 including tones). Relatively simple phonological constraints can sufficiently describe the way in which many available syllables are excluded as being valid ones in Mandarin Chinese.

In addition to the specific phonological and phonetic properties of spoken Chinese outlined above, the special characteristics in its signal properties consist of tonality and fundamental frequency variations that signal the lexical identity in the language in addition to paralinguistic information. Speech analysis techniques for fundamental frequency or pitch extraction are therefore more important for Chinese than for the non-tonal languages such as English. Recent research has provided both the production and perceptual accounts for tonal variations in spoken Chinese, where the articulatory constraint on the perception processing has been quantified. To understand the underlying science for the speech processing techniques, we will first present the human mechanisms in speech production and perception.

2. Speech Production Mechanisms

2.1. *Speech Organs*

Many speech analysis techniques are motivated by the physical mechanisms by which human speech is produced. The major organs of the human body responsible for producing speech are the lungs, the larynx (including the vocal cords), the pharynx, the nose and the mouth (including the velum, the hard palate, the teeth, the tongue, and the lips), which are illustrated by the midsagittal view shown in Figure 1. Together, these organs form a complicated "tube" extending from the lungs to the lips and/or the nostrils. The part of the tube superior to the vocal cords is called the vocal tract. During speech production, the shape of the vocal tract varies extensively by movements of the tongue, jaw, lips, and the velum. These organs are named the articulators and their movement is known as articulation.

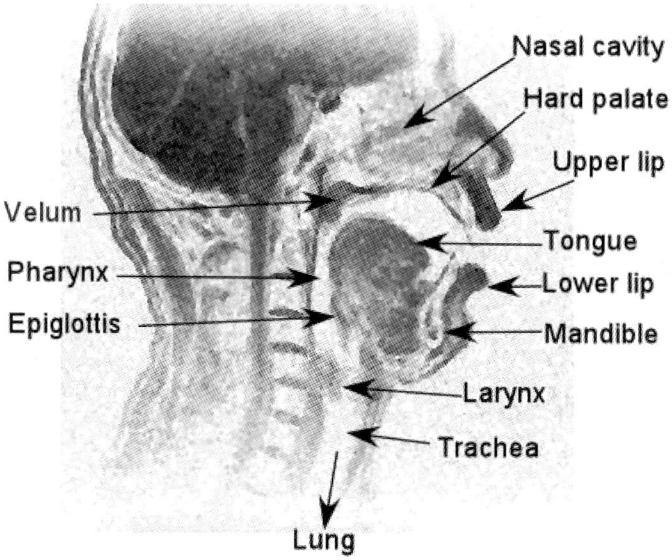

Fig. 1. MRI-based midsagittal view of the human head, showing the vocal organs.

2.2. *Acoustic Filtering in Speech Production*

In speech production, a time-varying vocal tract is formed by articulation. Each specific vocal tract shape has its inherent resonances and anti-resonances corresponding to its shape, and functions as a filter.[1,2] Although both the resonances and anti-resonances are decisive factors for generating sound, the former one is of prime importance in determining the properties of speech sounds. For this reason, in speech analysis, we often treat the vocal tract as an all-pole filter. The principal resonant structure, particularly for vowels, is the essential characteristics for distinguishing one from another. That is, if a specific vocal tract with a proper source is given, the sound is uniquely determined. Note that there are many vocal tract shapes that are able to generate a given sound. This is called the inverse problem in speech processing.

To illustrate the relation between the geometry of the vocal tract and the resonance structure of vowels, we show the midsagittal view of the vocal tract shape obtained in pronouncing the Chinese vowels /a/, /i/, /u/ and /ə/ in Figure 2, which are located in the top-left, the lower-left, the top-right, and the lower-right panels, respectively. The geometric difference between vowels is clearly seen in the vocal tract. For instance, there is a wide opened cavity in the anterior part of the vocal tract with a lower tongue position for /a/, while for /i/ the posterior part is widely opened with a higher tongue position. According to the geometric structure, vowel /a/ is called *open vowel* or *low vowel*, while vowel /i/ is referred to as a *closed vowel* or *high vowel*. Geometrically, a key part in the vocal tract for determining the vowel properties is the narrowest portion of the vocal tract, namely the *constriction*. The location of constrictions is most crucial for producing a sound, and is used to describe the articulation of the vowels. As shown in the lower-right panel of Figure 2, the constrictions of /a/, /i/ and /u/ are located at the vertices of the triangle and /ə/ is in its center. Note that the constriction of the vocal tract is not as tight for vowels as that for consonants. For vowels, the location of the constriction is usually approximated using the highest position of the tongue body, namely the tongue height.

The resonances of the vocal tract are heavily dependent on the location of the constriction in the vocal tract, which can be used for distinguishing vowels. If there is no noticeable constriction in the vocal tract such as production of /ə/, the vocal tract can be roughly thought as a uniform tube whose resonances will appear at around 500 Hz, 1500 Hz, and so on, which are a multiple of the sound velocity over four times the tube length. If the constriction is located in the anterior part of the vocal tract such as the vowel /i/, the first resonance lowers down and the second one goes up, where the typical values are around 250 Hz and 2100 Hz. If the constriction is located in the anterior part of the vocal tract such as /a/, the first resonance moves upward to about 700 Hz and the second one reduces to about 1200 Hz. The resonant system of the vocal tract can be considered as a filter that shapes the spectrum of the sound source to produce speech. After a voiced source is modulated by the vocal tract filter, a vowel sound would be obtained from the lip radiation, where the resonant modes are known as *formants*. According to convention, formants are numbered from the low-frequency end, referred to as F1, F2, F3, etc. F1 and F2 roughly determine the major phonetic properties of the vowels, and the other formants mainly give the detailed information on timbre and individual differences.

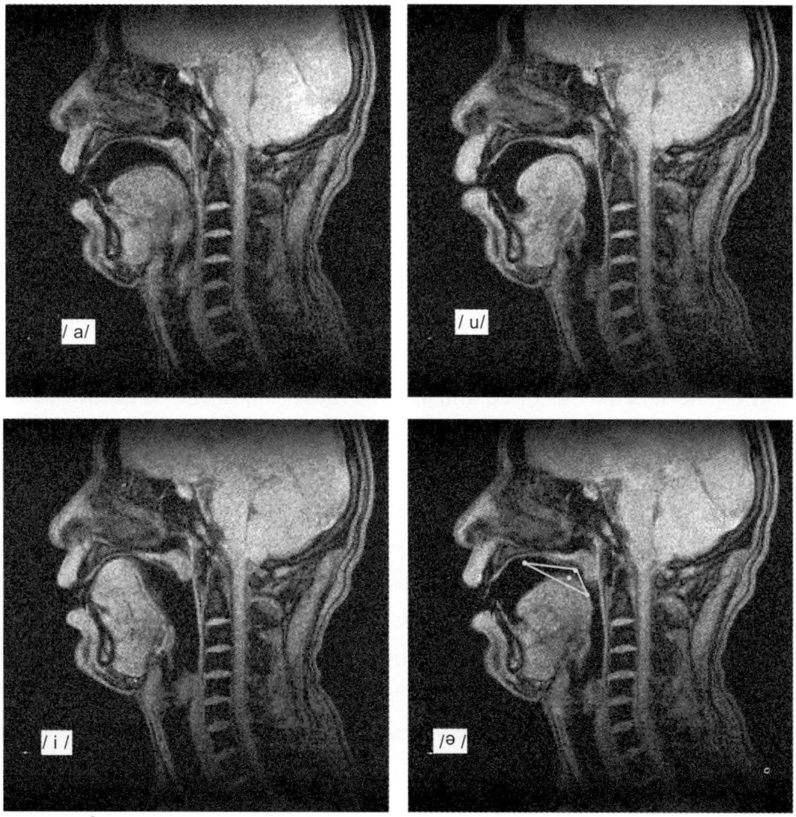

Fig. 2. Midsagittal view of the vocal tract in producing Chinese vowels: /a/ top-left, /i/ lower-left, /u/ top-right, and /ə/ lower-right. Constrictions of /a/, /i/ and /u/ are located in the vertexes of the triangle and /ə/ in the center.

2.3. *Excitation Source in Speech Production*

To understand speech production, especially the production of consonants, we also need to understand the sources of the sounds in addition to filters. The source or energy for speech production is the steady stream of air that comes from the lungs as we exhale. This air flow is modulated in a variety of ways and is transformed to the acoustic signal in the audio frequency range. In generating speech sounds, such energy can be classified to three different types of sources: quasi-periodical pulse train for vowels, turbulence noise for fricatives, or burst for plosives. Although the different source types may be combined with one another, the quasi-periodical pulse is the major source for voiced sounds (i.e., vowels or voiced consonants). In voiced sounds, the number of circles per second in the quasi-periodical pulse train is referred to as *fundamental frequency*, or F0, which is perceived as a pitch that describes how high a tone is. Since Chinese is a tone language, the fundamental frequency and its variance are very important for understanding Chinese words. We now describe in some detail the voiced sound source, where the speech organ, the larynx, plays a central role.

The glottis, which is the airspace inside the larynx, is opened by the separation of the left and right folds during normal breathing, where the air stream is inaudible. When the vocal folds get closer to one another, the air pressure in the subglottal part increases, and then the air stream becomes an audible pulse train due to vocal folds' vibration. The vocal folds are soft tissue structures contained within the cartilaginous framework of the larynx. The location of the larynx has been shown in Figure 1 and the structure of the larynx is shown in Figure 3, where (a) shows a side view and (b) is the top view. The anterior parts of the vocal folds are attached together at the front portion of the thyroid cartilage, while the posterior parts connect to the arytenoid cartilages on the left and right sides separately. To produce a sound, the arytenoid cartilages adduct (move together) the vocal folds and make the point of division between the subglottal and supraglottal airways. This action sets the vocal folds into rapid vibration as the air pressure in the subglottal part increases, and thus makes the air flow audible, namely *phonation*. For stopping the phonation the arytenoid cartilages abduct (move apart) the vocal folds, as the shape shown in Figure 3(b).

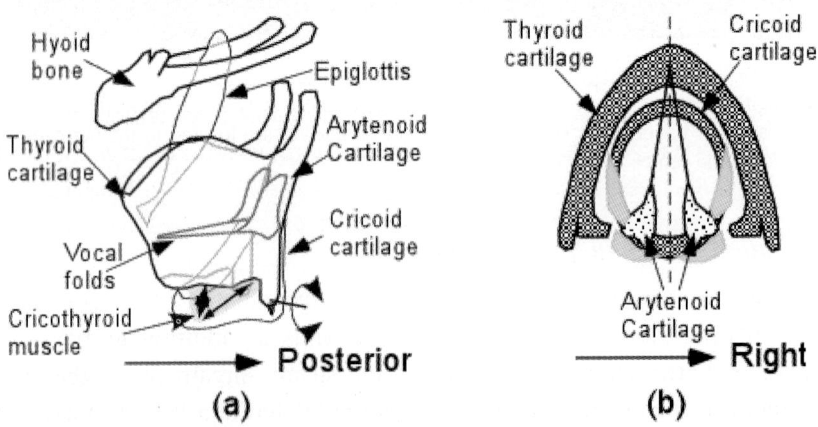

Fig. 3. The structure of the larynx (a) a side view and (b) the top view.

The structure of the vocal folds is often described by the cover–body concept. It suggests that the vocal folds can be roughly divided into two tissue layers with different mechanical properties. The cover layer is comprised of pliable, non-contractile mucosal tissue that serves as a sheath around the body-layer. In contrast, the body layer consists of muscle fibers (thyroarytenoid) and some ligamentous tissue. For a phonation, the arytenoid cartilages move the vocal folds together, the vocal folds start a rapid vibration as the air pressure in the subglottal part increases. Suppose in the initial state the vocal folds on the left and right sides are in contact and the airway is closed. An idealized cycle of vocal fold vibration begins with a lateral movement of the inferior portion of the cover surface which continues until the left and right sides separate, thereby opening the airway. Once the maximum lateral displacement is achieved, the lower portion of the vocal folds begins to move medially with the upper portion following. Eventually, the lower portions on the left and right sides collide with each other and again closing the airway. Medial displacement continues as the upper portions also collide. The entire process then repeats itself cyclically at the fundamental frequency of vibration (F0). Once in vibration, the vocal folds effectively convert the steady air flow from the lungs into a series of flow pulses by periodically opening and closing the air space between the vocal folds. This stream of flow pulses provides the sound source for the excitation of the vocal tract resonances in vowels. That is, the vocal folds are capable of converting a steady, flowing stream of air into vibratory motion.

One of the methods for controlling the F0 is manipulating the lung pressure. In general, the F0 increases as the lung pressure increases, and vice versa. For a tone language such as Chinese, there is a large scale change in the F0 within a syllable. An easy way to generate Chinese tones, especially for a low tone, is by manipulating the lung pressure.

The second major source of sound in speech production is the air turbulence that is caused when air from the lungs is forced through a strict constriction in the vocal tract. Such constrictions can be formed in the region of the larynx, as in the case of [h] sounds in English (in Chinese, constrictions are around the velar location), and at many other places in the tract, such as between various parts of the tongue and the roof of the mouth, between the teeth and lips, or between the lips. The air turbulence source has a broad continuous spectrum, and the spectrum of the radiated sound is affected by the acoustics of the vocal tract, as in the case of voiced sounds. Sustainable consonant sounds that are excited primarily by air turbulence, such as [s, f], are known as *fricatives*, and hence the turbulent noise is often referred to as *frication*.

The third type of sound source results from the build-up of pressure that occurs when the vocal tract is closed at some point for a stop consonant. The subsequent plosive release of this pressure produces a transient excitation of the vocal tract which causes a sudden onset of sound. If the vocal folds are vibrating during the pressure build-up, the plosive release is preceded by a low-level sound, namely a *voice bar*, which is radiated through the walls of the vocal tract. If the vocal folds are not vibrating during the closure, it needs time to build up a pressure difference between the supraglottal and subglottal portions by exhausting the stored air behind the closure. The time from releasing the closure to vocal folds vibration is called as the voice onset time (VOT). Since Mandarin Chinese has no voiced stop consonant, the VOT seems to be more crucial for perceiving Chinese stop consonants. The plosive release approximates a step function of pressure, with a consequent −6 dB/octave spectrum shape, but its effect is very brief and the resultant excitation merges with the turbulent noise at the point of constriction, which normally follows the release. Note that although there is no concept of VOT for fricatives, the length of the frication is an important cue for perceiving such consonants.

In connected speech, muscular control is used to bring all of these sound sources into play. This is accomplished with just the right timing for them to combine, in association with the appropriate dimensions of the resonant system, to produce the complex sequence of sounds that we recognize as a linguistic message. For many sounds (such as [v, z]), voiced excitation from the vocal folds occurs simultaneously with turbulent excitation. It is also possible to have turbulence generated in the larynx during vowel production to achieve a breathy voice quality. This quality is produced by not closing the arytenoids quite so much as in normal phonation, and by generating the vibration with a greater air flow from the lungs. There will then be sufficient random noise from air turbulence in the glottis combined with the periodic modulation of the air flow to produce a characteristic breathiness that is common for some speakers. If this effect is taken to extremes, a slightly larger glottal opening, tense vocal folds and more flow will not produce any phonation, but there will then be enough turbulence at the larynx to produce whispered speech.

Comprehensive and classical descriptions of the source mechanisms in speech production can be found in references.[3–5]

3. Speech Perception Mechanisms

3.1. *Hearing Organs*

Figure 4 illustrates the structure of the human ear, which is the "front-end" of hearing and speech perception. The outer ear consists of the pinna, which is the visible structure of the ear, and the passage known as the auditory canal. The ear canal, an air-filled passageway, is open to the outside world at one end. At its internal end, it is closed off by the eardrum (the tympanic membrane). Acoustic waves falling on the external ear travel down the auditory canal to reach the eardrum, or tympanic membrane, where the pinna plays a significant role of collecting the sound due to the effect of reflections from the structures of the pinna. This effect is confined to frequencies above 3 kHz as it is only at these high frequencies that the wavelength of the sound is short enough for it to interact with the structures of the pinna. An outstanding enhancement by the pinna is seen in frequency region around 6 kHz. The pinna also plays a role in judging the direction of a sound source, especially in the vertical direction.

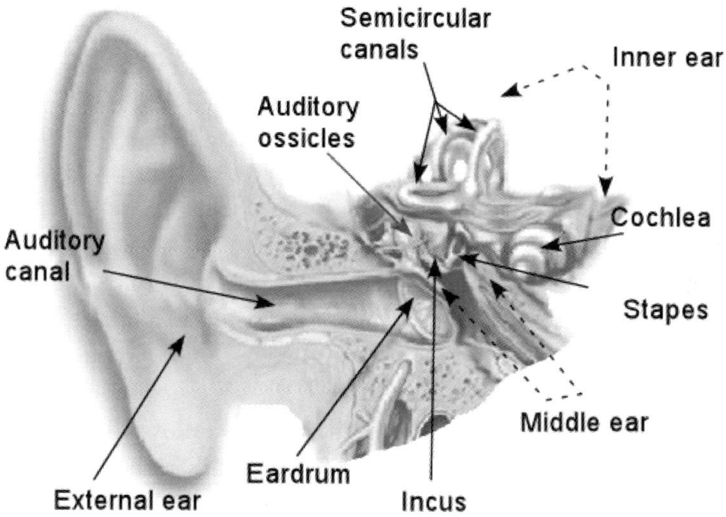

Fig. 4. A view of the outer, middle, and inner ear.

The auditory canal, with a length slightly more than two centimeters, forms an acoustic resonator with a rather heavily damped main resonance at about 3.5 kHz that is corresponding to its length. Some slight secondary resonances take place at higher frequencies. The principal effect of this resonant behavior is to increase the ear's sensitivity to sounds in the 3–4 kHz range. Thus, the pressure at the eardrum for tones near this resonance may be as much as 10 times greater than the pressure at the entrance to the ear canal. This effect enables us to detect sounds that would be imperceptible if the eardrum were located at the surface of the head.

The eardrum is driven by the impinging sound to vibrate. The vibrations are transmitted through the middle ear by the malleus (hammer) to the incus (anvil) which, in turn, is connected to the stapes (stirrup). The footplate of the stapes covers the oval window, which is the entrance to the fluid-filled cavity that makes up the inner ear. The cochlea is the main structure of the inner ear. The ossicles vibrate with a lever action, and enable the small air pressure changes that vibrate the eardrum to be coupled effectively to the oval window. In this way the ossicles act as a transformer, to match the low acoustic impedance of the eardrum to the higher impedance of the input to the cochlea.

Although the pinna and the ossicles of the middle ear play an important role in the hearing process, the main function of processing sounds is carried out within the inner ear, also known as the cochlea, and in higher levels of neural processing.

As shown in Figure 5, the cochlea is a coiled, tapered tube containing the auditory branch of the mammalian inner ear. At its end there are the semicircular canals, that has the main function of balance control, and not hearing. Figure 5 shows a section through one turn of the spiral, and it is divided along its length into three parts by two membranes, where the core component is the organ of Corti, the sensory organ of hearing. The three parts are known as the scala vestibuli, the scale media and the scala tympani. The interior of the partition, the scala media, is filled with endolymph, a fluid similar in composition to the fluid within body cells. The scala vestibuli lies on one side of the partition, and the scala tympani on the other. Both regions are filled with perilymph, a fluid similar in composition to the fluid surrounding body cells. The helicotrema, an opening in the partition at the far, or apical, end of the cochlea, allows fluid to pass freely between the two cavities. One of the membranes, Reissner's membrane, is relatively wide, and serves to separate the fluids in the seals media and the scala vestibuli but has little effect acoustically. The other membrane, the basilar membrane (BM), is a vital part of the hearing process. As shown in the figure, the membrane itself occupies only a small proportion of the width of the partition between the scale media and the scala tympani. The remainder of the space is occupied by a bony structure, which supports the organ of Corti along one edge of the BM. Rather surprisingly, as the cochlea becomes narrower towards the helicotrema, the basilar membrane actually becomes wider. In humans, it is typically 0.1 mm wide at the basal end, near the oval window, and is 0.5 mm wide at the apical end, near the helicotrema.

The stapes transmits to the oval window on the outside of the cochlea, which vibrates the perilymph in the scala vestibuli. If the stapes is given an impulsive movement, its immediate effect is to cause a distortion of the basal end of the BM. These initial movements are followed by a traveling wave along the cochlea, with corresponding displacements spreading along the length of the BM. However, the mechanical properties of the membrane in conjunction with its environment cause a resonance effect in the membrane movements; the different frequency components of the traveling wave are transmitted differently, and only

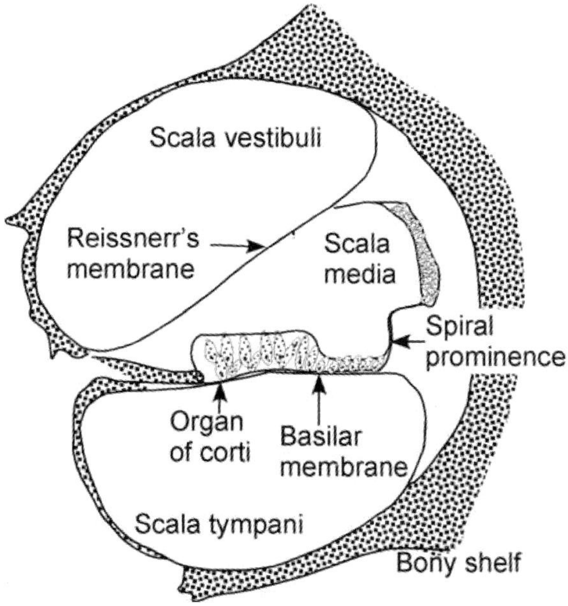

Fig. 5. Cross-section of one turn of the cochlear spiral.

the lowest audio frequency components of the wave cause any significant movement at the apical end. For very low frequencies (below 20 Hz), the pressure waves propagate along the complete route of the cochlea - up the scala vestibuli, around the helicotrema and down the scala tympani to the round window. These low frequencies do not activate the organ of Corti and are below the threshold for hearing. Higher frequencies do not propagate to the helicotrema but are transmitted through the endolymph in the cochlea duct to the perilymph in the scala tympani. Note that a very strong movement of the endolymph due to very loud noise may cause hair cells to die.

For the purpose of hearing, the frequency-selective BM movements must be converted to a neural response. This transduction process takes place by means of the inner hair cells in the organ of Corti. Research over the last couple decades has resulted in a detailed biophysical understanding of how the hearing receptors of the inner ear function. It is the hair cells, particularly the inner hair cells that convert mechanical vibrations of the basilar membrane into electrical signals that are carried by neurons of the auditory nerve to higher levels of the central nervous system. This remarkable process is controlled by a unique structural feature of the hair cell. The bottom of each hair cell rests on the basilar membrane, while the stereocilia extend from the top of the hair cell. The stapes vibrates the endolymph in the scala media, thus causing movements of the hair bundles of the hair cells, which are acoustic sensor cells that convert vibration into electrical potentials. The hair cells in the organ of Corti are tuned to certain sound frequencies, being responsive to high frequencies near the oval window and to low frequencies near the apex of the cochlea. However, the frequency selectivity is not symmetrical: at frequencies higher than the preferred frequency the response falls off more rapidly than for lower frequencies. The response curves obtained by von Bekesy were quite broad, but more recent measurements from living animals have shown that in a normal, healthy ear each point on the BM is in fact sharply tuned, responding with high sensitivity to a limited range of frequencies. The sharpness of the tuning is dependent on the physiological condition of the animal. The sharp tuning is generally believed to be the result of biological structures actively influencing the mechanics of the cochlea. The most likely structures to play this role are the outer hair cells, which are part of the organ of Corti. The magnitude of the BM response does not increase directly in proportion with the input magnitude: although at very low and at high levels the response grows roughly linearly with increasing level, in the mid-range it increases more gradually. This pattern shows a compressive non-linearity, whereby a large range of input sound levels is compressed into a smaller range of BM responses.

The ear as the "front-end" of hearing and speech perception system described above provides the input to the "back-end" or higher levels of the human auditory system. We now provide a functional overview of this "back-end".

3.2. *Perception of Sound*

Much of the knowledge we gained in the area of sound perception, including both speech and non-speech sounds, has been based on psychoacoustic experiments where human subjects are exposed to acoustic stimuli through earphones or a loudspeaker, and then these subjects tell something about the sensations these stimuli have produced. For instance, we can expose the subject to an audible sound, gradually decreasing its intensity and ask for an indication of when the sound is no longer audible. Or we may send a complex sound through the headphone to one ear and ask the subject to adjust the frequency of a tone entering the other ear until its pitch is the same as that of the complex sound.

In speech perception, one of the most famous experiments has been that on the McGurk effect.[6] In the experiment, a video is made by composing a talking head with a sound of "BA", where the video of the talking head was producing sound "GA". The subjects are asked to alternate between looking at the talking head while listening, and listening with their eyes closed. Most adult subjects

(98%) think they are hearing "DA" when they are looking at the talking head. However, they are hearing the sound as "BA" when closing their eyes. The above McGurk effect has a few interesting implications regarding sound and speech perception:

(i) Listening and perception are carried out at different levels. The subjects perceive a sound not only according to the acoustic stimuli but also based on additional information. (Regarding the nature of such "additional information", some researchers claim that the objects of speech perception are articulatory gestures while others argue that the objects are auditory in nature.)

(ii) The same general perceptual mechanisms underlie the audio-visual interactions dealing with speech or with other multi-sensory events.

(iii) The McGurk effect has been considered by the protagonists of the motor theory of speech perception as supporting the idea of a specialized perceptive module, independent of the general auditory module.

(iv) The McGurk effect is often taken as evidence for gestural approaches to speech perception because it provides an account for why the auditory and visual information are integrated during perception.

3.3. *Pitch and Fundamental Frequency*

Pitch is defined as the aspect of auditory sensation in terms of which sounds may be ordered on a scale running from "low" to "high". Pitch is chiefly a function of the frequency of a sound, but it also depends on the intensity and composition. At the sound pressure level (SPL) of 40 dB, the pitch of a 1,000 Hz sinusoid is 1,000 Hz. The half of the pitch is 500 Hz and the twice of the pitch is 2,000 Hz. In the frequency region above 1,000 Hz, the pitch unit (Mel) is almost proportional to the logarithm of the frequencies. That is why the Mel scale is extensively used in many applications of the signal processing such as the Mel Frequency Cepstrum Coefficient (MFCC) in speech analysis and recognition.

Although we have defined a pitch scale in terms of pure tones, it is obvious that more complex sounds, such as musical notes from a clarinet, spoken words, or the roar of a jet engine, also produce a more or less definite pitch. Following the Fourier series, we can consider complex waveforms to be made up of many components, each of which is a pure tone. This collection of components is called a spectrum. For speech sounds, for example, the pitch depends on the frequency of the spectrum's lowest component. In most cases, the pitch is used to describe the fundamental frequency of a voiced sound, which is the vibration frequency of the vocal folds.

Strictly speaking, the pitch is a subjective quantity, while the fundamental frequency is a physical quantity. They should be used distinctively because they are not always consistent with each other even in their values. As mentioned above, pitch is not only a function of the frequency of a sound, but also dependent on the intensity and composition. This phenomenon is clearly seen in producing and perceiving Chinese tones. For instance, you can produce a low tone (Tone 3) of Mandarin Chinese by lowering the power of the sound instead of the fundamental frequency. Experiments have shown that many foreign students who can pronounce good Chinese tones often manipulate the sound power when generating the low tone.

4. Relationship between Speech Production and Perception Mechanisms

Producing and perceiving speech sounds are basic human activities in speech communication. A speaker can be considered as an encoder in a speech production system and a listener as a decoder to accomplish speech perception. Further, speech information is exchanged not only between the speaker and a listener but also internally within the human brain because a speaker also acts as a listener of his own speech. This is the case especially in acquiring a new language. During such a learning process, the loop in the human brain between speech production and perception must be closed, as a type of internal "speech chain".

4.1. *Speech Chain*

The concept of a speech chain[7] is a good place to start thinking about speech and the relationship between its production and perception. This chain includes the following links in which a thought is expressed in different forms as it is born in a speaker's mind and eventually giving rise to its understanding in a listener's mind. The various components of the speech chain are illustrated in Figure 6.

In the speech production side of the speech chain, the speaker first decides to say something. This event takes place in the higher level of the mind/brain. The desired thought passes through the language center(s) of the brain where it is given expression in words which are assembled together in the proper order and given final phonetic, intonational, and durational form. The articulation-motor center of the brain is planning a speech motor program which executes over time by conveying firing sequences to the lower neurological level, which in turn impart motion to all of the muscles responsible for speech production:

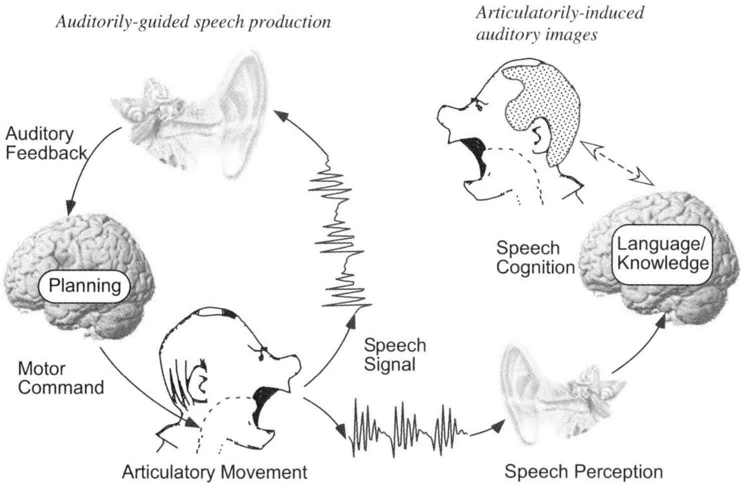

Fig. 6. The speech chain linking speaker and listener.

the muscle contractions, a stream of air emerges from the lungs, passes through the vocal cords where a phonation type (e.g. normal voicing, whispering, aspiration, creaky voice, or even no shaping at all) is developed, and receives its final shape in the vocal tract before radiating from the mouth and the nose and through the yielding wall of the vocal tract. The vibrations caused by the vocal apparatus of the speaker radiate through the air as a sound wave.

In the the side of speech perception, the sound wave eventually strikes the eardrums of listeners as well as of the speaker himself/herself, and is first converted to mechanical vibration on the surface of the tympanum membranes, and then is transformed to fluid pressure waves in the medium via the ossicles of the middle ear, which bathes the basilar membrane of the inner ear, and finally to firings in the neural fibers which combine to form the auditory nerve. The lower centers of the brainstem, the thalamus, the auditory cortex, and the language centers of the brain all cooperate in the recognition of the phonemes which convey meaning, the intonational and durational contours which provide additional information, and the vocal quality which allows the listener to recognize who is speaking and gain insight into the speaker's health, emotional state, and intention in speaking. The higher centers of the brain, both conscious and subconscious, bring to this incoming auditory and language data, all the experience of the listener in the form of previous memories and understanding of the current context, allowing the listener to "manufacture" in his or her mind a more or less faithful "replica" of the thought which was originally formulated in the speaker's consciousness and to update the listener's description of the current state of the world. The listener may in turn become the speaker, and vice versa, and the speech chain will then operate in reverse.

Actually, in speech communication, a speaker is also playing the role of a listener, which forms another loop besides that between the speaker and the listener as shown in Figure 6. For many years, a number of experiments have been conducted to investigate such a relationship between speech production and perception in order to explore the nature of the speech chain.

4.2. *Hypothesis of Articulatory-Auditory Linkage*

Speech production can be considered as a forward process in the speech chain while speech perception is an inverse process. In these two processes, speech production and perception are interlinked with each other at both the motor planning and acoustic transmission levels. In addition to the traditional use of electromyography (EMG), a number of new technologies such as functional Magnetic Resonance Imaging (fMRI), Magnetoencephalography (MEG), and Positron Emission Tomography (PET) were developed in the last decades to discover the brain functions in speech production and perception. The research in this area has found curious resemblance of motor and acoustic patterns of the vowel sounds in speech. This not only provides physiological evidence that the motor pattern of vowel articulation is compatible with the acoustic pattern, but also suggests an important aspect of high-level speech organization in the brain: Vowel representations in the motor and auditory spaces are also compatible.

As a general assumption, the high-level motor organization utilizes sensory information as a guide to motor control. This sort of sensori-motor integration typically accounts for visually-aided hand movements, where the object's coordinates in the visual space are mapped into kinematic parameters in the motor space. Although speech articulation does not always undergo the same scheme, there may be a case for the claim that articulatory control is guided with reference to auditory input. The assumption of motor-to-auditory compatibility may not be unreasonable in such a situation. Therefore, at least as far as vowels are concerned, the compatibility of the sensori-motor patterns can be considered as a unique underlying characteristic of speech processes. This view provides an extended account for the earlier motor theory of speech perception.[8,9]

In summary, human speech processing is a closed-loop control in which articulatorily-induced auditory images and sensory-guided motor execution communicate in the brain during speech. Due to this linkage, humans have a robust capability to adapt them in adverse environments and to extract the relevant linguistic and paralinguistic information. Many engineering techniques for analyzing speech have been motivated, directly or indirectly, by the speech production and/or perception mechanisms discussed in this section.

5. Introduction to Speech Analysis

The previous sections in this chapter focused on how humans process speech. The remaining sections will address one area of applications where computers are used to automatically extract useful information from the speech signal. This is called speech analysis. One main theme of this chapter is that the commonly used speech analysis techniques, which we will describe in the remainder of this chapter, can be provided with a new angle based on how they are motivated by and corrected to the human speech production and/or perception mechanisms. The basic material in the remaining sections of this chapter comes from references [10,11] with extensive re-organization and re-writing.

Speech analysis is sometimes called (linguistically independent) speech parameter or feature extraction, which is of direct use to other areas of speech processing applications such as coding and recognition. From the knowledge gained in human production that articulators are continuously moving over time, it is clear that a speech signal changes its characteristics continuously over time as well, especially when a new sound is encountered. Therefore, speech analysis cannot be performed over the entire stretch of time. Rather, it is carried out on short windowed segments during which the articulators and the resulting vocal tract shape are relatively stable. We call this type of analysis, motivated directly by the nature of speech production, short-time analysis.

Within each window, the analysis proceeds in either the time or frequency domain, or by a parametric model. In this section, we discuss only the time-domain analysis, deferring other more intricate analyses to later sections.

5.1. *Short-Time Analysis Windows*

Speech is dynamic or time-varying. Sometimes, both the vocal tract shape and pertinent aspects of its excitation may stay fairly constant for dozens of pitch periods (e.g., to 200 ms). On the other hand, successive pitch periods may change so much that their name "period" is a misnomer. Since the typical phone averages only about 80 ms in duration, dynamic coarticulation changes are more the norm than steady-state sounds. In any event, speech analysis usually presumes that signal properties change relatively slowly over time. This is most valid for short time intervals of a few periods at most. During such a short-time window of speech, one extracts parameters or features, each representing an average over the duration of the time window. As a result of the dynamic nature of speech, we must divide the signal into many successive windows or analysis frames, allowing the parameters to be calculated frequently enough to model dynamic vocal-tract features. Window size is critical to good modeling. Long vowels may allow window lengths up to 100 ms with minimal loss of detail due to the averaging, but stop explosions require much shorter windows (e.g., 5–10 ms) to avoid excess averaging of rapid spectral transitions. In a compromise, typical windows last about 20–30 ms, since one does not know *a priori* what sound one is analyzing.

Windowing means multiplication of a speech signal by a window, yielding a set of new speech samples weighted by the shape of the window. The simplest window has a rectangular shape, which gives equal weight to all samples of the speech signal and limits the analysis range to width of the window. A common is the Hamming window, which is a raised cosine pulse, or the quite similar Hanning window. Tapering the edges of the window allows its periodic shifting (at the update frame rate) along without having large effects on the resulting speech parameters due to pitch period boundaries.

5.2. *Short-Time Average Zero-Crossing Rate*

Speech analysis that attempts to estimate spectral features usually requires a Fourier transform. However, a simple measure called the zero-crossing rate (ZCR) provides basic spectral information in some applications at low cost. For a speech signal, zero crossing takes place whenever the waveform crosses the time axis (i.e., changes algebraic sign). For all narrowband signals (e.g., sinusoids), the ZCR can accurately measure the frequency where power is concentrated.

The ZCR is useful for estimating whether speech is voiced. Voiced speech has mostly low-frequency power, owing to a glottal excitation spectrum that falls off at about −12 dB per octave. Unvoiced speech comes from broadband noise excitation exciting primarily high frequencies, owing to the use of shorter vocal tracts (anterior to the constriction where noise is produced). Since speech is not narrowband, the ZCR corresponds to the average frequency of primary power concentration. Thus high and low ZCR (about 4,900 and 1,400 crossings/sec) correspond to unvoiced and voiced speech, respectively.

5.3. *Short-Time Autocorrelation Function*

Another way to estimate certain useful features of a speech signal concerns the short-time autocorrelation function. Like the ZCR, it serves as a tool to access some spectral characteristics of speech without explicit spectral transformations. As such, the autocorrelation function has applications in F0 estimation, voiced/unvoiced determination, and linear prediction. In particular, it preserves spectral amplitude information in the speech signal concerning harmonics and formants, while suppressing (often undesired) phase effects.

For F0 estimation, an alternative to the autocorrelation is the average magnitude difference function (AMDF). The AMDF has minima for the interval value near multiples of the pitch period (instead of the peaks for the autocorrelation function).

6. Speech Analysis Based on Production Mechanisms

6.1. *Introduction to LPC*

The most prominent method in speech analysis, linear predictive coding (LPC), has been directly motivated by our understanding of the physical properties of the human speech production system. LPC analysis has had a successful history for more than 30 years. The term "linear prediction" refers to the mechanism of using a linear combination of the past time-domain samples to approximate or to "predict" the current time-domain sample, using a compact set of LPC coefficients. If the prediction is accurate, then these coefficients can be used to efficiently represent or to "code" a long sequence of the signal (within each window). Linear prediction expressed in the time-domain is mathematically equivalent to modeling of an all-pole resonance system. This type of resonance system has been a rather accurate model for the vocal tract when vowel sounds are produced.

LPC is the most common technique for low-bit-rate speech coding and its popularity derives from its simple computation and reasonably accurate representation of many types of speech signals. LPC as a speech analysis tool has also been used in estimating F0, formants, and vocal tract area functions. One drawback of LPC is its omission of the zero components in several types of speech sounds with glottal source excitation and multiple acoustic paths in nasals and unvoiced sounds.

The most important aspect of the LPC analysis is to estimate the LPC coefficients from each of the windowed speech waveforms. The estimation technique has been well-established and can be found in any standard textbook on speech processing. Briefly, a "normal equation" is established using the least-squares criterion. Then highly-efficient methods are used to solve it to obtain the estimated LPC coefficients.

6.2. *Choice of the LPC Order*

The choice of the LPC order in speech analysis reflects a compromise of representation accuracy, computation time, and memory requirement. It can be shown that a perfect representation can be achieved in the limiting case where the order approaches infinity. This is only of theoretical interest, since the order rarely goes very high, due to increasingly excessive cost of computation. In practical applications, the LPC order is chosen to assign enough model poles to represent all formants (at two poles per resonance) in the bandwidth of the input speech signal. An additional 2–4 poles are usually assigned (e.g., the standard for 8 kHz sampled speech is 10 poles) to account for windowing effects and for weaknesses in the all-pole model. The all-pole model ignores zeros and assumes an infinitely-long stationary speech sound; thus assigning only enough poles to model the expected number of formants risks the case that poles may be used by the model to handle non-formant effects in the windowed spectrum (such is seen often in LPC modeling). The non-formant effects derive mostly from the vocal-tract excitation (both glottal and fricative) and from lip radiation. In addition, zeros are regularly found in nasalized sounds. Nasal sounds theoretically have more resonances than vowels, but we rarely increase the LPC order to handle nasals, because most nasals have more than one resonance with little energy (due to the effects of zeros and losses).

The prediction error energy can serve as a measure of the accuracy of an LPC model. The normalized prediction error (i.e., the energy in the error divided by the speech energy) decreases monotonically with LPC order (i.e., each additional pole in the LPC model improves its accuracy). With voiced speech, poles in excess of the number needed to model all formants (and a few for zero effects) add little to modeling accuracy but such extraneous poles add increasingly to the computation.

6.3. *Introduction to Voicing Pitch Extraction*

Fundamental frequency F0 or pitch parameters associated with voiced speech characterize the most important aspect of the source mechanism in human speech production. F0 is especially relevant to tone languages such as spoken Chinese, since it provides the informational basis for linguistic and lexical contrast.

Although automatic F0 estimation appears fairly simple at first glance, full accuracy has so far been elusive, owing to the non-stationary nature of speech, irregularities in vocal cord vibration, the wide range of possible F0 values, interaction of F0 with vocal tract shape, and degraded speech in noisy environments. F0 can be estimated either from periodicity in the time-domain or from harmonic spacing in frequency. Spectral approaches generally have higher accuracy than time-domain methods, but they need more computation.

Because the major excitations of the vocal tract occur when the vocal cords close for a pitch period, each period starts with high amplitude and then has an amplitude envelope that decays exponentially with time. Since the very lowest frequencies dominate power in voiced speech, the overall rate of decay is usually inversely proportional to the bandwidth of the first formant. The basic method for pitch period estimation is a simple search for amplitude peaks, constraining the peak-to-peak interval to be consistent in time (since F0 varies slowly as constrained by articulators). Because speakers can range from infants to adult males, a large pitch-period range from about 2 ms to 20 ms is possible.

Input speech is often low-pass-filtered to approximately 900 Hz so as to retain only the first formant, thus removing the influence of other formants, and simplifying the signal, while retaining enough harmonics to facilitate peak-picking. F0 estimation in the time domain has two advantages: efficient calculation and direct specification of pitch periods in the waveform. This is useful for applications when pitch periods need to be manipulated. On the other hand, F0 values alone (without explicit determination of the placement of pitch periods) suffice for many applications, such as vocoders.

When F0 is estimated spectrally, the fundamental itself and, more often, its equally-spaced harmonics can furnish the main clues. In time-domain peak-picking, errors may be made due to peaks corresponding to formants (especially F1), misinterpreting the waveform oscillations due to the F1 as F0 phenomena. Spacing between harmonics is usually more reliable as an F0 cue. Estimating F0 directly in terms of the lowest spectral peak in the speech signal can be unreliable because the speech signal is often bandpass filtered (e.g., over telephone lines). Even unfiltered speech has a weak first harmonic when F1 is at high frequency (as in low vowels). While often yielding more accurate estimates than time-domain methods, spectral F0 detectors require much more calculation due to the required spectral transformation. Typical errors include: 1) misjudging the second harmonic as the fundamental and 2) the ambiguity of the estimated F0 during aperiodicities such as in voice creak. A given estimation method often performs well on some types of voice but less so for other types.

6.4. *Pitch Estimation Methods*

We estimate F0 either from periodicity in the time domain or from regularly-spaced harmonics in the frequency domain. Like many pattern recognition algorithms, most pitch estimators have three components: a preprocessor to simplify the input signal (eliminate information in the signal that is irrelevant to F0), a basic F0 extractor to form the F0 estimate, and a postprocessor to correct errors. The preprocessor serves to focus the remaining data towards the specific task of F0 determination, reducing data rates by eliminating much formant detail. Since the basic pitch estimator, like all pattern recognizers, makes errors, a postprocessor may help to clean up the time series of output pitch estimates (one per frame), e.g., imposing continuity constraints from speech production theory, which may not have been applied in the basic F0 extractor often operating independently on each speech frame.

The pitch detection algorithm tries to locate one or more of the following features in the speech signal or in its spectrum: the fundamental harmonic F0, a quasi-periodic time structure, an alternation of high and low amplitudes, and signal discontinuities. The intuitive approach of looking for harmonics and periodicities usually works well, but fails too often to be relied upon without additional support. In general, pitch detectors trade off complexities in various components; e.g., harmonic estimation requires a complex preprocessor (e.g., often including a Fourier transform) but allows a simple basic extractor that just does peak-picking. The preprocessor is often just a low-pass filter, but the choice of the filter's cutoff frequency can be complicated by the large range of F0 values possible when accepting speech from many different speakers.

Frequency-domain methods for pitch detection exploit correlation, maximum likelihood, and other spectral techniques where speech is analyzed during a short-term window for each input frame.

Autocorrelation, average magnitude difference, cepstrum, spectral compression, and harmonic-matching methods are among the varied spectral approaches. Spectral methods generally have greater accuracy than time-domain methods, but require more computation.

To provide results in real-time for many applications, F0 estimators must work with little delay. Delays normally arise in part from the use of a buffer to accumulate a large frame of speech to analyze, since pitch can only be detected over intervals corresponding to pitch periods (unlike spectral envelope information, like formants, which can succeed with much shorter analysis frames). Time-domain F0 estimators often incur less delay than frequency-domain methods. The latter mostly require a buffer of speech samples prior to their spectral transformation. Many of the F0 detectors with less delay sacrifice knowledge about the timing of the pitch periods; i.e., they estimate the lengths of pitch periods without explicitly finding their actual locations. While most F0 estimators do not need to locate period times, those that do locate them are more useful in certain applications (e.g., to permit pitch-synchrounous LPC analysis).

7. Speech Analysis Methods Based on Perception Mechanisms

7.1. *Filter Bank Analysis*

As we have seen from Section 1.3, one basic function of the ear is to decompose the impinging sounds into a bank of outputs along the BM spatial dimension. Each point along this dimension is a filter with band-pass-like frequency selectivity. The outputs from the BM are analogous to those in the traditional filter bank analysis technique.

Filter bank analysis consists of a set of band-pass filters. A single input speech signal is simultaneously passed through these filters, each outputting a narrowband signal containing amplitude (and sometimes phase) information about the speech in a narrow frequency range. The bandwidths normally are chosen to increase with center frequency, thus following decreasing human auditory resolution. They often follow the auditory Mel scale, i.e., having equally-spaced, fixed bandwidths below 1 kHz, then logarithmic spacing at higher frequencies.

Such a filter-bank analysis tries to simulate very simple aspects of the human auditory system, based on the assumption that human signal processing is an efficient way to do speech analysis and recognition. Since the inner ear apparently transfers information to the auditory nerve on a spectral basis, the filter banks discussed above approximate this transfer quite roughly.

7.2. *Auditory-Motivated Speech Analysis*

Other speech analysis methods go further than filter-bank analysis in the hope that improved approximation to perception mechanisms may occur. Many of these alternative approaches use auditory models where the filtering follows that found in the cochlea more precisely.

One example of auditory-motivated analysis is that of modulation spectrogram, which emphasizes slowly-varying speech changes corresponding to a rate of approximately 4 per second. Such 250 ms units conform roughly to syllables, which are important units for perceptual organization. Modulation spectrogram displays show less rapid detail than standard wideband spectrograms. In a sense, they follow the idea of wavelets, which allow time and frequency resolution in automatic analysis to follow that of the ear.

Part of the auditory processing of sounds is adjusting for context. Since human audition is always active, even when people are not specifically listening, it is normal to ignore ambient sounds. People pay attention to unexpected auditory information, while ignoring many predictable and thus useless aspects of sounds. These adjustments come naturally to humans, as part of the maturation of their hearing systems. In computer sound processing, however, one must explicitly model this behavior. A number of speech analysis methods used successfully in environment-robust automatic speech recognition do simulate the human auditory mechanisms to adjust to the acoustic environment (e.g., noise, use of telephone, poor microphone or loudspeaker).

Since automatic speech recognition involves comparing patterns or models, environmental variations can cause major acoustic differences which are superfluous for the recognition decision, and which human audition normalizes for automatically. Basic speech analysis methods such as filter-bank analysis, LPC, and cepstra, cannot execute such normalization. The filtering effects of RASTA provide one way to try to implement normalization and to improve the results of analysis for noisy speech. In another common approach, a mean spectrum or cepstrum is subtracted from that of each speech frame (e.g., as a form of blind deconvolution), to eliminate channel effects. It is unclear over what time range this mean should be calculated. In practice, it is often done over several seconds, on the assumption that environmental conditions do not change more rapidly. This, however, may impose a delay on the speech analysis; so the channel conditions are sometimes estimated from prior frames and imposed on future ones in their analysis. Calculating such a mean may require a long-term average for efficiency, which is difficult for real-time applications. Often the mean is estimated from a prior section of the input signal that is estimated to be (noisy) silence (i.e., non-speech). This latter approach requires a speech detector and assumes that pauses occur fairly regularly in the speech signal. As the channel changes with time, the mean must be updated.

Speech analysis methods that can simulate auditory properties and normalize the acoustic environments accordingly are still an active research area.

8. Speech Analysis Methods Based on Joint Production-Perception Mechanisms

8.1. *Perceptual Linear Prediction Analysis*

As we discussed earlier in this chapter, LPC analysis is based primarily on speech production mechanisms, where the all-pole property of the human vocal tract is used as the basic principle to derive the analysis method. It can be shown that LPC analysis is equivalent to a type of spectral analysis where the linear frequency scale is involved.

However, auditory processing of sounds in the ear exploits the Mel instead of linear frequency scale. Further, various nonlinear properties in the ear are not exploited in the LPC analysis. Some of these auditory properties have been incorporated into the LPC analysis, resulting in the analysis method called perceptual linear prediction (PLP). PLP modifies the basic LPC using a critical-band or Mel power spectrum with logarithmic amplitude compression. The spectrum is multiplied by a mathematical curve modeling the ear's behavior in judging loudness as a function of frequency. The output is then raised to the power 0.33 to simulate the power law of hearing. Seventeen bandpass filters equally spaced in Bark or Mel scale (i.e., critical bands) map the range 0–5 kHz, for example, into the range 0–17 Bark. Each band is simulated by a spectral weighting. One direct advantage of the PLP is that its order is significantly less than orders generally used in LPC.

PLP has often been combined with the RASTA (RelAtive SpecTrAl) method of speech analysis. RASTA bandpasses spectral parameter signals to eliminate steady or slowly-varying components in the speech signal (including environmental effects and speaker characteristics) and rapid noise events. The bandpass range is typically 1–10 Hz, with a sharp zero at 0 Hz and a time-constant of about 160 ms. Events changing more slowly than once a second (e.g., most channel effects, except in severe fading conditions) are thus eliminated by the highpass filtering. The lowpass cutoff is more gradual, which smoothes parameters over about 40 ms, thus preserving most phonetic events, while suppressing noise.

8.2. *Mel-Frequency Cepstral Analysis*

Another popular speech analysis method that jointly exploits speech production and perception mechanisms is Mel-frequency cepstral analysis. The results of this analysis are often called Mel-frequency cepstral coefficients (MFCCs). To introduce MFCCs, we first introduce the (linear frequency) cepstral analysis method which has been primarily motivated by speech production knowledge.

The basic speech-production model is a linear system (representing the vocal tract) excited by quasi-periodic (vocal-cord) pulses or random noise (at a vocal-tract constriction). Thus the speech signal, as the output of this linear system, is the convolution of an excitation waveform with the vocal-tract's impulse response. Many speech applications require separate estimation of these individual components; hence a deconvolution of the excitation and envelope components is useful. Producing two signals from one in such a deconvolution is generally nondeterministic, but has some success when applied to speech because the relevant convolved signals forming speech have a unique time-frequency behavior.

Cepstral analysis or cepstral deconvolution converts a product of two spectra into a sum of two signals. These may be separated by linear filtering if they are sufficiently different. Let speech spectrum be S = EH, where E and H represent the excitation and vocal-tract spectra, respectively. Then, log S = log (EH) = log (E) + log (H). Since H consists mostly of smooth formant curves (i.e., a spectrum varying slowly with frequency) while E is much more active or irregular (owing to the harmonics or noise excitation), contributions due to E and H can be separated. Inverse Fourier transform of log spectrum (log S) gives the (linear frequency) cepstrum. It consists of two largely separable components, one due to the vocal tract excitation and another due to the vocal tract transfer function.

To incorporate the perceptual mechanism of Mel-spaced frequency analysis, the (linear frequency) cepstral analysis has been modified to produce MFCCs, which are widely used as the main analysis method for speech recognition. MFCCs combine the regular cepstrum with a nonlinear weighting in frequency, following the Bark or Mel scale so as to incorporate some aspects of audition. It appears to furnish a more efficient representation of speech spectra than other analysis methods such as LPC.

In computing MFCCs, a power spectrum of each successive speech frame is first effectively deformed both in frequency according to the Mel scale and in amplitude on the usual decibel or logarithmic scale. The power spectrum can be computed either via the Fourier transform or via the LPC analysis. Then the initial elements of an inverse Fourier transform are obtained as the MFCCs, with varying orders from the zero-th order to typically a 15th order.

The zero-th order MFCC simply represents the average speech power. Because such power varies significantly with microphone placement and communication channel conditions, it is often not directly utilized in speech recognition, although its temporal derivative often is. The next first-order MFCC indicates the balance of power between low and high frequencies, where a positive value indicates a sonorant sound, and a negative value a frication sound. This reflects the fact that sonorants have most energy at low frequencies, and fricatives the opposite. Each higher-order MFCC represents increasingly finer spectral detail. Note that neither MFCCs nor LPC coefficients display a simple relationship with basic spectral envelope detail such as the formants. For example, using a speech bandwidth with four formants (e.g., 0–4 kHz), a high value for the second-order MFCC corresponds to high power in the F1 and F3 ranges but low amounts in F2 and F4 regions. Such information is useful to distinguish voiced sounds, but it is difficult to interpret physically.

8.3. *Formants and their Automatic Extraction*

The main objective of speech analysis is to automatically extract essential parameters of the acoustic structure from the speech signal. This process serves the purpose of either data reduction or identification and enhancement of information-bearing elements contained in the speech signal. To determine what such information-bearing elements are, one needs to have sufficient knowledge about the physical nature of the speech signal. Such knowledge is often provided by a production model that describes how the observed speech signal is generated as the output of a vocal-tract digital filter given an input source. This type of production model decomposes the speech waveform into two independent source and filter components. Formants comprise a very important set of the information-bearing elements in view of the source-filter model, since they form the resonance peaks in the filter component of the model. At the same time, formants are also the information-bearing elements in view of speech perception, because the auditory system not only robustly represents such information, but also exploits it for distinguishing different speech sounds. Before describing the formant extraction methods, we first elaborate the concept of formants in detail.

Formants characterize the "filter" portion of a speech signal. They are the poles in the digital resonance filter or digital resonator. Given the source-filter model for voiced speech that is free of nasal coupling, the all-pole filter is characterized by the pole positions, or equivalently by the formant frequencies, F1, F2, …, Fn, formant bandwidths, B1, B2, …, Bn, and formant amplitudes, A1, A2, …, An. Among them, the formant frequencies or resonance frequencies, at which the spectral peaks are located, are the most important. A formant frequency is determined by the angle of the corresponding pole in the discrete-time filter transfer function.

The normal range of the formant frequencies for adult males is F1 = 180–800 Hz, F2 = 600–2500 Hz, F3 = 1200–3500 Hz, and F4 = 2300–4000 Hz. These ranges have been exploited to provide constraints for automatic formant extraction and tracking.

The average difference between adjacent formants of adult males is about 1,000 Hz. For adult females, the formant frequencies are about 20% higher than for adult males. The relationship between male and female formant frequencies, however, is not uniform and the relationship deviates from a simple scale factor. When the velum is lowered to create nasal phonemes, the combined nasal+vocal tract is effectively lengthened from its typical 17 cm vocal-tract length by about 25%. As a result, the average spacing between formants reduces to about 800 Hz.

Formant bandwidths are physically related to energy loss in the vocal tract, and are determined by the distance between the pole location and the origin of the z-plane in the filter transfer function. Empirical measurement data from speech suggest that the formant bandwidths and frequencies are systematically related. Formant amplitudes, on the other hand, vary with the overall pattern of formant frequencies as a whole. They are also related to the spectral properties of the voice source.

LPC analysis models voiced speech as the output of an all-pole filter in response to a simple sequence of excitation pulses. In addition to major speech coding and recognition applications, LPC is often used as a standard formant extraction and tracking method. It has limitations in that the vocal-tract filter transfer function, in addition to having formant poles (which are of primary interest for speech analysis), generally also contains zeros due to sources located above the glottis and to nasal and subglottal coupling. Furthermore, the model for the voice source as a simple sequence of excitation impulses is inaccurate, with the source actually often containing local spectral peaks and valleys. These factors often hinder accuracy in automatic formant extraction and tracking methods based on LPC analysis. The situation is especially serious for speech with high pitch frequencies, where the automatic formant-estimation method tends to pick harmonic frequencies rather than formant frequencies. Jumps from a correctly-estimated formant in one time frame to a higher or a lower value in the next frame constitute one common type of tracking error.

The automatic tracking of formants is not trivial. The factors rendering the formant identification process complex include the following. The ranges for formant center-frequencies are large, with significant overlaps both within and across speakers. In phoneme sequences consisting only of oral vowels and sonorants, formants smoothly rise and fall, and are easily estimated via spectral peak-picking. However, nasal sounds cause acoustic coupling of the oral and nasal tracts, which lead to abrupt formant movements. Zeros (due to the glottal source excitation or to the vocal tract response for lateral or nasalized sounds) also may obscure formants in spectral displays. When two formants approach each other, they sometimes appear as one spectral peak (e.g., F1–F2 in back vowels). In obstruent sound production, a varying range of low frequencies is only weakly excited, leading to a reduced number of formants appearing in the output speech.

Given a spectral representation S(z) via the LPC coefficients, one could directly locate formants by solving for the roots of the denominator polynomial in S(z). Each complex-conjugate pair of roots would correspond to a formant if the roots correspond to a suitable bandwidth (e.g., 100–200 Hz) at a frequency location where a formant would normally be expected. This process is usually very precise, but quite expensive since the polynomial usually requires an order in excess of 10 to represent 4–5 formants. Alternatively, one can use phase to label a spectral peak as a formant. When evaluating S(z) on the unit circle a negative phase shift of approximately 180 degrees should occur as the radiant frequency passes a pole close to the unit circle (i.e., a formant pole).

Two close formants often appear as a single broad spectral peak, a situation that causes many formant estimators difficulty, in determining whether the peak corresponds to one or two resonances. A method called the chirp-z transform has been used to resolve this issue.

Formant estimation is increasingly difficult for voices with high F0, as in children's voices. In such cases, F0 often exceeds formant bandwidths, and harmonics are so widely separated that only one or two make up each formant. A spectral analyzer, traditionally working independently on one speech frame at a time, would often equate the strongest harmonics as formants. Human perception, integrating speech over many frames, is capable of properly separating F0 and the spectral envelope (formants), but simpler computer analysis techniques often fail. It is wrong to label a multiple of F0 as a formant center frequency, except for the few cases where the formant aligns exactly with a multiple of F0 (such alignment is common in songs, but much less so in speech).

9. Conclusion

In this chapter we have provided an overview of speech analysis from the perspectives of both speech production and perception, emphasizing their relationship. The chapter starts with a general introduction to the phonological and phonetic properties of spoken Mandarin Chinese. This is followed by descriptions of human speech production and perception mechanisms. In particular, we present some recent brain research on the relationship between human speech production and perception. While the traditional textbook treatment of speech analysis is from the perspective of signal processing and feature extraction, in this chapter we take an alternative, more scientifically-oriented approach in treating the same subject, classifying the commonly-used speech analysis methods into those that are more closely linked with speech production, speech perception, and joint production/perception mechanisms. We hope that our approach to treating speech analysis can provide a fresh view of this classical yet critical subject and help readers understand the basic signal properties of spoken Chinese that are important in exploring further materials in this book.

References

1. M. Chiba, and T., Kajiyama, *The Vowel: Its Nature and Structure*, Phonetic Society of Japan.
2. G. Fant, *Acoustic Theory of Speech Production*, Mouton, The Hague, (1960).
3. R. Titze, "On the Mechanics of Vocal Fold Vibration," *J. Acoust. Soc. Am.*, vol. 60, (1976), pp. 1366-1380.
4. K. N. Stevens, "Physics of Laryngeal Behavior and Larynx Modes," *Phonetica*, vol. 34, (1977), pp. 264-279.
5. K. Ishizaka and J. Flanagan, "Synthesis of Voiced Sounds from a Two-mass Model of the Vocal cords," *Bell Sys. Tech. J*, vol. 512, (1972), pp. 1233-1268.
6. H. McGurk and J. MacDonald, "Hearing Lips and Seeing Voices," *Nature*, vol. 264, (1976), pp. 746-748.
7. P. Denes and E. Pinson, *The Speech Chain*, 2nd Ed., New York: W.H. Freeman and Co., (1993).
8. A. M. Liberman and I. G. Mattingly, "The Motor Theory of Speech Perception Revised," *Cognition*, vol. 21, (1985), pp. 1-36.
9. J. Dang, M. Akagi and K. Honda, "Communication between Speech Production and Perception within the Brain -Observation and Simulation-," *J. Computer Science and Technology*, vol. 21, (2006), pp. 95-105.
10. L. Deng and D. O'shaughnessy, *Speech Processing --- A dynamic and optimization-oriented approach*, Mercel-Dekker, New York, (2003).
11. D. O'shaughnessy, *Speech Communications: Human and Machine*, IEEE Press, Piscataway, NJ, (2000).

CHAPTER 2

PHONETIC AND PHONOLOGICAL BACKGROUND OF CHINESE SPOKEN LANGUAGES

Chih-Chung Kuo

Industrial Technology Research Institute, Hsinchu
E-mail: cck@itri.org.tw

This chapter provides the phonetic and phonological background of Chinese spoken languages, Mandarin especially. Before going into the main theme of the chapter, a brief clarification of the distinction between phonetics and phonology is provided for readers of non-linguistic background. After generally describing the major features of spoken Chinese, standard Mandarin, among other dialects, is chosen as a typical example to explore in detail the unique syllable structure of spoken Chinese. Both traditional initial-final analysis and modern linguistic analysis approaches such as phonetics, phonemics, and phonotactics are described with the goal of examining Mandarin syllables and phonemes in detail. Hopefully, this chapter can help lay the linguistic foundations of Chinese spoken language processing (CSLP) for both Chinese and non-Chinese speaking researchers and engineers.

1. Introduction

The written form of Chinese, the Chinese characters has been in existence for almost 2000 years without radical changes until the adoption of font simplification in mainland China around 50 years ago. The image on the right shows part of a famous inscription called shíménsòng[a] (石門頌/石门颂[b] "Rock Gate Eulogy") carved on rock in AD 148. The four Chinese characters shown here are 鑿通石門[c]/凿通石门 (záotōng shímén, "to dig through Rock Gate"), which are legible to modern Chinese readers, especially those who have learned traditional fonts.

[a] The Romanization for Mandarin Chinese used in this chapter is Hanyu Pinyin.
[b] All Chinese text in this chapter is presented as "traditional fonts/simplified fonts" if the two forms are different.
[c] They are in clerical script (隸書/隶书 lìshū), which was invented in Qín Dynasty (221 BC–206BC) and mature in Han Dynasty (206 BC–AD 220), and is still used today as the font shown here.

In contrast, spoken Chinese has been varied across the different geographical regions since ancient times. Pronunciations also changed over time and likely to have been influenced by alien languages. In spite of mutual unintelligibility among the spoken forms of Chinese, referred to as dialectal variations, there is only one type of orthography that developed. Hence, considerable gap between the spoken and written form has always existed. Despite that, the major features and basic structure of spoken Chinese has remained almost the same. This is evidenced by the current form of existing Chinese dialects, the abundant amount of poetry and lyrics from the past thousands of years, and even by some ancient rhyme dictionaries like qiēyùn (切韻/切韵, 601 AD) or guǎngyùn (廣韻/广韵, 1011 AD),[d] which are still being studied today.

Although the many variants of spoken Chinese may be too different to be mutually comprehensible, they do share some common features such that they can be regarded as "one language" (however this is still a controversial point especially when compared to the similarities that exist across the languages under the Romance language family). In Section 3, several distinctive characteristics of spoken Chinese are described. It can be shown that the major feature of spoken Chinese is the specific structure of tonal syllables that corresponds to the pronunciation of a character in written Chinese.

The six major dialects/variants of spoken Chinese, in order of speaker population[1] size, are given in the table below.

Table 1. Major dialects/variants of spoken Chinese.

No.	Name	Name in Chinese	Population	Important member
1	Mandarin	guānhuà (官話/官话)	800 million	Standard Mandarin
2	Wu	wú (吳/吴)	90 million	Shanghainese
3	Cantonese	yuè (粵/粤)	70 million	
4	Min	mǐn (閩/闽)	50 million	Taiwanese
5	Xiang	xiāng (湘)	35 million	
6	Hakka	kè(jiā) (客(家))	35 million	

The term *Guānhuà* (官話/官话, "official speech") was used since the Ming Dynasty (1368–1644) to refer the speech used in the courts. The term *Mandarin* coming directly from the Portuguese, was first used to call the Chinese officials (i.e., the mandarins), and then following that, the word was used to refer to the spoken language that these officials used amongst themselves (i.e., guānhuà).

[d] Historically, Chinese has a rich tradition of studying sound systems although the pronunciation was usually based on the authors' own dialects or the most commonly used dialect of the time.

Now linguists use Guānhuà or Mandarin to refer to the biggest category of related Chinese dialects spoken across most of northern and sounthwestern China.

Standard Mandarin[2] was originally a sub-dialect of Mandarin as spoken around Beijing and was chosen to be the standard spoken Chinese in 1909 in the Qīng Dynasty, when it is called *guóyŭ* (國語/国语 or "national language"). This name remained and the standardization process continued after 1912, and until today in Taiwan. In 1955, standard Mandarin was renamed *pŭtōnghuà* (普通話/普通话 or "common speech") in mainland China after 1949. Today, standard Mandarin, as an official language used in China, Taiwan, and Singapore, is the most commonly spoken language in the world due to both the world's largest population in China, and to the power of modern education and mass media.

Although Mandarin is the superset of standard Mandarin, and is the larger dialect group, it has become common and (also in this chapter hereafter) that standard Mandarin is simply called Mandarin for short. For a deeper understanding of the unique characteristics of the syllable structure of spoken Chinese, Mandarin will be used as a typical example and described in detail in both Sections 4 and 5. The traditional view of Mandarin syllables being a combination of initials and finals is detailed in Section 4. In contrast, the Mandarin syllable is examined phonetically and phonologically from the linguistic perspective in Section 5. But before these, a brief explanation is given in Section 2 to introduce the concept of phonemes in phonology, in contrast to phones in phonetics.

2. Phonological Phonemes vs. Phonetic Phones

2.1. *Phonetics and Phonology in Linguistics*

Linguistics[3–5] is the science of human language, including the science of speech. The field of linguistics is very broad containing several important sub-fields as shown in Table 2. These sub-fields are listed in the order of higher-level concepts

Table 2. Linguistic sub-fields analogous to networking layers.

Linguistics	Study of	Layer	Networking
Stylistics	linguistic styles	7	Application
Pragmatics	language uses	6	Presentation
Semantics	meanings	5	Session
Syntax	sentence patterns	4	Transport
Morphology	word structures	3	Network
Phonology	speech sound system	2	Data Link
Phonetics	speech sounds	1	Physical

to lower-level sounds, which is somewhat analogous to the seven layers of computer networking. It is interesting to associate data/packet communication between computers with language/speech communication between humans. For spoken language processing, phonetics and phonology[6] are the most relevant of all the sub-fields in linguistics.

Phonetics[6–8] is the study of sounds and human voice. It deals with the speech sounds (phones) themselves rather than the meaning they convey in the language. From the aspects of physics, physiology, and psychology, the study of phonetics is mainly divided into the following three branches.

- *articulatory phonetics*: the study of speech production such as the positions of speech organs and manners of sound production;
- *acoustic phonetics*: the study of the acoustic properties of speech such as waveforms, speech spectra/signals, formants, pitch contours, etc.;
- *auditory phonetics*: the study of speech perception, principally how the ears receive and transform speech into perceptual representations in the brain.

Phonology[5,6] is the study of the sound system of a specific language. The sound system includes sound units and sound patterns, among which several important topics in phonology are:

- *Phonemics*: the study of the abstract sound units (phonemes) of a specific language; i.e. the smallest speech segment that causes *meaning contrast*.
- *Distinctive Features*: the study of the most basic unit of phonological structure; i.e. the smallest feature that causes a class of sounds to be distinct from others (i.e. *natural class* of segments).
- *Phonotactics*: the study of valid sound patterns in a specific language; i.e. the permissible combinations of phonemes including syllable structure, consonant clusters, vowel sequence, etc.
- *Phonological Rules*: the study of how phonemes are realized into practical phones in specific phonetic contexts; i.e., the rules of transformation from phonemic representation to phonetic representation of sound units.

2.2. *Phonemes vs. Phones*

It is very important to distinguish between phonemes and phones. Linguists try to study and define a set of the smallest speech units, which are called *phonemes*, for a specific language. The phoneme is an abstract unit of phonology and not necessarily the actual pronunciation of the physical speech segment (i.e. the *phone*) it represents. It is a mental abstraction of a speech segment, which can cause meaning contrast with others in the same phonetic context.

For example, in English, the unvoiced plosive [pʰ][e] in [pʰu] will cause a perception of the word "poo" in contrast to other words (or nonsense-words) with other phones (sound) in the same phonetic context (i.e., before [u]). Similarly, the voiced plosive [b] can also cause meaning contrast in English (like [bu] for the word "boo"). Therefore, both /pʰ/[f] and /b/ are phonemes in English. Yet another bilabial plosive [p], is however not a phoneme in English because it does not cause meaning contrast although it does exist in words like "spoon" [spun] in English. Therefore, in English the unaspirated plosive [p] can be regarded as a variant phone of the aspirated plosive [pʰ] when it directly follows the fricative [s] in the same syllable. These variant phones of a phoneme are called *allophones* of that phoneme.

Two phones are usually judged as separate phonemes by the use of *minimal pairs*, which pairs of words that are identical except for a phone. The words, "poo" and "boo", form a minimal pair such that /pʰ/ and /b/ are separate phonemes in English. On the contrary, there is no minimal pair for [p] and [pʰ] in English (e.g. there is neither a word sounding [pu] with meaning different from "poo" nor a word sounding [spʰun] with meaning different from "spoon"), so they are regarded as allophones of the same phoneme rather than two separate phonemes in English.

Phonemes are spoken-language specific. Table 3 shows the three bilabial plosives in three different spoken languages. It has been mentioned that /pʰ/ and /b/ are phonemes in English. In Mandarin, however, /p/ and / pʰ/ are phonemes. Taiwanese has all the three phones as phonemes because there exists all the minimal pairs in Taiwanese (three different words with identical pronunciation except for the plosive consonant).

Table 3. Three bilabial plosives form different phoneme sets in different spoken languages.

Bilabial Plosives			Words	English	Mandarin	Taiwanese[g]
unvoiced	unaspirated	/p/	[pu]		不 bù, "no"	孵 pū, "to hatch"
	aspirated	/pʰ/	[pʰu]	poo	舖/铺 pù, "a shop"	浮 phû, "to float"
voiced		/b/	[bu]	boo		舞 bú, "to dance"

[e] *International Phonetic Alphabet* (IPA)[9] is used in this Chapter to specify more precise pronunciation. In this example, [ʰ] is an IPA diacritic indicating the aspirated feature.

[f] Note that in common linguistic notation a phoneme is specified within slashes (virgules, / /) and a phone is specified by a symbol within square brackets ([ ]).

[g] The Romanization for Taiwanese used in this chapter is Pe̍h-ōe-jī (POJ) (白話字/白话字 báihuà zì), aslo called Church Romanization (教會羅馬字/教会罗马字)[10,11]

2.3. *Transcription of Speech*

There are quite a few ways to transcribe speech even for the same language. They can be classified into two relative categories as follows:

- Narrow (phonetic) transcription
- Broad (phonemic) transcription

Narrow or phonetic transcription is to specify the pronunciation with as much detail as possible so that the speech can be phonetically reproduced without any ambiguity. On the other hand, broad or phonemic transcription is used mainly for phonemic representation of words in a specific language. Therefore, phonemic transcription is just an abstract symbolic representation in use for a specific language, where the native speakers of the language know how to enunciate correctly according to this minimal transcription forms. In fact, the writing systems of most alphabetic languages are originally the phonemic transcriptions of their languages.

Some of the symbols in broad (phonemic) transcription are misleading for non-native speakers who may mistake these phonemic symbols either for phonetic symbols, or for the sounds that the same symbols represent in their mother tongues. For example, because [p] and [p^h] are allophones in English, the symbol "p" alone is usually used for the unvoiced plosive phoneme in contrast with the symbol "b" for the voiced plosive. On the contrary, in Mandarin /p/ and /p^h/ are two separate phonemes and the voiced plosive [b] is not a phoneme, so in Hanyu Pinyin the symbol "b" is used for the phoneme /p/ and "p" is for /p^h/. Therefore, some Chinese speakers may mistakenly think that the English word "bay" sounds identical to the sound of the Chinese character 北 (běi, "north"). Similarly, an English speaker might wrongly perceive that the first syllable in the word "Beijing" (北京běi-jīng, "north capital") starts with a voiced stop [b] like in the English word "bay". Furthermore, most English speakers may also erroneously regard the second syllable in the word "Taipei" (台北tái-běi, "Taiwan's north"), as a syllable beginning with an aspirated stop [p^h], as in the English word "pay". In fact, it is an unaspirated stop [p] represented by the same character 北 (běi) as in "Beijing", but transcribed by an older Romanization system of Mandarin, the Wade-Giles, in which /p/ and /p^h/ are represented by /p/ and /p'/, respectively.[h]

IPA is the most authoritative speech transcription system, but it should be noted that IPA can be used both for phonetic and phonemic transcriptions. It all depends on how narrow the transcription is, that is, how much details are

[h] "Peking", the old name for "Beijing", is another example that reflects the broad transcription of the same word.

transcribed (e.g. by IPA diacritics or suprasegmentals). For example, some linguists[5] have argued that the alveolar fricative /s/ in Mandarin is more dental-oriented (apical-dental) and should be transcribed more precisely as [s̪] in contrast to the laminal-alveolar fricative [s] in English. In practice, there should be a variety of phonetic nuances for the same IPA-transcribed phoneme in different languages.

3. Major Features of Spoken Chinese Languages

3.1. *Monosyllabic Character*

The most evident fact in all the varieties of spoken Chinese languages is that all of them share the same apparent written form—the Chinese characters. Also, the pronunciation of each Chinese character, regardless of the language variety, is in the form of one tonal syllable, although the actual pronunciation could vary extremely across the different dialects. In addition, the basic shape and structure of Chinese syllables is similar in all the dialects. In traditional Chinese linguistics, a syllable is divided into two parts: *initial* and *final*. Each initial is a consonant or void, which is called empty initial or zero onset.[12] Each final is composed in the sequence of an optional glide (or approximant), a vowel, and an optional coda consonant, which is either a nasal or a stop. The syllable structure of standard Mandarin will be described in detail in Sections 4 and 5, demonstrating its distinctive shape and structure in spoken Chinese.

3.2. *Single-character Word*

Another related and interesting fact is that almost every Chinese character is also a word, especially in *literary Chinese* (文言文 *wényánwén*). Even though in modern written Chinese—*Vernacular Chinese* (白話文/白话文 *báihuàwén*), which is closer to spoken Chinese—there are a lot of two- or three-character words in the linguistic sense, the word boundary in Chinese is still rather vague and indefinite. Therefore, in an extreme sense, each character can be regarded as a word and a multi-character word as a compound word or a phrase.[i] For example, the three characters, 白話文/白话文 (báihuàwén), may be regarded as a word meaning "vernacular"; or they may be regarded as three consecutive words as "plainly (白) word (話/话) text (文)".

---

[i] In traditional Chinese there is no analogous sense and word for the "character" like that in an alphabetical language. In practice, the usual translation (without linguistic precision) of "word" in Chinese is 字 (zì), which in fact indicates Chinese character. Likewise, "phrase" is usually translated (again, imprecision in linguistics) into 詞/词 (cí), which is used in Chinese to indicate a single-character or multi-character word.

In principle, there is no inherent word boundary in written Chinese and only the character constitutes the inherent boundary. This is why word segmentation has been a basic problem in Chinese text processing for applications like text-to-speech (TTS) synthesis.[13] The feature of the Chinese character in morphology is similar to the feature of the Chinese syllable in phonetics. In other words, the character is an inherent unit in written Chinese just like the syllable is an inherent unit in spoken Chinese (although it may not be the smallest unit).

3.3. *Syllable-Timed Language*

This may be a natural result of the above two features. Chinese, as a *syllable-timed* language, produces rhythm in a sentence with the syllable as the rhythmic unit. In other words, each Chinese syllable (corresponding to one character/word) is uttered with roughly the same amount of time. In comparison, for a *stress-timed* language, syllables may take different amounts of time and the unit of rhythm (known as *beat*) is the duration between two consecutive stressed syllables. English is a typical stress-timed language and this is why native Chinese usually speak English with a different rhythm—by segmenting and producing each syllable clearly with relatively equal amounts of stress. On the other hand, a native English speaker who learns Chinese as a second language usually utters a Chinese sentence by prolonging (i.e. stressing) certain syllables while shortening others.

A related feature is that cross-syllable linking does not occur in spoken Chinese as it does in English. This phenomenon is possibly related to the above discussions that each syllable (character) is regarded as an inherent unit both in phonetics and morphology. Examples of inter-syllabic contrasts in Mandarin can be demonstrated in the following:

a1.	/çi/	(惜	xí)	"to cherish"
a2.	/çi.i/	(西夷	xī yí)	"western savage"
b1.	/çin.i/	(心儀/心仪	xīn yí)	"to admire in the heart"
b2.	/çi.ni/	(稀泥	xī ní)	"sparse mud"
b3.	/çin.ni/	(新泥	xīn ní)	"fresh mud"

If inter-syllable linking is realized in the same way as in English, a1 would sound like a2 and the pronunciations of b1, b2 and b3 could not be distinguished from each other. A Chinese speaker can distinguish each of the above cases because there is no inter-syllable linking that could cause ambiguity. Which acoustic features is this inter-syllable perception based on? Is it a phonetic contrast or a prosodic feature or even both that causes these meaning contrasts?

These still constitute the problems areas to be studied. One possible resolution is that proposed by Duanmu[14] who argues that

- Every syllable has an obligatory onset, thus the syllable /i/ should actually be /ji/.
- Every rime has two X slots, thus the vowel /i/ should become /iː/.

Therefore, the above cases can all be distinguished phonetically as follows.

a1'.	/çiː/	(惜	xí)	"to cherish"
a2'.	/çiː.jiː/	(西夷	xī yí)	"western savage"
b1'.	/çin.jiː/	(心儀/心仪	xīn yí)	"to admire in the heart"
b2'.	/çiː.niː/	(稀泥	xī ní)	"sparse mud"
b3'.	/çin.niː/	(新泥	xīn ní)	"fresh mud"

3.4. *Tonal Language*

Chinese is well known as a tonal language. In phonetics, the tone is mainly correspondent to and recognized by a specific pitch contour of the syllable vowel. In Mandarin (as well as other Chinese dialects), the precise pronunciation of each character is transcribed not only by a syllable but also by a tone. This is because the meaning contrast caused by the tone is as explicit as that by the syllable. A classic example of the 4 tones[j] in Mandarin is given as follows:

Table 4. Tones of Mandarin with exemplar syllable /ma/.

tone	Name	Pitch Contour	IPA		Pinyin		Example	Meaning
1st	Yin-Ping	high level	mɐ̋	mɐ˥	mā	ma1	媽/妈	mother
2nd	Yang-Ping	high rising	mɐ᷄	mɐ˧˥	má	ma2	麻/麻	hemp
3rd	Shang	low falling-rising	mɐ᷉	mɐ˨˩˦	mǎ	ma3	馬/马	horse
4th	Qu	high falling	mɐ᷇	mɐ˥˩	mà	ma4	罵/骂	scold
5th	Qing	neutral	mɐ	mɐ	ma	ma5	嗎/吗	question particle

Note that there are two ways of tone transcription both in IPA and Hanyu Pinyin. For Hanyu Pinyin, a diacritic mark above the nucleus vowel symbolizing the pitch contour of the tone or a tone number following the syllable is used.

The number and patterns of tones vary from one dialect to another. However, all tones can be generally classified into 4 basic types: *Ping* (平 ping2), *Shang* (上 shang3), *Qu* (去 qu4), and *Ru* (入 ru4). Each type can be further divided into two registers: *Yin* (陰/阴 yin1) and *Yang* (陽/阳 yang2). Therefore, there should

[j] The last (neutral) tone is used in a shortened and weakened syllable, which does not have a definite pitch contour. Therefore, some consider it an exceptional case and not a true tone type.

be eight tones for a complete set of Chinese tones. In rare case, more tones may exist for a particular dialect. For example, there are 9 tones in Cantonese, where an extra Ru tone called the Mid-Ru (中入 zhong1ru4) is derived from the Yin-Ru tone.

But in most cases, the number of tones reduces due to merging of two registers or the lost of some types of tones. For example, the remaining tones in Mandarin today are Yin-Ping, Yang-Ping, Shang, and Qu. Obviously, the Yin-Shang and Yang-Shang merged, as well as the Yin-Qu and Yang-Qu. As for Ru tones, Mandarin no longer contains them and the characters that were originally with Ru tones in ancient times or from other dialects, are assigned to other tones. This makes it inappropriate to recite ancient Chinese poems in Mandarin because the poetic rhythm would be wrong or lost with the reassignment of Ru tone characters into Ping tones.[k]

3.4.1. Tone Sandhi

Tones of syllables might change when forming words, and this phenomenon is referred to as *tone sandhi*. The complexity of tone sandhi rules varies from dialect to dialect. In Mandarin, the only systematic rule is the change of the 3rd tone to the 2nd tone when the 3rd tone is followed by another 3rd tone in a word. For example, the most common greeting, *ni3hao3* (你好), is pronounced *ni2hao3* in practice.

Some other Chinese dialects have more complex sandhi rules. For example, there are 7 tones in Taiwanese (or Southern Min) and each tone would change to another tone if it is not the last syllable of a word. A rather systematic sandhi rule, however, exists for Taiwanese tones. For example, a circular changing rule as 3 →2→1→7→3 exists for the 4 tones (the 3rd, 2nd, 1st, and 7th tone).[15] Observe the following examples of two-character words in Taiwanese.[11] All of the words end with the character 車/车 (IPA /t͡ɕʰia_1/[l], "vehicle"). The first syllable of each word is the same, /xuei/, but with different tones.

貨/货 /xuei_3/ "goods", 貨車/货车 [xuei_2 t͡ɕʰia_1] "a goods wagon"
火/火 /xuei_2/ "fire", 火車/火车 [xuei_1 t͡ɕʰia_1] "a train"
花/花 /xuei_1/ "flower", 花車/花车 [xuei_7 t͡ɕʰia_1] "a festooned vehicle"
會/会 /xuei_7/ "meet", 會車/会车 [xuei_3 t͡ɕʰia_1] "(two cars) crossing each other"

---

[k] Ping tones are long tones (平聲/平声 píngshēng) with longer duration and the other three types of tones are classified as short tones (仄聲/仄声 zìshēng) being shorter in duration.

[l] Note that for convenience here the number after underscore is the tone ID in Taiwanese, e.g., _1 means the 1st tone.

The single characters (left) bear their original (phonological or *canonical*) tones and the two character words (right) are specified by the changed (phonetic) tones. Thus, words with tone sandhi are more prosodic words than lexical words. As mentioned before, the word boundary in Chinese text is not at all definite. However, for dialects like Southen Min, prosodic words can be more clearly defined by judging the spoken utterance according to tone sandhi rules.

4. Traditional Syllable Structure of Mandarin

The traditional initial-final view of the Mandarin syllable structure is described in this section.

4.1. *Initial-Final Structure*

The traditional initial-final structure of Mandarin syllables is shown in Figure 1. A syllable consists of an optional *initial* (聲母/声母 shēngmǔ) and a *final* (韻母/韵母 yùnmǔ). A final in turn consists of an optional *medial* (介音 jièyīn) and a *rime* (韻/韵 yùn). The medial is also called the *rime-head* (韻頭/韵头 yùntóu), which is ahead of the *rime-belly* (韻腹/韵腹 yùnfù) and *rime-tail* (韻尾/韵尾 yùnwěi) in sequence. The rime-belly and the optional rime-tail make up the rime, which is similar to but not exactly the same as the sense of *rhyme* in linguistics (see Section 5.1).

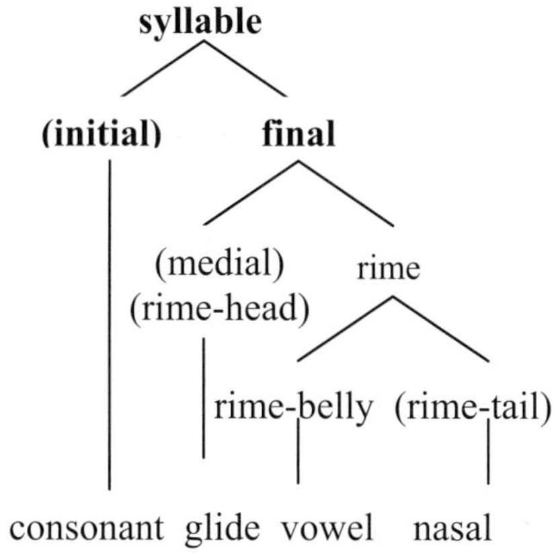

Fig. 1. Traditional initial-final structure of Mandarin syllables. The part contained in parentheses is optional. Each terminal node is a single phone if existed.

4.2. *Initials*

The initial is one of 21 consonants, which are shown below in their traditional order.

Table 5. Initials of Mandarin.

Zhuyin	ㄅ	ㄆ	ㄇ	ㄈ	ㄉ	ㄊ	ㄋ	ㄌ	ㄍ	ㄎ	ㄏ
Pinyin	b	p	m	f	d	t	n	l	g	k	h
IPA	p	p^{h}	m	f	t	t^{h}	n	l	k	k^{h}	x
Zhuyin	ㄐ	ㄑ	ㄒ	ㄓ	ㄔ	ㄕ	ㄖ	ㄗ	ㄘ	ㄙ	
Pinyin	j	q	x	zh	ch	sh	r	z	c	s	
IPA	t͡ɕ	t͡ɕ^{h}	ɕ	t͡ʂ	t͡ʂ^{h}	ʂ	ʐ/ɻ	t͡s	t͡s^{h}	s	

* ʐ and ɻ are two alternate IPA representations of the initial r.

Each consonant is specified by Zhuyin, Pinyin, and IPA. *Zhuyin* (注音 zhùyīn) is an older transcription system for Mandarin using special symbols derived from Chinese characters. Each Zhuyin symbol represents either an initial, a medial, or a rime. It must be noted that the Zhuyin system is a broad sense of phonemic transcription, which is not phonetically precise enough especially for capturing the phonetic realizations of finals. Zhuyin is till taught and formally used in Taiwan and in a few overseas Chinese communities.

4.3. *Finals*

Initials are simple and clear, while the composition of finals is more complex. Traditionally, according to the structure in Figure 1, all finals are grouped into the following classes (Numbers in parentheses indicate the number of items in the class. There are a total of 39 finals in all):

Non-compound finals (17): finals without medial

- **Mono-rime** (單韻/单韵 dānyùn) (9): monophthong without a rime-tail

Table 6. Mono-rimes of Mandarin finals.

	close (high) vowel				non-close (mid & open) vowel				
Zhuyin	ㄭ	ㄧ	ㄨ	ㄩ	ㄚ	ㄛ	ㄜ	ㄝ	ㄦ
Pinyin	i	i	u	ü	a	o	e	e	er
IPA	ɯ	i	u	y	ɐ	o	ɤ	ɛ̝	ɚ

- **Double-rime** (複韻/复韵 fùyùn) (4): diphthong

Table 7. Double-rimes of Mandarin finals.

end glides	i		u	
Zhuyin	ㄞ	ㄟ	ㄠ	ㄡ
Pinyin	ai	ei	au	ou
IPA	aɪ̯	ei̯	ɑʊ̯	ou̯

- **Nasal-rime** (聲隨韻/声随韵 shēngsuí yùn) (4): rime with a rime-tail

Table 8. Nasal-rimes of Mandarin finals.

Rime-tail	n		ŋ	
Zhuyin	ㄢ	ㄣ	ㄤ	ㄥ
Pinyin	an	en	ang	eng
IPA	an	ən	ɑŋ	əŋ

Compound finals (22): finals with a medial

There are 3 medials (rime-heads) in Mandarin:

Table 9. Medials of Mandarin.

Zhuyin		ㄧ	ㄨ	ㄩ
Pinyin	with initial	i	u	ü
	w/o initial	y	w	yu
IPA	semivowel	i̯	u̯	y̯
	approximant	j	w	ɥ
amount of compound finals		10	8	4

In most cases, the medial acts as a non-syllabic vowel (semi-vowel or pre-vowel glide) that is indicated by the IPA diacritic [̯] below each close vowel. However, some linguists regard medials as approximants especially when there is no initial ahead.[14] This is also manifested in Pinyin, in which the medials are represented by approximant-like symbols when there is no initial ahead. In most cases, however, the medial symbols used in Zhuyin and Pinyin could cause confusion because they are overlapped with the close vowels of mono-rimes (see Table 6).

Table 10. Compound finals of Mandarin (each with 3 rows in order of Zhuyin, Pinyin, and IPA).

Medial	Mono-rime				Double-rime				Nasal-rime			
	ㄚ	ㄛ	ㄜ	ㄝ	ㄞ	ㄟ	ㄠ	ㄡ	ㄢ	ㄣ	ㄤ	ㄥ
ㄧ	ㄧㄚ	ㄧㄛ		ㄧㄝ	ㄧㄞ		ㄧㄠ	ㄧㄡ	ㄧㄢ	ㄧㄣ	ㄧㄤ	ㄧㄥ
i	ia	*yo*		ie	*yai*		iao	iu	ian	in	iang	ing
i̯	i̯ɐ	i̯o		i̯ɛ	i̯aɪ̯		i̯ɑʊ̯	i̯oʊ̯	i̯ɛn	in	i̯ɑŋ	iŋ
ㄨ	ㄨㄚ	ㄨㄛ			ㄨㄞ	ㄨㄟ			ㄨㄢ	ㄨㄣ	ㄨㄤ	ㄨㄥ
u	ua	uo			uai	ui			uan	un	uang	ong*
u̯	u̯ɐ	u̯o			u̯aɪ̯	u̯ei̯			u̯an	un	u̯ɑŋ	oŋ*
ㄩ				ㄩㄝ					ㄩㄢ	ㄩㄣ		ㄩㄥ
ü				üe					üan	ün		iong
y				yɛ					yæn	yn		i̯oŋ

*ong ([oŋ]) becomes weng ([u̯oŋ]) if the initial is empty.

A compound final is composed by one of the 3 medials and one of the non-compound finals except for the 4 close vowels and /ɚ/ of the mono-rimes. The 22 compound finals are listed in Table 10. The Zhuyin symbols can be written in vertical order for their Chinese character-like feature. Note that the IPA transcription listed in the table is a phonetic representation, which may not be totally agreed upon by all linguists. However, the difference between the phonemic representation (Zhuyin) and the phonetic representation (IPA) is obvious, especially for the compound finals of nasal-rimes with schwa. There are at least three special cases for the phoneme to phone transformation as follows.

- Deletion of schwa
  For most cases the medial acts as a non-syllabic vowel but there are cases where the medial acts as a syllabic vowel in finals ([in] [un] [yn] [iŋ]) due to the deletion of original soft vowel [ə] in [ən] and [əŋ]. Take the case /ㄧㄣ/ for example:
  /i̯ ən/ → [in]
- Transformation for the case of /ㄨㄥ/
  /u̯ əŋ/ → [u̯oŋ], if the initial exists
  → [oŋ], if the initial is empty
- Transformation for the case of /ㄩㄥ/
  /y əŋ/ → [i̯oŋ]

It is interesting to note that the Pinyin is more phonetically precise than Zhuyin even though it is still coarse relative to IPA. The apparent number of compound finals are 22, however the practical number could be 23 if the different pronunciations of /ㄨㄥ/ with and without initial are regarded as two separate finals.

5. Linguistic Syllable Structure of Mandarin

A general linguistic view of the Mandarin syllable structure is described in this section.

5.1. *Onset-Rime Structure*

Two possible linguistic structures of Chinese syllables are depicted in Figure 2. The major difference is how the medial is considered in a syllable. It may be regarded as a pre-vowel glide (semivowel)[m] that acts as the head of a diphthong or triphthong, where it is classified as a nucleus (Figure 2(a)). On the other hand, a medial can also be regarded as a consonant (approximant) such that it would be grouped into the onset (Figure 2(b)). The differences between these two types of structure may be more phonological than phonetic mainly because the phonetic difference between semivowels and approximants is not noticeable in actual

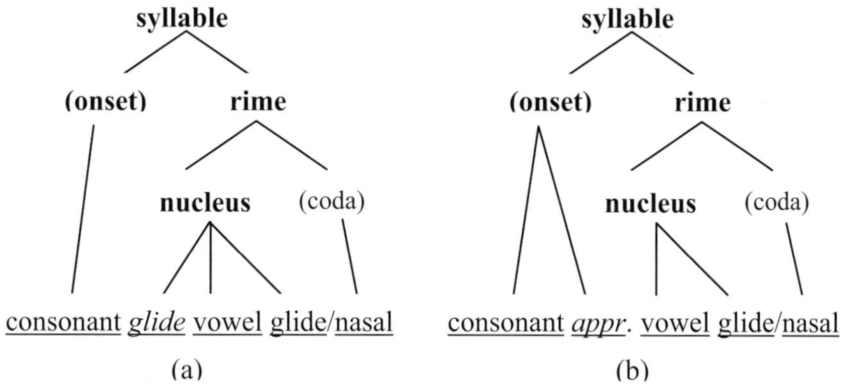

Fig. 2. Linguistic structure of Mandarin syllables. (a) A medial is regarded as a pre-vowel glide, which is a part of a nucleus (a diphthong or a triphthong). (b) A medial is regarded as an approximant, which is a part of onset with other consonants.

---

[m] Semivowels (also called semiconsonants or glides) are non-syllabic vowels that form diphthongs or triphthongs with syllabic vowels. They may be contrasted with approximants, which are similar to but closer (of mouth) than vowels or semivowels and behave as consonants.

5.2. *Consonants*

The Mandarin consonants in the well-known IPA chart[16,17] are shown in Table 11. In addition to the initial consonants, there may be three medial approximants (/j/, /w/ and /ɥ/) and one coda nasal (/ŋ/). Besides, there are only four voiced initial consonants: /m/, /n/, /l/ and /ʐ/. Also, do take note of the common non-aspirated/aspirated pairs of plosives and affricates.

Table 11. Mandarin consonants in IPA chart.

	Bilabial	Labio-dental	Alveolar	Retro-flex	Alveolo-Palatal	Palatal	Velar	Glottal
Nasal	m	ɱ	n	ɳ		ɲ	ŋ	
Plosive	p b		t d	ʈ ɖ		c ɟ	k g	ʔ
(aspirated)	p^h		t^h				k^h	
Affricate			t͡s	t͡ʂ	t͡ɕ			
(aspirated)			t͡s^h	t͡ʂ^h	t͡ɕ^h			
Fricative	ɸ β	f v	s z	ʂ ʐ*	ɕ ʑ	ç ʝ	x ɣ	h ɦ
Approximant		ʋ	ɹ	ɻ*		j	ɰ	
(labialized)						ɥ	w	
Lateral approximant			l	ɭ		ʎ	ʟ	

Where symbols appear in pairs, the one to the right represents a modally voiced consonant. Shaded areas denote articulations judged impossible. Light grey letters are other IPA symbols but not Mandarin consonants. ʐ and ɻ are two alternate representations of the voiced consonant □ /r.

5.2.1. *Zero Onset*

There has been much debate about whether the empty initial is a real phone segment. For example, Duanmu[14] argues that every syllable has an obligatory onset, which implies that the empty initial or zero onset is real. The embodiment of zero onset varies mainly according to the nucleus vowel. When the nuclei are high vowels, i.e. [i u y], the zero onset are corresponding approximants [j w ɥ], respectively. For the other nuclei, the zero onset has four variants:

- velar nasal [ŋ]
- velar fricative [ɣ]
- glottal stop [ʔ]
- glottal unaspirated continuant [ɦ]

The last three phones are shown in darker grey symbols in Table 11. Although the existence of these segments is not very clear if we observe actual speech waveforms or spectrograms, it is usually useful to assume an empty initial or zero onset for acoustic model training in speech recogniton, and this seems to result in better performance. However, to find out whether the zero onset segment actually exists requires a systematic study in acoustic phonetics.

5.3. *Vowels*

The Mandarin vowels in the IPA chart is shown in Table 12, where both vowels and semivowels are displayed. They can be grouped into three classes: close (including near-close), mid (including close-mid), and open (including near-open These names come from the initial lip-shapes of the vowels. Both stretched- and open-finals are of unrounded (or spread) lips. In contrast, both protruded- and compressed-finals are made with rounded lips. The compressed final is an endolabial rounding and the protruded final involves exolabial rounding with the lips pouted outwards. The columns of Table 13 reflect this traditional classification of finals.

Table 13 also displays a very systematic structure if we ignore the rarely-used finals (in grey), the derived transformations (in italics) and the special mono-rime final[n] /ɚ/.

Table 12. Mandarin vowels in IPA chart.

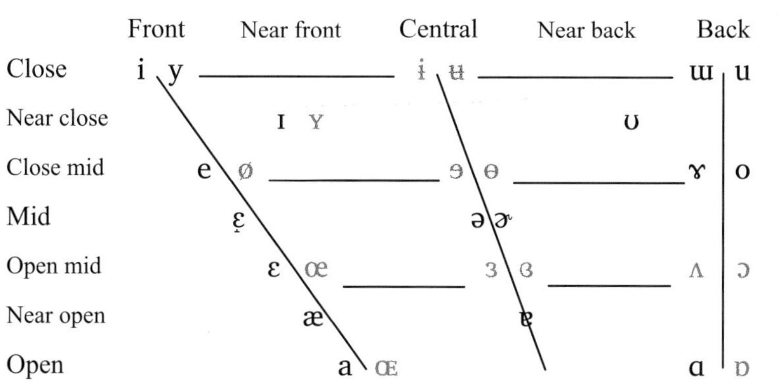

*Where symbols appear in pairs, the one to the right represents a rounded vowel.

[n] The final /ɚ/ (儿 er) is also a special syllable because no initials are allowed ahead of it.

Table 13. Mandarin finals classified by nucleus vowels (row) and lip-shapes (column).

Nucleus (Vowel)		Open			Stretched /i/			Protruded /u/			Compressed /y/			Coda	
		ZY	PY	IPA	ZY	PY	IPA	ZY	PY	IPA	ZY	PY	IPA		
Close	i	ㄭ	i	ɯ	ㄧ	i	i	ㄨ	u	u	ㄩ	ü	y	Ø	
Mid	ə	ㄛ	o	o	ㄧㄛ	io	i̯o	ㄨㄛ	uo	u̯o				Ø	
		ㄜ	e	ɤ											
		ㄝ	e	ɛ	ㄧㄝ	ie	i̯ɛ				ㄩㄝ	üe	yɛ		
		ㄦ	er	ɚ											
		ㄟ	ei	ei̯				ㄨㄟ	ui	u̯ei̯				i̯	G
		ㄡ	ou	ou̯	ㄧㄡ	iu	i̯ou̯							u̯	
		ㄣ	en	ən	ㄧㄣ	in	in	ㄨㄣ	un	un	ㄩㄣ	ün	yn	n	N
		ㄥ	eng	əŋ	ㄧㄥ	ing	iŋ	ㄨㄥ	ueng	u̯oŋ				ŋ	
		ㄨㄥ	*ong*	*oŋ*	*ㄩㄥ*	*iong*	*i̯oŋ*								
Open	a	ㄚ	a	ɐ	ㄧㄚ	ia	i̯ɐ	ㄨㄚ	ua	u̯ɐ				Ø	
		ㄞ	ai	aɪ	ㄧㄞ	iai	i̯aɪ̯	ㄨㄞ	uai	u̯aɪ̯				i̯	G
		ㄠ	ao	ɑʊ̯	ㄧㄠ	iao	i̯ɑʊ̯							u̯	
		ㄢ	an	an	ㄧㄢ	ian	i̯ɛn	ㄨㄢ	uan	u̯an	ㄩㄢ	üan	y̯æn	n	N
		ㄤ	ang	ɑŋ	ㄧㄤ	iang	i̯ɑŋ	ㄨㄤ	uang	u̯ɑŋ				ŋ	
Count		15			12			9			4			40	

* The finals in grey are rarely used. The finals in italics are derived transformations.

5.4. *Phoneme Set*

The definition of the Mandarin phoneme set may vary among different linguists. The major difference lie in how the three medials and the vowel variants in compound finals are viewed and treated. If the medials are regarded as consonants, and vowel variants as allophones, there could be as little as 39 phonemes in Mandarin as in following (where V and G stand for vowel and glide):

- 26 consonants
  21 initials + 1 zero onset + 1 coda nasal + 3 medial approximants
- 13 vowels
  9 monophthongs (mono-rimes, V) + 4 diphthongs (double-rimes, VG)

This is the traditional view of Mandarin phonemes. Note that the presence/absence of the zero onset makes the phoneme sets differ by one phoneme.

If the three medials are regarded as semivowels and all vowel variants as phonemes, the size of the phoneme set would be up to 52, as follows:

- 23 consonants
  21 initials + 1 zero onset + 1 coda nasal
- 29 vowels
  9 monophthongs (mono-rimes, V)
  15 diphthongs: 4 VG (double-rimes) + 6 GV (/i̯ɐ i̯ɛ i̯o u̯ɐ u̯o y̯ɛ/)
  + 3 GV-n (/i̯ɛ u̯a y̯æ/) + 2 GV-ŋ (/i̯ɑ u̯ɑ/)
  5 triphthongs: GVG (/i̯aɪ̯ u̯aɪ̯ u̯ei̯ i̯ɑʊ̯ i̯ou̯/)

The phoneme sets also vary in relation to the different judgments regarding allophones and phones. For example, the vowel /æ/ in /y̯æn/ (ㄩㄢ, üan) can be regarded as an extra phoneme or it may be regarded as an allophone of /a/ in /an/ (ㄢ, an).

One debatable phoneme is the mono-rime final (or unrounded back close vowel) /ɯ/, which is traditionally called *empty rime* (空韻/空韵 kōngyùn) because its Zhuyin symbol ㄭ is usually omitted in writing. However, the omission is because the only syllables it can form are connected by the following two classes of seven initials.

In fact, the symbol ㄭ itself is derived from the upside-down ㄓ of the first item in this initial group. Therefore, the syllable /ㄓㄭ/ is usually simplified as /ㄓ/, /ㄔㄭ/ as /ㄔ/, and so on. Many Sinologists used to divide the empty rime into two contrastive phonemes:

- /ʐ̩/ (old non-standard symbol /ʅ/): apical retroflex unrounded vowel, which is connected only to the retroflex class of initials in Table 14.
- /z̩/ (old non-standard symbol /ɿ/): apical dental unrounded vowel, which is connected only to the alveolar class of initials in Table 14.

Table 14. Two initial classes for the empty rime /ɯ/.

Class	Retroflex				Alveolar		
Zhuyin	ㄓ	ㄔ	ㄕ	ㄖ	ㄗ	ㄘ	ㄙ
Pinyin	zh	ch	sh	r	z	c	s
IPA	t͡ʂ	t͡ʂʰ	ʂ	ʐ/ɻ	t͡s	t͡sʰ	s

Table 15. Triplex sets in Mandarin initial.

	Alveolar	Retroflex	alveolo-palatal	Velar
unaspirated	t͡s	t͡ʂ	t͡ɕ	k
aspirated	t͡sʰ	t͡ʂʰ	t͡ɕʰ	kʰ
fricatives	s	ʂ	ɕ	x

However, some linguists[5] argue that these are two allophones of a single phoneme, with different phonetic characteristics due to their assimilation with the different classes of initials.

Another well-known example in linguistics is the set of alveolo-palatal consonants, /t͡ɕ t͡ɕʰ ɕ/ (/ㄐㄑㄒ/; /j q x/), which connect only to stretched finals (/i/ column in Table 13) and compressed finals (/y/ column in Table 13). On the contrary, the other similar triplexes shown in Table 15 (see also Table 11) appear in a complementary context, i.e., they only connect to open finals and protruded finals. Therefore, the alveolo-palatal triplex may be regarded as allophones of the other three triplexes. For example, /ɕ/ is regarded as the allophone of /s/ because the original alveolar fricative /s/ is palatalized due to the following palatal glides or vowels (/j/ /ɥ/ or /i/ /y/, i.e., the stretched- or compressed-finals) such that it is transformed phonetically into the alveolo-palatal fricative /ɕ/.

Finally, even /o ɤ ɛ̞/ (/ㄛㄜㄝ/; /o e e/) might be regarded as allophones if the rare cases of contrast syllables: (i) [o] vs. [ɤ] vs. [ɛ̞], (ii) [mo] vs. [mɤ], (iii) [lo] vs. [lɤ], and (iv) [i̯o] vs. [i̯ɛ̞], are ignored and only one syllable exist for each case.[o]

[o] This could be possible because [ɛ̞], [lo], and [i̯o] are rarely-used syllables (see Table 16) and the characters of [o] and [mɤ] are either rarely-used or onomatopoeic words, which may be replaced by other syllables.

5.5. *Number of Syllables*

The syllabification in English is usually ambiguous, which causes the number of syllables in English rather hard to determine. Contrary to English, the number of syllables in Chinese is definite due to the monosyllabic feature of the language. Furthermore, since the syllable structure in English is far more complicated than Chinese (largely due to a variety of consonant clusters before and after the nucleus vowel), the number of syllables in English is over 10 times as many as in Mandarin.

Since there are 22 initials (including empty initial/zero onset) and 39 finals, the maximum number of possible syllables in Mandarin is 858 (22*39). However, there are *systematic gaps* (for example, the complementary positions of the triplexes described in above) as well as *accidental gaps* (for example, the syllable /ʂoŋ/ ㄕㄨㄥ shong). The maximum number of Mandarin (non-tonal) syllables appearing in publications is as high as 417. However, there are at least 14 syllables that correspond only to one Chinese character each (Table 16). These syllables are also rarely used. Therefore, the syllables used in practice usually range from 403 to 413 in both speech recognition and synthesis.

Table 16. Rare Mandarin syllables and their corresponding Chinese characters.

Character	誒	诶	鞥	唷	咯	塞	剋	忒	扽	嗲	淋	欻	覅	勠
Zhuyin	ㄝˋ	ㄟˊ	ㄥ	ㄧㄛ	ㄌㄛ˙	ㄙㄟ	ㄎㄟ	ㄊㄟ	ㄉㄣˋ	ㄉㄧㄚˇ	ㄌㄩㄣˊ	ㄔㄨㄚ	ㄈㄥˋ	ㄈㄧㄠˋ
Pinyin	è	éi	ēng	yō	lo	sēi	kēi	tēi	dèn	diă	lǘn	chuā	fòng	fiào
IPA	ɛ̯	e̯i	əŋ	i̯o	lo	sei	kei	tei	dən	di̯ɐ	lyn	t͡ʂʰɥ̯ɐ	foŋ	fi̯ɑʊ

6. Conclusion

As a speech technology researcher and a native Chinese speaker, the author tried to describe the Chinese spoken language from the phonetic and phonological point of view. Therefore, this chapter simply provides an elementary review of the linguistic characteristics of spoken Chinese, including tone, syllable, initial and final, phoneme and phone. The linguistic concepts and jargons introduced in this chapter may be too simplified and arbitrary for linguists on one hand, but yet seem too abstract and non-quantitative to engineers on the other hand. This in fact manifests that there is a gap between linguistic knowledge and speech technology. Hopefully, this chapter can begin to play a role in filling the gap, so that a new direction of knowledge-rich speech technology[18] could be realized and begin to break new ground in CSLP research.

Acknowledgements

This work is a partial result of projects conducted by ITRI under the sponsorship of the Ministry of Economic Affairs of Taiwan. The author would like to thank Professor Chiu-yu Tseng who has been most earnest in bridging the gap between researchers of linguistics and engineering backgrounds. Her advice and encouragement motivated the writing of this chapter and helped in its improvement.

References

1. http://en.wikipedia.org/wiki/Chinese_Language
2. http://en.wikipedia.org/wiki/Standard_Mandarin
3. http://en.wikipedia.org/wiki/Linguistics
4. V. Fromkin, R. Rodman, and N. Hyams, *An Introduction to Language (7th Edition)*, Thomson Heinle, (2003).
5. J. Kwock-Ping Tse, *Yŭyánxué Gàilùn, (Overview of Linguistics),* (in Chinese), SanMin Book Co., Ltd., Taipei, (謝國平：語言學概論, 臺北, 三民書局), (1985).
6. J. Clark and C. Yallop, *An Introduction to Phonetics & Phonology*, Basil Blackwell, (1990).
7. D. O'Shaughnessy, *Speech Communication: Human and Machine*, New York: IEEE Press, (2000).
8. W. Shi-Yuan Wang, *Yŭyán Yŭ Yŭyīn, (Language and Speech),* (in Chinese), Crane Publishing Co., Taipei, (王士元：語言與語音, 臺北, 文鶴), (1988).
9. Official IPA Homepage, http://www2.arts.gla.ac.uk/IPA/ipa.html
10. http://en.wikipedia.org/wiki/Pe%CC%8Dh-%C5%8De-j%C4%AB
11. R. L. Cheng and S. S. Cheng, *Phonological Structure and Romanization of Taiwanese Hokkian* (in Chinese), Student Book Co., Ltd., Taipei, (鄭良偉/鄭謝淑娟：台灣福建話的語音結構及標音法，台灣學生書局), (1987).
12. Y. R. Chao, *A Grammar of spoken Chinese.* Berkeley, University of California Press, (1968).
13. C.-C. Kuo and K.-Y. Ma, "Error Analysis and Confidence Measure of Chinese Word Segmentation," *Proceedings of the 5th International Conference on Spoken Language Processing* (ICSLP'98), Sydney Australia, (1998).
14. S. Duanmu, *A Formal Study of Syllable, Tone, Stress and Domain in Chinese Languages,* Doctoral dissertation, MIT, Cambridge, Mass, (1990).
15. W.-H. Tsai, *Huìyīn Jiān Zìdiăn, (Phonemics and Lexicon),* (in Chinese), Ming-Shan Publishing Co., Taichung, Taiwan. (蔡文徽：彙音兼字典，台中名山事業行), (1972).
16. Online IPA chart with keyboard, http://www.linguiste.org/phonetics/ipa/chart/keyboard/
17. Online IPA chart with keyboard and sound, http://webmasterei.com/en/tools/ipa
18. C.-H. Lee, "From knowledge-ignorant to knowledge-rich modeling: a new speech research paradigm for next generation automatic speech recognition," in *Proc. ICSLP*, (2004).

19. http://www.ling.sinica.edu.tw/member/fulltime_08EN.html

CHAPTER 3

PROSODY ANALYSIS

Chiu-yu Tseng

Institute of Linguistics, Academia Sinica,
Academia Road 115, Taipei
E-mail: cytling@sinica.edu.tw

This chapter discusses why Mandarin speech prosody is not simply about tones and intonation, and how additional but crucial prosodic information could be analyzed. We present arguments with quantitative evidences to demonstrate that fluent speech prosody contains higher-level discourse information apart from segmental, tonal and intonation information. Discourse information is reflected through relative cross-phrase prosodic associations, and should be included and accounted for in prosody analysis. A hierarchical framework of Prosodic Phrase Grouping (PG) is used to explain how in order to convey higher-level association individual phrases are adjusted to form coherent multiple-phrase speech paragraphs. Only three PG relative positions (PG-initial, -medial and -final) are required to constrain phrase intonations to generate the prosodic association necessary to global output prosody which independent phrase intonations could not produce. The discussion focuses on why the internal structuring of PG forms prosodic associations, how global prosody can be accounted for hierarchically, how the key feature to speech prosody is cross-phrase associative prosodic templates instead of unrelated linear strings of phrase intonations; and how speech data type, speech unit selection, and methods of analysis affect the outcome of prosody analysis. Implications are significant to both phonetic investigations as well as technology development.

1. Introduction

By definition prosody is an inherent supra-segmental feature of human speech that carries stress, intonation patterns and timing structures of continuous speech. From the supra-segmental perspective, given that Mandarin tones are lexical, then by definition tone is lexical prosody. Given that intonation are syntactic, defining simple phrase and/or sentence types as an intonation unit (IU), by definition intonation is syntactic prosody. Much discussion in the literature has been devoted to tones and intonation as well as their interaction. However, in the following discussion we will argue why fluent speech prosody is not simply about tones and intonation and how fluent continuous speech prosody is in fact discourse prosody that exists in addition to and above tones and intonation. Our aim is to show how to capture and account for discourse information in addition to tones and intonation when analyzing prosody as well as the implications of discourse prosody.

What is the role of discourse in speech prosody? Our earlier investigations of Mandarin Chinese fluent spontaneous speech revealed that only 36% of syllables possess one-to-one phonological-to-phonetic correlations,[1] that is, with identifiable tone contours. The results suggest that (1) tonal specifications are not always realized in connected speech, and (2) lexical prosody makes up less than half of the output F0 contours. The same study also compared phrase intonation of identical simple declarative sentences first extracted from spontaneous conversational speech, then produced in isolated read form later. It was found that in spontaneous conversation only 20% of the declarative sentences possess declination contour patterns, 45% of them with terminal fall only, and the remaining 35% with unidentifiable contour patterns. When read as isolated single sentences, 50% of these declaratives were produced with declination contours, 27.5% with terminal falls and 22.5% with unidentifiable contour patterns.[1] Results further suggest that syntactic specifications are not always realized in connected speech either. Why are both tones and intonations so distorted in continuous speech? Rather than treating the above results as tonal and intonation variations, we argue alternatively from a top-down perspective that higher-level discourse information is involved in continuous speech and also contributes to final output prosody. In other words, instead of treating intonation units (IU) as the ultimate prosodic unit and looking for variation patterns of tones and intonations themselves, we argue that tone information (lexical prosody) and intonation patterns (syntactic prosody) combined are actually insufficient to account for fluent speech prosody. The question then is: what do discoursal information signify, how do they contribute to output prosody and how do we analyze and account for them?

Consider first what conditions would call for fluent continuous speech production. Typically, it involves expressions, narrations and/or discussions that require more than one single sentence to convey. This phenomenon is identified as an intonation group in the literature of discourse analysis. Nevertheless, the key feature of an intonation group is often not discussed. That is, intonation group is not simply unrelated intonations connected into strings, but a coherent multiple-phrase speech paragraph. It can be either a small discourse by itself or part of a larger discourse. The element that connects these sentences/phrases has to reflect their coherence; the relative between-phrase semantic association that cannot be expressed by unrelated single sentences must somehow be expressed. Therefore, some additional devices must be available in speech production for speakers to express this semantic association in order to form the coherence that connects between and among sentences. That same device is also used by the listeners to process, derive and recover intended coherence. This is essentially what speech communication is about, apart from lexical and syntactic information. Therefore, we argue that fluent speech prosody is basically about between-phrase coherence and association aside from tone and intonation. Higher-level discourse information is the governing constraint of speech prosody above lexical specifications of tones and syntactic specifications of individual phrases. Additional global semantic association is expressed not through each and every phrase intonation, but through cross-phrase global associations. Therefore, issues to be discussed are higher level discourse information, semantic coherence and cross-phrase relative associations.

However, methodological caution must be exercised to analyze prosody. Note that elicited single phrases produced in isolation (one at a time, with a full stop at the end of each phrase) would always yield nothing more than tones and canonical intonations. This is because such phrases contain no discourse information and bear no associative relationship with other phrases. Similarly, single phrases lifted out of continuous speech and studied as independent IUs only complicate the matter because they contain fragments of overall discourse prosody that canonical intonations could not accommodate. By analogy, a jigsaw puzzle could never be fully reconstructed unless both relatively large and small scales of reference are used. Likewise, fluent speech prosody is clearly NOT merely strings of independent tones and intonation, but how tones and intonations are systematically structured and modified into coherent speech paragraphs. From this more holistic and top-down perspective, we now need to tackle the following three problems: (1) identify where additional prosodic information is located in the speech signals, (2) separate discourse prosody from tones and intonation in prosody analysis, and (3) account for these through quantitative analysis.

Our previous corpus studies of read discourses have demonstrated that intonation groups in continuous speech are actually structured into three relative discourse positions to yield higher-level information, namely how and where speech paragraphs begin, continue and end. Through a multiple-phrase prosody hierarchy called Prosody Phrase Grouping (PG),[2,3] whereby PG stands for the prosodic organization that groups specified phrases through three PG-related positions: PG-initial, PG-medial and PG-final. Corresponding statistical analysis of speech corpora revealed how layered contributions cumulatively accounted for output prosody. These quantitative evidences confirm the existence of cross-phrase prosodic associations in fluent, continuous speech, and explain how higher-level discourse information is realized in cross-phrase associations. Evidences of cross-phrase templates for syllable duration patterns, intensity distribution patterns, and boundary breaks as well as a systematic account of layered contributions have been reported elsewhere.[2, 3] Hence in the following discussion we will only present analysis of F0 contour patterns to illustrate discourse prosody. Fluent speech prosody, continuous speech prosody and discourse prosody are used interchangeably. The term *prosody,* italicized, will be used in this chapter as an abbreviation to refer to all three prosody-types.

2. Phrase Grouping: Organization and Framework of Speech Paragraph

The following are prerequisites for an investigation on *prosody*. (1) Only fluent continuous speech should be used for *prosody* analysis so that the associative relationships between and among units within each grouping are available in the speech data. (2) Corpus-based approaches are preferred in order to better accommodate speech variations and facilitate quantitative analyses. (3) A top-down rather than bottom-up perspective of segmenting speech data is preferred in order for coherent, multiple-phrase speech paragraphs to emerge and better reflect the necessary prosodic associations. (4) Speech units above the IU should be available in the analysis so that analysis would not focus on individual phrase behavior. (5) Finally, methods of quantitative analysis and predictions should accommodate associative relationship and layered contributions. In other words, speech data type, speech data quantity, segmentation perspective, speech domain type, prosodic units, as well as the quantitative approach would all affect the results of prosody analysis.

The concept of phrase grouping is not just specific to Mandarin. It has been well accepted that utterances are phrased into larger constituents; together they (utterances and larger constituents) are hierarchically organized into various domains at different levels of prosodic organization.[4–6] Unfortunately this hierarchical organization is often ignored, as the necessary distinction between syntactic prosody (intonation) and discourse prosody (*prosody*) often goes unclarified. In particular, how the phrases of a PG within a hierarchy are associated and what roles IU and intonation have in *prosody,* have not received due attention.

Our other corpus studies demonstrated clearly that by adopting a top-down perspective to dissect spoken discourse, it was more than significant to take clearly audible and identifiable multiple-phrase speech paragraphs as prosodic units and work from there, instead of taking one IU at a time. By postulating speech paragraph as a higher-order node of IU, quantitative evidences of layered contributions could be found whereby corresponding cross-phrase acoustic templates could also be derived.[2,7] Our PG hierarchy specifies that lower-level units are subject to higher-level constraints while both local (phrase/sentence) and higher (discourse/global) levels of supra-segmental information contribute cumulatively to output *prosody*. *Prosody* is therefore a package of globally associated multiple phrases rather than unrelated strings of IUs. Our simple prosody framework states explicitly that by adding a higher PG level/node above phrases/IU,[7] the respective prosodic roles of PG phrases can be defined by simply three PG positions, namely, PG-initial, -medial and -final. These positions implicitly indicate the way a multiple-phrase begins, continues and ends. Compared to other attempts of automatic prosodic segmentation for continuous speech that proposed the classification of phrases into eight phrase types,[8,9] the PG framework may appear somewhat simplistic on the surface. However, the major difference lies in the sufficiency of only three PG relative positions to capture and explain cross-phrase associations in relation to higher-level discourse information; whereas the eight types remain arbitrary numbers that still assume phrases as independent, unrelated prosodic units without any relationship to each other.

Our PG framework not only specifies phrases as immediate subordinate units, but also by default specifies phrases at the same layer as subjacent sister constituents. By the same logic, PGs can further be extended as immediate constituents of a yet higher node, the discourse. Figure 1 is a schematic illustration of the framework that also includes the node *Discourse* above PGs. The 6-layer framework is from a prior work[10] and it is based on the perceived units located within different levels of boundary breaks across the speech flow. The same framework is also used for tone modeling elsewhere in this volume. The units used were perceived prosodic entities. The boundaries (not shown in Figure 1 to keep the illustration less complicated), annotated using a ToBI-based self-designed labeling system,[11] marked small to large boundaries with a set of 5 break indices (BI), B1 to B5, purposely making no reference to either lexical or syntactic properties in order to be able to study possible gaps between these different linguistic levels and units. Phrase-grouping related evidences were found both in adjustments of perceived pitch contours, and boundary breaks

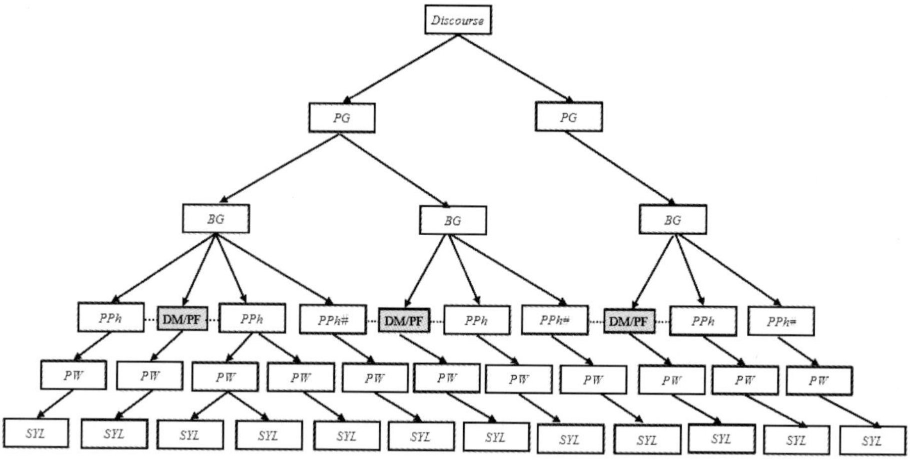

Fig. 1. A schematic representation of how PGs form spoken discourse and where DM (Discourse Marker) and PF (Prosodic Filler) are additional associative linkers.

within and across phrases, with subsequent analyses of temporal allocations and intensity distribution.[12-14]

Looking at Figure 1 from bottom up, the layered nodes are syllables (SYL), prosodic words (PW), prosodic phrases (PPh) or utterances, breath groups (BG), prosodic phrase groups (PG) and Discourse. Optional discourse markers (DM) and prosodic fillers (PF) between phrases are linkers and transitions within and across PGs, whereby DMs function as attention callers and PFs as parenthetical speech units. These constituents are, respectively, associated with break indices B1 to B5. B1's denote syllable boundaries and may not correspond to silent pauses; B2's are perceived minor breaks between PWs; B3's are breaks between PPhs; B4's, are points when the speaker takes in a full breath upon running out of breath, and also breaks at the BG layer; and B5's denote perceived trailing-to-a-final ends that occur followed by the longest break. In the framework, an IU is usually a PPh. When a speech paragraph is relatively shorter and does not exceed the speaker's breathing cycle, the top two layers BG and PG collapse into the PG layer. Both BGs and/or PGs can be immediate subjacent units of a discourse.

The most significant features of the PG framework are how it explains and accounts for variations in intonation across the speech flow and higher-level contributions to *prosody*. The multi-layer framework presented assumes an independent higher level that reflects the scope and unit of online discourse planning and processing. Put simply, the PG framework accounts for why *prŏsody* denotes *global package* prosody and how that it is formed. Hence it is feasible to assume corresponding canonical and default global templates contribute to the planning within and across units before and during speech production, very similar to cadence templates in music pieces. They also entail that the scope of cross-phrase planning and anticipation is far-reaching and does affect physiologically conditioned articulatory maneuvers at the segmental, tonal, and intonation levels. The additive and trading relationships between tones and sentence intonation were described over half a century ago as "…small ripples riding on large waves"[15] and have been well-known to the Chinese linguistic community. Our framework simply assumes that larger and higher layer(s) exist and may further be superimposed over intonation and tones as tides over both waves and ripples; the reason is to supply more and higher levels of information and discourse association.

In addition, by considering higher-level discourse information with regard to global package prosody, we are able to explain how and why global cross-phrase prosody involves an internal structuring that treats the IUs within as subjacent sister constituents, thus global prosody is therefore systematic and predictable. The framework also implies how the most significant features of discourse information dwell not in individual IUs, but in cross-phrase associations between and among them. Thus either treating *prosody* as strings of unrelated intonations or deliberating on IU behaviors regardless of their relative prosodic context would result in missing the picture of *prosody* completely.

2.1. *Speech Melody: Global F0 Patterns of PG*

A cadence template of perceived *prosody* melody is presented in Figure 3, the trajectory denotes a 5-phrase PG, preceded and followed by B4 or B where phrases within are separated by B3's. Note that a PG is featured by how it begins, holds and ends.[16] The unit of the template is a PPh, or an IU.

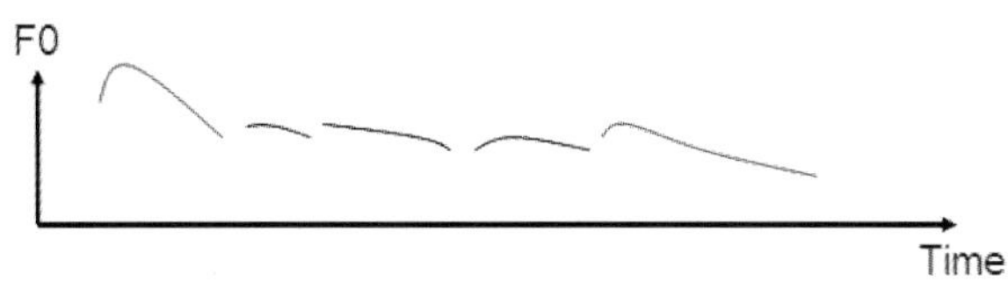

Fig. 2. Schematic illustration of the global trajectory of perceived F0 contours of a 5-PPh PG preceded and followed by B4 or B5. Within-PG units are PPh's and separated by boundary breaks B3's.

The following experiments illustrate how to analyze *prosody* from speech data.

2.1.1. *Speech data*

Mandarin Chinese speech data from Sinica COSPRO 08 were used.[17] A 30-syllable, 3-phrase complex sentence representing a short PG was constructed as a carrier paragraph with target single syllables embedded in three PG positions, namely, "△是一個常見的字，一般人常把△字掛在嘴邊，講話時動不動就會提到△. (Translation: △ is a frequently used word, people often use the word △ in their speech, and make mention of △ from time to time quite frequently.)". △ denotes the target syllable. The PG-initial, -medial and -final phrases in the carrier PG consisted of 8, 11 and 11 syllables, respectively. Note that (1) the speech paragraph is designed to remove as much lexical and semantic focus as possible and renders canonical global PG patterns, (2) the target syllables were embedded into the 1st, 6th and last syllable of the first, second and third phrases, thereby occurring at the initial, medial and final locations of the PG-initial, -medial and -final positions respectively; and (3) in spoken discourse, a multiple-phrase PG usually exceeds three phrases indicating the PG-medial phrases are often more than one. Furthermore, when compared to the reading of text passages, although such a 3-phrase complex sentence contains relatively minimal *prosody*, we believe it would still contain discourse information and at the same time offer repetitions of syllables in a uniform context for tone-*prosody* investigations. Speech data from a male (M054C) and a female (F054C) native speaker of Mandarin Chinese spoken in Taiwan were recorded in sound proof chambers. Both were instructed to read 1,300 speech paragraphs at their normal speaking rate with natural focus into microphones. The speaking rates are 289 and 308 ms/syllable for M054C and F054C, respectively. 60 files from F054C with target syllables of tone 1 were analyzed to illustrate PG effects. Analyses and predictions of F0 values were performed via parameters of the Fujisaki model (*Ap*, *Aa*).[16,18-21]

2.1.2. *Speech Data Annotation*

The speech data were manually labeled by independent transcribers for perceived boundaries and breaks (pauses), using a 5-step break labeling system corresponding to Figure 1. Pair-wise consistency was obtained from the transcribers.

2.1.3. *Higher-Level Discourse Information in Prosody Analysis*

The goal of the following two experiments is to look for phrase components and accent components that also contain additional higher-level information from the

PG hierarchy. The Fujisaki model operates on IU to derive F0 curve tendency of both the syllables and the phrase.[16,18-21] Therefore, the three phrases are first analyzed independently then compared in relation to their relative PG positions. Accent components (Aa) and phrase components (Ap) are first separated by a lowpass-filter[22-24] then calculated independently, whereby Aa predicts more drastic local F0 variations over time and Ap predicts smoother global F0 variations over time. The steps involved are first, analyzing these two components at the PPh level, that is, F0 curve tendency of individual phrases. Next, the same two components are analyzed in relation to higher-level PG information, that is, PPh's are classified by the three PG positions and analyzed respectively. Following that, a comparison of whether differences exist among the three PG positions is made. Lastly, we add contributions from the PPh level and the PG level to derive cumulative predictions and these predictions are then compared with speech data to test the validity.

2.1.3.1. Experiment 1

The aim of this experiment is to investigate (1) whether patterns of Ap could be derived from speech data, (2) whether there is evidence of interaction between Ap predictions from the PPh level and Ap predictions from higher-level PG positions, and (3) whether the evidence found could predict pitch allocation in the speech flow. Two levels of the PG framework are examined. According to the definition of PG hierarchy, all three PPh's at the PPh level are subjacent subordinate constituents of PG which are sister constituents to each other; each PPh is still an independent IU without any higher-level PG information. At the immediate upper PG level, each PPh is then assigned a PG role in relation to the three PG positions. Thus, at the PPh level, each of the three phrases is assumed as an independent prosodic unit. The magnitude of Ap's is generalized and assigned to predict the Ap within, while ignoring higher-level PG information. Next, at the PG level, the PG effects are considered where different values of Ap are assigned to predict phrase components according to where each of the three PPh's is located in PG-positions. Finally, prediction accuracy between PPh's with and without PG effects are compared with the original speech data for validity.

First, speech data are analyzed to provide prediction references. Ap values are extracted from the speech data and their characteristics examined. The respective range and distribution of extracted Ap values in each PG-position from the speech data are illustrated in Figure 2 and Table 1. Next, the characteristics of distribution in each PG-position are generalized and used for subsequent Ap predictions. Using a step-wise regression technique, a linear model is developed and modified for Mandarin Chinese to predict Ap. The hierarchical PG organization of prosody levels (the aforementioned system of boundaries and units) is used to classify Ap at the levels of the framework. Moving from the PPh level upwards to the PG level, we examine how much was contributed by the PG level. All of the data are analyzed using DataDesk™ from Data Description, Inc. Two benchmark values are used to evaluate how close predicted values are when compared with values derived from original speech data. The first benchmark is percentage of sum-squared errors at the lower PPh layer. The PG framework assumes that errors at a lower level are due to lack of information from higher levels. Therefore, residual errors (RE), defined as the percentage of sum-squared residues (the difference between prediction and original value) over sum-squared values of original speech data, are then included into the immediate higher-level for further predictions. If predictions improve from a lower level upward, the difference between two subjacent levels are considered as contributions from the immediate higher level.

Table 1. Range of values of Ap from phrases produced by female speaker F054C in three PG-related positions.

PG Position	Ap range
-Initial	0.959 ~ 0.499
-Medial	0.615 ~ 0.04
-Final	0.678 ~ 0.093

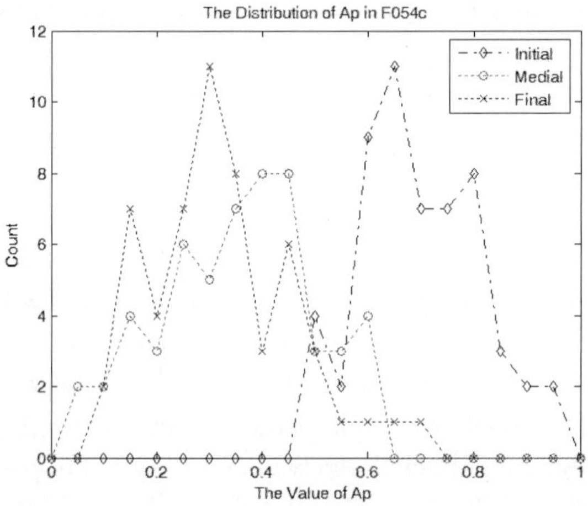

Fig. 3. A schematic representation of the distribution of the Ap's of speaker F054C where the horizontal axis represents values of Ap and the vertical axis represents number of Ap occurrence.

Results

Table 2 illustrates the coefficients of Aps from PPhs in a PG. At the PPh level, when each PPh is treated as an independent prosodic unit, the expected cell mean is at 0.4595. However, at the PG level, where the PPh's were classified by the three PG positions, namely, PG-initial, -medial and -final, the expected cell mean with PG effects are 0.6984, 0.3536 and 0.3265, respectively. In contrast to PG-initial PPh, the Ap of PG-final PPh is shortened. The coefficients reflect a clear distinction between PG-initial and PG-final prosodic phrases.

Table 2. The expected cell mean of predictions with and without the PG effect. The top row shows the expected cell mean value when PG effects are ignored. The bottom row displays the expected cell mean values when PG effect is considered.

Expected Cell Mean at the PPh level (without PG effects):	0.4595		
Expected Cell Mean at the PG level (with PG effect):	*PG Initial*	*PG Medial*	*PG Final*
	0.6984	0.3536	0.3265

When each IU (PPh in our framework) is analyzed independently, results revealed that correct predictions were only 40.15% and 59.85% were errors. After considering PG effects one level upward of the prosodic hierarchy, predictions were improved by 24.84%. Cumulative prediction accuracy was 65%. Ap adjustments with respect to PG positions provide further evidence of how prosodic units and layers function as constraints on the Ap in the speech flow and how higher-level prosodic units may be constrained by factors that differ from those constraining lower-level units. If higher-level information is ignored, inputs of prediction would be insufficient.

Finally, by adding up the predictions of the PG layer, we are able to derive a prediction of F0 curve allocation for all three phrases. Comparisons between predictions with and without PG effects are then made with the original speech data. Figures 4 and 5 show these comparisons. The final cumulative predictions indicate that patterns of F0 allocation in Mandarin speech flow cannot be adjusted by the PPh level alone. Input from the PG level must be included. Moreover, these results are also evidence demonstrating that the PPh is constrained and governed by higher-level information (PG). As illustrated in Figure 5, the distinction between PG-initial and PG-final is most obvious. If PG effect is neglected, the accuracy will diminish.

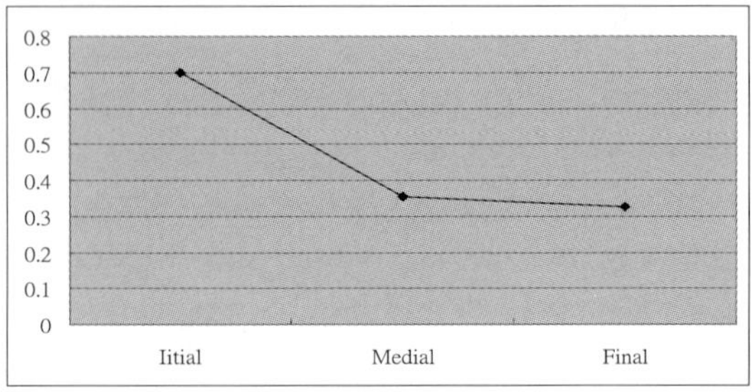

Fig. 4. A schematic representation of the patterns of phrases after PG effect is taken into consideration. Note how the PG-initial and PG-final groups possess the sharpest distinction.

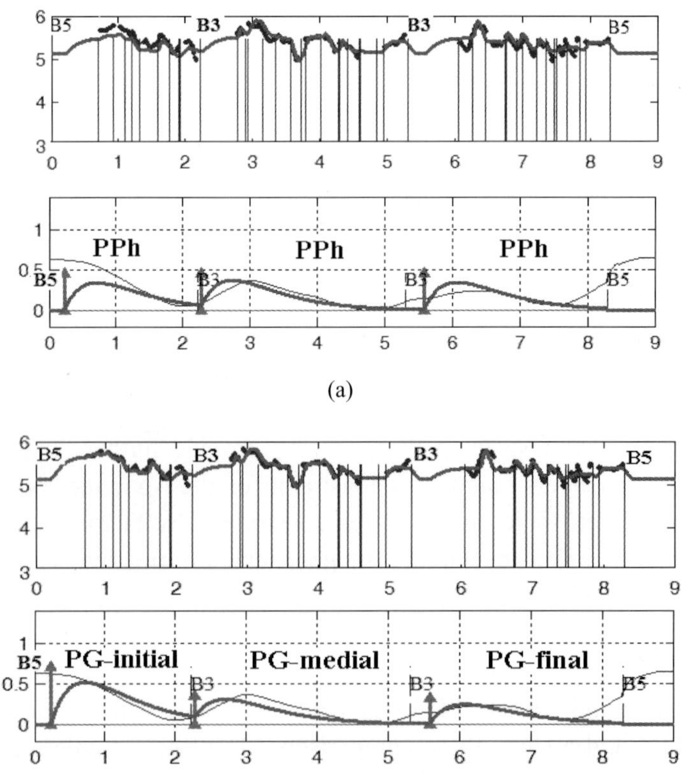

Fig. 5. Comparisons of Ap predictions without PG-effect (a) and with PG-effects (b) to the original speech data. The darker line in the upper panels shows F0 plotting of 3 phrases, while the lighter line indicates 3 predicted F0 curves; vertical lines denote syllable boundaries. In the lower panels, the thin line shows comparisons of lowpassed F0 curve, while the thicker line indicates predicted phrase components. Each arrow on the lower panels denotes an Ap.; their heights represent Ap values. In each panel, the vertical axis represents logarithmic value of F0 curve; while the horizontal axis represents temporal code.

In summary, the PPh layer only constitutes around 40% of the prosody output while higher-level discourse information at the PG layer puts in an additional 25%. Together, the PPh and PG layer make up a total of 65% of prosody output. Note however, that since the PG layer is higher in the prosody hierarchy and commands all phrases under it, its effect is not to be ignored. Without it, there would be no discourse prosody. By definition of the PG hierarchy, the remaining 35% of contributions should come from the lower syllabic (tonal) and word (both lexical and prosodic) levels. Working upwards in the prosody hierarchy, tonal information certainly is not the most significant contributor of fluent speech prosody.

2.1.3.2. Experiment 2

We assume that accent components (Aa, in the Fujisaki model) are also governed by the PG hierarchy as specified by our PG framework. Hence, the SYL, PW and PPh levels in the PG framework should all contribute to output prosody, respectively. The aim of this second experiment is to investigate the contributions of the SYL to PPh prosodic levels from an analysis of Aa. A similar regression technique is used to calculate contributions from each prosodic level to the final output in terms of magnitude of Aa from the SYL, PW and PPh levels.

At the syllable layer, the method adopted is to approach the F0 curve of each syllable by one accent component. In other words, each syllable is connected to one Aa, which makes us unable to extract SYL Aa accurately at the current stage. Nevertheless, the SYL, PW and PPh level models are postulated as follows:

The SYL Layer Model:

$$\text{Aa} = \text{constant} + \text{SYL} + Delta1. \tag{1}$$

SYL in the above represents syllable type. Factors considered include 23 syllable categories (excluding target syllables), and 5 tones (4 lexical tones and 1 neutral tone).

The PW Layer Model:

$$Delta1 = f(PWLength, PWSequence) + Delta2. \tag{2}$$

Each syllable is labeled with a set of vector values; for example, (3, 2) denotes that the unit under consideration is the second syllable in a 3-syllable PW. The co-efficient of each entry is then calculated using linear regression techniques identical to those of the preceding layer.

The PPh Layer Model:

$$Delta2 = f(PPhLength, PPhSequence) + Delta3. \quad (3)$$

Each syllable is labeled with a set of vector values; for example, (8, 4) denotes that the unit under consideration is the fourth syllable in an 8-syllable PPh. The coefficient of each entry is calculated using linear regression techniques identical to those of the preceding layer.

Results

Table 3 shows contributions and cumulative prediction accuracy at each prosodic level from Aa analyses.

Table 3. Cumulative accuracy of Aa predictions from SYL, PW and PPh levels.

Prosodic Level	Contribution	Cumulative Accuracy
SYL	19.89%	19.89%
PW	1.1%	20.99%
PPh	5.07%	25.16%

If the factors considered include only 5 tones without syllable categories, the accuracy of Aa prediction is about 12.5%. When syllable categories are included, the cumulative accuracy is improved to a cumulative 19.89%. From the SYL layer upwards to the PW level, cumulative prediction is improved to 20.99%. Finally at the PPh level, the cumulative accuracy of Aa prediction is 25.16%.

2.2. *Speech Rhythm, Intensity Distribution and Boundary Breaks.*

In addition to analysis of speech melody presented in the F0 analyses in Section 2.1, we have reported elsewhere similar systematic and layered contributions from the PG hierarchy to global *prosody* in speech rhythm, intensity distribution and boundary break investigations with quantitative evidences.[2,7,14,25-27] In Chapter 4, syllable duration patterns are based on patterns derived at both the SYL and PW levels from our PG framework. Detailed discussions of cross-phrase syllable duration templates exhibiting similar pre-boundary lengthening-shortening pattern of the last pentameter at the PPh and PG levels are available.[2,7,14,27] The pentameters are also PG-position conditioned, consistent across Taiwanese Mandarin and Beijing Putonghua,[28] where cumulative contributions were accounted for using the same modified linear regression analyses.[2,25–27] That is, quantitative evidences provided a global cross-phrase rhythmic pattern with three templates for PG-initial, -medial and -final PPh's, respectively; the patterns interact with syllable durations at PPh/IU, PW and SYL levels and cumulatively add up to output speech rhythm. Relative intensity distribution patterns were found significant only from the PPh level and above, i.e., the longer an IU/PPh is, the more energy it requires initially. Significant difference in intensity distribution patterns were found between PG-initial and PG-final PPh.[2,25–27] Finally, we found similar PG effects across boundary breaks as well,[2,25–27] thus proving why pauses across speech flow are PG-conditioned and therefore constitute systematic and significant prosody information. Without discourse context, pauses are at best concomitant syntactic components of major and minor phrases. With higher-level discourse constraints, at least three degrees of pauses and boundary effects are necessary. Discourse boundary breaks are systematic and predictable as well.[14]

3. Discussion

The most important features of the PG framework are (1) how it captures cross-phrase prosodic associations, (2) the way it explains why tones and independent intonation contours are insufficient to account for *prosody*, and (3) the way it accounts for why discourse information is crucial. Through the PG hierarchy and only three relative PG positions – the PG-initial, -medial and -final – the hierarchy specifies subjacent individual PPhs their respective but relative prosodic roles to generate the necessary coherence in multiple-phrase speech paragraphs. We note from the experiments presented above that once a PPh becomes a PG constituent, it is no longer an independent IU but is required to adjust its intonation contour pattern to convey discourse association. The PG-initial and PG-final positions specify two respective PPhs to retain intonation contours differing in relative starting point, slope, with boundary effects and boundary breaks. However, though both the PG-initial and PG-final PPhs may exhibit declination, the degree and slope of relative declination differs and final-lengthening-and-weakening only occurs at the PG-final PPh; the PG-medial position specifies all other PPhs in between to flatten intonation signaling a continuation. The relative positions are dependent on each other and the specifications are a package. Hence the phrases in continuous speech must be considered collectively in relation to one another instead of individually one at a time. The PG framework also explains systematically why intonation variations in fluent continuous speech are not random at all, but predictable in addition to lower-level syntactic specifications, why speech melody cannot be one intonation declination followed by another, and why pair-wise contrast between the PG-initial and -final phrases is significant. The global melodic pattern is only present when all PPhs under a grouping are present in the specified linear order; reverting the intonations of the PG-initials and PG-finals would not render acceptable *Prosody*. Note also that in the experiments presented above, the selected 3-PPh complex sentence represents a relative unmarked representation of a canonical prosodic group but still provides a default PG prototype on which a multiple-phrase paragraph of up to 12 PPhs (as in COSPRO) could be extended. In other words, between a PG-initial and -final PPh, depending the speaking rate, up to 10 PPhs could be accommodated with relatively flatter intonation to signal continuation. This explains why only 20% to 50% of intonation contours could be identified from read and spontaneous speech reported in Section 1.[1] The PG framework also presents a canonical form for multiple-phrase speech paragraphs while stress, focus, and emphasis could all be treated as subsequent add-ons. Without PG specifications, independent individual intonations from continuous speech are "distorted" to almost unlimited variations, even data driven classifications could be arbitrary by nature.[8,9]

The above results demonstrate that in fluent speech, higher-level information is involved in the planning of speech production; speech units are no longer discrete intonation units. Larger multi-phrase prosodic units reflecting higher-level discourse organization are in operation during the production of fluent speech. Hence methodologically, an IU produced without discourse context does not provide global prosody information. Removing fragments from fluent continuous speech and analyzing microscopic phonetic or acoustic details across segments and/or syllables would not yield systematic accounts towards the structures involved in the semantic coherence as a package, either. To test the validity of the PG framework, we have also constructed a mathematical modular acoustic model that could be used directly in text-to-speech development.[25,27]

Furthermore, we argue that though global melody and rhythm may differ from one language to another, higher-level discourse prosody is not language-specific. Any attempt at prosody organization and modeling should incorporate language-specific patterns of duration allocation and intensity distribution in addition to F0 contours, but maintain the discourse coherence and association.

4. Conclusion

From the evidence presented, we argue that Mandarin speech prosody is not simply about tones and intonation. Any prosody organization of fluent connected speech should go beyond intonation strings and instead accommodate higher-level discourse information above both lexical and syntactic prosody to account for the relative cross-phrase relationship of speech paragraphs. All three acoustic correlates, namely F0, duration and amplitude, should be accounted for with respect to phrase grouping, along with at least 3 degrees of boundary breaks. Global F0 contour patterns alone are NOT sufficient to represent and characterize the features of *prosody*. Rather, the roles of syllable duration adjustment with respect to temporal allocation over time as well as boundary effects, and intensity distribution with reference to overall cross-phrase relationships should also be included in prosody analysis. Boundary breaks across speech flow are also linguistically-significant components in spoken discourse and deserve a legitimate place in any *prosody* framework. We believe that together with cross-phrase F0 associations, syllable duration patterns, intensity distribution patterns and boundary breaks, a major part of speech melody, rhythm, loudness distribution as well as various degrees of lengthening and pauses, collectively reflect the domain, unit and to quite an extent, the strategies of how speech is planned and processed. In short, systematic template and boundary breaks are used by the speaker for planning in the speech production process, and as processing apparatuses by the listener as well. What speakers deliver through prosody, by maneuvering available acoustic vehicles, are also what listeners utilize to process and predict incoming speech signals. Furthermore, we suggest that both global cross-phrase template fitting and filtering as well as partial local unit recognition should be integrated to facilitate recognition of fluent speech.[2,3]

To summarize, the most significant features of the PG framework are the following: (1) the framework specifies how with three PG relative positions, PG-initial, -medial and -final, subjacent individual PPhs assume their respective places under a PG and adjust both lexical and syntactic specifications in order to generate global *prosody*. (2) The framework provides a crucial explanation as to why intonation variations in fluent continuous speech are not random, and to what extent PPhs may or may not preserve their phrase intonations. (3) PG effects are evidenced via quantitative analyses at all acoustic correlates, namely the F0 contour, syllable duration and intensity distribution. (4) Boundary breaks are also PG-governed, systematic and predictable, and are therefore legitimate units of discourse prosody as well. (4) Finally, each layer of the PG hierarchy contributes to output prosody and cumulatively adds up to the final prosody output.[2,3] Last but not least, the presented analysis and mathematical models[2,25,26] could also be applied to enhance technological and computational applications, in particular, speech synthesis and unlimited text-to-speech systems.

Future directions include on-going research and preliminary evidence regarding how, in addition to semantic coherence, speech paragraphs form a discourse through the associations of between-paragraph units.[10,29] These between-units include discourse markers (DM) and prosodic fillers (PF), as shown in the schematic representation of discourse prosody in Figure 1. In other words, an even higher node exists that conveys discourse information between and among paragraphs; the paragraphs in turn become subordinate subjacent discourse units.

Acknowledgements

This work was supported by the Academia Sinica Theme Project "New Directions for Mandarin Speech Synthesis: From Prosodic Organization to More Natural Output" (2003-2005). Experiments and statistical analyses were carried out by Zhao-Yu Su. Formatting was assisted by Yun-Ching Cheng.

References

1. C. Tseng, *An Acoustic Phonetic Study on Tones in Mandarin Chinese,* (2nd ed.) Institute of Linguistics, Academia Sinica, Taipei, Taiwan, (2006), CD-rom.
2. C. Tseng, S. Pin, Y. Lee, H. Wang and Y. Chen, "Fluent Speech Prosody: Framework and Modeling", *Speech Communication (Special Issue on Quantitative Prosody Modeling for Natural Speech Description and Generation)*, Vol. 46:3-4, (2005), pp.284-309.
3. C. Tseng, "Higher Level Organization and Discourse Prosody", Invited keynote paper, *TAL 2006 (The Second International Symposium on Tonal Aspects of Languages)*, April 27-29, 2006, La Rochelle, France, (2006), pp.23-34.
4. S. Shattuck-Hufnagel, A. Turk, "A prosody tutorial for investigators of auditory sentence processing", *Journal of Psycholinguist Research*, 25(2), (1996), p.193.
5. C. Gussenhoven, "Types of Focus in English?" In Daniel Buring, Matthew Gordon and Chungming Lee (eds.) *Topic and Focus: Intonation and Meaning: Theoretical and Crosslinguistic Perspectives*, Dordrecht: Kluwer, (1997).
6. E. Selkirk, "The interaction of constraints on prosodic phrasing", In Merle Horne (ed.) *Prosody: Theory and Experiment*, Dordrecht: Kluwer, (2000), pp.231-262.
7. C. Tseng, S. Pin, Y. Lee, "Speech prosody: issues, approaches and implications", in G. Fant, H. Fujisaki, J. Cao and Y. Xu Eds. *From Traditional Phonology to Mandarin Speech Processing, Foreign Language Teaching and Research Process*, (2004), pp.417-438.
8. H. Singer. and M. Nakai, "Accent Phrase Segmentation Using Transition Probabilities Between Pitch Pattern Templates", *Proc. EUROSPEECH'93*, (1993), pp.1767-1770.
9. M. Nakai, H. Singer, Y. Sagisaka. and H. Shimodaira, "Automatic prosodic segmentation by *F0* clustering using superpositional modeling", *ICASSP95*, (1995). 624–627.
10. C. Tseng, C. Chang, and Zh. Su, "Investigation F0 Reset and Range in relation to Fluent Speech Prosody Hierarchy", *Technical Acoustics,* Vol. 24, (2005), 279-284.
11. C. Tseng, and F. Chou, "A prosodic labeling system for Mandarin speech database" *Proceedings of the 14th International Congress of Phonetic Science,* (Aug. 1-7, 1999), San Francisco, California, (1999), 2379-2382.

12. C. Tseng, "The prosodic status of breaks in running speech: Examination and Evaluation", *Proceedings of the 1st International Conference on Speech Prosody 2002*, Aix-en-Provence, France, (2002.), pp.667-670.
13. C. Tseng, "Towards the organization of Mandarin speech prosody: Units, boundaries and their characteristics", *Proceedings of the 15th International Congress of Phonetic Science* (ICPhS-2003), Barcelona, Spain, (2003), pp.599-602.
14. C. Tseng, and Y. Lee, "Speech rate and prosody units: Evidence of interaction from Mandarin Chinese", *Proceedings of the International Conference on Speech Prosody 2004*, Nara, Japan, (2004), pp.251-254.
15. Y. R. Chao, *A Grammar of Spoken Chinese*, University of California Press, Berkeley and Los Angeles, California, (1968).
16. H. Fujisaki, S. Ohno, W. Gu, "Physiological and physical mechanisms for fundamental frequency control in some tone languages and a command-response model for generation of the F_0 contour", *Proceedings of International Symposium on Tonal Aspects of Languages with Emphasis on Tone Language*, (2004.), pp. 61-64.
17. C. Tseng, Y. Cheng and C. Chang, "Sinica COSPRO and Toolkit—Corpora and Platform of Mandarin Chinese Fluent Speech", *Proceedings of Oriental COCOSDA 2005*, Jakarata, Indonesia, (2005), pp.23-28.
18. H. Fujisaki, S. Ohno, O. Tomita, "Automatic parameter extraction of fundamental frequency contours of speech based on a generative model", *Proceedings of 1996 International Conference on Signal Processing*, vol. 1, (1996.) pp.729-732.
19. H. Fujisaki, S. Ohno, C. Wang, "A command-response model for F_0 contour generation in multilingual speech synthesis", *Proceedings of the 3rd ESCA/COCOSDA International Workshop on Speech Synthesis*, (1998.), pp.299-304.
20. C. Wang, H. Fujisaki, S. Ohno, T Kodama, "Analysis and synthesis of the four tones in connected speech of the Standard Chinese based on a command-response model", *Proceedings of the 6th European Conference on Speech Communication and Technology*, vol. 4, (1999), pp.1655-1658.
21. C. Wang, H. Fujisaki, R. Tomana, S. Ohno, "Analysis of fundamental frequency contours of Standard Chinese in terms of the command-Response model and its application to synthesis by rule of intonation", *Proceedings of the 6th International Conference on Spoken Language Processing*, vol. 3, (2000), pp.326-329.
22. H. Mixdorff, H. Fujisaki, "Automated Quantitative Analysis of F_0 Contours of Utterances from a German ToBI-Labeled Speech Database", *Proceedings of the '97 Eurospeech*, vol.1, (1997), pp.187-190.
23. H. Mixdorff, "A Novel Approach to the Fully Automatic Extraction of Fujisaki Model Parameters", *Proceedings of ICASSP 2000*, vol. 3, (2000), pp.1281-1284.
24. H. Mixdorff, Y. Hu, and G. Chen, "Towards the Automatic Extraction of Fujisaki Model Parameters for Mandarin", *Proceedings of Eurospeech 2003*, (2003).
25. S. Pin, Y. Lee, Y.Chen, H. Wang and C. Tseng, "Mandarin TTS system with an integrated prosody model", *Proceedings of the 4th International Symposium on Chinese Spoken Language Processing*, Hong Kong, (2004), pp.169-172.
26. C. Tseng and Y. Lee, "Intensity in relation to prosody organization", *Proceedings of the 4th International Symposium on Chinese Spoken Language Processing*, Hong Kong, (2004), pp.217-220.

27. C. Tseng and B. Fu, "Duration, Intensity and Pause Predictions in Relation to Prosody Organization", *Proceedings of Interspeech 2005*, Lisbon, Portugal, (2005), pp.1405-1408
28. 鄭秋豫、李岳凌、蔡蓮紅、鄭雲卿 （排印中）"兩岸口語語流韻律初探—以音強及音節時程分佈為例" *首屆海峽兩岸現代漢語問題學術研討會論文集*. 上海商務印書館.
29. C. Tseng, Z. Su, C. Chang, and C. Tai, "Prosodic filers and discourse markers—Discourse prosody and text prediction." *TAL 2006 (The Second International Symposium on Tonal Aspects of Languages)* April 27-29, La Rochelle, France, (2006).

CHAPTER 4

TONE MODELING FOR SPEECH SYNTHESIS

Sin-Horng Chen†, Chiu-yu Tseng‡, and Hsin-min Wang§

† *Department of Communication Engineering, National Chiao Tung University, Hsinchu*

‡ *Institute of Linguistics and §Institute of Information Science, Academia Sinica, Taipei*
E-mail: schen@mail.nctu.edu.tw, cytling@sinica.edu.tw, whm@iis.sinica.edu.tw

Tone modeling for speech synthesis aims at providing proper pitch, duration, and energy information to generate natural synthetic speech from input text. As speech processing technology progresses rapidly in recent years, some advanced tone modeling techniques for Mandarin text-to-speech (MTTS) are proposed. In this chapter, two modern tone modeling approaches for Mandarin speech synthesis are discussed in detail.

1. Introduction

Prosody is an inherent supra-segmental feature of human speech. It carries stress, intonation patterns and timing structures of continuous speech which, in turn, determine the naturalness and understandability of an utterance. For speech synthesis, the general prosody modeling approach is to build a model, done in a *training* phase that defines the relationship between the hierarchical linguistic structure of Chinese texts and the hierarchical prosodic structure of the corresponding Mandarin speech. In another phase, the *test* phase, this model is first used to map the hierarchical linguistic structure extracted from the input text onto the hierarchical prosodic structure, after which the model is used to generate prosodic features from prosodic structure training phase. This approach regards linguistic features as contributing factors that control the variations of prosodic features, and it is organized into different levels: first by using the hierarchical linguistic structure, and then mapping this to the hierarchical prosody structure. The employment of hierarchical linguistic structures in the creation of this type of model is common as it a well-grounded and conventional means of text analysis. The availability of many well-developed linguistic techniques and tools, such as lexicons, word and part of speech (POS) taggers, and parsers makes the adoption of this approach convenient. The linguistic structure hierarchy may be composed of various levels including character, lexical word, word chunk, phrase, clause, sentence, paragraph levels and so on. Complementing this is the hierarchical prosody structure which corrects the inappropriateness of directly using the linguistic structure to control the generation of prosodic features. A hierarchical prosody structure may contain the following levels[2]: syllable, prosodic word, intermediate phrase, intonational phrase/breath group, and prosodic phrase group levels.

In prosody modeling for Mandarin text-to-speech (MTTS), there are three main concerns. One is the hierarchical linguistic structure of Chinese text that describes the relationship between linguistic constituents of different levels. Currently, the sentence syntax of a language is generally accepted as the hierarchical linguistic structure of that language. Beyond these syntactic factors, semantics, emotional information, and higher-level factors such as discourse,[2] should be considered. Another concern is the mapping process from the hierarchical linguistic structure to the hierarchical prosody structure. This has been the major focus of prosody modeling for speech synthesis in recent years. Prosodic phrasing and break labeling are two related problems in this field.[14,22] The third concern is the generation of prosodic features from the hierarchical prosody structure. The approach employed most frequently at this time is to superimpose the patterns of the different hierarchy levels.[11] The pattern of each level can be obtained by simply assigning a deterministic average pattern extracted from a speech database or by using a linear/nonlinear regression method to combine the effects of the various influencing factors.

In the early days of MTTS, prosody modeling was performed using relatively simple linguistic and prosodic structures.[18] Only low-level linguistic features, like the syllable and the word, were used. The prevalent approach at that time was to find rules to map these low-level contextual features, extracted from the phonetic structure of the syllable, tone and word, to syllable/word-level prosodic features including pitch contour pattern, energy level pattern, initial/final or syllable duration pattern, and inter-syllabic pause duration. The estimated prosodic feature patterns were lastly superimposed with a sentence-level intonation pitch pattern selected from a pattern pool or assigned by rules. The generated synthetic speech typically sounds highly artificial and nothing like natural human speech.

In recent years, as speech processing technology progresses at a rapid pace, more sophisticated linguistic and prosodic structures have been made available. Along with this, a number of advanced prosody modeling techniques for MTTS have been proposed.[9,11,19–21] In the following sections, we discuss in detail two of these prosody modeling methods which are statistically based.

2. A Five-layer Tone Modeling Method for MTTS

Chapter 3 of this book demonstrates that phrase grouping is essential for characterizing the prosody of fluent Mandarin speech.[1] Figure 1 shows the hierarchical organization framework for multiple phrase grouping. Starting from the top, the layered nodes are: phrase groups (PG), breath groups (BG), prosodic phrases (PPh), prosodic words (PW), and syllables (SYL). These constituents are associated with the break indices B5 to B1, respectively.[2]

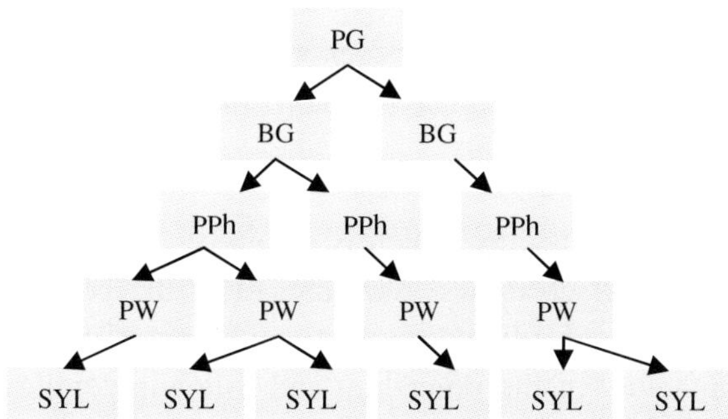

Fig.1. A schematic representation of the hierarchical organization for multiple phrase grouping of perceived units and boundaries.

Evidence of prosodic phrase grouping has been found in both the adjustments of F_0 contours and the temporal allocations within and across phrases. Thus, F_0, duration, and intensity should be considered simultaneously when modeling tone behavior in Mandarin speech. In this section, we discuss tone modeling for the synthesis of Mandarin speech and the development of an MTTS system that integrates prosody processing modules, such as duration modeling, F_0 modeling, intensity modeling, and break predictions.

2.1. *Duration Modeling*

In Tseng,[3] the analysis of rhythmic patterns in Mandarin speech reveals that syllable duration is not only affected by the current syllable's constitution, but also by the prosodic structures of the upper layers of the hierarchy, namely PW, PPh, BG, and PG. These factors allow us to design a layered model for syllable duration.

The analysis is conducted on a corpus of female read speech of 26 long paragraphs and discourses in text form. This corpus consists of 11,592 syllables in total. Initially, the speech data are aligned automatically with Initial and Final phones using the hidden Markov model toolkit (HTK), and then labeled manually by trained transcribers to indicate the perceived prosodic boundaries or break indices (BI).

2.1.1. *Intrinsic Statistics of Syllable Duration*

A layered model is used to estimate syllable duration. At the SYL-layer, the following linear model is adopted:

$$\begin{aligned}\text{Syllable intrinsic duration} = {} & const_d + CTy + VTy + Ton + PCTy + PVTy \\ & + PTon + FCTy + FVTy + FTon \\ & + 2 - \text{way factors of the above factor} \\ & + 3 - \text{way factors of the above factor,}\end{aligned} \tag{1}$$

where $const_d$ is a reference value, which is dependent on the corpus; *CTy*, *VTy*, and *Ton* represent the offset values associated with the consonant type, vowel type, and tone of the current syllable, respectively; the prefixes *P* and *F* represent the corresponding factors of the preceding and following syllable, respectively; the 2-way factors consider the joint effect of two single-type factors; and the 3-way factors consider the joint effect of three single-type factors. There are C_2^9 (=36) 2-way factors in total. The 3-way factors that have a negligible influence on syllable duration are not considered. Therefore, only these three 3-way factors are considered – the combination of consonant types, the vowel types, and the tones of the preceding, current, and following syllables. As a result, there are 49 factors in total. As reported in Tseng,[3] the SYL-layer model can account for about 60% of syllable duration.

2.1.2. *The Effect of the Layered Prosodic Structure*

As shown in Figure 2, a syllable's duration is affected by its position within a PW. Note that the final syllable in the PW tends to be longer than the other syllables.

$$DurS = \text{Syllable's intrinsic duration} + f_{PW}\,(\text{PW length, position in PW}). \tag{2}$$

The PW-layer speeds up the rhythm by subtracting a value derived from Figure 2.

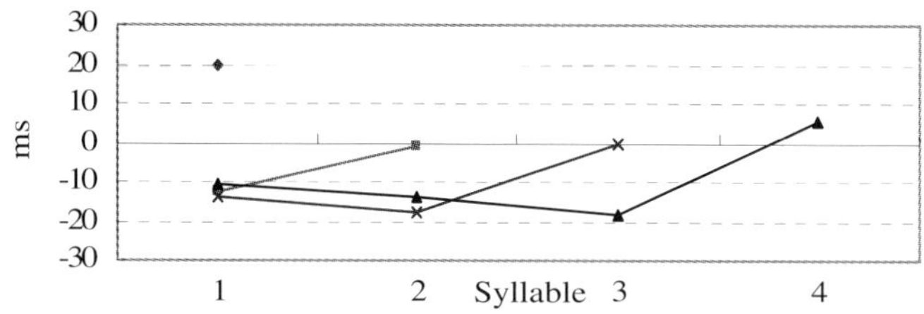

Fig.2. Rhythmic patterns in the PW-layer.

Similarly, the PPh-layer affects syllable duration in the way the PW-layer does. In the BG- and PG-layers, the length of the prosodic unit gets longer and more complicated, but the perceived significance only exists in the initial and final PPh units. Therefore, we model the BG-layer's effect as the effect of the initial and final PPhs in that layer. The overall model is thus formulated as:

$$\begin{aligned} DurS = &\text{ Syllable's intrinsic duration} + f_{PW}\text{(PW length, position in PW)} \\ &+ f_{PPh}\text{(PPh length, position in PPh)} \\ &+ f_{IFPPh}\text{(Initial/Final PPh length, position in PPh)}, \end{aligned} \quad (3)$$

where *DurS* denotes the modeled syllable's duration; and $f_{PW}(\cdot)$, $f_{PPh}(\cdot)$, and $f_{IFPPh}(\cdot)$ denote the portions of the syllable's duration affected by the function of the length of the PW, the PPh, and the initial or final PPh in the PG, respectively, together with the target syllable's position within them.

2.2. F_0 Modeling

In the literature, we find many F_0 models of sentence/phrasal intonation being proposed. Among these, we picked the well-known Fujisaki model as the production model for F_0.[4] The model connects the movements of the cricoid cartilage to the measurements of F_0 and is thus based on the constraints of human physiology. It is therefore reasonable to assume that the model can accommodate F_0 output in different languages. Successful applications of the model on many language platforms, including Mandarin, have been reported.[5,6]

In the case of Mandarin Chinese, *phrase* commands are used to produce intonation at the phrase level, while *accent* commands are used to predict lexical tones at the syllable level.[7] Phrasal intonations are superimposed on sequences of lexical tones. The interaction between these two layers does cause modifications of the F_0 during production of the final output. The superimposing of a higher level onto a lower level leaves room for even higher levels of F_0 specification to be superimposed and created. To handle this dynamism, we implement the hierarchical organization framework of phrase/intonation-grouping in the Fujisaki model by adding a PG layer over phrases.[8,9] The F_0 patterns of phrase grouping can hence be derived.

2.2.1. *Building the Phrasal Intonation Model*

A linear model for the phrase command of the Fujisaki model is adopted as follows:

$$\begin{aligned}\text{Phrase command Ap} = {} & const_{Ap} + \text{coeff1} \times \text{pause} \\ & + \text{coeff 2} \times pre\_phr + \text{coeff3} \times f_0\text{min} \\ & + f_{PPh}(\text{Phrase command position in PPh}) \\ & + f_{IFPPh}(\text{Initial/Medial/Final PPh}).\end{aligned} \tag{4}$$

where $const_{Ap}$ is a reference value, which is dependent on the corpus; *pause* is the preceding speechless portion associated with the current phrase command; *pre_phr* is the accumulated phrase command response of previous phrase commands, as the response of the current phrase command reaches its peak; f_0min is the minimum fundamental frequency of the utterance; $f_{PPh}(\cdot)$ reflects the position in PPh that the related phrase command occupies; and f_{IFPPh} is for the PG intonation which has a significant effect only on the first and last PPh units.

Figure 3 shows a comparison between the F_0 prediction/production of a PG and the original intonation.

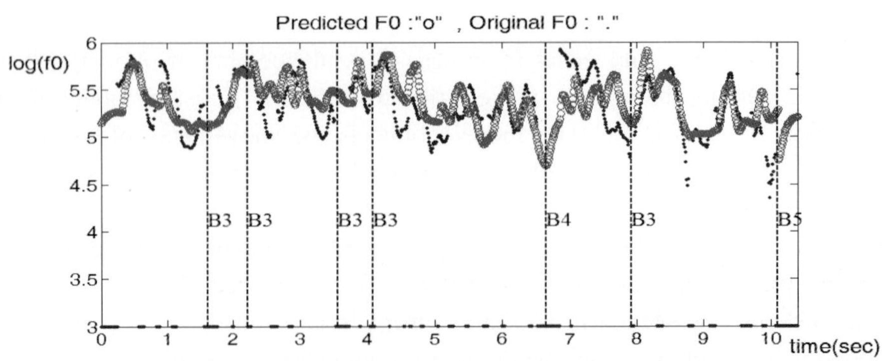

Fig. 3. The simulation result of global intonation modeling of a PG. The thin dotted line represents the original F_0 contour, while the thick line composed of circles represents the predicted contour.

2.3. *Intensity Modeling*

Segmental root mean square (RMS) values are first derived using the ESPS toolkit. For each initial and final phone in a syllable, the averaged RMS value is calculated by using 10 equally spaced frames in the target segment time span. To eliminate the difference in levels between paragraphs, possibly caused by slight changes during recording, the RMS values within each paragraph need to be normalized to NRMS (normalized RMS) values. Intensity modeling is much the same as duration modeling[10]:

$$\begin{aligned} IntS = &\ \text{Syllable's intrinsic intensity} \\ &+ f_{PW}\,(\text{PW length, position in PW}) \\ &+ f_{PPh}\,(\text{PPh length, position in PPh}) \\ &+ f_{IFPPh}\,(\text{Initial/Final PPh length, position in PPh}), \end{aligned} \tag{5}$$

where $f_{PW}(\cdot)$, $f_{PPh}(\cdot)$, and $f_{IFPPh}(\cdot)$ denote the portions of syllable intensity affected by the function of the length of PW, PPh, and initial or final PPh in PG, respectively, together with the target syllable's position within them. The syllable's intrinsic intensity is modeled by:

$$\begin{aligned} &\text{Syllable's intrinsic intensity} \\ &= const_i + CTy + VTy + Ton + PCTy + PVTy + PTon \\ &+FCTy + FVTy + FTon + 2 - \text{way factors of the above factor.} \end{aligned} \tag{6}$$

2.4. *The TTS System*

The above duration, F_0, and intensity modeling methods are not only useful for analyzing prosodic patterns in Mandarin speech, but can also be used to predict prosodic parameters for synthesizing speech according to text input. Given a large annotated speech database, the predicted duration, F_0, and intensity parameters can be used to select appropriate units for direct concatenation, and to minimize the signal processing requirement. Much research on unit selection have been published, most of which rely on the existence of large annotated speech databases. Since these huge databases are usually unavailable and difficult to obtain, rather than reviewing existing methods, we present a promising approach that rapidly adapts a TTS system to new voices by applying the above statistical analysis and modeling framework.

Two features of the Chinese writing system – that it consists of mono-syllabic logographic characters and that there are only 1,292 distinct tonal syllables – make syllables a convenient and reasonable choice as concatenative units.

However, the duration, F_0, and intensity models described above are based on the PG structure, and not the syllable structure. We therefore need a specially designed database so that the syllable-based TTS system can be implemented to use these models.[11] For this purpose, the time-domain pitch-synchronous overlap-add (TD-PSOLA)[12] method is used to perform prosody modification in the TTS system.

2.4.1. *Speech Database*

Recorded by a native female speaker in a sound-proof room, the database comprises 1,292*3 Mandarin tonal syllable tokens. Each of the 1,292 syllables is embedded in a phrase of a three-phrase *carrier* sentence (i.e. a PG of 3 PPhs) in the initial, medial, and final positions, respectively. So, for each syllable, three tokens were collected.

2.4.2. *Duration Adjustment*

Since the TTS database and the modeling corpus are obtained from different speakers, the absolute duration predicted by the duration model needs to be adjusted, while the rhythmic patterns in the PG organization should be retained. Because the initial, medial, and final syllables were originally collected from the same positions of the PG, their durations should not be changed. The duration of the remaining syllables, which were originally the first syllable of a PW at the medial position of a medial PPh of a 3-PPh PG, should be modified to satisfy the rhythmic pattern in PG organization. In this way, to synthesize a PG of m characters (or syllables), the duration of the i-th syllable is given by:

$$DurS_i^* = \begin{cases} OriDur(S_i), & i = 1, \frac{m}{2}, m \\ OriDur(S_i) - DF_i, & 1 < i < \frac{m}{2}, \frac{m}{2} < i < m, \end{cases} \tag{7}$$

where $OriDur(S_i)$ is the corresponding syllable-token's original duration, and DF_i is an offset factor calculated by:

$$\begin{aligned} DF_i = M_{TC}^d / M_{MC}^d \times [& f_{PW}(\text{PW length, position in PW}) - f_{PW}(2,1) \\ & + f_{PPh}(\text{PPh length, position in PPh}) - f_{PPh}(11,6) \\ & + f_{IFPPh}(\text{Initial/Final PPh length, position in PPh})], \end{aligned} \tag{8}$$

where M^d_{TC} and M^d_{MC} are, respectively, the mean of syllable duration in the TTS corpus and the training corpus; and $f_{PW}(\cdot)$, $f_{PPh}(\cdot)$, and $f_{IFPPh}(\cdot)$ are the same as those in Equation (3), which are estimated from the training corpus.

2.4.3. *F_0 Adjustment*

In the implementation of F_0 adjustment, the comparison is confined to the first F_0 peak of the predicted PG intonation and the average F_0 of the first syllable from the carrier sentence. The phrase control mechanism for phrase components in the Fujisaki model is defined as[4]:

$$G_p(t) = \begin{cases} \alpha^2 t \times \exp(-\alpha t), & \text{for } t \geq 0 \\ 0, & \text{for } t < 0. \end{cases} \tag{9}$$

In Equation (9), the time required to reach the maximum is $1/\alpha$. Therefore, the maximum value of the phrase response $Ap \times G_p(t)$ is:

$$P = Ap \times \alpha \times \exp(-1). \tag{10}$$

From Equation (10), it is clear that P is proportional to Ap when α remains a constant.

We can estimate the adjustment value ΔAp of Ap according to the difference between the average F_0, denoted as P_c, of the first syllable from the carrier sentence and the first F_0 peak, denoted as P_p, of the predicted PG intonation:

$$\Delta Ap = (P_c - P_p) \times \exp \times \alpha^{-1}. \tag{11}$$

Then, every predicted phrase command must be adjusted according to ΔAp. Note that the adjustment does not change the shape of the intonation, but the level moves closer to that of the carrier sentence database.

2.4.4. *Intensity Adjustment*

Intensity adjustment is realized in the same way as duration adjustment. If m syllables need to be synthesized, the intensity of the i-th syllable is given by

$$IntS_i^* = \begin{cases} OriInt(S_i), & i = 1, \frac{m}{2}, m \\ OriInt(S_i) - IF_i, & 1 < i < \frac{m}{2}, \frac{m}{2} < i < m, \end{cases} \tag{12}$$

where $OriInt(S_i)$ is the corresponding syllable-token's original intensity and IF_i is an offset factor calculated by

$$\begin{aligned} IF_i = M_{TC}^i / M_{MC}^i \times [& f_{PW}(\text{PW length, position in PW}) - f_{PW}(2,1) \\ & + f_{PPh}(\text{PPh length, position in PPh}) - f_{PPh}(11,6) \\ & + f_{IFPPh}(\text{Initial/Final PPh length, position in PPh})], \end{aligned} \tag{13}$$

where M_{TC}^i and M_{MC}^i are, respectively, the mean of the syllable intensity in the TTS corpus and the training corpus; and $f_{PW}(\cdot)$, $f_{PPh}(\cdot)$, and $f_{IFPPh}(\cdot)$ are the same as those in Equation (5), which are calculated from the training corpus.

2.4.5. *Break Prediction*

Prosodic boundaries and break indices are predicted by analyzing the syntactic structure of the text to be synthesized. Basically, the break indices can be predicted according to the punctuation. For a long PPh, we can insert an extra B3 to segment the PPh into two PPh units. PW is a fundamental prosodic unit, while the lexical word (LW) is a basic syntactic unit in the sentence structure. Therefore, PW prediction is the first step towards building a prosody model from a piece of text. According to Chen,[14] only 67.5% of PWs and LWs are found to be coincident in corpora tagged with prosodic structure information. The accuracy of predicting PWs by grouping LWs using statistical approaches is approximately 90%.

2.4.6. *System Flowchart*

Given a piece of text, the prosodic boundaries and break indices are predicted based on an analysis of the text's syntactic structure. The PG hierarchical structure and the pronunciation (i.e. the syllable sequence associated with the text) are also generated. The duration and intensity of all syllables are then assigned by the respective duration and intensity models, while the F_0 contours of all phrases are generated by the intonation model. The output of text processing is stored in a predefined XML document. Finally, the TD-PSOLA method is used to perform prosody modification, and the TTS system generates the concatenated waveform.

2.5. *Discussion and Conclusion*

The TTS system introduced in this section attempts to synthesize fluent speech in long paragraphs based on a specially-designed, moderate-sized, syllable-token database. It is believed that an integrated prosodic model that organizes phrase groups into related prosodic units to form speech paragraphs would significantly improve the naturalness of the output of an unlimited TTS system. The collection of mono-syllables to provide further prosodic information has also been shown.

3. A Tone Modeling Approach Using Unlabeled Speech Corpus

Traditionally, prosody modeling had been conducted using well-annotated speech corpora with all prosodic phrase boundaries and break indices being properly labeled in advance. This usually involved significant manual effort, making the process labor-intensive. Despite the effort, there is still the problem of inconsistency by human annotators, particularly if the databases are huge. So, most corpora used in prosody modeling are not large. Recently a number of alternative prosody modeling studies for syllable duration and pitch contour of Mandarin speech using unlabeled speech corpora were performed.[19–20] In this section, one method of statistical tone modeling for Mandarin pitch contour using an unlabeled speech corpus is discussed. This is an extension of the method proposed by Chiang.[21] Its basic idea is to use a statistical model to consider a few major factors that control the variation of syllable pitch contour. In this way, the relationship between the observed values of pitch contour patterns in the speech corpus and the major factors that affect it can therefore be created automatically.

3.1. *Review of Previous Works*

Two prosody modeling studies for Mandarin speech using unlabeled speech corpora were proposed recently.[19–21] One caters for syllable duration,[19] while the other for syllable pitch contour.[20] These are briefly reviewed in the following subsections.

3.1.1. *A Statistical Syllable Duration Model*[19]

The syllable duration model is designed based on the idea of taking each affecting factor as a multiplicative companding factor (CF) to control the compression and stretch of syllable duration. Five major influencing factors including tone, base-syllable, speaker-level speaking rate, utterance-level speaking rate, and prosodic state are considered. Prosodic state is conceptually regarded as the state in a prosodic phrase. The model is expressed by

$$Z_n = X_n \gamma_{t_n} \gamma_{y_n} \gamma_{j_n} \gamma_{l_n} \gamma_{s_n}, \tag{14}$$

where Z_n and X_n are the observed and normalized durations of the n-th syllable; γ_p is the CF of the affecting factor p; t_n, y_n, j_n, l_n and s_n correspondingly represent the lexical tone, prosodic state, base-syllable, utterance, and speaker of the n-th syllable; and X_n is modeled as a normal distribution with mean μ and variance v. Further considered in this model are the three Tone 3 patterns[15,16] of falling-rising, middle-rising and low-falling to increase the number of tones to 7. Trained by an expectation maximization (EM) algorithm with prosodic state being treated as hidden, this model is then validated by using a speech corpus containing paragraphic utterances of 5 speakers, leading to the following observations:

- The variance of syllable duration reduces significantly as the influences of these five affecting factors are eliminated.
- The influences of 7 tones and 411 base-syllables can be directly obtained from their CFs.
- The prosodic state is linguistically meaningful.
- The three Tone 3 patterns turn out to be well-labeled.
- The CFs of utterances show that long texts are always uttered quickly while short texts are less predictable and pronounced at arbitrary speeds.
- Both initial and final durations are propositionally related to syllable duration except when the syllable is largely shortened or lengthened. In these two extreme cases, the final duration is usually more significantly compressed or stretched.

3.1.2. *A Statistical Syllable Pitch Contour Model*[20]

The syllable pitch contour model is built based on the same principle as in syllable duration modeling. The mean and shape of syllable pitch contour are separately modeled by considering a different set of factors. For pitch mean, contributing factors considered include tones of the previous, current, and following syllables; the initial and final classes of the current syllable; the prosodic state of the current syllable; and the speaker's level shift and dynamic range scaling factors. For pitch shape, factors considered include lexical tone combinations,[15,16] the initial and final classes of the current syllable, the prosodic state for the effects of high-level linguistic features, and the pitch level shifting effect of speakers.

The same 5-speaker speech corpus is used to evaluate the pitch mean and shape models. The following conclusions were obtained:

- The variances of pitch mean and shape parameters reduce significantly as the effect of their respective influencing factors are eliminated.
- Many tone sandhi rules, including the famous 3-3 tone sandhi rule, can be observed from the CFs of tone combinations.

- The prosodic state is linguistically meaningful.
- A change of the prosodic state index, from large to small, indicates a possible phrase boundary. An effective rule-based method to detect minor and major prosodic phrase boundaries is therefore proposed.

3.2. F_0 Modeling

The proposed syllable pitch contour model considers the following three major influencing factors: lexical tone, prosodic state and inter-syllabic coarticulation. Here, prosodic state is used to account for the influences of all high-level linguistic features and can be conceptually regarded as the state of the current syllable remaining in a prosodic phrase.

3.2.1. *The Proposed Syllable Pitch Contour Model*

The model is formulated based on the assumption that all influencing factors are combined additively and can be expressed by

$$\mathbf{x}_{k,n} = \mathbf{y}_{k,n} + \chi_{t_{k,n}} + \chi_{p_{k,n}} + \chi^{f}_{c_{k,n-1},tp_{k,n-1}} + \chi^{b}_{c_{k,n},tp_{k,n}} \tag{15}$$

where $\mathbf{x}_{k,n}$ and $\mathbf{y}_{k,n}$ are vectors of four orthogonal expansion coefficients representing, respectively, the observed and normalized pitch contours of the n-th syllable in utterance k; $\chi_{t_{k,n}}$ is the affecting pattern of the current tone $t_{k,n} \in \{1,2,3,4,5\}$; $\chi_{p_{k,n}}$ is the affecting pattern of prosodic state $p_{k,n} \in \{0,1,2,\cdots,P\}$; $c_{k,n} \in \{0,1,2,\cdots,C,C+1\}$ is the coarticulation state of the inter-syllable location between syllables n and $n+1$ with $c_{k,-1}=0$ and $c_{k,N_k}=C+1$ representing the states of utterance beginning and ending, respectively; $tp_{k,n} \in \{(1,1),(1,2),\cdots,(5,5)\}$ is the tone pair $(t_{k,n},t_{k,n+1})$; $\chi^{f}_{c_{k,n-1},tp_{k,n-1}}$ is the forward affecting pattern of the tone pair $tp_{k,n-1}$ with coarticulation state $c_{k,n-1}$; $\chi^{b}_{c_{k,n},tp_{k,n}}$ is the backward affecting pattern of the tone pair $tp_{k,n}$ with coarticulation state $c_{k,n}$. Here, we note that $\chi^{f}_{c_{k,-1},tp_{k,n-1}} = \chi^{f}_{0,t_{k,1}}$ and $\chi^{b}_{c_{k,N_k},tp_{k,N_k}} = \chi^{b}_{C+1,t_{k,N_k}}$. Notice that we directly assign the prosodic state $p_{k,n}=0$ for those syllables whose F0 can not be detected. Figure 4 displays the relationship of syllable pitch contours and these influencing factors.

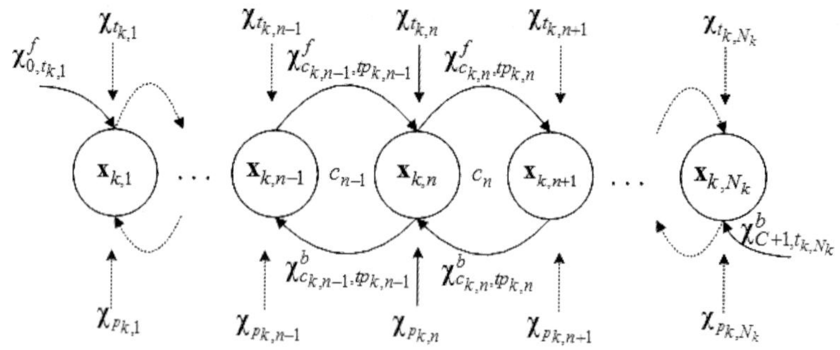

Fig. 4. The relationship of syllable pitch contours and influencing factors.

The normalized pitch shape $\mathbf{y}_{k,n}$ is modeled as a Gaussian distribution $N(\mathbf{y}_{k,n};\boldsymbol{\mu},\mathbf{R})$, or equivalently $\mathbf{x}_{k,n}$ is modeled by

$$N(\mathbf{x}_{k,n};\boldsymbol{\mu}+\chi_{t_{k,n}}+\chi_{p_{k,n}}+\chi^{f}_{c_{k,n-1},tp_{k,n-1}}+\chi^{b}_{c_{k,n},tp_{k,n}},\mathbf{R}). \tag{16}$$

Here, both the prosodic state, representing the prosodic feature variation in a prosodic phrase, and the coarticulation state, representing the degree of coupling between two consecutive syllables, are treated as hidden. To help determine these states, two additional probabilistic models are introduced. One is the coarticulation state model $P(\mathbf{i}_{k,n}\mid c_{k,n})$ which describes the relationship of the coarticulation state $c_{k,n}$ and a set of acoustic/linguistic features $\mathbf{i}_{k,n}$ extracted from the vicinity of the inter-syllable location following syllable n. Another is the prosodic state model $P(s_{k,n}\mid p_{k,n})$ which describes the relationship of the prosodic state $p_{k,n}$ and a set of syntactic features $s_{k,n}$ extracted from the syntactic tree of the sentence containing syllable n.

In this work, the model of $c_{k,n}$ involves four features and is expressed by

$$P(\mathbf{i}_{k,n}\mid c_{k,n})=P(PD_{k,n}\mid c_{k,n})P(PM_{k,n}\mid c_{k,n})P(IW_{k,n}\mid c_{k,n})P(IT_{k,n}\mid c_{k,n}) \tag{17}$$

where $\mathbf{i}_{k,n}=(PD_{k,n},PM_{k,n},IW_{k,n},IT_{k,n})$; $PD_{k,n}$ and $PM_{k,n}$ are the pause duration and punctuation mark following syllable n respectively; $IW_{k,n}$ indicates whether the inter-syllable location between syllables n and $n+1$ is an inter-word or intra-word location; and $IT_{k,n}$ is the general type of consonant of the $n+1$ syllable.

The prosodic state model describes the relationship of $p_{k,n}$ and some features representing the role of the current syllable n in the syntactic tree.[17] In this study, 31 syntactic features are selected based on the contextual information relating to the syllable. They are categorized according to the position of the current syllable in a word: beginning-of-word (BW), within-word (WW), ending-of-word (EW), and single-syllable-word (SW), as listed in Table 1. The model is then expressed by

$$P(\mathbf{s}_{k,n} \mid p_{k,n}) = P(\mathbf{s}_{k,n} = sr_i \mid p_{k,n}) \tag{18}$$

where sr_i is a syntactic role of the current syllable.

Table 1. The syntactic roles used in the modeling of $p_{k,n}$.

position in a word	• within-word (WW) • beginning-of-word (BW) • end-of-word (EW) • single-syllable-word (SW)
type of the preceding phrase at the same level in the tree	• single-syllable- word (PSW) • 2 or 3-syllable word (PW23) • 4 or more-syllable word (PW4) • phrase boundary without PM (PPB) • phrase boundary with PM (PPBPM)
type of the following phrase at the same level in the tree	• single-syllable- word (FSW) • 2 or 3-syllable word (FW23) • 4 or more-syllable word (FW4) • phrase boundary without PM (FPB) • phrase boundary with PM (FPBPM)
sr_i	(PSW| PW23| PW4| PPB| PPBPM)_BW 5 combinations
	EW_(FSW| FW23| FW4| FPB| FPBPM) 5 combinations
	(PSW| PW23| PW4| PPB| PPBPM)_SW _(FSW| FW23| FW4| FPB| FPBPM) 25 combinations
	WW 1 combination

3.2.2. *Experimental Results*

The performance of the proposed pitch modeling method is assessed using a Mandarin speech database containing the single-speaker read speech of a female professional announcer. Its texts are all short paragraphs composed of several sentences selected from the Sinica Tree-Bank Corpus.[17] All sentences of the Tree-Bank corpus are manually parsed to extract their syntactic tree structures. A total of 380 utterances with 52,192 syllables make up the entire database.

In the evaluation, we set the numbers of prosodic states and coarticulation states to be 16 and 8, respectively. After sufficiently good training, the covariance matrices of the original and normalized syllable pitch feature vectors were

$$\mathbf{R}_x = \begin{bmatrix} 2487 & -64 & -145 & 8 \\ -64 & 373 & 27 & -40 \\ -145 & 27 & 69 & -71 \\ 8 & -40 & -71 & 19 \end{bmatrix} \Rightarrow \mathbf{R}_y = \begin{bmatrix} 35 & -11 & 2 & -1 \\ -11 & 82 & 7 & -5 \\ 2 & 7 & 32 & 1 \\ -1 & -5 & 1 & 11 \end{bmatrix}$$

$$|\mathbf{R}_x| = 7.93\times10^8 \qquad |\mathbf{R}_y| = 8.90\times10^5$$

The determinant of the covariance matrix of the normalized pitch feature vector was reduced significantly as compared with that of the observed vector.

Figure 5 shows the affecting patterns and their F_0 mean values of 16 prosodic states, while Table 2 displays the state transition probabilities. Figure 6 illustrates three typical example sentences. As shown in Figure 5, States 1, 2, 3 and 4 have low and flat patterns and hence tend to be located at the trail of a prosodic phrase (because of the declination effect of F_0). High probabilities of $P(EW\_FPB\,|\,p)$ and $P(EW\_FPBPM\,|\,p)$ for p=2, 3 and 4, observed from the prosodic state model, also confirm that they appear very often at the ending portions of syntactic phrases and sentences. Moreover, high transition probabilities of 2-2, 2-3, 3-2, 3-3, 4-3 and 4-4 observed from the state transition table (Table 2) show that the low and flat trail patterns of prosodic phrases (as in Figure 6(c)) commonly appear. In contrast, States 15, 14 and 12 have high and rising-falling patterns and hence tend to be located at the beginning of prosodic phrases, demonstrating the reset phenomenon. This finding can be further confirmed by the high probabilities of

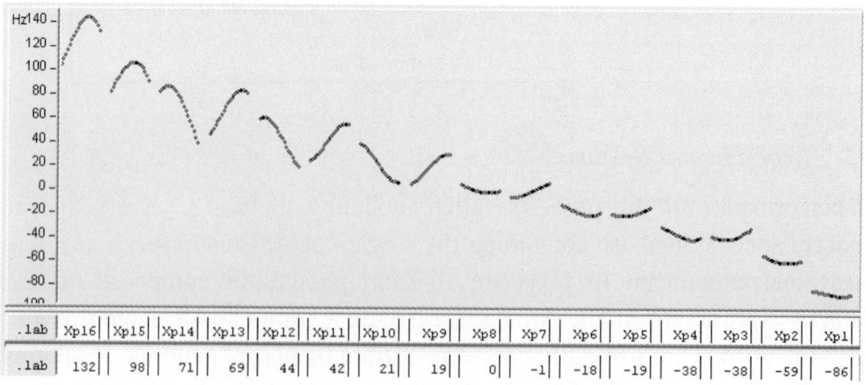

Fig. 5. The affecting patterns and their F0 mean values of 16 prosodic states.

Table 2. Prosodic state transition probability $P(p_n \mid p_{n-1})$.

Pn-1\Pn Bigram	0	1	2	3	4	5	6	7	8	9	10	11	12	13	14	15	16
0	0.02	**0.68**	0.02	0.02	0.05	0.02	0.03	0.02	0.02	0.02	0.02	0.02	0.02	0.02	0.02	0.02	0.02
1	0.08	**0.12**	**0.17**	0.10	0.05	0.10	0.02	**0.12**	0.02	0.10	0.01	0.04	0.01	0.02	0.00	0.01	0.01
2	0.00	0.08	**0.24**	**0.14**	0.09	**0.12**	0.02	0.10	0.02	0.08	0.01	0.05	0.01	0.02	0.01	0.01	0.00
3	0.00	0.04	**0.22**	0.09	**0.22**	0.09	0.10	0.06	0.04	0.03	0.02	0.02	0.02	0.02	0.01	0.00	0.00
4	0.00	0.02	0.09	**0.18**	0.04	**0.20**	0.02	**0.17**	0.01	**0.11**	0.02	0.06	0.02	0.02	0.01	0.01	0.00
5	0.00	0.02	**0.11**	0.07	**0.23**	0.09	**0.19**	0.06	0.08	0.04	0.04	0.03	0.02	0.01	0.01	0.01	0.00
6	0.00	0.01	0.06	**0.17**	0.03	**0.21**	0.02	**0.19**	0.02	0.11	0.02	0.06	0.03	0.03	0.02	0.02	0.01
7	0.00	0.01	0.04	0.04	**0.14**	0.07	**0.21**	0.05	**0.17**	0.05	0.07	0.04	0.04	0.03	0.02	0.01	0.00
8	0.00	0.01	0.04	**0.11**	0.06	**0.19**	0.07	**0.16**	0.06	0.10	0.03	0.07	0.03	0.03	0.02	0.02	0.01
9	0.00	0.01	0.02	0.02	0.06	0.05	**0.15**	0.06	**0.18**	0.07	**0.12**	0.06	0.07	0.05	0.05	0.04	0.01
10	0.00	0.01	0.04	0.07	0.09	**0.14**	**0.12**	**0.12**	0.10	0.09	0.05	0.05	0.04	0.04	0.02	0.02	0.01
11	0.00	0.00	0.02	0.02	0.04	0.04	0.09	0.05	**0.15**	0.05	**0.16**	0.06	**0.11**	0.06	0.07	0.07	0.02
12	0.00	0.01	0.03	0.06	0.08	**0.11**	**0.14**	0.09	**0.14**	0.08	0.09	0.05	0.04	0.04	0.02	0.03	0.01
13	0.00	0.00	0.01	0.01	0.03	0.03	0.08	0.02	**0.17**	0.03	**0.19**	0.04	**0.15**	0.04	**0.10**	0.06	0.03
14	0.00	0.00	0.02	0.03	0.05	0.08	**0.13**	0.09	**0.17**	0.07	**0.13**	0.05	0.07	0.03	0.03	0.03	0.01
15	0.00	0.00	0.01	0.01	0.01	0.03	0.06	0.04	0.13	0.04	**0.21**	0.05	**0.16**	0.05	**0.12**	0.06	0.03
16	0.00	0.00	0.02	0.02	0.01	0.02	0.03	0.03	0.08	0.03	**0.19**	0.06	**0.19**	0.02	**0.14**	**0.11**	0.04

$P(PPB\_BW \mid p)$ and $P(PPBPM\_BW \mid p)$ for p=15, 14 and 12 which show that they appear at the beginning portions of syntactic phrases and sentences very frequently. Also, the high transition probabilities of 15-10, 15-9, 15-13, 14-10, 14-9, 14-7, 12-9 and 12-7 show that the rising-falling reset pattern (see Figures 6(a) and (b)) of prosodic phrases commonly shows up. Close examination of frequently occurring prosodic state pairs or triplets reveals that most of them do form prosodic words.

Figure 7 shows the probabilities of prosodic state given syllables before and after comma and period, i.e., $P(p \mid PPBPM\_BW)$ and $P(p \mid EW\_FPBPM)$. It can be inferred from the figure that the beginning syllables of sentences remain, with high probabilities, at States 8, 11, 12, 14 and 15, while the ending syllables were probably associated with States 2, 3, 4 and 5.

Figure 8 displays the autocorrelations of the means of the original syllable pitch contour and the prosodic-state affecting patterns. With the exclusion of the more local influences of syllable tone and inter-syllable coarticulation, the prosodic-state affecting patterns have higher autocorrelation.

Table 3 shows displays the statistics of eight coarticulation states. We can deduce from this table that the first two states have higher hit rates to PMs (commas and periods) and have longer pauses. These correspond to major and minor breaks with no- or loosely-coupling coarticulation. On the other hand, the

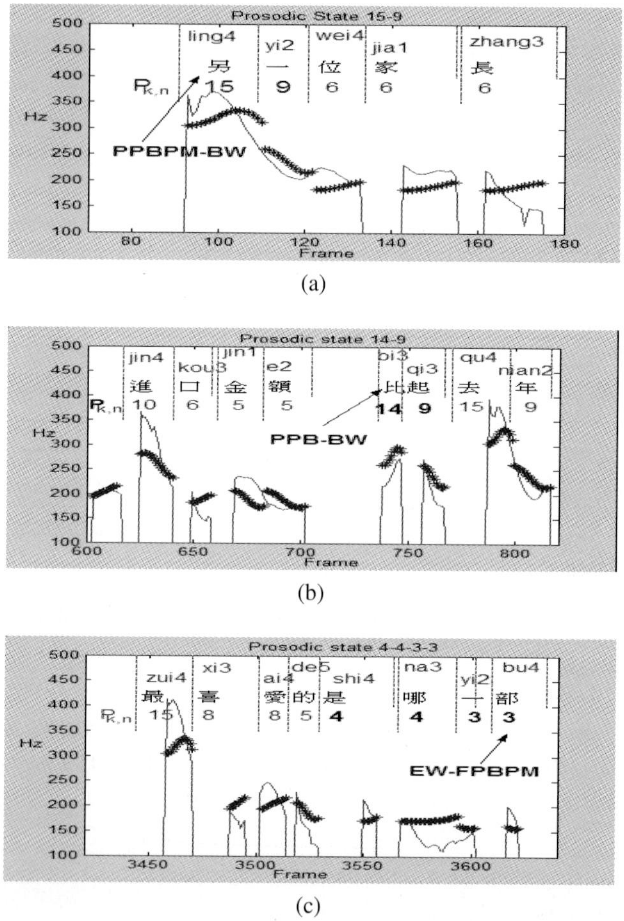

Fig. 6. Typical examples: (a) State pair 15-9 at the beginning of sentence, (b) 14-9 at the beginning of phrase, and (c) 4-3-3 at the end of sentence.

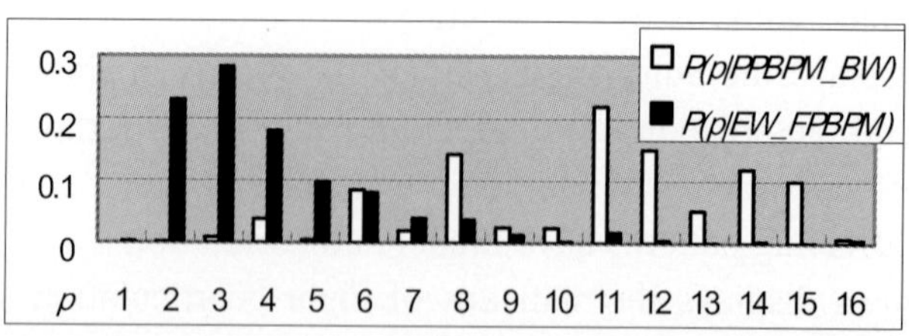

Fig. 7. The distributions of prosodic states at the beginning and ending locations of sentence.

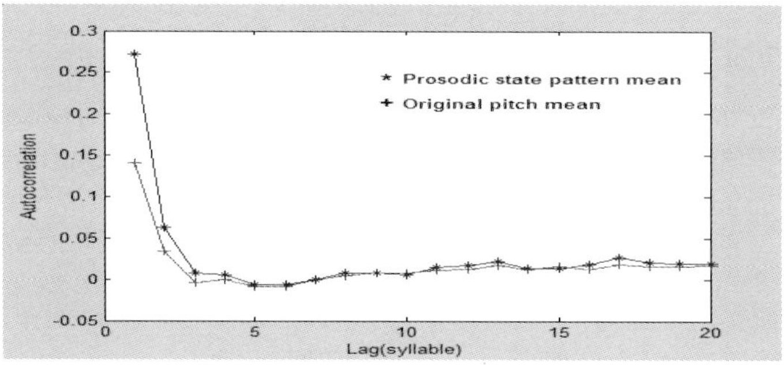

Fig. 8. The autocorrelations of the means of the original syllable pitch and the prosodic-state affecting patterns.

Table 3. Some statistics of eight coarticulation states.

C_n	1	2	3	4	5	6	7	8
P(inter| C_n)	0.85	0.72	0.70	0.67	0.48	0.38	0.32	0.35
P(intra| C_n)	0.15	0.28	0.31	0.33	0.52	0.62	0.68	0.65
P(comma| C_n)	0.32	0.07	0.04	0.04	0.02	0.03	0.02	0.02
P(period| C_n)	0.09	0.02	0.01	0.02	0.01	0.01	0.00	0.01
P(non-PM | C_n)	0.58	0.90	0.95	0.94	0.97	0.97	0.98	0.98
Average Pause duration (ms)	225	76	48	48	28	23	23	23

last four states have higher probabilities of intra-word and shorter pause durations. These in turn correspond to states of tightly-coupling coarticulation.

Figure 9 displays a typical example of the reconstructed 3-3 tone pattern. It can be seen from the figure that the second Tone 3, which was changed to a sandhi Tone 2, is well-reconstructed via the use of the coarticulation affecting pattern.

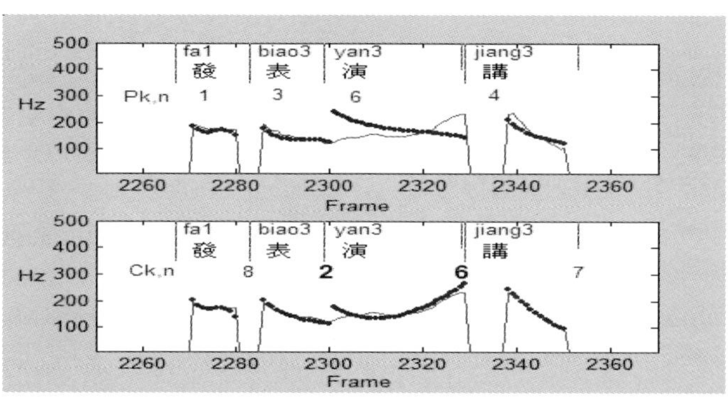

Fig. 9. A typical example of the reconstructed 3-3 tone pattern. Without (top) and with (bottom) the use of coarticulation affecting patterns.

Figure 10 displays a typical example of the reconstructed pitch contour and prosodic-state patterns of a sentence. The figure shows that the reconstructed pitch contour matches its original counterpart rather well. We also find the trajectory of the prosodic-state patterns to be smoother and more closely resembling a sequence of prosodic-word/phrase patterns. Moreover, a typical prosodic state pair of 15-13 (3-3) appears at the beginning (end) of the sentence.

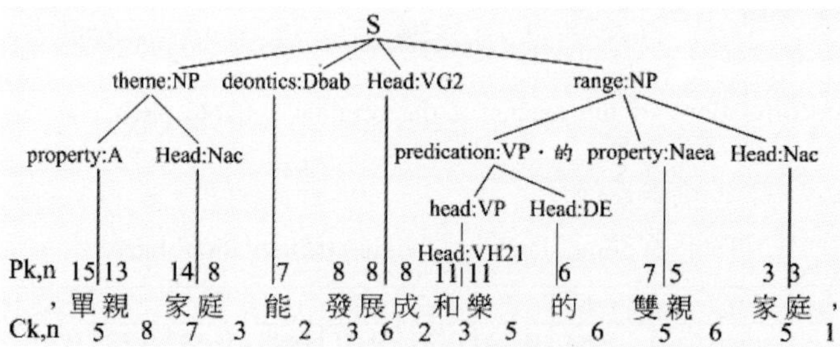

(a)

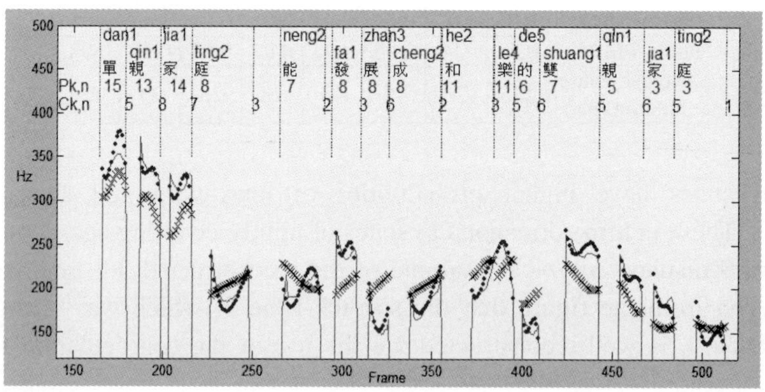

(b)

Fig. 10. A typical example: (a) the syntactic tree of a sentence and (b) the original (—) and reconstructed (···) pitch contours, and mean+prosodic-state patterns (xxx).

3.2.3. *Discussion and Conclusion*

A statistical syntax-prosody model of syllable pitch contour for Mandarin speech is discussed in this section. Experimental results show that the model performs well in separating the effects of several major influencing factors. Many prosodic cues, which are linguistically meaningful, are detected by the model. Not only are the individual prosodic and coarticulation states useful in constructing/analyzing the hierarchical prosody structure of Mandarin speech, but equally useful are the state sequences. In fact, it seems better to perform prosodic phrase analysis based on prosodic state sequences because they eliminate interference from locally affecting factors like base-syllable and tone.

With the capability of building explicit relationships between syntactic information and observed syllable pitch contour parameters, the model can be applied to assist MTTS in automatically annotating prosodic labels to large training corpora more consistently and accurately, in predicting prosodic phrase boundaries and breaks, and in generating other prosodic information for speech synthesis. This area is indeed worth further investigation.

4. Conclusion

It is believed that a sophisticated tone model would be effective in providing more relevant and appropriate prosodic information that can significantly improve the naturalness of the output of unlimited MTTS systems. In this chapter, two modern approaches to tone modeling for MTTS have been discussed. These methods involve the creation if computational models that analyze the relationship between hierarchical linguistic and prosodic structures in a quantitative way. Experimental results confirm their effectiveness.

References

1. C. Tseng, S. Pin, and Y. Lee, "Speech prosody: issues, approaches and implications," in Fant, G., H. Fujisaki, J. Cao and Y. Xu Eds, *From Traditional Phonology to Mandarin Speech Processing, Foreign Language Teaching and Research Process*, 417-438 (2004).
2. C. Tseng, and F. Chou, "A prosodic labeling system for Mandarin speech database," *in Proc. International Congress of Phonetic Sciences,* 2379-238 (1999).
3. C. Tseng, and Y. Lee, "Speech rate and prosody units: evidence of interaction from Mandarin Chinese," *in Proc. Speech Prosody*, 251-254 (2004).
4. H. Fujisaki and K. Hirose, "Analysis of voice fundamental frequency contours for declarative sentences of Japanese," *Journal of the Acoustical Society of Japan* (E) 5(4), 233-241 (1984).
5. H. Fujisaki, "Modeling in the study of tonal feature of speech with application to multilingual speech synthesis," *in Proc. SNLP-O-COCOSDA* (2002).
6. H. Mixdorff, "Quantitative tone and intonation modeling across languages," *in Proc. Int. Symp. on Tonal Aspects of Languages- with Emphasis on Tone Languages*, 137-142 (2004).
7. H. Mixdorff, Y. Hu, and G. Chen, "Towards the automatic extraction of Fujisaki model parameters for Mandarin," *in Proc. of European Conf. on Speech Communication*, (2003).
8. C. Tseng and S. Pin, "Mandarin Chinese prosodic phrase grouping and modeling - method and implications," *in Proc. Int. Symp. on Tonal Aspects of Languages- with Emphasis on Tone Languages*, 193-19 (2004).
9. C. Tseng and S. Pin, "Modeling prosody of Mandarin Chinese fluent speech via phrase grouping," *in Proc. ICSLT-O-COCOSDA* (2004).

10. C. Tseng and Y. Lee, "Intensity in relation to prosody organization," *in Proc. International Symposium on Chinese Spoken Language Processing*, 217-220 (2004).
11. S. Pin, Y. Lee, Y. Chen, H. Wang, and C. Tseng, "A Mandarin TTS system with an integrated prosodic model," *in Proc. ISCSLP* (2004).
12. M. J. Charpentier and M. G. Stella, "Diphone synthesis using an overlap-add technique for speech waveforms concatenation," *in Proc. IEEE ICASSP*, 2015-2018 (1986).
13. H. Mixdorff, "A novel approach to the fully automatic extraction of Fujisaki model parameters," *in Proc. IEEE ICASSP*, 1281-1284 (2000).
14. K. Chen, C. Tseng, H. Peng, and C. Chen, "Predicting prosodic words from lexical words – a first step towards predicting prosody from text," *in Proc. ISCSLP* (2004).
15. C. Shih, "Tone and Intonation in Mandarin," Working Papers of the Cornell Phonetics Laboratory, no. 3, pp.83-109, June (1988).
16. Z. J. Wu, "Can Poly-Syllabic Tone-Sandhi Patterns be the Invariant Units of Intonation in Spoken Standard Chinese," *in Proc. ICSLP*, pp.12.10.1–12.10.4 (1990).
17. Huang, Chu-Ren, Keh-Jiann Chen, Feng-Yi Chen, Keh-Jiann Chen, Zhao-Ming Gao and Kuang-Yu Chen, "Sinica Treebank: Design Criteria, Annotation Guidelines, and On-line Interface", *in Proc. of 2nd Chinese Language Processing Workshop*, 29-37 (2000).
18. L. Lee, C. Tseng, M. Ouh-young, "The Synthesis Rules in a Chinese Text-to-speech System," *IEEE Trans. on Acoustics, Speech and Signal Processing*, vol.37, no.9, pp.1309–1319 (1989).
19. S. H. Chen, W. H. Lai, and Y. R. Wang, " A New Duration Modeling Approach for Mandarin Speech," *IEEE Trans. on Speech and Audio Processing*, vol. 11, no. 4 (2003).
20. S. H. Chen, W. H. Lai, and Y. R. Wang, "A statistics-based pitch contour model for Mandarin speech," *J. Acoust. Soc. Am.*, 117 (2), pp.908-925 (2005).
21. C. Y. Chiang, S. H. Chen and Y. R. Wang, "On the inter-syllable coarticulation effect of pitch modeling for Mandarin speech", *in Proc. Interspeech*, Sept. (2005).
22. H. Dong, J. Tao and B. Xu, "Prosodic Word Prediction Using the Lexical Information," *in Proc. NLP-KE'05*, 189-193 (2005).

CHAPTER 5

MANDARIN TEXT-TO-SPEECH SYNTHESIS

Ren-Hua Wang[†], Sin-Horng Chen[‡], Jianhua Tao[§], Min Chu[*]

[†]*USTC iFlytek Speech Lab, University of Science & Technology of China, Hefei,*
[‡]*Speech Processing Lab, National Chiao Tung University, Hsinchu,*
[§]*NLPR, Institute of Automation, Chinese Academy of Sciences, Beijing,*
[*]*Speech Group, Microsoft Research Asia, Beijing*
E-mail: {rhw@ustc.edu.cn, schen@cc.nctu.edu.tw, jhtao@nlpr.ia.ac.cn, minchu@microsoft.com}

This chapter introduces Mandarin Text-To-Speech (MTTS) synthesis. Beginning with a brief review on the development history of MTTS and attributes of MTTS, three main constituents of the technology are presented: 1) Text processing: word segmentation, disambiguation of polyphones, and analysis of rhythm structure; 2) prosodic processing: features of Mandarin prosody, and prosody prediction, and; 3) speech synthesis: parametric synthesis and concatenative synthesis. Finally perspectives and applications for MTTS synthesis are discussed in the final sections.

1. Introduction

1.1. *Historical Review*

The development of Mandarin Text-To-Speech (MTTS) systems can be traced back to the seventies of the last century. Since the introduction of the first Mandarin speech synthesizer which used VOTRAX to generate speech from phonetic transcription in 1976,[1] we can roughly divide the development of MTTS technology into three stages.

In the early stage, the main focuses of research were on finding suitable speech synthesis techniques as well as in selecting proper synthesis units. The main concerns were the intelligibility of the synthetic speech and memory constraint. Formant synthesizers[2–5] and linear predictive coding (LPC)[6–8] were the two most popular techniques used in MTTS in the eighties. As for synthesis unit, both initial-final[6] and demisyllabic[7,9] schemes were often used. Systems developed in this early stage usually adopted simple, rule-based prosody control techniques[3,8,10] with input text in the form of phonetic transcription.[4] Most of these systems could produce highly intelligible speech for isolated words. But they could not generate natural-sounding speech for unlimited input texts because of the use of relatively simple text analysis and prosody generation rules.

The trend of speech synthesis techniques switched to the PSOLA (pitch synchronous overlap and add) methods[11–14, 20–24] in the nineties, while the trend in synthesis unit selection, from the late eighties, favored syllable-based concatenative systems.[8,12–14,18–24] A few other schemes, such as word-based[15] and diphone-based[4,11,16] techniques, were also proposed in the nineties. For prosody control, although more sophisticated rule-based methods[18,19] were reported, the trend changed to the data-driven approach in the nineties. In a data-driven approach, prosody generation rules were implicitly included in a statistical model[16,17,22,24] or an artificial neural network (ANN)[23] with parameters trained from a large, well-annotated speech database. Meanwhile, more sophisticated text analysis methods with electronically coded Chinese text input[11,12,17–20] were proposed in mid-nineties. Hierarchical prosody structures were exploited and applied to prosody generation.[17,19,20,24] Due to the uses of more sophisticated prosody generation schemes and the larger speech inventory of waveform templates, many MTTS systems developed in late nineties could produce good quality, natural-sounding synthetic speech.[17-24] A good review of the progress of MTTS technology and system developments in the early and middle stages was made by Shih and Sproat in 1996.[17]

From the late nineties, in the modern stage of MTTS development, corpus-based MTTS approaches[25–30] became the mainstream. The new approach uses sophisticated unit selection schemes to choose long speech segments with appropriate prosody from a large, single-speaker speech corpus, and concatenates these segments directly with little or no prosody modifications. The main focus of this approach lies in its unit selection technique. Usually, a prosody model or a rule-based method is needed to generate proper prosody targets for guiding the unit selection.[25,26] In this stage an approach without explicit prosody model and prosody modification was also proposed.[27] The synthetic speech of a corpus-based MTTS system has always been reported to be of high quality and very natural.

1.2. *Attributes of Mandarin TTS*

A TTS system typically contains three main components shown in Figure 1: text processing, prosody processing and speech synthesis. First, the text processing component converts any input text into corresponding phonetic notations with some other information needed for prosody processing. Then, the prosody processing component generates prosodic targets in symbolic format, such as ToBI,[31] or in numerical format, such as fundamental frequency (F0) curve and segment duration, or both. Lastly, the synthesis component outputs speech that matches the phonetic and prosodic specifications. The algorithms used in the prosody and synthesis components are normally language independent. However, the text processing component often contains language specific processes.

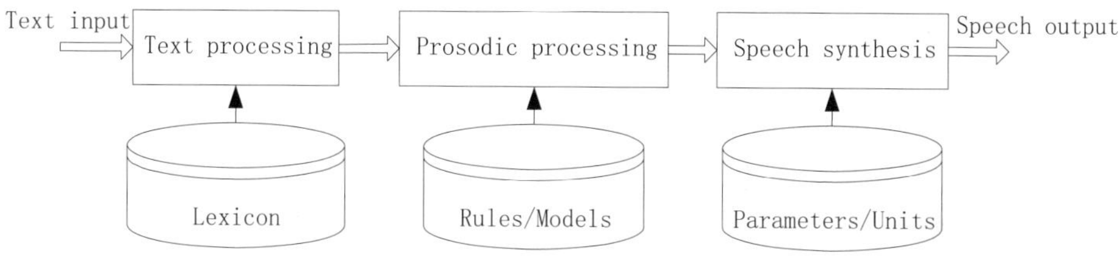

Fig. 1. Block-diagram of a TTS system.

1.2.1. *Characters and Syllables*

The base unit in written Chinese is the character. There are more than 70,000 different Chinese characters, but the 3,500 most frequently used characters can cover as much as 99.5% of actual occurrence.[32] For MTTS systems that do not aim to process ancient documents, handling up to 20,000 characters is enough.

Normally, one Chinese character corresponds to one syllable in speech. The only exception is in the case of a retroflexed syllable. For example, two characters, such as "玩儿" and "点儿", are converted to a single retroflexed syllable, pronounced as /wanr2/ and /dianr3/. The symbols between two slashes are modified Hanyu Pinyin (汉语拼音), which is the phonetic notation for Mandarin Chinese used in China and was adopted in 1979 by the International Organization for Standardization as the standard romanization system for modern Chinese. In Pinyin, 22 symbols are defined for initials (the consonants at the onset positions of Chinese syllables, one for zero-initial), 37 symbols for finals (the vowels plus coda consonants) and 5 symbols for the tones.

Theoretically, these 22 initials and 37 finals will generate 814 base syllables. Yet, in Mandarin, only about 410 syllables are valid. Also, since not all base syllables can go with all five tones, only about 1,338 tonal syllables can be found in an authoritative dictionary,[33] which keeps only the canonical pronunciations of each word. However, in continuous speech, more tonal syllables are used. There are three main sources for these additional syllables. The first source is tone sandhi. When two falling-rising tone syllables occur adjacently, the first one will be spoken with a rising tone. For example, /che2/ is not a valid syllable in Mandarin dictionaries. However, in the word "扯谎", the canonical pronunciation /che3 huang3/ is to be spoken as /che2 huang3/. The second source is neutralization. Although, only about 40 neutralized syllables are listed in most dictionaries, between 200–300 will be used in actual continuous speech. The third source is retroflex. Today, about 200–300 retroflexed syllables are used by people living in northern China. If all these additional syllables are considered, the total number of tonal syllables in Mandarin is close to 2,000.

1.2.2. *Lexical Word and Prosodic Word*

The word, rather than the character, is used as the basic unit in most Chinese processing systems because the usages and meanings of words are far more consistent in Chinese. In written Chinese, characters run continuously without visual cues to indicate word boundaries. Word segmentation becomes a basic requirement for almost all Chinese processing systems. Another particularly Chinese language problem lies in the identification of proper names (including person names and organization names).

Since most Chinese characters are themselves single-character words, many mono-syllabic words are detected as a result of word segmentation. Yet, in spoken Mandarin, there exists a disyllabic rhythm. A successive string of single-character words are often grouped into disyllabic rhythmic units, and long spoken words are normally chunked into several units as well. This basic unit of rhythm is known as a foot or a prosodic word in the literature.[34] To distinguish words listed in a lexicon from prosodic words in speech, words in a lexicon are referred to as lexical words. A prosodic word may contain one or more lexical words, or may even be part of a lexical word. Since prosodic words are formed dynamically according to context, it is impossible to list all prosodic words in a lexicon, as has been done for lexical words. Therefore, in a Mandarin TTS system, segmenting text into lexical words is not enough. Prosodic word segmentation is also needed.[35,36]

1.2.3. *Homophone and Polyphone*

In Chinese, there are many homophones. On average, about 15 characters share a syllable. This feature causes some difficulties in speech recognition, yet, it is not a problem in TTS. There are about 800 polyphones in Mandarin. In many cases, the pronunciation of a polyphonic character is fixed when it is used in a multi-character word. However, there are still some single-character words or multi-character words that have more than one pronunciation. Therefore, choosing the right pronunciation for a polyphone is a problem in TTS. If the most frequently used pronunciation of each polyphonic word is used, the error rate of character-to-syllable conversion is around 0.9%.[37] If a context model is used to disambiguate these possibilities, the error rate can be reduced to about 0.4%.[37–39]

Besides polyphonic words, there is no out-of-vocabulary problem in character-to-syllable conversion in Mandarin. Any new word can be converted simply by looking-up a character-to-syllable dictionary.

2. Text Processing in MTTS

The task of text processing is to process the input text and generate corresponding information for the later components, such as prosody modeling and speech synthesis. Text processing takes a very important role in TTS, because it not only determines the correctness of synthesized speech but also significantly influences the intelligibility and naturalness of the speech output.

To generate the Pinyin, rhythm, stress and other information corresponding to the input text, text processing in MTTS should include several processing steps to deal with the different problems in Chinese.

2.1. *Word Segmentation*

Automatic word segmentation is a fundamental and indispensable step in most Chinese processing tasks, including MTTS, due to the sole reason that there are no explicit word delimiters in Chinese text. By employing word segmentation, MTTS system can segment sentences (thereby paragraphs and articles) into words sequences, and so corresponding Pinyin, rhythm and part-of-speech information can be generated by looking up each word in a dictionary. The quality of word segmentation is critical for MTTS, but fortunately, Chinese word segmentation has been researched for tens of years, and significant progress has been achieved in each of the following four difficult problems.

Dictionary compilation is a preliminary but difficult task because there is no standard definition of what a word is in Chinese. In the last ten years, several high quality electronic dictionaries have been developed, with their sizes ranging from 60,000 to 270,000 entries. Research results show that higher segmentation performance can be achieved by incorporating more word entries.[40] To reduce the huge effort of dictionary compilation, many effective algorithms have been proposed to identify new word candidates from Chinese text corpus.

Given a dictionary, the most serious problem in Chinese word segmentation is the problem of segmentation ambiguity. For example, the sequence "尚未来(still not come)" can be segmented as "尚(still) 未来(future)" and "尚未(still not) 来(come)". Segmentation algorithms based on maximizing the probabilities of word sequences, prove to be able to reduce this problem to some degree. Some researchers analyze the segmentation ambiguity and find that only one of the segmentation paths is reasonable for more than 90% of the cases of ambiguous text. So saving the correct segmentation path for this kind of ambiguous texts is also a practical approach to improve segmentation performance.

Proper names must be identified in MTTS because rhythm and Pinyin information often need special processing in proper names, such as "曾"(/ceng2/) in surnames should be read as /zeng1/. Automatic proper name identification has been studied deeply in relation to many other Chinese processing[41] tasks and can be integrated into MTTS rather easily with some additional work in the area of rhythm and Pinyin information processing.

Another problem in word segmentation is the derivative word problem, such as "着了火"(have caught fire) derived from "着火"(catch fire), and "开开心心"(/kai1 kai1 xin1 xin1/), from "开心"(/kai1 xin1/). Chinese derivative words need to be identified so that correct rhythm and Pinyin information can be generated for these words. Research shows that most of the Chinese derivative words can be identified by adopting some tens of derivation rules, and the relationship between the characters within these words (such as verb-object relationship in "着火") is useful in Chinese derivative word identification.

Based on the segmentation research described above, the accuracy of a state-of-the-art Chinese word segmentation system is about 96%-98%, which satisfies the basic need of most MTTS systems.

2.2. *Part-Of-Speech Tagging*

Part-Of-Speech (POS) is a type of linguistic information that is widely used. The POS of a word also plays an important role in both the disambiguation of polyphone pronunciations and the analysis of rhythm structure. Therefore POS tagging is always carried out after or during word segmentation. Several POS categories have been proposed for Chinese, and the most commonly-adopted categorization is the one proposed by Yu[42] which includes 26 POS categories. The trigram POS tagging algorithm has been proven to be an effective method and the popular corpus annotated by Yu is often used to train POS trigram models. The tagging accuracy for Chinese is about 95%–97%.

2.3. *The Problem of Polyphones*

The polyphone problem is a particular issue of MTTS which needs to be handled almost exclusively by MTTS. To tackle this problem, listing as many words with polyphonic characters as possible, such as "中(zhong4)奖" and "行(hang2)长(zhang3)", into the dictionary is an approach commonly-employed in most MTTS systems. Detailed Pinyin information processing, after proper names and derivative words have been identified, can also help to solve part of the polyphone problem in MTTS.

Monosyllabic words, which are polyphones such as "长(chang2/zhang3)", "还 (hai2/huan2)", and "干 (gan1/gan4)", are often assigned with wrong pronunciations typically when the pronunciation selected is based only on the most frequent option after word segmentation. Several solutions have been proposed on this matter in recent years: summarizing pronunciation rules manually by human experts, applying machine learning methods on annotated corpus,[43] and introducing a hybrid method to integrate the strengths of both human and machine.[44]

As a result of the various efforts above, the accuracy of Pinyin generation on the whole is more than 99.8% in most MTTS systems.

2.4. *Rhythm Structure Analysis*

Beyond Pinyin, rhythm structure is another dimension of information which is introduced into MTTS, and this needs to be predicted from the input text too. And for Chinese, a widely applied rhythm structure definition consists of six layers:[35] syllable, prosodic word, minor prosodic phrase, major prosodic phrase breath group and sentence layers.

As discussed above, the lexical word sequence generated by word segmentation should be converted into a prosodic word sequence, and this conversion is often done through a series of human crafted chunking rules, such as the word "的 (/de/)" should always be grouped with its preceding word, and so on.

From the minor prosodic phrase layer to the breath group layer, each phrase or group is defined by the length of the phrase, and also the obviousness of the break at the boundaries of the phrase. The prediction of the rhythm structure from a text is an interesting but difficult research task. Rule-based methods were used for phrase break prediction in the early days, but recently, many researchers have been exploiting statistics-based methods[45,46] with part-of-speech and syllable number as the dominant features for this task and have achieved good performance. Syntactic parsing is assumed to contribute to rhythm structure prediction, but experimental results show that only shallow parsing, such as chunking, is effective.[47]

The accuracy of prosodic word generation is about 97%–99%, and about 82%–85% for predicted rhythm structure, which is regarded as acceptable.

There are also some other issues that should be handled in the text processing stage of MTTS, including text normalization,[48] and stress prediction. All these problems have been researched on but not explored here due to space constraints.

3. Prosody Processing in MTTS

3.1. *Features of Mandarin Prosody*

Prosody is an inherent supra-segmental feature of human speech. It carries stress, intonation patterns and timing structures of continuous speech which, in turn, determine the naturalness and intelligibility of an utterance. Prosody is even more important for Mandarin Chinese because Chinese is a tonal language. As the syllable is the basic pronunciation unit, the prosodic features in Chinese are known to include syllable pitch contours, syllable energy contours, syllable or initial/final durations, and inter-syllable durations. Hierarchical prosody structure can be formed by taking these elements as its basic building blocks.[49,50]

3.2. *Prosody Prediction*

The general approach of prosody prediction includes the following two steps: (1) extract some linguistic features from the input text, and (2) generate prosodic features from those linguistic features. Methods of prosodic feature generation can be classified into two general categories: rule-based and data-driven. The former approach is the more conventional one, involving the use of linguistic expertise to manually infer the phonological rules of prosody generation from a large set of utterances.[18–20] The main disadvantage of this approach lies in the difficulty of collecting enough rules without long-term dedication to the task. The data-driven approach tries to construct a prosody model from a large speech corpus, usually by statistical methods or artificial neural network (ANN) techniques.[21–23,51–53] The primary advantage of this approach is that it can be automatically realized from the training data set without the help of linguistic experts. As a result, the data-driven approach has gained popularity in recent years.

3.2.1. *F0 Prediction*

Although there are only five lexical tones, syllable pitch contour patterns in continuous Mandarin Chinese speech are highly varied and can deviate dramatically from their canonical forms. The factors that have major influences on pitch contours include the effects of neighboring tones, referred to as *sandhi* rules,[54] coarticulation, stress, intonation type, semantics, emotional status, and so on. F0 prediction therefore needs to consider not only the basic tone patterns, but also high-level factors from the hierarchical prosody structure.

(a) The rule-based approach

The method proposed by Wang[18] extends the four canonical tones of H, R, L, and F (i.e., high, rising, low, and falling) to $H^1 - H^3, R^1 - R^3, L^1 - L^3, F^1 - F^5$, and adds two kinds of light tones. Then, tone patterns of multi-syllable words are formed by the combinations of basic units of the proposed *monotonemes* with tone sandhi rules. Sentence intonation is realized by applying global modification rules. A formal evaluation confirmed that the resulting synthetic speech sounds very natural. In an improved method,[19] pitch generation is realized by building up a stable template at the prosodic word level and generating a base intonation contour. A subjective MOS test confirmed that the KD2000 Mandarin TTS system, which employed the F0 prediction method, performed better than KD863 which was ranked No.1 in the 1998 national assessment on the naturalness of synthesized speech.

Chou[20] assigns a pitch contour pattern to each word, and then superimposes the pattern with an intonation pattern of the major prosodic phrase level. At the word-level, the pitch contour patterns of all tone combinations are used and extracted from an isolated-word speech database. In the major prosodic phrase level, four global intonation patterns are applied depending on the type of punctuation mark, including sentence middle, comma, period and question mark. These four intonation pitch contour patterns are extracted from a sentence database. An informal test confirmed that the synthesized speech sounds indeed natural.

(b) The data-driven approach

Wu[22] built a word prosody tree to store both prosodic features and linguistic features of each word in a speech database. The tree contains two levels: word-length level and tone-combination level. In synthesis, it first calculates the sentence intonation to find the target pitch period of the first syllable. It then traverses the word prosody template tree by using word length and tone combination to extract some appropriate word template candidates. Lastly, cost functions considering the matching of linguistic features between the input word and these word template candidates are calculated and used to determine the word template. Experimental results showed that most synthesized pitch parameter sequences match quite well with their original counterparts.

In Yu's approach,[51] the syllable pitch contour pattern is generated by a linear regression method based on a 4-level hierarchical prosody structure containing the syllable, word, prosodic phrase, and utterance levels. Moreover, the predicted basic syllable pitch contour pattern is further refined by finding a syllable pitch contour pattern of real speech. A subjective test using a 10-scale MOS shows the results of 6.87 and 7.08 for the basic and modified methods, respectively.

In Chen's article,[23] an RNN-based method is proposed. It employs a three-layer recurrent neural network (RNN) to generate some prosodic features including the syllable pitch contour, syllable energy level, initial/final durations, and inter-syllable pause duration. The inputs of the RNN are syllable- and word-level linguistic features extracted from the input text. As one of the merits of RNN, the dynamic variations of syllable pitch contour can be automatically learned using only lower-level linguistic features without explicit information from high-level prosodic structural elements. Experimental results showed that all synthesized pitch contours resemble their original counterparts quite well. Moreover, many phonological rules, including the well-known tone sandhi rule for the 3-3 tone pair,[54] were automatic learned by the RNN.

The quantitative model has also been introduced to generate the pitch contour, such as the modified Fujisaki model.[18,46] A quantitative model allows us to analyze and represent the acoustic features of pitch contour more effectively. The model parameters can be extracted automatically based on a speech database. Experimental results have shown its feasibility in MTTS.

3.2.2. *Duration Prediction*

For MTTS, the task of duration prediction is to determine the duration of the whole syllable or the duration of its initial/final. A general approach to tackle this problem is to first identify important and relevant linguistic features, and then exploit rules or computational models to describe their relationships with syllable duration.

A two-level, rule-based syllable duration prediction method is proposed by Wang.[18] In both the lower word level and upper sentence level, a set of rules are derived.

Chou's method[20] generates syllable duration using a multiplicative model with the following four affecting factors considered: average syllable duration, tone, position, and break index.

An alternative RNN-based method for generating initial and final durations is also proposed[21] as discussed previously.

In Sun's method,[53] a duration prediction method based on a polynomial regression model is proposed. The method consists of three steps: linguistic features selection, polynomial model determination, and duration generation by nonlinear regression. The Eta-squared statistical concept is used to determine the most forceful linguistic features.

3.2.3. *Pause Duration Prediction*

A general rule-based approach of inter-syllable pause duration prediction is to first determine the break indices from high-level hierarchical prosody structure and then assign pause durations according to the estimated break indices. The pause duration of each inter-syllable location can be simply assigned a constant value according to its break index, and then added with a random perturbation.[20] An alternative data-driven approach[23] uses a 3-layer RNN to predict pause duration directly from some syllable and word level linguistic features.

4. Parametric Synthesis

The technology of speech synthesis dates back to the parametric techniques introduced by Homer Dudley in the late 1930's and early 1940's.[55] These methods are "parametric" in the sense that they construct a computational model of the acoustic properties of the human vocal tract, and then analyze speech by determining the values of the parameters of the model. Speech is then generated from the model controlled by time-varying parameter trajectories.

4.1. *Parametric Representation of Speech Signal*

4.1.1. *Formant Synthesizer*

The formant synthesizer uses a number of formant resonances which can be realized with a second-order IIR filter to represent functions of the vocal tract in speech production. A filter with several resonances can be constructed by cascading several second-order sections (cascade model) or by adding several such sections together (parallel model). Formants which are used in formant synthesizers can be generated by rules or be data-driven. Due to the complicated formant structures of compound vowels in Chinese, such as /iang, ian, iong/, etc., it is an even bigger challenge to develop a formant synthesizer for Chinese, compared to some other foreign languages. But despite that, there are still several very well-performing Chinese formant speech synthesizers.[56–60] In 1993, Lee[61] presented a set of improved tone concatenation rules to be used in a formant-based Chinese TTS system. A total of 14 representative tone patterns were defined for the five tones, and different rules about which pattern should be used under what kind of tone concatenation conditions were organized in detail. Preliminary subjective tests indicate that these rules actually produce better synthesized speech for a formant-based Chinese TTS system.

4.1.2. *Linear Predictive Coding*

Linear Predictive Coding (LPC) is a powerful method for speech analysis and synthesis. In recent years, several variations of linear prediction have been developed to improve the quality of the basic method.[62,63] These variations include Multi-pulse Linear Prediction Coding (MLPC), Residual Excited Linear Prediction (RELP), and Code Excited Linear Prediction (CELP).[64] A number of typical Chinese LPC synthesizers have been developed in the Institute of Acoustics, Chinese Academy of Sciences and the University of Science and Technology of China, where the speech code book method was integrated into their systems.[65,66]

Line Spectral Frequencies (LSF) serve as an equivalent representation of predictor coefficients. In practice, they are frequently used for their better quantization and interpolation properties. LSF can also be derived from the spectrum generated by other analysis methods, for example the STRAIGHT model to be described later, for parametric synthesis application.[67]

The Sinusoidal Model and the Harmonics Plus Noise Model have been proved effective for parametric synthesis due to the improvement of excitation.[68,69] But few reports are published regarding their application in MTTS.

4.1.3. *STRAIGHT Model*

The STRAIGHT (Speech Transformation and Representation using Adaptive Interpolation of weiGHTed spectrum) model[70] is a very high quality speech analysis-modification-synthesis method to represent and manipulate speech signals. It uses pitch-adaptive spectral analysis combined with a surface reconstruction method in the time and frequency region and consists of an F0 extraction using instantaneous frequency calculation based on a new concept called *fundamentalness*. The proposed procedures preserve the details of time and frequency surfaces while almost perfectly removing the fine structures resulting from signal periodicity and allow for over 600% manipulation of such speech parameters as pitch, vocal tract length, and speaking rate, while maintaining high reproductive quality. The flexibility of STRAIGHT may help promote research on the relation between physical parameters and perceptual correlates. The F0 extraction procedure also provides a versatile method for investigating quasiperiodic structures in arbitrary signals. This method has been successfully applied to Chinese TTS systems, such as database compression,[71] HMM-based parametric synthesis[67] and voice conversion.[72]

5. Concatenative Speech Synthesis

In concatenative speech synthesis, there is always a unit inventory that stores pre-recorded speech segments. During synthesis, suitable segments are selected and concatenated with or without signal processing. Four key problem areas include: defining a base unit set; choosing a prosody strategy; designing a unit selection scheme and collecting and annotating a speech corpus.

5.1. *Base Unit Set*

A base unit in a concatenative speech synthesizer is the lowest constituent in the unit selection process. There are many possible basic unit choices, such as phoneme, diphone, semi-syllable, syllable or even word. In order to obtain natural prosody and smooth concatenation in synthetic speech, for each base unit, rich prosodic and phonetic variations are often expected. This is easy to achieve when smaller base units are used. However, smaller units mean more units per utterance and more instances per unit, and this implies a larger search space for unit selection and thus a longer search time. Besides, smaller units do cause more difficulties in precise unit segmentation. It is found that longer base units are useful as long as enough instances are guaranteed to appear in the database.[73]

Mandarin has only about 410 base syllables and about 2,000 tonal syllables. Therefore, tonal syllable is a natural choice for the base unit in Mandarin and it is used in most state-of-the-art Mandarin TTS systems.[74-77] However, when the speech database is as small as 1 to 2 hours of speech, initials plus tonal finals are the alternative unit choice. When a moderate-sized speech corpus is available, defining a base unit set that contains all initials and finals as well as some frequently used syllables is a good, balanced solution.

5.2. *Prosody Strategy*

There are three typical choices for prosody control in a concatenative TTS:

Fully controlled: In many TTS systems, numerical targets for prosodic features like F0, segmental duration and energy, are predicted first. These targets are fully realized in the synthesized speech by adjusting prosodic features with signal processing algorithms, such as PSOLA[78] or HNM.[69] Such a prosody strategy has been widely adopted in late 80's and early 90's, when only one or a few instances of a unit are allowed to be stored in the unit inventory. On the one hand, this prosody model draws out such a limited range of prosodic variation, that there can be few unexpected or bad prosodic outputs in the synthetic speech. However, on the other hand, the generated prosody often has a rather flat intonation pattern and the speech sounds monotonous. Furthermore, signal processing used for pitch and time scaling often have side-effects that distort the speech quality. To reduce the extent of signal processing, a semi-controlled strategy is used.

Semi-controlled: Numerical prosody targets are predicted and embedded into the target cost for unit selection. If the prosodic features of a selected unit are close enough to the predicted targets, no signal processing is needed. Otherwise, signal processing is performed. The advantage of this strategy is that the degree of pitch and time scaling are constrained to small ranges in most of the cases. However, such an advantage can be achieved only when a large enough speech corpus is used. The resulting synthetic prosody is still rather monotonous.

Soft controlled: There is neither a numerical prosody model, nor any signal processing involved in this strategy. Instead, contextual features used in traditional prosody models are used to predict a cluster of speech instances that share similar prosodic features. Therefore, under the soft controlled strategy, acceptable regions of prosodic features, rather than the best path in the features space, are predicted by minimizing the probability of violating the invariant property in prosody. Normally, more than one valid path is kept in the acceptable regions. The final choice can be either random among all candidates, or the pattern that has the closest counterpart in the corpus. The advantage of the soft control strategy is that synthetic speech will have richer variations in prosody, sounding close to the original speaker. When there is a large enough speech corpus available, the soft control strategy works well in most cases and it has been successfully applied in many Mandarin TTS systems.[79] However, it still has the disadvantage that some unnatural utterances will be generated when improper units are selected, especially when the speech corpus is not large enough.

Among the three prosody strategies, there is no universal good or bad choice. It depends on the target task and the size of speech corpus available.

5.3. *Unit Selection*

Normally, the suitability of the instance sequence for a given text is described by two types of costs: the target cost and the smoothness cost.[80,81] Target cost describes the local goodness of an instance in relation to its target, and smoothness cost measures how smooth the synthesized utterance will be by concatenating these instances one by one.

Target cost: After text processing and prosody processing, each unit in the text to be synthesized has been assigned a specification that describes its target phonetic features and prosodic features. The same set of features has been derived for all speech segments in the unit inventory. If a speech segment in the unit inventory matches the specification of a target unit exactly, the target cost for selecting this speech segment is zero. Otherwise, there will be a positive penalty. In some TTS systems, especially those adopting fully-controlled or semi-controlled prosody strategies, numerical targets are predicted for prosodic features such as pitch, duration and intensity. While, in other systems, especially those adopting the soft-controlled prosodic strategy, categorical features, such as position in phrases, position in words, presence or absence of stress, are used and penalties for mismatch in these categories are decided experientially. Besides, penalties can be calculated from the segment likelihood to a target HMM[81] or from the similarity of the left and right phones of a segment in the unit inventory to the target unit.[80] Since Chinese is a tonal language, penalties are also derived from the similarity of the left and right tones of a unit.

Smoothness cost: A smoothness cost is needed to measure how smooth it will be if two speech segments are concatenated together. In some systems, the spectral distance across the concatenating boundary is used as the smoothness penalty. However, such a measurement is mostly suitable for systems that use diphone as the base unit, in which the concatenating point is at the stable part of a speech phoneme. For Mandarin TTS systems that use syllables as base units, concatenating boundaries are often at the parts with rapid changes. Therefore, spectral distance is not a good measure of the smoothness of concatenation. A very simple smoothness cost has been introduced.[27] If two segments are continuous in the original recording, the smoothness cost between them is zero. Otherwise, a non-zero value is assigned according to the type of concatenation.

With such a constraint, the continuous segments in the unit inventory tend to be selected and the unvoiced-unvoiced concatenation is preferred.

The final concatenation cost of an utterance is the weighted sum of target cost and smoothness cost. The weighting of the importance of all these penalties is still an open problem. They are often decided experientially. When subjective evaluation results are available, weights can be tuned to maximize the correlation between the subjective score and the penalty.[82]

5.4. *Resources Needed for Creating a TTS Voice*

The different TTS systems do share some common resource requirements. The functions and existing issues in the process of generating these resources are described below:

Script generation: The goal is to maximize the coverage of prosodic and phonetic variations of the base units in a limited amount of text script. Thus, at least three parameters, including the base unit set, the function for calculating coverage and the total amount of script to be recorded, are to be decided according to the characteristics of the target language and the target scenario. Normally, script generation is performed as a sentence selection problem with a weighted greedy algorithm. The relationship between the size of a speech database and voice quality has been studied.[83]

Speech recording: The recording process is normally carried out by a professional team in a sound-proof studio. The voice talent is carefully selected and well-trained. With such considerations, the recorded speech, generally, has good quality. Yet, it often has some mismatched words between the speech and the script. These mismatches are mostly caused by reading errors and the idiosyncratic pronunciation of the speaker. Detecting these mismatches automatically is still an unsolved problem.[84]

Text processing: When generating recording script and the corresponding phonetic transcription, many text processing functions, such as text normalization and grapheme-to-phoneme conversion are needed. These processes typically do generate more errors and again will cause the mismatch between speech and phonetic transcription, and therefore the generated transcription should be checked manually.

Unit segmentation: To make a speech corpus usable to a concatenative TTS, the phonetic transcriptions has to be aligned with the corresponding speech waveforms. The HMM-based forced alignment has been widely adopted for automatic boundary alignment. Post-refining is often performed to guide the boundaries moving toward the optimal locations for speech synthesis.[85] Besides, there are some improved approaches, such as discriminative training and explicit duration modeling, which have been introduced into HMM-based segmentation for Chinese speech.[86]

Prosody annotation: Prosody annotation is often performed on the speech corpus, either manually or automatically.[87] For Mandarin, the most important annotation is the break index.

6. Summary and Conclusion

6.1. *Perspective*

In the past years, there have been significant achievements in the field of speech synthesis research. Now that the intelligibility of synthetic speech is close approaching that of human speech, more diverse and more attractive research areas are possible, which will bring about more innovation and propagation to speech research. Among them, personalized speech synthesis (including speaker simulation/adaptation, expressive speech synthesis), HMM-based speech synthesis, and articulatory speech synthesis are the most active domains.

6.1.1. *Personalized Speech Synthesis*

A personalized TTS system is more expressive and valuable than a universal single voice/style and more appropriate for practical applications. It includes two parts: speaker simulation, which tries to synthesize a range of different voices that users can choose from, and Expressive Speech Synthesis (ESS), which tries to synthesize voices that contain more human expressions.

6.1.1.1. Speaker Simulation

Starting from a speech signal uttered by a speaker, speaker simulation, also called voice transformation, voice conversion (VC), or voice morphing, aims at transforming the characteristics of the speech signal in such a way that a person naturally perceives the target speaker's own characteristics in the transformed speech.[88] Most VC systems to date have been focusing on transforming the spectral envelope. Mapping codebooks,[90] linear regression and dynamic frequency warping (DFW),[91] and Gaussian mixture modeling (GMM)[89,92] are three popular mapping methods of spectral conversion. Because of the difficulty to extract and manipulate higher-level information with present speech technologies, prosodic features such as F0 contour, energy contour and speaking rate of the source speaker are often trivially adjusted to match the target speaker's average prosody.[89] At present, simulating F0 contour is the emphasis of prosody conversion, and the statistical model, the deterministic/stochastic model, piecewise linear mapping,[93] the CART model[72] and pitch target model[94] can be employed in the simulation of F0 contours.

Some attempts on Chinese have been made[72] and effective conversions achieved. However, VC is a complex task involving speech analysis, time alignment, mapping algorithm, speech synthesis, and other speech technologies. Based on that, a perfect VC system is still an unrealized application.

6.1.1.2. Expressive Speech Synthesis

ESS can offer a much more human-like scenario in human-machine interactions. Traditional methods on ESS consist of formant synthesis with rule based prosodic control, diphone concatenation and so on. But none of these methods can generate satisfying results. A number of new methods have been explored recently. These are unit selection based ESS and voice conversion based ESS.

(1) Expressive speech synthesis based on unit selection

The unit selection method is the most popular method in normal speech synthesis, which has been applied to ESS. Iida[95] constructed an emotional speech synthesis system based on unit selection, by recording three unit selection databases using the same speaker for three kinds of emotions: anger, joy and sadness. When synthesizing speech with these given emotions, only units from the corresponding database are selected. The evaluation experiment shows that 50-80% of the synthesized speech can be easily recognized. Another approach is to select the appropriate unit for the given emotion from only one database. This has been attempted by Marumoto and Campbell,[96] who used parameters related to voice quality and prosody as emotion-specific selection criteria. The results indicated a partial success: anger and sadness were recognized with up to 60% accuracy, while joy was not recognized above chance level.

(2) Expressive speech synthesis based on voice conversion

In this method, a neutral speech is converted to an emotional speech using mapping functions of a spectrum, F0 and other prosodic features. However, there is one big problem that needs to be resolved. Among these features, which ones are most important and which ones can be neglected.

Some researchers focus on voice quality. Kawanami[97] constructed an emotional speech synthesis system based on voice conversion, which used GMM and DFW to construct the mapping function for Mel-cesptrum derived from the STRAIGHT spectrum. As to the fundamental frequency, it was simply converted using the standard linear mean-variance transformation. However, other researchers believe that fundamental frequencies play the most important role. Kang *et al.*[94] used a parametric F0 model to explore underlying relations between source and target F0 contours for Mandarin ESS, and the pitch target model was selected for its capability of describing Mandarin F0 contour and its convenience for parametric alignment. The GMM and CART methods were used to build mapping functions for well-chosen pitch target parameters.

Although the systems mentioned above achieve good results, there is no conclusion about which feature is most important. It is possible that in different kinds of emotional speech, or in different languages, the same parameter plays different roles.

6.1.2. *HMM-based Speech Synthesis*

Hidden Markov processes are a powerful and tractable method of modeling non-stationary signals, which have been frequently used in speech recognition. Recently, a HMM-based synthesis system has been developed, where spectral and excitation parameters are extracted from a speech database and modeled by context-dependent HMMs. In the synthesis part of the system, spectral and excitation parameters are generated from the HMMs themselves. Then waveforms are generated based on a decoding process.[98] Compared with traditional method based on concatenation, this new system has many benefits:

(1) HMM-based systems can generate smooth and natural sounding speech, while there are always some inconsistencies at the concatenation points of the synthesized speech of concatenative systems.

(2) HMM-based systems can freely change the target voice characteristics by changing the parameters of the HMMs, while concatenation systems can only synthesize and generate the voice of only one speaker.

(3) HMM-based systems need comparatively smaller corpora compared to concatenative speech synthesis systems.

Although the speech quality from HMM-based systems is not as good as that of concatenative systems, this can be much improved by a high quality decoder, such as the STRAIGHT algorithm. Besides, there are some new criteria, such as the Minimum Generation Error,[99] which have been introduced into model training, achieving satisfactory improvements in the performance of Mandarin TTS.

6.1.3. *Articulatory Speech Synthesis*

Articulatory models can be divided into two and three dimensional models on one hand, and into geometric, statistical and biomechanical models on the other hand. Statistical 3D models have the advantage of having relatively few uncorrelated parameters. However, these models require huge amounts of MRI or CT (Computed Tomography) data for their construction and they are usually specific for a particular speaker. Biomechanical vocal tract models simulate the behavior of the articulators by means of finite element methods. They are especially suited to facilitate new insights into the relation between muscle activation and articulatory movements. On the other hand, they have many degrees of freedom, are difficult to control and require much computational power. Geometric vocal tract models are similar to statistical models in that their parameters define the vocal tract shape directly in geometrical terms, but the kinds and number of parameters are chosen *a priori* and fitted to particular data *a posteriori*. Therefore, the geometric vocal tract model has become the most popular method, achieving good results.[100]

6.2. *Applications*

With the rapid development of speech communication technology, TTS systems are being more widely applied in our daily lives.

(1) Call Centers

Since 2000, MTTS has been introduced to call centers on a large scale, to synthesize prompt sentences or queried information in interactive systems, especially dynamic information. InterPhonic,[101] a bilingual (Mandarin and English) TTS engine, now runs in most of the call centers in mainland China, including in the 168 information line, the voice portal of Unicom, the PICC countrywide call center, etc. Recently, China Telecom upgraded its 114 information service platform to the “Best Tone” (号码百事通) service which is powered by the InterPhonic engine. Mandarin TTS can significantly relieve the workload of human operators, or even substitute operators by being integrated with telephone-keyboard input or speech recognition technologies, along with simple (or even complex) dialogue management technologies.

(2) Mobile Phone Utility

With the advent of the information age, the use of mobile phones has become pervasive. Very natural speech can now be generated by state-of-the-art HMM-based MTTS with very limited resources. This means that MTTS systems can also be ported into mobile phones or other small devices. The phone can then read out short messages to you while you listen. Whenever there is a new call or scheduled item due, the caller's name or event can be read out to you, even before you see it on screen. In fact, the mobile phone may even serve as an online language learning device, or a translator.

(3) GPS Car Navigation Systems

The intelligent car has become a worldwide focus, and intelligent speech synthesis technology plays an important role in this technological pursuit. This navigation application involves the broadcasting of locations and directions of target destinations or stopovers, such as gas stations, parks, hotels, and so on. Integrated with wireless communication, the system can also broadcast real-time traffic, news, and weather forecast. In China, the ratio of speech-interfaced car navigation systems is only 2% of all car navigation systems, while it is 50% in Japan and 25% in America and Europe. The potential for wider MTTS deployment in this application area is therefore tremendous.

(4) Entertainment Industry

Recently, the application of speech synthesis system has entered the field of entertainment. For example, in games that involve voices, game characters can speak using the player's own voice. For users of e-books, listening to the book, instead of visually reading it, is possible with the integration of TTS, and even desirable when reading is an inconvenience or a hazard, such as in moving vehicles. Also, having your personal voice heard while text-chatting in cyberspace can add another dimension and color to your chat-identity.

With the integration of other speech technologies such as speech recognition and machine translation, the application of MTTS can be expanded to a much broader range than ever before.

References

1. C. Y. Suen, "Computer Synthesis of Mandarin", *IEEE ICASSP*, (1976), pp.698-700.
2. S. C. Lee, S. Xu and B. Guo, "Microcomputer-generated Chinese Speech", *Computer Processing of Chinese and Oriental Languages*, vol.1, no.2, (1983), pp.87-103.

3. J. Zhang, "Acoustic Parameters and Phonological Rules of a Text-to-Speech Systems for Chinese", *IEEE ICASSP*, (1986), pp.2023-2026.
4. C. Shih and M. Y. Liberman, "A Chinese Tone Synthesizer", *Technical Report, AT&T Bell Laboratories,* (1987).
5. S. A. Yang and Y. Xu, "An Acoustic-phonetic Oriented System for Synthesizing Chinese", *Speech Communication*, vol.7, (1988), pp.317-325.
6. T.-Y. Huang, C.-F. Wang and Y.-H. Pao, "A Chinese Text-to-Speech Synthesis System Based on an Initial-Final Model", *Computer Processing of Chinese and Oriental Languages*, vol.1, no.1, (1983), pp.59-70.
7. W. C. Lin and T.-T. Luo, "Synthesis of Mandarin by Means of Chinese Phonemes and Phonemes-pairs (JIFH)", *Computer Processing of Chinese and Oriental Languages*, vol.2, no.1, (1985) pp.23-35.
8. M. Ouh-Young, C.-J. Shie, C.-Y. Tseng and L.-S. Lee, "A Chinese Text-to-Speech System Based upon a Syllable Concatenation Model", *IEEE ICASSP*, (1986), pp.2439-2442.
9. H.-B. Chiou, H.-C. Wang and Y.-C. Chang, "Synthesis of Mandarin Speech Based on Hybrid Concatenation", *Computer Processing of Chinese and Oriental Languages*, vol.5, no.3/4, (1991), pp.217-231.
10. L.-S. Lee, C.-Y. Tseng and M. Ouh-Young, "The Synthesis Rules in a Chinese Text-to-Speech System", *IEEE Trans. on Acoustics, Speech, and Signal Processing*, vol.37, no.9, (1989), pp.1309-1320.
11. J. Choi, H.-W. Hon, J.-L. Lebrun, S.-P. Lee, G. Loudon, V.-H.g Phan and Yogananthan S. Yanhui, "A Software Based High Performance Mandarin Text-to-Speech System", *ROCLING VII*, (1994), pp.35-50.
12. L. Cai, H. Liu and Q. Zhou, "Design and Achievement of a Chinese Text-to-Speech System under Windows", *Microcomputer*, vol.3, (1995).
13. M. Chu and S. Lu, "High Intelligibility and Naturalness Chinese TTS System and Prosodic Rules", *the XIII Intenational Congress of Phonetic Sciences*, (1995), pp.334-337.
14. S.-H. Hwang, Y.-R. Wang and S.-H. Chen, "A Mandarin Text-to-Speech System", *ICSLP* (1996).
15. J. Xu and B. Yuan, "New Generation of Chinese Text-to-Speech System", *IEEE TENCON*, (1993), pp.1078-1081.
16. B. Ao, C. Shih and R.d Sproat, "A Corpus-Based Mandarin Text-to-Speech Synthesizer", *Proc. ICSLP*, (1994), pp.1771-1774.
17. C. Shih and R. Sproat, "Issues in Text-to-Speech Conversion for Mandarin", *Computational Linguistics and Chinese Language Processing*, vol.1, no.1, (1996), pp.37-86.
18. R.-H. Wang, Q. Liu and D. Tang, "A New Chinese Text-to-Speech System with High Naturalness", *ICSLP*, (1996) pp.1441-1444.
19. R.-H. Wang, Q. Liu, Y. Hu, B. Yin and X. Wu, "KD2000 Chinese Text-to-Speech System", *ICMI*, (2000), pp.300-307.
20. F.-c. Chou, C.-y. Tseng and L.-s. Lee, "Automatic Generation of Prosodic Structure for High Quality Mandarin Speech Synthesis", *Proc. ICSLP*, (1996) pp.1624-1627.
21. S. H. Pin, Y. Lee, Y.-c. Chen, H.-m. Wang and C.-y. Tseng, "A Mandarin TTS system with an Integrated Prosodic Model", *Proc. ISCSLP*, (2004), pp.169-172.
22. C.-H. Wu and J.-H. Chen, "Template-Driven Generation of Prosodic Information for Chinese Concatenative Synthesis", *IEEE ICASSP*, vol.1, (1999), pp.65-68.
23. S.-H. Chen, S.-H. Hwang and Y.-R. Wang, "An RNN-based Prosodic Information Synthesizer for Mandarin Text-to-Speech", *IEEE Trans. on Speech and Audio Processing*, vol.6, no.3, (1998), pp.226-239.

24. M.-S. Yu and N.-H. Pan, "A Statistical Model with Hierarchical Structure for Predicting Prosody in a Mandarin Text-To-Speech System", *Journal of the Chinese Institute of Engineers*, vol.28, no.5, (2005) pp.385-399.
25. F.-c. Chou and C.-y. Tseng, "Corpus-based Mandarin Speech Synthesis with Contextual Syllabic Units Based on Phonetic Properties", *IEEE ICASSP*, (1998), pp. 893-896.
26. F.-c. Chou, C.-y. Tseng and L.-s. Lee, "A set of corpus-based text-to-speech synthesis technologies for Mandarin Chinese", *IEEE Trans. on Speech and Audio Processing*, vol.10, no.7, (2002) pp.481-494.
27. M. Chu, H. Peng, Y. Zhao, Z. Niu and E. Wang, Microsoft Mulan – "A Bilingual TTS System", *IEEE ICASSP* (2003).
28. M. Dong, K.-T. Lua and H. Li, "A Unit Selection-based Speech Synthesis Approach for Mandarin Chinese", *Journal of Chinese Language and Computing*, vol.16, no.1 (2006).
29. R.-H. Wang, Z. Ma, W. Li and D. Zhu, "A Corpus-based Chinese Speech Synthesis with Contextual Dependent Unit Selection", *Proc. ICSLP*, vol.2, (2000), pp.391-394.
30. Z.-H. Ling, Y. Hu, Z.-W. Shuang and R.-H. Wang, "Decision Tree Based Unit Pre-selection in Mandarin Chinese Synthesis", *Proc. ISCSLP* (2002).
31. M. Beckman and G. Ayers Elam, *Guidelines for ToBI Labeling*, Version 3 (1997).
32. The list of frequently used characters in modern Chinese (《现代汉语常用字表》)[in Chinese] http://www.gmw.cn/content/2004-07/29/content_67735.htm.
33. Lexicography and Chinese dictionary compilation group in Institute of Linguistics, CASS, Ed (中国社会科学院语言所词典室词典编辑室编), The contemporary Chinese dictionary, the 5th edition(《现代汉语词典》) [in Chinese], *the commercial press* (2002).
34. Y. Qian, M. Chu and H. Peng, "Segmenting unrestricted Chinese text into prosodic words instead of lexical words", *IEEE ICASSP* (2001).
35. M. Chu and Y. Qian, "Locating boundaries for prosodic constituent in unrestricted Mandarin texts", *Computational Linguistics and Chinese Language Processing*, vol.6, no.1, p.61-82, (2001).
36. S. Zhao, J.H. Tao and L.H. Cai, "Prosodic phrasing with inductive learning", *ICSLP* (2002).
37. Z. R. Zhang, M. Chu and E. Chang, "An efficient way to learn rules for grapheme-to-phoneme conversion in Chinese", *Proc. ISCSLP*, Taipei (2002).
38. W. J. Wang, S. H. Hwang and S. H. Chen, "The broad study of homograph disambiguity for Mandarin speech synthesis", *Proc. ICSLP* (1996).
39. M. Zheng and L. H. Cai, "A new rule-based method of automatic phonetic notation on polyphones", *Proc. ICSP'04* (2004).
40. B.-F. Chen, G.-P. Hu and R.-H. Wang, "Large lexicon construction for TTS system", *Proc. ISCSLP* (2002).
41. H.-P. Zhang, Q. Liu, H.-K. Yu, X.-Q. Cheng and S. Bai, "Chinese Named Entity Recognition Using Role Model", *Computational Linguistics and Chinese Language Processing*, vol. 8, no. 2 (2003).
42. S. Yu, "Annotation for the Dictionary of Modern Chinese Grammar Information", *TsingHua University Press* (1998).
43. Z.-r. Zhang, M. Chu and E. Chang, "An Efficient Way to Learn Rules for Grapheme-to-Phoneme Conversion in Chinese", *Proc. ISCSLP* (2002).
44. G.-p. Hu, Z.-G. Chen and R.-H. Wang, "A Rule-Based Approach with SVM-Based Weight Estimation for Phoneme Disambiguation of Polyphone", *Proc. ICCPOL*, (2003), pp.599-605.
45. X. Shen and B. Xu, "A CART-based Hierarchical Stochastic Model for Prosodic Phrasing in Chinese", *Proc. ISCSLP* (2000).
46. J.-F. Li, G.-p. Hu and R.-h. Wang, "Chinese Prosody Phrase Break Prediction Based on Maximum Entropy Model", *Proc. ICSLP* (2004).

47. J.-F. Li, M. Fan, G.-P. Hu and R.-H. Wang, "Text Chunking for Intonational Phrase Prediction in Chinese", *Proc. NLP-KE*, (2003), pp.231-237.
48. Z.-G. Chen, G.-P. Hu and X.-F. Wang, "Text Normalization In Chinese Text-To-Speech System", *Journal of Chinese information processing*, vol.17, no.4, (2003), pp.45-51.
49. Y. R. Chao, *A Grammar of Spoken Chinese*, University of California Press (1968).
50. C.-y. Tseng, S.-h. Pin, Y.-l. Lee, H.-m. Wang and Y.-c. Chen, "Fluent speech prosody: framework and modeling", *Speech Communication*, vol.46, issues 3-4, *Special Issue on Quantitative Prosody Modelling for Natural Speech Description and Generation*, (2005), pp.284-309.
51. M.-S. Yu, N.-H. Pan and M.-J. Wu, "A Intonation Prediction Model that can Outputs Real Pitch Pattern", *Proc. Seventh Conference on Artificial Intelligence and Applications*, (2002), pp.784-788.
52. G.-p. Chen, Y. Hu, R.-H. Wang, "A Concatenative-Tone Model With Its Parameters' Extraction", *Speech Prosody 2004* (2004).
53. S. Lu, Y. Hu and R.-H. Wang, "Polynomial Regression Model for Duration Prediction in Mandarin", *Journal of Chinese Information Processing* (2005).
54. Z.-J. Wu, "Can Poly-Syllabic Tone-Sandhi Patterns be the Invariant Units of Intonation in Spoken Standard Chinese", *Proc. ICSLP*, (1990), pp.12.10.1-12.10.4.
55. S. Lemmetty, *Review of Speech Synthesis Technology*, Master thesis, Helsinki Univ. of Technology.
56. Z. Li, "合成无限词汇汉语语言的初步研究 " [in Chinese], *Chinese Journal of Acoustics*, vol.5, p.291-298.
57. J. Zhang, "汉语文语转换系统的语音规则和声学参数 " [in Chinese], *Chinese Journal of Acoustics*,vol.15, no.22, p. 113-120.
58. S.-a. Yang, *面向声学语音学的普通话语音合成技术* [in Chinese], Social Sciences Academic Press.
59. Shinan Lu and A. Almeida, "The Effects of Voice Disguise Upon Formant Transition", *IEEE ICASSP*, p.885-888, (1986).
60. S. Lu, J. Zhang and S. Qi, "Chinese text-to-speech system based on parallel formant synthesizer", *14th International Congress on Acoustics* (1992).
61. L. Lee, C. Tseng and C. Hsieh, "Improved tone concatenation rules in a formant-based Chinese text-to-speech system", *IEEE Trans. on Speech and Audio Processing*, vol.1, no.3, (1993), pp.287-294.
62. D. Childers and H. Hu, "Speech Synthesis by Glottal Excited Linear Prediction", *Journal of the Acoustical Society of America*, vol. 96 (4), (1994), pp.2026-2036.
63. R. Donovan, *Trainable Speech Synthesis*, PhD. Thesis. Cambridge University Engineering Department, England (1996).
64. G. Campos and E. Gouvea, "Speech Synthesis Using the CELP Algorithm", *Proc. ICSLP* (1996).
65. F. Mo, C. Li, H. Ni, J. Sun and T. Li, "Chinese All-Syllable Real Time Synthesis System", *Proc. International Conference on Signal Processing*, (1990), pp.369-372.
66. Q. Liu and R.-H. Wang, "A new synthesis method based on the LMA vocal tract model", *Chinese Journal of Acoustics*, vol.17, no.2, (1998), pp.153-162.
67. Y.-J. Wu and R.-H. Wang, "HMM-based trainable speech synthesis for Chinese" [in Chinese], *Journal of Chinese Information Processing*, accepted
68. R. J. McAulay and T. F. Quatieri, "Speech analysis/synthesis based on a sinusoidal representation", *IEEE Trans. on Acoustics, Speech, and Signal Processing*, vol. ASSP-34, no. 4, (1986), pp.744–745.

69. Y. Stylianou, "Applying the Harmonic Plus Noise Model in Concatenative Speech Synthesis", *IEEE Trans. on Speech and Audio Processing*, vol. 9, (2001), pp.21–29.
70. H. Kawahara, I. Masuda-Katsuse and A. de Cheveigne, "Restructuring speech representations using a pitch-adaptive time-frequency smoothing and an instantaneous-frequency-based F0 extraction: Possible role of a repetitive structure in sounds", *Speech Communication*, 27(3-4), (1999), pp.187-207.
71. Z.-H. Ling, Y.Hu, Z.-W. Shuang and R.-H. Wang, "Compression of Speech Database by Feature Separation and Pattern Clustering Using STRAIGHT", *Proc. ICSLP* (2004).
72. Z.-W. Shuang, Z.-X. Wang, Z.-H. Ling and R.-H. Wang, "A Novel Voice Conversion System based on Codebook Mapping with Phoneme-tied Weighting", *Proc. ICSLP* (2004).
73. Y. N. Chen, Y. Zhao and M. Chu, "Customizing Base Unit Set with Speech Database in TTS Systems", *Eurospeech* (2005).
74. M. Chu and S. N. Lu, "A Text-to-Speech System with High Intelligibility and High Naturalness for Chinese", *Chinese Journal of Acoustics*, vol.15, no.1, (1996), pp.81-90.
75. S. H. Hwang, S. H. Chen and Y. R. Wang, "A Mandarin Text-to-Speech System", *Proc. ICSLP* (1996).
76. M. Chu, H. Peng, H.-Y. Yang and E. Chang, "Selecting Non-uniform Units from a Very Large Corpus for Concatenative Speech Synthesizer", *IEEE ICASSP* (2001).
77. F. C. Chou, C. Y. Tseng and L. S. Lee, "A Set of Corpus-Based Text-to-Speech Technologies for Mandarin Chinese", *IEEE Trans. on Speech and Audio Processing*, vol. 10, issue 7, (2002), pp.481-494.
78. E. Moulines and F. Charpentier, "Pitch-Synchronous Waveform Processing Techniques for Text-to-Speech Synthesis Using Diphone", *Speech Communication*, vol. 9, (1990), pp.453-467.
79. M. Chu, Y. Zhao and E. Chang, "Modeling Stylized Invariance and Local Variability of Prosody in Text-to-Speech Synthesis", *Speech Communication*, vol. 48, (2006), pp.716-726.
80. A. Black and N. Campbell, "Optimizing Selection of Units from Speech Database for Concatenative Synthesis", *IEEE ICASSP*, (1996), pp.373-376.
81. H. Hon, A. Acero, S. Huang, J. Liu and M. Plumpe, "Automatic Generation of Synthesis Units for Trainable Text-to-Speech System", *IEEE ICASSP*, vol.1, p.293-296, (1998).
82. H. Peng, Y. Zhao and M. Chu, "Perpetually Optimizing the Cost Function for Unit Selection in a TTS System with One Single Run of MOS Evaluation", *Proc. ICSLP* (2002).
83. Y. Zhao, M. Chu, H. Peng and E. Chang, "Custom-Tailoring TTS Voice Font – Keeping the Naturalness When Reducing Database Size", *Proc. Eurospeech* (2003).
84. L. J. Wang, Y. Zhao, M. Chu, F. K. Soong and Z. G. Cao, "Phonetic Transcription Verification with Generalized Posterior Probability", *Proc. Eurospeech* (2005).
85. L. J. Wang, Y. Zhao, M. Chu, F. K. Soong, J. L. Zhou and Z. G. Cao, "Context-Dependent Boundary Model for Refining Boundaries Segmentation of TTS Units", *IEICE Trans. on Information and System*, vol. E89-D, no. 3, (2006), pp.1082-1091.
86. Y.-J. Wu, H. Kawai, J. Ni and R.-H. Wang, "Discriminative training and explicit duration modeling for HMM-based automatic segmentation", *Speech Communication*, vol. 47 (2005).
87. Y. N. Chen, M. Lai, M. Chu, F. K. Soong, Y. Zhao and F. Y. Hu, "Automatic Accent Annotation with Limited Manually Labeled Data", *Speech Prosody* (2006).
88. E. Moulines and Y. Sagisaka, "Voice conversion: State of the art and perspectives", *Speech Communication*, vol. 16, no. 2, (1995), pp.125–126.
89. A. B. Kain, *High Resolution Voice Transformation*, Ph.D. thesis, Oregon Health and Science Unitversity (2001).
90. M. Abe, S. Nakamura, K. Shikano and H. Kuwabara, "Voice conversion through vector quantization", *IEEE ICASSP*, (1988), pp.655-658.

91. H. Valbret and et al, "Voice transformation using psola technique", *Speech Communication*, vol. 11, no. 2-3, (1992), pp. 175–187.
92. Y. Stylianou and et al, "Continuous probabilistic transform for voice conversion", *IEEE Trans. on Speech and Audio Processing*, vol. 6, no. 2, (1998), pp.131– 142.
93. T. Ceyssens and et al, "On the construction of a pitch conversion system", *EUSIPCO*, (2002).
94. Y. Kang, J. Tao and B. Xu, "Applying Pitch Target Model to Convert F0 Contour for Expressive Mandarin Speech Synthesis", *IEEE ICASSP* (2006).
95. A. Iida, N. Campbell, S. Iga, F. Higuchi and M. Yasumura, "A Speech Synthesis System for Assisting Communication", *Proc. ISCA Workshop on Speech & Emotion*, (2000), pp.167-172,.
96. T. Marumoto and N. Campbell, "Control of speaking types for emotion in a speech re-sequencing system" [in Japanese], *Proc. Acoustic Society of Japan, Spring meeting*, (2000), pp.213-214.
97. H. Kawanami, Y. Iwami and T. Toda, "Gmm-based voice conversion applied to emotional speech synthesis", *Proc. Eurospeech*, (2003), pp.2401-2404.
98. T. Yoshimura, K. Tokuda, T. Masuko, T. Kobayashi, and T. Kitamura, "Simultaneous modeling of spectrum, pitch and duration in HMM-based speech synthesis", *Proc. Eurospeech*, (1999), pp. 2347-2350.
99. Y.-J. Wu and R.-H. Wang, "Minimum Generation Error Training for HMM-based Speech Synthesis", *IEEE ICASSP* (2006).
100. P. Birkholz and D. Jackèl, "Construction and Control of a Three-Dimensional Vocal Tract Model", *IEEE ICASSP* (2006).
101. http://www.iflytek.com

CHAPTER 6

LARGE VOCABULARY CONTINUOUS SPEECH RECOGNITION FOR MANDARIN CHINESE: PRINCIPLES, APPLICATION TASKS AND PROTOTYPE EXAMPLES

Lin-shan Lee

Department of Electrical Engineering, National Taiwan University, Taipei
E-mail: lslee@gate.sinica.edu.tw

This chapter very briefly reviews the area of Large Vocabulary Continuous Speech Recognition (LVCSR) for Mandarin Chinese, which is apparently a very important core technology in Chinese Spoken Language Processing. The overall framework and basic principles of LVCSR for Mandarin Chinese are briefly reviewed in this chapter considering the structural features of the Chinese language, serving as the introduction of the four following chapters of this book that focus on the four key modules of this framework: acoustic modeling, tone modeling, language modeling and pronunciation modeling. Evolution of application tasks and a very recent prototype example are then summarized, and some lessons learned in the development of LVCSR for Mandarin Chinese finally discussed.

1. Introduction

Large vocabulary continuous speech recognition (LVCSR) has long been the most important core technology in spoken language processing. In addition to its direct application to dictation and transcriptions tasks, almost all other applications such as spoken dialogues, spoken document processing, retrieval and summarization, speech-to-speech translation, computer-aided language learning, etc. have to rely on LVCSR as their first step. Even for text-to-speech synthesis, the most successful technologies of corpus-based approaches also use LVCSR technologies to perform initial processing on their corpora. Therefore in this chapter we first very briefly introduce the basic principles, application tasks and prototype examples of LVCSR for Mandarin Chinese. LVCSR for Mandarin Chinese actually include six key components: front-end processing and feature extraction, acoustic modeling, tone modeling, language modeling and lexicon generation, pronunciation modeling, search and decoding. Except for the first component, front-end processing and feature extraction, which is essentially language-independent, all the other five components have, more or less, to do with the special characteristics of Chinese languages. The first four components i.e., acoustic modeling, tone modeling, language modeling and lexicon generation, and pronunciation modeling will be briefly introduced later on in this chapter, while the details of these four components will be discussed in the following four chapters of this book. The last component, search and decoding, will be discussed only in this chapter. Extension of LVCSR to different application tasks and different prototype examples will also be very briefly described here, but these will be explored in much greater detail in various chapters in Parts II and III of this book.

2. Structural Features of Chinese Language Relevant to LVCSR

Chinese is quite different from most western languages in various structural features.[1,2] Here we briefly discuss those features which are related to LVCSR.

2.1. *Monosyllabic Structure and Tone Behavior*

Chinese is not alphabetic. Instead, the large number of Chinese characters are ideographic symbols. Almost every Chinese character is a morpheme with its own meaning. A *word* is composed of one to several characters, with its meaning sometimes related to the individual meaning of the component characters, but sometimes completely different from them. Thus, some words are *compositional*, i.e., the meaning of the word has to do with the meaning of the component characters, such as the characters "大 (big)" and "學 (learning)" forming a word "大學 (university)", but some other words are purely *ideographic*, such as the characters "和 (harmony)" and "尚 (prefer)" forming the word "和尚 (monk)", where the meaning of the word is completely different from the meaning of its component characters. An elegant feature is that all the characters are pronounced as monosyllables, and the total number of phonologically allowed syllables is rather limited, about 1,345 for Mandarin and other numbers for the other Chinese dialects. Chinese is also a tone language, in which each syllable is assigned a tone, and the tone carries lexical meaning. There are 4 lexical tones plus a neutral tone for Mandarin, and the number of tones can be slightly higher for some other dialects. When differences in tones are disregarded, the total number of syllables in Mandarin is reduced from about 1,345 to 416. A similar reduction in syllable numbers applies to some other dialects as well. The syllables differentiated by the different tones are referred to as *tonal* syllables, while the tone-ignored ones are known as *base* syllables. The small number of syllables also implies a large number of homonym characters sharing the same syllable sounds. For example, the number of commonly used Chinese characters may be 8,000 or 10,000, which is much larger than 1,345. As a result, each syllable very often represents many characters with different meanings, and the combination of these syllables (or characters) gives an unlimited number of words (between 80,000 to over 200,000 are actually commonly used) and sentences. This is referred to as the *monosyllabic structure* of Chinese. This structural feature leads to considerations in LVCSR which are different from the concerns of western alphabetic languages, not only in acoustic and language modeling or in the additional component of tone modeling, but also in the overall system structure as well.

2.2. *Flexible Wording Structure*

The wording structure in Chinese languages is extremely flexible. For example, a long word can be arbitrarily abbreviated, such as "台灣大學 (Taiwan University)" being abbreviated as "台大", using just the first and the third characters, and new words can be easily generated every day, such as the characters "電 (electricity)" and "腦 (brain)" forming a new word "電腦 (computer)". These have to do with the fact that every character has its own meaning and thus they can play certain linguistic roles very independently. Furthermore, there are no blanks or spaces in written or printed Chinese sentences serving as word boundaries. As a result, the *word* in Chinese languages is not very well-defined. The segmentation of a sentence into a string of words is definitely not unique, and a commonly-accepted lexicon has never existed. Such situations make LVCSR very special and indeed challenging. For western alphabetic languages, since words are well-defined by the blanks between the words in written or printed form, LVCSR is primarily word-based, such as based on a lexicon of words or on word (or word class) based language models. For Chinese, since words are not easily identified, special measures are usually needed.

2.3. *Flexible Word Ordering*

Another special feature of Chinese is its sentence structure. The degree of flexibilities in word ordering in sentences seems to be quite special. A good example is in Figure 1. When the several words or phrases, "我 (I)", "明天

(tomorrow)", "早上 (morning)", "六點半 (six thirty)", "要 (would like to)", "出發 (depart)", are put together into a sentence meaning, "I would like to depart at six thirty tomorrow morning", there is an unimaginable number of ways to permute those words or phrases to generate valid sentences.

明天	早上	六點半	我	要	出發
(tomorrow)	(morning)	(six thirty)	(I)	(would like to)	(depart)

明天早上六點半我要出發
我明天早上六點半要出發
我要明天早上六點半出發
明天我早上六點半要出發
明天我要早上六點半出發
明天早上我六點半要出發
明天早上我要六點半出發
我明天要早上六點半出發
明天我早上要六點半出發
□
□
□

Fig. 1. The flexibility in word ordering for Chinese sentences.

On the other hand, there certainly exists strong enough grammar rules governing the ways the words can be put together into valid sentences. This phenomenon also makes language modeling for Chinese languages rather special.

3. Some Historic Notes

The development of LVCSR for Mandarin Chinese has a long history. It is briefly reviewed here as there are indeed many lessons learned in the past which remain useful even today.

3.1. *From Isolated Syllable Recognition to LVCSR*

The research work on large vocabulary speech recognition for Mandarin Chinese started roughly in the mid 1980's by a few groups in mainland China and Taiwan. At that time, large vocabulary speech recognition technologies being explored were isolated-word-based even for English, and LVCSR for Mandarin Chinese was only a long-term vision, if not a dream. Considering the monosyllabic structure of the Chinese language mentioned above, recognition of the limited number of about 1,345 tonal syllables or 416 base syllables seems to be much more feasible than trying to recognize the very large number, at least 80,000, of commonly used words. The monosyllabic structure of Chinese also makes it less difficult, even if it does not seem natural, for the user to pronounce a Chinese sentence as a sequence of isolated syllables. This was the basic rationale for the paradigm of isolated-syllable-based large vocabulary Chinese speech recognition[3-10] in those years. Also, at that time, there was no Mandarin speech corpus available in the world, and the western research community was concentrated only on English. Thus all the research groups in mainland China and Taiwan had to create their own corpora by themselves, which was tremendously difficult. The difficulties in obtaining a corpus for developing LVSCR as well as the need of having one large enough for training the necessary acoustic models, are also reasons which delayed the progress of continuous speech recognition research.

As a result of the above, the early stages of large vocabulary speech recognition for Mandarin Chinese started with the input mode of using isolated syllables.[3-10] However, uttering a Chinese sentence as a sequence of isolated syllables is both awkward and slow. But LVCSR was a vision that was still remote, and even a large enough speech corpus for such purposes had not yet existed. A few intermediate approaches therefore emerged in the early 1990's. The first was the input mode of using isolated words, following the same approach of recognizing English speech in those years.[11] This worked very well for English, but not very successful for Chinese. The problem was the very flexible wording structure for Chinese as mentioned above. Not only the segmentation of a sentence into words was not unique, but there were always very large numbers of out-of-vocabulary (OOV) words regardless of how large the lexicon was, even if the sentence that was to be recognized did not include any special term or named entity. It was therefore very possible that a word produced by the user was not in the lexicon. For this reason, another mode of speech input using *prosodic segments*[12] emerged.

A prosodic segment is an utterance easily produced by the user as a breath group, which is usually composed of a few words and is linguistically bounded by syntactic or prosodic boundaries in the sentences.[12] The prosodic segmentation of a given sentence is again not unique. However, rules for construction of such prosodic segments using several words existed and could be found at least partially, even if in those early years the detailed prosodic structure of Chinese sentences had not been discovered yet. A good feature of this method is that it is natural for a native speaker to utter a sentence in the form a few prosodic segments. Prosodic segments are shorter in duration and simpler in structure, so it was easier to implement large vocabulary speech recognition in this way.

It then became feasible to develop LVCSR technologies in the mid 1990's.[13,14] But the unavailability of a speech corpus, which had long been a serious problem, remained a major obstacle. This was why the earliest prototypes were speaker dependent,[13,14] and speaker adaptation was specially emphasized in those years. At that time, it was still unknown to the research community how acoustic models can be adapted to a specific speaker for unseen acoustic units. Great efforts were thus made to generate a phonetically-balanced sentence set with minimum number of sentences,[15] such that a new speaker can have an adapted LVCSR system after producing the least number of utterances.

3.2. *Early Typical Prototypes: The Golden Mandarin Series*

Quite a number of prototype systems have been developed by different groups in mainland China[16-19] and Taiwan in the 1990's. The Golden Mandarin Series developed at the National Taiwan University and the Academia Sinica in Taipei are very good examples of what was available then, and probably the best-known to the rest of the world. In classical Chinese literature, it was said that the most beautiful sound in the world is that produced by knocking a piece of gold with a piece of jade. This sound is called "金玉之聲 (sound of gold and jade)". To researchers in this area, the most beautiful sound in the world must certainly be Mandarin speech, which is why these prototype systems were called the Golden Mandarin Series.

Golden Mandarin (I), openly demonstrated in Taipei in March 1991, was probably the first working, real-time large vocabulary Mandarin speech recognition system in the world.[20] It was implemented on an IBM PC/AT, connected to three sets of specially-designed hardware boards on which 10 TMS 320C25 chips operated in parallel. It was speaker-dependent without any adaptation functions. The speech input mode was isolated syllables. Golden Mandarin (II) was demonstrated to the public in September 1993[21] and implemented on a digital signal processor (DSP) card with a single-chip Motorola DSP 96002D and could be installed on any personal computer. The input mode was still in isolated syllables, but the hardware requirements were reduced from 10 DSP chips to 1 DSP chip, and various adaptation/learning functions were also implemented. The two earliest versions of Golden Mandarin (III) were first demonstrated in Taipei in March of 1995. Version (IIIa) was implemented on the same DSP card as was used for Golden Mandarin (II) with a single-chip Motorola DSP 96002D and could be installed on any personal computer, such as a 486, but its input mode was then in the form of isolated prosodic segments.[12] Version (IIIb), on the other hand, was implemented on a Sun SPARC 20 workstation, and the input mode was in continuous speech and complete sentences.[13,14] The Golden Mandarin (III) Windows 95 version was then publicly demonstrated and transferred to the industry in September 1996. Not long after, products were released and used by large numbers of users in 1997. It was improved from version (IIIb) and it had been downsized from the SPARC 20 to an ordinary Pentium PC using its standard sound card and implemented on MS Windows 95 (Chinese Version). Fast incremental speaker adaptation was implemented with a specially-developed user raining interface.

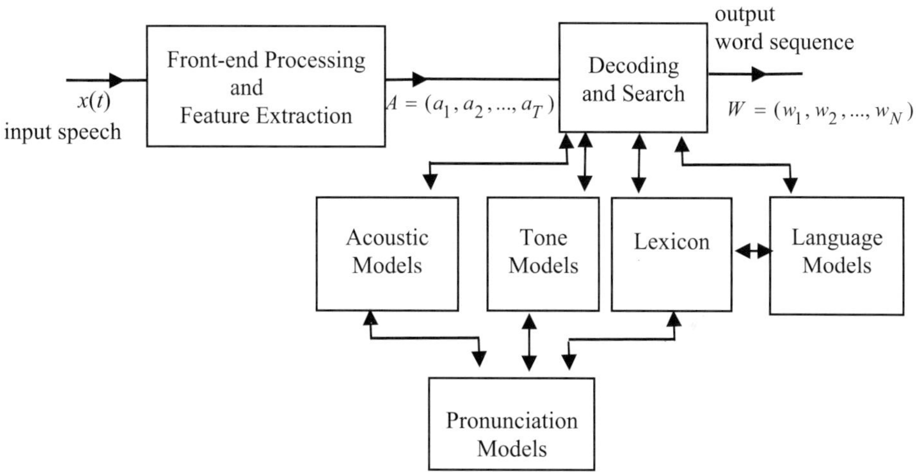

Fig. 2. General framework of LVCSR for Mandarin Chinese.

4. Basic Principles of LVCSR for Mandarin Chinese

The basic principles of LVCSR are in general language-independent, with the fundamental framework almost the same as that for all other languages including English,[22] as shown in Figure 2. The structural features of Chinese languages, however, lead to special approaches in most of the individual modules. As can be seen in Figure 2, the front-end processing and feature extraction first transform the input speech signal $x(t)$ into a sequence of feature vectors, $A = (a_1, a_2, \ldots, a_T)$, where a_t is the feature vector at time t, $1 \leqq t \leqq T$. The goal is to find the output word sequence, $W=(w_1, w_2, ..., w_N)$, where w_i is the *i*-th word in the sequence, $1 \leqq i \leqq N$, for the input signal $x(t)$. The most popular principle for LVCSR is the maximum a posterior (MAP) probability criterion,

$$W^* = \max_W \arg P(W \mid A) \tag{1}$$

where $P(W|A)$ is the a posterior probability of W given A, and Equation (1) indicates that the best output word sequence W^* is the one which maximizes $P(W|A)$. The probability $P(W|A)$ is usually evaluated by $P(W|A) = P(A|W)\,P(W)/P(A)$, and as a result Equation (1) can be reduced to

$$W^* = \max_W \arg[P(A \mid W)P(W)], \tag{2}$$

because $P(A)$ is the same for all possible output word sequence W. In Equation (2) $P(A|W)$ can be evaluated by acoustic models for all languages, but for Mandarin Chinese this probability is partially dependent on the tone models as well, while $P(W)$ can be evaluated by language models. In addition, the pronunciation models may lead to better lexicon and better acoustic models for all languages, and better tone models for Mandarin Chinese as well. So with the various modules as shown in Figure 2, the recognition process in Equation (2) is reduced to a search problem. Many new approaches have been developed for better front-end processing and feature extraction, but almost all of them are language-independent, requiring no further discussion of that module relating to Chinese. The rest of this section very briefly explains the other modules.

4.1. *Acoustic Modeling*

Hidden Markov models (HMMs)[22,23] have been widely used in acoustic modeling for most LVCSR systems, although there have been cases where some other approaches were used. In the acoustic modeling for Mandarin Chinese using HMMs, every acoustic unit is modeled as an HMM, in which a series of states is used to describe the statistical behavior of the feature vectors a_t mentioned in Equation (1). The time warping phenomena that usually happen in speech signals are taken care of by the state transition probabilities among the states, while the stochastic nature of the speech signals for a given state is modeled by a set of Gaussian mixtures. All the statistical parameters can be trained given a set of training corpus.

The first question we then face is what the acoustic unit for each HMM should be for Mandarin Chinese. In the early days of isolated syllable input, this acoustic unit may be the syllable. For continuous speech input, a better choice is evidently the so-called sub-syllabic unit. A very good choice of such sub-syllabic units are the *initial/finals*. Conventionally, each Mandarin syllable is decomposed in to an initial and a final. Here *initial* is the initial (or onset) consonant part of a syllable, while *final* is the part after that in the syllable which is usually made up of a vowel or diphthong plus an optional medial and an optional nasal ending. This initial/final framework fitted well with the monosyllabic structure of Mandarin Chinese. One approach for handling the context dependency in these initial/final models is to let the initial models be right context dependent on the following final, while the final models are context-independent. In this way, context dependency is properly simplified and handled only within a syllable, which is also in line with the monosyllabic structure of Mandarin Chinese. Experimental results have consistently indicated that the initial/final models developed in this way perform very well even today.[1,2,12-14] However, when more fluent or spontaneous speech was tested and more training data were available, even more co-articulation and context dependency needed to be considered. Some experimental results indicated that tri-phones, which are well-used for western alphabetic languages, seemed to offer slightly better performance, although the obtainable improvements were actually limited. In the tri-phone approach, each phoneme is an acoustic unit, and the same phoneme preceded or followed by different phonemes are considered as different units. This leads to a large number of tri-phone units to be trained, requiring a much larger training corpus, but it also brings in better capabilities of handling co-articulation and context dependency for more fluent or even spontaneous speech.[24-26] The probability $P(A|W)$ in Equation (2) can then be evaluated by all the HMMs for the component sub-syllabic units for the word sequence W. In recent years, more delicate acoustic models were also developed and used, for example the quin-phones. Chapter 7 explores this in greater detail.

4.2. *Tone Modeling*

Chinese is a tone language, with the different tones indicating different syllables and in turn different characters with different meanings. Modeling and recognition of tones is thus important for Mandarin Chinese. This is not the case for most western alphabetic languages, in which the pitch contours are in general not considered in speech recognition because they do not carry lexical information. Tones are, in general, patterns in pitch contours. In Mandarin, the four lexical tones have clear patterns in pitch contours, and the neutral tone has contour patterns which are unclear and highly dependent context. But these are true only for isolated syllables. For very fluent and spontaneous speech, the pitch contours vary significantly and tone behavior becomes very complicated.[27-29] Identifying tones directly from the pitch contours of fluent or spontaneous speech is very difficult, even for domain experts.

Recent works have shown that the prosody (including tones) of fluent or spontaneous speech acts as a whole. Durational features (e.g. syllable and pause durations), pitch contour features (e.g. level, slope and range of pitch contours), intersyllabic features (e.g. the relationships of durational and pitch contour features among adjacent syllables)[29] and others, all behave together making up the prosody of speech. Tones may thus be considered as partial information contributing to prosody. From this viewpoint, improved tone modeling and recognition can be achieved by considering all these different prosodic features together, as compared to using the pitch contour features alone. There have been studies which indicated that MFCC features, usually believed to represent the formant structures of speech signals, are also helpful in tone recognition. More details in this area can be found in Chapter 8.

4.3. *Language Modeling and Lexicon Generation*

The purpose of language models is to evaluate the prior probability P(W) of a word sequence W to be used in Equation (2). The most simplified general form of language models is the *n*-gram, or the probability $P(w_i \mid w_{i-n+1}, w_{i-n+2}, \ldots, w_{i-1})$ of observing the next word w_i given the previous *n*-1 words. For example, in the case of tri-gram ($n = 3$) language model, *P(W)* in Equation (2) for a word sequence $W = (w_{1,} w_2, \ldots w_N)$ can be estimated as follows:

$$P(W) = P(w_1)P(w_2 \mid w_1)\prod_{i=3}^{N} P(w_i \mid w_{i-2}, w_{i-1}), \tag{3}$$

where the first term on the right hand side is the uni-gram (n=1) for w_1, the second term the bi-gram ($n = 2$) for w_2, followed by tri-gram probabilities for the next several words. All these *n*-gram probabilities can be trained with a large text corpus.[30-32] Great efforts have been made to try to further improve the above general model. Important directions include clustering words into classes,[31] adaptation to different task domains and topics,[32-34] incorporating more linguistic or grammatical knowledge,[35,36].and so on.

The above general principle is word-based, or based on a set of well-defined words in the lexicon. For Chinese, this is difficult because, as mentioned above, there are no blanks or spaces in written or printed Chinese sentences that serve as word boundaries. A text corpus can be used to train *n*-gram language models only after it is segmented into sequences of words. But even the segmentation of a sentence into a sequence of words is not unique, and there has never been a commonly accepted lexicon of Chinese words. The basic principle to handle this problem is then as follows. First, we need an algorithm which can automatically extract frequently occurring patterns of segments of a few characters (e.g. special terms, named entities), and include them in the lexicon. A word segmentation algorithm can then be developed based on this lexicon and used to segment the corpus. The segmented corpus can then be used to train the language model.[33,34,37,38] We should note that some words in the lexicon are those frequently occurring patterns in the corpus, and not necessarily words linguistically. Thus they are generated dynamically for a given task domain defined by a corpus.

More details for this area, including improved language modeling techniques beyond *n*-grams and special approaches for handling Chinese languages are explored in Chapter 9 of this book.

4.4. *Pronunciation Modeling*

When people speak normally in real-world conditions, especially in the case of very fluent or spontaneous speech, very often the produced speech is different from "what it is supposed to be", and also different from the sequence of phonemes listed in the lexicon. Instead, the produced continuous speech is likely to contain different forms of a phoneme, or produced with some pronunciation variation. The "correct" (but may be unrealized pronunciation) form of the pronunciation of the speech unit is called the *base* form or canonical form, while forms found in actual speech that may vary from the canonical forms are called the *surface* forms. For example, in fluent or spontaneous speech, the bi-syllabic word "今天 (jiin-tien)" may be produced as a monosyllabic word "間 (jien)". Such variation in pronunciation inevitably cause serious problems to the recognition process.

The general approach to handle pronunciation variation is to try to model the pronunciation based on a large enough training corpus in order to describe how the pronunciation really behaves.[39-42] One way to do this is to develop a multiple-pronunciation lexicon, in which a word in the lexicon can have more than one pronunciation, each of which may have a probability. But the extra pronunciations also lead to added ambiguity in the recognition. The other way is to include such variation in the training of the acoustic models, which also leads to added ambiguity for the acoustic models. In either way, the pronunciation variation can be explicitly itemized, or expressed in terms of rules. The rule-based approach has the advantage of being able to handle some unseen pronunciation variations not occurring in the training corpus. However, this may also cause extra problems because those unseen pronunciation variation produced by the rules may not actually exist.[39-42] Another difficult problem for pronunciation modeling is that the pronunciation variation patterns are speaker dependent.

Pronunciation variation and modeling is very often language-dependent. For Mandarin Chinese, this variation also includes the variation in tones. Chapter 10 describes this area in greater detail.

4.5. *Decoding and search*

Even with the probabilities $P(A|W)$ and $P(W)$ in Equation (2) given, finding the best word sequence $W^* = (w_1^*, w_2^*, ..., w_N^*)$ is still a very difficult problem, because the total number of all possible word sequences $W = (w_1, w_2, ..., w_n)$ is huge, making the evaluation of Equation (2) for each of them simply impossible. Different approaches have been developed to handle this problem. Today, the most popular solution may be the time synchronous Viterbi search over the tree lexicon.[22] In this approach, the lexicon of all possible words are organized into a tree structure based on their component tri-phone units and the search process is constrained over this tree. In this way the search process over a certain section of speech signal for a certain tri-phone can be shared by many words, and the best path having the highest probability score is obtained at each time frame given the results of the previous frame. Beam search is very helpful here, in which only a limited number of possible paths with the highest scores are kept at each time frame.[22] Multi-pass search is very helpful as well, in which the search process is divided into two or more passes.[22] When less information is used in earlier passes to produce a much smaller search space for the later passes using much more information, the computational load can be significantly reduced.

For western alphabet-based languages, a word is simply the cascade of the component tri-phones, so the above search approach is very good. In Mandarin, there are two extra levels of linguistic units – the syllable and the character – between the tri-phone and the word. Several tri-phones are first concatenated to form a syllable. A syllable usually stands for at least several homonym characters. The cascade of several characters then gives us the word. Proper consideration and treatment of these additional syllable/character levels in the search process may produce better results than merely ignoring these extra levels and simply replicating what has been done for the western alphabetic languages.[43-45] These approaches were usually referred to as the syllable-based approaches. A good example is to obtain a syllable lattice in the first pass using only the acoustic model scores. Another example is that the tree lexicon is constructed using arcs of syllables. Extensions of such approaches have usually produced very good results, if the syllable/character structure of the language was properly considered.

In recent years, a search algorithm minimizing the word error rate (WER) using word-based consensus networks has been popularly used for western alphabet-based languages, producing better results than those obtained with the MAP principle of Equations (1) and (2). This is because with the MAP principle, it can be shown that the expected sentence error rate is minimized. However, in speech recognition it is usually the minimized word error rate (WER) rather than the minimized sentence error rate which is desired. This is why to explicitly minimize the WER is helpful, and a new WER minimization algorithm applicable to word lattices obtained in the first pass was thus developed for western alphabetic langauges.[46] In order to reduce the required computation, in this approach, the word lattice is first reduced to a word-based consensus network, which is the cascade of several properly-aligned segments, each of which includes several word hypotheses having consensus on their word entities (the same word or words with similar phonemic structures) and time spans (reasonably overlapping in time). By choosing the word hypotheses having the highest posterior probabilities in each segment, the final word string can be obtained with the expected WER minimized to a good extent.[45]

Recently, it was proposed that in the above word-based consensus network approach for minimizing the WER, considering the syllable/character structure of Chinese, character-based rather than word-based consensus networks should be used for Mandarin.[47] Extensive experimental results indicated that with this character-based consensus network improved recognition performance can be obtained as compared to the word-based consensus network, or the conventional one-pass or multi-pass search algorithms.[47] A similar concept of evaluating the character posterior probabilities, rather than the word posterior probabilities, has also been developed and proposed,[48] although from a different point of view. This is one recent example of a search approach that makes use of the syllable/character structure of the Chinese language.

5. Evolution of Application Tasks of LVCSR

The application tasks of LVCSR, for Mandarin Chinese and for all languages in general, have in fact evolved from dictation to a very wide variety of tasks. These are summarized below.

5.1. *From Dictation to Different Application Tasks*

In the early years of developing large vocabulary Chinese speech recognition, from the mid 1980's to the mid 1990's in both mainland China and Taiwan, the only task thought of was the input of Chinese characters into computers, or dictation applications. This was apparently because the input of Chinese characters into computers was a very difficult and unsolved problem at that time. Entering characters by voice was understandably very attractive that great efforts were made towards this goal.

In the mid 1990's, however, the achievable performance of speech recognition technologies has more or less crossed the threshold for practical applications. The Internet also brought a new platform of many possible applications. A much wider scope of application tasks thus emerged.[2,49] This expansion of tasks happened first to the western speech research community, but very soon followed by the Chinese speech research community. A typical application area was conversational interfaces or spoken dialogues, which led to the various new research issues such as speech understanding, user interaction, discourse analysis and dialogue management.[50-53] Further extensions of such conversational interfaces include voice portals, speech-enabled intelligent agents, etc. Another example of a typical application developed slightly later was audio indexing and spoken document retrieval.[54-60] Indexing and retrieval is still an active research area today, even for text documents. Mapping the relevant technologies for text to speech signals was not only challenging, but generated new problems primarily due to the uncertainty and errors in the speech recognition process. In more recent years two additional application tasks turned out to be very important among others, i.e., the speech-to-speech translation[61] and computer-aided language learning,[62] both promoted by globalization and the associated multi-lingual environment in our daily lives. The former needs to integrate machine translation with LVCSR, while the latter tries to integrate the profession of language education with LVCSR. There are also many other applications related to but not necessarily directly based on LVCSR, for example language identification and speaker verification.

5.2. *From User Interface to Content Analysis*

On the other hand, LVCSR has traditionally been considered as a technology for user interface. All application tasks mentioned above are in fact different types of user interfaces, from dictation to dialogues, from retrieval to translation. In recent years, however, the speech research community realized that there exists another huge area of application tasks for LVCSR which is actually different from user interface, but has to do with content analysis, or the analysis of the unlimited network content offered by the Internet.[63-65] In the future, digital content over the network will include all the information activities in our lives, from real-time information to knowledge archives, from working environments to private services. Today, most of these contents are in text form, and thus conveniently accessed by text-based processes. Not only do users enter their instructions by words or texts, but the network or search engine also offers text materials from which the users can browse and select. However, in the future with multimedia being the most attractive form of network content, speech information will also be a central concern. Speech information usually provides some insights to the subjects, topics, and concepts of multimedia contents. As a result, the spoken documents associated with the network content will be the key for users to utilize such content efficiently.

When considering the above network content access environment, we must keep in mind that unlike written documents, which are better structured with titles and paragraphs and thus easier to access, multimedia/spoken documents are merely video/audio signals. Examples include a three-hour video of a course lecture, a two-hour movie, or a one-hour news episode. They are not segmented into paragraphs and no titles are written for the paragraphs. Thus, they are much more difficult to access because the user simply cannot browse through each from the beginning to the end. As a result, better approaches are required for a better analysis of spoken documents (or their associated multimedia content) to make these contents more easily accessible. An approach in this area should include at least the following:[63]

(1) *Key term extraction from spoken documents.* To extract the key terms in the spoken documents (or the associated multimedia content) are the key to understanding the subject matters of the documents, although these key terms are usually difficult to extract from the spoken documents.

(2) *Spoken document segmentation.* Spoken documents (or the associated multimedia content) need to be automatically segmented into short paragraphs, each with a central concept or topic.

(3) *Information extraction for spoken documents.* This involves automatically extracting the key information (such as who, when, where, what, and how) for the events described in the segmented short paragraphs, which is very often the relationships among the key terms in the paragraphs.

(4) *Summary and title generation for spoken documents.* This is to automatically generate a title and a summary (in text or speech form) for each short paragraph of the spoken documents (or the associated multimedia content).

(5) *Topic analysis and organization.* This involves automatically analyzing the subject topics of the segmented short paragraphs of the spoken documents (or the associated multimedia content), clustering them into groups with topic labels, constructing the relationships among the groups, and organizing them into some hierarchical visual presentation easier for users to browse.

When all the above tasks can be properly performed, the spoken documents (or the associated multimedia content) can be automatically transformed into the form of short paragraphs, properly organized in some hierarchical visual presentation with titles/summaries/topic labels as references for efficient access. This whole area of application tasks is thus referred to as spoken document understanding and organization[63] here in this chapter. Spoken document summarization, currently explored by many research groups worldwide, is one important task in this area. Figure 3 illustrates this area as another different set of application tasks other than user interface. From this figure, it can also be seen that spoken document retrieval is in fact the application task capable of integrating both areas of user interface and content analysis.

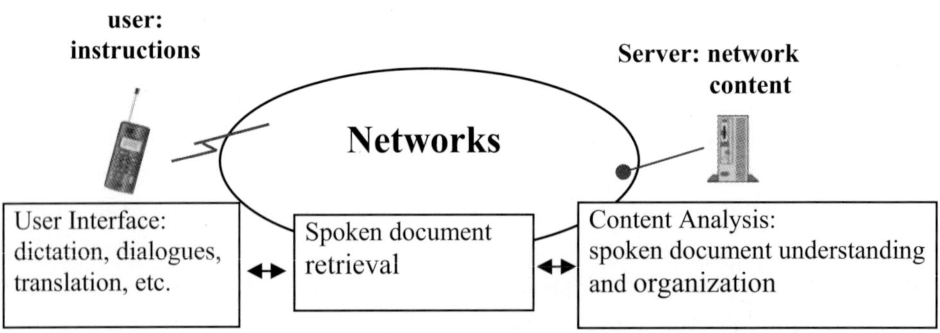

Fig. 3. The two major areas of application tasks: user interface and content analysis.

It should be noted that in the various user interface applications very often, technology developers find it difficult to satisfy the user, because in most cases humans can do better than the computer. To replace a person with a computer is always difficult. However, in the area of content analysis, very often only the computer can handle huge quantities of contents, even though the human can indeed do better if the quantity is small. This is also true for spoken document retrieval, which certainly involves significant content analysis as well. In fact, this clear advantage of the computer implies that those application tasks involving content analysis may be the areas where speech recognition technologies will become very useful in the future.

Good examples of the many application tasks of LVCSR mentioned in this section are explored in detail in various chapters in Part II and Part III of this book. In the next section of this chapter, we very briefly introduce one prototype example employing spoken document understanding and organization technologies.

6. A Prototype Example for Spoken Document Understanding and Organization

An initial prototype system for spoken document understanding and organization has been successfully developed in the National Taiwan University[66] and this system will be briefly described in this section. Broadcast news are taken as the example spoken/multimedia documents. The broadcast news archive consist of two sets, both in Mandarin Chinese. The first has approximately 85 hours of about 5,000 news stories, recorded from radio and TV stations in Taipei in the period from February 2002 to May 2003. No video signals were kept with them. The second set has roughly 25 hours of about 800 news stories, including the video signal parts, recorded from a TV station in Taipei from October to December 2005.

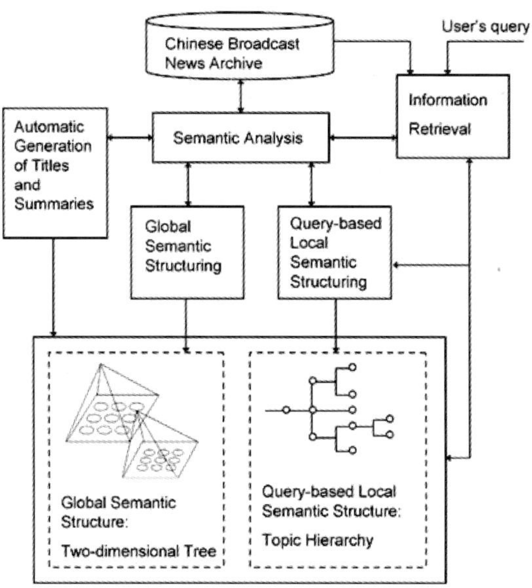

Fig. 4. The block diagram of the prototype example for spoken document understanding and organization.

The complete block diagram of the prototype system is shown in Figure 4. It includes three major parts: (1) Automatic Generation of Titles and Summaries for each of the news stories,[67,68] such that they become much more easier to access, (2) Global Semantic Structuring of the entire broadcast news archive, offering to the user a global picture of the semantic structure of the archive,[69] and (3) Query-based Local Semantic Structuring for the subset of the news stories retrieved by the user's query, providing the user a detailed semantic structure of the relevant news stories given the query he entered.[64] All three parts are based on a very useful semantic analysis framework for spoken documents, the Probabilistic Latent Semantic Analysis (PLSA). Below, these three parts are very briefly introduced first, followed by a summary of the functionalities of the system.

6.1. *Automatic Generation of Titles and Summaries*

The titles exactly complement the summaries for the user during browsing and retrieval. The user can easily select the desired document with a glance at the list of titles. He can then look through or listen to the summaries in text or speech form for the titles he selected. It was found that the sentences selected based on the topic entropy evaluated with PLSA mentioned above can be used to construct better summaries for the spoken documents.[68] For title generation, a new delicate scored Viterbi approach was developed, in which the key terms in the automatically generated summaries are carefully selected and sequenced by a Viterbi beam search using three sets of scores. This new delicate scored Viterbi approach was further integrated with the previously-proposed adaptive K-nearest neighbor approach[67] to offer better results.

6.2. *Global Semantic Structuring*

The purpose of global semantic structuring is to offer an overall knowledge of the semantic content of the entire spoken document archive through a kind of hierarchical structure with concise visual presentation to help the user to browse across spoken documents efficiently. In this system, we developed a new approach to analyze and structure the topics of the spoken documents in an archive into a two-dimensional tree structure or a multi-layered map.[69] The spoken documents are clustered by the latent topics they primarily address, obtained from semantic analysis, and the clusters are organized as a two-dimensional map. Every node can then be expanded into another two-dimensional map in the next layer with nodes representing finer topics.

6.3. *Query-based Local Semantic Structuring*

The global semantic structure mentioned above is useful, but not good enough for the user in relation to his special information needs, represented by the query he entered. The query given by the user is usually short and not specific enough, and as a result a large number of spoken documents are retrieved, including many *noisy* documents. However, spoken documents are very difficult to be shown on the screen and very difficult to browse. It is thus very helpful to construct a local semantic structure for the retrieved spoken documents for the user to identify what he really needs to go through, or to specify what he really wishes to obtain. This semantic structure is localized to the user's query, constructed from those retrieved documents only and thus needs to be much more delicate over a very small subset of the entire archive. This is why it is different from the global semantic structure mentioned above. In this system we used the Hierarchical Agglomerative Clustering and Partitioning algorithm (HAC+P) recently proposed to construct a very fine topic hierarchy for the localized retrieved documents. Every node on the hierarchy represents a small cluster of the retrieved documents, and is labeled by a key term as the topic of the cluster. The user can then click on the nodes or topics to select the documents he wishes to browse, or to expand his query by adding the selected topics onto his previous query.[64]

6.4. *Summary of the Functionalities of the Prototype Example*

In this prototype example, for those news stories with video signals, the video signals were also summarized using video technologies, such as video frames for human faces, moving objects and scene changes being regarded more important, and basing the length of the video summary on the length of the speech summary.[66]

For the global semantic structure, a total of six two-dimensional tree structures were obtained for six categories of news stories, e.g. world news, business news, sports news, etc. A 3x3 small map on the second layer of the tree for world news overlaid with the video signal is shown in Figure 5. This is a map expanded from a cluster in the first layer covering all disasters happening worldwide. As can be found on this map, one small cluster is for "airplane crash (墜機)" and others similar to it, one for "earthquake (地震)" and other similar disasters, one for "hurricane (颶風)", and so on. All the news stories belonging to each node of the two-dimensional tree are listed under the node by their automatically generated titles. The user can easily browse through these titles or

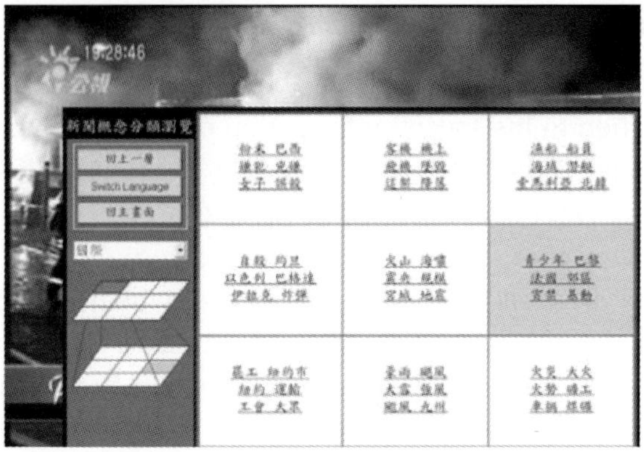

Fig. 5. A 3x3 map on the second layer expanded from a cluster on the first layer of the global semantic structure for world news.

Fig. 6. The result of query-based local semantic structuring for a query of "White House of United States."

click to view either the summaries or the complete stories. With this structure it is much more easier for the user to browse news stories either top-down or bottom-up.[66]

For the query-based local semantic structuring, the topic hierarchy constructed in real-time from the news stories retrieved by a query, "White House of United States (美國白宮)," is shown on the left lower corner of Figure 6, in which the three topics on the first layer are respectively "Iraq (伊拉克)", "US (美國)" and "Iran (伊朗)", and one of the nodes in the second layer below "US" is "President George Bush (布希)". When the user clicks on the node "President George Bush", the relevant news stories are listed on the lower right corner by their automatically generated titles. The user can then click the "summary" button to view the summary, or click the titles to view the complete stories. Such information are overlaid with the news video retrieved with the highest score.[66]

7. Lessons Learned in the Development of LVCSR for Mandarin Chinese

Many lessons were learned from the development of Mandarin Chinese LVCSR in the past years. Some of them are summarized very briefly below, although there must indeed be more than those listed here.

1. Even if the Chinese language has a structure quite different from that of western alphabetic languages such as English, the development of LVCSR for Mandarin Chinese turned out to be on par with that of the western languages, although very often with a propagation delay. Mandarin LVCSR started with isolated-syllable-based approaches, and later extended to continuous speech, just as western languages started with isolated-word-based approaches and so on. Application tasks started with dictation but evolved into a wide variety of tasks including both user interface and content analysis, for both Mandarin Chinese and western alphabetic languages in exactly the same way. This may imply that many of the technologies and application environment of LVCSR are intrinsically language-independent, and many of the linguistic behavior of speech signals are universal even if the surface structure carrying such behavior are quite different across these different languages.
2. With the above understanding, the structural features of Chinese languages did require special considerations in designing or implementing the individual modules to be used in the overall framework. Syllable structure in acoustic modeling, tone behavior and modeling, word segmentation and lexicon generation in language modeling, special variations in pronunciation modeling, and the extra levels of syllable/character in decoding and search are all good examples. Nonetheless, the basic principles behind these modules are actually language-independent in most cases. Some structural features may require special attention, for example tone modeling and word segmentation. Interestingly, the differences in the surface structure of languages seemed to be able to play more roles in earlier years of LVCSR. For example, when isolated syllables were used as the input mode, even special acoustic models quite different from hidden Markov models (HMMs) could be used and very good results were reported because of the relatively simple phonetic structure of isolated Mandarin syllables.[7] But such differences in surface structure seemed to decline in prominence when very fluent or spontaneous speech is considered. Probably these surface structures

themselves for the different languages become much closer to one another in very fluent or spontaneous speech. For example, the pitch contours for spontaneous Mandarin speech are very random and the tones are very difficult to identify in spontaneous speech. Human listeners can recognize the tones under such conditions very well probably because they use more context information rather than pitch contours alone. This is still unknown to us.

3. On the other hand, when different application tasks are considered, the differences in surface structures of the languages seem to play a bigger role when the tasks are extended to a much wider variety, especially those which are more culturally oriented, such as network content. For example, when broadcast news or course lectures are to be analyzed, summarized or retrieved, the percentage of out-of-vocabulary (OOV) words, especially named entities and special terms, in such spoken documents due to the very flexible wording structure of Mandarin Chinese[38,64,70] are apparently much higher than in dictation applications for normal office use. The special treatment of these is the key to achieving better results.
4. With the significant advances in technology and the rapid development of the variety of application tasks, the achievable performance of LVCSR for Mandarin Chinese is still not satisfactory. More effort is apparently needed. For example, new recognition models or architectures, such as the detection-based approach,[71] new feature parameters, the use of new information such as speech prosody,[72] the consideration of the special problems of spontaneous speech,[73] and the use of many other approaches to attain more robust recognition technologies[74,75] are all very much encouraged. Many of these directions are again on par with the research activities on other languages in different parts of the world.[76,77] Closer interaction with these activities worldwide and learning lessons from them will certainly benefit the advances of Mandarin Chinese LVCSR technologies.

8. Conclusion

This chapter very briefly introduces the Large Vocabulary Continuous Speech Recognition (LVCSR) for Mandarin Chinese. Structural features of the language which have to do with LVCSR are first presented. Some historic notes are also mentioned, followed by a review of the overall framework and the basic principles of each individual module of LVCSR for Mandarin Chinese. The evolution of application tasks is also reviewed, followed by a summary of a very recent prototype example. The lessons learned in the development of LVCSR are finally discussed.

References

1. L.-s. Lee, "Voice Dictation of Mandarin Chinese", *IEEE Signal Processing Magazine*, vol. 14, No.4, (1997), pp.63-101.
2. L.-s. Lee, "Structural Features of Chinese Language – Why Chinese Spoken Language Processing is Special and Where We Are", keynote Speech, *Proc. International Symposium on Chinese Spoken Language Processing*, Singapore, (1998), pp.1-15.
3. C.-h. Hwang, Y.-m. Hsu, B.-c. Wang, C.-y. Tseng and L.-s. Lee, "Efficient Speech Recognition Techniques for the Finals of Mandarin Syllables," *International Journal of Pattern Recognition and Artificial Intelligence*, vol .2, No.1, (1988), pp.87-103.
4. P.-y. Ting, C.-y. Tseng and L.-s. Lee, "An Efficient Speech Recognition System for the Initials of Mandarin Syllables", *International Journal of Pattern Recognition and Artificial Intelligence*, vol. 4, No.4, (1990), pp.687-704.
5. L.-s. Lee, C.-y. Tseng, F.-h. Liu, C. H. Chang, H.-y. Gu, S. H. Hsieh, C. H. Chen, "Special Speech Recognition Approaches for the Highly Confusing Mandarin Syllables Based on Hidden Markov Models", *Computer Speech and Language*, vol. 5, No.2, (1991), pp.181-201.
6. F.-h. Liu, Y. Lee, and L.-s. Lee, "A Direct Concatenation Approach to Train Hidden Markov Models to Recognize the Highly Confusing Mandarin Syllables with Very Limited Training Data ", *IEEE Transactions on Speech and Audio Processing*, vol. 1, No.1, (1993), pp. 113-119.
7. R.-Y. Lyu, I-C. Hong, J.-L. Shen, M.-Y. Lee, L.-s. Lee, "Isolated Mandarin Syllable Recognition Based Upon the Segmental Probability Models (SPM)", *IEEE Trans. Speech and Audio Processing*, vol. 6, No. 3, (1998), pp.293-299.
8. L.-s. Lee, C.-y. Tseng, K. J. Chen, J. Huang, C.-H. Hwang, P.-Y. Ting, L.-J. Lin, and C. C. Chen, "A Mandarin Dictation Machine Based Upon A Hierarchical Recognition Approach and Chinese Natural Language Analysis", *IEEE Transactions on Pattern Analysis and Machine Intelligence*, vol. 12, No.7, (1990), pp.695-704.
9. L.-s. Lee, C.-y. Tseng, K. J. Chen and J. Huang, "A Mandarin Dictation Machine Based Upon Chinese Natural Language Analysis", *Proc. The 10th International Joint Conference on Artificial Intelligence*, AAAI, Milano, Italy, (1987), pp.619-621.
10. L.-s. Lee, C.-y. Tseng, H.-y. Gu, K.-J. Chen, F.-h. Liu, C. H. Chang, S. H. Hsieh, C. H. Chen, "A Real-time Mandarin Dictation Machine for Chinese Language with Unlimited Texts and Very Large Vocabulary", *Proc. International Conference on Acoustics, Speech and Signal Processing*, IEEE, Albuquerque, NM, USA, (1990), pp.65-68.
11. J.-K. Chen, L.-s. Lee and F. K. Soong, "Large Vocabulary Word-based Mandarin Dictation System", *Proc. 4th European Conference on Speech Communication and Technology*, ESCA, (1995), Madrid, Spain, pp.285-288.
12. R.-Y. Lyu, L.-F. Chien, S.-H. Hwang, H.-Y. Hsieh, R.-C. Yang, B.-R. Bai, J.-C. Weng, Y.-J. Yang, S.-W. Lin, K.-J. Chen, C.-Y. Tseng, and L.-s. Lee, "Golden Mandarin (III)-A User-Adaptive Prosodic-Segment-Based Mandarin Dictation Machine for Chinese Language with Very Large Vocabulary", *Proc. International Conference on Acoustics, Speech and Signal Processing*, Detroit, USA, (1995), pp. 57-60.
13. H.-m. Wang, J.-l. Shen, Y.-J. Yang, C.-Y. Tseng, and L.-s. Lee, "Complete Recognition Of Continuous Mandarin Speech for Chinese Language with Very Large Vocabulary But Limited

Training Data", *Proc. International Conference on Acoustics, Speech and Signal Processing*, Detroit, USA, (1995), pp. 61-64.
14. H.-m. Wang, T.-H. Ho, R.-C. Yang, J.-L. Shen, B.-R. Bai, J.-C. Hong, W.-P. Chen, T.-L. Yu and L.-s. Lee, "Complete Recognition of Continuous Mandarin Speech for Chinese Language with Very Large Vocabulary Using Very Limited Training Data", *IEEE Trans. Speech and Audio Processing*, vol. 5, No.2, (1997), pp.195-200.
15. J.-l. Shen, H.-m. Wang, R.-Y. Lyu, and L.-s. Lee, "Automatic Selection of Phonetically Distributed Sentence Sets for Speaker Adaptation with Application to Large Vocabulary Mandarin Speech Recognition", *Computer Speech and Language*, vol. 13, No. 1, (1999), pp.79-97.
16. Y. Gao, T. Huang, Z. Lin, B. Xu and D. Xu, "A Real-Time Chinese Speech Recognition System with Unlimited Vocabulary", *Proc. ICASSP*, (1991), pp.257-361.
17. B. Xu, B. Ma, S. Zhang, F. Qu, and T. Huang, "Speaker Dependent Dictation of Chinese Speech with 32K Vocabulary", *Proc. ICSLP*, (1996).
18. S. Gao, B. Xu and T. Huang, "A New Framework for Mandarin LVCSR based on onepass decoder", *Proc. ISCSLP*, Beijing, (2000), pp.49-52.
19. Z. Wang, J. Wu, et al., "Methods Towards the Very large Vocabulary Chinese Speech Recognition", *Proc. Eurospeech' 95*, Madrid, Spain, (1995), pp.215-218.
20. L.-s. Lee, C.-y. Tseng, H.-y. Gu, F.-h. Liu, C. H. Chang, Y. H. Lin, Y. Lee, S. L. Tu, S. H. Hsieh, C. H. Chen, "Golden Mandarin (I) - A Real-time Mandarin Speech Dictation Machine for Chinese Language with Very Large Vocabulary", *IEEE Transactions on Speech and Audio Processing*, vol. 1, No. 2, (1993), pp. 158-179.
21. L.-s. Lee, C.-y. Tseng, K.-J. Chen, I-J. Hung, M.-Y. Lee, L.-F. Chien, Y. Lee, R. Lyu, H.-m. Wang, Y.-C. Wu, T.-S. Lin, H.-y. Gu, C.-p. Nee, C.-Y. Liao, Y.-J. Yang, Y.-C. Chang, R.-c. Yang, "Golden Mandarin(II) - An Improved Single-Chip Real-Time Mandarin Dictation Machine for Chinese Language with Very Large Vocabulary," *Proc. International Conference on Acoustics, Speech and Signal Processing*, Minneapolis, MN, USA, (1993), pp. II-503-506.
22. X. Huang, A. Acero, and H.-W. Hong, *Spoken Language Processing—A Guide to Theory, Algorithm and System Development*, Prentice Hall, Inc., (2001).
23. L. Rabiner, and B.-H. Juang, *Fundamentals of Speech Recognition*, Prentice Hall Inc., (1993).
24. P.-y. Liang, J.-l. Shen, and L.-s. Lee, "Decision Tree Clustering for Acoustic Modeling in Speaker-Independent Mandarin Telephone Speech Recognition", *Proc. 1998 International Symposium on Chinese Spoken Language Processing*, Singapore, (1998), pp.207-211.
25. S. Gao, B. Xu, T. Huang, "Class-Triphone Acoustic Modeling Based on Decision Tree for Mandarin Continuous Speech Recognition", *Proc. ISCSLP'98*, Singapore, (1998), pp.44-48.
26. B. Ma, T. Huang, B. Xu, X. Zhang, and F. Qu, "Context-Dependent Acoustic Models in Chinese Speech Recognition", *Proc. ICASSP*, Atlanta, USA, (1996), pp.2320-2323.
27. T.-H. Ho, C.-J. Liu, H. Sun, M.-Y. Tsai, L.-s. Lee, "Phonetic State Tied-Mixture Tone Modeling for Large Vocabulary Continuous Mandarin Speech Recognition", *Proc. Sixth European Conference on Speech Communication and Technology*, Budapest, Hungary, (1999), pp. 883-886.
28. Y. Cao, Y. Deng, H. Zhang, T. Huang and B. Xu, "Decision Tree Based Mandarin Tone Model and Its Applications to Speech Recognition", *Proc. ICASSP'2000*, Istanbul, vol. 3, (2000), pp.1759-1762.
29. W.-y. Lin and L.-s. Lee, "Improved Tone Recognition for Fluent Mandarin Speech Based on New Inter-Syllabic Features and Robust Pitch Extraction", *IEEE 8th Automatic Speech Recognition and Understanding Workshop*, St. Thomas, US Virgin Islands, USA, (2003), pp.237-242.

30. H.-y. Gu, C.-y. Tseng and L.-s. Lee, "Markov Modeling of Mandarin Chinese for Decoding the Phonetic Sequence into Chinese Characters", *Computer Speech and Language*, vol. 5, No.4, (1991), pp.363-377.
31. Y.-J. Yang, S.-C. Lin, L.-F. Chien, K.-J. Chen and L.-s. Lee, "An Intelligent and Efficient Word-Class-Based Chinese Language Model for Mandarin Speech Recognition with Very Large Vocabulary", *Proc. International Conference on Spoken Language Processing*, Yokohama, Japan, (1994), pp.1371-1374.
32. S.-C. Lin, C.-L. Tsai, L.-F. Chien, K.-J. Chen and L.-s. Lee, "Chinese Language Model Adaptation Based on Document Classification and Multiple Domain-Specific Language Models", *Proc. 5th European Conference on Speech Communication and Technology*, Rhode, Greece, (1997), pp.1463-1466.
33. P.-C. Chang, S.-P. Liao, and L.-s. Lee, "Improved Chinese Broadcast News Transcription by Language Modeling with Temporally Consistent Training Corpora and Iterative Phrase Extraction", *Proc. 8th European Conference on Speech Communication and Technology, ISCA*, Geneva, Switzerland, (2003), pp.421-424.
34. P.-C. Chang and L.-s. Lee, "Improved Language Model Adaptation Using Existing and Derived External Resources", *IEEE 8th Automatic Speech Recognition and Understanding Workshop*, St. Thomas, US Virgin Islands, USA, (2003), pp.531-536.
35. L.-F. Chien, K.-J. Chen and L.-s. Lee, "A Best-first Language Processing Model Integrating the Unification Grammar and Markov Language Model for Speech Recognition Applications", *IEEE Transactions on Speech and Audio Processing*, vol. 1, No. 2, (1993), pp. 221-240.
36. L.-s. Lee, L.-f. Chien, L.-j. Lin, J. Huang and K. J. Chen , "An Efficient Natural Language Processing System Specially Designed for the Chinese Language", *Computational Linguistics*, vol. 17, No.4, (1991), pp.347-374.
37. K.-C. Yang, T.-H. Ho, L.-F. Chien, and L.-s. Lee, "Statistics-Based Segment Pattern Lexicon – A New Direction for Chinese Language Modeling", *Proc. International Conference on Acoustics*, Speech and Signal Processing, Seattle, WA, USA, (1998), pp.I-169-I-172.
38. Y.-C. Pan, Y.-Y. Liu, and L.-s. Lee, "Named Entity Recognition From Spoken Documents Using Global Evidences and External Knowledge Sources with Applications on Mandarin Chinese," *IEEE Automatic Speech Recognition and Understanding Workshop*, San Juan, (2005).
39. M.-y. Tsai, F.-C. Chou, and L.-s. Lee, "Pronunciation Variation Analysis with respect to Various Linguistic Levels and Contextual Conditions for Mandarin Chinese", *Proc. European Conference on Speech Communication and Technology*, Aalborg, Denmark, (2001), CD-ROM.
40. M.-y. Tsai, F.-c. Chou, L.-s. Lee, "Improved Pronunciation Modeling by Inverse Word Frequency and Pronunciation Entropy", *IEEE Automatic Speech Recognition and Understanding Workshop*, Madonna di Campiglio, Italy, (2001), CD-ROM.
41. M.-Y. Tsai and L.-s. Lee, "Pronunciation Variation Analysis Based on Acoustic and Phonemic Distance Measures with Application Examples on Mandarin Chinese", *IEEE 8th Automatic Speech Recognition and Understanding Workshop*, St. Thomas, US Virgin Islands, USA, (2003), pp.117-122.
42. M.-Y. Tsai, F.-C. Chou and L.-s. Lee, "Pronunciation Modeling with Reduced Confusion for Mandarin Chinese using a Three-stage Framework", to appear in *IEEE Transactions on Audio, Speech and Language Processing*.
43. T.-h. Ho, H.-m. Wang, L.-F. Chien, K.-J. Chen and L.-s. Lee, "Fast and Accurate Continuous Speech Recognition for Chinese Language with Very Large Vocabulary", *Proc. 4th European Conference on Speech Communication and Technology*, ESCA, Madrid, Spain, (1995), pp. 211-214.

44. H.-Y. Hsieh, R.-Y. Lyu and L.-s. Lee, "Use of Prosodic Information to Integrate Acoustic and Linguistic Knowledge in Continuous Mandarin Speech Recognition with Very Large Vocabulary", *Proc. 4th Int. Conf. on Spoken Language Processing*, Philadelphia, PA, USA, (1996), pp. 809-812.
45. T.-H. Ho, K.-C. Yang, K.-H. Huang, and L.-s. Lee, "Improved Search Strategy for Large Vocabulary Continuous Mandarin Speech Recognition", *Proc. International Conference on Acoustics, Speech and Signal Processing*, Seattle, WA, USA, (1998), pp. II-825-II-828.
46. L. Mangu, E. Brill, and A. Stolcke, "Finding Consensus in Speech Recognition: Word Error Minimization and Other Applications of Confusion Networks", *Computer Speech and Language*, vol.14, No.4, (2000), pp.373-400.
47. Y.-S. Fu, Y.-c. Pan, and L.-s. Lee, "Improved Large Vocabulary Continuous Chinese Speech Recognition by Character-based Consensus Networks", *Proc. International Symposium on Chinese Spoken Language Processing*, Singapore, (2006).
48. Y. Qian, F. K. Soong and T. Lee, "Tone-enhanced Generalized Character Posterior Probability (GCPP) for Cantonese LVCSR" *Proc. ICASSP,* (2006).
49. L.-s. Lee, and Y. Lee, "Voice Access of Global Information for Broadband Wireless: Technologies of Today and Challenges of Tomorrow" (invited paper), *Proc. IEEE*, vol.89, No.1, (2001), pp. 41-57.
50. B.-s. Lin, and L.-s. Lee, "Computer-aided Analysis and Design for Spoken Dialogue Systems Based on Quantitative Simulations", *IEEE Transactions on Speech and Audio Processing*, vol. 9, No.5, (2001), pp. 534-548.
51. Y.-J. Yang, L.-F. Chien and L.-s. Lee, "Speaker Intention Modeling for Large Vocabulary Mandarin Spoken Dialogues", *Proc. 4th Int. Conf. on Spoken Language Processing*, Philadelphia, PA, USA, (1996), pp. 713-716.
52. Y.-J. Yang, and L.-s. Lee, "A Syllable-Based Chinese Spoken Dialogue System for Telephone Directory Services Primarily Trained with A Corpus", *Proc. International Conference on Spoken Language Processing*, Sydney, Australia, (1998), CD-ROM.
53. C. Huang, X. Peng, X. Zhang, S. Zhao, T. Huang and B. Xu, "LODESTAR: A Mandarin Spoken Dialogue System for Travel Information Retrieval", *Proceedings of Eurospeech'99*, vol. 3, Budapest, Hungary, (1999), pp.1159-1162.
54. S.-C. Lin, L.-F. Chien, K.-J. Chen and L.-s. Lee, "Unconstrained Speech Retrieval for Chinese Document Databases with Very Large Vocabulary and Unlimited Domains", *Proc. 4th European Conference on Speech Communication and Technology*, ESCA, Madrid, Spain, (1995), pp. 1203-1206.
55. B.-R. Bai, L.-F. Chien and L.-s. Lee, "Very-Large-Vocabulary Mandarin Voice Message File Retrieval Using Speech Queries", *Proc. 4th Int. Conf. on Spoken Language Processing*, Philadelphia, PA, USA, (1996), pp. 1950-1953.
56. L.-F. Chien, S.-C. Lin, J.-C. Hong, M.-C. Chen, H.-m. Wang, J.-L. Shen, K.-J. Chen and L.-s. Lee, "Internet Chinese Information Retrieval Using Unconstrained Mandarin Speech Queries Based on A Client-Server Architecture and A PAT-Tree-Based Language Model", *Proc. IEEE Int. Conf. on Acoustics, Speech and Signal Processing*, Munich, Germany, (1997), pp. 1155-1158.
57. B. Chen, H.-m. Wang and L.-s. Lee, "Discriminating Capabilities of Syllable-based Features and Approaches of Utilizing Them for Voice Retrieval of Speech Information in Mandarin Chinese", *IEEE Transactions on Speech and Audio Processing*, vol. 10, No.5, (2002), pp.303-314.
58. B. Chen, H.-m. Wang, and L.-s. Lee, "A Discriminative HMM/N-gram-Based Retrieval Approach for Mandarin Spoken Documents", *ACM Transactions on Asian Language Information Processing*, vol. 3, No.2, (2004), pp.128-145.

59. B. Chen, H.-m. Wang, and L.-s. Lee, "Improved Spoken Document Retrieval by Exploring Extra Acoustic and Linguistic Cues", *Proc. European Conference on Speech Communication and Technology*, Aalborg, Denmark, (2001), CD-ROM.
60. C.-J. Wang, B. Chen, and L.-s. Lee, "Improved Chinese Spoken Document Retrieval with Hybird Modeling and Data-driven Indexing Features", *Proc. International Conference on Spoken Language Processing*, Denver, Co, USA, (2002), CD-ROM.
61. B. Xu, S. Zhang and C. Zong, "Statistical Speech-to-Speech Translation with Multilingual Speech Recognition and Bilingual-Chunk Parsing", *Proc. Eurospeech,* Geneva, Switzerland, (2003), pp.2329-2332.
62. M. Peabody and S. Seneff, "Towards Automatic Tone Correction in Non-native Mandarin", *Proc. International Symposium on Chinese Spoken Language Processing*, Singapore, (2006).
63. L.-s. Lee and B. Chen, "Spoken Document Understanding and Organization", *IEEE Signal Processing Magazine*, Special Issue on Speech Technology in Human-machine Communication, vol.22, No.5, (2005), pp.42-60.
64. Y.-C. Pan, C.-C. Wang, Y.-C. Hsieh, T.-H. Lee, Y.-S. Lee, Y.-S. Fu, Y.-T. Huang and L.-s. Lee, "A Multi-Modal Dialogue System for Information Navigation and Retrieval across Spoken Document Archives with Topic Hierarchies," *Proc. of IEEE Automatic Speech Recognition and Understanding Workshop*, San Juan, (2005).
65. Y.-c. Pan, J.-y. Chen, Y.-s. Lee, Y.-S. Fu, and L.-s. Lee, "Efficient Interactive Retrieval of Spoken Documents with Key Terms Ranked by Reinforcement Learning", *Proc. Interspeech*, Pittsburgh, USA, (2006).
66. L.-s. Lee, S.-y. Kong, Y.-c. Pan, Y.-S. Fu, and Y.-t. Huang, "Multi-layered Summarization of Spoken Document Archives by Information Extraction and Semantic Structuring", *Proc. Interspeech*, Pittsburgh, USA, (2006).
67. L.-s. Lee and S.-C. Chen, "Automatic Title Generation for Chinese Spoken Documents Considering the Special Structure of the Language", *Proc. 8th European Conference on Speech Communication and Technology*, ISCA, Geneva, Switzerland, (2003), pp.2325-2328.
68. S.-y. Kong, and L.-s. Lee, "Improved Spoken Document Summarization Using Probabilistic Latent Semantic Analysis (PLSA)", *Proc. International Conference on Acoustics, Speech and Signal Processing*, Toulouse, France, (2006).
69. T.-H. Li, M.-H. Lee, B. Chen, and L.-s. Lee, "Hierarchical Topic Organization and Visual Presentation of Spoken Documents Using Probabilistic Latent Semantic Analysis (PLSA) for Efficient Retrieval/Browsing Applications," *Proc. European Conference on Speech Communication and Technology*, Lisbon, (2005), pp.625-628.
70. L.-s. Lee, Y. Ho, J.-f. Chen, and S.-C. Chen, "Why Is the Special Structure of the Language Important for Chinese Spoken Language Processing- Examples on Spoken Document Retrieval, Segmentation and Summarization", *Proc. 8th European Conference on Speech Communication and Technology*, ISCA, Geneva, Switzerland, (2003), pp.49-52.
71. C.-H. Lee, "From Knowledge-ignorant to knowledge-rich Modeling: A New Speech Research Paradigm for Next Generation Automatic Speech Recognition", *Proc. International Conference on Spoken Language Processing*, plenary speech , Jeju, (2004).
72. J.-T. Huang, and L.-s. Lee, "Prosodic Modeling in Large Vocabulary Mandarin Speech Recognition", *Proc. Interspeech*, Pittsburgh, USA, (2006).
73. C.-K. Lin, and L.-s. Lee, "Improved Spontaneous Mandarin Speech Recognition by Disfluency Interruption Point (IP) Detection Using Prosodic Features," *Proc. European Conference on Speech Communication and Technology*, Lisbon, (2005), pp.1621-1624.
74. J.-w. Hung and L.-s. Lee, "Optimization of Temporal Filters for Constructing Robust Features in Speech Recognition", *IEEE Transactions on Speech and Audio Processing*, vol. 14, No.3, (2006), pp.808-832.

75. C.-w. Hsu and L.-s. Lee, "Higher Order Cepstral Moment Nomalization(HOCMN) for Robust Speech Recognition", *Proc. International Conference on Acoustics, Speech and Signal Processing*, Montreal, CA, (2004), pp.197-200.
76. "Special Issue on Spoken Language Processing", *Proceedings of the IEEE*, vol. 88, No.8, (2000).
77. "Special Section on Speech Technology in Human-Machine Communication", *IEEE Signal Processing Magazine*, vol. 32, No.5, (2005).

CHAPTER 7

ACOUSTIC MODELING FOR MANDARIN LARGE VOCABULARY CONTINUOUS SPEECH RECOGNITION

Mei-Yuh Hwang
Department of Electrical Engineering, University of Washington, Seattle
Email: mhwang@ee.washington.edu

After reviewing the history on Mandarin speech recognition in the previous chapter, we will now describe a few key technologies to build a highly accurate Mandarin Large Vocabulary Continuous Speech Recognition (LVCSR) system. LVCSR is the foundation for many useful speech-based applications, including keyword spotting, translation, voice indexing, etc. The core technologies developed on western languages are easily applicable to Chinese Mandarin. However, as noted in the previous chapter, we need to take care of the special characteristics of the Chinese language in order to achieve very high accuracy. Our emphasis will be on the differences and extra features used in the Mandarin system, with some brief summarization of the backbone technologies that are language independent. Finally we will present a state of the art Mandarin speech recognizer jointly developed by University of Washington (UW) and SRI International, and discuss unsolved challenges.

1. Introduction

Although English LVCSR had been proven feasible since the late 80s,[1] the Chinese research community did not start to tackle the problem directly until about a decade ago. One of the main constraints came from the lack of large speech and text corpora. With many researchers' advocacy and collaboration,[2] data is becoming less of an issue and Mandarin LVCSR is finally taking off.

Recently the Chinese and Arabic languages have been getting increasing attention in the United States due to economic and security reasons. Just to name a few, the EARS[3] and GALE[4] projects funded by the Defense Advanced Research Projects Agency (DARPA) push for high performance expectations on the recognition and translation of both languages. The Linguistic Data Consortium[5] (LDC) has been collecting and will soon be publishing hundreds to thousands of hours of Mandarin speech data and trillions of Chinese text words. Coupled with the advance in computer hardware, highly accurate, real-time Mandarin LVCSR is becoming a reality. We will focus on the steps and techniques to build such a system in this chapter. While limited-domain small vocabulary CSR with or without finite-state grammars is still useful in many applications, we will not be discussing it here.

Figure 1 illustrates a typical speech recognition system. When the speech wave enters, speech analysis is done first to represent the input wave with feature vectors that summarize the frequency spectrum of every short segment of speech (typically 10ms). A recognizer (decoder or search) utilizes an acoustic model (AM) and a language model (LM) to find the most likely sequence of words, W^*, given the input feature sequence $X = (x_1 x_2 \ldots x_T)$:

$$W^* = \arg\max_W P(W|X) = \arg\max_W P(X|W)P(W)$$
$$\approx \arg\max_W P(X|W)P(W)^\rho \quad (1)$$

where the language weight ρ is necessary to balance the contribution from two knowledge sources whose probabilities range in different orders of magnitude.

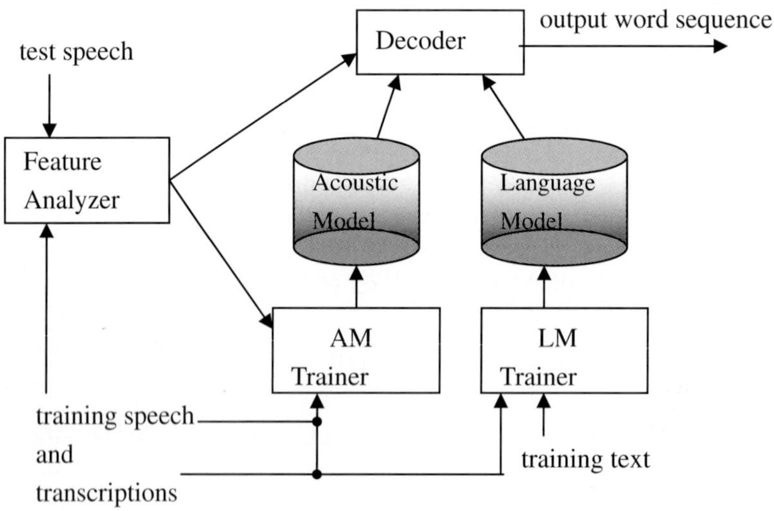

Fig. 1. Speech recognition system diagram.

The AM is usually modeled by HMMs whose parameters are trained beforehand with hundreds of hours of training data. One can treat the tone model in Figure 2 of Chapter 6 as one part of AM, or a separate module as an additional knowledge source to be applied at a different stage of the search process. Similarly, the LM for LVCSR is often an n-gram language model and is trained with millions of words. A lexicon (i.e. the vocabulary of the system) has to be defined before an n-gram can be trained. Therefore one can treat the lexicon as a part of LM.

Each word in the decoding lexicon and training lexicon has to be given at least a pronunciation in order to be modeled by the HMM. Pronunciations can thus be considered as a part of AM. Since all these components have to be integrated together to produce a highly accurate system, we will discuss briefly all the various components in this chapter, with particular emphasis on acoustic modeling. Chapter 8 will focus on the modeling of tone features, Chapter 9 on language modeling, and Chapter 10 on pronunciation modeling.

In evaluating the merits of a speech recognizer, the most prevailing metric is the word error rate (WER), which is the number of substitution, deletion, and insertion errors over the number of words in the correct transcription (i.e., minimum string editing distance):

WER = (substitution+deletion+insertion) / (# of reference words)

In Chinese language, since there is no clear definition of words and each character is written independently, character error rates (CER) make more sense to the end users:

CER = (substitution+deletion+insertion) / (# of reference characters)

CER is well used in the Chinese research community for measuring speech recognition systems and will also be adopted here.

2. Chinese Word Segmentation and Lexicon

Since there are only about 6000 frequently used Chinese characters, it seems to be easy to build a system with only these 6,000 characters as the lexicon. That is, each "word" in the recognition system is one individual character. A high-order character *n*-gram can be trained and used in decoding. A careful consideration (and many experiments) proves that this thinking is naïve. Defining each word as one single character implies high perplexity (number of branches) between words for the language model. For example, given character 不 (not), it can be followed by many different characters:

不幸 (unfortunately)
不是 (isn't)
不再 (not anymore)
不必 (not necessary)
...

On the other hand, if the above multi-character words are individual entries in the search lexicon, it will narrow down the word that can possibly follow them and thus make the search easier. A bigram of two two-character words allows you to see 4 characters in total: $P(\text{“}c_3c_4\text{”}|\text{“}c_1c_2\text{”})$. If single-character words are used in the lexicon exclusively, a 4-gram will be needed instead, to reach the same context: $P(c_4|c_1c_2c_3)$.

Equally as important, if not more important, is the acoustic modeling of individual words. First of all, using single-character words result in a high occurence of homophones in Mandarin Chinese. It would be impossible for the AM to distinguish homophones unless word-dependent acoustic models are used. Otherwise, one would need a very powerful language model which can utilize long-distance context to distinguish different characters. Secondly, since all Chinese characters are monosyllabic, there is little acoustic context to model within a "word" (which is a character in this case). We know Mandarin tones are highly contextual in continuous speech. However, cross-word contextual modeling is much more complicated than within-word contextual modeling, in terms of implementation and search space. To see a few characters away would mean to cross many word boundaries in the single-character lexicon. This imposes great difficulty in the design of the search algorithm. On the contrary, using multiple-character words as lexicon entries enables us to model within-word tone sandhi easily.

One can argue that a simple character-based CSR system without much word-boundary context can be built to output a character lattice first, followed by another search algorithm on the character lattice, using a high-level language model, to finalize the output character sequence. However, the second-stage search is not trivial. Furthermore, if the correct character sequence is pruned in the first search, there is no way to recover the error from the character lattice. If the character lattice is set to be big in order to be able to cover the correct character sequence, it may become too big to be efficient for the second stage search. For the above reasons, we will be focusing on word representation of lexicon and use a system paradigm that is as similar as possible to that used in western languages. In this way, we can capitalize on the language independent aspect of the technologies to the maximum extent.

There are a few Chinese word-lexicons available from LDC that one can use to start a system. Otherwise, the pointwise mutual information (PMI)[6] is a good way to create a "word" based lexicon automatically[7]:

1. Start from a lexicon where all words are single-character.
2. Compute the pointwise mutual information for every pair of words in the current lexicon:
   $PMI(w_1, w_2) = \log \frac{P(w_1 w_2)}{P(w_1)P(w_2)}$
   where $P(w_1 w_2)$ is the probability that w_1 is followed immediately by w_2, in a given training text corpus.
3. Choose the pair with the maximum PMI and merge the two words into a new longer word in the training text. Add the new longer word into the lexicon.
4. Go to step 2 to re-compute PMI, until a certain threshold is met.

The transcriptions of some Chinese speech corpora may not be segmented according to words. In that case, one would need to use his/her (or some other) lexicon to segment the transcription automatically (so is the text training data). A simple longest-first segmentation is proved to be reasonable.[8] Otherwise, an n-gram based maximum likelihood segmentation[7] is possibly better once an n-gram LM is available, since it contains guided information from the n-gram statistics. Very often Chinese word boundaries are ambiguous and in some instances even dependent on personal preferences (i.e. subjective). At times, the different segmentation possibilities produce sentences which are semantically different, as the following examples show:

民进党 / 和亲 / 民党 ... (The Green Party made peace with the Min Party via marriage...)
民进党 / 和 / 亲民党 ... (The Green Party and the Qin-Min Party...)
清楚 / 地表 / 明 /... (clear earth-crust bright...)
清楚 / 地 / 表明 /... (clearly showed that...)

N-gram based word segmentation often yields the right semantics.

Even though the literature has not shown much influence in CER with regards to the different word segmenters, we believe that a better segmenter will indeed help in language understanding, which in turn will benefit all other applications such as information retrieval and language translation. Chapter 9 will further elaborate on the issue of language modeling.

Since almost all speech corpora are not labeled with silence annotations in their transcriptions, it is necessary to allow an optional silence between words during AM training. For example, the sentence 星期一/恢复/上班/ (work schedule was resumed on Monday) should be trained in the following way:

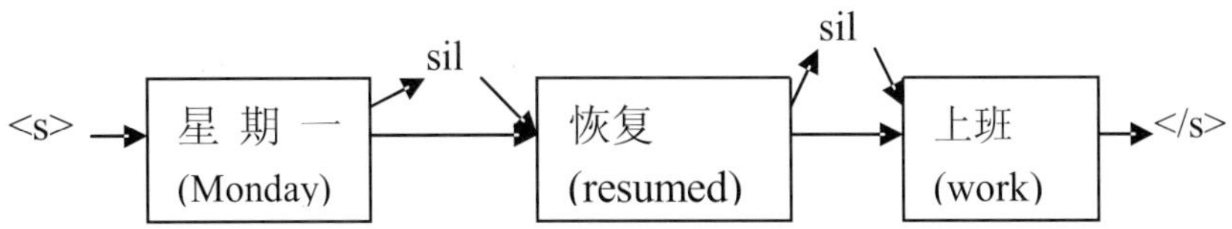

where each word in the above graph is modeled by a word HMM, which can be decomposed into phonetic or syllabic HMMs. $< s >$ represents the beginning silence in a sentence and $< /s >$ the ending silence. As one can see, the location of optional silence between words depends on the word segmentation, as we generally do not allow silence within a "word".

Another note about the lexicon is that in this era of globalization, it is fairly common to see English words embedded in a Chinese sentence. This scenario is called *code mixing*. For this reason, we often include frequent English words (mostly nouns which are content words and names) in a Chinese SR system. Another scenario, commonly referred to as *code switching*, happens when different languages are used across different sentences in the same speech context. For example, in a Chinese TV news program, one may hear the journalist speaking in Mandarin, followed by an interviewee speaking in English. For the case of code switching, multiple speech recognizers are needed in order to recognize the different spoken languages accurately. Code switching is outside the scope of this chapter.

3. Acoustic Feature Representation

3.1. *Cepstra and Normalization*

To begin with, a basic Mandarin CSR is often built with the same cepstral front end as western languages. Both the Mel-scale ceptral coefficients[9] and the PLP features[10] are equally effective in Mandarin CSR. Common parameters are one frame per 10ms with 25-ms Hamming windows, 12th-order cepstra and their delta and double delta. Together with the c_0 energy and its deltas, a common dimensionality of cepstrum features in SR is 39. Utterance-based, window-based, or speaker-based cepstral mean and variance normalization is commonly applied in order to reduce channel distortion:

$$\hat{x}_t = \frac{x_t - \mu}{\sigma} \sim N(0,1) \tag{2}$$

where N represents the Gaussian distribution and x_t is the 39-dim cepstrum feature for time frame t. Another common normalization technique is the vocal track length normalization[11] to compensate the difference in vocal-track sizes, especially between male and female, or between children and adults.

3.2. *Pitch Features*

As tones are important in Mandarin, pitch features are often extracted as an additional signal feature. The most commonly used package for pitch tracking is the get_f0 function[12] from the former Entropic Research Laboratory's signal processing system or ESPS.[13] Get_f0 implements a fundamental frequency estimation algorithm using the normalized cross correlation function and dynamic programming. It determines, every 10ms, if the input wave is voiced or unvoiced. If it is voiced, it estimates the fundamental frequency (F0). If unvoiced, it outputs zero. For HMM-based speech recognition, it is essential to make the voiced/unvoiced transition smooth or even to smooth out the whole pitch contour of the entire utterance. Chen proposed a mean-based pitch smoothing algorithm,[14] while Lei claimed a cubic spline smoothing was superior[15] for CSR.

After F0 is obtained for every frame, we often take log in order to make the feature more Gaussian-like, as the Gaussian density function is the prevailing probability density function used in HMM-based systems. Then we compute its delta and double delta, just as with cepstra. Furthermore, mean and variance normalization are also applied to these three dimensions. Variance normalization is especially important when the pitch feature is combined with other features, because delta pitches are usually close to zero. A Gaussian density value is inversely proportional to the scale of the input value:

$$\begin{aligned} \text{If X } &\sim N\left(\mu,\sigma^2\right) \text{ and } \text{Y} = a\text{X}, \\ \text{then Y } &\sim N\left(a\mu, a^2\sigma^2\right) \\ N\left(\text{y};\ a\mu, a^2\sigma^2\right) &= (1/a)\, N\left(\text{x}; \mu, \sigma^2\right) \end{aligned} \tag{3}$$

which would essentially make delta pitch features (Y with a very small a) more influential than other features such as cepstra, had the pitch features not been normalized.

After the pitch features are finalized, one can separate them as another independent feature stream,

$$\begin{aligned} x_t &= [c_t]\,[p_t] \\ P(x_t|\lambda) &= P(c_t|\lambda_c)\, P(p_t|\lambda_p)^\gamma \end{aligned} \tag{4}$$

where c_t is the 39-dimension cepstra and p_t is the 3-dimension pitch feature; λ_c is the Gaussian model for cepstra; λ_p model for pitch. When multiple feature streams are used in CSR, often there is a weighting parameter, γ, to optimize the contribution of different features. γ can be empirically tuned or learned from some acoustic training data with discriminative objective criteria.

Alternatively, appending the pitch features to cepstra in the same feature stream is more common:

$$x_t = \begin{bmatrix} c_t \\ p_t \end{bmatrix}$$

That is, we simply increase the dimensionality of the input feature. As all feature dimensions are variance normalized, it is safe to combine this new knowledge source in either of the above fashion. The latter is more popular for its simplicity and joint optimization of cepstra and pitch. Adding pitch features often result in 10% relative CER reduction.

In some Mandarin CSR systems, a separate tone recognition module using pitch and other prosodic features was built. Another separate module was responsible for base syllable recognition. These two outputs were then combined to generate the most likely tonal syllable sequence or character sequence. However, we believe in joint-optimization by incorporating pitch features as part of the feature representation and tones as part of the word/phonetic model, as described below. Chapter 8 will elaborate on tone modeling for Mandarin SR.

3.3. *Multi-layer Perceptron (MLP) based Discriminative Features*

In recent years, MLP (or neural network) has been successfully generating useful discriminative features to be combined with cepstra,[16–18] based on analysis of critical frequency bands. Because this technique is mainly developed in the International Computer Science Institute, Berkeley, it is often referred to as the ICSI-feature. This has been demonstrated to be just as successful for Mandarin systems.[19,20] We will briefly describe the essence of using MLP to analyze critical band information.

The motivation behind MLP-based features comes from speech perception and the fact that cepstra are only short-term analysis. Warren *et al.*[21] and Greenberg *et al.*[22] have shown that different critical frequency bands affect the human perception of the different phones, suggesting that each critical band does carry critical information for different phones. Furthermore, the standard cepstra and pitch feature analysis are both short-term information (usually around 10-20ms). Using longer-term (0.5-1s) critical band information will help capture temporal patterns in the underlying speech signal, hence the original name TRAPS. After a decade of research and investigation, the final winning MLP feature for LVCSR is the HATS (hidden activation TRAPS) feature. We will focus on the description of the HATS feature here.

Figure 2 illustrates the concept of the HATS feature. There are two stages of MLP involved. The first stage contains multiple MLPs, while the second stage only one MLP. Each block in the figure represents one MLP.

First of all, we compute the log critical band energies (15 critical bands shown in the figure) for every short window (e.g. 10ms). Then we concatenate 0.5-1s of each band to be the input of the first-stage MLP. In the figure, the previous 25 frames and the future 25 frames of the same band with that of the current time frame are concatenated, forming 51 input units for each of the 15 MLPs at the first stage. The goal of each MLP is to identify the posterior likelihood of the current frame being a certain phone: $P(P_j|x_t)$. Hence each output unit of an MLP represents one phone in the speech recognition system. As these MLPs provide phoneme posteriors for discriminating phones, the feature rendered offers phone discriminative power for speech recognition. The figure shows that the system has 72 phones (output units). The summation of all outputs of an MLP is 1. Therefore a softmax output function is applied at the output unit:

$$y_j = \sum_i w_{ij} x_{ij}$$
$$z_j = \frac{e^{y_j}}{\sum_i e^{y_i}} \quad (5)$$

where x_{i^*} is the input coming from the hidden unit i; w_{ij} the weight connecting the hidden unit i to the output unit j; z_j is the MLP output as the phoneme posterior. The hidden unit uses the sigmoid function to constrain its output to be between 0 and 1.

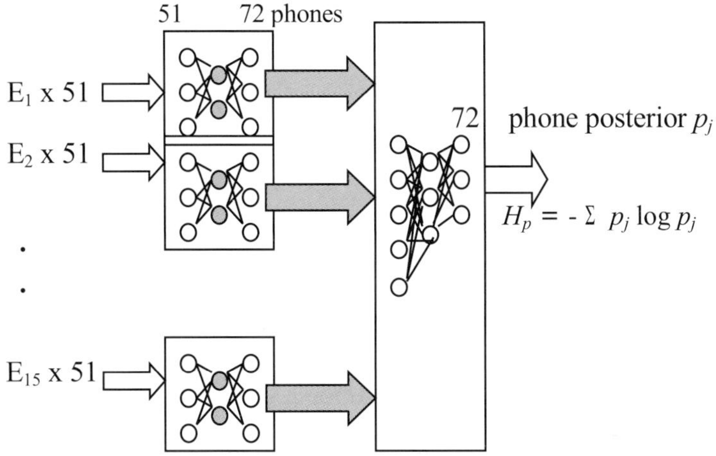

Fig. 2. Illustration of the HATS feature.

Since each critical band is responsible for the different phones, the output of each 1st stage MLP provides critical information about these different phones. The purpose of the 2nd-stage MLP is then to combine all critical band information for the final decision on the current frame's identity. From various experiments, it is shown that the most successful configuration for LVCSR is to take the output from *the hidden layer* (not the output layer) of the 1st-stage MLPs as the input for the 2nd stage MLP. This is perhaps because the softmax at the 1st stage makes all outputs from the 1st stage to be in the same order of magnitude and thus smears out the distinguishing power across all the MLPs at the first stage. As the input of the 2nd stage comes from the output of the hidden units at the 1st stage, the name of hidden activation TRAPS (or HATS) arises. Therefore the number of input units of the 2nd stage MLP is $15h$ where h is the number of hidden units in each of the 1st stage MLP. Although the output units from the first-stage MLPs are not used by the

2nd stage of MLP, they are still necessary during the training of the 1st stage MLPs. Lastly, we can compute the entropy (or uncertainty) of the phoneme posteriors from the 2nd stage MLP by H_p as the figure shows.

A more powerful MLP-based feature is to combine the HATS posteriors with a simple medium-term MLP-based feature, as shown in Figure 3.

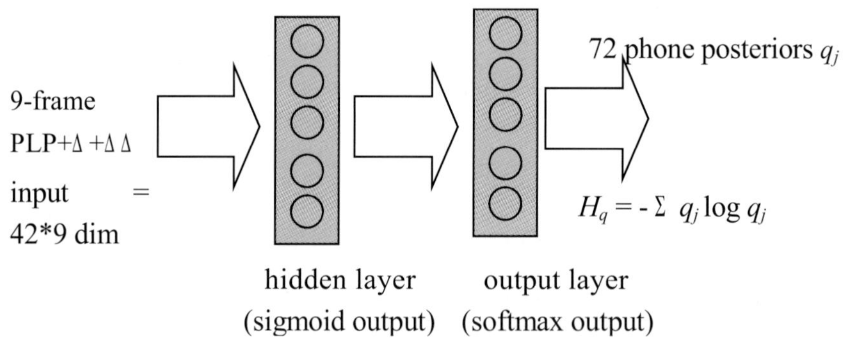

Fig. 3. Medium-term based MLP feature.

In Figure 3, there is only one MLP with 378 input units which include the standard short-term static and dynamic cepstra and pitch across 9 neighboring frames. To maximize the amount of new information, PLP cepstra is used in the MLP network if MFCC is used as the regular HMM input feature, and vice versa. The hidden units still use the sigmoid function and output units softmax posteriors. Similarly, we can compute the entropy of this simple MLP output.

With these two sets of MLP systems, we have two sets of phoneme posteriors for each time frame. The posteriors are combined with an inverse entropy weighting scheme to obtain the final phoneme posterior vector $[r_1 r_2 \ldots r_{72}]$:

$$r_j = \alpha p_j + (1-\alpha) q_j$$

$$\alpha = \frac{H_q}{H_p + H_q} \tag{6}$$

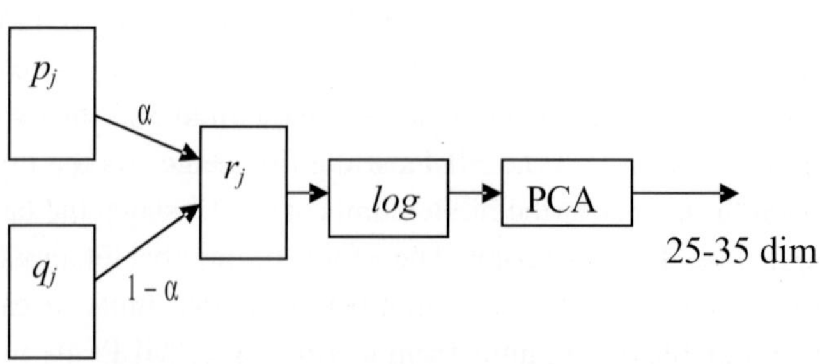

Before appending the final posterior vector r into the cepstral feature, we first take log to make it more Gaussian-like and then principal component analysis[23] (PCA) or the Karhunen-Loeve transform is often used to reduce the dimensionality and to make each individual dimension independent of each other, as Gaussian density functions are often assumed to have diagonal co-variances for simplicity. Again, these additional features are usually mean and variance normalized, for the same reason as the pitch feature. This final feature containing about 70 dimensions ($42 + 25 = 67$, $42 + 35 = 77$) is the ICSI-feature, and has been demonstrated to be a superior feature for HMM-based LVCSR.

4. Acoustic Units and Pronunciations

As it is impossible to sufficiently cover all possible words in the training data, sub-word modeling is usually used for LVCSR. For Mandarin, the concept of initials and toneless/tonal finals has been widely used in the Asian community, as mentioned in the previous chapter. Recently, Chen[24] proposed the idea of main vowels, which is now the winning strategy in many Mandarin LVCSR systems. The key idea behind main vowels is to decompose a final or diphthong into medial, main vowel, and nasal three parts if necessary. Tones are associated with the main vowel only. That is, the same main vowel with a different tone represents a different phone. For example, Table 1 lists a possible decomposition of some finals. Each of the symbols (case sensitive) in the "phonetic pronunciation" column represents one phone and is modeled by one HMM with usually 3-5 states.

Decomposing the finals makes it easier to share the phonetic units across different syllables. Attaching tones to only main vowels reduces the number of phones needed and thus reduces the number of triphones or any other contextual consideration. This results in better decision trees for HMM state tying. With this idea, the number of distinct phones for Mandarin is reduced to 70-80, depending on how many neutral tones are modeled. Although this is still bigger than the English phone set (around 50), it is more manageable to apply the standard English speech techniques than the traditional initial/tonal-final approach.

It is also very useful to design a phone set such that the decomposition of a word's pronunciation into a sequence of syllables is unique, so that it is easy to find syllable boundaries and map each component character to its syllable pronunciation. The syllabification is a simple table lookup with about 400 entries, one for each base syllable. This easy syllabification turns the problems of pronunciation verification, syllabic modeling, text-to-speech, etc., into simple tasks.

To achieve unique syllabification, one may have to distinguish the following three phones in syllable final vs. non-final: /n, y, w/ vs. /N, Y, W/. As shown in Table 1, we use uppercase for these three phones at syllable final positions. For example, had /w/ and /W/ not been distinguished, there would be ambiguity in the following syllabification:

教安 j y a4 w / a1 n ("sincerely", used to sign off letters to teachers)

架弯 j y a4 / w a1 n ("the frame is tilted")

Finally as mentioned earlier, within-word tone sandhi can be easily applied in a word-based lexicon, such as:

总统 z o2 NG t o3 NG

where the 1st third tone is changed to 2nd tone.

Table 1. Illustration of main vowels. Phones are case sensitive.

Example character	Pinyin	Phonetic pronunciation
爱	ai	a4 Y
对	dui	d w E4 Y
要	yao	y a4 W
又	you	y o4 W
南	nan	n a2 N
饿	e	e4
恩	en	e1 N
况	kuang	k w a4 NG
夜	ye	y E4

For the few English words in a Mandarin SR system, one can use the Mandarin phone set to simulate the English pronunciations by rules. Alternatively, one may add a few English-only phones such as /v/, /th/, /dh/, etc., if there is enough acoustic training data for them.

5. Acoustic Training

Either by choosing the main vowel or the initial-final concept for the basic acoustic unit, all the standard HMM training and adaptation techniques used in English systems can be easily extended to Mandarin. However, with the main vowel strategy, it is even easier to apply all the context-dependent modeling techniques, as the basic number of phones remains small.

5.1. *Parameter Sharing*

As speech is context-dependent and co-articulation happens within words and across words, it is essential to model context dependency (CD) if high recognition accuracy is targeted. Modeling triphones or quinphones would be difficult if the basic number of phones is too big. Despite the fact that the number of tonal syllables (1,300 or so) in Mandarin is a few order smaller than that of English, considering cross-word contexts and with possibly English words mixed in Chinese sentences, the number of triphones and quinphones can increase very quickly. For example, with a 60K-word lexicon, the possible number of within-word and cross-word triphones needed for any sequence of these words is 20K and 225K respectively, using a phone set of 70 basic phones. A bigger phone set would result in an unmanageable number of CD phones. A huge number of CD phones takes up huge memory space, increases program thrashing between RAM and hard disks during training and/or recognition, and slows down the training and recognition process. More importantly, there will be many CD models which are rarely trained. These models are necessary to build the senonic decision tree[25] for HMM state tying, which allows parameter sharing and thus makes the model more robust against new test data. The name of "senones" comes from the contrast with "fenones"[26] which represents frame-level labels. "Senones", on the other hand, represent Markov state-level labels. They can both be used to describe the pronunciation of a word, just like phonemes.[26,27]

Reducing the number of basic phones and CD phones is thus the main motivation behind the main-vowel idea. While building the senonic decision tree, one should allow parameter sharing across different tones of the same base vowel and different state locations within one HMM. Tonal questions should be included, in addition to linguistic categorical questions. Figure 3 illustrates the top few levels of a decision tree for phone /w/ and /W/ in one of the Mandarin CSR systems built at the University of Washington. The left subtree answers "yes" to its parent's question. In this system, word initial phone /w/ and word final phone /W/ were both in the same class. That is, they were allowed to share HMM Gaussian densities if they were indeed similar. The tree showed that they were so different that even in the first question they were split up into two subtrees. Furthermore, /W/ was used for diphthong /aw/ and /ow/ only (see Table 1). We see the question of "is the left-context phone any /a/ phone?" was asked immediately after a state-location question. Similarly, /w/ is often preceded by an initial and indeed the tree asked an appropriate question soon.

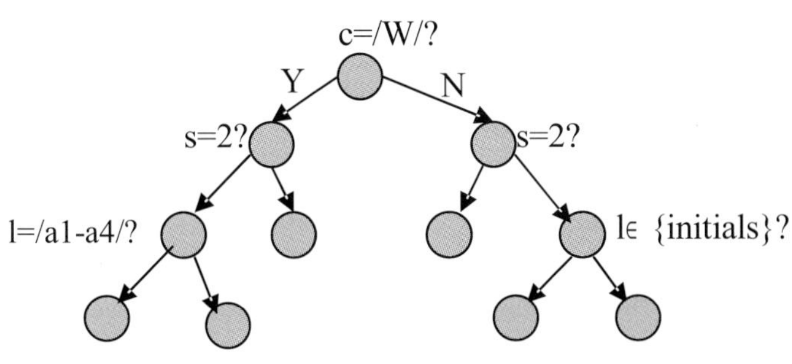

Fig. 4. An example decision tree to cluster all the triphones with center phone either /w/ or /W/. All left subtrees answer yes to their parents' questions.

In another study,[25] composite questions were found to be somewhat helpful. If composite questions are not used during the construction of senonic decision trees, various combinations of simple questions should be manually created and added into the question set to be asked during tree construction. Alternatively, Beulen *et al.*[28] and Chien[29] have proved effective ways of creating the question set automatically.

5.2. *Estimation of HMM Parameters*

In this section, we will describe the concepts of some popular training objective functions. Readers are encouraged to look up the references for their details and implementation.

5.2.1. *Maximum Likelihood Estimation (MLE)*

The easiest and most common algorithm of estimating the HMM parameters, λ, is the Baum-Welch algorithm,[30,31] based on maximizing the likelihood of generating the training data, given the correct transcription:

$$\max F_{MLE}(\lambda) = \log P(X|\lambda) = \sum_r \log P_\lambda(X_r|\lambda(s_r)) \tag{7}$$

where s_r is the correct transcription of the r-th training speech file X_r and is usually modeled by a concatenation of phonetic HMMs, $\lambda(s_r)$. The objective does not concern about the likelihood of the word string s_r itself. One reference[32] has a detailed description of the Baum-Welch algorithm.

5.2.2. *Discriminative Training: MMIE and MPE*

The objective of MLE training is to maximize the probability of the training data, given the correct transcription. This may not be the best goal for recognition since maximizing the correct word sequence for training data does not guarantee a distant separation between the correct path and the incorrect ones. If we can train the HMM parameters to separate the correct word sequence as far away from the wrong word sequences as possible, it may ease the search process on unseen test data and thus increase recognition accuracy. This is the idea behind corrective training.[33,34]

Another discriminative training criterion is the minimum classification error (MCE)[35,36] training which minimizes sentence error rates and therefore is more suitable for isolated-word recognition or small vocabulary tasks. On the other hand, maximum mutual information[37,38] (MMI) objective is to maximize the posterior probability (after the data X_r is seen) of the correct word string s_r:

$$\max F_{MMI}(\lambda) = \sum_r \log P_\lambda(s_r|X_r) = \sum_r \log \frac{P_\lambda(s_r, X_r)}{P_\lambda(X_r)}$$
$$\approx \sum_r \log \frac{P_\lambda(X_r|s_r)^\kappa P(s_r)^\kappa}{\sum_u P_\lambda(X_r|u)^\kappa P(u)^\kappa}, \tag{8}$$

where $P(u)$ is the language model probability, after the language weight ρ and word insertion penalty, etc. are all applied, for word sequence u. $P(.|u)$ is the acoustic probability given the sentence HMM for u. The MMIE objective function concerns both the acoustic and lexical likelihoods. Following Schluter and Macherey,[39] the constant scale κ is important empirically to lead to improved performance using MMI training. κ is usually set to be around $1/\rho$. The procedure to estimate MMI parameters thus becomes to maximize the numerator for the correct transcription (similar to the MLE estimation) and simultaneously minimize the denominator for all possible transcriptions, using the extended Baum-Welch algorithm.[40,38] The calculation of the denominator terms directly is computationally very expensive and therefore word lattices generated by a recognizer are usually used to approximate the denominator model.[41]

A very successful discriminative training paradigm for LVCSR now is the minimum phone error (MPE) training.[42,43] MPE targets at minimizing phone errors which are defined by word sequences, rather than any random phone loop. Like MMIE, MPE also maximizes the posterior probability. But unlike MMIE, which is more like corrective training, it considers all possible transcriptions instead of only the correct transcription. Each possible transcription for each training sample is then weighted by the resemblance to the correct phone sequence:

$$\max F_{MPE}(\lambda) = \sum_r \sum_s P_\lambda(s|X_r)^\kappa A(s, s_r)$$
$$= \sum_r \sum_s \frac{P_\lambda(X_r|s)^\kappa P(s)^\kappa A(s, s_r)}{P_\lambda(X_r)^\kappa}$$
$$= \sum_r \frac{\sum_s P_\lambda(X_r|s)^\kappa P(s)^\kappa A(s, s_r)}{\sum_u P_\lambda(X_r|u)^\kappa P(u)^\kappa}, \tag{9}$$

where $A(s, s_r)$ is the phone accuracy of sentence s, compared with the correct sentence s_r. Like MMIE, the set of all possible word sequences (both u and s) is generated by running the recognizer on the training data to dump a word/phone lattice per training utterance. As the scale κ becomes large, the MPE criterion for each utterance approaches the value of $A(s, s_r)$ for the most likely transcription s of that utterance. As κ becomes smaller, the criterion increasingly takes into account the accuracy of less likely sentences. This improves the ability of the trained system to generalize to unseen data, by taking into account more alternative paths.

5.2.3. *Feature Space MPE (fMPE) Transforms*

Dovey *et al.*[44] extended the MPE training criterion to the feature domain, hence the name of fMPE. The motivation of fMPE comes from a quick search to identify which Gaussians of the AM an input frame x_t is more likely to belong to. For that, we define the vector of Gaussian probabilities, $P_1^n(x_t)$, assuming there are n Gaussians in the system HMM (usually n is in the order of tens to hundreds of thousands):

$$P_1^n(x_t) \cong \begin{bmatrix} P(x_t|N_1) \\ P(x_t|N_2) \\ \cdots \\ P(x_t|N_n) \end{bmatrix}. \tag{10}$$

To have an even better estimate, we concatenate the Gaussian probability vectors of neighboring frames for the current frame:

$$h_t = \begin{bmatrix} P_1^n(x_{t-3}) \\ P_1^n(x_{t-2}) \\ P_1^n(x_{t-1}) \\ P_1^n(x_t) \\ P_1^n(x_{t+1}) \\ P_1^n(x_{t+2}) \\ P_1^n(x_{t+3}) \end{bmatrix}. \tag{11}$$

This h_t vector has a very high dimension. If n is 100,000, taking 3 neighboring frames gives h_t a dimension of 700k. We then apply a transformation matrix M to h_t, so that we can add the transformed result to the input vector x_t:

$$y_t = x_t + M\,h_t\,, \tag{12}$$

where the dimensions of M are around 42×700k for Mandarin systems. y_t has the same dimensionality as x_t, yet contains some information about the quick search result, which we hope will provide useful information during decoding.

To learn M, we first assume there exists an HMM λ_1. Use λ_1 to compute h_t and estimate M with the MPE criterion with the model λ_1 fixed:

$$\max F_{MPE}(M) = \sum_r \sum_s P_\lambda(s|Y_r)^\kappa A(s, s_r)\,. \tag{13}$$

Since M is MPE-learned, the y feature is thus called a discriminative feature. After M is learned, we then apply M, with λ_1 to compute h_t, to all the training data and MPE-train a new set of HMMs, λ_2, with the y feature. During decoding, M, with λ_1 to compute h_t, is also used to compute the y feature for the test speech, for decoding with model λ_2 .

Notice h_t is a sparse vector. Keeping that in mind will simplify the matrix computation greatly. Also to speed up the computation, λ_1 is usually a smaller model than λ_2.

5.3. *Lightly or Unsupervised Acoustic Training*

The above sections all assume the availability of transcribed corpora (see Figure 1). As careful transcription is labor-intensive, time-consuming, and expensive, there is much more acoustic data that are either not transcribed at all or containing only closed captions.

If there is no transcription at all, one can run an existing recognition system to get a rough transcription. The rough transcription can be used to collect a separate sufficient statistics to interpolate with or adapt the existing model trained on careful manual transcriptions. This is particularly useful if the un-transcribed data is in-domain and contains unseen microphone channels. The extra in-domain and channel information can compensate the existing model, despite of the inaccurate transcription. Once a real application is deployed, it is easy to log and collect real user data for this purpose.

If closed caption is available, one can use the closed caption to wisely choose a subset of quality data for training. This is known as lightly-supervised training.[45] One way to filter out bad transcription is to run a recognizer on the acoustic data with a general-purpose LM adapted by the closed caption and then compare the recognition result with closed caption.[46,47] High consistency implies high quality. Alternatively, one can construct a word graph from closed caption for each utterance, and allow a garbage word to be inserted between the words indicated by closed caption and allow any closed-caption word to be deletable.[48] This greatly simplifies the search space for each utterance. Once more, high consistency between the Viterbi-path word sequence and closed caption implies that the closed caption is reliable.

5.4. *Acoustic Model Adaptation*

There are many successful adaptation techniques that work well and are language independent.

5.4.1. *Maximum a posteriori (MAP) Adaptation*

The MAP approach[49,50,51] assumes that the HMM parameter vector λ is a random vector with a prior distribution function $g(\lambda)$. The goal is to maximize the posterior probability of the acoustic model λ (not the word string) after seeing the data:

$$\begin{aligned} \lambda_{MAP} &= \arg\max_{\lambda} P(\lambda|X) \approx \arg\max_{\lambda} P(X|\lambda) P(\lambda) \\ &\approx \arg\max_{\lambda} \sum_{r} \{\log P_{\lambda}(X_r|\lambda(s_r)) + \log P(\lambda(s_r))\} \end{aligned} \tag{14}$$

Similar to MLE training, the lexical probability of sentence s_r is not concerned. Assume λ is $N(m, \sigma^2)$ (for simplicity, assume m and σ are the only parameters in λ and they are scalars). Furthermore, assume σ is fixed while m is a random variable with distribution $N(\mu, \theta^2)$ which is given somehow:

$$\begin{aligned} \lambda &\propto N\left(m, \sigma^2\right) \\ g(m) &\propto N\left(\mu, \theta^2\right). \end{aligned} \tag{15}$$

Notice the only variable to be optimized is m since we assume σ is fixed across different speakers. With these assumptions, when the data X from a new speaker arrives, the MAP solution for the mean of the new speaker is[52]

$$\begin{aligned} \hat{m} &= a\bar{x} + (1-a)\mu \\ a &= \frac{T}{T + (\sigma^2/\theta^2)}, \end{aligned} \tag{16}$$

where T is the number of training samples in the SD data and $\bar{x}$ is the data average. When there is no SD data, $T = 0 = a$ and $\hat{m} = \mu$. As there are more and more SD data available, $\hat{m}$ eventually becomes the ML mean based on the SD data. Also the choice of θ^2 decides how fast the SD statistics is going to dominate the estimation. If θ^2 is small, it means strong confidence in the prior and will take a long time for SD data to make influence. If $\theta^2 \to \infty$, it is equivalent to no prior (m can be anything equally likely). Then the MAP estimation of the SD mean is the same as the ML estimation.

To choose the prior (μ, θ^2) in the context of speaker adaptation, we can build n speaker dependent (SD) models, $\lambda_1 = (m_1, \sigma_1^2), \lambda_2, \ldots, \lambda_n$, from a speaker independent (SI) corpus. Then use the count weighted mean and variance to be our prior:

$$\lambda \propto N\left(m, \sigma_{SI}^2\right)$$
$$g(\lambda) \propto N\left(\mu_{SI}, \sum_i w_i \sigma_i^2\right)$$
$$\mu = \sum_i w_i m_i = \mu_{SI}$$
$$\theta^2 = \sum_i w_i \sigma_i^2 \leq \sigma_{SI}^2 = \sum_i w_i \left[\sigma_i^2 + (m_i - \mu_{SI})^2\right], \quad (17)$$

where the weights $w_i = c_i/(\Sigma c_i)$ and c_i is the number of training samples for each Gaussian m_i.

The disadvantage of MAP adaptation is that it only touches the parameters that occur in the SD data. Therefore it is usually used when a moderate amount of SD data is available.

5.4.2. *Maximum Likelihood Linear Regression (MLLR) Adaptation*

Another very successful adaptation technique is the MLLR adaptation, where each regression class shares the same linear transform. It assumes the speaker dependent mean is a linear transformation of the speaker independent one:

$$\mu_{SD} = A\mu_{SI} + b. \quad (18)$$

Plugging the above formula into $F_{MLE}(\lambda)$ will give you a close form solution.[53] The advantage of MLLR adaptation is the tying of regression classes. All the parameters in the same regression class are modified. Therefore MLLR is usually applied even on a small amount of SD data. The less data one has, the fewer classes one will use. When more and more SD data are available, we can then afford to increase the number of transforms. For this reason, a decision tree is often used to dynamically decide on the number of MLLR regression classes, as a function of the amount of SD data.

MLLR and MAP can also be combined for the best adaptation performance, regardless of the amount of SD data.

5.4.3. *Speaker Adaptive Training (SAT)*

Inspired by MLLR, the motivation of SAT was to apply the model-space MLLR in the training process.[54] Later researchers have successfully applied the 1-class constrained MLLR[55,56] to the feature domain as one way of speaker adaptive training, also called feature-space SAT. The procedure is to first learn the 1-class constrained

MLLR for each test speaker,

$$\hat{\mu} = A\mu + b$$
$$\hat{\Sigma} = A\Sigma A^t\,, \tag{19}$$

where μ and Σ are from the speaker-independent model. The constraint comes from the fact that the transformation on the covariance matrix is constrained by the same transform, A, used by the mean. Using one regression class makes sure all Gaussians in the system use the same transform for the same speaker. Then the Gaussian density value of test data x, given the adapted model is

$$N\left(x; A\mu + b, A\Sigma A^T\right) = \parallel A \parallel^{-1} N\left(A^{-1}(x-b); \mu, \Sigma\right). \tag{20}$$

The constant term, $\parallel A \parallel^{-1}$, does not affect the relative log likelihood of any search path (every path is absolutely affected by $-T \log \parallel A \parallel$ where T is the number of frames in the input speech file). Therefore we can discard the constant term during decoding, and apply the transform to the feature domain without touching the SI model:

$$y = \left(A^{-1}\right)x + \left(-A^{-1}b\right). \tag{21}$$

Notice that the transform A and b are speaker dependent.

Similarly the constant term does not affect the sufficient statistics during HMM training. Therefore we can apply the feature transform during model training as a way of speaker normalization:

- For each training speaker i, compute his/her feature domain transform $(A_i^{-1}, -A_i^{-1}b_i)$ using a pre-trained SI model.
- Apply the speaker-dependent linear feature transform to the SD data while collecting the sufficient statistics for updating the SI model.
- Collect all statistics from all training speakers and update the SI model.

Usually we use the same SI model to compute feature transforms for all training speakers and test speakers. As the above algorithm shows, feature-space SAT is a lot more efficient in computation than model-space SAT, while achieving the same recognition performance. In another work,[7] we found that the improvement from the feature-space SAT was additive to that from cross-word triphone modeling for LVCSR.

5.4.4. *Cross Adaptation*

When unsupervised SD adaptation is applied, it is helpful to use the recognition output from another system to adapt the current system. This is because most of the current adaptation techniques are based on the ML criterion. When one system adapts to itself, it will tend to fall into the local optimum and make the same error again. On the other hand, different systems have different error behaviors. Using the output from another comparable system, one can integrate the knowledge and strength from the other system into the first system. Typical cross adaptation happens between two systems with two different front ends, such as one with MFCC and the other with PLP.

6. Multi-pass Decoding

First of all, for LVCSR a tree-representation of the lexicon has been well-adopted for its efficiency.[57–59] The n-gram probabilities have to be distributed across the arcs in the tree, in order to achieve efficient pruning.

Secondly, multi-pass decoding is often used. The reasons for multiple passes are:

- to ease the integration of more advanced technologies such as more complicated AMs or LMs. Earlier passes usually use simpler models.
- to provide transcription for adaptation on the models used in later passes.
- to execute cross adaptation.
- to be able to perform rover[60] (Recognizer Output Voting Error Reduction) or confusion-network-based combination.[61] They are both effective ways of improving recognition accuracy via combining the recognition outputs from multiple recognizers.

7. State of the Art and Challenges

In the GALE[4] project, where Mandarin broadcast news transcription is an important aspect, researchers have demonstrated highly-accurate Mandarin LVCSR[8,7,20,62,63] systems. The vocabulary size is around 64,000 words. With multiple-pass unsupervised cross adaptation on MPE-trained acoustic models, 5-gram language models, and confusion network combination between an MFCC-pitch system and an ICSI-feature system, the UW-SRI team achieved 3.7% of CER on the 2004 broadcast news development set and 12.2% of CER on the 2004 evaluation test set.[20,64] The other teams all performed in the same range of error rates.

Although the CER looks promising, there remain many unsolved problems:

- Conversational speech. All systems performed fairly well on careful announcement from journalists. However, spontaneous speech and other disfluency quickly deteriorate the accuracy. Despite the extra efforts of modeling disfluency in the n-gram, the improvement is still not satisfactory.
- Unseen microphone channels. Outdoor field interviews are extremely difficult, due to the unseen channels and background noises.

- Overlapped speech. When multiple people talk at the same time, speech separation is almost impossible without multiple microphones.
- Speech with music background. Although the degradation is not as much as speech over speech, it is nevertheless serious enough to deserve attention.
- Accent. Being one of the most spoken languages on earth, the Mandarin accent variation due to geographical locations is much bigger than that of English within the United States. In some cases, it is similar to the difference between American English and British English. Either data from different regions need to be collected to train accent dependent models or a powerful adaptation algorithm needs to be designed.
- Foreign languages. As mentioned earlier, the problems of code mixing and code switching need to be taken care of carefully.
- Machine translation. If the ultimate goal is translation rather than dictation, CER may not be the best measurement for SR. Recognizing keywords and optimizing the interface with the translation module are perhaps more important than recognizing some unimportant function words.

It is our goal to advance and expand our research expertise in every possible way to solve as many problems as possible. With the global collaboration and the availability of large amount of data, it is our hope that this goal is getting closer each day.

References

1. K. Lee, *Automatic Speech Recognition [The Development of the SPHINX System].* (Kluwer Academic Publishers, Norwell, Massachusetts, 1989).
2. Chinese corpus consortium. [Online]. Available: http://www.d-ear.com/ccc/
3. Effective, affordable, reusable speech-to-text. [Online]. Available: http://www.darpa.mil/ipto/Programs/ears/
4. Global autonomous language exploitation. [Online]. Available: http://www.darpa.mil/ipto/programs/gale/
5. The linguistic data consortium. [Online]. Available: http://www.ldc.upenn.edu/
6. T. Cover and J. Thomas, *Elements of Information Theory.* (John Wiley & Sons, 1991).
7. M. Hwang, X. Lei, W. Wang, and T. Shinozaki, "Investigation on Mandarin Broadcast News Speech Recognition," *Interspeech*, (2006).
8. B. Xiang, L. Nguyen, X. Guo, and D. Xu, "The BBN Mandarin Broadcast News Transcription System," *Interspeech*, pp. 1649–1652, (2005).
9. S. B. Davis and P. Mermelstein, "Comparison of Parametric Representation for Monosyllabic Word Recognition in Continuously Spoken Sentences," *IEEE Transactions on Acoustics, Speech and Signal Processing*, vol. 28, pp. 357–366, (1980).
10. H. Hermansky, "Perceptual Linear Predictive (PLP) Analysis of Speech," *Journal of the Acoustic Society of America*, vol. 87, pp. 1738–1752, (1990).
11. J. Cohen, T. Kamm, and A. Andreou, "Vocal Track Normalization in Speech Recognition: Compensating for Systematic Speaker Variability," *Journal of Acoustic Society America*, vol. 97, pp. 3246–3247, (1995).

12. D. Talkin, *Speech Coding and Synthesis [A robust algorithm for pitch tracking (RAPT)].* (NL: Elsevier Science, Amsterdam, 1995).
13. [Online]. Available: http://www.speech.kth.se/software/
14. C. J. Chen, "New Methods in Continuous Mandarin Speech Recognition," in *Proc. Eurospeech*, vol. 3, (1997), pp. 1543–1546.
15. X. Lei, M. Siu, M. Hwang, M. Ostendorf, and T. Lee, "Improved Tone Modeling for Mandarin Broadcast News Speech Recognition," *Interspeech*, (2006).
16. H. Hermansky and S. Sharma, "TRAPS - Classifiers of Temporal Patterns," in *Proc. International Conference on Spoken Language Processing*, (1998).
17. N. Morgan, B. Chen, Q. Zhu, and A. Stolcke, "TRAPping Conventional Speech: Extending TRAP/Tandem Approaches to Conversational Telephone Speech Recognition," in *Proc. International Conference on Acoustics, Speech, and Signal Processing*, (2004).
18. B. Chen, Q. Zhu, and N. Morgan, "Learning Long-term Temporal Features in Lvcsr Using Neural Networks," in *Proc. International Conference on Spoken Language Processing*, (2004).
19. X. Lei, M. Hwang, and M. Ostendorf, "Incorporating Tone-related MLP Posteriors in the Feature Representation for Mandarin ASR," *Interspeech*, (2005).
20. M. Hwang, X. Lei, J. Zheng, O. Cetin, W. Wang, G. Peng, and A. Stolcke, "Progress on Mandarin Broadcast News Speech Recognition," in *Proc. International Conference on Acoustics, Speech and Signal Processing*, (2007).
21. R. M. Warren, K. R. Riener, J. A. Bashford, and B. S. Brubaker, "Spectral redundancy: Intelligibility of sentences heard through narrow spectral slits," *Perception and Psychophysics*, vol. 57, pp. 175–182, (1995).
22. S. Greenberg, T. Arai, and R. Silipo, "Speech intelligibility derived from exceedingly sparse spectral information," in *International Conference of Spoken Language Processing*, (1998).
23. I. T. Jolliffe, *Principal Component Analysis.* (Springer-Verlag, Berlin, 1986).
24. C. J. Chen, H. Li, L. Shen, and G. K. Fu, "Recognize Tone Languages Using Pitch Information on the Main Vowel of Each Syllable," in *Proc. International Conference on Acoustics, Speech and Signal Processing*, vol. 1, (2001), pp. 61–64.
25. M. Y. Hwang, X. D. Huang, and F. Alleva, "Predicting Unseen Triphones with Senones," in *Proc. International Conference on Acoustics, Speech, and Signal Processing*, (1993), pp. 311–314.
26. G. Rigoll, "BaseformAdaptation for Large Vocabulary Hidden Markov Model Based Speech Recognition Systems," in *Proc. International Conference on Acoustics, Speech and Signal Processing*, (1990), pp. 141–144.
27. M. Y. Hwang and X. D. Huang, "Subphonetic Modeling with Markov States — Senones," in *Proc. International Conference on Acoustics, Speech and Signal Processing*, (1992).
28. K. Beulen and H. Ney, "Automatic Question Generation for Decision Tree Based State Tying," in *Proc. International Conference on Acoustics, Speech and Signal Processing*, vol. 2, (1998), pp. 805–808.
29. J. T. Chien, "Decision Tree State Tying Using Cluster Validity Criteria," *IEEE Transactions on Speech and Audio Processing*, vol. 13, pp. 182– 193, (2005).
30. L. E. Baum, "An Inequality and Associated Maximization Technique in Statistical Estimation for Probabilistic Functions of Markov Processes," *Inequalities*, vol. 3, pp. 1–8, (1972).
31. L. E. Baum, T. Petrie, G. Soules, and N. Weiss, "A Maximization Technique Occurring in the Statistical Analysis of Probabilistic Functions of Markov Chains," *Ann. Math. Statist.*, vol. 41, pp. 164–171, (1970).
32. L. Rabiner and B. H. Juang, *Fundamentals of Speech Recognition.* (Englewood Cliffs NJ: PTR Prentice Hall (Signal Processing Series), ISBN 0-13-015157-2) (1993).
33. L. R. Bahl, P. F. Brown, P. de Souza, and R. L. Mercer, "A New Algorithm for the Estimation

of Hidden Markov Model Parameters," in *Proc. International Conference on Acoustics, Speech and Signal Processing*, (1988), pp. 493–496.

34. K. Lee and S. Mahajan, "Corrective and Reinforcement Learning for Speaker-Independent Continuous Speech Recognition," *Computer Speech and Language*, (1990).
35. W. Chou, C. H. Lee, and B. H. Juang, "Minimum Error Rate Training Based on N-Best String Models," in *Proc. International Conference on Acoustics, Speech, and Signal Processing*, (1993), pp. 652–655.
36. B. H. Juang, W. Chou, and C. H. Lee, "Minimum Classification Error Rate Methods for Speech Recognition," *IEEE Transactions on Speech and Audio Processing*, vol. 5, pp. 266–277, (1997).
37. L. R. Bahl, P. F. Brown, P. V. de Souza, and R. L. Mercer, "Maximum Mutual Information Estimation of Hidden Markov Model Parameters for Speech Recognition," in *Proc. International Conference on Acoustics, Speech and Signal Processing*, (1986), pp. 49–52.
38. Y. Normandin, *Hidden Markov Models, Maximum Mutual Information Estimation and the Speech Recognition Problem*. (Ph.D. Thesis, McGill Unversity, Montreal, 1991).
39. R. Schluter and W. Macherey, "Comparison of Discriminative Training Criteria," in *Proc. International Conference on Acoustics, Speech and Signal Processing*, (1998), pp. 493–496.
40. P. S. Gopalakrishnan, D. Kanevsky, A. Nías, and D. Nahamoo, "An Inequality for Rational Functions with Applications to Some Statistical Estimation Problems," *IEEE Transaction on Information Theory*, vol. 37, pp. 107–113, (1991).
41. V. Valtchev, J. J. Odell, P. C. Woodland, and S. J. Young, "MMIE Training of Large Vocabulary Speech Recognition Systems," *Speech Communication*, vol. 22, pp. 303–314, (1997).
42. D. Povey and P. C. Woodland, "Minimum Phone Error and I-Smoothing for Improved Discriminative Training," in *Proc. International Conference on Acoustics, Speech, and Signal Processing*, (2002).
43. J. Zheng and A. Stolcke, "Improved Discriminative Training Using Phone Lattices," *Interspeech*, pp. 2125–2128, (2005).
44. W. K. Lo, P. C. Ching, T. Lee, and H. Meng, "fMPE: Discriminatively Trained Features for Speech Recognition," in *Proc. International Conference on Acoustics, Speech and Signal Processing*, (2005).
45. L. Lamel, J. L. Gauvain, and G. Adda, "Lightly Supervised Acoustic Model Training," in *Proc. IEEE Automatic Speech Recognition and Understand Workshop*, (2000), pp. 150–154.
46. L. Nguyen, N. Duta, J. Makhoul, S. Matsoukas, R. Schwartz, and D. X. B. Xiang, "The BBN RT03 BN English System," in *Proc. Rich Transcription Workshop*, (2003).
47. H. Y. Chan and P. C. Woodland, "Improving Broadcast News Transcription by Lightly Supervised Discriminative Training," in *Proc. International Conference on Acoustics, Speech, and Signal Processing*, (2004), pp. 737–740.
48. A. Venkataraman, A. Stolcke, W. Wen, D. Vergyri, V. Gadde, and J. Zheng, "An Efficient Repair Procedure for Quick Transcriptions," *Interspeech*, (2004).
49. C. H. Lee, C. H. Lin, and B. H. Juang, "A Study on Speaker Adaptation of the Parameters of Continuous Density Hidden Markov Models," *Proc. IEEE Transactions on Signal Processing*, vol. 39, pp. 806–814, (1991).
50. C. H. Lee and J. L. Gauvain, "Speaker Adaptation Based on MAP Estimation of HMM Parameters," in *Proc. International Conference on Acoustics, Speech, and Signal Processing*, (1993), pp. 558–561.
51. C. H. Lee, F. Soong, and K. Paliwal, *Automatic Speech and Speaker Recognition [Advanced Topics]*. (Kluwer Academic Publishers, 1996).
52. M. DeGroot, *Optimal Statistical Decisions*. (McGraw-Hill, 1970).
53. C. Leggetter and P. Woodland, "Speaker Adaptation of HMMs Using Linear Regression," *Cambridge University Technical Report CUED/F-INFENG/TR. 181*, (1994).

54. T. Anastasakos, "A Compact Model for Speaker Adaptive Training," in *Proc. International Conference on Spoken Language Processing*, (1996).
55. V. Digalakis, D. Rtischev, and L. G. Neumeyer, "Speaker Adaptation Using Constrained Estimation of Gaussian Mixtures," *IEEE Transactions on Speech and Audio Processing*, vol. 3, pp. 357–366, (1995).
56. M. Gales, "Maximum Likelihood Linear Transformations for HMM-based Speech Recognition," *Computer Speech and Language*, vol. 12, (1998).
57. H. Ney, R. Haeb-Umbach, B. Tran, and M. Oerder, "Improvements in Beam Search for 10000 Word Continuous Speech Recognition," in *Proc. International Conference on Acoustics, Speech and Signal Processing*, (1992).
58. F. Alleva, X. D. Huang, and M. Y. Hwang, "An Improved Search Algorithm for Continuous Speech Recongition," in *Proc. International Conference on Acoustics, Speech, and Signal Processing*, (1993).
59. J. Odell, *The Use of Context in Large Vocabulary Speech Recognition.* (PhD thesis, University of Cambridge, United Kingdom, 1995).
60. J. G. Fiscus, "A Post-Processing System to Yield Reduced Word Error Rates: Recognizer Output Voting Error Reduction (ROVER)," in *Proc. IEEE Automatic Speech Recognition and Understanding Workshop*, (1997), pp. 347–352.
61. L. Mangu, E. Brill, and A. Stolcke, "Finding Consensus in Speech Recognition: Word Error Minimization and Other Applications of Confusion Networks," *Computer Speech and Language*, pp. 373–400, (2000).
62. M. Gales, A. Liu, K. C. Sim, P. C. Woodland, and K. Yu, "A Mandarin STT System with Dual Mandarin-English Output," in *Proc. GALE PI Meeting*, (2006).
63. Y. Qin, Q. Shi, Y. Liu, H. Aronowitz, S. Chu, H. Kuo, and G. Zweig, "Advances in Mandarin Broadcast Speech Transcription at IBM under the DARPA GALE Program," in *Proc. International Symposium on Chinese Spoken Language Processing*, (2006).
64. J. Zheng, O. Cetin, M. Y. Hwang, X. Lei, A. Stolcke, and N. Morgan, "Combined Discriminative Training for Large Vocabulary Speech Recognition," in *International Conference on Acoustics, Speech and Signal Processing*, (2007).

CHAPTER 8

TONE MODELING FOR SPEECH RECOGNITION

Tan Lee[†] and Yao Qian[‡]

[†]*Department of Electronic Engineering*
The Chinese University of Hong Kong
Shatin, New Territories, Hong Kong

[‡]*Microsoft Research Asia*
5th floor, Beijing Sigma Center, 49 Zhichun Road
Haidian, Beijing 100080
E-mail: tanlee@ee.cuhk.edu.hk

Tone is an important linguistic component of spoken Chinese. For Chinese speech recognition, tone information is useful to differentiate words. This chapter is about automatic tone recognition for Chinese and its usefulness in automatic speech recognition. Our discussion focuses on Cantonese and Mandarin, which are the representatives of Chinese dialects that have been studied extensively. The key problematic issues in tone recognition are addressed and the major approaches in tone modeling are described. We also introduce various techniques of integrating tone recognition into state-of-the-art large vocabulary continuous speech recognition systems.

1. Introduction

Chinese languages are tone languages, in which pitch of voice is used to distinguish one word from another.[1,2] In many Chinese dialects, including Mandarin and Cantonese, each basic lexeme that corresponds to a written Chinese character is pronounced as a monosyllable with a specific lexical tone. If the tone changes, the lexeme has a different meaning. In Cantonese, for example, the syllable */fuː/*[a] with different tones can mean "husband (夫)," "tiger (虎)," "rich (富)," "symbol (符)," "woman (妇)," or "father (父)". Similarly, in Mandarin, */pau tʂaŋ/* can mean "newspapers (报章)," "protection (保障)," "rise sharply (暴涨)," or "render an account (报帐)," depending on the tones of the two syllables.

[a]In this introductory section, the International Phonetic Alphabet (IPA) is used to label the pronunciations to make them comprehensible to general readers. In the subsequent sections, Mandarin syllables are transcribed using Hanyu Pinyin, and Cantonese syllables are transcribed using Jyut Ping.[3] Jyut Ping is also known as the LSHK system.

Given the contrastive function of tone, it is believed that tone information plays a vital role in automatic speech recognition (ASR) of Chinese languages. ASR is a computational process that converts an acoustic speech signal into a sequence of words. It is formulated as a problem of searching for the best word sequence among many possibilities. If the tones are known, the number of word candidates is much reduced. By restricting the search space, the performance of an ASR system can be improved in terms of both accuracy and efficiency.

Tone is described by the pitch contour of a syllable. Pitch can be measured acoustically in terms of the fundamental frequency (henceforth abbreviated as F0), which quantifies the periodicity of a speech signal. For example, there are four basic tones in Mandarin, which are characterized by distinctive patterns of pitch movement. Automatic tone recognition is a pattern classification process that determines the tone identities of individual syllables based on their F0 contours. The major challenge comes from the great variability of F0 in natural speech, which is caused by multifarious linguistic and non-linguistic factors. There have been many studies on automatic tone recognition and the use of tone information in ASR. We divide the approaches into two categories: embedded tone modeling and explicit tone recognition. In the embedded approach, tone recognition is done as an integral part of the existing framework of hidden Markov model (HMM) based phoneme recognition. F0-related feature parameters are appended to the conventional spectral feature vectors as additional components or as a separate feature stream for acoustic modeling.[4,5] Tone identity is treated as a special type of phonetic context and the phoneme models are tone-dependent.[6,7] In this way, tone information is embedded implicitly in the phoneme recognition result. In the approach of explicit tone recognition, tones are independently modeled and recognized in parallel with phoneme recognition.[8] Either there is a process by which the tone carried by each syllable is explicitly determined,[9,10] or at least the tone posterior probability is computed.[11] The results of tone recognition are used for post-processing of the phoneme recognition output,[12,8] or integrated directly into the search process.[13,11]

This chapter is intended to address the major problematic issues in automatic tone recognition and related topics. The state-of-the-art approaches to these problems are described. Our discussion mostly concerns Cantonese tone modeling and recognition, which has been the authors' research focus for many years. Relevant work on Mandarin tone modeling and recognition will also be discussed.

2. Phonological and Acoustic Properties of Tones in Chinese

2.1. *Phonological Functions*

The basic unit of written Chinese is the ideographic character. In both Cantonese and Mandarin, each character is pronounced as a tonal syllable, and is the smallest meaningful unit (morpheme) of the language. A spoken word may consist of one or more syllables. A spoken sentence is thus a sequence of continuously uttered syllables. There are thousands of different Chinese characters. They are used to form tens of thousands of words. A character may have multiple pronunciations, and a syllable typically corresponds to a number of different characters.

Each syllable is divided into two parts: the initial or onset, and the final or rhyme (also written as *rime*).[14] In Cantonese, the initial is a consonant, whereas the final typically consists of a vowel nucleus and a coda. The initial and the coda are optional. Tone is a supra-segmental component that spans the entire syllable. There are 19 initials and 53 finals in Cantonese. The finals can be divided into five categories: vowels (long), diphthongs, vowels with a nasal coda, vowels with a stop coda, and syllabic nasals. In Cantonese, the stop codas /p/, /t/, and /k/ are unreleased.[2] A Mandarin syllable can also be described by the initial-final structure. There are 22 initials and 37 finals in Mandarin.[15] Mandarin has a number of retroflex initial consonants that are not found in Cantonese. The number of finals in Mandarin is much less than that in Cantonese. Cantonese has six different consonant codas (/m/, /n/, /ng/, /p/, /t/, /k/) but Mandarin has only two (/n/, /ng/).

Each Chinese dialect has its own tone system, which defines a specific set of lexical tone categories. Cantonese is often said to have nine tones while Mandarin has four. Figure 1 compares the tone systems of Cantonese and Mandarin. Each tone is illustrated by a two-dimensional sketch of pitch movement, in which the vertical dimension shows the pitch height and the horizontal dimension indicates the length of the tone. Cantonese tones are distributed across three pitch levels: high, mid, and low. At each level, the tones are further classified according to the shape of the pitch contour. "Entering tone" is a historically defined tonal category that generally refers to abrupt and short tones. Cantonese is one of the existing Chinese dialects that preserve entering tones.[16] In Cantonese, entering tones occur exclusively with "checked" syllables, i.e. syllables ending in an occlusive coda /p/, /t/ or /k/.[17] They are contrastively shorter than non-entering tones. In terms of pitch level, each entering tone coincides roughly with one of the non-entering tones. Many linguistic researchers have suggested treating the three entering tones as abbreviated versions of their non-entering counterparts.[2] Jyut Ping defines only six distinctive tones, labeled from 1 to 6 as in Figure 1. The four basic tones of Mandarin are characterized by distinctive contour shapes, namely high-level, mid-rising, falling-rising and high-falling.[18] In addition, there is a neutral tone (labeled as tone 0) that goes with "lightly" or casually articulated syllables.[15] In Mandarin, when a pair of tone 3 (falling-rising) syllables occur in succession, the first would change to tone 2 (mid-rising). This is known as tone sandhi.[17]

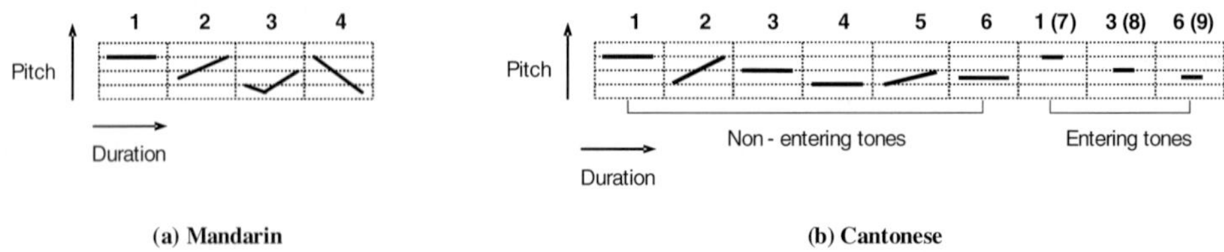

Fig. 1. Tone systems of Mandarin and Cantonese. In both Hanyu Pinyin (for Mandarin) and Jyut Ping (for Cantonese), tones are labeled by numbers. For Cantonese, the numbers in the bracket are used in the nine-tone system.

Table 1 compares the syllable inventories of Cantonese and Mandarin.[3,19] "Base syllable" refers to a tone-independent initial-final combination. "Tonal syllable" refers to a base syllable carrying a specific tone. There are approximately 50% more base syllables and 20% more tonal syllables in Cantonese than in Mandarin. On average, the number of tones that can be associated with a base syllable is 2.8 for Cantonese and 3.5 for Mandarin. Cantonese has over 600 legitimate base syllables and nearly 1,800 tonal syllables, which cover the pronunciations of more than 10,000 Chinese characters. Each syllable typically corresponds to a number of different characters (homophones). The average number of homophonous characters per base syllable and per tonal syllable are 17 and 6 respectively. By knowing the tone identity, the number of candidate characters can be greatly reduced.

Table 1. Comparison between the syllable inventories of Cantonese and Mandarin.

	Cantonese	Mandarin
Total number of base syllables	625	420
Total number of tonal syllables	1,761	1,471
Average number of tones per base syllable	2.8	3.5
Average number of base syllable pronunciations per character	1.1	1.6
Average number of tonal syllable pronunciations per character	1.2	2
Average number of homophonous characters per base syllable	17	31
Average number of homophonous characters per tonal syllable	6	8

2.2. *Acoustic Properties*

Syllable-wide F0 contours have been widely used as the basis of acoustic analysis of tones in various tone languages.[20,18,21] The tone contour of an uttered Cantonese syllable can be visualized by a plot of continuously varying F0 over the entire duration of the syllable. Figure 2 shows the measured F0 contours of the Cantonese tones. They were computed from about 1,800 isolated tonal syllables uttered by a male native speaker. These syllables form a nearly complete syllabary of today's Hong Kong Cantonese. Each contour shown in the figure is the average over all syllables that carry the respective tone. For the ease of comparison, all contours are aligned to have the same length. The tone contours of isolated syllables reflect the schematic pitch patterns in Figure 1 very well. Tones 1, 3, 4 and 6, have either flat or slightly falling F0 contours, which can be viewed as level-pitch tones at different levels. It can also be seen that the time-aligned F0 contours of an entering tone and its non-entering counterpart are similar.

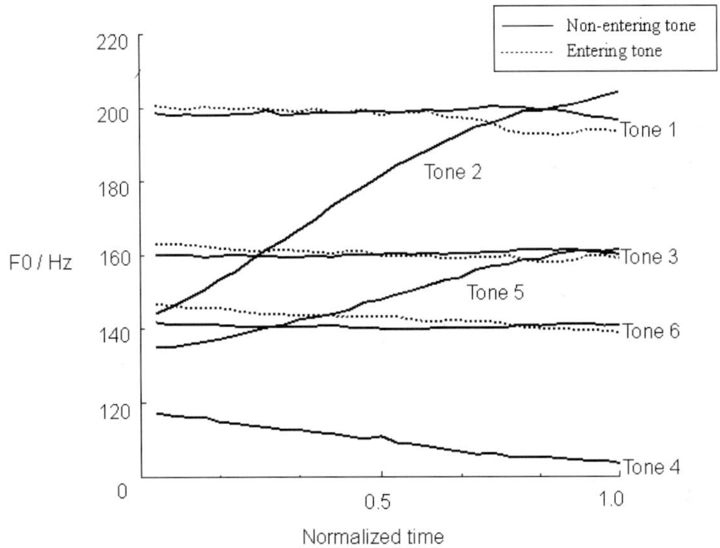

Fig. 2. F0 contours of Cantonese tones uttered in isolation.

F0 is determined by both the physical and the linguistic aspects of speech production. Obviously each speaker has a specific range of F0 variation. Even for the same speaker, the actual range of F0 changes from time to time because of a variety of physical, emotional, semantic or stylistic factors. In natural speech, intonation and co-articulation are the major factors that cause tone contours to deviate from their canonical patterns.[22,21] Figure 3 shows the waveform and the F0 contour of a Cantonese sentence spoken by a male native speaker. The sentence consists of 19 tonal syllables. The numeral at the end of each syllable transcription is the tone identity. For each syllable, an average value of F0 is computed from the middle one-third section of its tone contour. It is shown at the bottom of the F0 plot to represent the pitch level of the respective syllable. It can be seen that the F0 contours of individual syllables deviate greatly from their canonical patterns. The sentence contains six syllables of tone 1 (high level). Some of them have falling pitch contours while the others have flat contours. Apparently, this may be caused by tone co-articulation, e.g., between /hei1/ and /mong6/ (the 14th and the 15th syllables). The F0 values vary greatly even among the syllables with the same tone in the same sentence. For example, the F0 levels of the six syllables with tone 1 range from 123 Hz to 196 Hz. They seem to be related to the positions of these syllables in the sentence.

Figure 4 shows the statistical variation of the six tones of Cantonese as observed from a large amount of speech data. About 10,000 utterances from 34 male speakers are used for the analysis.[23] Each utterance contains a complete sentence of 6 to 20 syllables. The F0 contour of each syllable is divided into three even sections. The average logarithmic F0 value of each section is computed. It can be seen that the F0 ranges of different tones overlap largely with each other. The confusion is particularly severe between tone 3 and tone 6, and between tone 6 and tone 4.

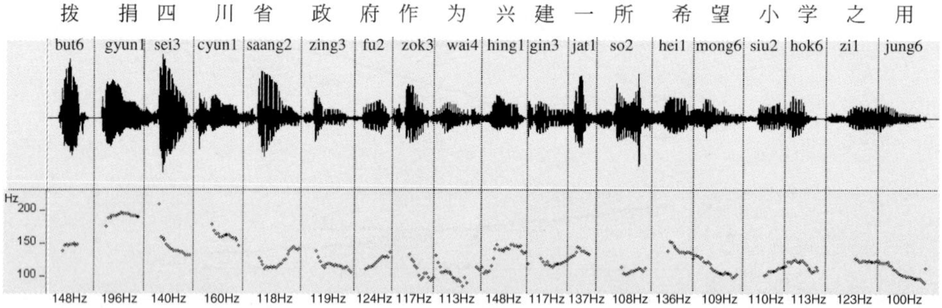

Fig. 3. The F0 contours of a continuous Cantonese sentence spoken by a male speaker. The upper panel shows the waveform and the lower panel gives the corresponding F0 plot. The content of the sentence is given in both Chinese characters and their Jyut Ping transcriptions. The numbers at the bottom are the average F0 values computed from the middle one-third section of each syllable.

The six tones of Cantonese can be roughly categorized as level tones or rising tones, according to the shapes of tone contours. This is unlike Mandarin, in which all the four basic tones have distinctive contour shapes. Discrimination between the level tones of Cantonese relies more on the heights than on the shapes of the pitch contours. Bauer and Benedict[2] pointed out that the height of a tone is a relative and not an absolute feature. It is the relative pitch difference, rather than the absolute pitch heights, which make the tones identifiable and distinguishable. Given the large variation in pitch, it is questionable whether tones can retain their distinctive pitch patterns in natural speech.

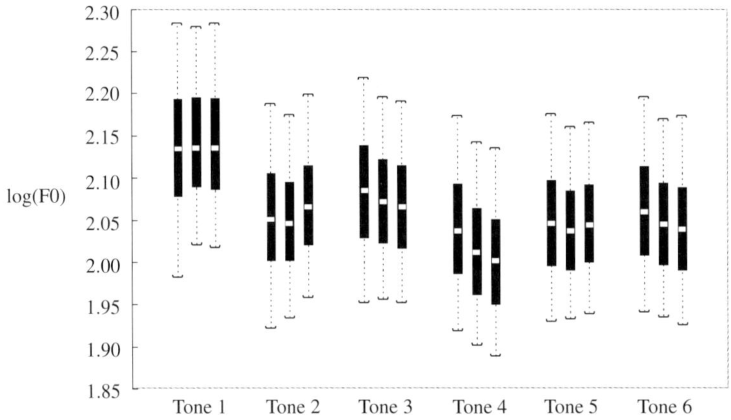

Fig. 4. Statistical variation of the F0 contours of the six Cantonese tones uttered by 34 male speakers. The white strip indicates the median. The thick solid bar extends from the 25th to the 75th percentile. The thin dashed line extends from the 5th to the 95th percentile.

Consider an arbitrary pair of syllables and compare their pitch heights. If the syllables are not in neighboring positions, their relative pitch heights may not follow the order of height as shown in Figures 1(b) and 2. In the example in Figure 3, the third syllable, which carries tone 3, has a noticeably higher F0 than the eighteenth syllable, which carries tone 1. However, from the same example it can be seen that the relative pitch heights are mostly preserved for neighboring tones. It is very unlikely, if not impossible, that a tone 4 syllable would have a higher F0 than a tone 3 syllable in its near neighborhood.

3. Usefulness of Tone Information in ASR

Despite the linguistic significance of tones, it is not inarguable that tone information is "absolutely essential" for Chinese ASR. There has been an opinion that, by using powerful language models, high-performance ASR can be done without considering tones at all. In this section, we try to address this issue from various perspectives.

The output of a Chinese ASR system is in the form of a sequence of Chinese characters. Conceptually, the recognition process involves the conversion from acoustic observations to phonetic (syllable) symbols, and the conversion from phonetic representation to orthographic text (Chinese characters). Tone information can be made contributive to resolve ambiguities in these two conversion processes.

For small-vocabulary applications, the usefulness of tone information can be easily understood. For example, in Cantonese digit recognition, the vocabulary is limited to ten digits: "0 (/ling4/)," "1 (/jat1/)," "2 (/ji6/)," "3 (/saam1/)," "4 (/sei3/)," "5 (/ng5/)," "6 (/luk6/)," "7 (/cat1/)," "8 (/baat3/)," and "9 (/gau2/)". Only the digit "0" carries tone 4 and only "9" carries tone 2. They can be recognized simply by their tone identities. If a digit is known to carry tone 3, there are only two possible candidates, i.e., "3" and "8".

In a large-vocabulary task, a syllable, depending on its lexical context, may carry up to six different tones. The effect of phonological constraints on syllable-tone combinations becomes less obvious. Nevertheless, it is observed that nearly 30% of the base syllables of Cantonese are allowed to carry only one specific tone and more than 50% of them carry at most two different tones.[24] If the tone is known, the number of syllable candidates would be much reduced. In Cantonese, there is a tendency that the tones in the "high" group (tones 1, 2 and 3) co-occur with the same base syllable, and so do the tones in the "low" group (tones 4, 5 and 6).

Large-vocabulary continuous speech recognition (LVCSR) systems deal with fluently spoken speech with a vocabulary size of several thousands of words or more.[25] The key components of a state-of-the-art LVCSR system are acoustic models, a pronunciation lexicon, and language models.[26] The acoustic models are a set of HMMs that characterize the statistical variation of input speech features. Each HMM represents a specific phoneme. The pronunciation lexicon and language models are used to define and constrain the way in which these phonemic units can be concatenated to form words and sentences. In Wong *et al.*[27] and Choi *et al.*,[28] we presented a baseline Cantonese LVCSR system, which does not use any tone information. The disambiguation among homophones relies on the lexicon and the language models. This system has a character accuracy rate of 84%. It is found that about 30% of the errors can be rectified if the correct tones are given.[24]

The baseline LVCSR system mentioned above uses a pronunciation lexicon of about 6,400 words. The pronunciations can be in the form of either base syllable or tonal syllable. A word may have multiple pronunciations while the same pronunciation may be shared by a number of different words. A specific word with a specific pronunciation is treated as a distinct entry of the lexicon. Table 2 compares the number of base syllable and tonal syllable entries. The inclusion of tone information leads to a significant increase of the number of one-to-one mapping entries, i.e., pronunciations that correspond to only one word, and a substantial reduction on the average number of homophonous words.

The potential contribution of tone information to Cantonese LVCSR can also be seen via an oracle experiment on syllable-to-character conversion. Given a sequence of Cantonese syllables, we can convert it into a character sequence. The process is very much like LVCSR with perfect acoustic models that can recognize all syllables correctly. In the experiment, true transcriptions of the test utterances

Table 2. Analysis of a 6,400-word Cantonese pronunciation lexicon.

	Base syllable transcriptions	Tonal syllable transcriptions
Total number of entries	7,168	7,456
No. of one-to-one mapping entries	3,747	4,568
Average number of homophonous words	5.4	3.5

are used. If tone is not included as part of the transcription, the accuracy of conversion is 90.7%. If tone information is given, the accuracy can be improved to 95.8%.

In summary, we believe that tone information, if acquired accurately and utilized effectively, contributes positively to Chinese ASR. The next two sections are dedicated, respectively, to the techniques of tone recognition and the effective incorporation of tone information into the existing LVCSR framework.

4. Explicit Tone Recognition

4.1. *Feature Extraction and Normalization*

Tone recognition is a typical pattern recognition task. It is accomplished in two steps: feature extraction and pattern classification. Feature extraction aims at deriving a compact parametric representation from the input speech, which contains useful and discriminative tone-related information. Syllable-wide F0 contours are considered to be the most important acoustic representation of tones. Other commonly-used supplementary features are the energy or amplitude contours and the duration of syllables.

To obtain the F0 contour of a syllable, the beginning and ending times of the syllable need to be known in advance. For isolated syllables, a simple energy-based end-point detection algorithm can be used.[9] For continuous speech in which syllables are closely co-articulated, syllable boundaries are often provided by an independent HMM-based ASR system.[8] Since the ultimate goal of tone recognition is to improve ASR performance, there is usually an ASR system running side by side, from which syllable alignments are obtained as a by-product of the recognition process.

F0 is defined only for voiced speech. The F0 contour of a Cantonese syllable may or may not cover the initial consonant. It is arguable whether we should make a tone contour "complete" by F0 interpolation over the voiceless initial segment, or simply ignore any voiceless initial consonant. Acoustic-phonetic studies also revealed that voiceless initial consonants can cause local F0 perturbation.[29] So far both approaches have been used and there seems to be no conclusive difference between them in terms of tone recognition performance. Automatic determination of instantaneous F0 values can be done by exploiting the quasi-periodic properties of speech signals in either time domain, frequency domain or both.[30] Various post-processing techniques have been developed to improve the accuracy of pitch extraction, among which dynamic programming based pitch tracking is most successful.[31]

As shown in Section 2.2, F0 is subject to inter-speaker, intra-speaker and even intra-utterance variation. The extracted F0 contours are contaminated with tone-irrelevant information. F0 normalization aims at reducing such undesirable variation and making the tone contours comparable. In general, the normalization is performed in two steps[8]:

(i) obtain a normalization factor, which serves as a reference of the speaker's F0 range, and
(ii) divide raw F0 values by this normalization factor (or subtract on the logarithmic scale).

The determination of a proper normalization factor plays a key role in the normalization. Ideally, the normalization factor should be not only speaker-specific, but also utterance-specific and position-specific. Some of the commonly-used methods will be described in the following sections.

4.2. *Tone Recognition for Isolated Syllables*

Early efforts on tone recognition started with syllables uttered in isolation. In this case, the effect of tone co-articulation is assumed to be minimal and the syllable boundaries can be clearly located. In Yang *et al.*,[32] Chang *et al.*[33] and Hon *et al.*,[34] tone recognition for isolated Mandarin syllables were studied. Yang *et al.*[32] used HMMs to model the normalized F0 contours. The normalization was done with a pre-computed "pitch base". Chang *et al.*[33] described the height and curvature of a tone contour with a few feature parameters and used multi-layer perceptron (MLP) for classification. Hon *et al.*[34] performed quadratic curve fitting so that each tone contour was represented by only four coefficients.

In another work, we presented a neural network based classifier for the nine tones of Cantonese.[9] To deal with syllables of different durations, a time warping procedure was employed to produce fixed-length tone contours. The voiced portion of each syllable was divided into 16 even segments and for each segment, an F0 value was obtained. On the basis of extensive statistical measurement and analysis, it was concluded that F0 levels at the beginning and the end of a syllable, as well as the degree of temporal F0 rising (or falling), are most useful for identifying the non-entering tones. Accordingly, three feature parameters, namely the initial pitch, the final pitch and the pitch rising index, were defined. F0 normalization was found to be extremely important for Cantonese. We proposed to determine the F0 normalization factor based on the initial pitch values of tones 2, 4, 5 and 6, which were found to be relatively stable. The normalization factor was computed off-line for each individual speaker, via an enrollment procedure in which the speaker was asked to read a set of pre-selected syllables. Two additional feature parameters were used to differentiate entering tones from non-entering tones. They are the duration of the syllable's voiced portion and the energy drop rate. Since an entering tone syllable ends with an unreleased stop consonant, the signal energy drops abruptly at the end of the syllable. The energy drop rate measures how fast the short-time energy decreases. We used a three-layer feed-forward neural network to classify the 5-dimensional tone feature vector. The nine-tone recognition accuracy was 87.6% for 5 male and 5 female native speakers. Tone 1 gave the highest accuracy because of its distinctively high F0 level. Tone 2, being characterized by a significant rise of F0, was also easily separated from other tones. There was noticeable confusion between tones 3, 4 and 6, which have similar contour shapes and close F0 levels.

4.3. *Tone Recognition for Continuous Speech*

4.3.1. *General Overview*

Tone recognition for continuous speech is much more difficult than that for isolated syllables. There are three problematic issues to be addressed:

- **Tone co-articulation**. In continuous speech, the tone contour of a syllable is heavily influenced by its neighboring tones. The feature parameters proposed for recognizing isolated tones are no longer effective.
- **Online F0 normalization**. Intonation is realized by sentence-level F0 movement. The speaker's pitch varies substantially in a long utterance. It would be inadequate to use a fixed normalization factor as in the case of isolated syllables.
- **Syllable boundary detection**. The automatic detection of syllable boundaries in running speech is prone to errors. The tone recognition algorithm needs to be robust against such errors.

Context-dependent phoneme models have been effectively used to deal with phonetic co-articulation. Wang *et al.*[12] proposed to use context-dependent tone models for tone recognition in continuous Mandarin speech. That is, the same tone with different tonal contexts are modeled separately. Cao *et al.*[35] used the data-driven decision tree approach to build context-dependent tone models. It was suggested that, while the identities of neighboring tones are the most important contextual factors, the phonetic composition and the syllable position also play a role.

Zhang *et al.*[36] proposed the method of tone-nucleus-based modeling, and exploited the pitch contrast between neighboring tones.

To alleviate inter-speaker variability, online F0 normalization can be done based on the average F0 value over the entire utterance.[37] The approach of moving average has been found very effective for Mandarin speech.[5,38] The raw F0 value at a particular time instant is normalized by the average F0 over a window that covers a few neighboring syllables. Wang and Seneff[39] assumed the same intonation movement for similar types of utterances, i.e., digit strings, and used a fixed F0 downdrift pattern for normalization.

In the following sub-sections, we will describe our work on context-dependent modeling and supra-tone modeling for continuous Cantonese speech.

4.3.2. *Context-Dependent Tone Modeling for Cantonese*

For Cantonese LVCSR, initials and finals have been used as the fundamental units for acoustic modeling.[27] With these acoustic models, speech segmentation at initial-final level can be obtained. This segmentation not only indicates the syllable boundaries but also provides useful information about the voiced/voiceless boundaries within individual syllables. On the other hand, a binary voicing classification can be obtained by the pitch tracking algorithm.[31] These two sources of information supplement each other in locating the voiced portion of a syllable.

For each 10-ms frame of voiced speech, a feature vector is formed by the instantaneous F0 value, the signal energy, and their first- and second-order time derivatives. F0 is computed using the robust algorithm for pitch tracking (RAPT).[31] For voiceless and silence frames, F0 is not available and the feature components are assigned fixed values that far exceed the dynamic ranges of the corresponding parameters in voiced speech. Moving-window normalization (MWN) is applied to capture localized F0 features. Each syllable is associated with a window that extends to a few neighboring tones. The average F0 over this window is used as the normalization factor for that particular syllable. As the window moves, the normalization factor adapts to the sentential intonation.

Treating "silence" as a special kind of context, a total of 294 ($7 \times 6 \times 7$) context-dependent tone models (CDTM) are needed to cover both left and right tonal contexts. Each tone model is a left-to-right HMM with 4 emitting states. The first state is designated to the voiceless part of a syllable and hence can be skipped. The other states correspond to the voiced part. In addition, there is a silence model with one emitting state. Speaker-independent tone recognition experiments are carried out using CUSENT, which is a large-scale Cantonese continuous speech database developed at the Chinese University of Hong Kong.[23] The training data consists of about 20,000 phonetically-rich sentences uttered by 34 male and 34 female speakers. The average sentence length is approximately 10 syllables. Tone recognition was performed as a one-pass forward Viterbi search, which produced the most probable sequence of tone models. The test data comprised 1,200 unseen sentences uttered by 6 male and 6 female speakers. A recognition accuracy of 66.4% was attained using the CDTMs. It is observed that, for MWN, an asymmetric window including two preceding tones and the four succeeding tones gives the best recognition performance. Tones 1, 2 and 4 are the best recognized tones. Tones 3, 5 and 6, which reside at the middle pitch range, are difficult to recognize. Tone 3 is easily confused with either higher or lower tones (tones 1 and 6), while tone 6 is often confused with the lowest tone (tone 4) and tone 3, which are just next to it. Confusion between the two rising tones (tones 2 and 5) is also noticeable.

4.3.3. *Supra-tone Modeling for Cantonese*

As discussed in Section 2, Cantonese tones are characterized by their distinctive pitch levels. These levels are defined in a relative sense. Although the absolute pitch level of a specific tone may vary substantially in different contexts, the relative heights of different tones with respect to each other remain largely invariant. Such invariance is well preserved between abutting tones in the same utterance. To effectively recognize a tone in continuous Cantonese speech, it is not only the F0 contour of the current syllable that is useful. Those of its neighboring syllables play an important role in serving as references of pitch height. This motivates us to extend the scope of tone modeling beyond the scope of a single syllable.

A supra-tone unit refers to the concatenation of multiple tones in succession. Currently we focus on di-tone and tri-tone units. A di-tone unit is composed of two tones. It covers not only the individual F0 contours of the two syllables, but also the transition between them. Similarly, a tri-tone unit is made up of three neighboring tones. The notion of supra-tone modeling is fundamentally different from that of context-dependent tone modeling. A context-dependent tone model is defined based on the phonetic context, rather than the acoustic context. The term "context" refers to the categorical identities of neighboring tones, and the exact acoustic realization of these tones is not considered. A supra-tone model captures the tonal contextual effect by using not only the tone identities, but also the acoustic features, i.e., the F0 contours, of the neighboring syllables. In this way, the tonal context can be characterized more precisely than by simply relying on the linguistically-defined tone categories.

The feature extraction process for di-tone modeling is shown as in Figure 5. Given a continuous speech utterance, a sequence of F0 values are computed on a short-time basis. The F0 contour of each syllable is divided evenly into three sections, and the average logarithmic F0 value of each section is computed. Thus, each tone contour is represented by three coarsely-sampled points. In di-tone and tri-tone modeling, the feature vector is composed of 6 and 9 components, respectively. As shown in the figure, each pair of neighboring tones forms a di-tone unit. To cover all of the tonal transitions in the utterance, the di-tone units are overlapped. There are several advantages of such overlapping. Firstly, for the same utterance, the number of overlapping di-tone units is approximately double what it would be without overlapping. This is desirable for the statistical modeling of tones, especially when the amount of training data is limited. Secondly, the overlap provides an additional constraint to the tone recognition process. For example, given that there are only four distinct level tones in Cantonese, it is not permitted to have more than three successive di-tone units with an upward change of pitch level.

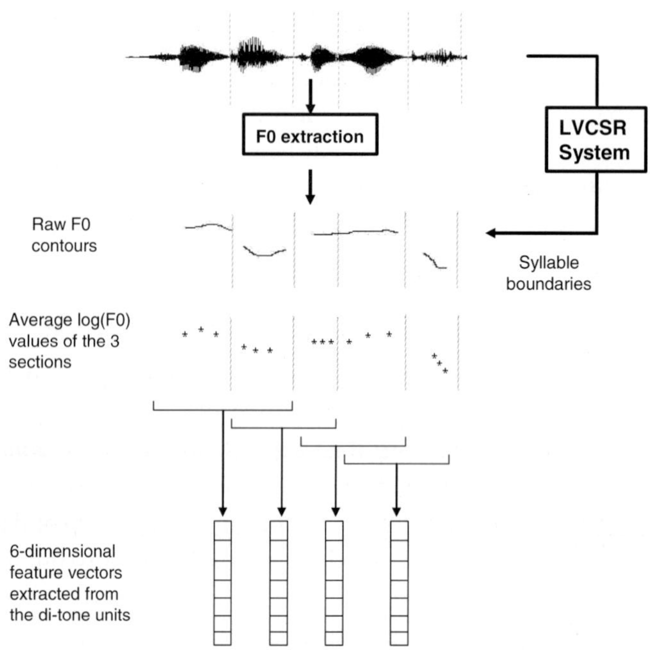

Fig. 5. The process of extracting feature vectors for di-tone modeling.

Each supra-tone unit is modeled by a dedicated Gaussian mixture model with a diagonal covariance matrix. The model parameters, which include the mixture weights, mean vectors, and covariance matrices, are estimated by the expectation-maximization (EM) algorithm with a large number of supra-tone feature vectors. The process of tone recognition is formulated as a problem of searching for the most likely sequence of di-tone models. The di-tone models form a search space. The transition between a pair of di-tone units is allowed only if they overlap with the same tone. From all of the candidate paths, the one with the highest probability is selected as the result of tone recognition. Phonological constraints are exploited in the search process so that the output would be linguistically meaningful. The LVCSR system that is used to generate syllable boundaries provides a sequence of hypothesized base syllables. In the process of searching for the best tone sequence, if the combination of a tone and a hypothesized base syllable is not allowed phonologically, this tone will have no chance of being included in the optimal path.

Speaker-independent tone recognition experiments are carried out using CUSENT. With the syllable boundaries automatically generated by the LVCSR system, the overall accuracy of tone recognition using di-tone models is 74.68%, which is significantly better than the context-dependent tone models as reported in Section 4.3.2. More reliable segmentation can be obtained in a supervised way through the forced alignment technique. With this improved syllable segmentation, the tone recognition accuracy increases to 79.18%, which can be considered to be the performance upper bound that the method of di-tone modeling can attain. Table 3 shows the confusion patterns among the six tones obtained with supervised syllable segmentation. Similar patterns are observed when the syllable boundaries are generated by unconstrained LVCSR search. Among the six tones, the highest and the lowest accuracy, 96.40% and 58.94%, are attained for Tone 1 and Tone 5, respectively.

Table 3. Confusion matrix and overall accuracy of tone recognition using di-tone models and supervised syllable segmentation.

Input Tone	**Recognized tone**						**Accuracy**
	Tone 1	Tone 2	Tone 3	Tone 4	Tone 5	Tone 6	
Tone 1	2061	6	35	4	3	29	96.40%
Tone 2	49	1008	66	33	47	76	78.81%
Tone 3	96	64	1192	17	56	215	72.68%
Tone 4	14	43	57	1399	51	227	78.11%
Tone 5	7	117	21	44	399	89	58.94%
Tone 6	54	69	232	101	79	1552	74.37%

The performance of tone recognition can be analyzed in terms of the percentage of correctly recognized di-tone units. The di-tone accuracy is 68.29% with supervised syllable segmentation. Table 4 lists the most frequent di-tone errors. They occur mostly between di-tone units that have the same direction of pitch movement, e.g., a high tone followed by a low tone. There are very few cases of confusion between di-tone units that have opposite directions of pitch movement. For example, there is only one case of confusion between the units "6-3" and "3-6", although tone 3 and tone 6 are highly confusable individually.

Table 4. The 10 most frequently occurring di-tone recognition errors found in the experiment with supervised syllable segmentation. "1-3→1-6" means that the unit "1-3" (tone 1 followed by tone 3) is recognized as "1-6".

10 most frequent di-tone recognition errors									
1-3	6-1	1-6	6-4	1-4	4-1	3-1	3-4	6-6	4-6
↓	↓	↓	↓	↓	↓	↓	↓	↓	↓
1-6	3-1	1-3	3-4	1-6	6-1	6-1	6-4	6-3	4-3

Using tri-tone models, the tone recognition accuracy improves to 75.59%. Tri-tone units have a longer time span than di-tone units. A pair of neighboring tri-tone units overlap each other by two tones. In other words, there is an overlap between three consecutive tri-tone units. This imposes more stringent constraints for recognition. However, given the same amount of speech data, the number of training tokens available for each tri-tone model is much smaller than that for a di-tone model. This may affect the effectiveness of statistical modeling, and thus limit the performance of the tri-tone models.

5. Integrating Tone Recognition into LVCSR

In an LVCSR system, different knowledge sources are integrated to form a search space, from which the most likely word sequence is determined. When high-level knowledge sources like high-order language models and prosody are considered, it would be computationally impractical to make decisions in a single pass. Instead, multi-pass search strategies are commonly adopted in state-of-the-art systems. Computationally efficient exploitation of short-term knowledge sources can be implemented in earlier passes, which produce a reduced search space. High-level knowledge sources are applied to the reduced search space in the later passes.

We have developed a number of different approaches to integrating the results of explicit tone recognition into a Cantonese LVCSR system. The baseline system uses context-dependent initial-final models. Each initial model is an HMM with 3 emitting states while each final model consists of 3 or 5 states, depending on its phonetic composition. Each HMM state is represented by 8-Gaussian mixture components. The acoustic feature vector has 26 components, including 12 MFCCs, energy and their first-order derivatives. The HMMs were trained with 20,000 utterances from CUSENT (see Section 4.3.2). The language models are word bi-grams built on a lexicon of 6,449 Chinese words. The training text contains 98 million Chinese characters from the one-year's editions of five local newspapers. For the 1,200 test utterances of CUSENT, a character accuracy of 75.4% was attained without using tone information.

5.1. *Syllable Lattice Expansion*

In Lee *et al.*,[8] a two-pass approach was adopted for integrating tone information into a Cantonese LVCSR system. As shown in Figure 6, the first pass is done by a forward Viterbi search to generate a syllable lattice based only on the acoustic models. The search space is made up of all phonologically legitimate combinations of initials and finals. Whenever the search reaches the end of a syllable, a syllable record is created. The output syllable lattice is made up of the top N syllable records kept at every time frame. The second pass is a backward search over the syllable lattice. It generates the best character sequence as the ultimate recognition output. The search is directed by a suffix lexical-tree using a cost function that combines the acoustic score from the syllable lattice and the language model probabilities.

The N-best output of tone recognition is used to augment the base syllable lattice produced by the first pass of search and produce a tonal syllable lattice for subsequent character decoding in the second pass. Each base syllable hypothesis is associated with the tone hypotheses that have the maximum percentage overlap in duration with the syllable. If the combination between a base syllable and a tone does not correspond to a legitimate tonal syllable, it will be treated simply as a base syllable and all possible tones are permitted. Each tonal syllable candidate is assigned a new score, which is a weighted sum of the acoustic score of the base syllable and the tone score. The weighting factors are determined empirically.

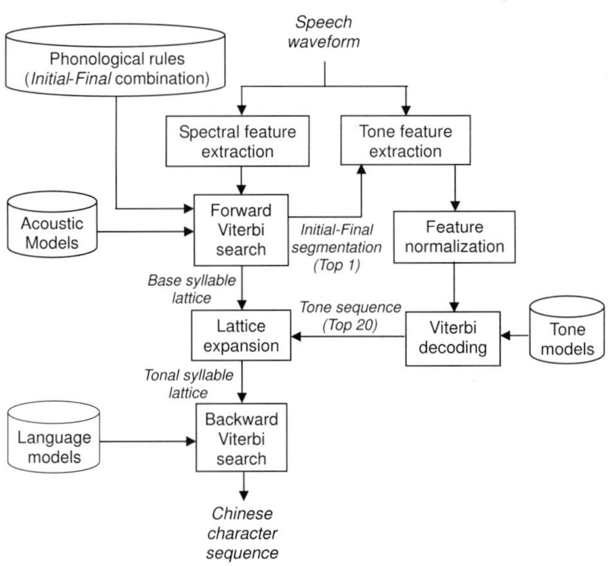

Fig. 6. Integrating tone information into Cantonese LVCSR by syllable lattice expansion.

Tones carry useful information for linguistic disambiguation. However, erroneous tone information may lead to performance degradation. To make sure that the incorporated tone information is reliable, four broad classes of tones are formed so that those easily confused tones are not differentiated. Tones 3, 4 and 6 are grouped into one class, while each of the other tones forms a class by its own. With the broad-class tone information, the accuracy of the LVCSR system improves from 75.4% to 76.6%. The maximum potential contribution of tone information can be examined by assuming 100% accuracy of tone recognition. This gives a character accuracy of 82.1% with the same acoustic models and language models.

5.2. *Tone-enhanced Generalized Posterior Probability*

A newer version of our baseline Cantonese LVCSR system adopts a different two-pass search strategy. The first pass is a time-synchronous, beam-pruned Viterbi token-passing search with cross-word acoustic models, a word-conditioned prefix lexical tree and bi-gram language models. It generates a word graph, which is a compact summary of the reduced search space. A word graph is an acyclic, directed graph connected by arcs, each of which represents a particular word. The second pass of search is an A* stack decoder. It performs re-scoring in the word graph with tri-gram language models to generate either the best word sequence or an N-best list. In Qian *et al.*,[11] we proposed to integrate the di-tone models as described in Section 4.3.3 into an improved second-pass decoding algorithm that operates on the word graph. The algorithm employs a decision criterion that explicitly minimizes character error rate, based on estimated character-level posterior probability.

Posterior probability is defined as the conditional probability of a linguistic unit given the acoustic observation. It provides a quantitative assessment of the correctness of speech recognition output. The posterior probability of a hypothesized word can be estimated as the summation of the posterior probabilities of all sentence hypotheses that contain the word with the same starting and ending time. In practice, these sentence posterior probabilities are obtained from a word graph.[40] Generalized word posterior probabilities (GWPP) were proposed by Soong *et al.*[41] to address various limitations of conventional word posterior probabilities (WPP). It is designed to incorporate automatically-trained optimal weights to equalize the dynamic ranges of acoustic models, language models as well as segmentation ambiguities.

For Cantonese LVCSR, the word graph is first converted into a character graph from which the generalized character posterior probabilities (GCPP) are computed. The character graph is further converted into a character confusion network, which is a concatenation of time-aligned character confusion sets.[42] Minimum character error rate decoding can be done straightforwardly on the confusion network.[43] To incorporate tone information, the likelihood scores produced by supra-tone models are included in the computation of GCPP. The use of tone-enhanced GCPP improves the character recognition accuracy from 83.82% to 86.14%. More details of this method can be found in Qian's PhD thesis.[43]

5.3. *Embedded Tone Modeling*

Embedded tone modeling refers to the approaches that treat tones as a special phonetic context and attempt to model tone-related acoustic features under the HMM-based ASR framework. It requires minimal redevelopment effort on an existing non-tonal LVCSR system and thus has been adopted in many commercial systems. Seide and Wang[13] gave a very good description of different ways of implementing embedded tone modeling in Mandarin LVCSR systems. In particular, the single-stream and two-stream approaches were compared. The single-stream approach, as presented by Chen *et al.*,[4] uses tone-dependent sub-word acoustic models and an augmented feature vector that contains both spectral and tone features. The two-stream approach was first proposed by Ho *et al.*[44] It separates spectral and tone features into two different streams for acoustic modeling. Stream-specific state dependencies and parameter sharing are used to address the different nature of spectral and tonal variations. When the sub-word units become both context-dependent, i.e., with specific left and right phonetic context, and tone-dependent, e.g., tonal finals or tonemes,[4] the number of models may be too large to be practically feasible. Zhou *et al.*[6] and Zhang *et al.*[7] proposed effective techniques of optimizing the phoneme set for Mandarin LVCSR.

The effectiveness of the embedded approach has been demonstrated in many studies on Mandarin LVCSR. However, we were not able to attain similar improvement on Cantonese LVCSR.[8] The embedded approach imposes a fixed time resolution for both segmental spectral features and supra-segmental pitch features. In other words, it assumes that these two types of features are in synchrony with each other. This assumption is not appropriate because supra-segmental features generally span over multiple segments. In the approach of explicit tone recognition, tone models are built separately and independently. They can have a tailor-made design that takes the supra-segmental characteristics of tones into account.

6. Conclusion

We believe that tone information can serve as a useful knowledge source in automatic speech recognition of Chinese languages. Automatic tone recognition is a difficult problem because many aspects of tone-relevant and tone-irrelevant information are co-encoded in the single-dimension feature of F0. Raw F0 measurements would not be meaningful tone features unless they are normalized with respect to properly established references. Despite the practical convenience of embedded tone modeling, we believe that explicit tone modeling should be the right direction to go, because we can have tailor-made design of the tone models to take into account the supra-segmental nature of tones. It is not realistic to expect a perfect (or nearly perfect) performance of tone recognition. When integrating tone recognition into a speech recognition system, we must be able to assess the reliability or confidence of a recognized tone, and make sure that the use of tone information would not introduce extra recognition errors. The contribution of tone information in speech recognition has not been fully exploited and further investigation is certainly needed.

Acknowledgements

Our research has been supported by a number of Earmarked Grants from the Hong Kong Research Grants Council.

References

1. K. L. Pike, *Tone Languages*, (University of Michigan Press, 1948).
2. R. S. Bauer and P. K. Benedict, *Modern Cantonese Phonology (Trends in Linguistics: Studies and Monographs; 102)*, (Mouton de Gruyer, 1997).
3. Linguistic Society of Hong Kong, *Hong Kong Jyut Ping Characters Table*, (Linguistic Society of Hong Kong Press, 1997).
4. C. J. Chen, R. A. Gopinath, M. D. Monkowski, M. A. Picheny, and K. Shen, "New Methods in Continuous Mandarin Speech Recognition," *Proc. Eurospeech*, (1997), pp. 1543–1546.
5. H. Huang and F. Seide, "Pitch Tracking and Tone Features for Mandarin Speech Recognition," *Proc. ICASSP*, (2000), pp. 1523–1526.
6. J. Zhou, Y. Tian, Y. Shi, C. Huang, and E. Chang, "Tone Articulation Modeling for Mandarin Spontaneous Speech Recognition," *Proc. ICASSP*, 1, (2004), pp. 997–1000.
7. J.-S. Zhang, X.-H. Hu, and S. Nakamura, "Automatic Derivation of a Phoneme Set with Tone Information for Chinese Speech Recognition Based on Mutual Information Criterion," *Proc. ICASSP*, 1, (2006), pp. 337–340.
8. T. Lee, W. Lau, Y. W. Wong, and P. C. Ching, "Using Tone Information in Cantonese Continuous Speech Recognition," *ACM Trans. on Asian Language Information Processing*, 1 (1), (2002), pp. 83–102.
9. T. Lee, P. C. Ching, L. W. Chan, B. Mak, and Y. H. Cheng, "Tone Recognition of Isolated Cantonese Syllables," *IEEE Trans. SAP*, 3 (3), (1995), pp. 204–209.
10. Y. Qian, T. Lee, and Y. Li, "Overlapped Di-tone Modeling for Tone Recognition in Continuous Cantonese Speech," *Proc. Eurospeech*, (2003), pp. 1845–1848.
11. Y. Qian, F. K. Soong, and T. Lee, "Tone-Enhanced Generalized Character Posterior Probability (GCPP) for Cantonese LVCSR," *Proc. ICASSP*, 1, (2006), pp. 133–136.
12. H.-M. Wang, T.-H. Ho, R.-C. Wang, J.-L. Shen, B.-R. Bai, J.-C. Hong, W.-P. Chen, T.-L. Yu, and L.-S. Lee, "Complete Recognition of Continuous Mandarin Speech for Chinese Language with Very Large Vocabulary using Limited Training Data," *IEEE Trans. SAP*, 5 (2), (1995), pp. 195–200.
13. F. Seide and N. J.-C. Wang, "Two-Stream Modelling of Mandarin Tones," *Proc. ICSLP*, (2000), pp. 495–518.

14. O.-K. Y. Hashimoto, *Studies in Yue Dialects 1: Phonology of Cantonese*, (Cambridge University Press, 1972).
15. Y. R. Chao, *A Grammar of Spoken Chinese.* (Berkeley and Los Angeles: University of California Press, 1968).
16. J. Yuan, *Hanyu Fangyan Gaiyao [An Introduction to Chinese Dialectology]*, (Wenzi Gaige Chubanshe, Beijing, 1960).
17. M. Y. Chen, *Tone Sandhi: Patterns across Chinese Dialects*, (Cambridge University Press, 2000).
18. Y. Xu, "Contextual Tonal Variation on Mandarin," *J. of Phonetics*, 25, (1997), pp. 61–83.
19. CCDICT: *Dictionary of Chinese Characters, Version 3.0*, (2000). [Online : http://www.chinalanguage.com/CCDICT/]
20. C.-Y. Tseng, *An Acoustic Phonetic Study on Tones in Mandarin Chinese*, (Institute of History & Philology, Academic Sinica, Taipei, 1990).
21. Y. Li, T. Lee, and Y. Qian, "Analysis and Modeling of F0 Contours for Cantonese Text-to-Speech," *ACM Trans. on Asian Language Information Processing*, 3, (2004), pp. 169–180.
22. Y. Xu, "Sources of Tonal Variations in Connected Speech," *Journal of Chinese Linguistics, Monograph Series*, 17, (2001), pp. 1–31.
23. T. Lee, W. K. Lo, P. C. Ching, and H. Meng, "Spoken Language Resources for Cantonese Speech Processing," *Speech Communication*, 36, (2002), pp. 327–342.
24. Y. Qian, T. Lee, and F. K. Soong, "Tone Information as a Confidence Measure for Improving Cantonese LVCSR," *Proc. ICSLP*, (2004).
25. J. L. Gauvain and L. Lamel, "Large-Vocabulary Continuous Speech Recognition: Advances and Applications," *Proc. IEEE*, 88, (2000), pp. 1181–1200.
26. X.-D. Huang, A. Acero, and H.-W. Hon, *Spoken Language Processing – A Guide to Theory, Algorithm, and System Development*, (Prentice-Hall, 2001).
27. Y. W. Wong, K. F. Chow, W. Lau, W. K. Lo, T. Lee, and P. C. Ching, "Acoustic Modeling and Language Modeling for Cantonese LVCSR," *Proc. Eurospeech*, (1999), pp. 1091–1094.
28. W. N. Choi, Y. W. Wong, T. Lee, and P. C. Ching, "Lexical-Tree Decoding with a Class-Based Language Model for Chinese Speech Recognition," *Proc. ICSLP*, (2000), pp. 174–177.
29. C. X. Xu and Y. Xu, "F0 Perturbations by Consonants and their Implications on Tone Recognition," *Proc. ICASSP*, 1, (2003), pp. 456–459.
30. W. Hess, *Pitch Determination of Speech Signals*, (Springer-Verlag, 1983).
31. A. D. Talkin, "A Robust Algorithm for Pitch Tracking (RAPT)," in *Speech Coding and Synthesis*, W. B. Kleijn and K. K. Paliwal, Eds., (Elsevier Science B.V., Amsterdam, 1995), pp. 495–518.
32. W.-J. Yang, J.-C. Lee, Y.-C. Chang, and H.-C. Wang, "Hidden Markov Model for Mandarin Lexical Tone Recognition," *IEEE Trans. ASSP*, 36 (7), (1988), pp. 988–992.
33. P.-C. Chang, S.-W. Sun, and S.-H. Chen, "Mandarin Tone Recognition by Multi-Layer Perception," *Proc. ICASSP*, 1, (1990), pp. 517–520.
34. H.-W. Hon, B. Yuan, Y.-L. Chow, S. Narayan, and K.-F. Lee, "Towards Large Vocabulary Mandarin Chinese Speech Recognition," *Proc. ICASSP*, 1, (1994), pp. 545–548.
35. Y. Cao, Y. Deng, H. Zhang, T. Huang, and B. Xu, "Decision Tree Based Mandarin Tone Model and its Application to Speech Recognition," *Proc. ICASSP*, 3, (2000), pp. 1759–1762.
36. J.-S. Zhang, S. Nakamura, and K. Hirose, "Tone Nucleus-Based Multi-Level Robust Acoustic Tonal Modeling of Sentential F0 Variations for Chinese Continuous Speech Tone Recognition," *Speech Communication*, 46, (2005), pp. 440–454.
37. S.-H. Chen and Y.-R. Wang, "Tone Recognition of Continuous Mandarin Speech Based on Neural Networks," *IEEE Trans. SAP*, 3 (2), (1995), pp. 146–150.
38. Y. W. Wong and E. Chang, "The Effect of Pitch and Tone on Different Mandarin Speech Recognition Tasks," *Proc. Eurospeech*, (2001), pp. 1517–1521.

39. C. Wang and S. Seneff, "Improved Tone Recognition by Normalizing for Co-articulation and Intonation Effects," *Proc. ICSLP*, (2000), pp. 83–86.
40. F. Wessel, R. Schluter, K. Macherey, and H. Ney, "Confidence Measures for Large Vocabulary Continuous Speech Recognition," *IEEE Trans. SAP*, 9 (3), (2001), pp. 288–298.
41. F. K. Soong, W. K. Lo, and S. Nakamura, "Generalized Word Posterior Probability (GWPP) for Measuring Reliability of Recognized Words," *Proc. SWIM*, (2004).
42. L. Mangu, E. Brill, and A. Stolcke, "Finding Consensus in Speech Recognition: Word Error Minimization and Other Applications of Confusion Networks," *Computer Speech and Language*, 14 (4), (2000), pp. 373–400.
43. Y. Qian, *Use of Tone Information in Cantonese LVCSR Based on Generalized Character Posterior Probability Decoding*, PhD Thesis, The Chinese University of Hong Kong, (2005).
44. T.-H. Ho, C.-J. Liu, H. Sun, M.-Y. Tsai, and L.-S. Lee, "Phonetic State Tied-Mixture Tone Modeling for Large Vocabulary Continuous Mandarin Speech Recognition," *Proc. Eurospeech*, 2, (1999), pp. 883–886.

CHAPTER 9

SOME ADVANCES IN LANGUAGE MODELING

Chuang-Hua Chueh, Meng-Sung Wu and Jen-Tzung Chien
Department of Computer Science and Information Engineering,
National Cheng Kung University,
No. 1, University Road, Tainan
E-mail: jtchien@mail.ncku.edu.tw

Language modeling aims to extract linguistic regularities which are crucial in areas of information retrieval and speech recognition. Specifically, for Chinese systems, language dependent properties should be considered in Chinese language modeling. In this chapter, we first survey the works of word segmentation and new word extraction which are essential for the estimation of Chinese language models. Next, we present several recent approaches to deal with the issues of parameter smoothing and long-distance limitation in statistical n-gram language models. To tackle long-distance insufficiency, we address the association pattern language models. For the issue of model smoothing, we present a solution based on the latent semantic analysis framework. To effectively refine the language model, we also adopt the maximum entropy principle and integrate multiple knowledge sources from a collection of text corpus. Discriminative training is also discussed in this chapter. Some experiments on perplexity evaluation and Mandarin speech recognition are reported.

1. Introduction

Language models (LM) are used to characterize the regularities in natural language and have been widely employed in machine translation,[1] document classification, information retrieval (IR),[2] speech recognition and many other applications. When building retrieval systems, each document serves as a source to build its corresponding language model. This model represents the specification of word occurrences in the document. The similarities or retrieval scores are then calculated according to the probabilities of generating query from these document sources. In a speech recognition task, a language model is trained based on the whole corpus to explore the prior probability of word sequence for maximum *a posteriori* (MAP) decision as shown in Figure 1.

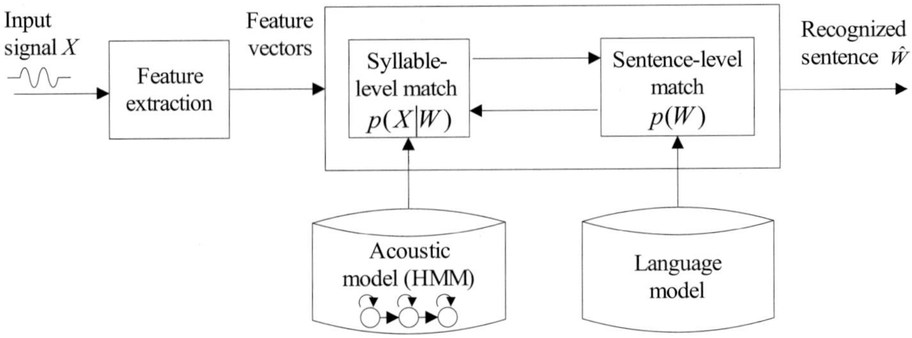

Fig. 1. Typical procedure of an automatic speech recognition system.

In the literature, there are various language models that are able to extract linguistic regularities in natural language. The structural language model extracts the relevant syntactic regularities based on predefined grammar rules.[3] Also, a large-span semantic language model allows us to exploit the document-level semantic regularities.[4] Nevertheless, the statistical n-gram model has been effective in capturing the more local lexical regularities. Due to the efficiency and popularity of n-gram models, in this chapter, we address some issues of n-gram modeling, e.g., smoothing methods, long-distance information incorporation and discriminative training. In addition, we focus on building Chinese language models for Mandarin speech recognition. Some properties of Chinese language are also studied.

1.1. *Statistical N-Gram Models*

When considering n-gram modeling, the probability of word sequence W is computed using a product of probabilities of individual words conditional on their histories

$$\begin{aligned} p(W) = p(w_1, w_2, \ldots, w_L) &\cong \prod_{i=1}^{L} p(w_i | w_{i-n+1}, \ldots, w_{i-1}) \\ &= \prod_{i=1}^{L} p\left(w_i | w_{i-n+1}^{i-1}\right) \end{aligned} \tag{1}$$

where w_{i-n+1}^{i-1} represents the historical word sequence for word w_i. We refer to the value n of an n-gram model as its *order*, which comes from the area of Markov models. Particularly, an n-gram model can be interpreted as a Markov model of order n-1. If the word depends on the previous two words ($n = 3$), we have a *trigram*: $p(w_i|w_{i-2}, w_{i-1})$. Similarly, we can have *unigram* ($n = 1$): $p(w_i)$, or *bigram* ($n = 2$): $p(w_i|w_{i-1})$ models. Usually, the n-gram parameter $p\left(w_i|w_{i-n+1}^{i-1}\right)$ is obtained via maximum likelihood (ML) estimation:

$$p\left(w_i|w_{i-n+1}^{i-1}\right) = \frac{c\left(w_{i-n+1}^{i}\right)}{c\left(w_{i-n+1}^{i-1}\right)} \tag{2}$$

Here, $c\left(w_{i-n+1}^{i}\right)$ is the number of occurrences of word sequence w_{i-n+1}^{i} in the training data.

1.2. *Language Model Smoothing*

Smoothing is one of fundamental techniques for compensating insufficient data in statistical language modeling. Generally speaking, the higher the order an n-gram model uses, the better predictive ability or resolution it has. However, the most critical problem of constructing high order n-grams is the problem of data sparseness. A huge amount of training data is required to estimate model parameters. For example, when building a trigram model using a lexicon with 80,000 words, we have $80,000 \times 80,000 \times 80,000$ parameters to be estimated. The demand of training data increases rapidly as the order n increases. No occurrence will happen in many trigrams. This makes probability calculation intractable. With limited amount of data, some smoothing techniques have been proposed to solve this problem.

1.2.1. *Additive Smoothing*

One intuitive and simple method is additive smoothing.[5] To avoid a zero probability, a small value δ was added in parameter estimation:

$$p_{\text{Add}}\left(w_i|w_{i-n+1}^{i-1}\right) = \frac{\delta + c\left(w_{i-n+1}^{i}\right)}{\delta V + c\left(w_{i-n+1}^{i-1}\right)} \tag{3}$$

where V is lexicon size. This approach assigns the same count to the n-grams with zero count.

1.2.2. *Deleted Interpolation Smoothing*

Generally, it is useful to combine higher-order n-gram models with lower-order n-gram models.[6] In case of insufficient data, parameters of higher-order models cannot be reliably estimated. Lower-model provides useful information. Deleted interpolation smoothing or Jelinek-Mercer smoothing performs the combination based on linear interpolation method. The probability is smoothed by

$$p_{\text{DI}}\left(w_i|w_{i-n+1}^{i-1}\right) = \alpha_{w_{i-n+1}^{i-1}}\, p\left(w_i|w_{i-n+1}^{i-1}\right) + \left(1 - \alpha_{w_{i-n+1}^{i-1}}\right) p_{\text{DI}}\left(w_i|w_{i-n+2}^{i-1}\right) \tag{4}$$

Linear interpolation coefficient can be determined using the expectation-maximization (EM) algorithm. It represents the history-dependent interpolation weight. Using this approach, the n-th-order parameters are interpolated with $(n-1)$-th-order smoothed parameters recursively.

1.2.3. *Katz Backoff Smoothing*

Another attractive smoothing method is the backoff method. The Katz smoothing model[7] based on the Good-Turing estimate[8] is a canonical backoff approach. The Good-Turing method adapts the number of occurrences of contexts to avoid assigning a zero probability. It partitions n-grams into groups according to their frequencies. For any n-gram occurring r times, we adapt it using r^* times:

$$r^* = (r+1)\frac{n_{r+1}}{n_r} = \text{discount}(r) \tag{5}$$

where n_r is the number of n-grams that occur r times in the training data.

Katz smoothing adopts Good-Turing estimate and the combination of higher-order models with lower-order ones. The smoothed Katz model is calculated by

$$p_{\text{Katz}}\left(w_i|w_{i-n+1}^{i-1}\right) = \begin{cases} \frac{\text{discount}\left(c\left(w_{i-n+1}^{i}\right)\right)}{c\left(w_{i-n+1}^{i-1}\right)} & \text{if } c\left(w_{i-n+1}^{i}\right) > 0 \\ \alpha\left(w_{i-n+1}^{i-1}\right) p_{\text{Katz}}\left(w_i|w_{i-n+1}^{i-1}\right) & \text{otherwise} \end{cases} \tag{6}$$

Here, $\alpha\left(w_{i-n+1}^{i-1}\right)$ is calculated by

$$\alpha\left(w_{i-n+1}^{i-1}\right) = \frac{1-\sum_{w_i:c\left(w_{i-n+1}^{i}\right)>0} p_{\text{Katz}}\left(w_i|w_{i-n+1}^{i-1}\right)}{1-\sum_{w_i:c\left(w_{i-n+1}^{i}\right)>0} p_{\text{Katz}}\left(w_i|w_{i-n+2}^{i-1}\right)} \tag{7}$$

1.2.4. *Class N-gram*

Another way to handle the data sparseness problem is through a class-based language model. Generally, a word belongs to multiple classes. For simplification, we assume each word belongs to only a single class. N-gram model can be calculated depending on the preceding n-1 classes

$$p\left(w_i|w_{i-n+1}^{i-1}\right) \cong p\left(w_i|c_i\right) p\left(c_i|c_{i-n+1}^{i-1}\right) \tag{8}$$

where $p\left(w_i|c_i\right)$ denotes the probability of word w_i given class c_i in the current position, and $p\left(c_i|c_{i-n+1}^{i-1}\right)$ denotes the probability of class c_i given the class history. The number of parameters is considerably reduced. Accordingly, parameter estimation becomes reliable.

1.3. *Evaluation of Language Models*

The most intuitive way to evaluate a language model is to test the system performance based on its application. For example, we can calculate word error rate to evaluate a speech recognition system. However, it requires implementation of a speech recognizer with acoustic matching. Alternatively, we can evaluate a language model based on cross-entropy known as *perplexity* without involving acoustic matching. The cross-entropy of a model emitting the word sequence W can be approximated as

$$H(W) = -\frac{1}{N_W}\log_2 p(W) \tag{9}$$

where N_W denotes the amount of words in W. The perplexity of a language model $p(W)$ is defined by

$$\text{Perplexity} = 2^{H(W)} \tag{10}$$

which can be roughly interpreted as the geometric mean of the branching of the text generated by the language model. In general, a model with lower perplexity contains less uncertainty or equivalently less confusion in prediction. Such model matches test data better.

In the next section, we focus on the issues relating to building a Chinese language model. Some linguistic properties of the Chinese language are introduced. In Section 3, we address the topics of improving language modeling for speech recognition. Two fundamental problems of statistical n-gram models, namely data sparseness and long distance limitation, are discussed. We explore the associations between word sets and predicted word for association pattern language modeling. Also, we propose methods to incorporate semantic information into n-gram models based on latent semantic analysis.

2. Chinese Language Processing and Modeling

When establishing a Chinese language model, we first discuss some properties and structural features of the language.[9,10] Chinese is quite different from western languages. It is non-alphabetic, and a large number of characters are ideographic and monosyllabic. A Chinese word is constructed by one or several characters, and a Chinese character is itself a tonal syllable. Every syllable is represented in writing by multiple characters, and the different tones along with this syllable represent the different meanings. The structure of Chinese language is shown in Figure 2. Totally, there are 408 syllables and 1,345 tonal syllables with four lexical tones and one neutral tone in Chinese.

Different from western languages, there are no blank spaces in a Chinese sentence. Word boundary is unknown and not unique. One particular issue of Chinese language modeling is to determine reliable word segmentation. Different segmentations illustrate different realizations of a sentence, which affects the performance of language models significantly. One way is to build language models based on

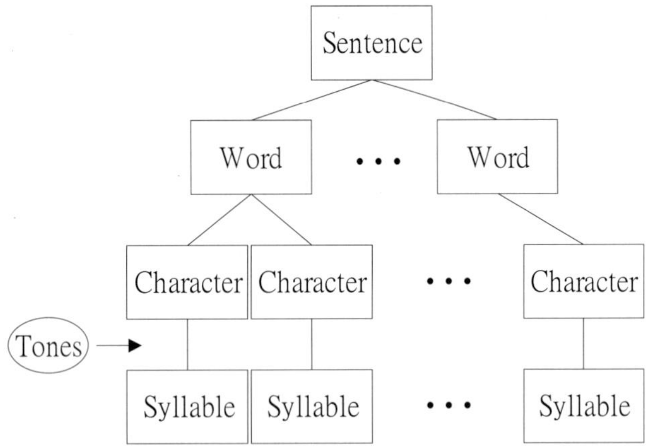

Fig. 2. Hierarchical structure of Chinese is composed of syllables, characters, words and sentences.

characters.[11] In this way, word segmentation is unnecessary and the basic units for language modeling can be changed from about 80,000 words to 10,000 characters. The number of model parameters is accordingly reduced. Higher-order n-gram models can be reliably estimated using the limited amount of data. Although character-based models are desirable, it has been shown that word-based language models can achieve better performance than character-based language models.[12] Undoubtedly, characters still provide some additional information embedded in words. It is thus useful to combine character-based and word-based models. Also, PAT-tree[13] is an efficient data structure for indexing and has been successfully used in the area of information retrieval.[14] Using this approach, all possible character segments are stored without requirement of word boundaries. Also, a segment can be a word or a sequence of words, so that compound words can be considered. There have been many approaches implemented to deal with this problem. In this study, we focus on general techniques for word segmentation and new word extraction.

As shown in Figure 3, the procedure of building Chinese language models is composed of two parts. The language processing part produces the possible segmented sentences from training texts. A word segmentation algorithm and a new word extraction technique are applied. The second process receives the output of the first process to build language models. It can be a recursive procedure. If the feedback arrow from model estimation to language processing is active, lexicon and model parameters can be optimized simultaneously[15,16] and the language model can be refined.

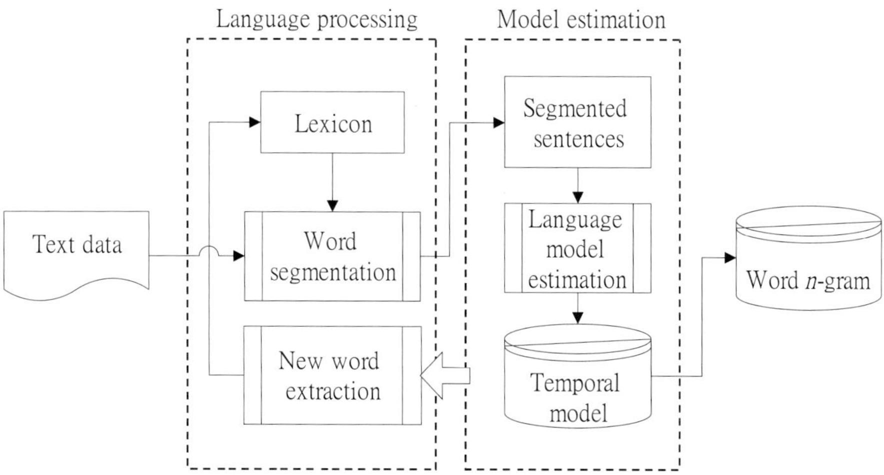

Fig. 3. Construction of word n-gram models is illustrated.

2.1. *Word Segmentation*

Before estimating a word-based Chinese language model, we should determine the word boundaries of the text data by referring to a dictionary. Several approaches were developed for word segmentation.[17,18,19,20,21] Dictionary-based approaches adopt the *longest matching rule* to obtain the desirable word combination.[22] Some heuristic rules also help to further refine word segmentation. In the work of Ma and Chen[23], the matching approach considered the next two words. Possible words were seen as word chunks. The disambiguation for these three word chunks are applied as follows. For example, in a sentence with three words "中文 語言 處理" (meaning, Chinese language processing), the first word can be "中" or "中文" according to the given lexicon. All possible combinations of these three word chunks are taken into consideration. The algorithm selects the first chunk as the current segmented word according to the following heuristic rules.[23]

Possible word chunks of sentence "中文語言處理":

中 文 語言

中文 語 言

中文 語言 處理

…

Longest Matching Rule The most plausible segmentation is the three-chunk sequence with the longest length. In the above example, the longest matching result is "中文 語言 處理". The first word is then segmented as "中文". Experiments show that this rule achieves accuracy as high as 99.69%.[23] The following rules can be further applied to refine word segmentation.

Word Length Rule
Select the three-chunk sequence with the smallest standard deviation in length of these three chunks.

Probability Rule
Select the three-chunk sequence with the highest frequency of producing these three chunks.

Readers may refer to Ma and Chen's work[23] for other rules relevant for Chinese word segmentation. The Chinese Knowledge and Information Processing (CKIP) group in the Academia Sinica, Taiwan, has developed a complete word segmentation system.[24] This system is helpful for conducting related research on Chinese language processing.

2.2. *New Word Extraction*

Prior to word segmentation, a Chinese dictionary is required for extracting possible chunks. The basic dictionary provided by the CKIP group is an open-source.[25,26] It contains more than 80,000 words. However, one property of the Chinese language is its *open vocabulary* characteristic.[9] People can easily create a new word by combining characters or existing words. Also, new words and compound words are created everyday. The number of Chinese words is infinite. The vocabularies in all existing dictionaries would still be insufficient. Accordingly, the out-of-vocabulary (OOV) problem does happen in real applications. We should therefore create a dynamic dictionary. Generally, compound words and proper names are two major types of unknown words. New word extraction techniques allow us to explore new words from data according to some heuristic or theoretical methods. New word extraction methods using statistical and knowledge-based approaches are surveyed in rest of this section.

Statistical approaches adopt mutual information, entropy, relative frequency, etc., as features to extract candidate words.[16,27,28] Next, new words are chosen and added into the dictionary so as to minimize the perplexity. Lai and Wu[29] extracted phrase-like units (PLU) according to PLU-based likelihood ratio. The meaningful terms were then explored. Yang *et al.*[12] adopted the average Kullback-Leibler distance to exploit segment patterns and proposed a forward-backward algorithm to integrate the processing of sentence segmentation and parameter estimation. An iterative procedure with two phases of lexicon generation and lexicon pruning was also proposed.[30] In the first phase, mutual information was first used to extract candidate new words. The undesirable words were then removed based on relative frequency and context dependency. In the second phase, words which could not significantly reduce model perplexity were removed from the lexicon. Such a method is effective and efficient. However, statistical approaches require a large amount of training data in order to obtain reliable features. Thus, a method based on *strict phrase likelihood ratio* (SPLR) was specially designed for a small training corpus. This method is practical for a real application.[31]

On the other hand, knowledge-based approaches[32,33,34] analyze the characteristics of new words using linguistic features, such as morphology, syntax and semantics. Sun *et al.*[34] used prefixes and suffixes to identify property names. Tseng *et al.*[35] applied semantic knowledge from HowNet to detect unknown verbs. Lin *et al.*[36] used morphological rules and statistical models to identify unknown words and provided a preliminary study of unknown word identification. Chen and Lee[37] used morphological rules and contextual information to identify the names of organizations. However, it is difficult and time-consuming to define a complete set of rules. To automatically extract rules, Chen and Bai[38] proposed a corpus-based method to derive syntactic rules for unknown word detection, although tagged data is still required to derive these rules or even the hand-crafted rules. Also, statistical and knowledge-based methods reveal different levels of information for new word extraction. It is beneficial to combine these two approaches. There are works[39,40] where the hybrid method of combining statistical and contextual information are presented. Li *et al.*[41] used support vector machines (SVMs) to identify new words, where the syntactic and statistical features were merged. In general, new word extraction is a pre-requisite in Chinese language processing tasks. An effective extraction algorithm is in high demand.

3. Robust and Discriminative Language Modeling

There is no doubt that a statistical n-gram model plays a critical role in many applications. Using n-gram models, local lexical regularities can be efficiently characterized. However, the n-gram model suffers from the problems of data sparseness and insufficient long-distance information. In addition, the model's discriminative ability is not guaranteed for speech recognition. System performance is degraded accordingly. In this chapter, we introduce some new approaches to handle these problems. For the issue of data sparseness, we present a solution based on *latent semantic smoothing*.[42] To compensate the insufficiency of long-distance information, we address the *association pattern language modeling*.[43] Besides that, we also address the *maximum entropy language modeling* by integrating topic information from the text corpus.[44] Finally, we present the *discriminative language modeling* via the minimum classification error criterion for improving speech recognition performance.

3.1. *Latent Semantic Modeling and Smoothing*

Latent semantic analysis (LSA)[45,46] is useful to analyze the relations between documents and words. In the work of Bellegarda,[4] LSA was first applied for language modeling. The resulting perplexity and word error rate were substantially reduced. However, this work has poor representation of history at the beginning of the text document. Here, we represent the historic words based on a retrieval framework. Furthermore, we resolve the data sparseness problem and estimate unseen model parameters using the k-nearest neighbor words. Neighbor words are identified according to their closeness in the LSA space.

LSA is a dimension reduction technique that projects words and documents into a common semantic space. The first stage of LSA is to construct an $M \times D$ word-by-document matrix $\mathbf{A}$. Here, M and D denote the vocabulary size and the number of training documents, respectively. The expression[4] for (i, j) entry in matrix $\mathbf{A}$ is

$$a_{i,j} = (1 - \varepsilon_i)\frac{c_{i,j}}{n_j} \tag{11}$$

where $c_{i,j}$ is the number of times word w_i appears in document d_j, n_j is the number of words in d_j, and ε_i is the normalized entropy of w_i, computed by

$$\varepsilon_i = -\frac{1}{\log D}\sum_{j=1}^{D}\frac{c_{i,j}}{t_i}\log\frac{c_{i,j}}{t_i} \tag{12}$$

where t_i is the total number of times w_i appears in the training corpus. In the second stage, we perform singular value decomposition (SVD) to project words and documents into a lower dimensional space

$$\mathbf{A} = \mathbf{U}\Sigma\mathbf{V}^T \approx \mathbf{U}_R\Sigma_R\mathbf{V}_R^T = \mathbf{A}_R \tag{13}$$

Here, Σ is a reduced $R \times R$ diagonal matrix with singular values and $R < \min(M, D)$. $\mathbf{U}_R$ is an $M \times R$ matrix whose columns are the first R eigenvectors derived from the word-by-word correlation matrix $\mathbf{A}\mathbf{A}^T$, and $\mathbf{V}_R$ is a $D \times R$ matrix whose columns are the first R eigenvectors derived from the document-by-document correlation matrix $\mathbf{A}^T\mathbf{A}$. After the projection, each column of $\Sigma_R\mathbf{U}_R^T$ and $\Sigma_R\mathbf{V}_R^T$ characterizes the location of a particular word and document in the reduced semantic space, respectively.

3.1.1. *LSA Parameter Modeling*

N-gram models can be improved by employing LSA for large span prediction of word occurrence. The LSA language model[4] is expressed by

$$p\left(w_i|h_{i-1}^{(l)}\right) = p\left(w_i|\mathbf{d}_{i-1}\right) \tag{14}$$

where $\mathbf{d}_{i-1}$ denotes the *pseudodocument* vector of historical words H_{i-1}. We can obtain the vector $\mathbf{d}_{i-1}$ recursively via

$$\mathbf{d}_{i-1} = \frac{n_{i-1}-1}{n_{i-1}}\mathbf{d}_{i-2} + \left[0\cdots0\frac{1-\varepsilon_{i-1}}{n_{i-1}}0\cdots0\right]^T \tag{15}$$

Then, we can obtain the coordinate of pseudodocument $\mathbf{d}_{i-1}$ in the LSA space by $\mathbf{U}_R^T\mathbf{d}_{i-1}$. However, it is difficult to capture long-distance dependencies to calculate $p(w_i|\mathbf{d}_{i-1})$ when the number of historical words is small. As shown in Figure 4, we aim to retrieve the most likely relevant document $\hat{\mathbf{d}}_{i-1}$ from the training documents so as to represent the pseudodocument vector $\mathbf{d}_{i-1}$. Accordingly, the relevant document $\hat{\mathbf{d}}_{i-1}$ is retrieved using

$$\hat{\mathbf{d}}_{i-1} = \arg\max_{\mathbf{d}_j} p\left(\mathbf{d}_j|\mathbf{d}_{i-1}\right), \quad \text{for } j = 1,\ldots,D \tag{16}$$

The probability $p(\mathbf{d}_j|\mathbf{d}_{i-1})$ is calculated according to the angle between the vectors of documents in the LSA space:

$$p\left(\mathbf{d}_j|\mathbf{d}_{i-1}\right) = \cos\left(\mathbf{U}_R^T\mathbf{d}_j, \mathbf{U}_R^T\mathbf{d}_{i-1}\right) = \frac{\mathbf{d}_j\mathbf{U}_R\mathbf{U}_R^T\mathbf{d}_{i-1}^T}{||\mathbf{U}_R^T\mathbf{d}_j||\cdot||\mathbf{U}_R^T\mathbf{d}_{i-1}||} \tag{17}$$

When the number of historical words increases, the more likely relevant document $\hat{\mathbf{d}}_{i-1}$ with the closest semantic content can be retrieved to represent the corresponding historical context.

In this work, the LSA language model is adopted to integrate the effects of histories obtained from the conventional n-gram $h_{i-1}^{(n)} = w_{i-n+1}^{i-1}$ and LSA $h_{i-1}^{(l)} = \hat{\mathbf{d}}_{i-1}$. The new language model is calculated by

$$\begin{aligned} p(w_i|h_{i-1}) &= p\left(w_i|h_{i-1}^{(n)}, h_{i-1}^{(l)}\right) = \frac{p\left(w_i|h_{i-1}^{(n)}\right)p\left(h_{i-1}^{(l)}|w_i, h_{i-1}^{(n)}\right)}{\sum_{w_j} p\left(w_j|h_{i-1}^{(n)}\right)p\left(h_{i-1}^{(l)}|w_j, h_{i-1}^{(n)}\right)} \\ &= \frac{p\left(w_i|w_{i-n+1}^{i-1}\right)p\left(\hat{\mathbf{d}}_{i-1}|w_i\right)}{\sum_{w_j} p\left(w_j|w_{i-n+1}^{i-1}\right)p\left(\hat{\mathbf{d}}_{i-1}|w_j\right)} = \frac{p\left(w_i|w_{i-n+1}^{i-1}\right)\frac{p(w_i|\hat{\mathbf{d}}_{i-1})}{p(w_i)}}{\sum_{w_j} p\left(w_j|w_{i-n+1}^{i-1}\right)\frac{p(w_j|\hat{\mathbf{d}}_{i-1})}{p(w_j)}} \end{aligned} \tag{18}$$

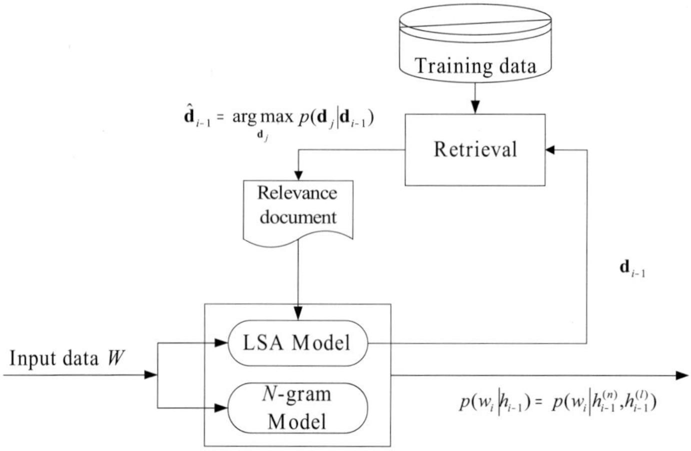

Fig. 4. Procedure of LSA semantic language modeling. The most relevant document is retrieved according to the LSA probability for representing historical words.

Here, we assume that $p\left(h_{i-1}^{(l)}|w_i, h_{i-1}^{(n)}\right) = p\left(\hat{\mathbf{d}}_{i-1}|w_i\right)$ which is computed using LSA probability

$$p\left(w_i|\hat{\mathbf{d}}_{i-1}\right) = \cos\left(\mathbf{u}_i\Sigma^{1/2}, \hat{\mathbf{v}}_{i-1}\Sigma^{1/2}\right) = \frac{\mathbf{u}_i\Sigma\hat{\mathbf{v}}_{i-1}^T}{||\mathbf{u}_i\Sigma^{1/2}|| \cdot ||\hat{\mathbf{v}}_{i-1}\Sigma^{1/2}||} \tag{19}$$

3.1.2. *LSA Parameter Smoothing*

In real-word applications, training data are always insufficient to train high-order n-grams. With this concern, language models should be smoothed so as to reliably estimate parameters of seen as well as unseen word combinations. The smoothing is done by merging word relations to k-nearest neighbors. The LSA n-gram explores the word relation between predictive word w_i and the words semantically-related to its preceding word w_{i-1}. The k nearest words $\hat{w}_j^{i-1}$ to word w_{j-1} are selected based on the LSA probabilities

$$p(w_{i-1}|w_j) = \cos(\mathbf{u}_{i-1}\Sigma_R, \mathbf{u}_j\Sigma_R) = \frac{\mathbf{u}_{i-1}\Sigma_R^2\mathbf{u}_j^T}{||\mathbf{u}_{i-1}\Sigma_R|| \cdot ||\mathbf{u}_j\Sigma_R||}, \quad 1 \le j \le M \tag{20}$$

The smoothed model is calculated by

$$\tilde{p}(w_i|h_{i-1}) = \alpha_i p(w_i|h_{i-1}) + (1-\alpha_i)\sum_{j=1}^{k} \beta_j^i p\left(w_i|\hat{w}_j^{i-1}\right) \tag{21}$$

where the interpolation weights are estimated using the EM algorithm[47]

$$\beta_j^i = \frac{p\left(w_i|\hat{w}_j^{i-1}\right)}{\sum_{j=1}^{k} p\left(w_i|\hat{w}_j^{i-1}\right)} \tag{22}$$

and

$$\alpha_i = \frac{p\left(w_i|h_{i-1}\right)}{p\left(w_i|h_{i-1}\right) + \sum_{j=1}^{k} \beta_j^i p\left(w_i|\hat{w}_j^{i-1}\right)} \tag{23}$$

Different from conventional smoothing methods using maximum likelihood language model, the proposed smoothing technique is combined with the LSA framework, and the probabilities $p\left(w_i|h_{i-1}\right)$ and $p\left(w_i|\hat{w}_j^{i-1}\right)$ are computed via the LSA approach.

3.1.3. *System Evaluation*

To evaluate the proposed LSA n-gram model, two databases are used. The first database is the CKIP balanced corpus.[26] It is used to train baseline n-gram model. We randomly selected 9,148 documents from our collected Chinese news documents to train the LSA model and another 224 documents for testing. Our lexicon is composed of 32,941 words. In this study, we find that an LSA dimension of 25 is appropriate to construct the semantic space for this training corpus. In the experiments, we investigate the proposed LSA modeling and LSA smoothing. We evaluate the perplexities using different numbers of nearest neighbors k and found that $k = 5$ is desirable. Here, the Witten-Bell smoothing[48] is brought in for comparison. The results are illustrated in Table 1. We can see that the proposed LSA n-gram model outperforms conventional n-grams. The LSA smoothing method achieves better performance than the Witten-Bell smoothing.

Table 1. Comparison of perplexity using different modeling and smoothing methods.

Language Model		**Perplexity**
Modeling Method	*Smoothing Method*	
Baseline N-gram	Witten-Bell Smoothing	122.6
LSA N-gram	Witten-Bell Smoothing	108.7
Baseline N-gram	LSA Smoothing	102
LSA N-gram	LSA Smoothing	81

3.2. *Association Pattern Language Modeling*

In n-gram modeling, each word is predicted according to the preceding $n-1$ words. The dependencies to the words out of this window are missing. Siu and Ostendorf constructed a variable n-gram model, which uses various values n for different contexts.[49] By allowing contexts of various lengths, long-distance regularity were merged. Furthermore, they extended variable n-grams by adopting skips and context-dependent classes for modeling conversational speech characteristics. Their experiments showed that the variable n-grams capturing 4-gram context with less than half the standard trigram parameters achieve better perplexity and recognition accuracy. Gao and Suzuki also presented studies on linguistically-motivated word skipping and predictive clustering for language modeling.[50] Applying the word skipping technique, functional words were skipped in historical contexts and the word probability was calculated conditioned on its previous content words or headwords. Also, the predictive clustering approach was presented to build a class-based n-gram model. This method achieved desirable improvement in recognition accuracy. Chen[51] applied latent topical information to build a topic mixture model. In this model, the mixture weights are dynamically adopted based on the historical context. The statistics of long-distance context is considered as well. The trigger pair language model[52] was also merged with the associations from trigger pairs extracted according to their average mutual information. Trigger pairs are effective to explore long-distance regularities for language modeling. However, this approach only considers the associations from two distant associated words. Here, we present the association pattern language model by combining the information from association patterns which are represented by a sequence of related words.[43]

3.2.1. *Mining of Association Patterns*

The procedure of mining association patterns is done by recursively *identifying frequent word subsets* and *performing subset unification*. In the beginning, we develop the frequent one-word subset $L_1 = \{w_a\}$ based on the frequency of each word in the database. Then, we unify the different words in L_1 and generate the candidate two-word subset $C_2 = \{w_a \bigcup w_b\}$. We select the frequent two-word subset $L_2 = \{w_a \rightarrow w_b\}$ from C_2 based on average mutual information (AMI)

$$\begin{aligned}\mathrm{AMI}(w_a;w_b) = {} & p(w_a,w_b)\log\frac{p(w_b|w_a)}{p(w_b)} + p(w_a,\overline{w}_b)\log\frac{p(\overline{w}_b|w_a)}{p(\overline{w}_b)} \\ & + p(\overline{w}_a,w_b)\log\frac{p(w_b|\overline{w}_a)}{p(w_b)} + p(\overline{w}_a,\overline{w}_b)\log\frac{p(\overline{w}_b|\overline{w}_a)}{p(\overline{w}_b)} \qquad (24)\end{aligned}$$

where $p(w_a, \overline{w}_b)$ denotes the probability of occurring w_a but without w_b afterward in the predefined window. Four types of occurrences including $p(w_a, w_b)$, $p(\overline{w}_a, w_b)$, $p(w_a, \overline{w}_b)$ and $p(\overline{w}_a, \overline{w}_b)$ are calculated by scanning all sentences. The frequent d-word subset L_d can be recursively generated from frequent $(d-1)$-word subset L_{d-1}. Let W_{d-1}^a be an association pattern in L_{d-1} and we use W_{d-1}^a as the trigger sequence to predict the future word w_b. The frequent d-word subset is built by fulfilling the following two passes.

Join pass: We scan the subset L_{d-1} and pick up the pattern W_{d-1}^b, where the preceding $d-2$ words are identical to those of W_{d-1}^a. The last word w_b of pattern W_{d-1}^b is appended to W_{d-1}^a. The unification $W_{d-1}^a \bigcup w_b$ is formed. Accordingly, the candidate d-word subset $C_d = \{W_{d-1}^a \bigcup w_b\}$ is generated.

Prune pass: Two prune stages are performed. First, we delete the unification $W_{d-1}^a \bigcup w_b$ from C_d when some $(d-1)$-word subset of the d-word sequence is not in L_{d-1}. The candidate subset is refined to $\tilde{C}_d$, $\tilde{C}_d \subseteq C_d$. Furthermore, we prune the unification $W_{d-1}^a \bigcup w_b \in \tilde{C}_d$ via AMI between trigger sequence W_{d-1}^a and word w_b. Association patterns (frequent d-word subset) are finally selected by

$$\begin{aligned} L_d &= \left\{W_{d-1}^a \bigcup w_b \in \tilde{C}_d \middle| \text{AMI}\left(W_{d-1}^a; w_b\right) \geq \text{minimum AMI}\right\} \\ &= \left\{W_{d-1}^a \rightarrow w_b\right\} \end{aligned} \tag{25}$$

To reduce the search space, we define an upper bound d_{up} for the number of words in selected association patterns. The complete association pattern set Ω_{AS} is constructed by $\bigcup_{d=2}^{d_{\text{up}}} L_d$. We search the occurrences of association patterns $W_{d-1}^{s,a} \rightarrow w_b^s$ within a sentence W^s. The words in association patterns are order-dependent and semantically related. These patterns are referred here as the *sequential patterns*. Furthermore, we merge the features provided by Ω_{AS} to estimate the *association pattern n-gram*.

3.2.2. *Association Pattern N-gram*

Here, we perform linear interpolation combination for association pattern n-gram modeling. When linear interpolation is applied, we combine the mutual information of all association patterns

$$\text{MI}\left(W_{d-1}^a \rightarrow w_b\right) = \log \frac{p\left(W_{d-1}^a, w_b\right)}{p\left(W_{d-1}^a\right) p\left(w_b\right)} \tag{26}$$

into language modeling to yield the association pattern model

$$\log p_{\mathrm{AS}}(W) = \sum_{i=1}^{T} \log p(w_i) + \sum_{s=1}^{S} \sum_{W_{d-1}^{s,i} \to w_j^s \in \Omega_{\mathrm{AS}}} \mathrm{MI}\left(W_{d-1}^{s,i} \to w_j^s\right) \tag{27}$$

We estimate linear interpolation (LI) association pattern n-gram by combining the association pattern model $p_{\mathrm{AS}}(W)$ and the static n-gram model $p(W)$ according to

$$\log p_{\mathrm{LI}}(W) = \eta \log p_{\mathrm{AS}}(W) + (1-\eta) \log p(W) \tag{28}$$

3.2.3. *System Evaluation*

In the experiments, an n-gram model was trained using the CKIP balanced corpus collected by the Academia Sinica in Taiwan. We also collected 9,372 news documents from 2001 to 2002 from the websites of CNA (cna.com.tw), ChinaTimes (news.chinatimes.com) and UDNnews (undnews.com.tw). We randomly selected 2,232 news documents for the training of the association pattern model. Witten-Bell smoothing[48] was applied. The benchmark MAT-400 speech database was used to train speaker-independent HMMs. Test 500 comprised of 500 sentences from a new set of 30 speakers, beyond the training set, serving as a test set. Each feature vector was composed of twelve Mel-frequency cepstral coefficients, one log-energy and their first derivatives. The syllable error rates are reported in Table 2. When trigger pairs are incorporated into the n-gram model, the syllable recognition rate is improved from 57.8% to 58.9%. Further, the association pattern n-gram model achieves higher recognition rate than the trigger-pair n-gram model.

Table 2. Comparison of syllable recognition rates (%) using different language models.

Language models	**Syllable recognition rate** (%)
Baseline N-gram	57.8
Trigger Pair N-gram	58.9
Association Pattern N-gram	59.1

3.3. *Maximum Entropy Semantic Topic Modeling*

Representation of long-distance information is crucial for language modeling. Here, we present another method where long-distance topic information is extracted via the LSA framework and applied for knowledge integration via the maximum entropy (ME) approach. Wu and Khudanpur[53] integrated statistical n-gram and topic unigram using the ME approach. Topic information was extracted by clustering the document vectors in the original document space. However, the original document space is generally sparse and full of noise caused by polysemy and synonymy.[45] To explore representative topic information, we introduce a new knowledge source by adopting the LSA approach. Because the occurrence of a word is highly correlated with the topic of the current discourse, the subspace of semantic topic is constructed via k-means clustering of document vectors generated from the LSA model. Next, the semantic information is merged into the n-gram model through the ME approach.[44] The proposed procedure of ME semantic topic modeling is illustrated in Figure 5.

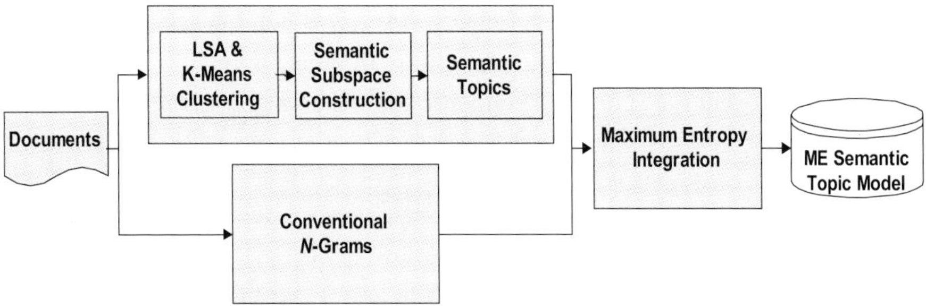

Fig. 5. Implementation procedure for ME semantic topic modeling.

3.3.1. *Construction of Semantic Topics*

Using the LSA procedure discussed in Section 3.1, we can find the location of a particular document in the R-dimensional semantic space spanned by columns of $\Sigma_R \mathbf{V}_R^T$. Also, we can perform document clustering in the semantic space. Each cluster consists of semantically-related documents and reflects a particular semantic topic. During document clustering, we measure the similarity of documents and topics in the LSA space by cosine measure

$$\mathrm{sim}\left(\mathbf{d}_j, \mathbf{t}_k\right) = \cos\left(\mathbf{U}_R^T \mathbf{d}_j, \mathbf{U}_R^T \mathbf{t}_k\right) = \frac{\mathbf{d}_j^T \mathbf{U}_R \mathbf{U}_R^T \mathbf{t}_k}{||\mathbf{U}_R^T \mathbf{d}_j|| \cdot ||\mathbf{U}_R^T \mathbf{t}_k||} \tag{29}$$

where $\mathbf{d}_j$, $\mathbf{t}_k$ are the vectors constructed by document j and document cluster k, respectively. $\mathbf{U}_R^T \mathbf{d}_j$ and $\mathbf{U}_R^T \mathbf{t}_k$ are the projected vectors in the semantic space. After assigning topics to different documents, we incorporate the topic-dependent unigram $p\left(w_i|\mathbf{t}_k\right)$ into the n-gram model. Here, we present the linear interpolation (LI) and maximum entropy (ME) approaches to carry out the semantic topic n-gram. To find LI semantic topic n-gram model, we first construct a pseudodocument vector from a particular historical word set h_{i-1}. Using the projected vector, we adopt the nearest neighbor rule to detect the closest semantic topic $\mathbf{t}_k$ corresponding to h_{i-1}. The LI model is calculated by

$$\log p_{\mathrm{LI}}\left(w_i|h_{i-1}\right) = \eta \log p\left(w_i|h_{i-1}\right) + (1-\eta)\log p\left(w_i|\mathbf{t}_k\right) \tag{30}$$

The EM algorithm can be applied to dynamically determine the interpolation coefficient by maximizing the overall perplexity.

3.3.2. *ME Semantic Topic N-gram*

In addition to LI integration, we perform an integration based on the ME principle. The underlying idea of the ME principle is to completely model what we know and assume nothing about what we do not know. With the ME model, we can combine different knowledge sources for language modeling. Each knowledge serves as a set of features used to build the ME constraints. In what follows, we define feature functions to represent the scopes of semantic topic and n-gram features by

$$f_{i,k}^{\mathrm{t}}(h,w) = \begin{cases} 1, & \text{if } h \in \mathbf{t}_k \text{ and } w = w_i \\ 0, & \text{otherwise} \end{cases} \tag{31}$$

and

$$f_{w_{i-n+1}^{i}}^{\mathrm{n}}(h,w) = \begin{cases} 1, & \text{if } h \text{ ends in } w_{i-n+1}^{i} \text{ and } w = w_i \\ 0, & \text{otherwise} \end{cases} \tag{32}$$

Using the combined features $f_i = \{f^{\mathrm{n}}, f^{\mathrm{t}}\}$, the constraints are typically expressed as marginal distributions. Because the target distribution is designed to encapsulate all the information provided by these features, we specify these constraints by calculating expectations with respect to empirical distribution $\tilde{p}(h,w)$ and target conditional distribution $p(w|h)$

$$\begin{aligned} \tilde{p}(f_i) &= \sum_{h,w} \tilde{p}(h,w) f_i(h,w) \\ &= \sum_{h,w} \tilde{p}(h) p(w|h) f_i(h,w) = p(f_i) \end{aligned} \qquad \text{for } i = 1,\ldots,F, \tag{33}$$

Using these constraints, we maximize the conditional entropy or uniformity of distribution $p(w|h)$. Lagrange optimization is adopted to solve this constrained optimization problem. Objective function is yielded by

$$H = -\sum_{h,w} \tilde{p}(h) p(w|h) \log p(w|h) + \sum_{i=1}^{F} \lambda_i [p(f_i) - \tilde{p}(f_i)] \tag{34}$$

Accordingly, the target ME solution is estimated as a Gibbs distribution

$$p(w|h) = \frac{1}{Z(h)} \exp\left(\sum_{i=1}^{F} \lambda_i f_i(h,w)\right) \tag{35}$$

with normalization term

$$Z(h) = \sum_{w} \exp\left(\sum_{i=1}^{F} \lambda_i f_i(h,w)\right) \tag{36}$$

The generalized iterative scaling (GIS) or improved iterative scaling (IIS) algorithm[54,55] can be used to find Lagrange parameters λ_i. The IIS algorithm is briefly described as follows.

Input: Feature functions $f_1, f_2, \cdots, f_F$ and empirical distribution $\tilde{p}(h,w)$
Output: Optimal Lagrange multiplier $\hat{\lambda}_i$

(1) Start with $\lambda_i = 0$ for all $i = 1,2,\cdots,F$
(2) For each $i = 1,2,\cdots,F$
- Let $\triangle\lambda_i$ be the solution to

$$\sum_{h,w} \tilde{p}(h)\, p(w|h)\, f_i(h,w) \exp\left(\triangle\lambda_i F(h,w)\right) = \tilde{p}(f_i) \tag{37}$$

where $F(h,w) = \sum_{i=1}^{F} f_i(h,w)$
- Update the value of λ_i according to $\lambda_i = \lambda_i + \triangle\lambda_i$

(3) Go to Step (2) if some λ_i have not converged.

After estimating optimal parameters $\{\hat{\lambda}_i\}$, we can calculate the ME semantic topic n-gram by using 35 and 36.

It is also interesting to note the relation between conventional maximum likelihood (ML) language model and the ME language model. The relation between these two estimations is illustrated in Table 3. Basically, the ME model is equivalent to an ML model when adopting Gibbs distribution.[55]

Table 3. Relation between ML and ME language models.

Objective function	$L(p_\lambda)$	$H(p)$
Criterion	Maximum Likelihood	Maximum Entropy
Distribution assumption	Gibbs distribution	No assumption
Type of search	Unconstrained optimization	Constrained optimization
Search space	$\lambda \in$ real values	p satisfied with constraints
Solution	λ_{ML}	p_{ME}
	$p_{\lambda_{\mathrm{ML}}} = p_{\mathrm{ME}}$	

3.3.3. *System Evaluation*

In this study, we evaluated the ME semantic topic n-gram model by measuring perplexity and character error rate in continuous speech recognition. The baseline n-gram model was implemented. The ME language model proposed by Wu and Khudanpur[53] was carried out for comparison. In the experiments, the training corpus for language modeling was constructed by 5,500 documents from TDT2 Corpus, which were collected by the Xinhua News Angency[56] from January to June in

1998. The dimensionality of LSA space was reduced to $R = 100$. To evaluate perplexity, we selected an additional 734 documents from the XinHua News Agency, which consisted of 244,573 words, as test data. Here, we fixed the length of history h at 50 to determine the corresponding topic. The results of perplexity are shown in the brackets in Table 4. This table details the perplexities for baseline bigram and semantic models using different number of topics C. The results demonstrate that incorporation of semantic information can significantly improve the perplexity of the n-gram model, and the ME combination outperforms the LI combination. In the evaluation of speech recognition, the initial speaker-independent hidden Markov models were trained by the benchmark Mandarin speech corpus TCC300.[57] Each Mandarin syllable was modeled by right context-dependent states with, at most, 32 Gaussian mixtures. Each feature vector was composed of twelve Mel-frequency cepstral coefficients, one log-energy and their first derivatives. Maximum *a posteriori* (MAP) adaptation[58] was performed on the initial HMMs using 83 sentences (about 10 minutes long) from the Voice of America (VOA) news in the TDT2 corpus. The additional 49 sentences selected from VOA news were used for speech recognition evaluation. The character error rates using Wu's and proposed methods are summarized in Table 4. In the case of $C = 50$, the proposed LI model can achieve an error rate reduction of 8.5% compared to baseline n-gram model, while the proposed ME model attains a 16.9% error rate reduction. Generally, the proposed method here achieves lower error rates compared to Wu's method.

Table 4. Comparison of character error rate and perplexities (in brackets) for baseline N-gram and different LI and ME semantic language models.

	Baseline N-gram	**Wu's method**		**Proposed method**	
		LI	ME	LI	ME
$C = 30$	41.4 (451.4)	38.9 (444.7)	36.4 (399)	36.7 (441)	34.9 (393.7)
$C = 50$		38.1 (442.9)	36.8 (402)	37.9 (438)	34.4 (394.8)
$C = 100$		38.3 (437)	36.5 (397.2)	37.3 (435.7)	36.1 (401.2)

3.4. *Discriminative Language Modeling*

Discriminative training is an important issue in the area of pattern recognition. Different from ML distribution estimation, discriminative estimation aims to realize estimation procedure by considering the information of competing hypotheses. In the literature, minimum classification error (MCE)[59] and maximum mutual information (MMI)[60] have been proposed for acoustic modeling as well as language modeling. In MCE training, a misclassification measure for observed speech data

X_i is defined by

$$d(X_i) = -g(X_i, W_i) + G\left(X_i, W_1^i, \dots, W_K^i\right) \tag{38}$$

where W_i and $\{W_1^i, \dots, W_K^i\}$ denote the true transcription and K competing hypotheses for X_i, respectively. Discriminant function g is calculated using weighted combination of acoustic and language model scores

$$g(X_i, W_i) = \eta \log p(X_i|W_i) + \log p(W_i) \tag{39}$$

and

$$G\left(X_i, W_1^i, \dots, W_K^i\right) = \log\left(\frac{1}{K}\sum_{k=1}^{K}\exp\left[g\left(X_i, W_K^i\right)\kappa\right]\right)^{\frac{1}{\kappa}} \tag{40}$$

κ is a positive weight parameter for different hypotheses. To build a smooth and differentiable criterion, the sigmoid function can be used to determine the *class loss function*

$$l(X_i) = \frac{1}{1 + \exp(-\gamma d(X_i) + \theta)} \tag{41}$$

with slope and shift factors γ and θ, respectively. The MCE criterion minimizes the expected loss

$$E[l(X)] = \sum_{i=1}^{R} l(X_i) \tag{42}$$

to estimate discriminative parameters. Recently, Gao *et al.* proposed a minimum sample risk method for language modeling.[61] Kuo performed minimum word error based discriminative training of language models.[62] Subsequently, we present a discriminative ME language model by incorporating discriminative acoustic features.[63] According to the concept of whole-sentence exponential model[64], we define n-gram feature by

$$f^{\mathrm{n}}_{w_{i-n+1}^{i}}(W) = count\left(w_{i-n+1}^{i}|W\right) \tag{43}$$

In addition to original n-gram features, we merge acoustic features using sentence-level log-likelihood ratio of competing and target sentences for each training sentence

$$f_X^{\mathrm{a}} = \begin{cases} \log\frac{p(X|W)}{p(X|W_X)} & \text{if } W \in \text{ competing sentence of } X \\ 0 & \text{if } W \in \text{ target sentence of } X \end{cases} \tag{44}$$

where W_X denotes the corresponding transcription of X. By assigning feature parameters λ_X^{a} by

$$\lambda_X^{\mathrm{a}} = \begin{cases} 1 & \text{if } X \in \text{training set} \\ 0 & \text{otherwise} \end{cases} \tag{45}$$

we obtain discriminative language model parameters by performing the ME procedure. We also construct the connection to MMI estimation. The discriminative ME (DME) objective function is represented by

$$\hat{\lambda} = \arg\max_{\lambda}\{\wedge_{\mathrm{DME}} = \sum_{i=1}^{R} \log p_{\mathrm{DME}}(W_i)\}$$
$$= \arg\max_{\lambda} \sum_{i=1}^{R} \log \frac{\exp\left(\sum_{j=1}^{F} \lambda_j^{\mathrm{n}} f_j^{\mathrm{n}}(W_i) + \lambda_{X_i}^{\mathrm{a}} f_{X_i}^{\mathrm{a}}(W_i)\right)}{\sum_{W'} \exp\left(\sum_{j=1}^{F} \lambda_j^{\mathrm{n}} f_j^{\mathrm{n}}(W') + \lambda_{X_i}^{\mathrm{a}} f_{X_i}^{\mathrm{a}}(W')\right)} \tag{46}$$

Using the assignment of 44 and 45, we obtain

$$\wedge_{\mathrm{DME}} = \sum_{i=1}^{R} \log \frac{\exp\left(\sum_{j=1}^{F} \lambda_j^{\mathrm{n}} f_j^{\mathrm{n}}(W_i) + \log p(X_i|W_i)\right)}{\sum_{W'} \exp\left(\sum_{j=1}^{F} \lambda_j^{\mathrm{n}} f_j^{\mathrm{n}}(W') + \log p(X_i|W')\right)}$$
$$= \sum_{i=1}^{R} \log \frac{p(X_i|W_i)\exp\left(\sum_{j=1}^{F} \lambda_j^{\mathrm{n}} f_j^{\mathrm{n}}(W_i)\right)}{\sum_{W'} p(X_i|W')\exp\left(\sum_{j=1}^{F} \lambda_j^{\mathrm{n}} f_j^{\mathrm{n}}(W')\right)}$$
$$= \sum_{i=1}^{R} \log \frac{p(X_i|W_i)\,p(W_i)}{\sum_{W'} p(X_i|W')\,p(W')} = \wedge_{\mathrm{MMI}} \tag{47}$$

Accordingly, this ME language model is inherent with discriminative power.

3.4.1. *System Evaluation*

In the experiments, we adapted the seed speaker-independent HMMs trained by TCC300 to the environment of broadcast news transcription task using the Mandarin Across Taiwan Broadcast News (MATBN) corpus.[65] Totally, 1,060 conversations were selected for MAP adaptation of HMMs and corrective training of the DME language model. Another 250 sentences, about 30 minutes, were used for testing. The seed baseline *n*-gram model was trained using the CKIP balanced corpus. We report the syllable, character and word error rates in Table 5. Experimental results show that the proposed DME language model can alleviate the confusion of target and competing hypotheses in speech recognition compared to the baseline *n*-gram model.

Table 5. Recognition error rates (%) using baseline and DME language models.

	SER (%)	CER (%)	WER (%)
Baseline N-gram	29.1	36.8	48.9
DME N-gram	28.6	35.3	46.9

4. Conclusion

We have presented several new approaches to tackle difficulties in building a Chinese language model. For Chinese, word boundaries in the sentence are unknown. Different segmentations result in different realizations of a sentence. The reliable determining of word boundaries is thus important for Chinese language modeling. Furthermore, the vocabulary size of Chinese is unlimited. New words are created everyday. New word extraction techniques are required to complete the dictionary. In this chapter, we have discussed the significant properties of the Chinese language and surveyed several studies and their solutions to related problems. After discussing the issues of Chinese language processing, we focused on developing new Chinese language models. We have also presented several approaches for language model smoothing, long-distance association compensation and discriminative model training to improve the performance of the statistical n-gram model which has been used in numerous applications. These approaches can attain discriminative ability and robustness in language modeling. However, we believe that there are still other good ideas that can bring language modeling to greater heights. We are looking forward to see even better performance of Chinese systems through the application of these new language models.

References

1. P. F. Brown, J. Cocke, S. D. Pietra, V. D. Pietra, F. Jelinek, J. D. Lafferty, R. L. Mercer, and P. S. Roosin, "A Statistical Approach to Machine Translation," *Computational Linguistics*, vol. 16, pp. 79–85, (1990).
2. J. Ponte and W. Crofte, "A Language Modeling Approach to Information Retrieval," in *Proc. ACM SIGIR on Research and Development in Information Retrieval*, (1998), pp. 275–281.
3. C. Chelba and F. Jelinek, "Structured Language Modeling," *Computer Speech and Language*, vol. 14, pp. 283–332, (2000).
4. J. Bellegarda, "Exploiting Latent Semantic Information in Statistical Language Modeling," in *Proc. IEEE*, vol. 88, (2000), pp. 1279–1296.
5. G. J. Lidstone, "Note on the General Case of the Bayes-Laplace Formula for Inductive or Posteriori Probabilities," *Transactions of the Faculty of Actuaries*, vol. 8, pp. 182–192, (1920).
6. F. Jelinek and R. L. Mercer, "Interpolated Estimation of Markov Source Parameters from Sparse Data," in *Proc. Workshop on Pattern Recognition in Practice*, (1980), pp. 381–397.
7. S. M. Katz, "Estimation of Probabilities from Pparse Data for the Language Model Component of a Speech Recognizer," *IEEE Trans. Acoustics & Speech and Signal Processing*, vol. 35, pp. 400–401, (1987).

8. I. J. Good, "The Population Frequencies of Species and the Estimation of Population Parametersn," *Biometrika*, vol. 40, pp. 237–264, (1953).
9. L. S. Lee, "Voice Dictation of Mandarin Chinese," *IEEE Signal Processing Magazine*, vol. 14, pp. 63–101, (1997).
10. ——, "Structural Features of Chinese Language: Why Chinese Spoken Language Processing is Special and Gwhere We Are," in *Keynote Speech, Proc. International Symposium on Chinese Spoken Language*, (Singapore, 1998), pp. 1–15.
11. H. Y. Gu, C. Y. Tseng, and L. S. Lee, "Markov Modeling of Mandarin Chinese for Decoding the Phonetic Sequence into Chinese Characters," *Computer Speech and Language*, vol. 5, (1991), pp. 363–377.
12. K. C. Yang, T. H. Ho, L. F. Chien, and L. S. Lee, "Statistics-based Segment Pattern Lexicon- A New Direction for Chinese Language Modeling," in *Proc. ICASSP*, (1998), pp. 169–172.
13. C. L. Chen, B. R. Bai, L. F. Chien, and L. S. Lee, "PAT-Tree-Based Language Modeling with Initial Application of Chinese Speech Recognition Output Verification," in *Proc. International Symposium on Chinese Spoken Language Processing*, vol. 1, (1988), pp. 139–144.
14. G. Gonnet, R. A. Beaza-Yates, and T. Arrays, "New Iondices for Text: Pat Trees and Pat Arrays," *Proc. Information Retrieval data Structure and Algorithms*, pp. 66–82, (Prentice Hall, 1992).
15. J. Gao, H. F. Wang, M. Li, and K. F. Lee, "A Unified Approach to Statistical Language Modeling for Chinese," in *Proc. ICASSP*, (Istanbul, Turkey, 2000).
16. Y. Li, T. Lee, and Y. Qian, "Toward a Unified Approach to Statistical Language Modeling for Chinese," *ACM Trans. on Asian Language Information Processing*, vol. 1, pp. 3–33, (2002).
17. Z. Wu and G. Tseng, "Chinese Text Segmentation for Text Retrieval Achievements and Problems," *Journal of the American Society for Information Science*, vol. 44, pp. 532–542, (1993).
18. M. Sun, D. Shen, and B. K. Tsou, "Chinese Word Segmentation without Using Lexicon and Hand-Craft Training Data," in *Proc. COLING-ACL*, (1998), pp. 1265–1271.
19. R. Sproat, C. Shih, W. Gale, and N. Chang, "A Stochastic Finite-State Word- Segmentation Algorithm for Chinese," in *Proc. The 32nd conference on Association for Computational Linguistics*, (1994), pp. 66–73.
20. D. D. Palmer, "A Trainable Rule-Based Algorithm for Word Segmentation," in *Proc. The 35th conference on Association for Computational Linguistics*, (1997), pp. 321–328.
21. R. Sproat and C. L. Shih, "A Statistical Method for Finding Word Boundaries in Chinese Text," *Computer Processing of Chinese and Oriental Languages*, vol. 4, pp. 336–351, (1993).
22. J. J. Chen, *An Experimental Parsing System for Chinese Sentence*. MS. Thesis.(National Taiwan University, Taipei, 1985).
23. W. Y. Ma and K. J. Chen, "Introduction to CKIP Chinese Word Segmentation System for the First International Chinese Word Segmentation Bakeoff," in *Proc. ACL, Second SIGHAN Workshop on Chinese Language Processing*, vol. 1, (2003), pp. 168–171.
24. [Online]. Available: http://ckipsvr.iis.sinica.edu.tw/
25. C. K. I. P. Group, *Technical Report No. 93-02*. (Institute of Information Science, Academia Sinica, Taipei).
26. [Online]. Available: http://rocling.iis.sinica.edu.tw/CKIP/
27. Y. Xiong and J. Zhu, "Toward a Unified Approach to Lexicon Optimization and Perplexity Minimization for Chinese Language Modeling," in *Proc. International Conference on Machine Learning and Cybernetics*, vol. 6, (2005), pp. 3824–3829.
28. S. He and J. Zhu, "A Bootstrap Method for Chinese New Words Extraction," in *Proc. ICASSP*, vol. 1, (2001), pp. I–581.
29. Y. S. Lai and C. H. Wu, "Meaningful Term Extraction and Discriminative Term Selection in

Text Categorization via Unknown-Word Methodology," *ACM Trans. on Asian Language Information Processing*, vol. 1, pp. 34–64, (2002).
30. J. Zhao, J. Gao, E. Chang, and M. Li, "Lexicon Optimization for Chinese Language Modeling," in *Proc. International Symposium on Chinese Spoken Language Processing*, (2000).
31. T. H. Chang and C. H. Lee, "Automatic Chinese Unknown Word Extraction Using Small-Corpus-Based Method," in *Proc. International Conference on Natural Language Processing and Knowledge Engineering (NLP-KE)*, (2003), pp. 459–464.
32. W. Y. Ma and K. J. Chen, "A Bottom-Up Merging Algorithm for Chinese Unknown Word Extraction," in *Proc. ACL workshop on Chinese Language Processing*, (2003), pp. 31–38.
33. H. P. Zhang, Q. Liu, H. Zhang, and X. Q. Cheng, "Automatic Recognition of Chinese Unknown Words Based on Role Tagging," in *Proc. the 1st SIGHAN Workshop on Chinese Language Processing*, (2002), pp. 71–77.
34. M. Sun, D. Shen, and C. Huang, "SCeg&Tag1.0: a Practical Word Segmenter and POS Tagger for Chinese Texts," in *Proc. Fifth Conference on Applied Natural Language Processing*, (1997), pp. 119–126.
35. H. H. Tseng, C. L. Liu, Z. M. Gao, and K. J. Chen, "Automatic Classification of Chinese Unknown Verbs," in *Proc. Research on Computational Linguistics Conference XIV (ROCLING XIV)*, (Tainan, 2001), pp. 16–17.
36. M. Y. Lin, T. H. Chiang, and K. Y. Su, "A Preliminary Study on Unknown Word Problem in Chinese Word Segmentation," in *Proc. Research on Computational Linguistics Conference VI (ROCLING VI)*, (1993), pp. 119–137.
37. H. H. Chen and J. C. Lee, "The Identification of Organization Names in Chinese Texts," *Communication of Chinese and Oriental Languages Information Processing Society*, vol. 4, pp. 131–142, (1994).
38. K. J. Chen and M. H. Bai, "Unknown Word Detection for Chinese by a Corpus-Based Cearning Method," *International Journal of Computational linguistics and Chinese Language Processing*, vol. 3, pp. 27–44, (1998).
39. J. Y. Nie, M. L. Hannan, and W. Jin, "Unknown Word detection and Segmentation of Chinese Using Statistical and Heuristic Knowledge," *Communications of COLIPS*, vol. 5, pp. 47–57, (1995).
40. C. S. Khoo and T. E. Loh, "Using Statistical and Contextual Information to Identify Two-and Three-Character Words in Chinese Text," *Journal of the American Society for Information Science and Technology*, vol. 53, pp. 365–377, (2002).
41. H. Li, C. N. Huang, J. Gao, and X. Fan, "The Use of SVM for Chinese New Word Identification," in *Proc. The First International Joint Conference on Natural Language Processing*, (2004), pp. 497–504.
42. J. T. Chien, M. S. Wu, and H. J. Peng, "Latent Semantic Language Modeling and Smoothing," *International Journal of Computational Linguistics and Chinese Language Processing*, vol. 9, pp. 29–44, (2004).
43. J. T. Chien, "Association Pattern Language Modeling," *IEEE Trans. Audio, Speech and Language Processing*, vol. 14, (2006), pp. 1719–1728.
44. C. H. Chueh, H. M. Wang, and J. T. Chien, "A Maximum Entropy Approach for Semantic Language Modeling," *International Journal of Computational Linguistics and Chinese Language Processing*, vol. 11, pp. 37–56, (2006).
45. S. Deerwester, S. Dumais, G. Furnas, T. Landauer, and R. Harshman, "Indexing by Latent Semantic Analysis," *Journal of the American Society of Information Science*, vol. 41, pp. 391–407, (1990).
46. M. Berry, S. Dumais, and G. OBrien, "Using Linear Algebra for Intelligent Information Retrieval," *SIAM Review*, vol. 37, pp. 573–595, (1995).

47. A. Dempster, N. Laird, and D. Rubin, "Maximum Likelihood from Incomplete Data via the EM Algorithm," *Journal of the Royal Statistical Society*, vol. 39, pp. 1–38, (1977).
48. I. H. Witten and T. C. Bell, "The Zero-Frequency Problem: Estimating the Probabilities of Novel Events in Adaptive Text Compression," *IEEE Trans. Information Theory*, vol. 37, pp. 1085–1094, (1991).
49. M. Siu and M. Ostendorf, "Variable *n*-grams and Extension for Conversational Speech Language Modeling," *IEEE Trans. Speech and Audio Processing*, vol. 8, pp. 63–75, (2000).
50. J. Gao and H. Suzuki, "Capturing Long Distance Dependency in Language Modeling: A Empirical Study," in *Proc. International Joint Conference on Natural Language Processing*, (2004).
51. B. Chen, "Dynamic Language Model Adaptation Using Latent Topical Information and Automatic Transcripts," in *Proc. 9th Western Pacific Acoustics Conference (WESPAC IX 2006)*, (2006).
52. R. Rosenfeld, "A Maximum Entropy Approach to Adaptive Statistical Language Modeling," *Computer Speech and Language*, vol. 10, pp. 187–228, (1996).
53. J. Wu and S. Khudanpur, "Building a Topic-Dependent Maximum Entropy Model for Very Large Corpora," in *Proc. ICASSP*, vol. 1, (2002), pp. 777–780.
54. J. Darroch and D. Ratcliff, "Generalized Iterative Scaling for Log-Linear Models," *The Annals of Mathematical Statistics*, vol. 43, pp. 1470–1480, (1972).
55. A. Berger, S. D. Pietra, and V. D. Pietra, "A Maximum Entropy Approach to Natural Language Processing," *Computational Linguistics*, vol. 22, pp. 39–71, (1996).
56. C. Cieri, D. Graff, M. Liberman, N. Martey, and S. Strassel, "The PTDT-2 Text and Speech Corpus," in *Proc. The DARPA Broadcast News Workshop*, (1999).
57. J. T. Chien and C. H. Huang, "Bayesian Learning of Speech Duration Model," *IEEE Trans. Speech and Audio Processing*, vol. 11, pp. 558–567, (2003).
58. J. L. Gauvain and C. H. Lee, "Maximum a Posteriori Estimation for Multivariate Gaussian Mixture Observation of Markov Chain," *IEEE Trans. Speech and Audio Processing*, vol. 2, pp. 291–298, (1994).
59. H. J. Kuo, E. Fosloer-Lussier, H. Jiang, and C. Lee, "Discriminative Training of Language Models for Speech Recognition," in *Proc. ICASSP*, (2002), pp. 325–328.
60. Y. Normandin, R. Cardin, and R. D. Mori, "High-Performance Connected Digit Recognition Using Maximum Mutual Information Estimation," *IEEE Trans. Speech and Audio Processing*, vol. 2, pp. 299–311, (1994).
61. J. Gao, H. Yu, W. Yuan, and P. Xu, "Minimum Sample Risk for Language Modeling," in *Proc. HLT/EMNLP*, (2005).
62. J. W. Kuo and B. Chen, "Minimum Word Error Based Discriminative Training of Language Models," in *Proc. INTERSPEECH*, (2005), pp. 1277–1280.
63. C. H. Chueh, T. C. Chien, and J. T. Chien, "Discriminative Maximum Entropy Language Model for Speech Recognition," in *Proc. INTERSPEECH*, (2005), pp. 721–724.
64. R. Rosenfeld, S. Chen, and X. Zhu, "Whole-Sentence Exponential Language Models: A Vehicle for Linguistic-Statistical Integration," *Computer Speech and Language*, vol. 15, pp. 55–73, (2001).
65. H. Wang, B. Chen, J. W. Kuo, and S. S. Cheng, "MATBN: A Mandarin Chinese Broadcast News Corpus," *International Journal of Computational Linguistics and Chinese Language Processing*, vol. 10, pp. 219–236, (2005).

CHAPTER 10

SPONTANEOUS MANDARIN SPEECH PRONUNCIATION MODELING

Pascale Fung and Yi Liu
Human Language Technology Center, Department of Electronic & Computer Engineering, Hong Kong University of Science & Technology
Clear Water Bay, Kowloon, Hong Kong
E-mail: {pascale,eeyliu}@ee.ust.hk

Pronunciation variations in spontaneous speech can be classified into *complete changes* and *partial changes*. Complete changes are the replacement of a canonical phoneme by an alternative phone. Partial changes are variations within the phoneme such as nasalization, centralization and voicing. We propose a solution for modeling both complete changes and partial changes in spontaneous Mandarin speech. We use the decision tree based pronunciation modeling to predict alternate pronunciations with associated probabilities in order to model complete changes. To avoid lexical confusion with the augmented pronunciation dictionary, we propose using a likelihood ratio test as a confidence measure. In order to model partial changes, we propose partial change phone models (PCPMs) and acoustic model reconstruction. We treat PCPMs as hidden models and merge them into the pre-trained baseform model via model reconstruction through decision tree merging. It is shown that our phone level pronunciation modeling results in an absolute 0.9% syllable error rate reduction, and the acoustic model reconstruction approach results in a significant 2.39% absolute syllable error rate reduction in spontaneous speech.

1. Introduction

Mandarin speech recognition has been gaining ever-increasing attention from the research community at large, mainly due to the strategic global position of the Chinese economy. 872 million people speak Mandarin natively, compared to 308 million native English speakers.[1] The research and development of Mandarin spoken language systems have brought to the foreground a number of significant issues distinct from English systems, which have been hitherto the focus of the automatic speech recognition (ASR) community

First, Chinese in its written form is represented by characters, not phonetic or alphabetic symbols. Orthographically, Mandarin is unique among the world's languages. Written Chinese is ideographic and is a poor reference of pronunciation information. Since the pronunciation of a word is separated from and not linked to the word structure and form, the pronunciation differences between the Chinese dialects and standard Mandarin (Putonghua) are indeed significant. This is an even bigger problem in Mandarin spontaneous speech because spontaneously spoken Mandarin tends to be pronounced more casually and flexibly, with larger acoustic variability.

The pronunciations of Chinese characters are distinct in different Sinitic languages. Despite the fact that Mandarin Chinese is the language spoken by the largest number of native speakers (872 million) and fluent speakers (178 million), most Mandarin speakers do not adhere to the standard canonical pronunciation found in a dictionary, nor to that used by radio announcers and television anchor persons. This presents a unique challenge to Mandarin speech recognition, where pronunciation variation is a major hurdle to the widespread market application of speech recognition systems.

The standard pronunciation of a word is typically called its *baseform*, whereas the actual phonetic realization by a speaker is known as its *surface form*. When base and surface forms differ, then we say a pronunciation variation has taken place. Pronunciation variations in Mandarin can be largely divided into two types: *complete changes* and *partial changes*. Complete changes are the replacement of a canonical phoneme by another alternate phone, such as an expected /b/ being pronounced as /p/. Partial changes are the variations within the phoneme such as nasalization, centralization, voicing and rounding. There is a third type of pronunciation variation, namely tone changes, which can be considered as a subset of complete changes as tonal information is supra-segmental rather than sub-phonetic.

Human transcribers can be quite confounded by pronunciation variations and usually cannot agree with each other on what was actually said.[2] In addition, ASR performance suffers a severe degradation when phoneme/phone models are used for recognizing spontaneous speech. Mixture distribution in the phoneme/phone models of read speech are insufficient in capturing the acoustic variability that leads to partial changes within phoneme units. Therefore, a more powerful acoustic model is required to deal with the phonetic confusions caused by partial changes. The acoustic model for spontaneous speech should be different from that of read speech: it should be robust enough to cover the rich pronunciation variations in spontaneous speech as well as have enough discriminative ability for partial changes. In this chapter, we describe how to model both complete changes and partial changes in spontaneous Mandarin speech.

2. Decision Tree Based Pronunciation Modeling for Complete Changes

Complete changes are the replacement of a canonical phoneme by an alternate phone, such as /b/ being pronounced as /p/, or /zh/ as /z/. For complete changes, we use alternative phone units or a concatenation of phone units to represent pronunciation variations. To predict from phonemes to phones, we take a phoneme string as input and produce phonetic realizations as output along with their likelihoods.

Let $B = b_1 b_2 \cdots b_m$ be the baseform phonemic string and $S = s_1 s_2 \cdots s_n$ the corresponding surface form phonetic string. The most general form of our predictor is $\hat{P}(S|B)$, where $\hat{P}$ is the probability that the phone sequence S is the realization of the phoneme sequence B. To simplify the computation, we decompose this into one phone prediction at a time, such that

$$P(S|B) = p_n(s_n|B, s_1 \cdots s_{n-1})\, p_{n-1}(s_{n-1}|B, s_1 \cdots s_{n-2}) \cdots p_1(s_1|B) \tag{1}$$

and

$$p_k(s_k|B, s_1 \cdots s_{k-1}) = p(s_k|b_{k-r} \cdots b_{k-1} b_k b_{k+1} \cdots b_{k+r}, s_1 \cdots s_{k-1}) \tag{2}$$

For practicality, we assume the k-th phone does not depend on any of the previous phones:

$$\begin{aligned} &p(s_k|b_{k-r} \cdots b_{k-1} b_k b_{k+1} \cdots b_{k+r}, s_1 \cdots s_{k-1}) \\ &\quad = p(s_k|b_{k-r} \cdots b_{k-1} b_k b_{k+1} \cdots b_{k+r}) \end{aligned} \tag{3}$$

A less stringent assumption would be that the k-th phone depends only on the immediately preceding phone:

$$\begin{aligned} &p(s_k|b_{k-r} \cdots b_{k-1} b_k b_{k+1} \cdots b_{k+r}, s_1 \cdots s_{k-1}) \\ &\quad = p(s_k|b_{k-r} \cdots b_{k-1} b_k b_{k+1} \cdots b_{k+r}, s_{k-1}) \end{aligned} \tag{4}$$

In this case the phone string is a first-order Markov chain given the phonemic context.

The most straightforward procedure for estimating the phoneme-to-phone mapping probabilities is to collect n-gram statistics from training data. However, phoneme n-grams are not ideal for this task since the contextual effects are often class-based (e.g., the pronunciation of a phone is different, depending on whether the preceding phoneme is a vowel or not). In addition, in most practical cases, we would only have a limited amount of hand-labeled surface form transcriptions which are usually insufficient for phoneme n-gram estimation. Class-based phoneme n-grams are more compact, less sparse, and more effective.[3,4] Following this, we adopt a decision tree based pronunciation modeling approach, originally developed for English spontaneous speech,[4,5,6] for Mandarin spontaneous speech. Furthermore, we propose a novel method of using *cross-domain* unlabeled data to refine the initial pronunciation model trained from a small set of annotated data as a bootstrap. In addition, we propose using a *likelihood ratio test* as a confidence measure to obtain phoneme-to-phone mapping pairs that we can reliably believe to be due to pronunciation variations, and not due to decoder confusion.

2.1. *Phoneme-to-Phone Mapping Generation*

The flow chart of generating decision tree based pronunciation modeling is shown in Figure 1.

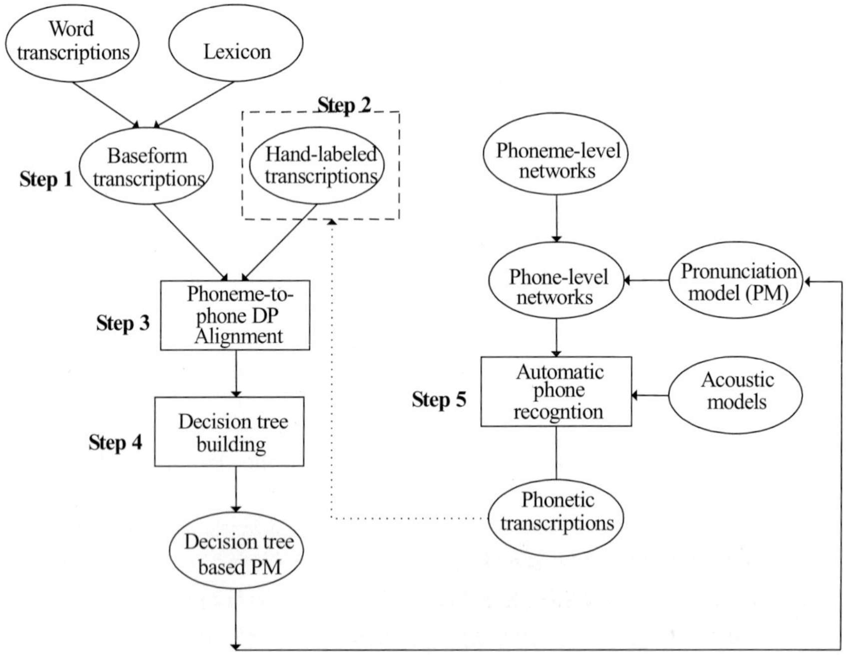

Fig. 1. Building a Decision-Tree based Pronunciation Model.

(1) **Obtain baseform phonemic transcriptions** from a standard word-to-syllable dictionary.
(2) **Generate initial surface form phonetic transcriptions** from hand-labeled phonetic labels or, if the amount of hand-labeled transcriptions is insufficient, use automatic phone recognition to generate phonetic sequence as in Step 5.
(3) **Align phonemic and phonetic transcriptions** by dynamic programming (DP) with flexible local edit distance measure.[7]
(4) **Decision tree based pronunciation model estimation**. A decision tree is constructed for each reference phoneme to predict its surface form by asking

questions about its phonemic context. This context includes information on the phoneme stream itself (such as stress, position and classes of neighboring phones), or the output history of the tree (including the identities of surface phones to the left of the current phone). For each leaf in the tree, we obtain a maximum likelihood estimate via the empirical probability distribution of the samples that fall into that leaf. Our decision tree based pronunciation model thus assigns probabilities to alternative surface form realizations of each phone according to its context.

(5) **Automatic phone recognition with pronunciation model** finds the most likely phone sequence from the phone network which is then regarded as the surface form transcription. This procedure is shown on the right hand side of Figure 1. With this surface form transcription, the alternative pronunciations of Chinese words or syllables can be extracted through the forced alignment between the surface form sequence and baseform sequence with the word/syllable boundary information.

Hand-labeled transcriptions are used to train the initial pronunciation model. This initial set of pronunciation models are then used to generate pronunciation networks using more training data. Automatic phone recognition is performed using the generated networks to get the most likely phone sequence which is then regarded as the surface form transcription. This process is then iterated.

In addition, we propose using a likelihood ratio test as a confidence measure to evaluate the phonetic confusion between phonemes and phones, and find an optimum set of alternative pronunciations. Without such a confidence measure, the extended phone set can cause additional lexical confusion, undermining any improvement that might have been brought by pronunciation modeling. We use the conventional maximum likelihood estimates for p, p_1 and p_2, and write c_1, c_2 and c_{12} for the number of occurrences of b, s and b_s in the training set, where b is the phoneme unit of the baseform sequence, s is the phone unit of the surface form sequence and b_s is the phoneme-to-phone aligned pair. We have

$$p = \frac{c_2}{N}, \quad p_1 = \frac{c_{12}}{c_1}, \quad p_2 = \frac{c_2 - c_{12}}{N - c_1} \tag{5}$$

where N is the total number of phonetic units in the training data. The log of the likelihood ratio λ is then as follows:

$$\begin{aligned} \log\lambda &= \log L(c_{12}, c_1, p) + \log L(c_2 - c_{12}, N - c_1, p) \\ &\quad - \log L(c_{12}, c_1, p_1) + \log L(c_2 - c_{12}, N - c_1, p_2) \end{aligned} \tag{6}$$

where $L(k,n,x) = x^k (1-x)^{n-k}$ is a binomial distribution. In general, we use $-2\log\lambda$ instead of λ for practicality.[8] According to Equation 6, we calculate the likelihood ratio for each aligned pair b_s and use it to evaluate the degree of phonetic confusion between b and s. The higher the likelihood ratio, the more confusable b and s are. For lexical augmentation, we only keep the alternative pronunciations that pass the likelihood ratio test.

2.2. *Experimental Results of Modeling Complete Changes*

We use an acoustic training set consisting of 10 hours of speech (10,483 utterances, which include about 183,513 syllables) selected from the first two CDs in the Linguistic Data Consortium 1997 Mandarin Broadcast News corpus. Three hours of hand-labeled transcriptions from the CASS[2] (Chinese Annotated Spontaneous Speech) corpus are used as bootstrap material to train the initial pronunciation model. The testing data consists of two parts: the first test set (test_set1) includes 865 spontaneous utterances with 11,512 syllables in total. The second test set (test_set2) is used for performance comparison, consisting of clean utterances (F0 condition) from the 1997 and 1998 Hub4NE evaluation sets.[9] The set test_set2 contains 1,263 utterances, with about 15,535 syllables. The hidden Markov model (HMM) topology is a three-state, left-to-right model without skips. The acoustic features are $13MFCC$ (Mel-frequency Cepstral Coefficients), $13\Delta MFCC$ and $13\Delta\Delta MFCC$. 27 standard initials (include 6 zero initial symbols) and 38 finals are used to generate context-independent HMMs, then the HMM Toolkit (HTK) flat-start procedure is used to build the 10-Gaussian triphone model of state-clustered HMMs with 2,904 states. The baseline system in the experiments uses 2,094 tied-state triphone models with 10 Gaussians trained on baseform standard phonemic transcriptions.

The effectiveness of using the reweighted and augmented dictionary with respect to the number of new pronunciations introduced is shown in Table 1. The

Table 1. Performance of using the reweighted and augmented dictionary with alternative pronunciations.

Number of New Pronunciations	**Syllable Error Rate %**	
	(*test_set1*) Spontaneous speech	(*test_set1*) Planned speech
0	42.23	30.92
1536	42.53 (+0.30)	31.3 (+0.38)
503	41.71 (−0.52)	30.74 (−0.18)
290	42.10 (−0.13)	30.8 (−0.12)
803	41.82 (−0.41)	31.15 (+0.23)
474	**41.66 (−0.57)**	30.72 (−0.2)
278	42.10 (−0.13)	30.85 (−0.07)
1023	42.40 (+0.17)	31.1 (+0.18)
426	41.71 (−0.52)	**30.64 (−0.28)**
189	42.18 (−0.05)	30.76 (−0.16)

lowest syllable error rate (SER) in spontaneous speech (test_set1), 41.66%, is achieved with 474 alternate pronunciations, which gives an absolute 0.57% SER reduction compared to the baseline. In addition, when the number of newly-introduced pronunciations is 426, a slight 0.28% SER reduction in planned speech (test_set2) is obtained.

We then used a likelihood ratio test as a confidence measure to optimize the 2,988 initially extended pronunciations. The results show that the lowest SER, 41.33%, on test_set1 is achieved when 426 new alternative pronunciations are introduced, providing an encouraging 0.9% absolute SER reduction compared to the baseline, and an additional 0.33% SER reduction with respect to the best performance of using conventional methods. Moreover, there is even an absolute 0.41% SER reduction on the clean speech in test_set2. This shows that the likelihood ratio test leads to an efficient and reliable selection of the extended alternative pronunciations in modeling complete changes for spontaneous Mandarin speech. In addition, we found that, on average, each syllable has just one additional pronunciation. The computation time for decoding, using such a dictionary, is comparable to using a standard dictionary with single, canonical pronunciations.

3. Acoustic Model Reconstruction for Partial Changes

Partial changes are variations within the phoneme. When partial changes occur, a phone is not completely substituted, deleted or inserted. Figure 2 illustrates the phonetic confusion caused by partial changes in spontaneous speech. Suppose A is a subword unit and B is a relevant subword unit that is often confused with A, and their acoustic samples are X_A and X_B, respectively. It has been shown that the

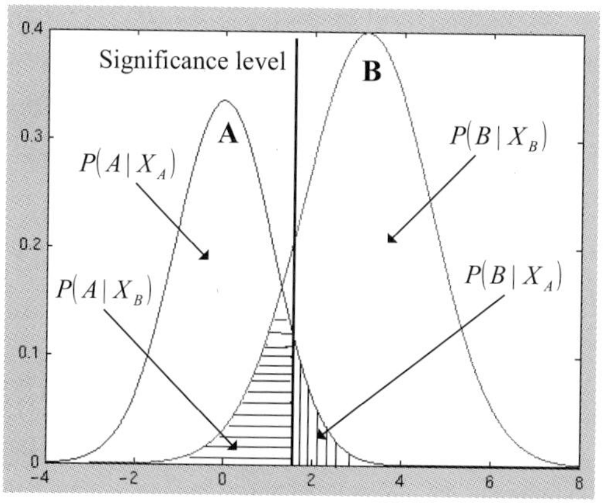

Fig. 2. Partial changes.

acoustic samples related to partial changes which are expected to be recognized as A but are mis-classified as B, lie between the average realization of A and the average realization of B and can be assigned to either $P(B|X_A)$ or $P(A|X_B)$.

Compared to complete changes, partial changes are hard to capture using conventional phonetic units.[6,10,11] Saraclar[6] proposed the state-level pronunciation model (SLPM) and investigated different levels of pronunciation variations by using different HMM topologies. However, the current SLPM may introduce additional model confusions because the same phone set is used to represent both the baseform and surface form models. We need to address two challenges in modeling partial changes: (1) how to identify partial changes in spontaneous speech; and (2) how to improve the acoustic model ability without model confusion. In this section, we introduce our proposed approach of acoustic model reconstruction for this purpose.

3.1. *Partial Change Phone Models*

Motivated by phoneme-to-phone aligned mappings discussed in Section 2.1, we propose *partial change phone models* (PCPMs) to describe partial changes between the canonical and alternative pronunciations. Instead of phone models, PCPMs are established from the samples obtained through the alignment between the baseform and surface form transcriptions.

We start from the recognition formula and deduce the representation of PCPMs. In current ASR systems, where words are represented by the concatenation of small subword units (e.g., phonemes or phones), the decoding formula is

$$\hat{B}_1^N = \arg\max_{B_1^N} P\left(X_1^T|B_1^N\right) P\left(B_1^N\right) \tag{7}$$

where $X_1^T = x_1, x_2, \cdots, x_T$ is the input speech vector, $B_1^N = b_1, b_2, \cdots, b_N$ is the baseform phoneme sequence, N is the number of phonemes in the utterance.

Suppose a word can be pronounced in several alternative ways, and assuming $S_1^N = s_1, s_2, \cdots, s_N$ is one possible sequence of a pronunciation — the surface form — the decoder formula then becomes

$$\begin{aligned}\hat{B}_1^N &= \arg\max_{B_1^N} \sum_{S_1^N} P\left(B_1^N, S_1^N|X_1^T\right)\\ &= \arg\max_{B_1^N}\left[P\left(B_1^N\right)\sum_{S_1^N} P\left(X_1^T|B_1^N, S_1^N\right) P\left(S_1^N|B_1^N\right)\right]\end{aligned} \tag{8}$$

Now $P\left(B_1^N\right)$ is the language model, $P\left(X_1^T|B_1^N, S_1^N\right)$ is the acoustic model and $P\left(S_1^N|B_1^N\right)$ is the pronunciation model. In general, the acoustic model training procedure assumes that

$$P\left(X_1^T|B_1^N,S_1^N\right)=P\left(X_1^T|B_1^N\right) \tag{9}$$

If surface form transcriptions are available, the acoustic model training can be expressed as

$$P\left(X_1^T|B_1^N,S_1^N\right)=P\left(X_1^T|S_1^N\right) \tag{10}$$

Ideally, both the baseform and surface form should be taken into account for acoustic model estimation. The acoustic probability $P\left(X_1^T|B_1^N,S_1^N\right)$ can be factorized into successive contributions. Let t_{i-1} and t_i-1 denote the start and end time of the realization of each unit. We then obtain

$$P\left(X_1^T|B_1^N,S_1^N\right)=\prod_{i-1}^{N}P\left(X_{t_i-1}^{t_i-1}|b_i,s_i\right) \tag{11}$$

$P\left(X_{t_i-1}^{t_i-1}|b_i,s_i\right)$ is called the *partial change phone model* (PCPM), which takes both the baseform and the surface form into consideration for acoustic model training.

3.1.1. *Partial Change Phone Model Generation*

The procedures of generating the baseform/surface form phone pair transcriptions and PCPM inventory are shown as follows. Steps 1- 4 below are similar to the steps described in Section 2.1.

(1) **Obtain baseform phonemic representations** from a standard dictionary.
(2) **Generate surface form phonetic transcriptions** from hand-labeled data or by phone recognition.
(3) **Refine surface form transcriptions** using cross-domain data.
(4) **Align baseform and surface form transcriptions** using dynamic programming (DP).
(5) **Obtain the inventory of PCPMs** based on the mapped baseform/surface form phone pair obtained through DP alignment.
(6) **Generate baseform/surface form phone pair transcriptions** using the alignment results between the phoneme and phone transcriptions. If a phoneme in the baseform transcription has a related alternate phone in the surface form transcription, and this phoneme-to-phone pair can be found in the inventory of PCPM, the phoneme in the baseform transcription is replaced by the phone pair unit.
(7) **Train acoustic model of PCPMs.** The initial parameters of PCPM are cloned from related baseform models and re-estimated using the Baum-Welch (BW) algorithm with phone pair transcriptions.

In the next section, we discuss how to use these PCPMs in acoustic model reconstruction for modeling partial changes.

3.2. *Acoustic Model Reconstruction for Modeling Partial Changes*

3.2.1. *Generating Auxiliary Decision Trees for PCPM Triphones*

Current ASR systems tend to use context-dependent triphone models to achieve higher recognition accuracy. Decision tree based state clustering is commonly used.[12] In our system, triphones for PCPM are similar to conventional triphones except for the central phone. A triphone of a PCPM is in the form of $[b_{i-1}, b_i\_s_i, b_{i+1}]$. The trees for PCPM triphones are called *auxiliary decision trees*, while trees for standard triphone models are called *standard decision trees*. However, auxiliary decision trees are only used during the state-tying procedure for PCPM triphone models, but not in the acoustic model estimation and decoding. This is because each leaf node of a decision tree represents a tied-state after acoustic model reconstruction. The auxiliary decision trees will be merged with standard decision trees and will not appear in the subsequent steps.

3.2.2. *Triphone Model Reconstruction through Decision Tree Merge*

We would like to reconstruct the pre-trained baseform triphone models using the generated PCPM triphones to improve the model resolution for covering partial changes. In order to avoid model confusion and parameter size inflation, we apply acoustic model reconstruction through a decision tree merging process to infuse the pre-trained model with the ability obtained from PCPM triphones to accommodate partial changes.

The nodes between auxiliary decision trees and the relevant standard decision tree are mapped according to the Minimum Gaussian Distance Measure between two tied states as described by Young.[12] Leaf nodes of auxiliary decision trees are merged into the relevant nodes of standard decision trees as shown in Figure 3. After tree merging, the baseform models are reconstructed to include both its own Gaussian mixtures as well as those from the PCPMs. For example, in Figure 3, the leaf node, i.e., tied state "ST_4_3" of the standard decision tree includes the nodes from different auxiliary decision trees in order to model different pronunciation changes, e.g., $b \rightarrow f$ and $b \rightarrow p$.

In our approach, one auxiliary decision tree can only be used by a single conventional or standard decision tree, so no model confusion is introduced. On the other hand, the reconstructed model has acquired the ability from PCPMs to model partial variations. Therefore, without introducing the model confusion, the model resolution is improved.

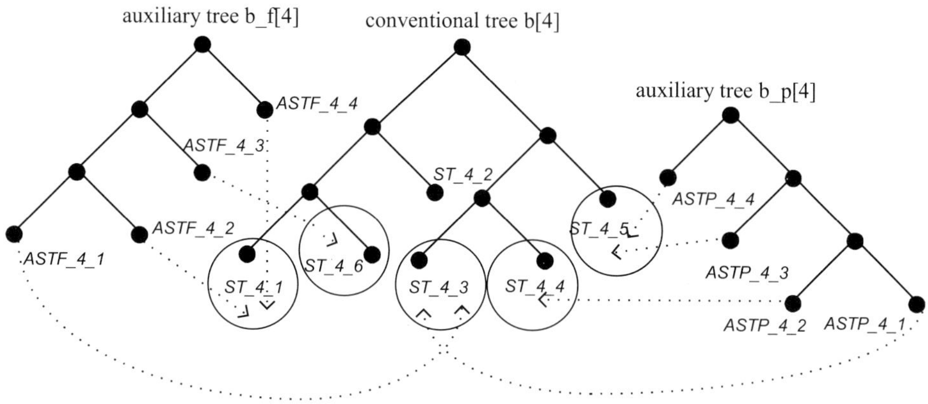

Fig. 3. Decision tree merging.

3.2.3. *Formulation of Acoustic Model Reconstruction*

We now show the formulation of acoustic model reconstruction focusing on continuous density HMMs[a]. Let x, b and s be input vectors, baseform state and surface form state, respectively. $P(x|b)$ is the original output distribution of the baseform model b, and $P(s|b)$ is the state-level pronunciation model that can be determined using state-to-state alignment or frame-to-state mapping.[13] In general, the state output distribution is a mixture of Gaussians:

$$P(x|b) = \sum_{k=1}^{K} w_{bk} \mathrm{N}\left(x; \mu_{bk}, \Sigma_{bk}\right) \tag{12}$$

where w_{bk} is the mixture weight of the k-th mixture component. In the following equations, $\mathrm{N}_{bk}(\cdot)$ is used to represent $\mathrm{N}(x; \mu_{bk}, \Sigma_{bk})$ for simplification.

Let $P'(x|b)$ be the new output distribution of a state after model reconstruction. Since partial changes are represented by the PCPMs, we have

$$P'(x|b) = \lambda P(x|b) + (1-\lambda) P(x|b,s) P(s|b) \tag{13}$$

where λ can be regarded as a linear interpolation coefficient for combining the different acoustic models. It is determined by the probability of the baseform state being recognized as itself. For instance, if "p[2]" has 70% probability to be recognized as "p[2]" and 30% for other variations from the training data, then $\lambda = 0.7$. Since partial changes can be derived from different PCPM triphone models, the above equation is then reformulated accordingly as

$$P'(x|b) = \lambda P(x|b) + (1-\lambda) \sum_{i} P(x|b,s_i) P(s_i|b) \tag{14}$$

[a]For semi-continuous HMMs, the reader is referred to the formulation in the work by Liu and Fung.[14]

where $i = 1, 2\cdots, N$, and N is the total number of merged states from PCPMs during acoustic model reconstruction. If the state of the baseform model has no mapping states from PCPMs, then $N = 0$ and $\lambda = 1$. Substituting Equation 12 into Equation 14, we have

$$\begin{aligned} P'(x|b) &= \lambda \sum_{k=1}^{K} w_{bk}\mathrm{N}_{bk}(\cdot) + (1-\lambda)\sum_{i=1}^{N} P(s_i|b) \sum_{l=1}^{K} w_{(b,s_i)l}\mathrm{N}_{(b,s_i)l}(\cdot) \\ &= \sum_{k=1}^{K} w'_{bk}\mathrm{N}_{bk}(\cdot) + \sum_{i=1}^{N}\sum_{l=1}^{K} w'_{(b,s_i)l}\mathrm{N}_{(b,s_i)l}(\cdot) \end{aligned} \tag{15}$$

where k and l are the indices of mixture components, w'_{bk} and $w'_{(b,s_i)l}$ are the new mixture weights in the reconstructed model. They are

$$\begin{aligned} w'_{bk} &= \lambda \cdot w_{bk} \\ w'_{(b,s_i)l} &= P(s_i|b) \cdot (1-\lambda) \cdot w_{(b,s_i)l} \end{aligned} \tag{16}$$

The parameters of reconstructed output distribution can be further estimated in much the same way as conventional state-tying parameters are estimated using the BW algorithm. Pronunciation model parameters can be re-estimated as

$$\hat{P}(s|b) = \frac{\sum_t \gamma_t(b,s)}{\sum_t \sum_s \gamma_t(b,s)} \tag{17}$$

where

$$\gamma_t(b,s) = P\left(S_t = s, B_t = b | X_1^T; \Phi\right) \tag{18}$$

is the probability of being in state b and s at time t. That is,

$$\gamma_t(b,s) = \gamma_t(b) \cdot \frac{P(s|b) \cdot P(x|s)}{\sum_{s'} P(s'|b) \cdot P(x|s')} \tag{19}$$

where $\gamma_t(b) = P\left(B_t = b | X_1^T; \Phi\right)$ is the probability of being in state b at time t. This can be efficiently computed by the forword-backword algorithm.[15] Φ is the HMM set.

The re-estimation of the parameters of a reconstructed model is similar to that of the re-estimation in Rabiner *et al.*,[15] except that the quantity of $\gamma_t(b,k)$ is modified to $\gamma_t(b,s,k)$, which is the probability of being in state b, s and the k-th mixture component at time t, given the model Φ and the observation sequence X_1^T. Hence,

$$\hat{\mu}_{bk} = \frac{\sum_t \sum_s \gamma_t(b,s,k)\, x_t}{\sum_t \sum_s \gamma_t(b,s,k)} \tag{20}$$

and

$$\hat{\sum}_{bk} = \frac{\sum_t \sum_s \gamma_t (b,s,k) (x_t - \hat{\mu}_{bk}) (x_t - \hat{\mu}_{bk})^t}{\sum_t \sum_s \gamma_t (b,s,k)} \tag{21}$$

where

$$\gamma_t (b,s,k) = \gamma_t (b) \cdot \frac{P(s|b) \cdot w_{(s,b)k} P(x|s,k)}{\sum_{s'} \sum_{k'} P(s'|b) w_{(s',b)k'} P(x|s',k')} \tag{22}$$

In the above equations, k indexes all the Gaussian components in the reconstructed model. According to Equation 15, such Gaussian components include the original Gaussian components from the pre-trained baseform model as well as those from the PCPMs.

3.3. *Experimental Results of Modeling Partial Changes*

The resources and baseline used for the experiments shown here are the same as those described in Section 2.1. The total number of context-independent PCPMs is 145, which covers a majority of the partial changes in spontaneous Mandarin speech. On average, there are 2.5 phone pairs for each initial and 2.0 for each final. 818 leaf nodes (i.e., tied-states) are generated for PCPM triphones. Our reconstructed model (*Model 2* in Table 2) includes 37,229 $((2904+818)*10)$ Gaussians and each state has 12.8 Gaussians on average, with an increase of 28.2% in parameter size. A comparison was also made to an enhanced acoustic model (*Model 3* in Table 2) with 13 Gaussians per state. Moreover, a Gaussian mixture sharing model (*Model 4*) according to the SLPM with 13.1 Gaussian components per state on average is also generated for comparison.

Table 2. Recognition performance of using the reconstructed acoustic models for partial change modeling compared to other pronunciation modeling approaches

HMM	Syllable Error Rate %	
	(test_set1) Spontaneous speech	(test_set2) Planned speech
Baseline (*Model 1*) (10 Gau. per state)	42.23	30.92
Enhanced model (*Model 3*) (13 Gau. per state)	41.57	30.58
SLPM by Gaussian mixture sharing (*Model 4*) (13.1 Gau. per state)	41.29 (−0.94)	30.05 (−0.87)
Reconstructed model using PCPM triphones (*Model 2*) (12.8 Gau. per state)	**39.84 (−2.39)**	**29.68 (−1.24)**

Table 2 shows that our reconstructed model yields a significant 2.39% SER absolute reduction on test_set1 compared to the baseline. There is an encouraging 1.24% absolute SER reduction on the clean (or planned) speech test data. Moreover, the reconstructed acoustic model gives an additional 1.45% SER reduction in spontaneous speech with respect to that of the SLPM with Gaussian mixture sharing across phonetic models. The reason for the higher efficiency of pronunciation modeling through acoustic model reconstruction lies in the fact that (1) we use PCPM triphones to distinguish different types of partial changes, while the SLPM approach uses the same unit inventory for both the baseform and surface form acoustic models and thus cannot efficiently describe partial changes, and (2) in our approach, one auxiliary decision tree can only be used by one standard decision tree during tree merges, therefore no model confusion is introduced. Our model also achieves an additional 1.73% absolute SER reduction with respect to the enhanced acoustic model.

4. Conclusion

The high error rate in spontaneous speech recognition is due in part to the poor modeling of pronunciation variations. Pronunciation variations in spontaneous Mandarin speech include both complete changes and partial changes. In order to model complete changes, we introduced decision tree based phone-level pronunciation modeling to predict alternate pronunciations and their associated probabilities. To resolve data sparseness in pronunciation model training, we proposed using cross-domain data to estimate pronunciation variability. To discard the unreliable alternative pronunciations, we used a likelihood ratio test as a confidence measure to evaluate the degree of confusions between the aligned phoneme-to-phone mappings. Finally, we generated a reweighted, augmented dictionary with selected multiple pronunciations and their associated probabilities. Using such a dictionary in decoding gives an absolute 0.9% SER reduction on spontaneous speech compared with the baseline.

We also proposed PCPMs to differentiate partial changes and acoustic model reconstruction for modeling partial changes. In addition, in order to avoid model confusion, we generated auxiliary decision trees for PCPM triphones, and applied decision tree merging for acoustic model reconstruction on context-dependent acoustic models. Using these reconstructed acoustic models on spontaneous speech resulted in a significant 2.39% SER absolute reduction, compared with 0.9% SER reduction using phone-level pronunciation modeling, and a 0.94% SER reduction with the SLPM. Moreover, our method produces significant improvements in spontaneous speech tasks without sacrificing the performance of read speech tasks.

More recently, researchers have used pronunciation modeling on accented speech[16,17] or dialectal speech,[11,18,19] as special cases of spontaneous speech recognition. The pronunciation modeling approach we introduced in this chapter has also been applied successfully to accented speech recognition.[20,21,22,23,24] All these works have taken steps toward the goal of creating a better model for pronunciation variations.

Acknowledgements

This work was partially supported by grants CERG#HKUST6206/03E of the Hong Kong Research Grants Council, and DAG03/04.EG30 of the Hong Kong University of Science & Technology.

References

1. Wikipedia http://en.wikipedia.org/wiki/List_of_languages_by_number_of_native_speakers
2. A. Li, F. Zheng, W. Byrne, P. Fung, T. Kamm, Y. Liu, Z. Song, U. Ruhi, V. Venkataramani, and X. Chen, "CASS: A Phonetically Transcribed Corpus of Mandarin Spontaneous Speech," *Proc. ICSLP'00*, (2000).
3. M. Riley and A. Ljolje, "Automatic Generation of Detailed Pronunciation Lexicons," *Automatic Speech and Speaker Recognition: Advanced Topics*, (Kluwer Academic Press, Boston, 1996), pp. 285–302.
4. W. Byrne, M. Finke, S. Khudanpur, J. Mcdonough, H. Nock, M. Riley, M. Saraclar, C. Wooters and G. Zavaliagkos, "Pronunciation Modeling using a Hand-labeled Corpus for Conversational Speech Recognition," *Proc. ICASSP'98*, (Seattle, 1998), pp. 313–316.
5. M. Finke, J. Fritsch, D. Koll and A. Waibel, "Modeling and Efficient Decoding of Large Vocabulary Conversational Speech," *Proc. Eurospeech'99*, (Budapest, Hungary, 1999), pp. 467–470.
6. M. Saraclar, *Pronunciation Modeling for Conversational Speech Recognition*, PhD thesis, The Johns Hopkins University, (Baltimore, MD, 2000).
7. P. Fung, W. Byrne, F. Zheng, T. Kamm, Y. Liu, Z. Song, V. Venkataramani, and U. Ruhi, "Pronunciation Modeling of Mandarin Casual Speech," in Final Report, The Johns Hopkins University Summer Workshop, (2000).
8. D. C. Manning and H. Schutze, *Foundations of Statistical Natural Language Processing*, (The MIT Press, Cambridge, Massachusetts, 1999).
9. W. Byrne, V. Venkataramani, T. Kamm, F. Zheng, P. Fung, Y. Liu, and U. Ruhi, (2001). "Automatic Generation of Pronunciation Lexicons for Mandarin Spontaneous Speech," *Proc. ICASSP'01*, (Salt Lake City, USA, 2001).
10. M, Saraclar, H. Nock, and S. Khudanpur, "Pronunciation Modeling by Sharing Gaussian Densities across Phonetic Models," *Computer Speech and Language*, 14, (2000), pp. 137–160.
11. Y. Zheng, R. Sproat, L. Gu, I. Shafran, H. Zhou, Y. Su, D. Jurafsky, R. Starr and S.-Y. Yoon, "Accent Detection and Speech Recognition for Shanghai-Accented Mandarin," *Proc. Eurospeech'05*, (2005).
12. S. Young, *The HTK book*, (Entropic Cambridge Research laboratory, 1999).
13. Y. Liu and P. Fung, "Modeling Partial Pronunciation Variations for Spontaneous Mandarin Speech Recognition," *Computer Speech & Language*, 17, 4, (2003), pp. 357–379.
14. Y. Liu and P. Fung, "State-dependent Phonetic Tied Mixtures with Pronunciation Modeling for Spontaneous Speech Recognition", in *IEEE Transactions on Speech and Audio Processing*, 12, 4, (2004) pp. 351–364.

15. L. Rabiner and B. H. Juang, *Fundamentals of Speech Recognition*, (Prentice-Hall, Englewood Cliffs, NJ, 1993).
16. M. Liu, B. Xu, T. Huang, Y. Deng and C. Li, "Mandarin Accent Adaptation Based on Context-Independent/Context-Dependent Pronunciation Modeling," *Proc. ICASSP'00*, (Istanbul, Turkey, 2000), pp. 1929–1932.
17. C. Huang, E. Chang, J. Zhou, and K. Lee, "Accent Modeling Based on Pronunciation Dictionary Adaptation for Large Vocabulary Mandarin Speech Recognition," *Proc. ICSLP'00*, (Beijing, China, 2000).
18. J. Li, T. F. Zheng, W. Byrne and D. Jurafsky, "A Dialectal Chinese Speech Recognition Framework," *Journal of Computer Science and Technology*, (2005).
19. P. Kam, and T. Lee, "Modeling Pronunciation Variation for Cantonese Speech Recognition," *Proc. ISCA ITR-Workshop on Pronunciation Modeling and Lexicon Adaptation*, (Colorado, USA, 2002).
20. P. Fung, and Y. Liu, "Triphone Model Reconstruction for Mandarin Pronunciation Variations," *Proc. IEEE International Conference on Acoustic, Speech and Signal*, (Hong Kong, 2003).
21. P. Fung, and Y. Liu, "Effects and Modeling of Phonetic and Acoustic Confusions in Accented Speech," *Journal of the Acoustical Society of America*, 118, 5, (2005), pp. 3279–3293.
22. Y. Liu and P. Fung, "Partial Change Accent Models for Accented Mandarin Speech Recognition," *Proc. IEEE Workshop on Automatic Speech Recognition and Understanding*, (St. Thomas, U.S. Virgin Islands, 2003).
23. Y. Liu and P. Fung, "Acoustic and Phonetic Confusions in Accented Speech Recognition," *Proc. Interspeech 2005 - Eurospeech*, (Lisbon, 2005).
24. Y. Liu and P. Fung, "Multi-Accent Chinese Speech Recognition," *Proc. Interspeech 2006*, (Pittsburgh, 2006).
25. Y. Liu and P. Fung, "Decision Tree-Based Triphones are Robust and Practical for Mandarin Speech Recognition," *Proc. Eurospeech'99*, (Budapest, Hungary, 1999), pp. 895–898.
26. Y. Liu and P. Fung, "Rule-Based Word Pronunciation Networks Generation for Mandarin Speech Recognition," *Proc. ISCSLP'00*, (Beijing, China, 2000), pp. 35–38.
27. X. Luo and F. Jelineck, "Probabilistic Classification of HMM States for Large Vocabulary Continuous Speech Recognition," *Proc. ICASSP'99*, (Phoenix, USA, 1999), pp. 353–356.
28. M. Riley, W. Byrne, M. Finke, S. Khudanpur, A. Ljolje, J. Mcdonough, H. Nock, M. Saraclar, C. Wooters, and G. Zavaliagkos, "Stochastic Pronunciation Modeling from Hand-Labeled Phonetic Corpora," *Speech Communication*, 29, (1999), pp. 209–224.
29. M. Saraclar and S. Khudanpur, "Pronunciation Ambiguity vs Pronunciation Variability in Speech Recognition," *Proc. ICASSP'00*, (Istanbul, Turkey, 2000), pp. 1679–1682
30. M. Tsai, F. Chou and L. Lee, "Pronunciation Variation Analysis with Respect to Various Linguistic Levels and Contextual Conditions for Mandarin Chinese," *Proc. Eurospeech'01*, (Aalborg, Denmark, 2001), pp. 1445–1448.
31. F. Zheng, Z. Song, P. Fung and W. Byrne, "Modeling Pronunciation Vvariation using Context-Dependent Weighting and B/S Refined Acoustic Modeling," *Proc. Eurospeech'01*, (Aalborg, Denmark, 2001), pp. 57–60.

CHAPTER 11

CORPUS DESIGN AND ANNOTATION FOR SPEECH SYNTHESIS AND RECOGNITION

Aijun Li[†] and Yiqing Zu[‡]

[†] *Institute of Linguistics, Chinese Academy of Social Sciences*
No. 5, JianNeiDaJie,Beijing
[‡] *Motorola China Research Center*
1168 Nanjing Rd. W., 38F, PC: 200041, Shanghai
E-mail: yiqing.zu@motorola.com, liaj@cass.org.cn

In this chapter we focus our attention primarily on Chinese speech corpora design, collection and annotation, oriented to speech synthesis, recognition and fundamental speech research. Speech corpora are referred to not only as speech signals per se, but they include relevant documents, metadata, annotations and all related specifications. A complete corpus would be ready for use in the development of speech application systems and available for distribution to more than one research team in the community.

1. Introduction: Chinese Speech Corpus

A speech corpus is the basis for both the analysis of the characteristics of speech signals, and the development of speech synthesis and recognition systems. The corpus content becomes more and more complicated and its size larger and larger along with the development of computational power. For example, in the early Chinese parametric speech synthesis system, which is a rule-based synthesis system,[1] the speech corpus, as we call it today, was a small amount of speech recorded in a laboratory and used for acoustic analysis and parameter extraction. In today's corpus-based synthesis, the size of a corpus reaches around several gigabytes covering a myriad of phonetic and linguistic constituents, such as Chinese tonal syllables, frequently used words and phrases and other special speech units. For speech recognition, the quality of the speech corpus used is one of the crucial aspects in the training of an acoustic model.

Spoken Chinese comprises many regional variants, called *dialects*. Although they all employ a common written form, they are mutually unintelligible. There are 10 major dialects in China: *Guan, Jin, Wu, Hui, Xiang, Gan, Hakka, Yue*, *Min* and *PingHua*. Guan (Mandarin) is referred to as a common language which covers very large regional areas from north east to south west of China, with over 800 million speakers. A Chinese speech corpus can be categorized according to its content, speaking style, channel property, phonetic coverage, dialectal accent or application area, as follows:

- Spontaneous speech vs. read speech;
- Monologue vs. dialogue;
- Dialect vs. Standard Chinese vs. regional accented speech corpus;
- Fixed line telephone vs. mobile phone vs. VoIP speech corpus;
- Speech synthesis vs. speech recognition vs. voice print recognition vs. speech evaluation corpus
- …

In mainland China, speech corpus production receives long term support from various national funds. For instance, the RASC863, a Chinese speech corpus with ten regional accents, was supported by the 863 Hi-tech Research fund.[2] Moreover, almost all of the speech research and development affiliations are developing their own speech corpora.

There are so many different kinds and such large amounts of Chinese speech corpora that it is rather important to be able to conveniently share these to avoid wastages of time and money, making the research work more efficient. One of the main problems hindering the sharing of these corpora is the lack of general specifications on corpus collection, annotation and distribution.

It is the improvement of phonetic research and the advancement of speech technology that stimulates and inspires the need for building good quality speech corpora and the standardization of their relative specifications.

Generally speaking, the process of corpus production can be divided into 9 steps:[3] determining the various specifications, preparing for collection, pre-collecting, pre-validation, starting the actual collection, annotating, compiling lexical dictionaries or lexical frequency tables, post validation and distribution. It is not necessary to follow every one of these steps. Some of them can be carried out simultaneously, such as collecting and annotating, some can be skipped in a specific task; in fact, other additional steps can be also introduced by the producer.

2. Specifications of Corpus Collection

Table 1 shows the major specifications in producing a speech corpus. The technical parameters of recording define the acoustic features, which are summarized and listed in Table 2.

Table 1. Primary specifications of speech corpus.

Specifications	Comments
Specification of speakers	Describing the speaker's features such as age, gender, educational background, voice quality, language and accent.
Specification of corpus design	Describing the corpus organization and contents. For instance, the detail information or scripts (prompts) organization of read and spontaneous speech, dialogues or monologues, elicited spontaneous speech (answering questions, etc.), expressive speech. Introduction to the phonetic or linguistic coverage and the algorithm used for selecting the corpus scripts.
Specification of recording	Describing the recording technical specifications on recording equipments, environmental conditions, the recording platform and the data storage strategy such as sampling rate, speech wave format...
Specification of annotation	Describing the annotation conventions of sound to characters transcription, phonetic annotation or other information such as syntactic annotation.
Validation criteria	Explicitly setting the criteria that the corpus should fulfill. Giving an overview of the features to be checked and the criteria employed to accept or reject the corpus.
Specification of distribution	Describing the distribution plan, principles and the storage medium.

Corpus validation criteria are the final validation steps after pre-validation, and after the completion of the whole corpus production. So the manual of validation specification must describe the detailed method of evaluation and define every validation data. If there are more than one transcribers transcribing or annotating the collected data simultaneously, the agreement and consistency of their annotations should be checked first. A sample of cross-transcriber annotations agreement rates is listed here for your reference in Table 3.

3. Chinese Speech Corpus Design

The aim of speech corpus design is to determine what is to be recorded and to obtain or create the necessary scripts. Whether or not a particular corpus requires designated scripts before collection is determined by the corpus type and corpus content. There are corpora related to unplanned, spontaneous speech within some domain or topic, while there are others involving read speech whose scripts must be carefully controlled and prepared. For example, lecture speeches belong to the unscripted, unprompted corpus design category. The corpus for a data-driven speech synthesis or speech recognition system falls under the second design type whose scripts and prompts need comprehensive phonological, phonetic and linguistic coverage. The following sections describe the principles of corpus design, and the whole procedure of creating a fundamental speech corpus as well as corpora for speech recognition and synthesis.

Table 2. List of the technical parameters of recording.

Recording Technical Parameters	Attribute	Comments
Acoustic Environment	Recording scenarios	Public, office, entertainment, home or vehicle…
	Acoustic space	For each scenario, detailed information should be described, such as room area, vehicle size/type/speed/, equipment at home, etc.
	Speakers' gestures	Including the direction to which the speaker faces, such as facing the wall, facing another speaker, or back against the wall
	Background noise	Type and level of the background noise
Microphone	Type	Types and the manufacturers should be listed.
	Technical details of each microphone	Frequency response, directional pattern, supply voltage…
	Microphone numbers	
	Microphone mounting positions	The distance of each microphone to the speaker and to the wall(s)
Channels	Channel number	
	Signal in the channel	
Signal	Sampling rate	For normal cases: 16KHz, 22KHz or higher; for telephone: 8KHz; Glottal signal (Laryngograph EGG): same as speech; EMA (Electromagnetic Articulograph): 200HZ
	Speech coding	Sampling type and width. Such as ALAW (world)/ULAW (US) PCM/ADPCM… 8bit/16bit/22bit/48bit/96bit….
	Format of signal	Signal file format of each channel should be given, such as raw, wave…
	S/N	Sometimes to control the speech quality, S/N range for each speech channel is required, which is often automatically operated by recording tools.

Table 3. Agreement among transcribers (partly after Florian Schiel, Christoph Draxler, 2003)[3].

Chinese character for read speech:99%
Chinese character for spontaneous speech:95–97%, depending on background noise.
Syllable for spontaneous telephone speech: 80%
Initials and finals of spoken speech recorded in sound proof room: 94%
Segmental boundary of initials and finals: (read/ spontaneous):+/-20ms
Average prosodic boundary and stress: 60–70%

3.1. *Fundamental Speech Corpus Design*

Here, a fundamental speech corpus primarily refers to the read speech corpus for acoustic-phonetic analysis on the theoretical phonetic issues associated with speech technology. There are many fundamental speech corpora which commonly used, for example, the Standard Chinese monosyllable corpus, tone and tonal combination speech corpus, sentence corpus with various structures, speech act corpus, and so on.

3.2. *Corpus Design for Speech Synthesis*

Generally speaking, there are two approaches of text-to-speech (TTS) synthesis: concatenative speech synthesis and parametric speech synthesis. Concatenative speech synthesis[4] selects pre-recorded, naturally uttered human speech segments to concatenate and generate speech output. So far, the trend favors the use of a large-sized corpus in concatenative TTS due to its more natural-sounding output. For parametric speech synthesis, such as formant synthesis,[5, 6] the speech corpus is used for parameter extraction. Whichever synthesis approach is used, speech corpus is clearly a fundamental issue. A key concern is phonetic coverage on both the segmental and supra-segmental, or prosody, levels.

3.2.1. *Phonetic Coverage*

In a typical corpus-based, variable-length speech unit concatenation TTS system, a rather large speech corpus is required, and this needs to be finely designed. The discussion on corpus design in this section centers on this kind of speech synthesis because it involves careful design of the speech corpus which needs to cover an abundance of phonetic and linguistic phenomena.

3.2.2. *Speech Unit Coverage*

(1) *Syllable coverage*: Chinese is a tonal language and each tone is carried by a syllable. There are 10 major dialects in China as described in the first section,

and they may differ in the number of consonants, vowels and even tones. However, there is no significant difference in the numbers of syllables between these dialects based on a rough analysis of their respective phonetic structures. It is reasonable to use the syllable as the speech unit for Chinese speech systems because the number of syllables in many of these Chinese languages or dialects is limited, ranging between 1,200 and 15,000.

(2) *Word coverage*: Zipf's law says that the relationship between word frequency P_r and its rank r in a large text corpus can be expressed as:

$$P_r = Cr^{-1} \tag{1}$$

where C is a constant. The word having the highest frequency ranks first. Applied to English data, C is determined to be about 0.1.

$$\sum_{i=1}^{N} P_i = 1 \tag{2}$$

$$\sum_{r=1}^{N} Cr^{-1} = 1 \tag{3}$$

Where N is an integer that stands for number of words. If $C = 0.1$, then

$$0.1 \times \sum_{r=1}^{N} r^{-1} = 1 \tag{4}$$

Using the approximate approach,[7, 8] N is found to be roughly 12,366. That is to say, when the number of words is about 12,366, the sum of these word frequencies is 1. Applying this result to Chinese text, the entropy of the Chinese word would no longer increase when 12,366 words appear. From various recent years' resources on the internet, we gathered word occurrence statistics in three domains: technology, finance and entertainment. The figures obtained demonstrate a confirmation of this rule (see Figure 1–Figure 3). In each domain, 12,366 words will cover more than 99% of the text.

3.2.3. *Prosody Coverage*

Prosodic structure in an utterance may have some relationship with syntactic, semantic and physiological constraints. It phrases an utterance into groups. The boundary of the prosodic group is called a *break* and is signaled by a pause, pre-lengthening/final-lengthening, pitch movement or F0 reset.[9,10,35,36] Some

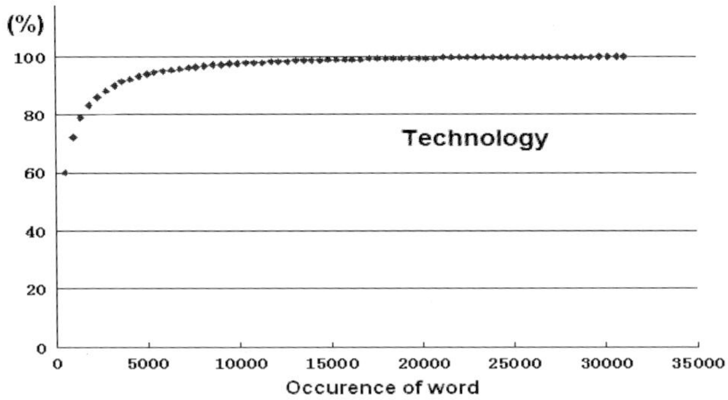

Fig. 1. Word occurrence and text coverage in domains of science and technology.

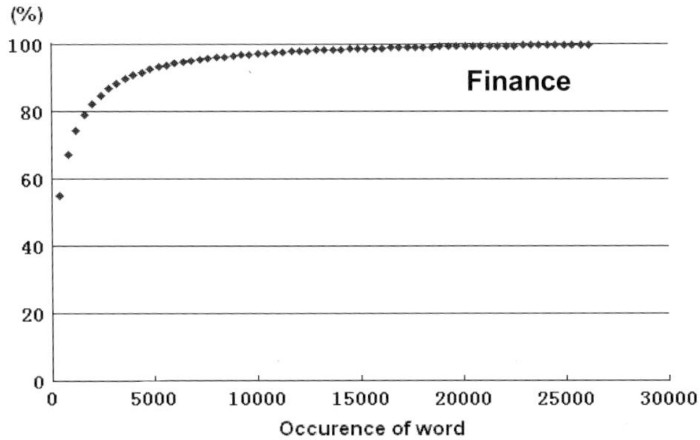

Fig. 2. Word occurrence and text coverage in the financial domain.

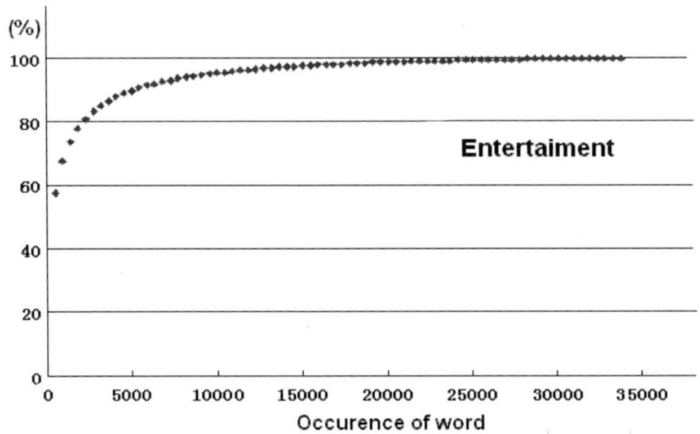

Fig. 3. Word occurrence and text coverage in the entertainment domain.

researchers revealed that pauses brought about by syntax occur at the boundaries of sentences or more complex structures.[11] This fact shows that pausing takes place at major prosodic boundaries. It can be further inferred that perceived breaks are not necessarily signaled by silence, but probably by other acoustic cues.

Unfortunately, at the text level, prosodic structure cannot be exactly predicted. When reading the same text, we may find different speakers applying different strategies to phrasing or breaking. A simple way to overcome this is to allow target speech units to appear in different positions in an utterance, such as in the initial, middle and final positions of utterances. More occurrences in sentence middle positions are helpful in achieving better coverage. The ideal corpus would be attained when all syllables and frequently used words occur in the different prosodic positions.

3.2.4. *Expressiveness and Linguistic Coverage*

To synthesize speech that is more varied and colorful, expressive sentences and linguistic variation coverage should be a focus as well. The major cases are as follows:

(i) *Statement sentence*: Most sentences in text are in the form of statements. These should make up the bulk of the corpus. Most phonetic occurrences can be captured within such statements.

(ii) *Interrogative sentence*: There are two kinds of interrogative sentences – those with and those without question words.

(iii) *Exclamatory sentence*: The expressive sentences are always characterized with exclamation point (!), and modal words, for instance, 哦 /o/, 哎/ai/, 呀/ya/,…

(iv) *Numbering*: There is a numbering prosodic structure when speakers read strings of digits. For example, telephone numbers will be grouped according to the country code, local area code, and so on.

(v) *Appellation*: "爸爸" (/ba4 ba0/ "father"), "妈妈" (/ma1 ma0/ "mother"),…

(vi) *Reduplicative syllable word*: there are three kinds of reduplicative words with different syntactic structures. For example: "轻轻(地)" (/qing1 qing1 de0/); "冷冰冰" (/leng3 bing1 bing1/); "明明白白" (/ming2 ming2 bai2 bai2/)…

(vii) *Retroflex*: The more frequently used retroflexed words include "玩儿" (/wanr2/), "一会儿" (/yi1 huir4/), "那儿" (/nar4/), "哪儿" (/nar3/), etc.

(viii) *Necessary neutral tone word*: "葡萄" (/pu2 tao0/), "西瓜" (/xi1 gua0/), etc.

3.2.5 *Scale of TTS Speech Corpus*

Script Selection Sentences in a large text corpus are segmented with the following punctuation marks: "。", "，", "；", "！", "？", "：". To ensure reading fluency, the length of a sentence is always limited, say within 15 or 20 syllables. Word segmentation aims to determine the pronunciation of polyphones, and the phonetic symbol set, e.g. Pinyin, is adopted to calculate phonetic coverage.

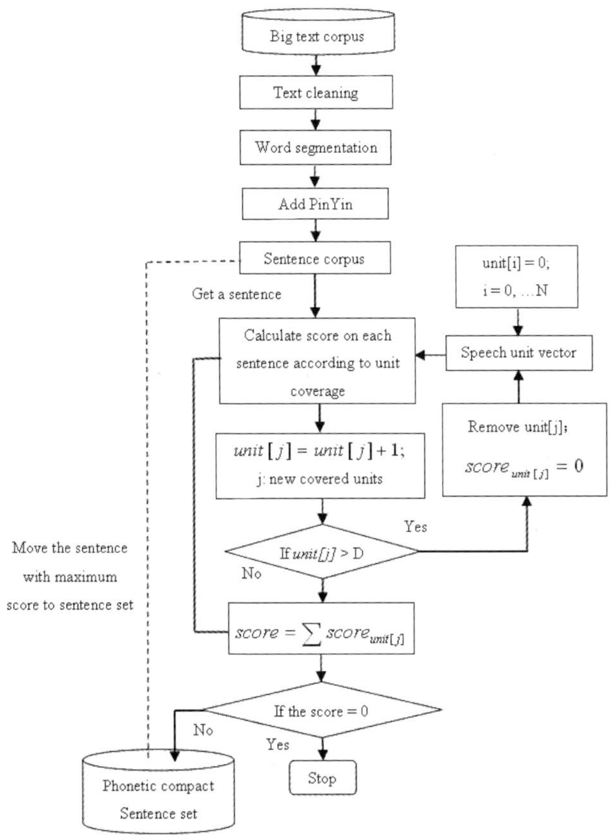

Fig. 4. Flowchart of a greedy algorithm.

The sentences are collected by counting the appearances of speech units according to a set of phonetic rules. The flowchart of a well-known greedy algorithm for sentence selection is shown in Figure 4.[12, 13] This algorithm has a very high computational cost.

There are other approaches to select sentences as part of corpus design conducted by various speech synthesis research and application groups.[14–16]

Qualitative Analysis of Chinese Text: A couple of questions need to be addressed when dealing with the scale of a corpus: Is the speech data sufficient enough to support corpus-based concatenative TTS synthesis? Is it true that the bigger the corpus, the better the quality? The statistical analysis of text corpus may be helpful to answer these questions.

(1) Length of sentence
Assuming that sentences are separated with any of these punctuations "。", "，", "；", "！", "？", or "：", the statistics on several hundred gigabytes of text data downloaded from the internet and other public servers, show that the average length of a sentence in news reports is about 10 to 12 characters; the length of a sentence in short messages is about 6 to 8 characters, while a typical sentence found in Blogs is around 8 to 10 characters. For general purposes, it is reasonable to limit the sentence length in TTS scripts to 20 characters.

(2) Size and coverage of TTS scripts
Many factors can influence the quantitative estimation of the size of a TTS corpus. Here we try to provide a qualitative analysis to clue readers in on what needs to be considered. There is a huge amount of words in Chinese. The coverage of the more frequently used words, phrases or syllable strings, greatly benefits the maximum matching of longer speech units, which is desired in a corpus-based concatenative TTS. If the average length of a Chinese word is 1.65, then 12,366 words or about 20,000 characters will cover enough information for Chinese. There are 6,723 simplified Chinese characters in GB encoding. Since there are a lot of homophones in Chinese, there are only about 1,200 tonal syllables in Mandarin speech. Among these 1,200 tonal syllables, there are 38 finals and 21 initials. Word coverage implies tonal syllable coverage, syllable initials and finals coverage, as well as context coverage. Using the greedy algorithm discussed in the previous section, sentence selection can also be conducted based on word coverage.

However, in natural texts, there are some constraints that we need to be aware of. The following factors should be taken into account for good word coverage:

(a) Sentence structure constraints
Semantic, syntax and word collocation rules will bring about redundancy when 12,366 words are reached. In the following formula, N_{98} is the number of words when all 12,366 words occur; N is 12,366; N_r is the number of the r-th word when 12,366 words are obtained.

$$N_{98} = \sum_{r=1}^{N} N_r \tag{5}$$

The statistics on the technology domain demonstrates that when 12,366 words are encountered, a total of 17,000 words were the actual input. The test data are approximately the same as the estimated data.

A test on word coverage may illustrate the scale of the sentence set in the technology domain. The number of targeted words is 12,366. According to the sentence length statistics in (1), the sentence length is limited to less than 15 characters. As shown in Figure 5(a), when 24,000 sentences occur naturally, about 45% of the target words occur. The greedy algorithm can reduce the number of frequently appearing words and increase the occurrence of rarely used words. Figure 5(b) shows that with only about 4,500 sentences, we can already cover nearly 90% of the target words. When it all 12,366 words are covered, a total of 25,000 sentences are selected. To cover units longer than the word, the number of sentences will increase significantly.

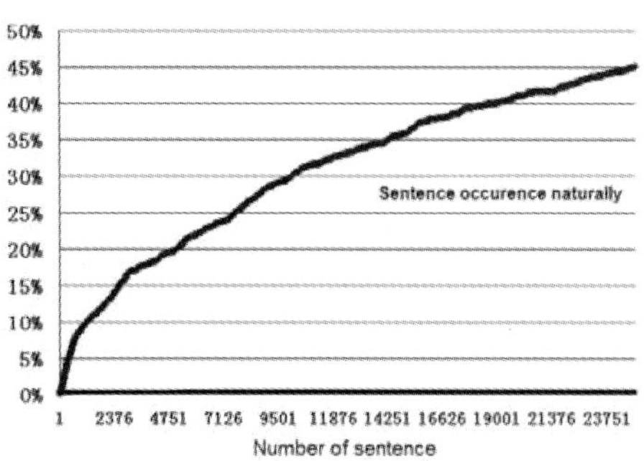

(a)

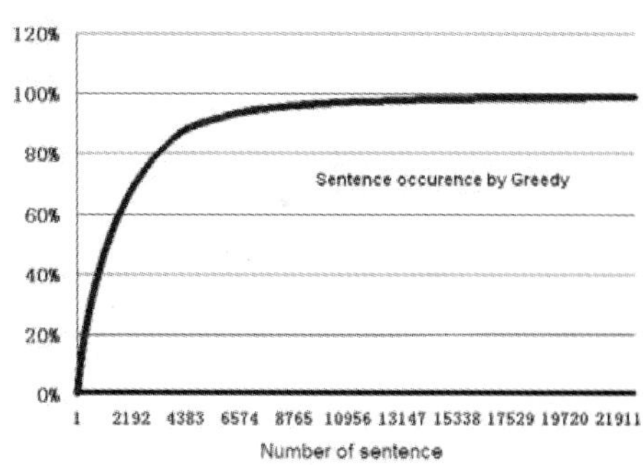

(b)

Fig. 5. (a) The distribution of word coverage when sentences occur naturally. (b) The distribution of word coverage with sentences obtained by the greedy algorithm.

(b) Constraints from prosody

Prosodic structure and linguistic structure are not identical.[17] Selkirk argues for a hierarchy of prosodic units, including phonological phrase, intonational phrase, and utterance. They do not correspond to syntactic phrases. To incorporate prosody into the corpus, each word and character should be put in different prosodic positions. If each target word is required to appear in different positions of sentences, the number of sentences selected will surely increase.

(c) Constraints from target word coverage
Words occurring in different domains have significant differences in their word frequencies. A statistical analysis of the three domains is displayed in Figure 6. The materials were selected from the technology, finance and entertainment domains from recent webpages. To cover 97% of words for all the three domains, about 19,000 words are needed. This fact implies that the 12,366 word-coverage rule can only serve a domain specific purpose, and not a general purpose.

(3) Co-articulation between words
Besides word coverage, word context coverage is also important. Both the co-articulation and tone contexts will indeed influence concatenation, particularly on voiced-to-voiced segment connections. In script design, it may not be practical to cover every possible word context. However, selecting repeated occurrences of the more frequently used words may be effective for better corpus coverage.

(4) Rare event
When the word entropy no longer increases at the text level, even when a rare event (word or any other unit) is not yet encountered, the corpus script could be said to carry sufficient information. Nevertheless, the absent, rarely-used cases will result in occasionally bad concatenation.

In Chinese, the most important source of rare event comes from rarely used syllables. These syllables are either used in ancient times or are found only in some dialects. An efficient method to include these syllables is to artificially create carrier sentences, instead of searching for their occurrences in a large corpus.

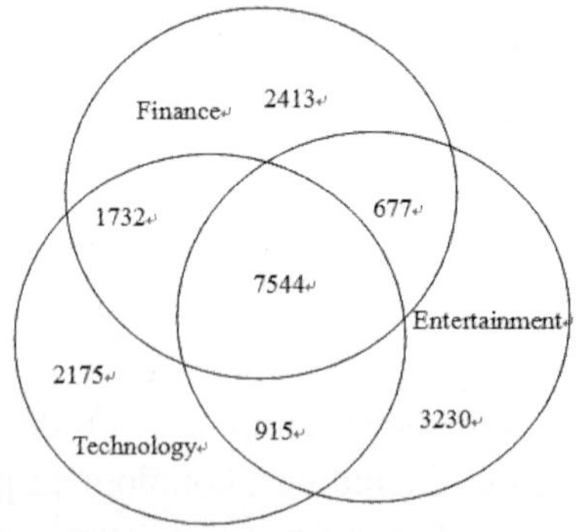

Fig. 6. The overlaps of words in three domains.

3.3. *Corpus Design for Speech Recognition*

Different from the needs of a TTS corpus, i.e. a single voice talent's speech data containing abundant prosodic details, the ASR (automatic speech recognition) speech corpus requires speech from a large number of speakers to cover as much speech segmental varieties as possible. Among the most commonly-used HMM approaches for ASR, many do avoid using pitch directly. Prosody coverage for the ASR speech corpus is therefore less important than it is for the TTS speech corpus. In ASR tasks involving speaker-independent recognition, capturing the different varieties of speakers' pronunciation is most important.

TIMIT, an English speech database for the purpose of training speech recognizers, considers acoustic-phonetic rules in connected speech.[18,19,20] The segments in this database were labeled automatically at first[21] and then in 1990s were hand-labeled by phoneticians.[22] In terms of prosody, a group of scientists and engineers with diverse backgrounds joined forces to develop a prosodic transcription system called Tone and Break Indices (ToBI).[23] With the aim of designing reading texts for a continuous speech database, the ASR corpus should cover as many phonetic phenomena across different speakers as possible in order to achieve high accuracy in the speech recognition task. There is a large amount of variability of speech unit in natural speech. With the rapid progress of speech technology, many Chinese ASR speech databases have been constructed by different research groups for their specific objectives, such as general-purpose read speech recognition, telephone channel speech recognition, spontaneous speech recognition, and so on.

3.3.1. *Phonetic Description for Mandarin Speech*

The most important issue in ASR speech corpus design is phonetic coverage. In many ASR speech corpora, such as the 863-database, the HKU-93 and the HKU-96, phonetic units of tri-phones and di-phones are taken into account.[24, 25] Since there are 38 finals and 21 initials in Mandarin speech, coverage of initial-final contexts is also easily incorporated.[26] The greedy algorithm is also useful in sentence selection.[15] In this section we detail the phonetic description of Standard Chinese (Mandarin).

Basic Phone

Thirty-seven phones, as well as their contexts, are proposed for Standard Chinese, and listed in Table 4, with their syllabic contexts in parentheses. Note that "sil" is an abbreviation for "silence", and only vowels /a, i, o, e/ can be realized as "sil" in some contexts to their left and right. There are three semi-vowels (/w, y, yv/)

in Mandarin speech. The reason why they not are listed in Table 4 is that they always occur as initials and are distinguishable from /u, i1, yv/ by their context.

Table 4. Consonant and vowel in Mandarin (in Pinyin).

Consonants	initial	b (ba,bu), c(ci,ca), ch(cha,chu), d(da,di), f(fa,fei), g(ge,gei), h(he,ha), j(ji,jin), k(ke,ka), l(la,lang), m(ma,mi), n(na,ni), p(po,pang), q(qi,qu), r(ri,rong), s(si,san), sh(shi,shui), t(te,ti), x(xia,xi), z(zi,zuo), zh(zhu,zhong)
	Nasal tail	n(an,en), ng(ong, qing)
Vowels in allophones	a1(ba,wa), a2 (an,ai), a3(ang,ao), e1(ge), e2(ei,ye), e3(en,eng), er(er) i1 (bi,xia), i2 (zi,ci,si), i3 (zhi,chi,shi), n, ng, o1(wo,po) ,o2 (ou), u(wan,bu), yv(jv,yve,yv,yvan)	
silence	sil	

There are broadly defined allophones for some vowels. For example, vowel [i] as three allophones: /i1/ as in “yi”, /i2/ as in syllables “zi, ci, si”, and /i3/ as in the syllables “zhi, chi, shi”. The low open vowel [a] is phonetically realized into three allophones: /a1/ in open syllables such as “ba”, /a2/ as in “ai, an”, and /a3/ as in “ang, ao”. Similarly, three allophones for vowel [ɤ], /e1/ as in “ge, he”, /e2/ as in “ei, ie, yve”, and /e3/ as in “en, eng”. The vowel [o], is /o1/ as in “uo”, and /o2/ as in “ou”. Within syllables, the contexts themselves will be able to identify the allophones for the above vowels. But when the influence from preceding consonants is taken into account, it is necessary to distinguish different allophones.

Diphones and Triphones

An utterance of continuous speech is structured by a series of syllables, and each syllable is made up of a series of phones. In continuous speech, each phone exists in the form of its allophones. The distinction between continuous speech and isolated words or connected words, is that these co-articulatory phenomena do not only occur between syllables but also between phrases. The connectivity of those syllables together in continuous speech is quite different from isolated syllables.

Phones are always influenced by their phonetic contexts, like syllable position, and these phones influence their adjacent phones as well. So diphones, triphones and semi-syllables have been introduced as speech units in continuous speech. Diphones capture the transitions between two adjacent segments. An inventory of several hundreds of diphones makes up a computationally manageable set. Triphones are larger alternative units that are successful in describing the variabilities and transitions in continuous speech. They were first used by the SPHNIX system in speech recognition.[7,27]

The spectrogram in Figure 7 below displays corresponding labels for phones, diphones, triphones (with the "*" indicating syllable boundaries), semi-syllables and the Pinyin transcription /la4 yue4 chu1 liu4/ (meaning, "the sixth day of the last month by the lunar calendar"). It can be seen that by using triphones as the basic unit, the two occurrences of the consonant /l/ in "la" and "liu", are labeled differently. They match different formant transition patterns when their phonetic context changes. This sample illustrates that a phonetic segment corresponds to a number of concatenating segments in a speech waveform.[28] In other words, one phonetic segment corresponds to more acoustic segments due to the existence of transitions.

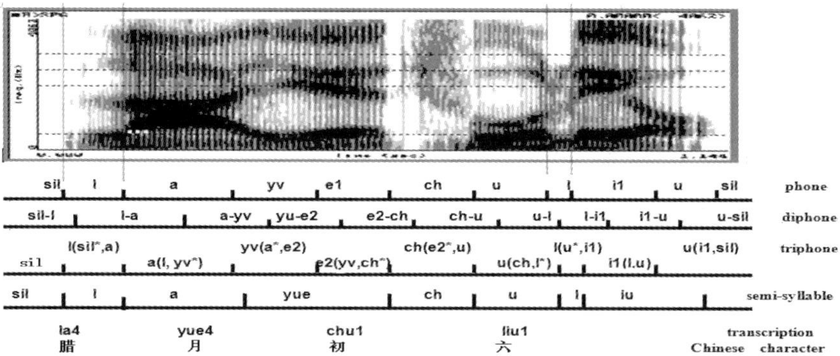

Fig. 7. Spectrogram of the utterance /la4 yue4 chu1 liu4/ and speech unit labels.

Variability in Continuous Speech

Variability in continuous speech is defined as the deviation of the phonetic characteristics of speech from their citation or canonical forms. At the segmental level, there are two kinds of variability which are either *context-dependent* variability (influenced by adjacent segments) or *context-independent* ones (originating from differences in speaking rate, style, mood, sentence patterns and the speaker's individual speech traits). At the prosodic level, variability refers to changes in fundamental frequency, duration and energy, as well as the interaction between the segment and prosody.

Continuous speech is cascaded by sequences of syllables and each of these syllables in turn consists of smaller units. To explore the phonetic phenomena in continuous speech, we must first define the basic elements of continuous speech in Standard Chinese. The phoneme is a distinctive unit in a language, and its various realizations are called allophones. Here, the phone is proposed as the minimal segment in continuous speech. In isolated words or connected words where words are separated by distinct pauses, the beginnings and ends of words are clearly marked. In continuous speech, however, word boundaries are blurred and words unfold and evolve smoothly in time with no distinct acoustic separation. This is when segmental variability emerges.

3.3.2 *The Phonetic Coverage*

Segmental Coverage

Based on the phonetic description and analysis in the previous section, the following speech units are suggested to be included in a Chinese speech corpus design.

(a) Syllables without tones;
(b) Inter-syllabic diphones;
(c) Inter-syllabic triphones;
(d) Inter-syllabic final-initial structures.

Phonetic Phenomena in Prosody

Prosody in speech plays an important role in boosting the accuracy of the continuous speech recognition, since it communicates the speaker's intentions and meanings. But the current level of prosody understanding does not enable us to manage it in the database design. We work on the assumption that prosody can be covered simply by including major sentence patterns with different syntactic structures. The relevant sentence patterns include: interrogative sentences, one word sentences, verbs + clauses, adjectives + clauses, and so on.

4. Speech Corpus Annotation

Speech corpus annotation includes preliminary annotation and extended annotation. Orthographic Chinese character transcription and orthographic tonal syllable transcription in Pinyin (or IPA) belong to the basic or preliminary annotation process. Time alignment segmentation, prosodic annotation or other kinds of annotation, such as expressive or emotional state annotation, fall under the class of extended annotation.

4.1. *Sound to Orthographic Character Transcription*

If the recorded speech is spontaneous and unscripted, Chinese characters should be transcribed with paralinguistic and non-linguistic information. Usually the transcribed characters do not need to be time-aligned with speech sound, but it is useful to align a short period of speech sound with its transcribed characters according to turns or long, silent pauses.

4.1.1. *Paralinguistic and Non-linguistic Events Transcription*

Correct paralinguistic and non-linguistic events transcription is very important in sound to orthographic character transcription. Table 5 lists some of the labels used in the RASC863 database. Contents between square brackets '[ ]' is the domain where the labeled phenomenon appears. These labels can be designed or expanded individually.

Table 5. Some examples of non-linguistic/paralinguistic phenomena labels used in RASC863.

	Phenomena	Labels	Examples
1	lengthening	[LE]	呃[MO][LE],还有那个[LE]保龄球,橄榄球等等,都是非常喜欢[SM].
2	breathing	[BR]	[BR]我的业余爱好是看书[BR].
3	laughing	[LA]	本来我也很想报那所[LA 学校].
4	crying	[CR]	[CR 他学历很高,是一名大学生]. [CR 我非常崇拜他写一手好字].
5	coughing	[CO]	[CO]到上海去看病也不会好[BR].
6	disfluency	[DS]	我跟我爱人是在一九[DS]七五年[DS]认识的.
7	noisy	[NS]	因为[NS],那里很多老鼠,爸妈就[DS],买了很多猫回来养.
8	silence (long)	[SI]	到了北京[SI],所谓的北京的几大名吃[BR],南方人吃起来,总觉得味儿不大对劲[BR].
9	modal/exclamation	[MO]	恩[MO][BR]哎[MO]我说的话题是上网的感觉.
10	smack	[SM]	天安门[SM]对面就是个高高的纪念碑,然后,往后就是毛主席的纪念堂.

4.1.2. *Accent or Dialect Annotation*

Regional accent degrees or dialectal distributions of the speakers must be correctly annotated. The accent level evaluation called the *PSC* (Putonghua Shuiping Pingce) is a Standard Chinese speaking skill test held by China's Ministry of Education. The accent levels are categorized into 3 major levels – L1: light, 'L2': medium, and 'L3': heavy – and within each level there are 2 sub-levels 'A' and 'B'. So there are 6 levels in all.

For dialect annotation, the primary dialect district or even the secondary dialectal category should be coded and labeled, such as SHD and XMD, referring to Shanghai and Xiamen dialects respectively.

4.1.3. *Dialogue Transcription*

In the transcription of dialogues, each speaker is assigned a code, for example, A, B, or C. These codes are used to indicate speaker turns, as shown below. Portions which overlap are transcribed in the form of [OV A:…; B:…].

A:怎么样？他现在考试,[OV A:成绩怎么样,啊[MO];
B:什么怎么样儿，迎春杯那初赛都没过。
[OV A:啊[MO][UC]初赛现在就[LE]赛完了哦，对,哪天;B:气死我了,赛完了已经,一月七号赛的。]

4.2. *Transcription File Format and Transcription Tools*

Format of the transcribed files can be in the form of plain text or XML format. Other than *Praat*, another recommended transcription tool is the *Transcriber* written by Claude Barras (DGA) (http://www.etca.fr/CTA/gip/Projets/Transcriber/). However, the corpus producer can develop their own transcription tools and even integrating them with more flexible functions such as characters-to-phoneme (G2P) transformation.

4.3. *Segmental Annotation*

There are two types of segmental annotation: phonetic transcription and phonetic segmentation. Phonetic transcription is often referred to as the segments transcribed phonetically without time-aligned information. The transcription has to annotate what the speaker actually said, including elisions, reductions and assimilations present in continuous speech. Phonetic segmentation refers to the annotation of the time-aligned boundaries of the segments and the annotation of sound variability of what the speaker really said.

The segmental annotation includes syllable, initial and final, and phoneme boundary identification and explicit marking of changes in the transcription caused by coarticulation between these segments (e.g. reduction or elision of vowels).

Chinese Pinyin is an effective way to transcribe Standard Chinese. But for a few reasons, it is not entirely a one-to-one mapping to the International Phonetic

Alphabet (IPA). For example, Pinyin 'i' in Standard Chinese represents the IPA sounds [i], [ʅ], [ɿ]. For accented Chinese or dialect transcription, the phonological system is primarily described in IPA. In this case, IPA is the appropriate set of symbols for labeling. For multilingual and multi-dialect speech research, several machine-readable phonetic symbols have been created to describe IPA symbols. For example, XSAMPA (http://www.phon.ucl.ac.uk/home/sampa/home.htm) and Worldbet (http://www.ling.ohio-state.edu/~edwards/worldbet.pdf) are the most widely used symbol sets. In many English speech systems, an English character or character-pair is introduced to describe an English phoneme, such as ARPAbet from the TIMIT speech corpus. For Chinese, the Institute of Linguistics, Chinese Academy of Social Sciences, has created the SAMPA-C (Chinese Speech Assessment Methods Phonetic Alphabet, http://ling.cass.cn/yuyin/product/product_9.htm) which is a Mandarin phonetic system based on the XSAMPA standard.[29] This set of phonetic symbols is a reference for creating a common symbol set for the various Chinese dialects. The symbols in C-SAMPA supports the labeling of continuous speech including the representation of consonants and vowels, tone charts, sound variations phenomena such as centralization, reduction, insertion, and so on.

However, there are shortcomings when programming with SAMPA. For instance, some special symbols used in this set, such as "\, _, !, …", can intervene with the program or cause some confusion in programming. You may design a concise phonetic symbol set for Chinese multi-dialect speech processing.

Do note that when annotating corpus for speech synthesis, if the signal of a given word is not suited for concatenative speech synthesis, the word should be preceded by the symbol '*'. Every word which presents an evident or potential problem for concatenative speech: noise (either from the speaker or external), mispronunciations, unintelligible words, word fragments, non-speech acoustic events, truncated waveforms, etc. should be annotated with the symbol '*'.

A segmental annotation example in Standard Chinese is shown in Figure 8, which includes 7 tiers or levels of information:

- HZ: Chinese orthographic characters,
- PY: orthographic tonal syllable in Pinyin,
- YJ: orthographic segmentation on tonal syllables,
- SY: phonetic segmentation on initials and finals,
- IPA: phonetic segmentation on initials and finals using IPA labels,
- SAM: phonetic segmentation on initials and finals using SAMPA-C labels,
- MIS: miscellaneous tier for paralinguistic and non-linguistic information.

An example of regional accent Chinese speech is shown in Figure 9, with four tiers of annotation: 1) HZ: Chinese character tier; 2) PY: Pinyin tier (labeled with orthographic Pinyin and tone transcription); 3) SY: Initial-final tier, labeled with the initial and final boundary of each syllable and their sound variations. The sound variations include sound addition, sound deletion, centralization, nasalization and phoneme variation. We annotated the sound variations, including phoneme and tone variation which are caused by dialectal accent with the symbol '#' in the tiers of Chinese character, syllable and initial-final; mispronunciations that are caused in other ways with the symbol '*'; and 4) MIS: miscellaneous tier for paralinguistic and non-linguistic information.

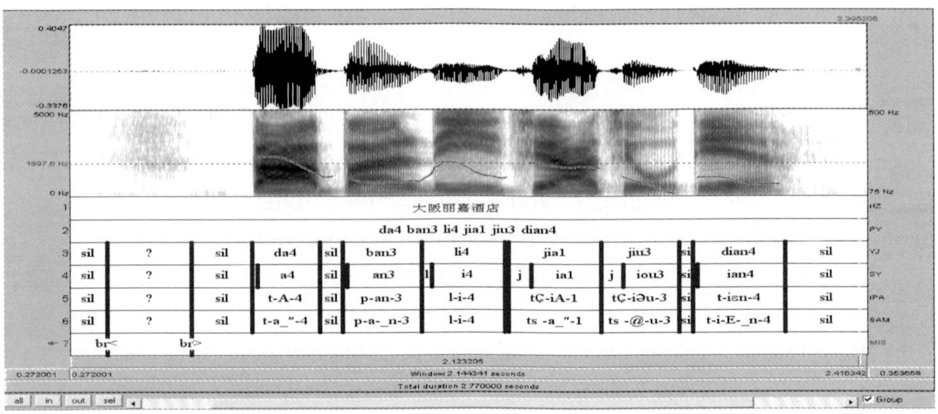

Fig. 8. An example of segmental annotation on standard Chinese with 7 tiers.

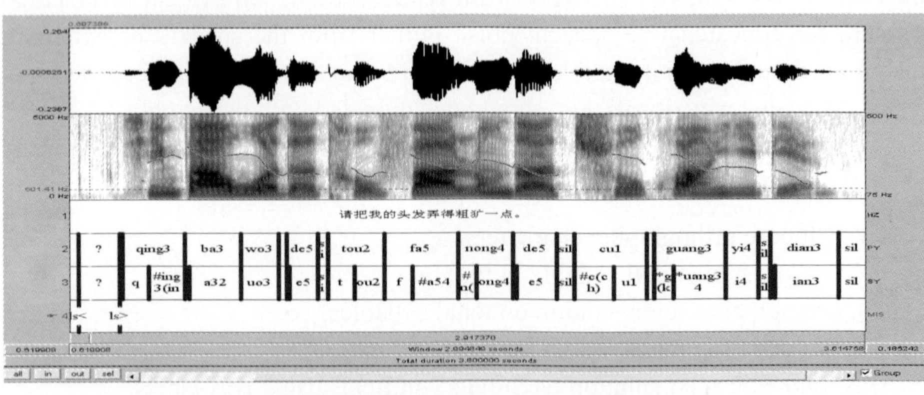

Fig. 9. An example for regional accented Chinese.

4.4. *Prosodic Annotation*

4.4.1. *Principles*

The phonetic features bearing linguistic meanings are phonologically labeled. Five principles of prosodic annotation are formulated as a guide and listed here: (a) Labeling the tonal variation, intonation, stress and prosodic structure that have linguistic functions. For example, tonal co-articulation between syllables is not labeled, while tonal co-articulation caused by stress is labeled. (b) Prosody is qualitatively annotated, while those quantitative prosodic features like duration and intensity are not annotated. (c) Uncertainty annotation is permitted to avoid providing the wrong information to the user. (d) The labels are machine-readable and the label-names easy to remember. (e) Agreement and consistency in the annotations of different transcribers should be high.

4.4.2. *Introduction to C-ToBI: A Chinese Prosodic Labeling System*

C-ToBI,[30] a ToBI-like prosodic transcription system is developed for Chinese prosodic annotation. Since 1991, when the English was created (http://www.ling.ohio-state.edu/~tobi/), many other language-specific ToBI systems have been proposed, such as J-ToBI for Japanese, K-ToBI for Korean, M-TOBI for Mandarin, and Pan-Mandarin ToBI.

The first Chinese ToBI-C system was developed in 1996 when prosodic labeling was carried out for 52 read dialogues in the 863 speech synthesis corpus.[31] But for the lack of a workable intonation theory for Chinese spontaneous speech, we had to employ different prosodic research results in our labeling system. The C-ToBI introduced here is the third version for both read and spontaneous speech labeling.

(a) *Pinyin tier*: Canonical Pinyin and tone for each syllable are labeled, e.g. 1, 2, 3 and 4, for the 4 canonical tones, and 0 for the neutral tone in Standard Chinese.
(b) *Initial and final tier*: The initial and final of each syllable are annotated in terms of sound variation by using IPA, Pinyin or SAMPA-C labeling set.
(c) *Tone and intonation tier* (T&IN): We did not have an existing, well-known intonation grammar at that time that can be used directly in our prosodic labeling activities. Intonation transcription is rather ambiguous in many Chinese prosodic labeling procedures and systems. In our system, tonal features, tonal register and range of intonation, boundary tones can be transcribed on this T&IN tier as shown in Table 6. Two examples are shown in Figures 10 and 11.

Table 6. Tone and intonation labels in C-ToBI(3.0).

Labels	Meaning
H-L, L-H, H-H L-L	Tonal features for four tones of Standard Chinese
H, L	Neutral tone features of Standard Chinese
L% H%; %L, %H	Final boundary tones; Initial boundary tones
&	Transition tone
^, !, ^^, !!	^ upstep, ^^ wide upstep; ! downstep, !! wide downstep
Re^() Re^^() Re!() Re!!()	For pitch register change, ( ) for the scope
Ra^() Ra^^() Ra!() Ra!!()	For global variation of pitch range, ( ) for the scope
H^^,H^,L!	For local variation of pitch range

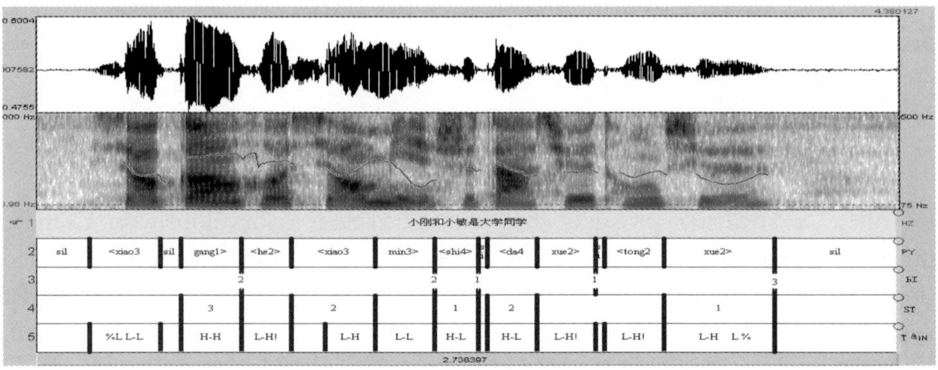

Fig. 10. An example with Pinyin (PY), break (BI), stress (ST), tone and intonation(T&IN) tiers.

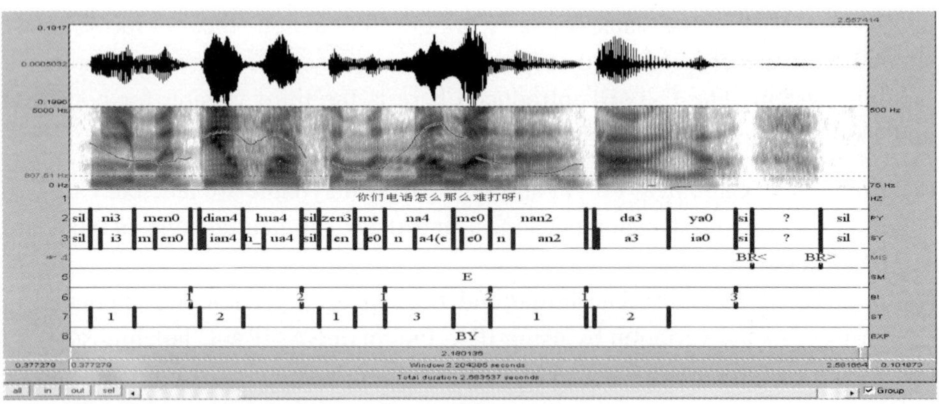

Fig. 11. An example for prosodic annotation from a spontaneous speech corpus
1- HZ: Chinese orthographic characters; 2- PY: orthographic tonal syllable in Pinyin;
3- SY: phonetic segmentation on initials and finals'
4- MIS: miscellaneous tier for paralinguistic and no-linguistic information;
5- SM: Sentence mode; 6- BI: Break index; 7- ST: Stress index;
8- EXP: expressiveness, BY stands for complaining expressions.

(d) *Break index tier*: Breaks are labeled accordingly between two syllables, whenever they are perceived by the transcriber. The location and duration of breaks are variable for the same text read by different speakers, or by the same speaker reading at different times. We define break levels into 5 categories according to the length of the perceived pause coded as the break index.
- break index = 0: the minimum break between syllables, usually breaks within a prosodic word;
- break index = 1: for prosodic word boundary;
- break index = 2: for minor prosodic phrase boundary;
- break index = 3: for major prosodic phrase (intonational phrase) boundary;
- break index = 4: for prosodic group boundary;
- 1p, 2p and 3p stand for the break produced by abnormal break like hesitation or some other acts like cough.
- "?" for uncertainty.

(e) *Stress index tier*: Stress index is coded into 4 levels (1 - 4) for hierarchical stresses corresponding to prosodic units for neutral read speech. In spontaneous speech, hierarchical stress structure can be organized as expressing various attitudes and emotions, so stress should be labeled according to the auditory and perceptual result which may be inconsistent with the prosodic structure. The symbol "@" is attached to the index for emphasis or contrastive stress.

(f) *Sentence function tier*: Four sentence types are annotated as interrogative, imperative, declarative and exclamation sentences.

(g) *Accent tier*: Regional accent is labeled with the acronym of the region, e.g. <ASH,ASH> for accented Shanghai Mandarin, and the Shanghai dialect can be annotated by <DSH,DSH>.

(h) *Turn taking tier*: Using <A A>, <B B>, ... to indicate the start and end points of each turn.

(i) *Miscellaneous tier*: Paralinguistic and non-linguistic phenomena are annotated by the symbols listed in Table 7.

4.5. *Other Associated Information Annotation or Transcription*

Besides the annotations introduced above, other information can be annotated according to the user's own needs, such as syntax, affectiveness annotation and pitch marking labeling.

For syntactic annotation, parts of speech (POS) or sentence types are often transcribed or annotated as done in speech synthesis systems. A popular tag set or annotation system for syntactic elements is postulated by Yu.[32] Annotations for speech acts, illocutionary acts or dialogue acts are typically made for dialogue corpus to explore and define the range of functional meanings associated with the utterances.[37]

Affectiveness usually consists of two subcategories: emotion and attitude. Emotion refers to the speaker's internal feeling, such as joy, anger, sadness, surprise, and so on. In contrast, attitude refers to the speaker's external behavior, such as being friendly, appreciative, apologetic, etc. The affective speech corpus incorporates two types of description – dimensional and categorical. Dimensional descriptions are associated with the emotional content as perceived by a particular subject in terms of an activation-evaluation space. A computer program called Feeltrace based on that representation allows users to generate time-varying descriptions of emotional content as they perceive it.[33] Categorical labels are decretive descriptions on the affectiveness of each clip (e.g. angry, happy etc.). In affective speech analysis and synthesis, speakers' attitudes or emotional states are often transcribed or annotated by these two descriptions. But, to date, there is no consistent affectiveness annotation framework for Chinese or other languages.

Finally, many systems also require pitch synchronous processing. For this reason, speech signals have to be labeled with pitch marks. The use of EGG signals (laryngograph) make pitch detection algorithms more reliable. Be sure that the synchronized speech and EGG signals are time-aligned, because speech signal is delayed with respect to the EGG signal due to the distance of the close-talking microphone from the larynx.

5. Conclusion

In this chapter, we described the primary principles for speech corpus design and annotation. New principles should be established and implemented because annotation conventions should be improved to keep up and cater for the development of speech technologies in the future.

References

1. S. Yang, *Mianxiang shengxue yuyinxue de putonghua yuyin hecheng jishu* (Techniques for Putonghua Phonetic Synthesis Aiming for Acoustic Phonetics), Beijing, Social Science Documentary Press, (1994).

2. A. Li , Z. Yin, et.al, "RASC863 - A Chinese Speech Corpus with Four Regional Accents", *Proceedings of ICSLT-o-COCOSDA*, New Delhi, India, (2004).
3. F. Schiel and C. Draxler, *Production and validation of speech corpora*, Bastard Verlag Munchen, Erstausgabe, (2003).
4. W. Black and N. Campbell, "Optimising selection of units from speech databases for concatenative synthesis", *Proceedings of Eurospeech 95*, vol. 1, Madrid, Spain, (1995), pp 581-584.
5. D. Klatt, "Review of text-to-speech conversion for English", *Journal of the Acoustical Society of America*, 82, (1987), pp. 737-793.
6. K. N. Stevens, "Toward formant synthesis with articulatory controls, Speech Synthesis", *Proceedings of 2002 IEEE Workshop on Speech Synthesis*, (2002), pp. 67 – 72.
7. F. Zhiwei, "Analysis of formation of Chinese terms in data processing", *Research Report in Fraunhofer Institute*, Stuttgart, (1988).
8. F. Zhiwei, *Mathematics and language*, Hu Nan Education press, (1988).
9. E. Blaauw, "The contribution of prosodic boundary marks to the perceptual difference between read and spontaneous speech", *Speech Communication* 14, (1994), pp.359-375.
10. G. Fant and Kruckenberg, "A. Preliminaries to the study of Swedish prose reading and reading style", *STL-QPSR* 2, (1989).
11. M. Rossi, "Is Syntactic Structure Prosodically Retrievable", *Proceedings of 5th European Conference of Speech Communication and Technology*, vol.1, (1997), pp. KN 1-8.
12. T. H. Cormen, C.E. Leiserson and R. L. Riverst, *Introduction to Algorithms*, The MIT Press, Cambridge, Massachussetts, (1990).
13. Jan P. H. van Santen and A. L. Buchsbaum, "Methods for Optimal Text Selection", *Proceedings of Eurospeech '97*, vol.2, (1997), pp. 557-561.
14. M. Chu, H. Peng, et.al, "Selecting non-uniform units from a very large corpus for concatenative speech synthesizer", *Proc. of ICASSP2001*, Salt Lake City, (2001).
15. L. Sun, Y. Hu, and R. Wang, "Corpus design for Chinese speech synthesis", *Proceedings of the 6th National Conference on Man Machine Speech Communication*, (2002), pp.313-317.
16. W. Zhu, W. Zhang, Q. Shi, F. Chen, H. Li, X. Ma and L. Shen, "Corpus building for data-driven TTS systems", *Proceedings of 2002 IEEE Workshop speech on Synthesis*, (2002), pp. 199- 202.
17. E. Selkirk, "On prosodic structure and its relation to syntactic structure", in: *Fretheim, T. (Ed.), Nordic Prosody 2*. TAPIR, Trodheim, (1978).
18. W. M. Fisher and G. R. Doddington, "The DARPA Speech Recognition Research Database: Specification and Status", *Proceedings of the DARPA Speech Recognition Workshop*. Palo Alto, CA, (1986), pp.93-99.
19. V. W. Zue, D. S. Cyphers, R. H. Kassel, D. H. Kaufman, H. C. Leung, M. A. Randolph, S. Seneff, J. E. Unverferth, M. and T. Wilson, "The Development: Design and Analysis of the Acoustic-Phonetic Corpus", *Proceedings of ICASSP-86*, Tokyo, Japan, (1986).
20. V. Zue, S. Seneff and J. Glass, "Speech database development at MIT: Timit and Beyond", *Speech Communication* Vol.9, No. 4, (1990), pp.351-356.
21. S. Seneff and V. Zue, "Transcription and Alignment of the TIMIT Database", *The Second Symposium on Advanced Man-Machine Interface through Spoken Language*, Oahu, Hawaii, (1988).
22. P. Keating, B. Blankenship, D. Byrd, E. Flemming, Y. Todaka, "Phonetic Analyses of the TIMIT Corpus of American English", *Proceedings ICSLP92*,vol.1, (1992), pp. 823-826.
23. K. Silverman, M. Beckman, J. Pitrelli, M. Ostendorf, C. Wightman, P. Price, J. Pierrehumbert, J. Hirschberg, "TOBI, A Standard For Labeling English Prosody", *Proceedings of the International Conference on Spoken Language Processing*, vol.2, (1992), pp.867-870.

24. W. Li, Y. Zu and C. Chan, "A Chinese Speech Database (Putonghua Corpus)", *Proceedings of SST-94*, (1994), pp.834.
25. Y. Zu, "Sentence Design for speech synthesis and speech recognition", *Proceedings of 5th European Conference of Speech Communication and Technology*, vol2., (1997), pp.743-746.
26. J. S. Sun, Z. Y. Wang, X. Wang and B. Li, "Constructing a word table for training of continuous speech", *In Proceedings of National Conference on Man Machine Speech Communication,* (Tsing Hua University Press), (in Chinese), (1995), pp.116-121.
27. K. F. Lee, *Automatic Speech Recognition: The Development of the SPHINX System*, Kluwer Academic Publishers, (1989).
28. G. Fant and J. Gauffin, *Speech Science and Technology*, translated by Zhang Jialu et. al, Commerial Press, (1994).
29. X. Chen, A. Li, et al., "An Application of SAMPA-C for Standard Chinese", *Proceedings of International Conference on Spoken Language Processing (ICSLP)*, Beijing, (2000).
30. A. Li, "Chinese Prosody and Prosodic Labeling of Spontaneous Speech", *Prosody Speech 2002*, AIX-EN-PROVENCE France, (2002).
31. A. Li, "A national database design for speech synthesis and prosodic labeling of standard Chinese", *Proceedings of oriental COCOSDA'99*, Taipei, Taiwan, (1999).
32. S. Yu, et al. *Xiandai hanyu yufa zixun cidian xiangjie* (A Thorough Interpretation of the Information on Modern Chinese Grammar), Beijing: Tsinghua University Press, (2003).
33. E. Douglas-Cowie, R. Cowie and M. Schröder, "A New Emotion Database: Considerations, Sources and Scope, In: E. Douglas-Cowie, Roddy Cowie, Marc Schröder:" *Proceedings of the ISCA Workshop on Speech and Emotion: A Conceptual Framework for Research*, Belfast, (2000), pp. 39-44.
34. C.-y. Tseng and F.-c. Chou, "A Prosodic Labeling System for Mandarin Speech Database", *XIVth International Congress of Phonetic Science,* (1999), pp.2379-2382.
35. F.-c. Chou and C.-y. Tseng, "The Design of Prosodically Oriented Mandarin Speech Database", *XIVth International Congress of Phonetic Science,* (1999), pp.2375-2377.
36. C.-y. Tseng, "Higher Level Organization and Discourse Prosody", *The Second International Symposium on Tonal Aspects of Languages (TAL 2006)*, La Rochelle, France,(2006), pp.23-34.
37. D. Gibbon, I. Mertins and R. K. Moore, *Handbook of Multimodal and Spoken Dialogue Systems*. Boston: Kluwer Academic Publishers, (2000).

Advances in Chinese Spoken Language Processing **Part II**

CSLP Technology Integration

CHAPTER 12

SPEECH-TO-SPEECH TRANSLATION

Yuqing Gao, Liang Gu and Bowen Zhou
IBM T. J. Watson Research Center
P.O. Box 218, Yorktown Heights, NY 10598
Email: {yuqing, lianggu, zhou}@us.ibm.com

In this chapter, the speech-to-speech translation problem is introduced and presented along with the research efforts and approaches towards a solution. Two different statistical approaches for speech-to-speech translation are described in considerable detail. The concept-based approach focuses on understanding, extracting the semantic meaning from the input speech, and then re-generating the same meaning in the output language. The approach uses requires a huge amount of human effort for linguistic information annotation, although the amount of annotated data needed is not very large (in our experiment only 10,000 sentences are annotated for each language). Detailed work on how to improve the natural language generation translation quality is presented. The second approach, a novel framework for performing phrase-based and finite-state transducer based approach, emphasizes both system development and search speed as well as memory efficiency. It is significantly faster and more memory efficient than existing approaches. The entire translation model is statically optimized with a single weighted finite-state transducer (WFST). The approach is particularly suitable for converged real-time translation on scalable computing devices, ranging from high-end servers to mobile PDAs. This approach exploits un-annotated parallel corpora at the cost of potential meaning loss and the requirement of large amount of parallel text data (in our experiment 240K sentences, in the order of millions of words for each language, are used).

1. Introduction

Automatic speech-to-speech translation (S2ST) aims to facilitate communication between people who speak different languages and due to the increasingly globalizing world economy, humanitarian services and national security, there is an ever-increasing demand for speech-to-speech translation capability. While substantial progress has been made over the past decades in each of the related research areas of Automatic Speech Recognition (ASR), Machine Translation (MT), Natural Language Processing and Text-To-Speech synthesis (TTS), multilingual natural speech translation remains a challenge for human speech and language technologies. Conventional translation technologies, designed for translation of written text, are not optimal when translating conversational speech, since casual spontaneous speech often contains strong disfluencies, imperfect syntax and no punctuations. The accurate recognition of spontaneous, conversational speech and speech with background noise are still major challenges. As a result, the outputs of speech recognizers often contain recognition errors, making robust and accurate speech translation even more difficult.

Significant amount of research effort has been devoted to automatic S2ST. Promising approaches have been proposed to tackle the specific problem of spoken language translation, although some efforts have been channelled towards integrating the translation component developed for written text translation into S2ST. The interlingua approach, which uses language-independent knowledge representations, i.e., interlinguas, to represent semantic meaning and facilitate translation, does have potential in speech translation. The use of interlinguas, to some extent, can mitigate the effects of speech recognition errors and ungrammatical inputs and disfluencies due to the language-independent nature of *semantic meaning representation*. As the development complexity of S2ST grows linearly with the number of languages involved, the interlingua approach potentially reduces the development effort for handling new languages. The approach has been explored extensively within the Consortium for Speech Translation Advanced Research (C-STAR) by CMU,[1,2] ATR,[3] ITC-IRST,[4] CAS,[5] and CLIPS,[6] to name a few. However, there still are significant practical issues with this approach due to the difficulty in building an efficient and comprehensive semantic knowledge representation formalism.[7] Two works[8,9] introduced statistical modeling approaches to learn concept representation from an annotated corpus.

Another approach with good potential is based on statistical MT methodology, originally proposed for written-text translation by an IBM group.[10] It was then applied to spoken language translation by the RWTH group[11,12,13] and used in the VerbMobil project.[14] This approach uses a channel-decoding model and thereby enables translation between arbitrary pairs of languages that is independent of individual language properties. The SMT approach is widely adopted in the recently-launched DARPA GALE program[15] for broadcast speech translation. Nevertheless, to maintain its translation accuracy, the statistical S2ST approach requires a large amount of spoken, conversational training data in the form of parallel bilingual corpora, which are usually very difficult to obtain, especially if the languages involved are low in language resources. There are also other methods such as the Spoken Language Translator (SLT)[16] and Finite-State Transducer based approaches,[17,18,19,20,21] and example-based approaches.[22]

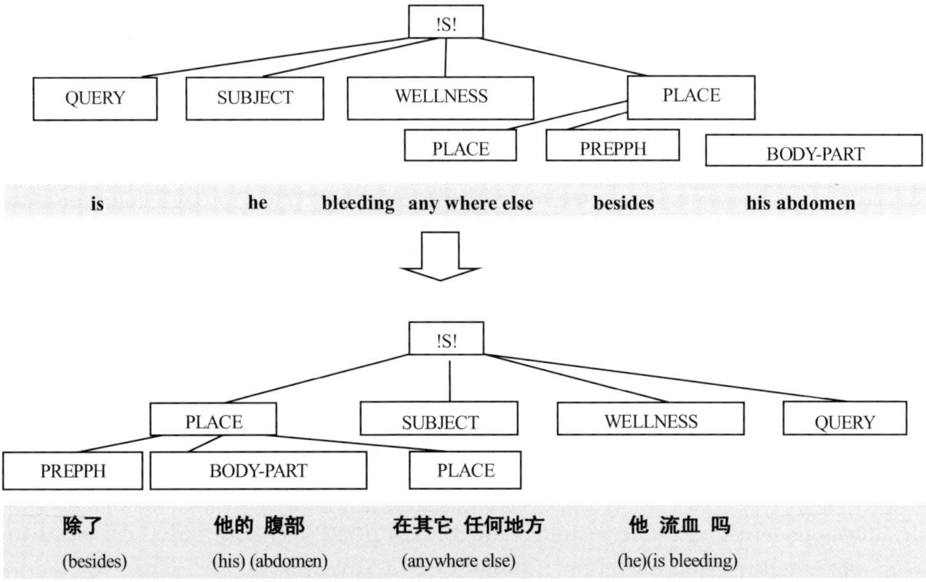

Fig. 1. Example of Concept-based English-to-Chinese Translation.

Research on speech translation from and into Chinese was started in late 1990's by the CAS group.[23,24,25] They investigated both template-based and interlingua-based translation approaches. They also used dialogue management to guide the translation, because in an interactive dialogue, a dialogue manager can help to disambiguate some ambiguous input speech.

We have worked on speech-to-speech translation between English and Mandarin Chinese in the DARPA CAST and DARPA TransTac programs. Through these projects, we developed two statistical approaches for S2ST.[26] One approach is based on tree-structured semantic/syntactic representations, or concepts, and the other is a phrase-based translation using finite-state transducers. The research work since 2001[8] also resulted in a high-performance S2ST system, MASTOR, short for Multilingual Automatic Speech-to-Speech Translator. Since MASTOR has been the test-bed for all the S2ST research work at IBM, we will present these two approaches, as well as the MASTOR system in this chapter.

1.1. *Summary of the Two Translation Approaches*

An example of English-to-Chinese translation using the statistical interlingua approach[9] is illustrated in Figure 1. The source English sentence and the corresponding Chinese translation are represented by a set of concepts - {PLACE, SUBJECT, WELLNESS, QUERY, PREPPH, BODY-PART}. Some of the concepts (such as PLACE, WELLNESS and BODY-PART) are semantic representations, while some others (such as PREPPH, representing prepositional phrases) are syntactic representations. There are also concepts (such as SUBJECT and QUERY) that represent both semantic and syntactic information. Note that although the source-language and target-language sentences share the same set of concepts, their tree structures could be significantly different because of the distinct nature of these two languages (i.e., English and Chinese). Therefore, in our approach, a natural language generation (NLG) algorithm, and in particular, a natural concept generation (NCG) algorithm, is required to transform the tree structures in the source language into appropriate tree structures in the target language, for a reliable source-to-target language translation.

Finite state methods have recently been widely applied in various speech and language processing applications.[27] Of particular interest are the recent efforts in approaching the task of machine translation using Weighted Finite State Transducers (WFST). Various translation methods have been implemented using WFST in the literature. Among them, Knight *et al.*[28] described a system based on word-to-word statistical translation models in the light of Brown *et al.*'s[10] work. Bangalore *et al.*[29] proposed to apply WFST to select and reorder lexical items, and Kumar *et al.*[30] implemented the alignment template translation models using WFST. One of the reasons why WFST-based approaches are favored is because of the availability of mature and efficient algorithms for general-purpose decoding and optimization. For the task of S2ST where our ultimate goal is to obtain a direct translation from source speech to target language, the WFST framework is even more attractive as it provides the additional advantages of integrating speech recognition and machine translation more coherently. In addition, the nature of WFST that combines cascaded models together as compositions offers an elegant framework that is able to incorporate heterogeneous statistical knowledge from multiple sources. This should be particularly valuable when the translation task is further complicated by the presence of disfluent, conversational speech and recognition errors. On the other hand, compared with word level SMT,[10] phrase-based methods explicitly take word contexts into consideration to build translation models. Koehn *et al.*[31] compared several schemes proposed by various researchers regarding how to establish phrase-level correspondences and they showed that all of these methods performed consistently better compared to word-based approaches. In this work, we propose a novel framework for performing phrase-based statistical machine translation using weighted finite-state transducers (WFST's) that is significantly faster than existing frameworks while still being memory-efficient. In particular, we represent the entire translation model with a single WFST that is statically optimized, in contrast to previous work that represents the translation model as multiple WFST's that must be composed on the fly. While the language model must still be dynamically combined with the translation model, we describe a new decoding algorithm[32] that can be viewed as an optimized implementation of dynamic composition.

2. Brief Description of the IBM MASTOR System

The general framework of our MASTOR system is illustrated in Figure 2.

The core speech recognition algorithms for both English and Mandarin are inherited from the IBM ViaVoice large-vocabulary dictation systems.[33,34] Both English and Mandarin baseline ASR systems are developed for large-vocabulary continuous speech and trained on over 200 hours of speech collected from over 2,000 speakers for each language. Phone-based hidden Markov models (HMMs) were used with approximately 3,000 context-dependent states and 40,000 Gaussian distributions. A cepstral feature vector was extracted every 10 ms as the acoustic features, followed by a transformation of linear discriminative analysis. Tri-gram language models (LMs) trained from millions of words of broad-domain text data are used for both languages as baseline language models. Domain specific, semantic class based language models trained over in-domain text corpus are combined with the general-purpose baseline LMs for higher recognition accuracy. While the domain-specific LMs try to capture the in-domain conversational style and enhance the coverage of the specific domain, the general-purpose LMs enlarge the system coverage and make the speech recognizers more robust by smoothing the domain-specific LMs.

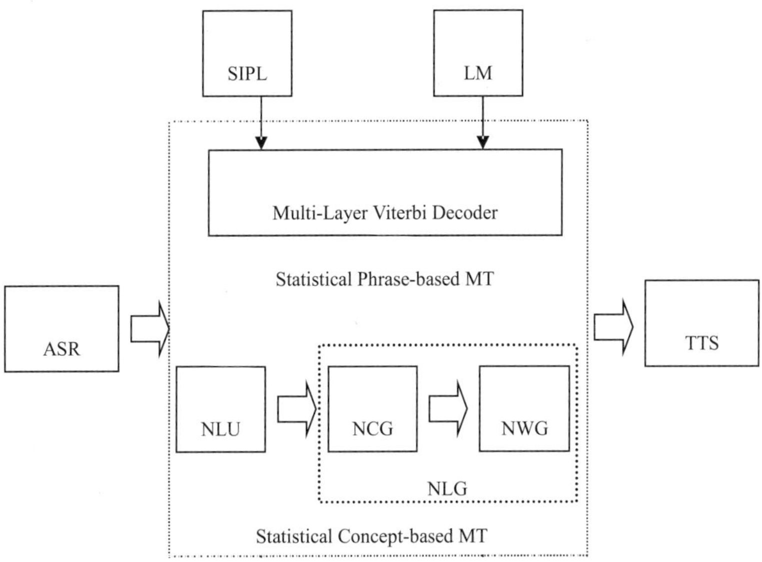

Fig. 2. General framework of IBM MASTOR system.

The core NLU engine was originally developed for the IBM Conversational Telephony system,[35] and later modified to accommodate the specific needs of S2ST tasks. A trainable, phrase-slicing and variable substitution TTS system is adopted from the IBM Phrase Splicing system[36] to synthesize Mandarin or English speech from translated sentences.

The statistical concept-based translation consists of three cascaded components: natural language understanding (NLU), natural concept generation (NCG) and natural word generation (NWG). The NLU process extracts the meaning of the sentence in the source language by evaluating a large set of potential parse trees based on pre-trained statistical models. The NCG generates a set of structural concepts in the target language according to the semantic parse tree derived from the NLU process in the source language.[9] The NWG process generates a word sequence in the target language using the structural concepts from NCG and a tag-based word-to-word translation dictionary or an annotated parallel corpus.[37] NCG and NWG together constitute the Natural Language Generation (NLG) process.

In parallel, an alternative is the statistical phrase-based approach. The target translation can be obtained from a multi-layer Viterbi search, given the Statistical Integrated Phrase Lattices (SIPL) and a statistical language model, which is a novel framework for performing phrase-based statistical machine translation.[32] An IBM-internal finite-state transducer toolkit[38] is used for the development.

3. Statistical Concept-Based Translation Approach Using NLU and NLG

3.1. *Statistical NLU Parser*

The NLU process in MASTOR is realized through a decision tree based statistical semantic parser.[39] Through this method, the statistical parser incorporates semantic information into the parsing model via a decision tree algorithm, and uses a hidden derivational model to maximize the amount of semantic information available. A stack-decoding algorithm is further applied to efficiently search through the immense space of possible parses. In our NLU analysis, the semantic parser examines the ASR output and determines the meaning of the sentence by evaluating a large set of potential trees in a bottom-up left-to-right manner. The parse hypothesis with the highest score according to the pre-trained statistical models is selected.

3.2. *Semantic Annotation and Treebank*

Both statistical NLU and NLG models are trained on treebanks, which are semantically annotated text corpora. The treebank in each language is utilized for the training of NLU and NLG models. For the translation from English to Mandarin, the NLU models are designed to analyze ASR-transcribed English sentences, while the NLG models are designed to generate Mandarin sentences as a translation of the input English. Similar schemes are applied in the other direction, where the NLU and NLG models are trained over Mandarin and English treebanks, respectively. Therefore, the annotation design needs to take both NLU and NLG modeling into account.

Current English and Chinese corpora include 10,000 sentences for each language in the domain of security and emergency medical care. 68 distinct labels and 144 distinct tags are used to capture the semantic information. An example of an annotated English sentence is illustrated in Figure 3. In this parse tree, "FOOD" is a semantic concept represented by one or a group of words, while "food" is a *tag* that refers to a semantic concept represented by only one word. Similar to the example in Figure 1, the concepts and tags in Figure 3 are not designed to exclusively represent semantic meanings and may represent syntactic information as well, such as those shown in the label of "SUBJECT" and the tag of "query". While the semantic information remains the main annotation target, syntactic-related labels and tags are used to group the semantically less important words into classes, which have been to be found very useful in the NLG procedure to deal with the serious data sparseness problem. In practice, the design and selection of language-

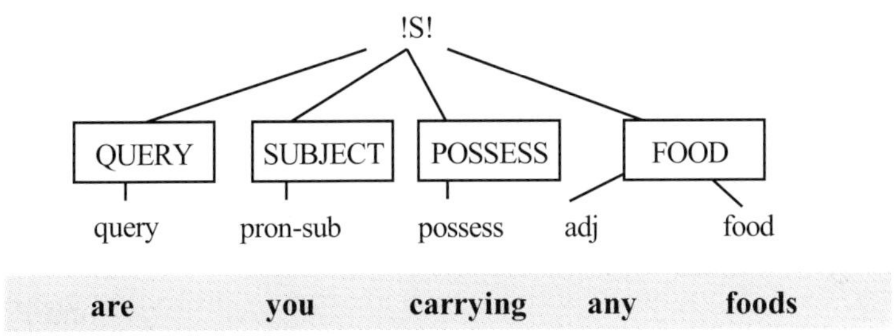

Fig. 3. Example of (Concept-based) Semantic Parse Tree.

independent concepts remain labor-intensive, time-consuming, yet very important in our concept-based approach, depending on the domain in which the translation system is used. The concepts have to be not only broad enough to cover all intended meanings in the source sentence, but also sufficiently informative so that a target sentence can be generated with the right word senses and in a grammatically correct manner. On the other hand, these concepts need to be defined as concisely as possible, since the smaller the total number of distinct concepts, the less the effort will be in the annotation procedure, and the greater the accuracy and robustness of the statistical NLU and NLG algorithms will be.

The current annotation process in MASTOR is performed manually to a large extent. Automatic annotation methods are under investigation and will be used for annotating the ever-expanding multilingual training corpora.

3.3. *NWG and Word Sense Disambiguation*

Word sense disambiguation (WSD) is a common and important issue in Natural Word Generation (NWG). Initial WSD in our system is accomplished by designing translation dictionaries that take into account the semantic meanings and senses of the words to be translated. In most cases, each distinguishable sense is represented by a distinct tag in the treebank as described in Figure 3. In our tag-based dictionary, the number of entries for a word equals the total number of distinct tags annotated to that word in the treebank, since we observed that in most cases different tag-represented word senses correspond to different translations in the target language. For example, the two most common senses for the word "leave" as a verb are "go_away" and "leave_behind". The corresponding Chinese translations of these two senses are "离开" and "留下", respectively. Hence, two entries are designed, along with other entries, for the verb "leave" in our English-to-Mandarin dictionary as shown in Table 1.

Table 1. Example of word sense disambiguation (WSD) using semantic tags.

English	Tag	Chinese
Leave	go_away	离开
Leave	leave_behind	留下

However, for a rather broad domain such as security protection and emergency medical care in the DARPA Babylon/CAST program, our semantic annotation is deliberately designed to be "unrefined" in order to maintain the simplicity of the annotation. As a result, the tag-based dictionary is not sophisticated enough to carry all the semantic information needed to disambiguate all the senses and the corresponding translations. Our compromise solution is to cluster all senses into classes, keep some dictionary entries with multiple translations corresponding to different word meanings, and leave some of the disambiguation task to a language model based post-processing approach proposed in Liu *et al.*.[40] In this approach, a domain-specific N-gram language model is derived from existing general N-gram language models as well as available domain-specific text data. This language model is then used to re-score all possible word translations in a post-processing manner and generate the best hypothesis as the selected word translation. More recently, we proposed a novel maximum-entropy based statistical natural word generation[37] that takes into account both the word level and concept level context information in the source and target languages.

3.4. *Advantages and Challenges in Statistical Concept-based Approach*

Our unique statistical concept-based translation approach translates an ASR output by understanding the meaning of the sentence. While the concepts are comparable to interlingua, our method is significantly different from typical interlingua-based speech translation methods. In our approach, the intended meanings are represented by a set of *language-independent* concepts (as in conventional interlingua approaches) but organized in a *language-dependent* tree structure (different from conventional interlingua approaches). While the total number of concepts may usually be limited to alleviate the impact of data sparseness (especially for new domains), there are no constraints on the structures of the conceptual trees. Therefore, compared to traditional interlingua-based speech translation approaches, our conceptual-tree-based approach could achieve more flexible meaning preservation with wider coverage and, hence, higher robustness and accuracy on translation tasks in limited domains. This, however, is at the cost of additional challenges in the appropriate transformation of conceptual trees between source and target languages.

One major challenge in concept-based S2ST is the generation of concepts in the target language via a *natural concept generation* (NCG) process. As the concept structures are language-dependent, errors in concept generation could greatly distort the meaning to be expressed in the target language, particularly in conversational speech translations where, in most cases, only a few concepts are conveyed in the messages to be translated. Therefore, accurate and robust NCG is viewed as an essential step towards high-performance concept-based spoken language translation.

While NCG approaches can be rule-based or statistical, we prefer the latter because of its trainability, scalability and portability. One such approach based on maximum-entropy (ME) criterion was preliminarily presented in our previous work.[8] A critical problem yet to be solved in our ME-based translation approach is feature selection. In theory, the principle of maximum entropy does not directly concern itself with the issue of feature selection.[41] It merely provides a framework to combine constraints of both source and target languages into a translation model. In reality, however, the feature selection problem is crucial to the performance of ME-based approaches, since the universe of possible constraints (or features) is typically in the thousands or even millions for natural language processing. Another crucial component of NCG is the generation process. The robustness of this process becomes a serious concern if more sophisticated features are applied to our ME-based generation framework.

4. Statistical Natural Language Generation

4.1. *Concept Generation*

Let C denote the structural concept set derived from NLU parser in the source language, and S denote the corresponding structural concept set in the target language, as both illustrated in Figure 1. If $p(S|C)$ denotes the probability that the structural concepts S occur in the translated sentence, given that C is the structural concepts in the input sentence, then the natural concept generation procedure should decide in favor of a structural concept set $\hat{S}$.

$$\hat{S} = \arg\max_{S} \; p(S|C) \tag{1}$$

That is, the statistical concept generator will pick the most likely structural concepts in the target language given the parsed structural concepts in the source language. $p(S|C)$ may be optimally selected by maximizing the conditional entropy:

$$H(p) \equiv -\sum_{(C,S)\in X} p(C)\,p(S|C)\log p(S|C) \tag{2}$$

where X is the training data that consists of pairs of structural concept sets in the source and target languages. If $\hat{S}$ is determined based on Equations 1 and 2, we refer to the corresponding generation procedure as a Maximum Entropy based (ME-based) NCG procedure.

Our proposed ME-based NCG procedure further consists of two closely related subroutines: 1) Concept sequence generation at each node of the source-language parse tree, and, 2) Generation of target-language semantic tree via recursive structural generation.

4.1.1. *Concept Generation at the Sequence Level*

The sequence level generation was proposed[8,42] as an extension of the "NLG2" algorithm described by Ratnaparkhi.[43] During natural concept sequence generation, the concept sequences in the target language are generated sequentially according to the output of the NLU parser. Each new concept is generated based on the local N-grams of the up-to-date generated concept sequence and the subset of the input concept sequence that has not yet appeared in the generated sequence.

Let us assume that the flat concept sequence produced from NLU parser in the source language is $C = \{c_1, c_2, \ldots, c_M\}$. Let $S = \{s_1, s_2, \ldots, s_N\}$ denote the corresponding concept sequence in the target language. Using the chain rule of probability theory, Equation 1 can be formally decomposed as

$$p(S|C) = \prod_{n=1}^{N} p(s_n|c_1, c_2, \ldots, c_M, s_1, s_2, \ldots, s_{n-1}), \tag{3}$$

where $p(s_n|c_1,c_2,\ldots,c_M,s_1,s_2,\ldots,s_{n-1})$ is the probability that s_n will be generated given that the concept sequence in the source language is $C=\{c_1,c_2,\ldots,c_M\}$ and that concept sequence $\{s_1,s_2,\ldots,s_{n-1}\}$ were generated previously.

In reality, the estimation of $p(s_n|c_1,c_2,\ldots,c_M,s_1,s_2,\ldots,s_{n-1})$ is difficult since $(c_1,c_2,\ldots,c_M,s_1,s_2,\ldots,s_{n-1})$ may occur only a few times or may never occur at all in the training corpora, and hence involves a severe data sparseness problem. Alternatively, one can use $(c_1,c_2,\ldots,c_M,s_{n-1},s_{n-2})$ to approximate it as in Equation 4.

$$p(S|C)=\prod_{n=1}^{N} p(s_n|c_1,c_2,\ldots,c_M,s_{n-2},s_{n-1}), \tag{4}$$

Under this approximation, in order to generate the next new concepts s_{n+1}, the conditional probability of a concept candidate is defined and computed as

$$p(s|c_m,s_n,s_{n-1})=\frac{\prod_k \alpha_k^{g\left(\vec{f}_k^{(4)},s,c_m,s_n,s_{n-1}\right)}}{\sum_{s'\in V}\prod_k \alpha_k^{g\left(\vec{f}_k^{(4)},s',c_m,s_n,s_{n-1}\right)}}$$
$$c_m\in C=\{c_1,c_2,\ldots,c_M\} \tag{5}$$

where s is the concept candidate to be generated, c_m is a concept in the remaining concept set in the source language, s_n and s_{n-1} are the previous two concepts in s. V is the set of all possible concepts that can be generated. $\vec{f}_k^{(4)}=\left(s_{+1}^k,c^k,s_0^k,s_{-1}^k\right)$ is the k-th four-dimensional feature consisting of uni-gram $\left\{c^k\right\}$ in the source concept sequence and tri-gram $\left\{s_{+1}^k,s_0^k,s_{-1}^k\right\}$ in the target sequence. α_k is a probability weight corresponding to each feature $\vec{f}_k$. The value of α_k is always positive and is optimized over a training corpus by maximizing the overall logarithmic likelihood, i.e.,

$$\alpha_k=\arg\max_{\alpha}\sum_{l=1}^{L}\sum_{s\in q_l}\sum_{m}\log\left[p(s|c_m,s_n,s_{n-1})\right] \tag{6}$$

where q_l is a concept sequence in the source language and $Q=\{q_l,1\le l\le L\}$ is the total set of concept sequences. The optimization process can be accomplished via the Improved Iterative Scaling algorithm using the maximum entropy criterion described in Ratnaparkhi.[43]

$g(\cdot)$ is a binary test function defined as

$$g\left(\vec{f}_k^{(4)},s,c_m,s_n,s_{n-1}\right)=\begin{cases}1 & \text{if } \vec{f}_k^{(4)}=(s,c_m,s_n,s_{n-1})\\ 0 & \text{otherwise}\end{cases} \tag{7}$$

Using Equations 5, 6 and 7, s_{n+1} is generated by selecting the concept candidate with highest probability, i.e.,

$$s_{n+1} = \arg\max_{s \in V} \left\{ \prod_{m=1}^{M} p\left(s \middle| c_m, s_n, s_{n-1}\right) \right\} \tag{8}$$

Please note that the re-ordering of a subset of concepts is only part of the generation procedure. The generated concept sequence may have a different number of concepts, i.e., there may be insertion and deletion of concepts in the generated sequences. Therefore, the number of concepts generated in S could be different from the number of concepts in the input sequence in the source language. To reduce computational complexity, we constrain the maximum number (denoted as N) of concepts that may be generated.

An example of primary-level (or main level) concept sequence generation is depicted in Figure 4 when translating the English sentence in Figure 1 into Chinese.

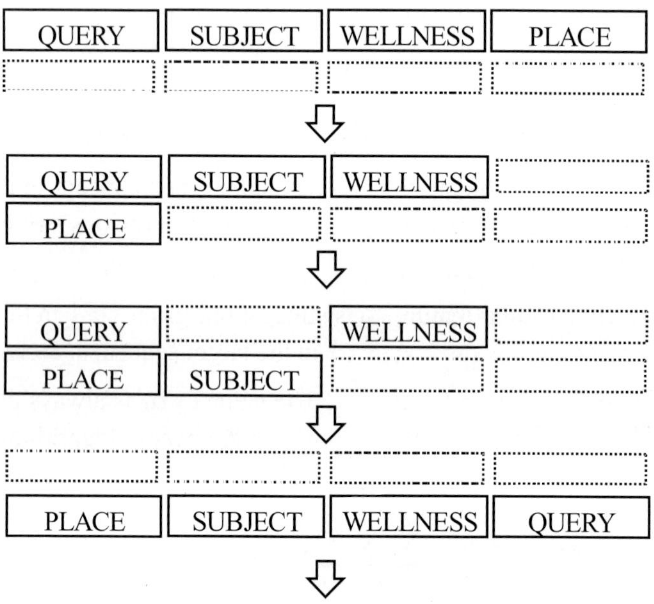

Fig. 4. Example of Concept Sequence Generation during translation of English sentence "is he bleeding anywhere else besides his abdomen" as illustrated in Figure 1.

4.1.2. *Structural Concept Sequence Generation*

The algorithms described above only deal with the concept generation of a single sequence. To generate multiple sequences at different structural levels, a recursive structural concept sequence generation algorithm is proposed as follows:

(1) Traverse each flat unprocessed concept sequence in the semantic parse tree in a bottom-up, left-to-right manner;
(2) For each unprocessed concept sequence in the parse tree, generate an optimal concept sequence in the target language based on the procedure described above; after each concept sequence is processed, mark the root-node of this sequence as "visited";
(3) Repeat step (2) until all parser branches in the source language are processed;
(4) Replace nodes with their corresponding output sequence to form a complete concept tree for the output sentence.

4.2. *Forward-Backward Modeling*

The concept generation model described in Equations 5–8 generates the concepts in the target language in a left-to-right (or *forward*) manner. This is a common statistical modeling strategy in many pattern recognition and signal processing applications where the left context information contributes the most to the system performance. One well-known example is the left-to-right HMM which is widely used in speech recognition.[44] However, in the concept generation process we discuss here, the left context information may not be dominant over the right context information. In many cases, the backward generation using right context information can be beneficial as observed from our generation experiments.

The concept sequence generation scheme described in Section 4.1 can be viewed as a forward generation model. Assume $C^{fwd} = \left\{c_1^{fwd}, c_2^{fwd}, \ldots, c_M^{fwd}\right\}$ is the remaining concept set in the source language and $S_n^{fwd} = \left\{s_1^{fwd}, s_2^{fwd}, \ldots, s_n^{fwd}\right\}$ is the set of n concepts in the target language that have already been generated. When generating the next new concept s_{n+1}^{fwd}, the conditional probability of a concept candidate in Equation 5 may be re-defined based on a forward generation model M_{fwd} as

$$p\left(s^{fwd}|M_{fwd}, c_m^{fwd}, s_n^{fwd}, s_{n-1}^{fwd}\right) = \frac{\prod_{k=1}^{K_{fwd}} \left\{ \left[\alpha_k^{fwd}\right]^{g\left(\vec{f}_k^{fwd}, s^{fwd}, c_m^{fwd}, s_n^{fwd}, s_{n-1}^{fwd}\right)} \right\}}{\sum_{s' \in V} \prod_{k=1}^{K_{fwd}} \left\{ \left[\alpha_k^{fwd}\right]^{g\left(\vec{f}_k^{fwd}, s'^{fwd}, c_m^{fwd}, s_n^{fwd}, s_{n-1}^{fwd}\right)} \right\}} \tag{9}$$

$$M_{fwd} = \left\{ \vec{f}_k^{fwd}, \alpha_k^{fwd} | 1 \le k \le K_{fwd} \right\} \tag{10}$$

where $\overrightarrow{f}_k^{fwd}$ and α_k^{fwd} are the k-th feature and its corresponding probability weight that are equivalent to those defined in Equations 7 and 6, respectively.

Using Equations 9 and 10, s_{n+1}^{fwd} may be selected via the forward generation model M_{fwd} as

$$s_{n+1}^{fwd} = \arg\max_{s \in V} \left\{ \prod_{m=1}^{M} p\left(s^{fwd} | M_{fwd}, c_m^{fwd}, s_n^{fwd}, s_{n-1}^{fwd} \right) \right\} \tag{11}$$

Similar to the above forward generation model, we propose a backward generation model M_{bwd} in which the generation direction is reversed. More specifically, assume $C^{bwd} = \{c_1^{bwd}, c_2^{bwd}, \ldots, c_M^{bwd}\}$ is the remaining concept set in the source language and $S_{N-n+1}^{bwd} = \{s_n^{bwd}, s_{n+1}^{bwd}, \ldots, s_N^{bwd}\}$ is the set of $N - n + 1$ concepts in the target language that have already been generated. To generate a new concept s_{n-1}^{bwd}, the conditional probability of a concept candidate based on a backward generation model M_{bwd} is defined as

$$p\left(s^{bwd} | M_{bwd}, c_m^{bwd}, s_n^{bwd}, s_{n+1}^{bwd} \right) = \frac{\prod_{k=1}^{K_{bwd}} \left\{ \left[\alpha_k^{bwd}\right]^{g\left(\overrightarrow{f}_k^{bwd}, s^{bwd}, c_m^{bwd}, s_n^{bwd}, s_{n+1}^{bwd}\right)} \right\}}{\sum_{\bar{s} \in V} \prod_{k=1}^{K_{bwd}} \left\{ \left[\alpha_k^{bwd}\right]^{g\left(\overrightarrow{f}_k^{bwd}, \bar{s}^{bwd}, c_m^{bwd}, s_n^{bwd}, s_{n+1}^{bwd}\right)} \right\}} \tag{12}$$

$$M_{bwd} = \left\{ \alpha_k^{bwd}, \overrightarrow{f}_k^{bwd} \, | 1 \le k \le K_{bwd} \right\} \tag{13}$$

The best candidate s_{n-1}^{bwd} is thus determined as

$$s_{n-1}^{bwd} = \arg\max_{s \in V} \left\{ \prod_{m=1}^{M} p\left(s^{bwd} | M_{bwd}, c_m^{bwd}, s_n^{bwd}, s_{n-1}^{bwd} \right) \right\} \tag{14}$$

To exploit both left and right context information, we propose a new statistical forward-backward modeling (FBM) method[9] based on the forward and backward models described above. Given the input concept sequence $C = \{c_1, c_2, \ldots, c_M\}$ in the source language, the conditional probability of a concept sequence candidate

$S = \{s_1, s_2, \ldots, s_N\}$ based on FBM is defined and computed as

$$
\begin{aligned}
p(S|C) &= p\left(M_{fwd}\right) \cdot p\left(S|C, M_{fwd}\right) + p\left(M_{bwd}\right) \cdot p\left(S|C, M_{bwd}\right) \\
&= \lambda_{fwd} \cdot p\left(S|C, M_{fwd}\right) + \lambda_{bwd} \cdot p\left(S|C, M_{bwd}\right) \\
&= \lambda_{fwd} \prod_{n=1}^{N} \prod_{m=1}^{M} p\left(s_n^{fwd} | M_{fwd}, c_m^{fwd}, s_{n-1}^{fwd}, s_{n-2}^{fwd}\right) \\
&+ \lambda_{bwd} \prod_{n=N}^{1} \prod_{m=1}^{M} p\left(s_n^{bwd} | M_{bwd}, c_m^{bwd}, s_{n+1}^{bwd}, s_{n+2}^{bwd}\right)
\end{aligned} \tag{15}
$$

where M_{fwd} and M_{bwd} are the forward and backward generation models, respectively. $p\left(M_{fwd}\right)$ and $p\left(M_{bwd}\right)$ are the corresponding prior probabilities and set as λ_{fwd} and λ_{bwd}, where $\lambda_{fwd} + \lambda_{bwd} = 1$.

A logarithmic variation of Equation 15 is further proposed below.

$$
\log p(S|C) \approx \lambda_{fwd} \cdot \log p\left(S|C, M_{fwd}\right) + \lambda_{bwd} \cdot \log p\left(S|C, M_{bwd}\right) \tag{16}
$$

The best concept sequence is generated in the target language by choosing the sequence candidate with the highest probability based on FBM, i.e.,

$$
\hat{S} = \arg\max_{S} p(S|C) \tag{17}
$$

4.3. *Improving Feature Selection*

In the feature set $\vec{f}_k^{(4)}$ defined in Equation 7, the order of concepts in the input sequence is discarded to alleviate performance degradation caused by sparse training data. However, there are cases where the same concepts need to be generated into two different sequences depending on the order of the input sequence, such as "move the vehicle (ACTION VEHICLE)" vs. "the vehicle moves (VEHICLE ACTION)". In these cases, generation errors are inevitable with the current feature used. We augment the feature set in Equation 7 with a new set of features proposed in Gu *et al.*[9] as $\vec{f}_k^{(5)} = (s_{+1}, c_0, c_{+1}, s_0, s_{-1})$, where c_0 and c_{+1} are two sequential concepts in the source language. Accordingly, the conditional probability of a concept candidate and the probability weights in Equations 5 and 6 are modified as

$$
p(s|c_m, c_{m+1}, s_n, s_{n-1}) = \frac{\prod_k \alpha_k^{g_k\left(\vec{f}_k^{(5)}, s, c_m, c_{m+1}, s_n, s_{n-1}\right)}}{\sum_{s' \in V} \prod_k \alpha_k^{g_k\left(\vec{f}_k^{(5)}, s', c_m, c_{m+1}, s_n, s_{n-1}\right)}} \tag{18}
$$

$$
\alpha_k = \arg\max_{\alpha} \sum_{l=1}^{L} \sum_{s \in q_l} \sum_{m=1} \log\left[p(s|c_m, c_{m+1}, s_n, s_{n-1})\right] \tag{19}
$$

To solve the resulting data sparseness issue, a combination of feature sets in Gu *et al.*[9] is proposed. Multiple feature sets are extracted with various dimensions and concept/word constraints. As an example, we combine features $\vec{f}_k^{(5)}$ and features $\vec{f}_k^{(7)}$ as

$$\alpha_k = \arg\max_{\alpha} \sum_{l=1}^{L} \sum_{s \in q_l} \sum_{m=1}^{M-1} \left\{ \log \frac{\prod_k \alpha_k^{g_k\left(\vec{f}_k^{(5)}, s, c_m, c_{m+1}, s_n, s_{n-1}\right)}}{\sum_{s' \in V} \prod_k \alpha_k^{g_k\left(\vec{f}_k^{(5)}, s', c_m, c_{m+1}, s_n, s_{n-1}\right)}} \right.$$

$$\left. + \log \frac{\prod_k \alpha_k^{g_k\left(\vec{f}_k^{(7)}, s, c_m, c_{m+1}, \bar{w}_m, \bar{w}_{m+1}, s_n, s_{n-1}\right)}}{\sum_{s'' \in V} \prod_k \alpha_k^{g_k\left(\vec{f}_k^{(7)}, s'', c_m, c_{m+1}, \bar{w}_m, \bar{w}_{m+1}, s_n, s_{n-1}\right)}} \right\} \quad (20)$$

To further reduce the impact of data sparseness, a confidence threshold parameter, β, is introduced in Gu *et al.*[9] on the conditional probability ratio defined as

$$r(s|c_m, c_{m+1}, s_n, s_{n-1}) = \frac{\prod_{m=1}^{M-1} p(s|c_m, c_{m+1}, s_n, s_{n-1})}{\prod_{m=1}^{M-1} p(c_1|c_m, c_{m+1}, s_n, s_{n-1})} \quad (21)$$

where c_1 is the first concept in the remaining source concept sequence. In Equation 21, the numerator and denominator represent the likelihood of generating concept s and c_1, respectively. Therefore Equation 21 indicates how likely concept s rather than concept c_1 will appear next in the target language when $(c_m, c_{m+1}, s_n, s_{n-1})$ is observed. The generation procedure in Equation 8 is modified as: $s_{n+1} = \begin{cases} \hat{s} & \text{if } r(\hat{s}|c_m, c_{m+1}, s_n, s_{n-1}) > \beta \\ c_1 & \text{otherwise} \end{cases}$. Empirically, $1 \leq \beta \leq e^{3.5}$.

5. Efficient and Fast Translation Using Statistical Integrated Phrase Lattices

5.1. *Problem Statement*

One of the "killer" applications for machine translation is a handheld device that can perform interactive machine translation on the spot. However, a large portion of MT research have been focusing on methods that require at least an order of magnitude more resources than are readily available on PDA's. In this research, we address the issues involved in making statistical machine translation (SMT) practical for small devices.

The central issue in limited-resource SMT is translation speed. Not only are PDA's much slower than PC's, but interactive applications require translation speeds at least as fast as real time. In practice, it may be difficult to begin translation until after the complete utterance has been entered (e.g., because speech recognition is using all available computation on the PDA). In this case, translation speeds of much faster than real time are needed to achieve reasonable latencies.

In this work, we use phrase-based statistical machine translation models implemented using weighted finite-state transducers (WFST's). In recent years, phrase-based statistical translation models have shown clear advantages over word-based models in many studies. In contrast to most word-level statistical machine translation,[10] phrase-based methods explicitly take word context into consideration when translating a word. In particular, Koehn *et al.*[31] compared several schemes for computing phrase-level correspondences, and showed that all of these methods consistently outperform word-based approaches.

Meanwhile, finite-state methods have been applied in a wide range of speech and language processing applications.[27] More importantly, it has been shown in the field of ASR that WFST-based decoding methods can be significantly faster than other types of systems.[45]

A number of translation methods have been implemented using WFST's in the literature. For example, Knight and Al-Onaizan[28] described a system based on word-to-word statistical translation models, and Bangalore and Riccardi[29] used WFST's to select and reorder lexical items. More recently, Zhou *et al.*[21] described a constrained phrase-based translation system using WFST's, where a limited number of frequent word sequences and syntactic phrases were automatically extracted from the training data. The DARPA GALE program[15] explored the use of WFST's in speech-to-speech translation. Kumar *et al.*[30] and Kanthak *et al.*[46] implemented alignment template translation models using phrase-based WFST's. One of the reasons why WFST-based approaches are favored is because of the availability of mature and efficient algorithms for general-purpose decoding and optimization that can facilitate the translation task.

Adopting the notation introduced by Brown *et al.*,[10] the task of statistical machine translation is to compute a target language word sequence $\hat{e}$ given a source word sequence f_1^J as follows:

$$\begin{aligned} \hat{e} &= \arg\max_{e_1^I} \; \Pr\left(e_1^I | f_1^J\right) \\ &= \arg\max_{e_1^I} \; \Pr\left(f_1^J | e_1^I\right) \Pr\left(e_1^I\right) \end{aligned} \tag{22}$$

In WFST-based translation, the above computation is expressed in the following way:

$$\hat{e} = \text{best-path}\left(S = I \; o \; M_1 \; o \; M_2 \; o \cdots o \; M_m\right) \tag{23}$$

where S denotes the full search lattice, I denotes the source word sequence expressed as a linear finite-state automaton, the M_i are component translation models, and "o" represents the *composition* operation. That is, it is possible to express the models used in Equation 22 in terms of a sequence of WFST's.

In ASR, it has been shown that this computation can be made much faster by computing $M_* = M_1 \; o \; M_2 \; o \; \cdots o \; M_m$ offline and by applying determinization and minimization to optimize the resulting machine. This has been done in the past for word-level or constrained phrase-level machine translation systems as shown in Zhou *et al.*.[21] However, because of the large number of phrases used in typical translation systems, previous WFST-based implementations of phrase-based SMT were unable to compute the entire M_* as a single FST due to computational issues.

Instead, M_* is expressed as the composition of at least three component transducers (two for the translation model $\Pr(f|e)$ and one for the language model $\Pr(e)$,[30,46] and these component transducers are composed on the fly for every input sentence I. There are several significant disadvantages to this scheme, namely the large memory requirements and heavy online computational burden for each individual composition operation, and the loss of the benefits from doing static optimization on the resulting transducers.

As a consequence, the translation speeds of existing WFST-based systems are significantly slower than those of other phrase-based SMT systems. For example, some previous FST systems translate at a speed of less than a word per second on a server,[30] which is substantially slower than the speeds of other SMT systems that can be as high as 100 to 1,600 words per second.[47] These speeds make it infeasible to deploy phrase-based WFST systems for interactive applications.

We introduce a novel phrase-based translation framework using WFST's that addresses the above issues. In the proposed framework, which we refer to as Statistical Integrated Phrase Lattices (SIPL's), we statically construct a single optimized WFST encoding the entire translation model. In addition, we describe a Viterbi decoder that can combine the translation model and language model FST's with the input lattice extremely efficiently, resulting in translation speeds of up to 4,000 words/second on a PC and 800 words per second on a PDA device.

This section is organized as follows: We first present the translation models and their WFST representations, including all issues related to training; next, we describe details of our new search algorithm; following that, a section that presents experimental results; and finally, we summarize our contributions.

5.2. *Translation Models and FST's*

5.2.1. *Overview*

While the task of statistical machine translation can be expressed using Equation 22, in practice the following decision rule often achieves comparable results:[33]

$$\hat{e} = \arg\max_{e_1^I} \; \Pr\left(e_1^I | f_1^J\right) \Pr\left(e_1^I\right) \tag{24}$$

As this formulation has some practical advantages, we use this equation instead.

Phrase-based translation models explicitly take word contexts into consideration when making a translation decision. Therefore, the foreign word sequence is segmented into K phrases, $\bar{f}_1^K$, where $1 \leq K \leq J$, and each "phrase" here simply indicates a consecutive sequence of words. We have:

$$\Pr\left(e_1^I | f_1^J\right) = \sum_{K.,\bar{f}_1^K} \Pr\left(e_1^I, \bar{f}_1^K, K | f_1^J\right) \tag{25}$$

By approximating the sum in Equation 25 with maximum, we can express the translation model as a chain of conditional probabilities as follows:

$$\begin{aligned} \Pr\left(e_1^I | f_1^J\right) \Pr\left(e_1^I\right) \approx \max_{\bar{f}_1^K} \{ \; & P\left(K | f_1^J\right) P\left(\bar{f}_1^K | K, f_1^J\right) \times \\ & P\left(\bar{e}_1^K | \bar{f}_1^K, K, f_1^J\right) \times \\ & P\left(e_1^I | \bar{e}_1^K, \bar{f}_1^K, K, f_1^J\right) \times \\ & P\left(e_1^I\right) \; \} \end{aligned} \tag{26}$$

The conditional probability distributions can be represented by finite-state machines (FSM's) that model the relationships between their inputs and outputs. Therefore, the right-hand side of Equation 25 can be implemented as a cascade of these machines that are combined using the composition operation. In particular, the translation task can be framed as finding the best path in the following FSM: $S = I \; o \; H$, where I represents the source sentence with possible reordering, and,

$$H = P \; o \; T \; o \; W \; o \; L \tag{27}$$

here P, T, W, and L refer to the transducers of source language segmentation, the phrase translation, the target language phrase-to-word, and the target language model, respectively.

In the following, we first describe how our translation models are trained, and then describe how we construct each component WFST in Equation 26 in turn.

5.2.2. *Bilingual Phrase Induction and Estimation*

A fundamental task in phrase-based translation is extracting bilingual phrase pairs and estimating their translation probabilities. For this step, we follow the procedure described in Och *et al.*[48] to extract bilingual phrases. First, bidirectional word-level alignment is carried out on the parallel corpus. Based on the resulting Viterbi alignments A_{e2f} and $A_{f2e'}$, the union, $A_{\cup} = A_{e2f} \cup A_{f2e'}$, is taken as the symmetrized word-level alignment.

Next, bilingual phrase pairs are extracted from $A_{\cup}$ using an extraction algorithm similar to the one described in Och *et al.*[48] Specifically, any pair of consecutive sequences of words below a maximum length M is considered to be a phrase pair if its component words are aligned only within the phrase pair and not to any other word outside. The resulting bilingual phrase pair inventory is denoted as BP.

Then, we make the assumption that phrases are mapped from the source to target language and are not reordered, and that each phrase is translated independently. While it is generally sensible to support phrase reordering during translation, this incurs a heavy computational cost and a preliminary investigation suggested that this would have a limited effect on translation accuracy in the domains under consideration. We also note that while we assume each phrase is translated independently, the language model will constrain the translations of neighboring phrases.

To estimate the phrase translation probabilities, we use maximum likelihood estimation (MLE):

$$P_{MLE}\left(\overline{e}|\overline{f}\right) = \frac{N\left(\overline{e},\overline{f}\right)}{N\left(\overline{f}\right)} \tag{28}$$

where $N\left(\overline{f}\right)$ is the occurrence count of $\overline{f}$ and $N\left(\overline{e},\overline{f}\right)$ is the co-occurrence count of $\overline{f}$ aligning with $\overline{e}$. These counts are all calculated from the BP.

5.2.3. *Source Language Segmentation FST*

The source language segmentation transducer explores all "acceptable" phrase sequences for any given source sentence. We assume a uniform distribution over all acceptable segmentations. By "acceptable", we mean that all phrases in resulting segmentations must belong to BP. In addition, the segmentation transducer forces the resulting segmentation to satisfy:

$$Concatenation\ \left(\overline{f}_1,\cdots,\overline{f}_K\right) = f_1^J \tag{29}$$

Using the WFST framework, the segmentation procedure is implemented as a transducer P that maps from word sequences to phrases. For example, Kumar *et al.*[30] describes a typical realization of P. However, in general, this type of realization is not determinizable and it is crucial that this transducer be determinized because this can radically affect translation speed. Not only can determinization greatly reduce the size of this FST, but determinization collapses multiple arcs with the same label into a single arc, vastly reducing the amount of computation required during search.

The reason why a straightforward representation of P is non-determinizable is because of the overlap between phrases found in BP; i.e., a single word sequence may be segmented into phrases in multiple ways. Thus, the phrase identity of a source sentence may not be uniquely determined after the entire sentence is observed, and such unbounded delays make P non-determinizable.[27] In our work, we introduce an auxiliary symbol, denoted EOP, marking the end of each distinct source phrase. See Figure 5 for a sample portion of the resulting transducer.

By adding these artificial phrase boundary markers, each input sequence in Figure 5 corresponds to a single segmented output sequence and the transducer becomes determinizable. Once we have determinized the FST, we can replace the EOP markers with empty strings in a later step as appropriate. As we assume a uniform distribution over segmentations, we simply set the cost (or negative log probability) associated with each arc to be zero.

5.2.4. *Phrase Translation Transducer*

The phrase translation model is implemented by a weighted transducer that maps source phrases to target phrases. Under the assumptions of phrase translation independence and monotonic phrase ordering, the transducer is a trivial one-state machine, with every arc corresponding to a phrase pair contained in BP. The cost associated with each arc is obtained based on Equation 27.

In order to be consistent with the other FST's in Equation 25, one more arc is added in this transducer to map EOP to itself with no cost. This transducer is denoted as T.

5.2.5. *Target Language Phrase-to-Word FST and Target Language Model*

After translation, the target phrases can be simply concatenated to form the target translation. However, in order to constrain translations across phrases, it is necessary to incorporate the effects of a target language model in the translation system. To achieve this, the target phrases must be converted back to target words.

It is clear that the mapping from phrases to word sequences is deterministic. Therefore, the implementation of this transducer is straightforward. Again, we need

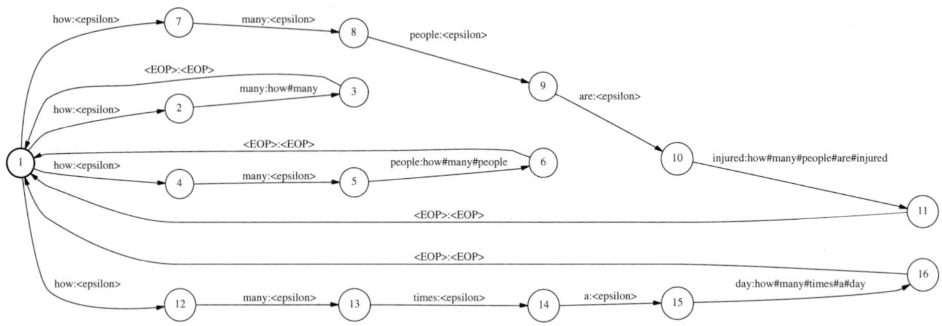

Fig. 5. A portion of source sentence segmentation transducer P. Each arc is labeled using the notation "*input:output*". The token "<epsilon>" (ε) denotes the empty string and "#" is used as a separator in multi-word labels.

to place the auxiliary token EOP on additional arcs to mark the ends of phrases. We denote this transducer as W.

The target language model can be represented by a weighted acceptor L that assigns probabilities to target language word sequences based on a back-off N-gram language model.[27]

5.3. *Search*

5.3.1. *Issues with Cascades of WFST's*

As mentioned earlier, the decoding problem can be framed as finding the best path in the lattice S given an input sentence/automaton I. Viterbi search can be applied to S to find its lowest-cost path.

To minimize the amount of computation required at translation time, it is desirable to perform as many composition operations in Equation 26 as possible ahead of time. The ideal situation is to compute H offline.

At translation time, one needs only to compute the best path of $S = I \circ H$. Applying determinization and minimization to optimize H can further reduce the computation needed. In the field of speech recognition, decoders that fall under this paradigm generally offer the fastest performance.[45]

However, it can be very difficult to construct H given practical memory constraints. While this has been done in the past for word-level and constrained phrase-level systems,[21] this has yet to be done for unconstrained phrase-based systems. In particular, the nondeterministic nature of the phrase translation transducer interacts poorly with the language model; it is not clear whether H is of a tractable size even after minimization, especially for applications with large vocabularies, long phrases, and large language models. Therefore, special consideration is required in constructing transducers for such domains.

Furthermore, even when one is able to compute and store H, the composition $I^\circ H$ itself may be quite expensive. To improve speed, it has been proposed that *lazy* or on-the-fly composition be applied followed by Viterbi search with beam pruning. In this way, only promising states in S are expanded on-demand. Nevertheless, for large H (e.g., consisting of millions of states and arcs), using such operations from general FSM toolkits can be quite slow.

5.3.2. *The SIPL and Multilayer Search Algorithm*

While it may not be feasible to compute H in its entirety as a single FSM, it is possible to separate H into two pieces: the language model L and the translation model M:

$$M = Min(Min(Det(P)\, o\, T)\, o\, W) \tag{30}$$

where *Det* and *Min* denote the determinization and minimization operation respectively. Here, the machine obtained from Equation 30 is entitled as the SIPL. In spite of the fact that T and W in 30 are not deterministic, and that minimization is formally defined on deterministic machines,[27] in practice, we often find that minimization can help reduce the number of states of non-deterministic machines. Due to the determinizability of P, M can be computed offline using a moderate amount of memory. We perform all operations using the tropical semiring as is consistent with Viterbi decoding, i.e., when two paths with the same labels are merged, the resulting cost is the minimum of the individual path costs. The cost associated with a transition is taken to be the negative logarithm of the corresponding probability. Minimization is performed following each composition to reduce redundant paths. It should also be noted that due to the determinizability of P, the SIPL, can be computed offline using a moderate amount of memory.

To address the problem of efficiently computing $I\ o\ M\ o\ L$, we have developed a multilayer search algorithm. The basic idea is that we perform search in multiple FSM's or layers simultaneously. Specifically, we have one layer for each of the input FSM's: I, L, and M. At each layer, the search process is performed via a state traversal procedure starting from the start state $\vec{s}_0$, and consuming an input word in each step in a left-to-right manner.

This can be viewed as an optimized version of on-the-fly or dynamic composition. However, this specialized decoding algorithm has the advantage of not only significant memory efficiency and being possibly many times faster than general composition implementations found in FSM toolkits, but they can also incorporate information sources that cannot be easily or compactly represented using WFST's. For example, the decoder can allow us to apply the translation length penalties and phrase penalties to score the partial translation candidates during search.

We represent each state $\vec{s}$ in the search space using the following 7-tuple: $\left(s_I, s_M, s_L, c_M, c_L, \vec{h}, \vec{s}_p\right)$, where s_I, s_M, and s_L record the current state in each input FSM; c_M and c_L record the accumulated cost in M and L in the best path up to this point; $\vec{h}$ records the target word sequence labeling the best path up to this point; and $\vec{s}_p$ records the best previous state. The initial search state $\vec{s}_0$ corresponds to being located at the start state of each input FSM with no accumulated costs.

At the beginning of the input sentence I, only the start state $\vec{s}_0$ is active. The active states at each position t in I are computed from the active states in the preceding position $t-1$ in the following way: For each active state $\vec{s}$ at position $t-1$, first advance s_I. Then, look at all outgoing arcs of s_M labeled with the current input word, and traverse one of these arcs, advancing s_M. Then, given the output label o of this arc, look at all outgoing arcs of s_L with o as its input, and traverse one of these arcs, advancing s_L. The set of all states $(s_I, s_M, s_L, \ldots,)$ reachable in this way is the set of active states at position t. The remaining state components c_M, c_L, $\vec{h}$, and $\vec{s}_p$ must be updated appropriately, and ε-transitions must be handled correctly as well.

The set of legal translation candidates are those $\vec{h}$ associated with states $\vec{s}$ where each component sub-state is a final state in its layer. The selected candidate is the legal candidate with the lowest accumulated cost.

For each active state, the hypothesis $\vec{h}$ is a translation of a prefix of the source sentence, and can conceivably grow to be quite large. However, we can store the $\vec{h}$'s for each state efficiently using the same ideas as used in token passing in ASR. In particular, the set of all active $\vec{h}$'s can be compactly represented using a prefix tree, and each state can simply keep a pointer to the correct node in this tree.

To reduce the search space, two active search states are merged whenever they have identical s_I, s_M, and s_L values; the remaining state components are inherited from the state with lower cost. In addition, two pruning methods, histogram pruning and threshold or beam pruning, are used to achieve the desired balance between translation accuracy and speed. To provide the decoder for a PDA, the search algorithm is implemented using fixed-point arithmetic.

6. Experimental Evaluations

We evaluate the proposed SIPL translation framework on a speech translation task from the government-sponsored TransTac program. This task is the two-way translation between English and Chinese. The objective of our speech translation system is to facilitate conversation between speakers of different languages in real time. Thus, both our training and test data are sentences transcribed from spontaneous speech rather than written text.

6.1. *Corpora and Setup*

The majority of the training corpus of the English-Chinese system was collected from simulated English-only doctor/patient interactions, and the dialogs were later translated into Chinese. As Chinese translations may not be representative of conversational Chinese, an additional 6,000 spoken sentences were collected directly from native Chinese speakers, to better capture the linguistic characteristics of conversational Chinese. After being transcribed and translated into English, this data set was also included in our corpus. In total, there are about 240K raw utterance pairs but with many repeated utterances. For concept translation approach, 10,000 sentences for each language (English and Chinese) are annotated. 68 distinct labels and 144 distinct tags are used to capture the semantic information.

The English-Mandarin recognition and translation experiments were done on the DARPA CAST Aug'04 offline evaluation data, which has an English script of 132 sentences and a Chinese script of 73 sentences for medical domain. Each script was read by 4 speakers. The recognition word error rate for English is 11.06%, while the character error rate for Mandarin is 13.60%, both are run on speaker-independent models.

Several dialogs were randomly selected to form a development set. Table 2 listed some statistics of the data sets used for the English-Chinese task.

Table 2. English-Chinese corpora statistics.

Data	**English**	**Chinese**
Training Set	240K utterances, 6.9 words/utt	240K utterances, 8.4 characters/utt
Vocabulary	9,690 words	9,764 words
Dev Set	300 utterances, 7.1 words/utt	582 utterances, 8.9 characters/utt
Test Set	132 utterances, 6.1 words/utt	73 utterances, 6.2 characters/utt

Table 3. ME-NCG Performance enhancement (sequence error rate / concept error rate) algorithms.

ME-NCG Methods	**Test-set**
feature on parallel corpora + confidence threshold + concept-word features + multiple feature selection	17.4 % / 11.8 %
+ FBM	15.8 % / 10.4 %

6.2. *Experiments on ME-based statistical NCG*

We evaluate the concept generation accuracy using ME-based statistical NCG. A primary concept sequence is extracted from each annotated sentence, which represents the top-layer concepts in the semantic parse tree. Concept sequences containing only one concept are removed as they are trivial to generate. To simplify the problem, we train and test on parallel concept sequences that contain the same set of concepts in English and Chinese. In this specific case, NCG is performed to generate the correct concept order in the target language. More general and complex experiments are performed and shown in the next sub-section.

According to the above criterion, about 5,600 concept sequences are selected as our experimental corpus. The average number of concepts per sequence is 3.94. During experimentation, this corpus is randomly partitioned into a training corpus containing 80% of the sequences and test corpus with the remaining 20%. (There is no sentence overlap between the training set and test set). This random process is repeated 50 times and the average performance is recorded. Two evaluation metrics were applied: sequence error rate and concept error rate. A concept sequence is considered to have an error during measurement of sequence error rate if one or more errors occur in this sequence. Concept error rate, on the other hand, evaluates concept errors in concept sequences such as substitution, deletion and insertion.

In the first experiment, various ME-based NCG methods were combined and compared on both the training and test corpus. The results are shown in Table 3.

6.3. *Experiments on FST Approach*

The sizes of the statically constructed translation model WFST's H are as following: 2.3 million states and 3.27 million arcs for English-to-Chinese and 1.9 million states and 2.78 million arcs for Chinese-to-English. While our framework can handle longer spans and larger numbers of phrases, bigger M did not produce significantly better results in this domain, probably due to the short sentence lengths. The development sets were used to adjust the model parameters and the search parameters (e.g., pruning thresholds).

For the results reported in Table 4, all decoding experiments have been conducted on a Linux machine with a 2.4 GHz Pentium 4 processor. The machine used for training (including the SIPL building) possesses a 4 GB memory. Since the decoding algorithm of the SIPL framework is memory efficient, the translation is performed on a machine with 512 MB memory (the actual memory requirement is less than 30 MB).

Experimental results are presented in Table 4 in terms of the BLEU metric.[49] Since the BLEU score is a function of the number of human references, we include these numbers in parentheses. Note that for English-Chinese translation, BLEU is measured in terms of characters rather than words. We observe from Table 4 that the proposed approach achieves encouraging results for all four translation tasks. Moreover, using our dedicated translation decoder, all tasks obtained an average

Table 4. Translation Performance.

	BLEU (%)	**Speed** (words/second)
English-to-Chinese (8)	59.67	1,894
Chinese-to-English (8)	32.98	2,246

decoding speed of higher than 1,800 words per second. The speed varies due to the complexity and structure of the lattices M and L. These speeds are competitive with the highest translated speeds reported in the literature.

More significantly, the complete system can run comfortably on a PDA as part of a complete speech-to-speech translation system. In this case, the translation component must run in about 20MB of memory, with the FSM's H and L stored on disk (typically taking a total of several hundred MB's) and paged in on demand. In this configuration, the same exact accuracy figures in Table 3 are achieved but at speeds ranging from 500 to 800 words/second. Because of these high translation speeds, translation component contributes almost nothing to the latency in the dialog interactive. To our knowledge, these are the first published MT results for a handheld device.

To illustrate the difference in speed between our optimized multilayer search as compared to using general on-the-fly composition and pruning operations from an off-the-shelf FSM toolkit,[38] we have an earlier toolkit-based SMT system that translated at around 2 words/second on comparable domains. While the translation models used are not comparable, this does give some idea of the possible performance gains from using our specialized decoder.

7. Summary and Conclusion

We described two different statistical approaches for speech-to-speech translation. The concept based approach focuses on understanding and re-generating the meaning of the speech input, while the finite-state transducer based approach emphasizes both system development and search speed and memory efficiency. The former approaches usually involve large amounts of human effort in the annotation of linguistic information, although the amount of annotated data needed is not very large (in our experiment only 10,000 sentences are annotated for each language). The latter approach, weighted FST, may exploit un-annotated parallel corpora at the cost of potential meaning loss and the requirement of large amount of parallel text data (in our experiment 240K sentences, in the order of millions of words for each language, are used).

Both approaches have shown comparable results.[26] The oracle scores show that if one can combine the translation results from these two different approaches, the accuracy can be further improved significantly. Currently we present two alternate translations to users in the real-time system to enhance the communications. It is very useful to notice that the translation results generated by our two approaches are always consistent in meaning.

In cases where under-studied languages (i.e., those low in resources) are involved in speech translation, the task would be more complex due to a number of reasons. Here are two particular concerns: 1) The lack of large amounts of speech data representative of the oral language spoken by the right target group of native speakers, consequently making traditional statistical translation approaches inapplicable and producing speech recognition error rates much higher than in popular languages like English and Chinese; 2) the lack of linguistic knowledge realization in annotated corpus. Therefore, neither linguistic knowledge based approaches (such as our concept-based approaches) nor pure statistical approaches (such as IBM model 1-5 and FST-based methods) are suitable for rapid development of applicable systems.

We believe that integration of the two research paradigms into a unified framework, e.g., in a unified FST composition, should be the right direction to go. A shallow semantic/syntactic parser is designed and implemented to enable statistical speech translation using knowledge-based shallow semantic/syntactic structures. This information is further utilized to process inevitable speech recognition errors and disfluencies in the colloquial speech. While the shallow-structure parser is initiated upon lightly annotated linguistic corpora and trained using statistical model, it can be greatly enhanced and expanded by applying machine learning algorithms on un-annotated parallel corpora. The integration of the two approaches should increase the system end-to-end performance, and reduces the amount of parallel text data required by the statistical algorithm.

References

1. A. Lavie, A. Waibel, L. Levin, M. Finke, D. Gates, M. Gavalda, T. Zeppenfeld, and P. Zhan, "JANUS-III: Speech-to-Speech Translation in Multiple Languages," in *Proc. ICASSP*, (Munich, Germany, 1997), pp. 99–10.
2. L. Levin, A. Lavie, M. Woszczyna, D. Gates, M. Gavalda, D. Koll, and A. Waibel, "The Janus-III Translation System: Speech-to-Speech Translation in Multiple Domains," *Machine Translation*, vol. 15, pp. 3–25, (2000).
3. S. Yamamoto, "Toward Speech Communications Beyond Language Barrier - Research of Spoken Language Translation Technologies at ATR," in *Proc. ICSLP*, (Beijing, 2000).
4. G. Lazzari, "Spoken Translation: Challenges and Opportunities," in *Proc. ICSLP*, (Beijing, 2000).
5. Y. Zhou, C. Zong, and B. Xu, "Bilingual Chunk Alignment in Statistical Machine Translation," in *Systems, Man and Cybernetics, 2004 IEEE International Conference*, vol. 2, (2004), pp. 1401 – 1406.
6. H. Blanchon and C. Boitet, "Speech Translation for French within the C-STAR II Consortium and Future Perspectives," in *Proc. ICSLP*, (Beijing, 2000).
7. L. Levin and S. Nirenburg, "The Correct Place of Lexical Semantics in Interlingual MT," in

COLING 94: The 15th International Conference on Computational Linguistics, (Kyoto, 1994), pp. 349–355.
8. Y. Gao, B. Zhou, Z. Diao, J. Sorensen, and M. Picheny, "MARS: A Statistical Semantic Parsing and Generation-based Multilingual Automatic Translation System," *Machine Translation*, vol. 17, pp. 185–212, (2002).
9. L. Gu, Y. Gao, F. Liu, and M. Picheny, "Concept-based Speech-to-Speech Translation using Maximum Entropy Models for Statistical Natural Concept Generation," *IEEE Transactions on Speech and Audio Processing*, vol. 14, pp. 377–392, (2006).
10. P. Brown, V. D. Pietra, S. A. D. Pietra, and R. L. Mercer, "The Mathematics of Statistical Machine Translation: Parameter Estimation," *Computational Linguistics*, vol. 19, pp. 263–311, (1993).
11. C. Tillmann, S. Vogel, H. Ney, and H. Sawaf, "Statistical Translation of Text, Speech: First Results with the RWTH System," *Machine Translation*, vol. 15, pp. 43–74, (2000).
12. H. Ney, S. Niessen, F. J. Och, H. Sawaf, C. Tillmann, and S. Vogel, "Algorithms for Statistical Translation for Spoken Language," *IEEE Translations on Speech and Audio Processing*, vol. 8, pp. 24–36, (2000).
13. H. Ney, "The Statistical Approach to Machine Translation and a Roadmap for Speech Translation," in *Proc. Eurospeech*, (2003).
14. W. Wahlster, Ed., *Verbmobil: Foundations of Speech-to-Speech Translation*. Springer, Berlin, (1999).
15. [Online]. Available: http://www.darpa.mil/ipto/programs/gale/index.htm
16. M. Rayner, D. Carter, P. Bouillon, V. Digalakis, and M. Wirén, *The Spoken Language Translator*. Cambridge University Press, (2000).
17. S. Bangalore and G. Riccardi, "Stochastic Finite-state Models for Spoken Language Machine Translation," *Machine Translation*, vol. 17, (2002).
18. I. Garcia-Varea, A. Sanchis, and F. Casacuberta, "A New Approach to Speech-Input Statistical Translation," in *Proc. 15th International Conference on Pattern Recognition*, vol. 3, (2000), pp. 907–910.
19. H. Alshawi, S. Bangalore, and S. Douglas, "Head-Transducer Models for Speech Translation and their Automatic Acquisition from Bilingual Data," *Machine Translation*, vol. 15, pp. 105–124, (2000).
20. F. Casacuberta, H. Ney, F. J. Och, E. Vidal, J. M. Vilar, S. Barrachina, I. García-Varea, D. Llorens, C. Martínez, S. Molau, F. Nevado, M. Pastor, A. S. D. Picó, and C. Tillmann, "Some Approaches to Statistical and Finite-state Speech-to-Speech Translation," *Computer Speech and Language*, vol. 18, pp. 25–47, (2004).
21. B. Zhou, S. Chen, and Y. Gao, "Constrained Phrase-based Translation using Weighted Finite-state Transducers," in *Proc. ICASSP*, (2005).
22. J. C. Amengual, J. M. Benedl, F. Casacuberta, A. Castano, A. Castellanos, V. M. Jimenez, D. Llorens, A. Marza, M. Pastor, F. Prat, E. Vidal, and J. M. Vilar, "The EuTrans-I Speech Translation System," *Machine Translation*, vol. 15, pp. 75–103, (2000).
23. H. Wu, T. Huang, C. Zong, and B. Xu, "Chinese Generation in a Spoken Dialogue Translation System," in *Proc. COLING*, (2000), pp. 1141–1145.
24. C. Zong, B. Xu, and T. Huang, "Interactive Chinese-to-English Speech Translation Based on Dialogue Management," in *ACL Workshop on Speech-to-Speech Translation*, (2002).
25. C. Zong, T. Huang, and B. Xu, "Technical Analysis on Automatic Spoken Language Translation Systems (in Chinese)," *Journal of Chinese Information Processing*, vol. 13, pp. 55–65, (1999).
26. Y. Gao, L. Gu, B. Zhou, R. Sarikaya, M. Afify, H.-K. Kuo, W. zhong Zhu, Y. Deng, C. Prosser, W. Zhang, and L. Besacier, "IBM MASTOR: Multilingual Automatic Speech-to-Speech Translator," in *Proc. ICASSP'06*, (2006).
27. M. Mohri, F. Pereira, and M. Riley, "Weighted Finite-state Transducers in Speech Recognition," *Computer Speech and Language*, vol. 16, pp. 69–88, (2002).

28. K. Knight and Y. Al-Onaizan, "Translation with Finite-state Devices," in *4th Conference of the Association for Machine Translation in the Americas*, (1998), pp. 421–437.
29. S. Bangalore and G. Riccardi, "A Finite-state Approach to Machine Translation," in *North American Chapter of the Association for Computational Linguistics*, (2001).
30. S. Kumar, Y. Deng, and W. Byrne, "A Weighted Rinite State Transducer Translation Template Model for Statistical Machine Translation," *Journal of Natural Language Engineering*, vol. 11, (2005).
31. P. Koehn, F. Och, and D. Marcu, "Statistical Phrase-based Translation," in *North American Chapter of the Association for Computational Linguistics/Human Language Technologies*, (2003).
32. B. Zhou, S. Chen, and Y. Gao, "Folsom: A Fast and Memory-Efficient Phrase-based Approach to Statistical Machine Translation," in *IEEE/ACL 2006 Workshop on Spoken Language Technology*, (2006).
33. C. Chen, R. Gopinath, M. Monkowski, M. Picheny, and K. Shen, "New Methods in Continuous Mandarin Speech Recognition," in *Proc. Eurospeech*, (1997), pp. 1543–1546.
34. Y. Gao, B. Ramabhadran, and M. Picheny, "New Adaptation Techniques for Large Vocabulary Continuous Speech Recognition," in *ISCA ITRW ASR2000 Automatic Speech Recognition: Challenges for the New Millenium*, (2000).
35. K. Davies, "The IBM Conversational Telephony System for Financial Applications," in *Proc. Eurospeech*, (1999), pp. 275–278.
36. R. Donovan, F. Franz, J. S. Sorensen, and S. Roukos, "Phrase Slicing and Variable Substitution using the IBM Trainable Speech Synthesis System," in *Proc. ICASSP*, (1999), pp. 373–376.
37. L. Gu and Y. Gao, "Use of Maximum Entropy in Natural Word Generation for Statistical Concept-based Speech-to-Speech Translation," in *Proc. InterSpeech 2005*, (2005).
38. S. Chen, *The IBM Finite-State Machine Toolkit*. Technical Report, IBM T. J. Watson Research Center, (2000).
39. D. Magerman, *Natural Language Parsing as Statistical Pattern Recognition*. PhD thesis, Stanford University, (1994).
40. F. Liu, L. Gu, Y. Gao, and M. Picheny, "Use of Statistical n-gram Models in Natural Language Generation for Machine Translation," in *Proc. ICASSP*, (2003).
41. A. Berger, V. J. D. Pietra, and S. A. D. Pietra, "A Maximum Entropy Approach to Natural Language Processing," *Computational Linguistics*, vol. 22, (1996).
42. B. Zhou, Y. Gao, J. Sorensen, Z. Diao, and M. Picheny, "Statistical Natural Language Generation for Trainable Speech-to-Speech Machine Translation Systems," in *Proc. ICSLP'02*, (2002).
43. A. Ratnaparkhi, "Trainable Methods for Surface Natural Language Generation," in *1st Meeting of the North American Chapter of the Association for Computational Linguistics*, (2000), pp. 194–201.
44. R. Bakis, "Continuous Speech Recognition via Centisecond Acoustic States," in *91st Meeting of the Acoustical Society of America*, (1976).
45. S. Kanthak, H. Ney, M. Riley, and M. Mohri, "A Comparison of Two LVR Search Optimization Techniques," in *International Conference of Spoken Language Processing*, (2002).
46. S. Kanthak, D. Vilar, E. Matusov, R. Zens, and H. Ney, "Novel Reordering Approaches in Phrase-based Statistical Machine Translation," in *ACL 2005 Workshop on Building and Using Parallel Texts: Data-Driven Machine Translation and Beyond*, (2005).
47. R. Zens and H. Ney, "Improvements in Phrase-based Statistical Machine Translation," in *Proc. HLT/NAACL'04*, (2004).
48. F. J. Och, C. Tillmann, and H. Ney, "Improved Alignment Models for Statistical Machine Translation," in *Proc. EMNLP/VLC'99*, (1999), pp. 20–28.
49. K. Papineni, S. Roukos, T. Ward, and W. J. Zhu, "Bleu: a Method for Automatic Evaluation of Machine Translation," in *Proc. ACL*, (2002).

CHAPTER 13

SPOKEN DOCUMENT RETRIEVAL AND SUMMARIZATION

Berlin Chen,[†] Hsin-min Wang[‡] and Lin-shan Lee[§]

[†]*National Taiwan Normal University, Taipei*

[‡]*Academia Sinica, Taipei*

[§]*National Taiwan University, Taipei*

E-mail: berlin@csie.ntnu.edu.tw, whm@iis.sinica.edu.tw, lslee@gate.sinica.edu.tw

Huge, continually increasing quantities of multimedia content including speech information are filling up our computers, networks and lives. It is obvious that speech is one of the most important sources of information for multimedia content, as it is the speech of the content that tells us of the subjects, topics and concepts. As a result, the associated spoken documents of the multimedia content will be key for content retrieval and browsing. Substantial efforts along with very encouraging results for spoken document transcription, retrieval, and summarization have been reported. This chapter presents a concise yet comprehensive overview of information retrieval and automatic summarization technologies that have been developed in recent years for efficient spoken document retrieval and browsing applications. An example prototype system for voice retrieval of Chinese broadcast news collected in Taiwan will be introduced as well.

1. Introduction

Speech is the primary and most convenient means of communication between humans.[1] In the future of networks, digital content over the network will include all the information relating to our daily life activities, from real-time information to knowledge archives, from work environments to private services. Naturally, the most attractive form of content is multimedia, including speech which carries the information that tells us of the subjects, topics and concepts of the multimedia content. As a result, the spoken documents associated with the network content will be key in retrieval and browsing activities.[2]

At the same time, the rapid development of network and wireless technologies is making it possible for people to access network content not only from offices and homes, but from anywhere, at any time with the use of small, hand-held devices such as personal digital assistants (PDAs) and cell phones. Today, our access to the network is primarily text-based. Users need to enter instructions by keying in words or texts, and the network or search engine in turn offers text materials for the user to select. These users therefore interact with the network or search engine and obtain the desired information via the text-based media. In the future, almost all text functions can be performed with speech. The users' instructions can be entered with speech just as well. Speech is a convenient user interface suitable for all the different kinds of devices and it is especially good for smaller, hand-held devices. The network content may be indexed, retrieved and browsed not only by text, but also by their associated spoken documents as well. Users may also interact with the network or the search engines by means of either text-based media or spoken, multi-modal dialogues. Text-to-speech synthesis can then be used to transform textual information in the content into speech when needed.

This chapter presents a concise yet comprehensive overview of the information retrieval and automatic summarization technologies that have been developed in recent years for efficient spoken document retrieval and browsing applications. An example prototype system for voice retrieval of Chinese broadcast news collected in Taiwan will be introduced as well.

2. Information Retrieval

We will start with a brief review of information retrieval (IR). In the past two decades, most of the research in IR focused on text document retrieval, and the Text REtrieval Conference[3] (TREC) evaluations in the nineties are good examples. In conventional text document retrieval, a collection of documents $D = \{d_i, i = 1, 2, \ldots, N\}$ are to be retrieved by a user's query Q. This retrieval is based on a set of indexing terms specifying the semantics of the documents and the query, which are very often a set of keywords, or even all the words used in all the documents. The document retrieval problem can thus be viewed as a clustering problem, i.e., selecting the documents out of the collection which are in the class relevant to the query Q. The documents are usually ranked by a retrieval model (or ranking algorithm) based on the relevance scores between each of the documents d_i and the query Q evaluated with the indexing terms. In this way, those documents on the top of the list are most likely to be relevant. The retrieval models are usually characterized by two different matching strategies, namely, literal term matching and concept matching. These two strategies are briefly reviewed below.

2.1. *Literal Term Matching*

The vector space model (VSM) is the most popular model for literal term matching.[4] In VSM, every document d_i is represented as a vector $\vec{d_i}$. Each component $w_{i,t}$ in this vector is a value associated with the statistics of a specific indexing term (or word) t, both within the document d_i and across all the documents in the collection D,

$$w_{i,t} = f_{i,t} \cdot \ln(N/N_t), \tag{1}$$

where $f_{i,t}$ is the normalized term frequency (TF) for the term (or word) t in d_i, used to measure the intra-document weight for the term (or word) t; while $\ln(N/N_t)$ is the inverse document frequency (IDF), where N_t is the total number of documents in the collection which include the term t, and N is the total number of documents in the collection D. IDF is to measure the inter-document discrimination ability for the term t, reflecting the fact that indexing terms appearing in more different documents are less useful in identifying the relevant documents. The query Q is also represented by a vector $\vec{Q}$ constructed in exactly the same way, i.e., with components $w_{q,t}$ in exactly the same form as in Equation 1. The cosine measure is then used to estimate the query-document relevance scores:

$$R(Q,d_i) = \left(\vec{Q} \cdot \vec{d_i}\right) / \left(\| \vec{Q} \| \cdot \| \vec{d_i} \|\right), \tag{2}$$

which apparently matches Q and d_i based on the terms literally. This model has been widely used because of its simplicity and satisfactory performance.

Literal term matching can also be performed with probabilities, the n-gram-based[5] and hidden Markov model (HMM)-based[6] approaches being good examples of this. In these models, each document d_i is interpreted as a generative model composed of a mixture of n-gram probability distributions for observing a query Q, while the query Q is considered as observations, expressed as a sequence of indexing terms (or words) $Q = t_1 t_2 \ldots t_j \ldots t_J$, where t_j is the j-th indexing term in Q and J is the length of the query, as illustrated in Figure 1. The n-gram distributions for the terms t_j, for example $P(t_j|d_i)$ and $P(t_j|t_{j-1}, d_i)$ for uni- and bigrams, are estimated from the document d_i and then linearly interpolated with the background uni- and bigram models estimated from a large outside (i.e., not part of the set used for training) text corpus C, $P(t_j|C)$ and $P(t_j|t_{j-1}, C)$. The relevance score for a document d_i and the query Q can then be expressed as, with uni- and bigram models,

$$P(Q|d_i) = [m_1 \cdot P(t_1|d_i) + m_2 \cdot P(t_1|C)] \cdot$$
$$\prod_{j=2}^{J} [m_1 \cdot P(t_j|d_i) + m_2 \cdot P(t_j|C) + m_3 \cdot P(t_j|t_{j-1}, d_i) + m_4 \cdot P(t_j|t_{j-1}, C)], \tag{3}$$

which again matches Q and d_i based on the terms literally. The uni- and bigram probabilities, as well as the weighting parameters, $m_1, \ldots, m_4$, can be further optimized, for example, by the expectation-maximization (EM) or minimum classification error (MCE) training algorithms, given a training set of query examples with the corresponding query-document relevance information.[7]

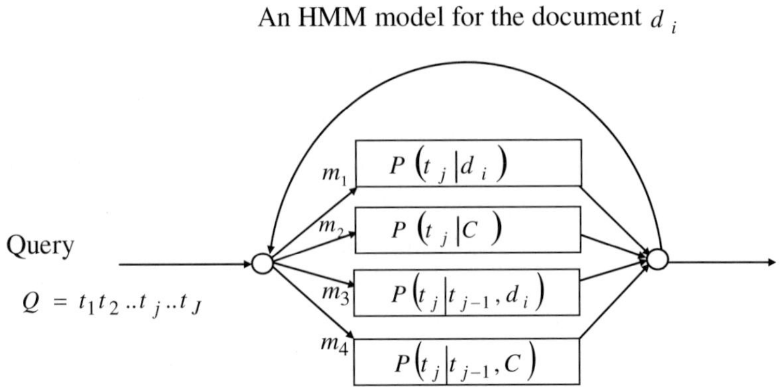

Fig. 1. An illustration of HMM-based retrieval model.

2.2. *Concept Matching*

Both approaches mentioned above are based on matching terms (or words), which makes them face the problem of word usage diversity (or vocabulary mismatch) very often. This happens when the query and its relevant documents are using rather different sets of words. In contrast, the concept matching strategy tries to discover the latent topical information inherent in the query and the documents on which the retrieval is to be done. The latent semantic indexing (LSI) model is a good example employing this strategy.[8,9] LSI starts with a "term-document" matrix W, describing the intra- and inter-document statistical relationships between all the terms and all the documents in the collection D, in which each term t is characterized by a row vector and each document d_i in D by a column vector of W. Singular value decomposition (SVD) is then performed on the matrix W in order to project all the term vectors and document vectors onto a single latent semantic space with significantly reduced dimensionality L:

$$W \approx \hat{W} = U \Sigma V^T \tag{4}$$

where $\hat{W}$ is the rank-L approximation to the "term-document" matrix W; U is the left singular matrix; Σ is the $L \times L$ diagonal matrix of the L singular values; V is the right singular matrix; and T denotes matrix transposition. In this way, the row/column vectors representing the terms/documents in the original matrix W can all be mapped to the vectors in the same latent semantic space with dimensionality L. As shown in Figure 2, in this latent semantic space, each dimension is defined by a singular vector and represents some kind of latent semantic concept. Each term t and each document d_i can now be properly represented in this space,

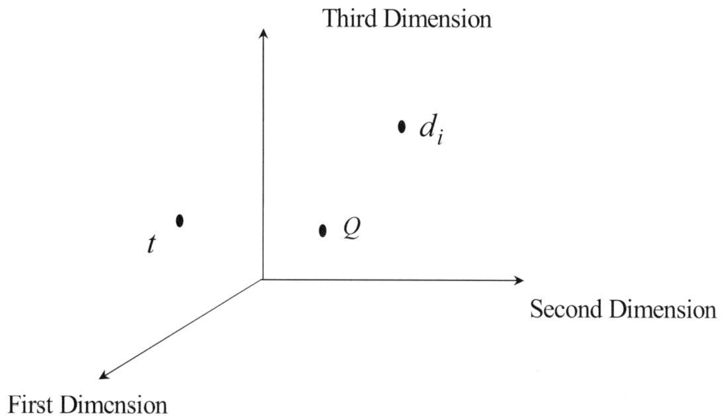

Fig. 2. Three-dimensional schematic representation of the latent semantic space and the LSI retrieval model.

with components in each dimension having to do with the weights of the term t and document d_i with respect to the dimension, or the associated latent semantic concept. While for the query Q or other documents that are not represented in the original analysis, they can be folded-in, i.e., similarly represented in this space, via some simple matrix operations. In this way, indexing terms describing related concepts will be close to each other in the latent semantic space even if they never co-occur in the same document, and the documents describing related concepts will be close to each other in the latent semantic space even if they do not contain the same set of words. So this is concept matching rather than literal term matching. The relevance score between the query Q and a document d_i is then estimated by computing the cosine measure between the corresponding vectors in this latent semantic space.

In recent years, new attempts have been made to establish probabilistic frameworks for the above latent topical approach. They include improved model training algorithms and the probabilistic latent semantic analysis (PLSA or aspect model),[10,11] which is often considered as a representative of this category. PLSA introduces a set of latent topic variables, $\{T_k, k = 1, 2, \ldots, K\}$, to characterize the "term-document" co-occurrence relationships, as shown in Figure 3. A query Q is again treated as a sequence of observed terms (or words), $Q = t_1 t_2 \ldots t_j \ldots t_J$, while the document d_i and a term t_j are both assumed to be independent conditioned on an associated latent topic T_k. The conditional probability of a document d_i generating a term t_j thus can be parameterized by

$$P(t_j|d_i) = \sum_{k=1}^{K} P(t_j|T_k) \cdot P(T_k|d_i) \tag{5}$$

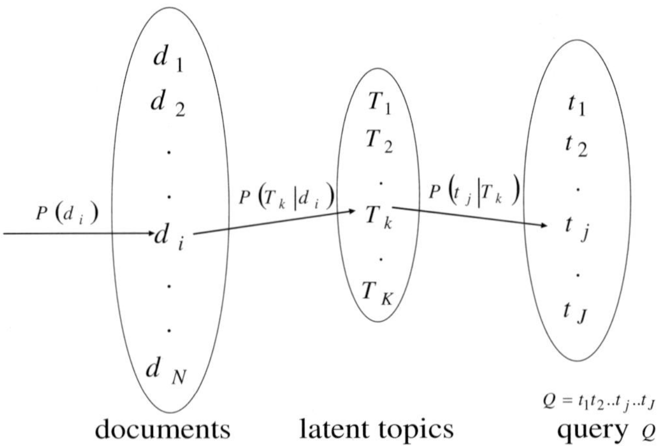

Fig. 3. Graphical representation of the PLSA-based retrieval model.

When the terms in the query Q are further assumed to be independent given the document, the relevance score between the query and document can then be expressed as:

$$P(Q|d_i) = \prod_{j=1}^{J} \left[\sum_{k=1}^{K} P(t_j|T_k) \cdot P(T_k|d_i) \right] \tag{6}$$

Notice that this relevance score is not obtained directly from the frequency of the respective query term t_j occurring in d_i, but instead through the frequency of t_j in the latent topic T_k as well as the likelihood that d_i generates the latent topic T_k. A query and a document thus may have a high relevance score even if they do not share any terms in common, which is therefore concept matching. The PLSA model can be trained in an unsupervised way by maximizing the total log-likelihood L_T of the document collection $\{d_i, i = 1, 2, \ldots, N\}$ in terms of the unigram $P(t_j|d_i)$ of all terms t_j observed in the document collection, using the EM algorithm:

$$L_T = \sum_{i=1}^{N} \sum_{j=1}^{N'} c(t_j, d_i) \cdot \log P(t_j|d_i) \tag{7}$$

where N is total number of documents in the collection, N' is the total number of different terms observed in the document collection, $c(t_j, d_i)$ is the frequency count for the term t_j in the document d_i, and $P(t_j|d_i)$ is the probability obtained above in Equation 5.

2.3. *Spoken Documents and Queries*

All the retrieval models mentioned above can in fact be equally applied to text or spoken documents with text or spoken queries. The additional, albeit important, difficulties for spoken documents and queries are the inevitable speech recognition errors: problems of spontaneous speech such as pronunciation variation as well as disfluencies, and the out-of-vocabulary (OOV) problem for words outside the vocabulary of the speech recognizer. A principal approach to the former, apart from the many approaches improving recognition accuracy, is to develop more robust indexing terms for audio signals. For example, multiple recognition hypotheses obtained from M-best lists, word graphs, or "sausages" can provide alternative representatives for the confusing portions of the spoken query or documents.[12] Improved scoring methods using different confidence measures, for example, posterior probabilities incorporating acoustic and language model likelihoods, or other measures considering relationships between the recognized word hypotheses,[13,14] as well as prosodic features including pitch, energy stress and duration measure,[15] can also help to weight the term hypotheses properly. The use of subword units – for example, phonemes for English[13] and syllables for Chinese,[12,16] or segments of them – rather than words as indexing terms mentioned above has also been shown to be very helpful. Special considerations of using syllable-level indexing features for Chinese spoken document retrieval will be discussed in the next section. In addition, another set of approaches try to expand the representation of the query and documents not only using conventional IR techniques such as pseudo relevance feedback,[17] but based on the acoustic confusion statistics and/or semantic relationships among the word- or subword-level terms derived from some training corpus, and these have been shown to be very helpful as well.[14]

3. Considerations Of Using Syllable-Level Indexing Features For Chinese Spoken Document Retrieval

3.1. *Characteristics of the Chinese Language*

In the Chinese language, because every one of the large number of characters (at least 10,000 commonly used) is pronounced as a monosyllable and is itself a morpheme with its own meaning, new words are very easily generated everyday by combining a few characters or syllables. For example, the combination of the characters "電 (electricity)" and "腦 (brain)" gives us the rather new Chinese word "電腦 (computer)", and the combination of "股 (stock)", "市 (market)", "長 (long)", and "紅 (red)" gives the business domain the word "股市長紅 (the market remains bullish for long)". In many cases, the meanings of these new words are somewhat related to the meaning of the component characters. Examples of such new words also include many proper nouns such as personal names and organization names which are simply arbitrary combinations of a few characters, as well as many domain-specific terms, like in the above examples. Many of such words are very often the focus in IR functions, because they typically carry the core information, or characterize the subject topic. But in many cases these important words for retrieval purposes are simply not included in any lexicon. It is therefore believed that the OOV problem is a particularly important issue for Chinese IR, and this makes using syllable-level statistical characteristics attractive, logical and even necessary to deal with this problem.

Actually, the syllable-level information makes great sense for the retrieval of Chinese information due to the largely monosyllabic structure of the language. Although there are more than 10,000 commonly used Chinese characters, an elegant feature of the Chinese language is that all its characters are monosyllabic and the total number of phonologically allowed Mandarin syllables is only 1,345. So a syllable is usually shared by many homonym characters with completely different meanings. Each Chinese word is then composed of one to several characters (or syllables), thus the combination of these 1,345 syllables actually gives an almost unlimited number of Chinese words. In other words, each syllable may stand for many different characters with different meanings, while the combination of several specific syllables very often gives only very few, if not unique, homonym polysyllabic words. As a result, comparing the input query and the documents to be retrieved based on the segments of several syllables may provide a very good measure of relevance between them.

In fact, there are other important reasons to use syllable-level information. We know that almost every Chinese character is a morpheme with its own meaning, and each of them have quite independent linguistic roles. As a result, the construction of Chinese words from its characters is indeed rather flexible. To illustrate this phenomenon, in many cases, different words describing the same or similar concepts can be constructed by slightly different combinations of characters. For example, both "中華文化 (Chinese culture)" and "中國文化 (Chinese culture)" have the same meaning, but the second characters in these two words are different. Another realization of this different-characters-same-meaning phenomenon is that a longer word can be arbitrarily abbreviated into shorter words, as in "國家科學委員會 (National Science Council)", which can be abbreviated into "國科會", with the same referent. The shorter word is made up of only the first, the third and the last characters of the first word. Furthermore, exotic words from foreign languages are very often translated into different Chinese words based on its pronunciation. To illustrate, "Kosovo" may be translated into "科索沃 /ke1-suo3-wo4/", "柯索佛 /ke1-suo3-fo2/", "克索夫 /ke1-suo3-fu1/," and so on, but these words usually have some syllables in common, or they can even have exactly the same syllables. Therefore, an intelligent IR system needs to be able to handle such word or terminological flexibilities, such that when the input queries include some words in one form, the desired spoken documents can be retrieved even if they include the corresponding words in different forms. The comparison between the spoken queries and the spoken documents directly at the syllable-level does allow for such flexibilities to some extent, since the "words" are not necessarily constructed during the retrieval processes, while the different forms of words describing the same or relevant concepts very often do have some syllables in common.

3.2. *Syllable-level Indexing Terms*

A whole class of syllable-level indexing terms were proposed by Chen *et al.*,[12] including overlapped syllable segments with length u $(A(u), u = 1,2,3,4,5)$ and syllable pairs separated by v syllables $(B(v), v = 1,2,3,4)$. Considering a syllable sequence of 10 syllables $s_1 s_2 s_3 \ldots s_{10}$, examples of syllable segments are listed on the upper half of Table 1, while examples of syllable pairs on the lower half of the same table. For example, syllable segments of length $u = 3$ include such segments as $(s_1\ s_2\ s_3), (s_2\ s_3\ s_4)$, etc., while syllable pairs separated by $v = 1$ syllables include such pairs as $(s_1\ s_3), (s_2\ s_4)$, etc.

Table 1. Various syllable-level indexing terms for an example syllable sequence $s_1\ s_2\ s_3 \ldots s_{10}$.

Syllable Segments	Examples
$A(u), u = 1$	$(s_1)(s_2)\ldots(s_{10})$
$A(u), u = 2$	$(s_1s_2)(s_2s_3)\ldots(s_9s_{10})$
$A(u), u = 3$	$(s_1s_2s_3)\ (s_2s_3s_4)\ldots(s_8s_9s_{10})$
$A(u), u = 4$	$(s_1s_2s_3s_4)\ (s_2s_3s_4s_5)\ldots(s_7s_8s_9s_{10})$
$A(u), u = 5$	$(s_1s_2s_3s_4s_5)\ (s_2s_3s_4s_5s_6)\ldots(s_6s_7s_8s_9s_{10})$
Syllable Pair Separated by v Syllables	Examples
$B(v), v = 1$	$(s_1s_3)\ (s_2s_4)\ldots(s_8s_{10})$
$B(v), v = 2$	$(s_1s_4)\ (s_2s_5)\ldots(s_7s_{10})$
$B(v), v = 3$	$(s_1s_5)\ (s_2s_6)\ldots(s_6s_{10})$
$B(v), v = 4$	$(s_1s_6)\ (s_2s_7)\ldots(s_5s_{10})$

Considering the structural features of the Chinese language, combinations of these indexing terms are beneficial for the retrieval process. For example, as mentioned previously, each syllable represents some characters with their respective meanings, and very often words with similar or relevant concepts have some syllables in common. Therefore syllable segments with length $u = 1$ makes sense in retrieval process. However, because each syllable is also shared by many homonymic characters, the syllable segments with length $u = 1$ may also cause ambiguity. Therefore it has to be combined with other indexing terms. On the other hand, more than 90% of most frequently used Chinese words are bi-syllabic,[12] so the syllable segments with length $u = 2$ definitely carry a plurality of linguistic information which are definitely useful as important indexing terms. Similarly, if longer syllable segments with $u = 3$ are matched between a document and the query, very often this brings about very important information for purposes of retrieval. On the other hand, because of the very flexible wording structure of Chinese, syllable pairs separated by v syllables are helpful in retrieval. For example, when the word "國家科學委員會 (National Science Council)" is abbreviated by including only the first, third and the last characters, syllable pairs separated by v syllables start to become useful. Furthermore, because substitution, insertion and deletion errors are inevitable and frequent during the recognition process, such indexing terms as syllable pairs separated by v syllables can also help to alleviate these problems.

3.3. *Information Fusion Using Word- and Syllable-Level Indexing Terms*

The characteristics of the Chinese language also lead to some special considerations for the spoken document retrieval task. That is, word-level indexing features possess more semantic information than syllable-level features; hence, word-based retrieval does enhance retrieval precision. Syllable-level indexing features behave more robustly in the areas of the Chinese word tokenization ambiguity issue, the abbreviation problem, the open vocabulary problem, and speech recognition errors, as mentioned above. Therefore, syllable-based retrieval enhances recall. Accordingly, there is good reason to fuse the information obtained from indexing the features of multiple levels. It has been shown that syllable-level indexing features are very effective for Chinese spoken document retrieval, and retrieval performance can be improved further by integrating information from word-level indexing features.[12,16]

4. Spoken Document Summarization

Spoken document summarization, which aims at distilling important information and removing redundant and incorrect information from spoken documents, enables us to efficiently review spoken documents and understand their associated topics quickly. Although research into the automatic summarization of text documents dates back to the early 1950s, for nearly four decades, research work suffered from a lack of funding. However, the development of the World Wide Web led to a renaissance in the field and summarization was subsequently extended to cover a wider range of tasks, including multi-document, multilingual and multimedia summarization.[18] Document summarization in general can be either *extractive* or *abstractive*. Extractive summarization tries to select a number of indicative sentences, passages or paragraphs from the original document according to a target summarization ratio, and then sequence them together to form a summary. Abstractive summarization, on the other hand, tries to produce a concise abstract of desired length that can reflect the key concepts of the document. The latter appears to be more difficult, and recent approaches have been focusing more on the former. The approaches for extractive spoken document summarization have been in principle developed on the basis of either statistical models or probabilistic generative models. These two kinds of models will be briefly reviewed below in Sections 4.1 and 4.2, respectively; while special considerations of spoken document summarization will be briefly discussed in Section 4.3.

4.1. *Statistical Models*

As one example, the vector space model (VSM), originally formulated for IR, can be used to respectively represent each sentence of the document, as well as the whole document, in a vector form. Within the VSM, each dimension specifies the weighted statistics associated with an indexing term (or word) in the sentence or document, and the sentences that have the highest relevance scores (e.g., in the cosine measure) to the whole document are selected to be included in the summary. When the intended summary aims to cover the more important concepts as well as the different ones within or among documents, after the first sentence with the highest relevance score is selected, indexing terms in that sentence can be removed from the document. The document vector is then reconstructed accordingly, based on which the next sentence can be selected, and so on.[19] The latent semantic analysis (LSA) model for IR is another example of a model that can be used to represent each sentence of a document as a vector in the latent semantic space for that document. This space is constructed by performing SVD on the "term-sentence" matrix for that document. The right singular vectors with larger singular values represent dimensions for more important latent semantic concepts in that document. Therefore, the sentences that have the largest index values in each of the top L right singular vectors are included in the summary.[19] A third statistical approach is carried out as follows: indicative sentences can be chosen from the document based on the sentence significance score (denoted as the *SenSig* model below). Given a sentence $S = \{t_1, t_2, \ldots t_j, \ldots t_J\}$ with length J, the sentence significance score $Sig(S)$ can be expressed using the following formula:

$$Sig(S) = \frac{1}{J} \sum_{j=1}^{J} [\beta_1 \cdot I(t_j) + \beta_2 \cdot F(t_j)] \tag{8}$$

where $I(t_j)$ is evaluated based on some statistical measure of term t_j (such as a product of term frequency (TF) and inverse document frequency (IDF)); $F(t_j)$ can be a linguistic measure of t_j (e.g., named entities and different parts-of-speech

(POSs) are given different weights, ignoring function words); and β_1 and β_2 are tunable weighting parameters.[20] These selected sentences in all the above cases can also be further condensed and shortened by removing the less important terms, if a higher compression ratio is desired.

4.2. *Probabilistic Generative Models*

Extractive document summarization also can be performed with probabilistic generative models.[21,22] For example, the HMM model originally formulated in IR can be applied to extractive spoken document summarization.[22] Each sentence S of a spoken document d_i is instead treated as a probabilistic generative model (or an HMM) consisting of n-gram distributions for predicting the document, and the terms (or words) in the document d_i are taken as an input observation sequence. The HMM model for a sentence can be expressed as the following using unigram modeling:

$$P_{HMM}(d_i|S) = \prod_{t_j \in d_i} [\lambda \cdot P(t_j|S) + (1-\lambda) \cdot P(t_j|C)]^{c(t_j, d_i)} \tag{9}$$

where λ is a weighting parameter, and $c(t_j, d_i)$ is the occurrence count of a term t_j in d_i. For each sentence HMM, the sentence model $P(t_j|S)$ and the collection model $P(t_j|C)$ can be simply estimated, respectively, from each sentence itself and a large text collection based on the maximum likelihood estimation (MLE). The weighting parameter λ can be further optimized by taking the document d_i as the training observation sequence and using the following EM training formula:

$$\hat{\lambda} = \frac{\sum_{t_j \in d_i} n(t_j, d_i) \cdot \frac{\lambda \cdot P(t_j|S)}{\lambda \cdot P(t_j|S) + (1-\lambda) \cdot P(t_j|C)}}{\sum_{t_j \in d_i} n(t_j, d_i)} \tag{10}$$

Once the HMM models for the sentences are estimated, they can thus be used to predict the occurrence probability of the terms in the spoken document, and the sentences with the highest probabilities are then selected and sequenced to form the final summary according to different summarization ratios.

In the sentence HMM, as previously shown in Equation 9, the sentence model $P(t_j|S)$ is linearly interpolated with the collection model $P(t_j|C)$ to have some probability of generating every term in the vocabulary. However, the true sentence model $P(t_j|S)$ might not be accurately estimated by the MLE, since the sentence consists of only a few terms and the portions of terms present in it are not the same as the probabilities of those terms in the true model. Therefore, we can explore the use of the relevance model (RM),[23,24] also originally formulated for IR, to get a more accurate estimation of the sentence model. In the extractive spoken document summarization task studied here, each sentence S of the document d_i to be summarized has its own associated relevant class R_s. This class is defined as the subset of documents in the collection that are relevant to the sentence S. The relevance model of the sentence S is defined to be the probability distribution $P(t_i|R_s)$, which gives the probability that we would observe a term t_j, if we were to randomly select a document from the relevant class R_s and then pick up a random term from that document.[23] Once the relevance model of the sentence S is constructed, it can be used to replace the original sentence model or to be combined with the original sentence model to produce a better estimated model. Because there is no prior knowledge about the subset of relevant documents for each sentence S, a local feedback-like procedure can be employed by taking S as a query and posing it to the IR system to obtain a ranked list of documents. The top L documents returned from the IR system are assumed to be the ones relevant to S, and the relevance model $P(t_j|R_s)$ of S can be therefore be constructed through the following equation:

$$P(t_j|R_s) = \sum_{d_i \in \{d\}_{\text{Top}L}} P(d_l|S) \cdot P(t_j|d_l) \tag{11}$$

where $\{d\}_{\text{Top}L}$ is the set of top L retrieved documents; and the probability $P(d_l|S)$ can be approximated by the following equation using Bayes' rule:

$$P(d_l|S) \approx \frac{P(d_l) \cdot P(S|d_l)}{\sum_{d_u \in \{d\}_{\text{Top}L}} P(d_u) \cdot P(S|d_u)} \tag{12}$$

A uniform prior probability $P(d_l)$ can be further assumed for the top L retrieved documents, and the sentence likelihood $P(S|d_l)$ can be calculated using an equation similar to Equation 3 once the IR system is implemented with the HMM retrieval model. Consequently, the relevance model $P(t_j|R_s)$ is linearly combined with the original sentence model $P(t_j|S)$ to form a more accurate sentence model:

$$\hat{P}(t_j|S) = \alpha \cdot P(t_j|S) + (1-\alpha) P(t_j|R_s) \tag{13}$$

where α is a weighting parameter. The final sentence HMM is thus expressed as:

$$\hat{P}_{HMM}(d_i|S) = \prod_{t_j \in d_i} \left[\lambda \cdot \hat{P}(t_j|S) + (1-\lambda) \cdot P(t_j|C)\right]^{c(t_j,d_i)} \tag{14}$$

A diagram of spoken document summarization jointly using the HMM and RM models is depicted in Figure 4.

4.3. *Spoken Documents*

The methods described above in Sections 4.1 and 4.2 are equally applicable to both text and spoken documents. However, spoken documents do involve extra difficul-

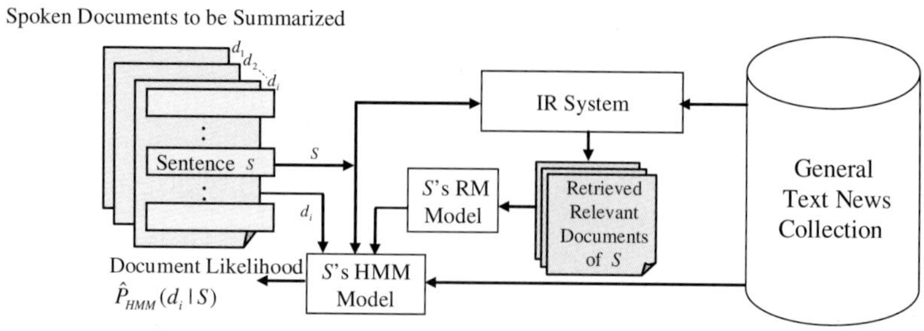

Fig. 4. A diagram of spoken document summarization jointly using the HMM and RM models.

ties like the handling of recognition errors, problems with spontaneous speech, and the lack of correct sentence or paragraph boundaries. In order to exclude the redundant and incorrect portions while selecting the important and correct information, multiple recognition hypotheses, confidence scores, language model scores and other grammatical knowledge have been utilized.[25] As an example, the above Equation 8 for the SenSig model may be extended as:

$$Sig(S) = \frac{1}{J}\sum_{j=1}^{J}\left[\beta_1 \cdot I(t_j) + \beta_2 \cdot F(t_j) + \beta_3 \cdot C(t_j) + \beta_4 \cdot G(t_j)\right] + \beta_5 \cdot H(S) \quad (15)$$

where $C(t_j)$ and $G(t_j)$ are obtained from the confidence score and n-gram score for the term t_j, $H(S)$ from the grammatical structure of the sentence S; and β_3, β_4 and β_5 are weighting parameters. In addition, prosodic features (e.g. intonation, pitch, energy, pause duration) can be used as important clues for summarization as well, although reliable and efficient approaches incorporating these features are still actively being studied.[25,26] The resulting summary of spoken documents can be generated in the form of either text or speech. Summaries in text have the advantage of easier browsing and further processing, but these are inevitably subject to speech recognition errors, as well as the loss of the speaker/emotional/prosodic information carried only by the speech signals. The speech form of summaries can preserve the latter information and is free from recognition errors, but it faces the difficult speech synthesis problem of smooth concatenation of speech segments.

5. A Prototype System of Chinese Spoken Document Retrieval and Summarization

5.1. *System Description*

A prototype system has been established in Taiwan that allows the user to search for Chinese broadcast news via the PDA using a spoken natural language query.[27]

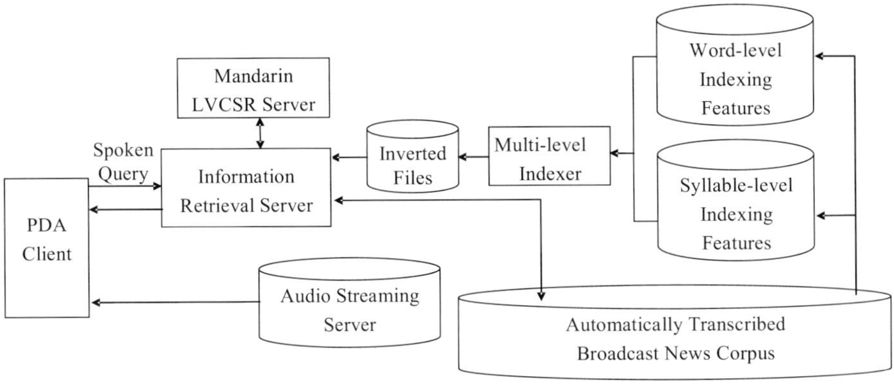

Fig. 5. The framework for voice retrieval of Chinese broadcast news.

The framework of the system is shown in Figure 5. There is a small client program on the PDA, as illustrated in Figure 6, which transmits the speech waveform or acoustic feature data of the spoken query to the information retrieval server. The information retrieval server then passes the speech waveform or acoustic feature data to the large vocabulary continuous speech recognition (LVCSR) server.[28] The recognition result is then passed back to the information retrieval server to act as the query to generate a ranked list of relevant documents. When the retrieval results are sent back to the PDA, the user can first browse the summaries of the retrieved documents, which were generated beforehand by jointly using the HMM and RM models, and then click to read the automatic transcript of the relevant broadcast news documents or play the corresponding audio files from the audio streaming server. On the other hand, a huge collection of broadcast news documents are recognized offline by the broadcast news transcription system, and the resultant transcripts are then utilized by the multi-scale indexer to generate the word-level and syllable-level indexing terms.[12] Only the VSM model for literal term matching of the spoken query and the spoken documents was implemented here for simplicity, although our previous experiments on Mandarin spoken document retrieval have demonstrated that the HMM retrieval model, and models with similar structure to the PLSA model, have superior retrieval performance over the VSM model.[7,11] The final retrieval indices, including the vocabularies and document occurrences of indexing terms of different types (word- and syllable-level indexing terms), are stored as inverted files[29] for efficient searching and comparison.

5.2. *Evaluation of Chinese Spoken Document Retrieval*

In order to evaluate the performance level of the retrieval system, a set of 20 simple queries with length of one to several words, in both text and speech forms, was man-

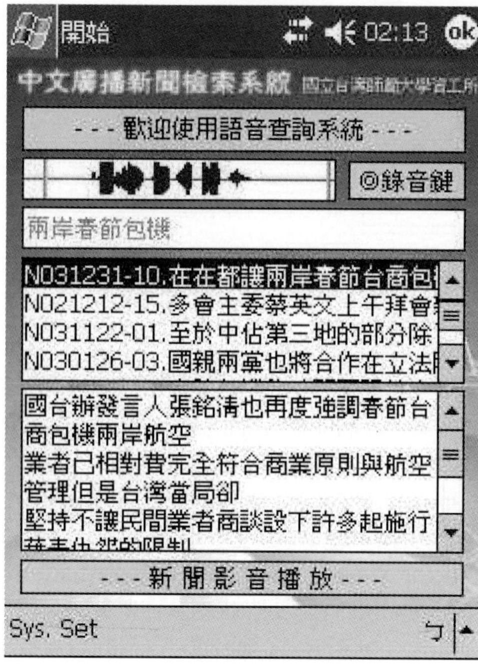

Fig. 6. A PDA-based broadcast news retrieval system that displays the retrieved broadcast news documents and their associated summaries for efficient browsing. The upper scrollable window lists the summaries of the retrieved documents, while the bottom one displays the automatic transcript of the selected document.

ually created. Four speakers (two males and two females) produced the 20 queries using an Acer n20 PDA with its original microphone in an environment with slight background noise. To recognize their spoken queries, another read speech corpus consisting of 8.5 hours of speech produced by an additional 39 male and 38 female speakers over the same type of PDA was used for training the speaker-independent acoustic models for recognition of the spoken queries. The character and syllable error rates for the spoken queries are 27.61% and 19.47%, respectively. The retrieval experiments were performed with respect to a collection of about 21,000 broadcast news stories. The final retrieval results are evaluated in terms of the mean average precision (mAP)[30] at different document cutoff values L, which computes the mean average precision when the top L documents have been presented to the user. The formula can be expressed as:

$$mAP_L = \frac{1}{E}\sum_{e=1}^{E}\frac{1}{N'_e}\sum_{i=1}^{N'_e}\frac{i}{r_{e,i}} \tag{16}$$

where E is the number of queries, N'_e is the total number of documents that are relevant to query Q_e appearing among the top L documents, and $r_{e,i}$ is the position of the i-th document that is relevant to query Q_e appearing among the top L documents, counting down from the top of the ranked list. The retrieval results are shown in Table 2. Columns 3, 4, 5 respectively show the results using

Table 2. The retrieval results evaluated in terms of the mean average precision at different document cutoff values.

		Word	Syllable	Word + Syllable
Document Cutoff: 10	Text Query	0.9309	0.8885	0.9580
	Spoken Query	0.5533	0.6036	0.6617
Document Cutoff: 30	Text Query	0.8838	0.8165	0.9224
	Spoken Query	0.5270	0.5435	0.6465
Document Cutoff: 50	Text Query	0.8656	0.7834	0.9065
	Spoken Query	0.5242	0.5212	0.6386

word-level indexing features, syllable-level indexing features and both of them, which are evaluated at different document cutoff values and with either text or spoken queries. As can be seen, the word-level indexing features are better than the syllable-level features for the text queries, while using both levels results in significant improvements over using any of them alone. Moreover, the retrieval results for the spoken queries are much worse than those of the text queries, but the combination of word-level and syllable-level features helps to reduce the performance gap between the spoken and the text queries.

5.3. *Evaluation of Chinese Spoken Document Summarization*

A set of 200 broadcast news documents (1.6 hours) collected in August 2001 were used in the summarization experiments. The average Chinese character error rate (CER) for the automatic transcripts of these broadcast news documents was 14.17%. Three human subjects were instructed to do human summarization, and this was taken to be the references for evaluation, in two forms: the first, simply to rank the importance of the sentences in the corresponding reference transcript of the broadcast news document from the top to the middle, and the second, to write

Table 3. The results achieved by jointly using the HMM and RM models, and by using other summarization models under different summarization ratios.

Summarization Ratio	HMM+RM	VSM	LSA-1	LSA-2	SenSig	Random
10%	0.3078	0.2845	0.2755	0.2498	0.2760	0.1122
20%	0.3260	0.3110	0.2911	0.2917	0.3190	0.1263
30%	0.3661	0.3435	0.3081	0.3378	0.3491	0.1834
50%	0.4762	0.4565	0.4070	0.4666	0.4804	0.3096

an abstract for the document manually by himself, with a length of about 25% of the original broadcast news document. Several summarization ratios were tested, which are the ratios of summary length to the total document length.[3] On the other hand, the ROUGE measure[31,32] was used to evaluate the performance levels of the proposed models and the other conventional models. It evaluates the summarization quality by counting overlapping units, such as the n-gram, word sequences and so forth, between the automatic summary and a set of reference (or manual) summaries. ROUGE-N is an n-gram recall measure which is defined as follows:

$$ROUGE-N = \frac{\sum_{S \in \mathbf{S}_R} \sum_{gram_n \in S} Count_{match}(gram_n)}{\sum_{S \in \mathbf{S}_R} \sum_{gram_n \in S} Count(gram_n)} \tag{17}$$

where N stands for the length of the n-gram; S is an individual reference (or manual) summary; $\mathbf{S}_R$ is a set of reference summaries; $Count_{match}(gram_n)$ is the maximum number of n-grams co-occurring in the automatic summary and the reference summary; and $Count(gram_n)$ is the number of n-grams in the reference summary. In this study, the ROUGE-2 measure that used word bigrams as the matching units was adopted.

The summarization results obtained by using the HMM and RM models jointly are shown in the second column of Table 3, and the corresponding ROUGE-2 recall rates are about 0.31, 0.33, 0.37, and 0.48 for summarization ratios of 10%, 20%, 30% and 50%, respectively. Then, we try to compare these results with those obtained by using the conventional VSM,[19] LSA, and SenSig[20] models. Two variants of LSA, i.e., the one mentioned in Section 4.1[19] (LSA-1) and the one proposed by Hirohata *et al.*[33] (LSA-2), were both evaluated here. For a spoken document, LSA-2 simply evaluated the score of each sentence based on the norm of its vector representation in the lower L-dimensional latent semantic space, and a fixed number of sentences having relatively large scores were therefore selected to form the summary. The value of L was set to 5 in our experiments, which is just the same as that suggested by Hirohata *et al.*[33] The results for these models are shown in Columns 3 to 6 of Table 3, and the results obtained by random selection (Random) is also listed for comparison. As can be seen, HMM+RM is substantially better than VSM and LSA at lower summarization ratios, and is significantly superior to SenSig as well, which provide some evidence that the probabilistic generative model (HMM+RM) is indeed a good candidate for extractive spoken document summarization tasks.

6. Conclusion

The ever-increasing storage capability and processing power of computers have made vast amounts of multimedia content available to the public. Clearly, speech is one of the most important sources of information for multimedia content, as it gives important, if not key, information regarding the content. Therefore, multimedia access based on associated spoken documents has been a focus of much active research. This chapter has presented a comprehensive overview of the information retrieval and automatic summarization technologies developed in recent years for efficient spoken document retrieval and browsing applications. An example prototype system for voice retrieval of Chinese broadcast news collected in Taiwan was also introduced.

References

1. B. H. Juang and S. Furui, "Automatic Recognition and Understanding of Spoken Languagełа First Step toward Natural Human-Machine Communication," in *Proc. IEEE 88(8)*, vol. 88(8), (2000), pp. 1142–1165.
2. L. S. Lee and B. Chen, "Spoken Document Understanding and Organization," *IEEE Signal Processing Magazine*, vol. 22(5), pp. 42–60, (2005).
3. Text retrieval conference (trec). [Online]. Available: http://trec.nist.gov/
4. G. Salton and M. E. Lesk, "Computer Evaluation of Indexing and Text Processing," *Journal of the ACM*, vol. 15(1), pp. 8–36, (1968).
5. J. M. Ponte and W. B. Croft, "A Language Modeling Approach to Information Retrieval," in *Proc. ACM SIGIR Conference on R&D in Information Retrieval*, (1998), pp. 275–281.
6. D. R. H. Miller, T. Leek, and R. Schwartz, "A Hidden Markov Model Information Retrieval System," in *Proc. ACM SIGIR Conference on R&D in Information Retrieval*, (1999), pp. 214–221.
7. B. Chen, H. M. Wang, and L. S. Lee, "A Discriminative HMM/N-Gram-Based Retrieval Approach for Mandarin Spoken Documents," *ACM Trans. on Asian Language Information Processing*, vol. 3, pp. 128–145, (2004).
8. G. W. Furnas, S. Deerwester, S. T. Dumais, T. K. Landauer, R. Harshman, L. A. Streeter, and K. E. Lochbaum, "Information Retrieval Using a Singular Value Decomposition Model of Latent Semantic Structure," in *Proc. ACM SIGIR Conference on R&D in Information Retrieval*, (1988), pp. 465–480.
9. J. R. Bellegarda, "Latent Semantic Mapping," *IEEE Signal Processing Magazine*, vol. 22(5), pp. 70–80, (2005).
10. T. Hofmann, "Probabilistic Latent Semantic Indexing," in *Proc. ACM SIGIR Conference on R&D in Information Retrieval*, (1999), pp. 50–57.
11. B. Chen, "Exploring the Use of Latent Topical Information for Statistical Chinese Spoken Document Retrieval," *Pattern Recognition Letters*, vol. 27(1), pp. 9–18, (2006).
12. B. Chen, H. M. Wang, and L. S. Lee, "Discriminating Capabilities of Syllable-Based Features and Approaches of Utilizing Them for Voice Retrieval of Speech Information in Mandarin Chinese," *IEEE Trans. on Speech and Audio Processing*, vol. 10, pp. 303–314, (2002).
13. K. Ng and V. W. Zue, "Subword-Based Approaches for Spoken Document Retrieval," *Speech Communication*, vol. 32, pp. 157–186, (2000).
14. S. Srinivasan and D. Petkovic, "Phonetic Confusion Matrix Based Spoken Document Retrieval," in *Proc. ACM SIGIR Conference on R&D in Information Retrieval*, (2000), pp. 81–87.
15. B. Chen, H. M. Wang, and L. S. Lee, "Improved Spoken Document Retrieval by Exploring Extra Acoustic and Linguistic Cues," in *Proc. European Conference on Speech Communication and Technology*, (2001), pp. 299–302.
16. E. Chang, F. Seide, H. Meng, Z. Chen, Y. Shi, and Y. C. Li, "A System for Spoken Query Information Retrieval on Mobile Devices," *IEEE Trans. on Speech and Audio Processing*, vol. l0, pp. 531–541, (2002).

17. A. Singhal and F. Pereira, “Document Expansion for Speech Retrieval,” in *Proc. ACM SIGIR Conference on R&D in Information Retrieval*, (1999), pp. 34–41.
18. I. Mani and E. M. T. Maybury, *Advances in Automatic Text Summarization*. (Cambridge. MA: MIT Press, 1999).
19. Y. Gong and X. Liu, “Generic Text Summarization Using Relevance Measure and Latent Semantic Analysis,” in *Proc. ACM SIGIR Conference on R&D in Information Retrieval*, (2001), pp. 19–25.
20. J. Goldstein, M. Kantrowitz, V. Mittal, and J. Carbonell, “Summarizing Text Documents: Sentence Selection and Evaluation Metrics,” in *Proc. ACM SIGIR Conference on R&D in Information Retrieval*, (1999), pp. 121–128.
21. B. Chen, Y. M. Yeh, Y. M. Huang, and Y. T. Chen, “Chinese Spoken Document Summarization Using Probabilistic Latent Topical Information,” in *Proc. IEEE International Conference on Acoustics, Speech, and Signal processing*, (2006), pp. 969–972.
22. Y. T. Chen, S. Yu, H. M. Wang, and B. Chen, “Extractive Chinese Spoken Document Summarization Using Probabilistic Ranking Models,” in *Proc. International Symposium on Chinese Spoken Language Processing*, (2006).
23. W. B. Croft and J. L. (Eds.), *Language Modeling for Information Retrieva*. (Kluwer-Academic Publishers, 2003).
24. M. D. Smucker, D. Kulp, and J. Allan, CIIR *Technical Report: Dirichlet Mixtures for Query Estimation in Information Retrieval*. (Center for Intelligent Information Retrieval, University of Massachusetts, 2005).
25. S. Furui, T. Kikuchi, Y. Shinnaka, and C. Hori, “Speech-to-Text and Speech-to-Speech Summarization of Spontaneous Speech,” *IEEE Trans. on Speech and Audio Processing*, vol. 12, pp. 401–408, (2004).
26. S. Maskey and J. Hirschberg, “Comparing Lexical, Acoustic/Prosodic, Structural and Discourse Features for Speech Summarization,” in *Proc. European Conference on Speech Communication and Technology*, (2005), pp. 621–624.
27. B. Chen, Y. T. Chen, C. H. Chang, and H. B. Chen, “Speech Retrieval of Mandarin Broadcast News via Mobile Devices,” in *Proc. European Conference on Speech Communication and Technology*, (2005), pp. 109–112.
28. B. Chen, J. W. Kuo, and W. H. Tsai, “Lightly Supervised and Data-Driven Approaches to Mandarin Broadcast News Transcription,” in *Proc. IEEE International Conference on Acoustics, Speech, and Signal processing*, (2004), pp. 777–780.
29. R. Baeza-Yates and B. Ribeiro-Neto, *Modern Information Retrieval*. (Addison-Wesley, 1999).
30. D. Harman, “Overview of the Fourth Text Retrieval Conference (TREC-4),” in *Proc. Fourth Text Retrieval Conference*, (1995), pp. 1–23.
31. C. Y. Lin. Rouge: Recall-oriented understudy for gisting evaluation (2003). [Online]. Available: http://www.isi.edu/ cyl/ROUGE/
32. ——, “Looking for a few Good Metrics: ROUGE and its Evaluation,” *Working Notes of NTCIR-4*, vol. Supl. 2, pp. 1–8, (2004).
33. M. Hirohata, Y. Shinnaka, K. Iwano, and S. Furui, “Sentence Extraction-Based Presentation Summarization Techniques and Evaluation metrics,” in *Proc. IEEE International Conference on Acoustics, Speech, and Signal processing*, (2005), pp. 1065–1068.

CHAPTER 14

SPEECH ACT MODELING AND VERIFICATION IN SPOKEN DIALOGUE SYSTEMS

Chung-Hsien Wu, Jui-Feng Yeh and Gwo-Lang Yan
Department of Computer Science and Information Engineering,
National Cheng Kung University,
No. 1, University Road, Tainan
E-mail: {chwu, jfyeh, glyan}@csie.ncku.edu.tw

Speech act, an essential element of conversation, underlies the principle that an utterance in a dialogue is an action being performed by a speaker. Since speech acts do convey speakers' intentions and opinions, it is key for the computer to identify and verify the speech act of a user's utterance in a spoken dialogue system. This chapter presents a few approaches to speech act identification and verification in Chinese spoken dialogue systems. Approaches using ontology-based partial pattern trees and semantic dependency graphs (SDGs) for speech act modeling are described. A verification mechanism using a latent semantic analysis (LSA) based Bayesian belief model (BBM) is adopted to improve the performance of speech act identification. Experimental results show the SDG-based approach outperforms the Bayes' classifier and the ontology-based partial pattern trees. By integrating discourse analysis into the SDG-based approach, the results show improvements obtained not only in the speech act identification accuracy rate, but also in the performance of semantic object extraction. Furthermore, LSA-based BBM for speech act verification further improves the performance of speech act identification.

1. Introduction

It would indeed be a tremendous achievement of computer technology to allow us to use natural spoken language to communicate with machines.[1,2] Understanding of spontaneous language is arguably the core technology of spoken dialogue systems, since the more accurate the information obtained by the machine is, the more possibilities there are to successfully complete a particular dialogue task.[3] Speech act theories proposed by Wittgenstein[4] and Austin[5] are now widely accepted in cognitive psychology. Searle[6] modified Austin's taxonomy of speech act[5] and suggested that all speech acts can be divided into five major classes. Some research extended speech acts to dialogue acts (also known as *dialogue moves* or *conversational moves*) that consist of figuring out the user's act and generating the system's output by integrating a grounding concept. In the realm of spoken language understanding, speech acts are used to represent the intentions of speakers. There is sufficient evidence to show that speech act theory is compatible with and effective for cognitive psychology.[4,5,6] Practical uses of speech act theories in spoken language processing have given both insight into and deeper understanding of verbal communication.[7,8,9] Shriberg *et al.*[10] and Woszczyna *et al.*[11] also applied speech act theory to facilitate comprehension of the speaker's utterance using a CART-style decision tree and hidden Markov models (HMMs) to capture speaker intentions, respectively.

In the last decade, several practical dialogue systems,[12] such as systems for air travel information service, weather forecast information, automatic banking services, automatic train timetable information, and the Circuit-Fix-it shop, have been developed to extract the user's semantic entities using semantic frames/slots and conceptual graphs. The dialogue management in these systems is able to handle the dialogue flow effectively. However, there are two essential issues which should be considered for augmenting dialogue systems in practical application: robustness of speech act identification and capability for multiple services. Due to the versatility of spontaneous speech, robust extraction of sentence patterns is crucial for speech act identification. Conventional task-specific dialogue management is not applicable to more complex applications such as a dialogue system that provides multiple services. As users switch directly from one service to another in the same dialogue exchange, a typical system fails in task-switching due to the absence of discourse analysis for precise speech act identification. Besides switching tasks, the successful completion of a service in dialogue systems also relies heavily on accurate speech act identification and semantic object extraction. Therefore, when considering the whole discourse, the relationship between the speech acts of the dialogue turns becomes extremely important.

This chapter presents two approaches to speech act identification: an ontology-based partial pattern tree for sentence pattern modeling and a semantic dependency graph (SDG) for discourse characterization. Finally, a Bayesian belief model (BBM),[13] based on latent semantic analysis (LSA),[14] is adopted to verify the potential speech acts and to determine the final speech act. For performance evaluation, a medical dialogue system with multiple services, including registration information, clinic information and FAQ information, is implemented. Experimental results show that the approach based on SDGs outperforms the Bayes' classifier and partial pattern trees. In addition, the LSA-based BBM for speech act verification further improves the performance of speech act identification.

2. Speech Act Identification

For speech act identification, this study firstly extracts the semantic words or concepts using latent semantic analysis (LSA). Based on these extracted semantic words and the domain ontology, a partial pattern tree is constructed to model the speech act of a spoken utterance.[15] The partial pattern tree is used to deal with the problem of ill-formed sentences in spoken dialogue systems. Concept expansion based on domain ontology is also adopted to improve system performance.

A novel approach to modeling the discourse of spoken dialogue is the use of semantic dependency graphs.[16] By characterizing the discourse as a sequence of speech acts, discourse modeling becomes the process of identifying speech act sequences. A statistical approach is adopted to model the relations between words in the user's utterance using the semantic dependency graphs. The dependency between the headword and other words in a sentence is detected by the semantic dependency grammar.

2.1. *Speech Act Identification Using Ontology-based Partial Pattern Tree*

In the task of identifying speech acts, word matching is not a directly applicable solution in spontaneous speech since word order is a very important aspect of sentence understanding. Consequently, in this study, a partial pattern tree (PPT) is used to partially match the words from ill-formed input utterances with the speech act patterns in the PPT for a more robust speech act identification. Two pre-processes, corpus collection and partial pattern tree construction, are essential for this ontology-based speech act identification.

Semantic Word Extraction based on Latent Semantic Analysis: In statistical approaches, the corpus generally plays an important role in both parameter estimation and model construction. Here, three methods of collecting corpus were employed – telephone recording followed by transcription, using the Wizard of Oz (WOZ) corpus and an on-line collection – as illustrated in Figure 1. The first set of corpus was obtained by recording service phone calls between users and the operator which are then transcribed. Via the WOZ corpus, dialogues between subjects and a system, which is monitored by a human via the internet, were recorded. In this method, users think they are talking to an automatic dialogue system. Following the creation of a prototype of the system, an on-line corpus was collected from actual on-line dialogues between users and an automatic dialogue system.

Latent semantic analysis (LSA) is a novel approach to automated document indexing based on a latent class model for factor analysis of count data. There are two motivations for using this analysis approach. First, semantic words extracted from LSA are more suitable for speech act representation, instead of manually-selected keywords. Secondly, LSA that projects higher dimensions into the latent semantic

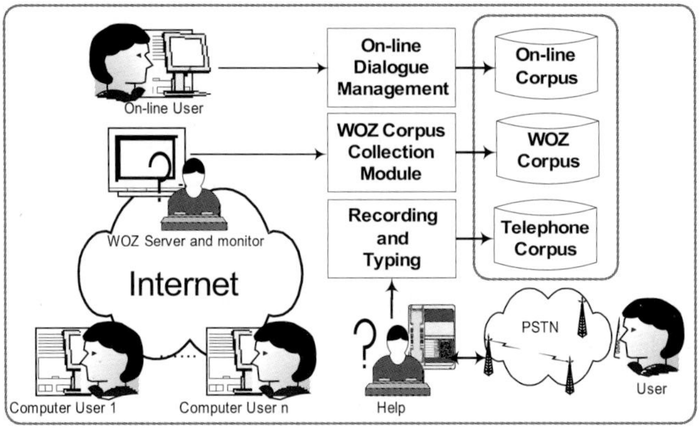

Fig. 1. Three methods of corpus collection.

space from the original space presents a method for dimensionality reduction. In this study, a SpeechAct-by-Word matrix is first constructed. The mapping is performed by decomposing the SpeechAct-by-Word matrix A into the product of three matrices, W, S, and SA using singular value decomposition.

$$A_{t\times d} = W_{t\times n}S_{n\times n}(SA_{d\times n})^T \approx W_{t\times r}S_{r\times r}(SA_{d\times r})^T = \tilde{A}_{t\times d} \tag{1}$$

where $n = \min(t,d)$. The matrices, W and SA, have orthonormal columns. This means that column vectors have unit length and all vectors are orthogonal to each other. In fact, these vectors are the eigenvectors. The diagonal matrix S contains the singular values of A in descending order. The i-th singular value indicates the number of variations along the i-th axis. The LSA approximation of A is computed by thresholding all but the largest r singular value in S. Besides dimensionality reduction, the LSA also keeps semantic words while filtering out irrelevant words.

Construction of Partial Pattern Tree: In general, each utterance can be represented as a sequence of function words and a semantic word from the key word set as $S_i = \{FP_1^i, FP_2^i, \cdots, FP_{NB}^i, SW^i, FP_{NB_{i+1}}^i, \cdots, FP_{NB_i+NA_i}^i\}$, where SW^i denotes the semantic word and FP_j^i denotes the j-th function word in the utterance S_i. NB_i and NA_i represent the number of function words before and after the semantic word, respectively. Therefore, $2^{NB_i+NA_i}$ partial pattern sequences containing the semantic word SW^i, will be generated according to the definition of PPT. As illustrated in Figure 2, the training sentence "I need a diagnosis" with a semantic word "diagnosis" will generate eight partial pattern sequences, such as "I need a diagnosis," "I need … diagnosis," "I … a diagnosis," "I … diagnosis," "… need a diagnosis," "… need… diagnosis," "… a diagnosis" and "… diagnosis." Each partial pattern is presented as a path in the PPT from root node to the leaf node that denotes the corresponding pattern as shown in Table 1. For practical implementation, the words

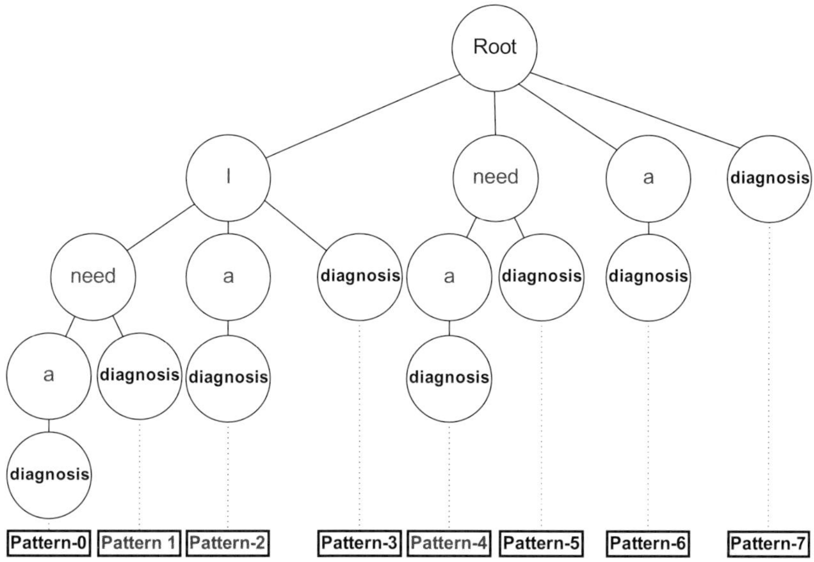

Fig. 2. An example of the partial pattern tree constructed from the sentence "I need a diagnosis." with "**diagnosis**" as its semantic word.

in the sequence excluding the semantic word are termed the "*don't care*" function words according to their positions in the utterances. Patterns are formed by ignoring function words, labeling the bit for the "*don't care*" function word as 1.

The PPT is basically an integrated tree structure of the partial pattern sequences generated from the training sentences. Each partial pattern sequence is tagged with one speech act. Each internal node representing a word in the partial pattern tree is denoted as $IN_i = \{PH_i, FR_i, Ns_i, Son_i\}$, where PH_i is the word in this internal node. FR_i is the frequency of the internal node, while Ns_i is the number of the descending internal nodes. Son_i is the pointer linked to the node's son (or child). Each external node represents one partial pattern sequence which corresponds to one speech act in the PPT. The data structure of the external node is defined as $EN_i = \{PP_i, Ptr_i, P\left(SA_i^k\right)\}$, where PP_i is the reference partial pattern sequence. Ptr_i, is the pattern pointer set. $P\left(SA_i^k\right)$ is the probability of the k-th speech act with respect to the i-th partial pattern sequence. The algorithm for constructing the PPT is described in another work.[15]

Speech Act Identification using Ontology-based PPT: Using the constructed PPT, speech act identification can be performed by matching the input utterance to the partial pattern sequence in the PPT. Dynamic programming algorithm is applied to deal with the problem of word order which is found to be important for detecting user intention. If the input utterance is $P_i = \{a_1, a_2, \ldots, a_I\}$ and $PP_j = \{b_1, b_2, \ldots, b_J\}$ is the external node representing the j-th partial pattern se-

Table 1. Illustration of partial patterns derived from the utterance "I need a diagnosis" with the semantic word "**diagnosis**".

	"Don't care" function words			**Partial Pattern**	**Description**
	b1	b2	b3		
Pattern-0	0	0	0	I need a **diagnosis**	Original sentence.
Pattern-1	0	0	1	I need ... **diagnosis.**	Neglecting the function word between "need" and "diagnosis."
Pattern-2	0	1	0	I ... a **diagnosis**	Neglecting the function word between "I" and "need."
Pattern-3	0	1	1	I ... **diagnosis**	Neglecting the function words between "I" and "diagnosis."
Pattern-4	1	0	0	... need a **diagnosis**	Neglecting the first function word.
Pattern-5	1	0	1	... need ... **diagnosis**	Neglecting the function words between "need" and "diagnosis" and the 1st word
Pattern-6	1	1	0	... a **diagnosis**	Neglecting the first two function words.
Pattern-7	1	1	1	... **diagnosis**	Neglecting all function words.

quence, the similarity of these two sequences can be obtained using the Needleman-Wunsch algorithm[17] shown in the following 3 steps:

(i) **Initialize**: Create a matrix with $I+1$ columns and $J+1$ rows. The first row and first column of the matrix can be initially filled with 0. That is,

$$Sim(i,j) = 0, \text{ if } i=0 \text{ or } j=0 \tag{2}$$

(ii) **Score pathways through array**: Assign the values to the remnant elements in the matrix as follows:

$$Sim(i,j) = \max \begin{cases} Sim(i-1,j-1) + Sim_{onto}(a_{i-1},b_{j-1}), \\ Sim(i-1,j) + Sim_{onto}(a_{i-1},b_j), \\ Sim(i,j-1) + Sim_{onto}(a_i,b_{j-1}) \end{cases} \tag{3}$$

(iii) **Construct alignment**: Determine the actual alignment with the maximum score $Sim(P_i, PP_j)$.

It is difficult to obtain an exact matching between an input utterance and its partial pattern sequence due to the versatility of spoken language, especially in the area of word sense. To solve this problem, an ontology is employed for measuring word similarity. Two basic word relations: hypernymy and synonymy are introduced. The similarity described in Equations 2 and 3 is defined as follows:

$$Sim_{onto}(a_i,b_j) = \begin{cases} 1 & \text{if } a_i = b_j \\ \left(\frac{1}{2}\right)^l & \text{if } a_i \text{ and } b_j \text{ are hypernyms} \\ 1-\left(\frac{1}{2}\right)^n & \text{if } a_i \text{ and } b_j \text{ are synonyms} \\ 0 & \text{otherwise} \end{cases} \tag{4}$$

where l is the number of levels between a_i and b_j. The variable n is the number of their common synonyms in the synonym set. Finally, the speech act for the input utterance P_i is determined according to the following equation.

$$SA^*(P_i) \equiv \arg\max_{k,j} \left\{ P\left(SA_j^k\right) \times Sim\left(P_i, PP_j\right) \right\} \tag{5}$$

where $P\left(SA_j^k\right)$ is the probability of the k-th speech act with respect to the j-th partial pattern sequence estimated in the construction of the PPT.

2.2. *Speech Act Identification using Semantic Dependency Graphs*

Since speech act theory can be applied to extracting the functional meaning of an utterance in a dialogue, discourse or history can be defined as a sequence of speech acts, $H^t = \{SA^1, SA^2, \ldots, SA^{t-1}, SA^t\}$. Accordingly, the speech act theory can be adopted for discourse modeling. Based on this definition, the analysis of semantics in discourse, using SDGs, tries to identify the speech act sequence in that discourse. Therefore, discourse modeling by means of speech act identification taking into consideration the discoursal history is shown in Equation 6. By introducing the hidden variable D_i, representing the i-th possible SDG derived from the word sequence W, the probability of hypothesis SA^t given word sequence W and history H^{t-1} can be described in Equation 6. According to the Bayes' rule, the speech act identification model can be decomposed into two components, $P\left(SA^t, |D_i, W, H^{t-1}\right)$ and $P\left(D_i, |W, H^{t-1}\right)$, described in the following.

$$\begin{aligned} SA^* &= \arg\max_{SA^t} P\left(SA^t | W, H^{t-1}\right) \\ &= \arg\max_{SA^t} \sum_{D_i} P\left(SA^t, D_i | W, H^{t-1}\right) \\ &= \arg\max_{SA^t} \sum_{D_i} P\left(SA^t | D_i, W, H^{t-1}\right) \times P\left(D_i | W, H^{t-1}\right) \end{aligned} \tag{6}$$

where SA^* and SA^t are the most probable speech act and the potential speech act at the t-th dialogue turn, respectively. $W = \{w_1, w_2, w_3, \ldots, w_m\}$ denotes the word sequence extracted from the user's utterance without considering stop words. H^{t-1} is the history representing the previous $t-1$ turns.

In this analysis, we apply semantic dependency, word sequence, and discourse analysis to the identification of an utterance's speech act. Since D_i is the i-th possible SDG derived from word sequence W, speech act identification with semantic dependency can be simplified as Equation 7.

$$P\left(SA^t | D_i, W, H^{t-1}\right) \cong P\left(SA^t | D_i, H^{t-1}\right) \tag{7}$$

According to Bayes' rule, the probability $P\left(SA^t|D_i,H^{t-1}\right)$ can be rewritten as:

$$P\left(SA^t|D_i,H^{t-1}\right) = \frac{P\left(D_i,H^{t-1}|SA^t\right)P\left(SA^t\right)}{\sum\limits_{SA_l} P\left(D_i,H^{t-1},|SA_l\right)P\left(SA_l\right)} \tag{8}$$

As history is defined as the functional sequence of speech acts, the joint probability of D_i and H^{t-1} given the speech act SA^t can be expressed as Equation 9. For the problem of data sparseness in the training corpus, the probability $P\left(D_i,SA^1,SA^2,\ldots,SA^{t-1},|SA^t\right)$, is hard to obtain and so the speech act bi-gram model is adopted for approximation.

$$\begin{aligned} P\left(D_i,H^{t-1}|SA^t\right) &= P\left(D_i,SA^1,SA^2,\ldots,SA^{t-1},|SA^t\right) \\ &\cong P\left(D_i,SA^{t-1}|SA^t\right) \end{aligned} \tag{9}$$

To combine both semantic and syntactic structures, the relations defined in HowNet serve as the basis of the syntactic dependency relations, while the hypernymical semantic relation between words is adopted according to the primary features of these words as defined in HowNet. Headword selection is determined by the algorithm based on part of speech (POS) proposed by the Academia Sinica in Taiwan. The probabilities of headwords are estimated according to the probabilistic context free grammar (PCFG) trained on the Chinese Treebank developed by the Academia Sinica.[18] That is to say, the headwords are extracted according to the syntactic structure and the semantic dependency graphs are constructed by the semantic relations defined in HowNet as shown in Figure 3.

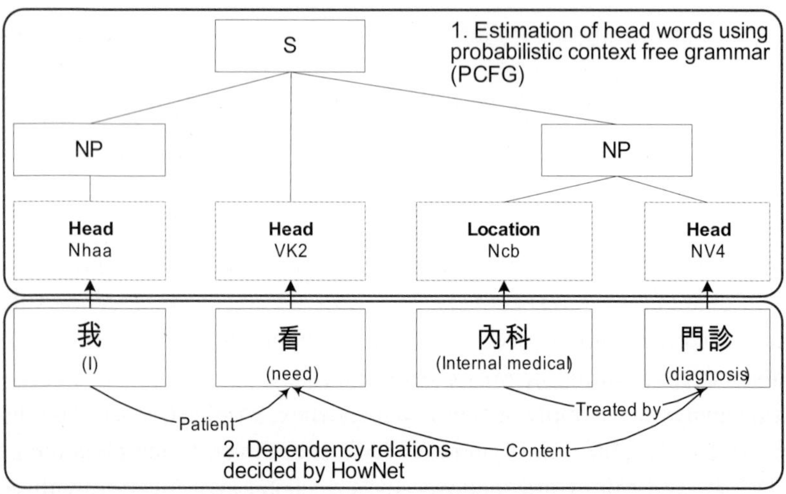

Fig. 3. The probabilities of the headwords are estimated according to the probabilistic context free grammar (PCFG). The headwords are extracted according to the syntactic structure and the semantic dependency graphs are constructed by the semantic relations defined in HowNet.

The dependency relation r_k, between word w_k and headword w_{kh} is extracted using HowNet and denoted as $DR(w_k, w_{kh}) \equiv r_k$. The SDG which is composed of a set of dependency relations in the word sequence W is defined as $D_i(W) = \{DR_1^i(w_1, w_{1h}), DR_2^i(w_2, w_{2h}), \ldots, DR_{m-1}^i(w_{m-1}, w_{(m-1)h})\}$.

According to the previous definition with the independent assumption and the bi-gram smoothing of the speech act model using the back-off procedure, we can rewrite Equation 9 into Equation 10.

$$\begin{aligned} & P\left(D_i, SA^{t-1}|SA^t\right) \\ & = \alpha \prod_{k=1}^{m-1} P\left(DR_k^i(w_k, w_{kh}), SA^{t-1}|SA^t\right) \\ & + (1-\alpha) \prod_{k=1}^{m-1} P\left(DR_k^i(w_k, w_{kh})|SA^t\right) \end{aligned} \tag{10}$$

where α is the mixture factor for normalization.

According to the conceptual representation of the word, the transformation function $f(\cdot)$, transforms the word into its hypernym defined as the semantic class using HowNet. The dependency relation between the semantic classes of two words will be mapped onto the conceptual space. The semantic roles between the dependency relations are also obtained. On the condition that SA^t, SA^{t-1} and the relations are independent, the equation becomes

$$\begin{aligned} & P\left(DR_k^i(w_k, w_{kh}), SA^{t-1}|SA^t\right) \\ & \cong P\left(DR_k^i(f(w_k), f(w_{kh})), SA^{t-1}|SA^t\right) \\ & = P\left(DR_k^i(f(w_k), f(w_{kh}))|SA^t\right) P\left(SA^{t-1}|SA^t\right) \end{aligned} \tag{11}$$

The conditional probability, $P\left(DR_k^i(f(w_k), f(w_{kh}))|SA^t\right)$ and $P\left(SA^{t-1}|SA^t\right)$, are estimated according to Equations 12 and 13, respectively.

$$P\left(DR_k^i(f(w_k), f(w_{kh}))|SA^t\right) = \frac{C\left(f(w_k), f(w_{kh}), r_k, SA^t\right)}{C(SA^t)} \tag{12}$$

$$P\left(SA^{t-1}|SA^t\right) = \frac{C\left(SA^{t-1}, SA^t\right)}{C(SA^t)} \tag{13}$$

where $C(\cdot)$ represents the number of events in the training corpus. According to the definitions in Equations 12 and 13, Equation 11 becomes practicable.

Although the discourse can be expressed in terms of the speech act sequence $H^t = \{SA^1, SA^2, \ldots, SA^{t-1}, SA^t\}$, the SDG D_i is determined mainly by W, instead of H^{t-1}. The probability that defines semantic dependency analysis using word sequence and discourse can be rewritten as the following:

$$P\left(D_i|W, H^{t-1}\right) = P\left(D_i|W, SA^{t-1}, SA^{t-2}, \ldots, SA^1\right) \cong P(D_i|W) \tag{14}$$

and

$$P(D_i|W) = \frac{P(D_i, W)}{P(W)} \tag{15}$$

Seeing that several SDGs can be generated from the word sequence W, by introducing the hidden factor D_i, the probability $P(W)$ can be the sum of the probabilities as expressed by Equation 16.

$$P(W) = \sum_{D_i:yield(D_i)=W} P(D_i, W) \tag{16}$$

Because D_i is generated from W, D_i is sufficient to represent W in semantics. We can estimate the joint probability $P(D_i, W)$ only from the dependency relations D_i. Further, the dependency relations are assumed to be independent of each other and therefore simplified as

$$P(D_i, W) = \prod_{k=1}^{m-1} P\left(DR_k^i(w_k, w_{kh})\right) \tag{17}$$

The probability of the dependency relation between words is approximated as the dependency relation between the concepts defined as the hypernyms of the words, and then the dependency rules are introduced. The probability $P(r_k|f(w_k), f(w_{kh}))$ is estimated from Equation 18.

$$\begin{aligned} P\left(DR_k^i(w_k, w_{kh})\right) &\equiv P\left(DR_k^i(f(w_k), f(w_{kh}))\right) \\ &= P(r_k|f(w_k), f(w_{kh})) \\ &= \frac{C(r_k, f(w_k), f(w_{kh}))}{C(f(w_k), f(w_{kh}))} \end{aligned} \tag{18}$$

According to Equations 16, 17 and 18, Equation 15 is rewritten as the following equation:

$$\begin{aligned} P(D_i|W) &= \frac{\prod_{k=1}^{m-1} P\left(DR_k^i(w_k, w_{kh})\right)}{\sum_{D_i:yield(D_i)=W} \prod_{k=1}^{m-1} P\left(DR_k^i(w_k, w_{kh})\right)} \\ &= \frac{\prod_{k=1}^{m-1} \frac{C(r_k, f(w_k), f(w_{kh}))}{C(f(w_k), f(w_{kh}))}}{\sum_{D_i:yield(D_i)=W} \prod_{k=1}^{m-1} \frac{C(r_k, f(w_k), f(w_{kh}))}{C(f(w_k), f(w_{kh}))}} \end{aligned} \tag{19}$$

where function $f(\cdot)$, denotes the transformation of the words into their corresponding semantic classes.

3. Speech Act Verification

Usually, the speech act of a spoken utterance is characterized by descriptive information which includes not only keywords but also the interactions between words, especially words that occupy semantic slots. This study presents an LSA-based BBM of the above characteristics, which is then used to verify the determined speech act.[19] The LSA-based BBM not only incorporates the relationship between keywords and a speech act, but also uses latent semantic analysis to discover the "hidden" interactions between keywords in a speech act.

Given a fragment sequence $W: w_1, w_2, \ldots, w_N$, a speech act can be verified by considering the combination of fragments in a sentence. An arbitrary number of mutually exclusive and exhaustive speech acts $SA_x\,(x = 1, \ldots, H)$, are assumed to partition the speech act universe. The verification is generalized as

$$P(SA_x|w_1w_2\ldots w_N) = \frac{P(SA_x) \times P(w_1w_2\ldots w_N|SA_x)}{\sum\limits_{i=1}^{H} P(w_1w_2\ldots w_N|SA_i) \times P(SA_i)} \tag{20}$$

Even though Equation 20 models the interaction between fragments in a speech act, the conditional probability $P(w_1w_2\ldots w_N|SA_x)$ is very difficult to calculate from the training corpus because the data are sparse. In practice, the Bayesian probability model[20] is often simplified by assuming that all fragments are statistically independent.

$$P(w_1w_2\ldots w_N|SA_x) = P(w_1|SA_x) \times P(w_2|SA_x) \times \cdots \times P(w_N|SA_x) \tag{21}$$

Based on this assumption, the Bayesian belief model can be used to represent the probabilistic and causal relationship because such a model is a directed acyclic graph in which the nodes (fragments) represent distinct pieces of evidence. The arcs represent causal relationships between these pieces of evidence. This model provides a clean, useful formalism for combining distinct evidence in support of the verification. However, applying the above independence assumption to the Bayesian probability model undermines the latent semantic information (inter-dependencies) between fragments in a speech act. The verification ability can be improved by capturing possible inter-dependencies between fragments. Therefore, the LSA is exploited to find the inter-dependencies between fragments in an input fragment sequence. The primary idea behind the exploration of latent semantic information is to convert the fragments and their corresponding sentences into a lower dimensional space. The starting point is the construction of an association matrix R between fragments and sentences for a speech act SA_x in the training corpus. Each sentence is associated with a row vector of dimension N (fragment number) in this matrix, and each fragment is associated with a column vector of dimension M (sentence number). The element R_{ij} in the association matrix R represents the number of occurrences of the i-th fragment in the j-th sentence. The association matrix R, constructed from the training corpus, is extremely large and typically very sparse. Singular value decomposition (SVD), a technique related to eigenvector decomposition and factor analysis,[21] is applied to decompose the association matrix R into three components. Consider that only the D largest singular values of S are kept along with their corresponding columns in U and V. The resultant matrix R_D is the matrix of rank D which is close to the original matrix R in the least square sense.

$$R \cong R_D = USV^T \tag{22}$$

where $U_{M\times D}$ is a left singular matrix with row vector $u_i\,(l \le i \le M)$. It is the matrix of eigenvectors derived from the fragment-to-fragment correlation matrix given by $R^T R$; $V_{N\times D}$ is a right-singular matrix with row vectors $v_j\,(l \le j \le N)$. This is the matrix of eigenvectors derived from the transpose of the sentence-to-sentence matrix given by RR^T; $S_{D\times D}$ is a $D\times D$ diagonal matrix of singular values. U and V are defined as orthonormal bases in the space of D dimensions; that is, $U^TU = V^TV = I_D$. The relationship between any two fragments in the reduced space of dimensionality D can be obtained from the $R^T R$ matrix,

$$\psi R_D{}^T R_D = \left(USV^T\right)^T USV^T = VSU^TUSV^T = VSSV^T = VS(VS)^T \tag{23}$$

The element $\psi = (i, j)$ quantifies the strength of the relationship between fragments w_i and w_j. The concurrent probability $P(w_iw_j|SA_x)$, which measures the inter-dependency between fragments w_i and w_j in the speech act SA_x, is defined as

$$P(w_iw_j|SA_x) = \frac{\psi(i,j)}{N_c(SA_x)} \tag{24}$$

where $N_c(SA_x)$ is the number of sentences in the speech act SA_x. The fragment pair w_iw_j is then defined as a compound fragment when the condition $P(w_iw_j|SA_x) \ge P(w_i|SA_x)\times P(w_j|SA_x)$ is satisfied. The process is performed recursively when the newly defined compound fragments replace the column elements of R.

Based on this concept, fragments "內科 (internal medicine)" and "診斷 (diagnosis)" for example, will form a compound fragment in which the probability P(內科 (internal medicine), 診斷 (diagnosis) $|SA_x)$ will replace the probabilities P(內科 (internal medicine) $|SA_x)$ and P(診斷 (diagnosis) $|SA_x)$ as shown in Equation 25 to assist in estimating speech act verification score more precisely. 1,812 compound fragments that contain two or three fragments are considered because a high-order fragment relationship is difficult to derive from a sparse corpus. These new relationships discovered by LSA are used to create concept nodes and form a new BBM. The following conditional probability is then redefined as

$$P(w_1w_2\ldots w_N|SA_x) = P(v_1v_2\ldots v_T|SA_x) = \prod_{t=1}^{T} P(v_t|SA_x) \tag{25}$$

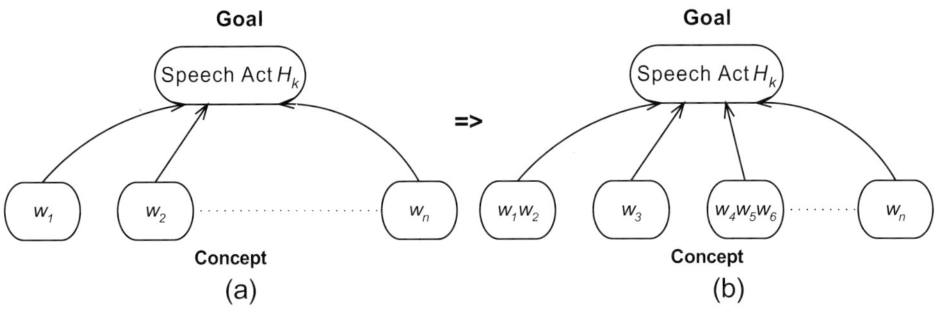

Fig. 4. (a) Topology of the Bayesian belief model. (b) Proposed topology of LSA-based Bayesian belief model.

where $v_1v_2\ldots v_T$ refers to the relationship that corresponds to $w_1w_2\ldots w_N$ for the speech act SA_x. Figure 4 displays an example. If compound fragments v_1, v_2, v_3, …, and v_T are derived from w_1w_2, w_3, $w_4w_5w_6$, …, and w_N, respectively, then the conditional probability is

$$P(w_1w_2\ldots w_6\ldots w_N|SA_x) = \prod_{t=1}^{T} P(v_t|SA_x)$$
$$= P(w_1w_2|SA_x) \times P(w_3|SA_x) \times P(w_4w_5w_6|SA_x) \times \cdots \times P(w_N|SA_x) \quad (26)$$

The estimated conditional probability is then integrated into the proposed system for speech act verification. The verification score from the LSA-based BBM for the identified speech act SA^* and the fragment sequence W^* is defined as follows:

$$VScore(W^*|SA^*;U) = \log(P(SA^*|w_1^*\ldots w_n^*\ldots w_N^*))$$
$$= \log\left(\frac{P(SA^*) \times P(v_1v_2\ldots v_T|SA^*)}{\sum_{i=1}^{H} P(SA_i) \times P(v_1v_2\ldots v_T|SA_i)}\right) \quad (27)$$

where w_n^* is the n-th fragment in the identified fragment sequence W^*. The speech act with the verification score $VScore\left(W^k|SA_{W^k}^*;U\right)$, above a selected threshold T is regarded as the final output. Conversely, any speech act candidate with a score below the threshold is rejected.

4. Experiments

In order to evaluate the proposed method, a multiple services spoken dialogue system for the medical domain was investigated. Three main services, registration information, clinic information, and FAQ information services were provided. This system mainly performs the function of on-line registration. For this goal, the health education documents are provided as the FAQ files. The inference engine regarding clinic information according to patients' syndromes was constructed based on a medical encyclopedia. To reach these goals, 12 speech acts are defined. Every service corresponds to the 12 speech acts with different probabilities.

4.1. *Analysis of Corpus*

The training corpus was collected via telephone recordings from the National Cheng Kung University Hospital in the first phase and by the WOZ method in the second phase. In total, there are 1,862 dialogues with 13,986 sentences in the corpus. The frequencies of the speech acts used in the system are shown in Figure 5.

The number of dialogue turns is also important to the success of the dialogue task. An observation of the corpus reveals that dialogues with more than 15 turns

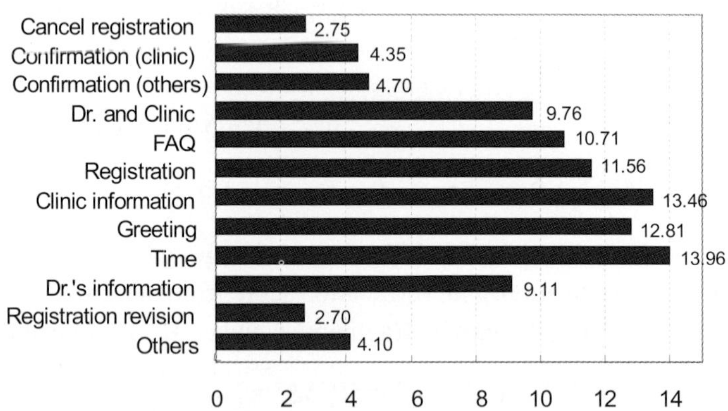

Fig. 5. Frequencies for each speech act in the corpus.

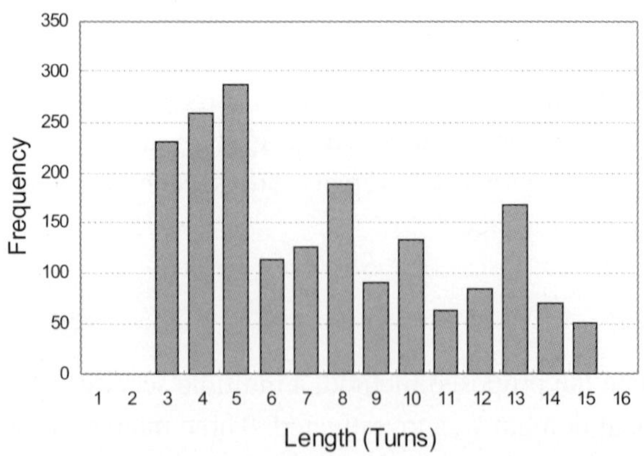

Fig. 6. The distribution of the number of turns per dialogue.

usually fail to complete the dialogue. That is to say, a common ground cannot be achieved. These failed dialogues were filtered out from the training corpus before conducting the following experiments. The distribution of the number of turns per dialogue is shown in Figure 6.

4.2. *Performance Analysis of Speech Act Identification*

To evaluate the performance, three systems – the Bayes' classifier,[22] the approaches based on PPT, and the semantic dependency graph – were separately developed to identify the speech acts of users' utterances and the results of these are compared. Since the dialogue discourse is defined as a sequence of speech acts, the prediction of the speech act of the new input utterance becomes the core issue for discourse modeling. The accuracy rates for speech act identification are shown in Table 2.

Based on the results, the SDG-based approach performs significantly better compared to the other approaches. The reason is that not only do meanings of words and concepts play a role in identifying speech acts, but so do the structural information and implicit semantic relations defined in the knowledge base. Besides, taking the flow of the discourse into consideration will improve the prediction of the speech act of the new or next utterance. The discourse model can thus improve the accuracy of the speech act identification. Discourse modeling can also help ascertain the user's desired intention, especially when his answer is very short. For example, the user may only say "yes" or "no" for confirmation. A misclassification of the short utterance's speech act is likely with only limited information. However, a better interpretation of this response by introducing semantic dependency relations as well as the discourse information can be obtained.

To obtain the single measurement, the average accuracy for speech act identification is shown in Table 2. The best approach is the SDG with discourse analysis,

Table 2. The accuracy (%) for speech act identification. The values in parentheses represent the numbers of speech acts tested or correctly identified speech acts using the respective approaches.

Speech act	**Semantic dependency graph**		**PPT**	**Bayes' Classifier**
	With discourse analysis	Without discourse analysis		
Dr. and Clinic (26)	100 (26)	96.1 (25)	88.0 (23)	92 (24)
Dr.'s information (42)	97.0 (41)	92.8 (39)	66.6 (28)	92.8 (39)
Confirmation (42)	95.0 (40)	95.0 (40)	95.0 (40)	95.0 (40)
Others (14)	57.1 (8)	50.0 (7)	43.0 (6)	38.0 (5)
FAQ (13)	70.0 (9)	53.8 (7)	61.5 (8)	46.0 (6)
Clinic information (135)	98.5 (133)	96.2 (130)	91.1 (123)	93.3 (126)
Time (38)	94.7 (36)	89.4 (34)	97.3 (37)	92.1 (35)
Registration (75)	100 (75)	100 (75)	86.6 (65)	86.6 (65)
Cancel registration (10)	90.0 (9)	80.0 (8)	60.0 (6)	80.0 (8)
Average Precision	**95.6**	**92.4**	**85**	**88.1**

Table 3. Comparisons of task completion rate and number of dialogue turns between different approaches.

	SDG(1)	SDG(2)	PPT	Bayes'
Task completion rate	87.2	85.5	79.4	80.2
Number of turns on average	8.3	8.7	10.4	10.5

SDG(1): With discourse analysis, SDG(2): Without discourse analysis.

Table 4. Accuracy rates for semantic object extraction.

	SDG(2)	PPT	Bayes'
Dr. and Clinic	95.0	89.5	90.3
Dr.'s information	94.3	71.7	92.4
Confirmation (Clinic)	98.0	98.0	98.0
Clinic information	97.3	74.6	78.6
Time	97.6	97.8	95.5

SDG(2):With discourse analysis.

directly reflecting that discoursal information do benefit speech act identification. The SDG-based approach employing the semantic analysis of words and their corresponding relations also outperforms the traditional approach.

The success of the dialogue lies on the achievement of a common ground between users and the system which is the most important issue in dialogue management. To compare the use of semantic dependency graph with earlier approaches, 150 individuals who have not been involved in the development of this project were asked to use the dialogue system with the goal of measuring the task success rate. A total of 131 dialogues were employed as the analysis data in this experiment, from which incomplete tasks were filtered out. The results are listed in Table 3. We find that the dialogue completion rate and the average length of the dialogues using the SDGs are better than those using the Bayes' classifier and the PPT approach. Two main conclusions are derived from this. First, the SDG does retain the most important information in a user's utterance, while in the semantic slot/frame approach, the semantic objects not matching the semantic slot/frame are generally filtered out. This filter enables us to skip repetition or similar utterances that would fill in the same information into different semantic slots. Second, the SDG-based approach does provide the inference to help in the interpretation of user intentions.

For the purpose of semantic understanding, correct interpretation of the information from user's utterances becomes crucial. Accurate speech act identification and correct extraction of semantic objects are both important issues for semantic understanding in spoken dialogue systems. Five main categories – medical application, clinic information, doctor's information, confirmation of the clinic's information, registration time and clinic inference – are analyzed in this experiment.

The results in Table 4 reflect that the worst-performing category is the query for doctor's information using the partial pattern tree. Here, the mis-identification of speech acts results in the unmatched semantic slots/frames. This mismatching will not occur with the SDG approach, since these graphs always retain the most important semantic objects according to their dependency relations in these semantic graphs, instead of just the semantic slots. Rather than filtering out the unmatched semantic objects, the SDG is constructed to keep the semantic relations in the utterance. This means that the system can preserve most of the user's information via the SDGs. This leads to the higher speech act identification from the SDG than that from the PPT and the Bayes' classifier approaches, as shown in Table 4.

4.3. *Experiment on Speech Act Verification*

In this experiment, singular value decomposition of the association matrix R is performed. Various numbers of singular values are considered and $D = 35$ is found to yield an acceptable reconstruction error. The experimental results presented in Figure 7 give the false acceptance rate (FAR) and false rejection rate (FRR) for various values of the threshold T. When threshold T is chosen as -1, the sentence rejection rate is approximately 5.1% and the lowest achieved total error rate is 25.8% with a false rejection rate of 2.8% and a false acceptance rate of 23.0%.

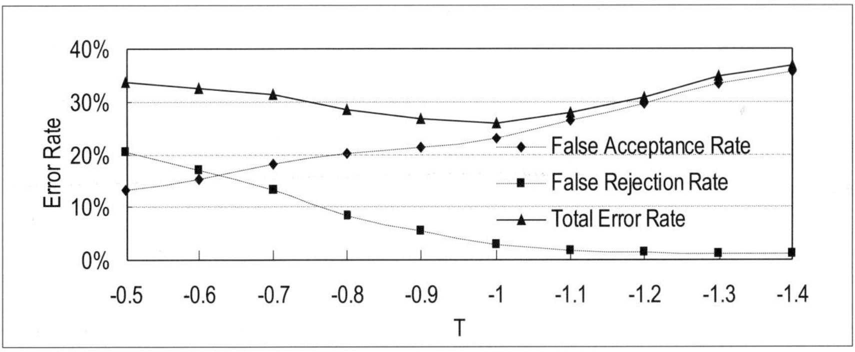

Fig. 7. Total error rate as a function of the threshold T in speech act verification.

The primary purpose of verification is to reject errors that have been accepted by the speech act identification system. Sometimes, the accepted sentences are grammatical. However, grammatical sentences do not necessarily imply that they are meaningful in a specific speech act and so should sometimes still be rejected. The best performances of the systems after verification are illustrated in Table 5. Notably, using LSA-based BBM for speech act verification further improves the performance of the system because more latent and salient dependencies between fragments are captured by the LSA-based BBM.

Table 5. The best performances of the systems after verification.

	SDG(1)	SDG(2)	PPT	Bayes'
Without verification	95.6	92.4	85.0	88.1
With verification	96.2	94.2	86.4	89.0
The ratio of improvement	0.63	1.95	1.65	1.02

SDG(1): With discourse analysis, SDG(2): Without discourse.

5. Conclusion

This chapter has presented novel approaches to speech act identification and verification for Chinese spoken dialogue systems. Ontology-based partial pattern trees and semantic dependency graphs are used for identifying the speech act of a speaker's utterance. A verification mechanism was adopted to improve the accuracy of speech act identification using the LSA-based BBM. The results of the experiments show that the semantic dependency graph outperforms both the Bayes' classifier and the PPT. By incorporating discourse analysis, results show improvements not only in speech act identification rate, but also in the extraction of semantic objects. Verification of speech acts can further improve speech act identification significantly.

References

1. X. Huang, A. Acero, and H.-W. Hon, *Spoken Language Processing*, (Prentice-Hall, 2001).
2. J. F. Allen, D. K. Byron, D. M. Ferguson, L. Galescu, and A. Stent, "Towards Conversational Human-Computer Interaction," *AI Magazine*, (2001).
3. R. Higashinaka, N. Miyazaki, M. Nakano, and K. Aikawa. "Evaluating Discourse Understanding in Spoken Dialogue Systems," *ACM Transactions on Speech and Language Processing (TSLP)*, vol. 1, (2004), pp. 1-20.
4. L. Wittgenstein, *Philosophical Investigations*, Translated by Anscombe, G.E.M., (Basil Blackwell, Oxford, 1953).
5. J. L. Austin, *How to Do Things with Words*, (Harvard University Press, Cambridge, MA, 1962).
6. J. R. Searle. *Speech Acts: An Essay in the Philosophy of Language*, (University Press, Cambridge, 1969).
7. A. Stolcke, K. Ries, N. Coccaro, E. Shriberg, R. Bates, D. Jurafsky, P. Taylor, R. Martina, M. Meteer, and C. V. Ess-Dykema, "Dialogue Act Modeling for Automatic Tagging and Recognition of Conversational Speech," *Computational Linguistics*, 26, (2000), pp. 339-371.
8. M. Walker and R. Passonneau, "DATE: A Dialogue Act Tagging Scheme for Evaluation of Spoken Dialogue Systems", in *Proc. Human Language Technology Conference*, (San Diego, 2001).
9. C.-H. Wu, J.-F. Yeh, and M.-J. Chen, "Speech Act Identification using an Ontology-Based Partial Pattern Tree," in *Proc. ICSLP'04*, (Jeju, Korea, 2004).
10. E. Shriberg, R. Bates, P. Taylor, A. Stolcke, D. Jurafsky, K. Ries, N. Coccaro, R. Martin, M. Meteer, and C. V. Ess-Dykema, "Can Prosody aid the automatic classification of dialog acts in conversational speech?," *Language and Speech*, 41 (3-4), (1998), pp. 439-487.
11. M. Woszczyna and A. Waibel, "Inferring linguistic structure in spoken language," in *Proc. ICSLP'94*, (1994), pp. 847-850.

12. M. F. McTear, "Spoken Dialogue Technology: Enabling the Conversational User Interface," *ACM Computer Surveys*, vol. 34 (1), (2000), pp. 90-169.
13. R. Baeza-Yates and B. Ribeiro-Neto, *Modern Information Retrieval*, (Addison-Wesley, Edinburgh Gate, Harlow, 1999), pp. 48-49.
14. J. R. Bellegarda, "Exploiting Latent Semantic Information in Statistical Language Modeling," in *Proc. IEEE*, vol. 88 (8), (2000), pp. 1279-1296.
15. C.-H. Wu and Y.-J. Chen, "Recovery of False Rejection Using Statistical Partial Pattern Trees for Sentence Verification," *Speech Communication*, vol. 43, (2004), pp. 71-88.
16. J.-F. Yeh, C.-H. Wu and M.-Z. Yang, "Stochastic Discourse Modeling in Spoken Dialogue Systems Using Semantic Dependency Graphs," in *Proc. COLING-ACL*, (2006).
17. C.-G. Nevill-Manning, C.-N. Huang, and D. L. Brutlag, "Pairwise Protein Sequence alignment using Needleman-Wunsch and Smith-Waterman Algorithms," *Personal Communication*, (2001).
18. K. J. Chen, C. R. Huang, F. Y. Chen, C. C. Luo, M. C. Chang, and C. J. Chen, "Sinica Treebank: Design Criteria, representational issues and implementation," in Anne Abeille, Ed., *Building and Using Syntactically Annotated Corpora*, (Kluwer, 2001), pp. 29-37.
19. C.-H. Wu and G.-L. Yan, "Speech Act Modeling and Verification of Spontaneous Speech with Disfluency in a Spoken Dialogue System," *IEEE Trans. Speech and Audio Processing*, vol.13, (2005), pp. 330-344.
20. D. W. Patterson, *Introduction to Artificial Intelligence & Expert System*, (Prentice Hall, Englewood Cliffs, New Jersey, 1990), pp. 107-125.
21. A. C. Rencher, *Multivariate Statistical Inference and Applications*, (John Wiely & Sons, 1998).
22. M. A. Walker, D. Litman, C. Kamm, and A. Abella, "PARADISE: A General Framework for Evaluating Spoken Dialogue Agents," in *Proc. ACL*, (1997), pp. 271-280.

CHAPTER 15

TRANSLITERATION

Haizhou Li[†], Shuanhu Bai[†], and Jin-Shea Kuo[‡]
[†]*Institute for Infocomm Research*
21 Heng Mui Keng Terrace, Singapore 119613
[‡]*Chunghwa Telecommunication Laboratories, Taoyuan*
E-mail: {hli, sbai}@i2r.a-star.edu.sg, jskuo@cht.com.tw

In speech and language processing, such as automatic speech recognition (ASR), text-to-speech (TTS), cross-lingual information retrieval (CLIR), and machine translation (MT), there is an increasing need to translate out-of-vocabulary words from one language into another, especially from Latin-scripted languages into ideographic graphemes of languages such as Chinese, Japanese or Korean (CJK). In practice, whenever semantic translation is not available, translation is done by transliteration. In general, transliteration refers to the method of translating from one language to another by preserving the way words sound in their original languages, also known as translation-by-sound. However, when translating from Latin-scripted words that are originally from Chinese and its dialects, Japanese, or Korean into Chinese, transliteration refers to the method of back-translating into their original ideographic graphemes, also known as back-transliteration. In this chapter, we will discuss an English to Chinese transliteration paradigm for proper nouns, in particular personal names, through the exploration of various transliteration and validation techniques.

1. Introduction

The study of transliteration may date back to the seventh century when Buddhist scriptures were translated into Chinese. The earliest bit of Chinese translation theory related to transliteration may be the principle of "Names should follow their bearers, while things should follow Chinese." In other words, names should be transliterated, while things should be translated according to their meanings. Xuan-zang[a] advocated the theory of *Five Untranslatables*, or five instances where

[a] 玄奘 (600-664), a Chinese Buddhist monk who was famous for his 17 year-long trip to India. When he returned, he brought with him some 657 Sanskrit texts. With the emperor's support, he set up a large translation bureau in Chang'an (present-day Xi'an), drawing students and collaborators from all over East Asia. He is credited with the translation of some 1,330 fascicles of scriptures into Chinese.

one should transliterate: esoteric words like religious *mantras*; polysemous words; words without Chinese equivalents; old, established terms; and, words with translations that reduce their referents' respect and righteousness. The same theory still holds today. In this chapter, we exlpore how the centuries-old transliteration problem can be approached by state-of-the-art techniques in computational linguistics.

In general, computational studies of transliteration fall into two categories: transliteration modeling (TM) and extraction of transliteration pairs (EX). There have been many studies on TM for different language pairs, such as English-Arabic,[1] English-CJK,[2–4] and French-Japanese.[5] Some other efforts are devoted to transliterating romanized CJK words back to ideographic graphemes, also known as back-transliteration.[6] The former approach (TM) models transliteration rules with a generative model that is trained from a large, bilingual transliteration lexicon, with the objective of translating unknown words on the fly in the open, general domain. The latter approach (EX) employs data-driven methods to extract actual, human-crafted transliteration pairs from a corpus, in an effort to construct a large, up-to-date transliteration lexicon from live text sources such as the Web. In this chapter, we focus on English-Chinese transliteration, in short, *E-C* transliteration. The techniques discussed there can be easily generalized to transliterations of other language pairs.

There are several problems unique to *E-C* transliteration. One of them is that Latin-scripted personal names may have first been derived from different language origins, such as from Chinese, Japanese or Korean. The language origin of a word does dictate the way we transliterate into Chinese. Furthermore, despite many standardization efforts, unfortunately diverse romanization systems still co-exist in the CJK languages due to historical reasons. This makes the transliteration task much more challenging. At the same time, transliteration is a difficult, artistic human endeavor, as rich as any other creative pursuit. Research on automatic transliteration has reported promising results for *regular* transliteration,[2,7,8] where transliterations follow rigid guidelines. The generative model works well as it is designed to capture regularities in terms of rules or patterns. However, in Web publishing, translators in different countries and regions may not observe common guidelines. People usually use wordplay to bring meanings into the translated words for various aesthetic effects, resulting in *casual* transliterations; for example, "Coca Cola" is transliterated into "可口可乐 /Ke-Kou-Ke-Le/"[b] as a sound equivalent in Chinese, which also literally means "happiness in the mouth". In such cases, the common generative models[2] fail to predict the desired transliterations most of the time. Therefore,

[b] *Pinyin* is used as the romanization convention in this chapter.

the EX approach sounds more appealing in constructing lexicons that cover both *regular* and *casual* transliterations.

The transliteration task can be considered as an extension to the traditional grapheme-to-phoneme (G2P) or phoneme-to-grapheme (P2G) conversions,[9] which have been much-researched topics in the field of speech processing. If we view the grapheme and phoneme as two symbolic representations of the same word in two different languages, then G2P is a transliteration task by itself. In other words, whatever algorithms that have been developed for G2P can be readily extended for transliteration. Despite G2P and transliteration are common in many ways, transliteration has its unique challenges, especially as far as *E-C* transliteration is concerned. First, we typically build a single G2P for each spoken language. However, we may need multiple transliteration models for Latin-scripted personal names due to different language origins and romanization schemes. Second, in G2P, the problem of homophones exists only in the grapheme level where one grapheme signals multiple phonemes, while every phoneme is unique. In other words, it is a many-to-one mapping problem. In transliteration, the graphemes in both languages suffer from the homophone problems. Therefore, the resolution to grapheme mapping becomes a many-to-many mapping problem.

Machine transliteration, in this full generality, can be seen as a subtask of statistical machine translation (SMT) as well. By treating a character as a word, and a grapheme unit as a phrase in SMT, one can easily apply a traditional SMT model, such as IBM generative model[10] or phrase-based translation model,[11] to transliteration. In transliteration, we will face similar issues as in SMT, such as lexical mapping, model training, alignment, and decoding. However, transliteration is also different from general translation tasks in many ways: 1) Unlike SMT where there are different word-ordering in the two languages, a word is always transliterated monotonously, in the same order; 2) In SMT, the source language is typically treated homogeneously. However, in transliteration, we have to concern ourselves with the genre of the words such as language origin, romanization system and gender of the personal names; 3) In target language generation, we have to consider transliteration styles such as regional variations and transliterations with different intended aesthetic effects.

2. Origins of Latin-scripted Personal Names

Simply speaking, transliteration is the process of rewriting a word from one language into a word in another language. Conversely, back-transliteration recovers the original word from its transliteration. For instance, we transliterate *Thatcher* to 撒切尔 (/Sa-Qie-Er/), and back-transliterate 撒切尔 (/Sa-Qie-Er/) to *Thatcher*. For language pairs like Spanish-English, the task is as simple as copying the same word over: a place name like *Colorado* gets translated as *Colorado*. However, the task becomes more complicated for language pairs involving different orthographic and sound systems, such as English-CJK. Although all English personal names are coded in 26 letters, these names can originate from non-English languages. By convention, we refer to all Latin-scripted words as English words, which might not usually be the case in *E-C* transliteration. In some instances, the origin of an English word is less important, for example, one might argue that *Colorado* is indeed an English word and translate it into 科洛拉多 (/Ke-Luo-La-Duo/). However, in some other cases, the origin of an English word is the key to a correct transliteration. For example, it would be wrong to translate the word *Hokkaido* which is of Japanese origin into 霍凯多 (/Huo-Kai-Duo/) as if it is an English word. The correct way would be to translate it into the Chinese equivalents of Japanese *kanji*, as 北海道 (/Bei-Hai-Dao/). The same principle applies to English words of Korean and Vietnamese origins as well.

Broadly, in this chapter, we consider five language origins as far as *E-C* transliteration is concerned. They are English, Chinese, Japanese, Korean, and Vietnamese. We consider words as having English origin if they follow English phonic rules, although they can originally come from other languages such as Arabic or Russian. The writing systems of Chinese, Japanese, Korean, and Vietnamese are partly or entirely based on Chinese characters - *hànzì* in Chinese, *kanji* in Japanese, *hanja* in Korean, and *chữ nôm* in Vietnamese. They are known as CJKV in the field of software and communications internationalization. Chinese requires at least 4,000 characters for a basic vocabulary and up to 40,000 characters for a reasonably complete coverage, whereas Japanese and Korean use fewer characters. Vietnamese used *chữ nôm* that is a variation of Chinese characters prior to adopting *quốc ngữ*. Therefore, even today, Vietnamese personal names are still translated into Chinese characters based on the older *chữ nôm* writing script.

2.1. *Language Origins and Romanization Systems*

Note that the language origin of a word implies a set of applicable transliteration rules. Identifying the origin of the word is just as important as the word's transliteration itself. Here are a few examples of English personal names of different origins.

English: *Heathtine*-赫塞尔廷, *Thatcher*-撒切尔
Chinese: *Hu Jintao*-胡锦涛, *Lee Kwan Yew*-李光耀
Japanese: *Sato*-佐藤, *Suzuki*-铃木, *Watanabe*-渡边
Korean: *Kim*-金, *Park*-朴, *Choi*-崔, *Lee*-李, *Roh*-卢
Vietnamese: *Nguyen*-阮, *Le*-黎, *Tran*-陈, *Ngo*-吴, *Pham*-范

Strictly speaking, in Chinese transliteration, it is regarded that a conversion from English is termed as transliteration, and a conversion from any of the CJKV language origins as back-transliteration. However, for simplicity, we refer to the process of conversion from romanized, or Latin-scripted, words of all origins into Chinese as *E-C* transliteration. We define back-transliteration as recovering the original Latin-scripted words from their Chinese transliterations.

Romanization system is another dimension of complexity in addition to language origin. Due to historical reasons, each of the CJK languages has several co-existing romanization systems. For example, a Chinese personal name can be presented in Latin script in different forms depending on the romanization system. For example, 董建华 can be shown in English text as *Dong Jianhua* (using *Hanyu Pinyin*) or *Tung Chien Hua* (using Mandarin *Wade-Giles*). To correctly translate a romanized word back to Chinese characters, identifying the romanization system is just as important as identifying the language origin. It is only when both the language origin and the romanization system are correctly identified that the exact Chinese characters can be recovered. Next are some of the more popular romanization systems for the CJK languages:

Chinese: *Hanyu Pinyin*, Mandarin *Wade-Giles*, Cantonese *Yale*, and Cantonese *Jyutping*

Japanese: *Hepburn, Kunrei*

Korean: *McCune-Reischauer*, Korean *Yale*

We refer to the language of origin as well as the romanization system used to represent a name, as the *romanization source*.

2.2. *Identify the Romanization Sources*

For Latin-scripted text documents, identifying the language which a particular text is written in, is no longer considered an unsolved problem with the use of *n*-gram language models. However, language identification for personal names is less straightforward because only very few name-words, compared to non-names, are available in any given corpus or text. In a related work, Meng *et al.*[7] studied the use of *Pinyin* and *Wade-Giles* coding to parse unknown English names. Qu and Grefenstette[12] proposed using *n*-gram language models (LM) LM to identify language origins.

Let us begin by formulating the identification task in a language modeling framework. In Latin-scripted text, we have an inventory of 27 symbols – 26 English letters plus a white space as the delimiter. An English word D can be represented as a sequence of Ω grapheme units $\hat{T} = t_1, \ldots, t_\pi, \ldots, t_\Omega$, with each unit drawn from the inventory of 27 alphabets, $t_\pi \in l_1, l_2, \ldots l_{27}$. One is able to train an n-gram language model for each romanization source. In the case of a bigram model, we have $p(i|j) = p(t_\pi = l_i | t_{\pi-1} = l_j)$.

Entropy is a measure of information. It can be used as a metric for how well a given grammar matches a given corpus, or for how predictive a given n-gram grammar is about the next n-gram token. In other words, given several n-gram grammars and a corpus, we can use entropy to tell us which grammar better matches the corpus. This can be achieved by measuring the *cross-entropy* between the n-gram model of interest Θ, and the actual distribution in a sample text D of size Ω. Taking the bigram model as an example,

$$H(D,\Theta) = -\frac{1}{\Omega}\sum\nolimits_{i,j} z_{i,j} \log p(i|j) \tag{1}$$

is described as an empirical estimate of the *cross-entropy* of the true data distribution $z_{i,j}$, the count of substring $l_i l_j$, with regard to the model Θ. The match between a LM and a corpus is often reported in terms of perplexity

$$PP(D,\Theta) = 2^{H(D,\Theta)} \tag{2}$$

The perplexity can be interpreted as the average token branching factor of the romanization system according to the model. It is a function of both the model and the test corpus. As a function of model, it measures how well the model matches the corpus. As a function of the corpus, it estimates the entropy or complexity of that corpus.

Notice that there are two informative clues that help identify the origin of a word. One is the phonetic and phonotactic structure of a language, such as its phonetic composition or its syllable structure. For example, English has unique consonant clusters such as /-str-/ and /-ks-/ that the CJK languages do not have. Another is the lexical structure of a romanization system, for example, *Pinyin*, *Wade-Giles* or *Hepburn* each has a finite set of syllable inventory. A romanized word is basically a sequence of pre-defined syllable entries. Some earlier work[7,13] used left-to-right longest match lexical segmentation to parse an English word. In this way, the romanization system is identified if it gives rise to a successful parse of the test word. However, this method only works when discriminating romanization systems that have a finite set of syllable inventory. For the general task of identifying the language origin and romanization system, the data-driven *cross-entropy* approach as given in Equations 1 and 2 appears more attractive.

2.3. *Experiments*

We now look into how the *cross-entropy* approach works in identifying the romanization source. First, a database is collected from publicly-accessible sources, consisting of personal names of Japanese (Data-I[c]), Chinese (Data-II[d] and -III), and English (Data-IV[14] and Data-V[e]) origins. They are all bilingual transliteration lexicons except Data-V, which is a monolingual English name database. Table 1 lists their details.

Table 1. A collection of personal name database.

Origin	*Data*	*Corpus*	*Number of Entries*	*Romanization System*
Japanese	I	ENAMDICT	123,239	*Hepburn*
Chinese	II	Hao's	115,879	*Pinyin* (Mandarin)
	III	Hao's	115,739	*Jyutping* (Cantonese)
English	IV	Xinhua	37,674	English
	V	US Names	88,799	English

Both closed-set and open-set tests are conducted on Data-I, -II, -III and -V for the identification of romanization sources. In the closed tests, trigram language models are trained on 27 English graphemes for the four romanization sources respectively, $\Theta_1, \Theta_2, \Theta_3$ and Θ_4. All the entries were used for both training and testing. In open tests, we randomly select 90% of the entries for training and the remaining 10% for testing. During the test, the romanization source classifier is defined as:

$$\hat{k} \equiv \arg\min_k PP(D, \Theta); \tag{3}$$

where $\hat{k}$ represents the romanization source that generates the test English word with the lowest perplexity. The confusion matrix and accuracy (Acc%) are reported in Tables 2 and 3. In Figure 1, we illustrate the distributions of perplexity scores of over 8,969 randomly selected romanized Chinese names (see Table 3) tested on four different language models. We can see that the Chinese *Pinyin* test samples clearly identify themselves from others if we apply Equation 3.

The Data-I, -II, -III and -V of Table 2 and 3 are the same databases used in Qu's work.[15] It is shown that the *cross-entropy* approach outperforms the previously-reported results on the same tasks.[15] A crucial finding is that the *cross-entropy* approach does not only distinguish the language origins, but also identifies Chinese *Pinyin* (Mandarin) and from *Jyutping* (Cantonese) well. Comparing the results in Tables 2 and 3, we also find that the *cross-entropy* approach is robust in open tests.

The performance for English is slightly worse than others. This can be explained by the fact that, in the US Census dataset, many of the American names

[c]The Electronic Dictionary Research and Development Group, Monash University, http://www.csse.monash.edu.au/~jwb/enamdict_doc.html

[d]Chih-Hao Tsai's Technology Page, http://technology.chtsai.org/namelist/

[e]US Census site, http://www.census.gov/genealogy/names/dist.all.last

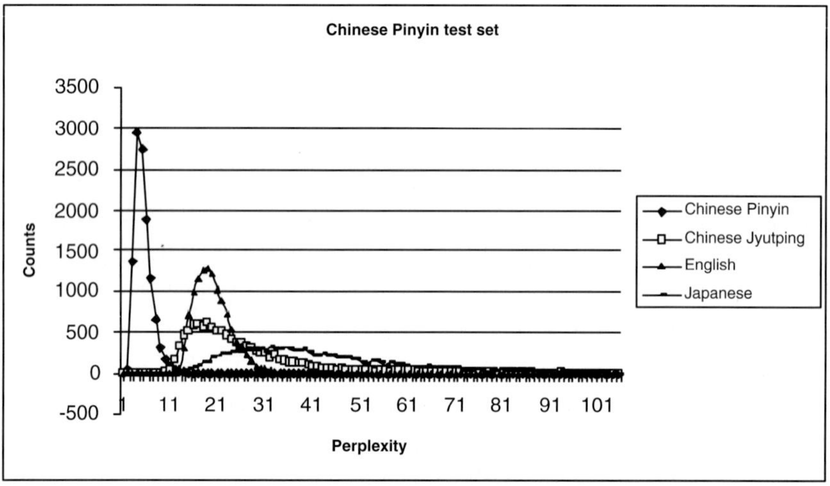

Fig. 1. Evaluating personal names in Chinese *Pinyin* on four trigram language models.

Table 2. Closed-test confusion matrix and accuracy using trigram *cross-entropy* on 4 data sets.

Romanization Sources	*Data*	*# Test Entries*	*As* JAP	*As* CHI_PY	*As* CHI_JY	*As* ENG	Acc%
Japanese	I	110,806	105,572	1,018	705	3,511	95.3%
Chinese *Pinyin*	II	104,370	390	102,086	1,750	144	98.0%
Chinese *Jyutping*	III	104,121	111	1,407	102,565	38	98.5%
English	V	79,830	2,708	571	696	75,855	95.0%

Table 3. Open-test confusion matrix and accuracy using trigram *cross-entropy* on 4 data sets.

Romanization Sources	*Data*	*# Test Entries*	*As* JAP	*As* CHI_PY	*As* CHI_JY	*As* ENG	Acc%
Japanese	I	12,433	11,838	106	79	410	95.2%
Chinese *Pinyin*	II	11,509	39	11,246	207	17	97.7%
Chinese *Jyutping*	III	11,618	7	175	11,432	4	98.4%
English	V	8,969	316	71	77	8,605	94.8%

are of different origins including Chinese and Japanese. For simplicity, we treat them all as English names.

In summary, romanization source identification can be achieved by a generative model such as an inexpensive *n*-gram grapheme language model. The identification performance also suggests that it is possible to consider a transliteration task as two sequential subtasks: romanization source identification followed by source-dependent transliteration.

3. Generative Modeling

Machine translieration is typically formulated as a generative process, which takes a character string in the source language as the input, and generates a character string in the target language as the output. It can be seen conceptually as two levels of decoding: segment the source string into grapheme units; and relate the source grapheme units with units in the target language by resolving different combinations of alignments and unit mappings. A grapheme unit could be a character in Chinese, or a monograph, a digraph or a trigraph and so on in English.

In *E-C* transliteration, we can simply define transliteration as finding sound equivalents for Latin-scripted words. We aim to decode the Chinese character sequence from an input English word. A popular approach is known as the phoneme-based method, where we first convert English graphemes to English sounds, then to Chinese sounds and finally into Chinese characters. This approach has been widely adopted in CJK transliteration.[3,8] Recently, a direct orthographical mapping approach, known as the grapheme-based approach, has attracted attention.[2] The grapheme-based approach has been shown to be an effective technique for *regular* transliteration.

Given a source word E in English which is to be translated into a target word C in Chinese, where $E = x_1^M = x_1, x_2 \dots x_M$ and $C = y_1^N = y_1, y_2 \dots y_N$ are strings of characters in the respective languages. Among all possible target strings, we will choose the string with the highest probability which is given by the Bayes decision rule.[10]

$$\begin{aligned}\hat{C} &= \underset{y_1^N, a_1^M}{\arg\max} \Pr(E, C) \\ &= \underset{y_1^N, a_1^M}{\arg\max} \left\{ \Pr(y_1^N, a_1^M, x_1^M) \right\}\end{aligned} \tag{4}$$

In Equation 4, $\Pr(y_1^N, a_1^M, x_1^M)$ is the string translation model which models both the alignment of grapheme units: $a_1^M = a_1, a_2 \dots a_M$, $m \to n = a_m$, and grapheme mapping.[f] The arg max operation denotes the search problem, i.e. the generation of the transliteration in the target language. As a result of the search decoding, we not only arrive at a string of transliterated graphemes, but also a set of optimal alignment. This process is similar to the Viterbi decoding in HMM-based speech recognition,[16] where a_m refers to the time alignment path of state sequence.

One of the key issues in modeling the unit mapping probability is defining the correspondence between the graphemes across the source and target languages.

[f]This is equivalent to the lexical model in SMT. For simplicity, we disallow *null* alignment between a grapheme unit and *null* unit, although the generalization to include *null* is straightforward and of practical use.

	R	O	B	E	R	T
罗	■	■				
伯			■	■	■	
特						■

Fig. 2. Monotonous alignment between *Robert* and 罗伯特.

Because of the monotonous nature of alignment, grapheme alignment can be represented as a character substring alignment as indicated by the boxes in Figure 2. It is important to note that the translation-by-sound principle implies that we can always find a phonetic alignment between bilingual grapheme units. Suppose that we derive K aligned grapheme units from one of the alignment $\alpha \in A(E,C)$, we can express the English word as $E = e_1^K = e_1, e_2 \dots e_K$ and the Chinese word as $C = c_1^K = c_1, c_2 \dots c_K$. The probability of such an alignment is denoted as:

$$\Pr(\alpha) = \Pr(e_1, e_2 \dots e_K, c_1, c_2 \dots c_K) \tag{5}$$

In this way, we have,

$$\Pr(E,C) = \sum_{\alpha \in A(E,C)} \Pr(\alpha) \tag{6}$$

where the alignment and grapheme mapping can be seen as an unified operation of lexical mapping. Combining Equations 4 and 6, we formulate the transliteration task,

$$\hat{C} = \arg\max_{C} \sum_{\alpha \in A(E,C)} \Pr(\alpha) \tag{7}$$

In decoding, we search over the space of all possible alignments $A(E,C)$ that can be generated. In practice, the summation in Equation 6 is usually replaced by maximization,

$$\Pr(E,C) = \arg\max_{\alpha \in A(E,C)} \Pr(\alpha) \tag{8}$$

Therefore,

$$\hat{C} = \arg\max_{C,\alpha} \Pr(\alpha) \tag{9}$$

A typical solution to the Equation 9 is Viterbi decoding. Next we study different ways of modeling $\Pr(\alpha)$.

The problem of modeling $\Pr(\alpha)$ has been studied extensively in the paradigm of the noisy channel model (NCM).[10] For a given English name E as the observed output from a noisy channel, Equation 9 attempts to recover the most likely Chinese transliteration C as the input, that aligns to E with α. In the NCM paradigm, Equation 5 is rewritten by applying Bayes' rule,

$$\Pr(\alpha) = \Pr(e_1^K | c_1^K) \times \Pr(c_1^K) \tag{10}$$

To do so, we are left with modeling two probability distributions: $\Pr(e_1^K|c_1^K)$, the probability of transliterating c_1^K to e_1^K through a noisy channel, also known as the lexical mapping rules, and $\Pr(c_1^K)$, the probability distribution of c_1^K, known as the target language model.

In Equation 10, the lexical mapping rules, $\Pr(e_1^K|c_1^K)$, ensure the faithfulness while $\Pr(c_1^K)$ measures how appropriate a transliteration is from the cultural and aesthetic point of view, which typically involves avoiding offensive and irritating words and sounds. One evidence demonstrating this rule is that only 374 out of few thousand common Chinese characters are selected for foreign name transliteration according to the *Xinhua* guidelines.[14] Yan Fu[g] placed faithfulness as the first of his three-word principle on translation: faithfulness, smoothness, and elegance. The same principle applies to transliteration as well.

A theory, generally credited to Vauqois,[17] summarizes translation approaches in a pyramid-structure framework, representing direct, transfer and interlingua translation relations. Direct translation applies lexical transfer on the surface without much semantic analysis. The transfer approach views translation as a three-stage process: 1) analysis of the input into a source-language syntactic structure representation; 2) transfer of that representation into the corresponding target-language structure; 3) synthesis, or generation, of the output from that structure. The deeper the analysis is, the less transfer is needed, the ideal case being the interlingua approach in which there is no transfer at all. The idea of interlingua is to treat translation as a process of extracting the meaning of the input and then expressing that meaning in the target language. It is especially effective in multilingual environments where many languages need to be cross-translated. The interlingual representation is an abstract representation of the meaning of the source text, capturing all and only the linguistic information necessary to generate an appropriate target text showing no undue influence from the original text. Motivated by the pyramid diagram, we can present the transliteration problem in Figure 3.

The idea of interlingua in machine transliteration is to represent a source language in language-independent, international phonetic inventories like Sampa[18] or

[g]严复 (1853–1921), a Chinese scholar and translator who is famous for introducing Western thoughts, including Darwin's ideas of "natural selection" and "survival of the fittest", into China during the late 19th century.

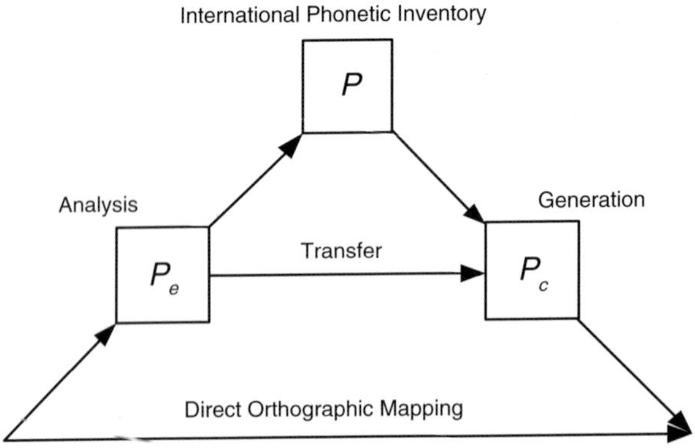

Fig. 3. Diagram suggesting 3 different transliteration techniques, IPA interlingua, Transfer and Direct Orthographic Mapping, in analogy to Vauqois's pyramid diagram of machine translation.

IPA.[19] It seems to be an obvious choice if multi-way transliteration is needed. However, the choice becomes less obvious in view of the fact that the analysis and generation processes in the pyramid are not entirely independent of the languages or language pairs, as far as transliteration is concerned. The choice of target words is typically influenced by the source text. For example, we typically choose different Chinese characters for Japanese names as opposed to English names. From a practical point of view, transfer and direct approaches provide closer coupling between the analysis and generation processes between the pair of languages. This is perhaps the reason why transfer and direct approaches have been widely discussed in the literature.

3.1. *Transfer Approach: Phoneme-based Transliteration*

The phoneme-based approach is motivated by the transfer formalism. Inspired by research results of grapheme-to-phoneme research in speech synthesis,[20] many have suggested phoneme-based approaches to resolving $\Pr(e_1^K|c_1^K)$. These approaches approximate the probability distribution by introducing an intermediate phonemic representation,[7] following the idea of the interlingua machine translation model. In this way, we convert the personal names in the source language, say e_k, into English phonemes P_E, and then Chinese phonemes P_C and then to the target language grapheme, say Chinese characters c_k. In *E-C* transliteration, the phoneme-based approach can be formulated as a generative process,

$$p(e_k|c_k) = p(e_k|P_E) \times p(P_E|P_C) \times p(P_C|c_k) \tag{11}$$

Thus,

$$\Pr(e_1^K|c_1^K) = \prod_{k=1}^{K} p(e_k|c_k) \tag{12}$$

where we have three probability distributions to describe different steps of conversion as illustrated in the Transfer path of Figure 3.

(1) $p(e_k|P_E)$ - Map English English graphemes to English phonemes
(2) $p(P_E|P_C)$ - Transfer English phonemes to Chinese phonemes
(3) $p(P_C|c_k)$ - Map Chinese phonemes to Chinese graphemes

In Equation 10, $\Pr(c_1^K)$ is usually estimated using n-gram language models.[21] Thus,

$$\Pr(\alpha) = \Pr(e_1^K|c_1^K) \times \Pr(c_1^K)$$
$$= \prod_{k=1}^{K} p(e_k|c_k)p(c_k|c_{k-n+1}^{k-1}) \qquad (13)$$

Several phoneme-based transfer approaches have been proposed in the recent past for machine transliteration, for example, one using a transformation-based learning algorithm[7] and another using a finite state transducer that implements transformation rules,[3] where both handcrafted and data-driven transfer rules have been studied. However, the phoneme-based approaches are limited by two major constraints, which could compromise the precision of transliteration.

First, none of the three generative steps guarantees perfect conversion. The overall performance of the generative model depends greatly on the quality of the individual probability estimates. A conversion error in one of the steps can easily lead to an overall error. Multiple sequential, suboptimal decoding steps pose great challenges to the decoder at run-time. This approach might have an advantage that allows modeling each step separately, with the help of linguistic knowledge. However, if this incorporation is of great cost to system performance, then it is not a worthwhile pursuit.

The second constraint is that obtaining Chinese orthography requires two further steps: 1) conversion from generic phonemic representation to Chinese *Pinyin*; 2) conversion from *Pinyin* to Chinese characters. Each step introduces a level of imprecision. It was reported[22] that 8.3% absolute accuracy drops when converting from *Pinyin* to Chinese characters, due to homophone confusion. Unlike Japanese *katakana* or Korean alphabets, Chinese characters are more ideographic than phonetic. To arrive at an appropriate Chinese transliteration, one cannot therefore rely solely on the intermediate phonemic representation.

3.2. *Direct Approach: Grapheme-based Transliteration*

Addressing problems of the phoneme-based approach, a grapheme-based framework was proposed by Li *et al.*[2] in implementing Equation 10. This grapheme-based approach, also known as direct orthographic mapping (DOM), is inspired by the direct translation model in machine translation that estimates $\Pr(\alpha)$ directly without interlingua representation. The DOM framework aims to alleviate the imprecision introduced by the multiple-step phoneme-based decoding as illustrated in Figure 3.

Replacing the three steps of the generative process in phoneme-based solutions, DOM converts the English graphemes into Chinese graphemes in one single step. This can be achieved by estimating the probability $p(e_k|c_k)$ in Equation 12 directly. Then the DOM approach can be implemented in the NCM framework.

The joint source-channel model (JSCM)[2] suggests another solution to DOM. In JSCM, we estimate $\Pr(\alpha)$ by a source-channel joint n-gram transliteration model. The model benefits from the monotonous property of transliteration pairs, where both source and target transliteration units are in the same ordering. Thus, the current transliteration is conditioned not only on its source language, but also its previous transliteration pairs.

Suppose that we have $e_1^K = e_1, e_2 \ldots e_K$ and $c_1^K = c_1, c_2 \ldots c_K$ in which e_k and c_k are aligned grapheme units $< e, c >_k$. For K aligned transliteration units, we have

$$\begin{aligned} \Pr(\alpha) &= \Pr(e_1, e_2 \ldots e_K, c_1, c_2 \ldots c_K) \\ &= \Pr(< e,c >_1, < e,c >_2 \ldots < e,c >_K) \\ &= \textstyle\prod_{k=1}^{K} p(< e,c >_k \mid < e,c >_{k-n+1}^{k-1}) \end{aligned} \tag{14}$$

where an n-gram transliteration model is defined as the conditional probability, or transliteration probability, of a transliteration pair $< e,c >_k$ depending on its immediate n predecessor pairs.

Equation 14 provides a grapheme-based alternative solution to Equation 11. Unlike the NCM, the JSCM does not try to capture how source personal names can be mapped to target names, but rather how source and target names can be generated simultaneously. In other words, we estimate a joint probability model that can be easily marginalized in order to yield conditional probability models for both transliteration and back-transliteration.

A group of machine learning methods have been studied for phoneme-based transliteration, grapheme-based transliteration or a mix of the two, such as decision trees,[23] the maximum entropy model and memory-based learning[8] with different successes. The idea behind these approaches is to learn rules from the statistics available in a parallel corpus.

3.3. *Comparative Studies*

We use the *Xinhua* database, which is a bilingual dictionary[14] edited by Xinhua News Agency and has been considered the *de facto* standard for personal name

Table 4. Modeling Statistics.

# close set bilingual entries (full data)	37,674
# unique Chinese transliteration (close)	28,632
# training entries for open test	34,777
# test entries for open test	2,897
# unique transliteration pairs T	5,640
# total transliteration pairs W_T	119,364
# unique English units E	3,683
# unique Chinese units C	374
# JSCM bigram $P(< e,c >_k \mid < e,c >_{k-1})$	38,655
# NCM Chinese bigram $P(c_k \mid c_{k-1})$	12,742

transliteration in today's Chinese press in mainland China. The database includes a collection of 37,674 unique English entries and their official Chinese transliterations. In this database, each English entry has only one *regular* Chinese transliteration. To conduct comparative studies, we use *Xinhua* database as the *gold standard* (GS), which is also called Xinhua GS hereafter.

The database is initially randomly distributed into 13 subsets. In the open test, one subset is put aside for testing while the remaining 12 subsets are used as training data. This process is repeated 13 times to yield an average result, and is called the 13-fold open test. After the experiments, we found that each of the 13-fold open tests gave consistent error rates with less than 1% deviation. Therefore, for simplicity, we randomly select one of the 13 subsets, which consists of 2,897 entries, as the standard open test set to report our results. In the closed test, all data entries are used for training and testing.

The alignment of transliteration units and training of the *n*-gram language model are carried out in an *Expectation-Maximization* process.[24] To model the boundary effects, we introduce two extra units <s> and </s> for the start and end of each name in both languages. The statistics are shown in Table 4 as a result of the model training.

3.3.1. *JSCM vs. NCM*

As suggested in Section 2, *cross-entropy* $H(D,\Theta)$ represents the match between the a model Θ and a corpus D. What makes the *cross-entropy* useful is that the *cross-entropy* is the upper bound of the entropy $H(D)$. For any model Θ, $H(D) \leq H(D,\Theta)$. This means that we can use some simplified model such as *n*-gram to help estimate the true entropy of a sequence of symbols in D. The more accurate Θ is, the closer the *cross-entropy* $H(D,\Theta)$ will be to the true entropy $H(D)$. Thus, between two models, the more accurate model will be the one with the lower *cross-entropy* or perplexity.[21] It is easy to understand that a closed test will always give lower perplexity than an open test.

In general, the *cross-entropy* or perplexity of two language models is comparable if they use the same vocabulary. We examine the perplexity of the JSCM and NCM models over the aligned *Xinhua* database as reported in Table 5, where we use 5,640 transliteration pairs to form a vocabulary. The $\Pr(\alpha)$ are estimated based on Equations 13 and 14.

Table 5. Perplexity study of the *Xinhua* database.

	JSCM open	**NCM open**	**JSCM closed**	**NCM closed**
1-gram	670	729	655	716
2-gram	324	512	151	210
3-gram	306	487	68	127

It is shown that the JSCM consistently gives lower perplexity than NCM in open and closed tests. We have good reason to expect JSCM to provide better transliteration performance. To validate the findings from the perplexity study, we conduct both open and closed tests for JSCM and NCM models under the DOM paradigm. Error rates in terms of whole-word and Chinese character are reported in Tables 6 and 7.

Table 6. Transliteration error rates using n-gram JSCM.

	open (word)	**open** (char)	**closed** (word)	**closed** (char)
1-gram	45.6%	21.1%	44.8%	20.4%
2-gram	31.6%	13.6%	10.8%	4.7%
3-gram	29.9%	10.8%	1.6%	0.8%

Table 7. Transliteration error rates using n-gram NCM.

	open (word)	**open** (char)	**closed** (word)	**closed** (char)
1-gram	47.3%	23.9%	46.9%	22.1%
2-gram	39.6%	20.0%	16.4%	10.9%
3-gram	39.0%	18.8%	7.8%	1.9%

In the word error report, a word is considered correct only if an exact match happens between transliteration and the reference in Xinhua GS. The character error rate is the sum of deletion, insertion and substitution errors. Not surprisingly, one can see that JSCM, which benefits from the joint source-channel model (JSCM) coupling both source and target contextual information into the model, is superior to NCM in all the test cases. The improved performance of JSCM can be credited to a larger number of parameters than NCM. Therefore, we will typically need more training data for JSCM than NCM training. In NCM training, typically we rely on a small set of bilingual parallel corpus to establish the lexical mapping $\Pr(e_1^K|c_1^K)$ and a larger set of monolingual corpus for the language model $\Pr(c_1^K)$. In JSCM, we count on a single bilingual parallel corpus to provide sufficient statistics for training of the joint probability model $\Pr(<e,c>_1,<e,c>_2 \ldots <e,c>_K)$.

3.3.2. *JSCM vs. Decision Tree*

Decision tree learning is one of the well-studied methods for inductive inference. In this method, given a learning vector of fixed size, we used top-down induction trees to predict the corresponding output. Here we implement ID3[23] algorithm to construct a decision tree which contains questions and return values at terminal nodes. Cast in the framework of Figure 3, decision tree is considered an alternative of direct orthographic mapping.[2,8] Similar to *n*-gram language modeling, for unseen personal names in a open test, ID3 has backoff smoothing, which lies on the default case which returns the most probable value as its best guess for a partial tree path according to the learning set.

We first define a letter in English and a character in Chinese as the grapheme unit. We form a learning vector of 6 attributes by combining 2 left and 2 right letters around the letter of focus e_k and 1 previous Chinese character c_{k-1}. The process is illustrated in Table 8, where both English and Chinese contexts are used to infer a Chinese character. An aligned bilingual dictionary is needed to build the decision tree. To minimize the effects due to alignment variation, we use the same alignment results from Section 3.3. ID3 results are reported in Table 9.

Table 8. ID3 decision tree for transliterating Nice to 尼斯(<NI,尼> <CE,斯>).

e_{k-2}	e_{k-1}	e_k	e_{k+1}	e_{k+2}	c_{k-1}		c_k
_	_	N	I	C	_	>	尼
_	N	I	C	E	尼	>	_
N	I	C	E	_	_	>	斯
I	C	E	_	_	斯	>	_

Table 9. *E-C* transliteration: Word error rate ID3 vs. 3-gram JSCM.

	Open Test	**Closed Test**
ID3	39.1%	9.7%
JSCM	29.9%	1.6%

We can observe that the JSCM consistently outperforms ID3 decision tree across the tests. This could be attributed to three factors: 1) English transliteration unit size ranges from 1 letter to 7 letters.[2] The fixed size windows in ID3 obviously find it difficult to capture the dynamics of the various ranges. JSCM seems to have captured the dynamics of transliteration units in a better way; 2) The back-off smoothing of the JSCM is more effective than that of ID3; 3) Unlike n-gram JSCM, ID3 requires a separate alignment process for bilingual dictionary. The resulting alignment may not be optimal for tree construction. Nevertheless, ID3 presents another successful implementation under the DOM framework.

3.3.3. *N-Best*

The Viterbi algorithm produces the best choice by maximizing the overall probability, $\Pr(E,C)$. We can also derive N-best results using a stack decoder[25] in both JSCM and NCM experiments. In CLIR or multilingual corpus alignment, N-best results is very helpful to increase chances of correct hits. Furthermore, N-best choices also allow us to apply external knowledge for refining the results.

In Table 10, a transliteration is considered correct if the Xinhua GS reference is found on the N-best list. The word error rates are reduced significantly at the 10-best level. This implies that potential error reduction is attainable by using a secondary knowledge source, as will be discussed in Section 4.

Table 10. *E-C* transliteration: N-best word error rates using 3-gram JSCM.

	Open Test	**Closed Test**
1-best	29.9%	1.6%
5-best	8.2%	0.94%
10-best	5.4%	0.90%

4. Validation of Transliteration

We can consider the transliteration model as the primary knowledge source that generates the N-best choices. Although the N-best choices are ranked in the order of likelihood scores, the correct answers do not always top the lists. Moreover, transliteration can be a one-to-many mapping, especially in the case of *casual* transliteration. There are multiple valid answers in the N-best choices.

In the statistical approaches that we discuss in this chapter, it is always possible for us to arrive at a N-best list with likelihood ranking. However, in some other studies where rule-based approaches are adopted, transliteration rules are applied to generate a collection of equiprobable transliteration candidates.[15] In the latter case, validation becomes one of the necessary steps in finding an appropriate transliteration. Fortunately, transliteration knowledge is present in other sources as well, for example, in the form of external monolingual or bilingual databases. If the external databases, also referred to as secondary knowledge, provide additional information, then it can be used for the validation of the transliteration candidates.

Two typical validation sources have been explored in the literature, the static corpus and the Web. The static corpus, or lexicons, are carefully-designed databases. Sometimes, only a smaller bilingual lexicon is required, like in the training of a statistical model, such as an NCM or JSCM, for N-best decoding. A bigger monolingual lexicon, which is more accessible than a bilingual one, is used to validate the N-best results further. For example, Qu and Grefenstette[15] used a monolingual corpus to validate *katakana* transliterations. Knight and Graehl[3] used lexicon frequency to rank transliteration candidates. The Web contains a much larger collection of language samples than any manually collected corpus. It has become a common platform for publishing up-to-date articles and textual communication, thus serving as a rich and live information source for transliterations. Grefenstette *et al.*[12] successfully explored query results to rank the transliterations by raw page counts.

Let us revisit the validation techniques using the *E-C* transliteration as an example. Suppose that N-best ranking is available. The validation can be carried out in two ways: 1) by validating the adequacy of candidates in a top-down manner in the order of N-best. In this way, we give priority to the original ranking. This is the approach often taken when validating against a static corpus; and, 2) by re-ranking the N-best according to the secondary knowledge source. The same technique is applicable to the post-processing of N-best speech recognition results.

4.1. *Corpus Validation*

In general, we assume that a reasonably large database is available for corpus validation. Here we utilize an LDC release (LDC2003E01) of 1,013,807 *E-C* translation/transliteration pairs. It is an *E-C* bilingual name entity list that is compiled by LDC, referred to as the LDC GS.

To illustrate how corpus validation works, we continue the open test experiment in Section 3.3. Out of the 2,897 English entries, 2,810 can be found in the LDC GS. We form a test subset by the 2,810 English entries. The whole test set and the subtest set are called T-2897 and T-2810 repectively, hereafter.

Suppose that we have a N-best list of transliteration candidates $\{C_1,\ldots, C_n,\ldots,C_N\}$ resulting from an English personal name E, which are rendered in descending order of likelihood scores. We take the N-best candidates resulting from the experiments in Section 3.3.3 and carry out two validation experiments. In the first experiment, we validate the Chinese transliterations against the LDC GS. The validation process traverses the N-best list from C_1 in a top-down manner until a transliteration C_n is found in the LDC GS. Then C_n is considered as being accepted. In this way, we only make use of the Chinese entries of the LDC GS. In the second experiment, we validate the *E-C* pairs against the LDC GS in the same manner as

Table 11. Acceptance rates when validating the *N*-best results against the LDC GS.

	1-best *E-C* pair	1-best Chinese-only	20-best *E-C* pair	20-best Chinese-only
T-2897	1,636 (56.5%)	2,186 (75.5%)	2,446 (84.4%)	2,803 (96.7%)
T-2810	1,636 (58.2%)	2,140 (76.1%)	2,446 (87.0%)	2,733 (97.3%)

in the first experiment. Only when the exact bilingual pairing is found in the LDC GS, the transliteration is accepted. The validation results are reported in terms of the number of hits and the acceptance rate in Table 11 where the acceptance rate is defined as the hits divided by the total number of trials.

As in Table 6, we note that the Xinhua GS suggests a 29.9% error rate or a 70.1% acceptance rate. When 1-best result is used, LDC GS suggests lower acceptance rates than Xinhua GS does for *E-C* pair validation, and higher acceptance rates for Chinese-only validation. However, when we validate using the 20-best results, the acceptance rates improve dramatically in both *E-C* pair and Chinese-only cases.

The corpus validation demonstrates an effective way to exploit independent knowledge sources for transliteration. It relies on a creditable source for transliteration screening. By validating the *E-C* pairing, instead of just the monolingual transliteration, this imposes a more rigid matching criterion, resulting in less hits. The rigid matching criterion ensures the quality of validation. For example, in the LDC GS, one can find the pairing of "Bushe-布希 (/Bu-Xi/)" and "Bush-布什 (/Bu-Shi/)," but not "Bush-布希 (/Bu-Xi/)", although "Bush-布希 (/Bu-Xi/)" is considered a valid transliteration. In a Chinese-only validation, both "布希(/Bu-Xi/)" and "布什 (/Bu-Shi/)" are accepted for "Bush". However, in the *E-C* pair validation, "Bush-布希 (/Bu-Xi/)"is ruled out.

In terms of precision and recall, one can expect an almost 100% precision but a lower recall from the *E-C* pair validation because some valid transliterations in the LDC GS may not form the exact pairings with their corresponding English counterparts. On the other hand, one perhaps gets a higher recall from the Chinese-only validation perhaps with a lower precision. As a monolingual corpus is more accessible than a bilingual corpus, the Chinese-only validation is indeed a lower-cost validation strategy.

4.2. *Web Validation*

The corpus validation requires the existence of large-scale parallel texts, which are hard to come by and can be expensive to construct. The Web is a source that provides low-cost access to texts that reflect documented as well as up-to-date transliteration usages. Web search engines[26] are designed to retrieve relevant documents.

By submitting queries to search engines, we get query results which are in the form of summarized abstracts of text documents, commonly referred to as snippets. A snippet typically has a document title, a window of the text document containing the query, and a URL address, which can direct users to the whole document. From the title and the text window, the user gets a quick glance and an idea of the return document. The same information is useful for transliteration validation as well, through a process known as Web validation.

As in corpus validation, we can validate either the transliteration alone, or the transliteration pair using the Web. Grefenstette *et al.*[12] proposed validating transliteration candidates using only raw page count (RPC), while Kuo[27] studied transliteration pair validation. In fact, there are several informative clues that are available from the query results. For example, the RPC represents the number of pages that the engine has indexed that contain the query terms. We can approximately see RPC as the document frequency in the Web space. The snippet-based pair count (PR) represents the number of pairings discovered in the snippets. The PR can be considered as the term frequency in the query results.

Given a collection of transliteration pairs, we can easily rank them by the RPC or PR scores. To illustrate how it works, we take 5-best results from the experiments of Section 3.3.3. We shuffle them by discarding their likelihood scores, then apply the Web statistics to re-establish their relevance ranking. In practice, we submit the transliteration pairs one by one to the search engine and rank the 5-best according to the RPC or PR values. For computational efficiency, we only retrieve the first 100 snippets for each query when estimating the PR. In Figure 4, we summarize the experiment results from two validation schemes: corpus validation against the Xinhua GS and the LDC GS, Web validation based on RPC and PR ranking.

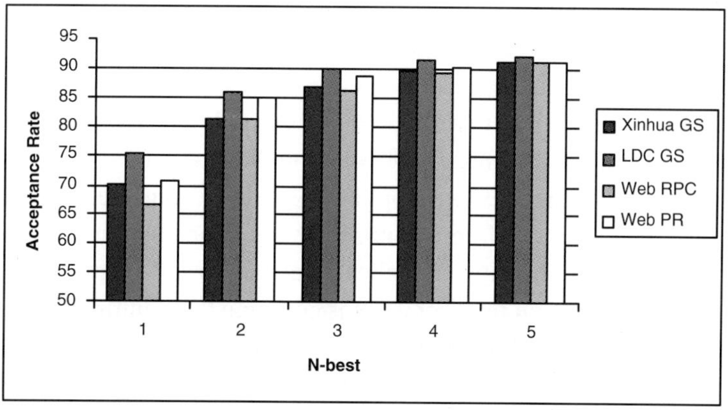

Fig. 4. Web validation vs. corpus validation.

In the Xinhua GS validation, we assume that there is only one correct transliteration for an English perosnal name. In the LDC GS and Web validations, variants of transliteration are accepted. As expected, the acceptance rate increases as N-best choices grow from 1 to 5. In Figure 4, one can also find that, given a random ranking of N-best, the Web validation re-establishes a N-best relevance ranking that is similar to that of corpus validation. Not only does the Web supplies the largest, exploitable collection of transliteration usages, but also provides statistics that are comparable with manually-prepared corpora. Web validation is especially useful when the ranking of a collection of transliteration candidates is not available, such as in the case of rule-based transliteration. It is also an effective approach for constructing transliteration lexicons at low cost. It is beyond the scope of this chapter to discuss extraction of transliteration pairs. Interested readers can refer to the work of Kuo *et al.*[28] for details.

5. Conclusion

This chapter has presented an overview of the various techniques in automatic machine transliteration. *E-C* transliteration has been used as an example illustrating how these techniques work. After considering different aspects of transliteration, we have focused on three active areas of transliteration: identification of word origin, the generative model of transliteration, and the validation of transliterations.

Among prior related studies, research on identification of word origin was not given much attention. This chapter highlights the important issues of a word's language origin and romanization source, as well as provides a solution to these problems. In practice, there are other factors that can influence transliteration as well, such as the gender of personal names and the different aesthetic accommodations to the Chinese transliterations. In *E-C* transliteration, some Chinese characters are reserved only for female English personal names. The same *cross-entropy* approach discussed here can be extended for gender identification as well.

From our study of generative models, we consider the transliteration challenge as analogous to the traditional machine translation problem. We classified existing work into two categories, the phoneme-based and the grapheme-based approaches. Note that the same techniques are applicable to both transliteration and back-transliteration. Without loss of generality, only *E-C* transliteration is explored in this chapter for reasons of brevity. We believe that back-transliteration is a more difficult task than transliteration in general.[2] It is common that multiple English names are mapped into the same Chinese transliteration. In Table 4, we see only 28,632 unique Chinese transliterations existing for 37,674 English entries, meaning that some phonemic evidence is lost in the process of transliteration. To better understand the task, let us compare the complexity of the two languages presented in the bilingual lexicon as in Table 1. The 5,640 transliteration pairs are cross-mappings between 3,683 English and 374 Chinese units. In other words, on average, for each English unit, we have 1.53 = 5,640/3,683 Chinese correspondences. In contrast, for each Chinese unit, we have 15.1 = 5,640/374 English back-transliteration units! Confusion is increased tenfold going backwards.

For validation of transliteration, we have studied two common approaches, corpus validation and Web validation, making a distinction between corpus – manually-prepared lexicon – and the Web, which is a source of rich, unstructured corpora. In fact, any free-form text corpora can be used as the gold standard, in a way similar to Web validation. The N-best decoding followed by validation technique is considered as one of the generate-and-probe techniques, which is readily applicable to speech recognition of proper nouns as well.

Desipte much promising results in these decades of research, machine transliteration remains a problematic area. We have presented the grapheme-based direct orthographic mapping and the phoneme-based transfer approaches. Practical transliteration systems today, however, typically combine ideas from these models. This chapter serves as an introduction to the interesting field of transliteration processing and is a good launching pad for any future work in this area.

References

1. Y. Al-Onaizan and K. Knight, "Translating Named Entities using Monolingual and Bilingual Resources," in *Proc. of 40th Annual Meeting of the Association for Computational Linguistics*, (2002), pp. 400–408.
2. H. Li, M. Zhang, and J. Su, "A Joint Source-Channel Model for Machine Transliteration," in *Proc. of 42nd Annual Meeting of the Association for Computational Linguistics*, (2004), pp. 159–166.
3. K. Knight and J. Graehl, "Machine Transliteration," *Computational Linguistics*, vol. 24, pp. 599–612, (1998).
4. J. S. Lee and K. S. Choi, "English to Korean Statistical Transliteration for Information Retrieval," *Computer Processing of Oriental Languages*, vol. 12, pp. 17–37, (1998).
5. K. Tsuji, B. Daille, and K. Kageura, "Extracting French-Japanese Word Pairs from Bilingual Corpora based on Transliteration Rules," in *Proc. of 3rd LREC*, (2002), pp. 499–502.
6. W.-H. Lin and H.-H. Chen, "Backward Machine Transliteration by Learning Phonetic Similarity," in *Proc. of 6th Conference on Natural Language Learning*, (Taipei, 2002), pp. 139–145.
7. H. Meng, W.-K. Lo, B. Chen, and K. Tang, "Generating Phonetic Cognates to Handle Named Entities in English-Chinese Cross-Language Spoken Document Retrieval," in *Proc. of Automatic Speech Recognition and Understanding Workshop*, (2001), pp. 311–314.
8. J.-H. Oh and K. S. Choi, "An Ensemble of Grapheme and Phoneme for Machine Transliteration," *Natural Language Processing - IJCNLP, LNAI 3651*, pp. 450–461, (Springer 2005).
9. L. Galescu and J. F. Allen, "Bi-directional Conversion between Graphemes and Phonemes using a Joint N-gram Model," in *Proc. 4th ISCA Tutorial and Research Workshop on Speech Synthesis*, (Scotland, 2001).

10. P. F. Brown, S. A. D. Pietra, V. J. D. Pietra, and R. L. Mercer, "The Mathematics of Statistical Machine Translation: Parameter Estimation," *Computational Linguistics*, vol. 19, pp. 263–311, (1993).
11. J. M. Crego, M. R. Costa-jussa, J. B. Mario, and J. A. R. Fonollosa, "N-gram-based versus Phrase-based Statistical Machine Translation," in *Proc. of International Workshop on Spoken Language Translation*, (2005), pp. 177–184.
12. G. Grefenstette, Y. Qu, and D. A. Evans, "Mining the Web to Create a Language Model for Mapping between English Names and Phrases and Japanese," in *Proc. of IEEE/WIC/ ACM International Conference on Web Intelligence, WI'04*, (2004), pp. 110–116.
13. J.-S. Kuo and Y.-K. Yang, "Generating Paired Transliterated-cognates using Multiple Pronunciation Characteristics from Web Corpora," in *Proc. of 18th PACLIC*, (2004), pp. 275–282.
14. *Xinhua News Agency, Chinese Transliteration of Foreign Personal Names*. The Commercial Press, (1992).
15. Y. Qu and G. Grefenstette, "Finding Ideographic Representations of Japanese Names Written in Latin Script via Language Identification and Corpus Validation," in *Proc. of 42nd Annual Meeting of the Association for Computational Linguistics*, (2004), pp. 183–190.
16. L. Rabiner and B.-H. Juang, *Fundamentals of Speech Recognition*. Prentice Hall, (1993).
17. B. Vauqois, "A Survey of Formal Grammars and Algorithms for Recognition and Transformation in Machine Translation," *IFIP Congress-68*, vol. reprinted *TAO: Vingt-cinq Ans de Traduction Automatique - Analectes* in C. Boitet, Ed., pp. 201–213, 1988.
18. C. J. Wells, "Computer-coded Phonemic Notation of Individual Languages of the European Community," *Journal of the International Phonetic Association*, vol. 19, pp. 32–34, (1989).
19. IPA, "The International Phonetic Association: IPA Chart," *Journal of the international phonetic association*, vol. 23, (1993).
20. H. Meng, "A Hierarchical Lexical Representation for Bidirectional Spelling-to-Pronunciation Pronunciation-to-Spelling Generation," *Speech Communication*, pp. 213–239, (2001).
21. F. Jelinek, "Self-organized Language Modeling for Speech Recognition," *Readings in Speech Recognition*, vol. A. Waibel and Lee K. F, Eds., (Morgan Kaufmann, 1991).
22. P. Virga and S. Khudanpur, "Transliteration of Proper Names in Cross-Lingual Information Retrieval," in *Proc. of ACL Workshop on Multilingual and Mixed-language Named Entity Recognition*, (2003), pp. 57–64.
23. J. R. Quinlan, C4.5 P*rograms for* Ma*chine* Le*arning*. Morgan Kaufmann, (1993).
24. A. P. Dempster, N. M. Laird, and D. B. Rubin, "Maximum Likelihood from Incomplete Data via the EM Algorithmn," *Journal of the Royal Statistical Society*, vol. 9, Ser. B, pp. 1–38, (1977).
25. R. Schwartz and Y. L. Chow, "The N-best Algorithm: An Efficient and Exact Procedure for Finding the N most Likely Sentence Hypothesis," in *Proc. ICASSP*, (1990), pp. 81–83.
26. S. Brin and L. Page, "The Anatomy of a Large-scale Hypertextual Web Search Engine," in *Proc. of 7th International World Wide Web Conference*, (1998), pp. 107–117.
27. J.-S. Kuo, "Generating Term Transliterations using Context Information and Validating Generated Results using Web Corpora," in *Proc. of Asia Information Retrieval Symposium*, (2005), pp. 659–665.
28. J.-S. Kuo, H. Li, and Y.-K. Yang, "Learning Transliteration Lexicons from the Web," in *Proc. of 44th Annual Meeting of Association for Computational Linguistics*, (2006), pp. 1129–1136.

CHAPTER 16

CANTONESE SPEECH RECOGNITION AND SYNTHESIS

P. C. Ching[†], Tan Lee[†], W. K. Lo[‡] and Helen M. Meng[‡]
[†]*Department of Electronic Engineering*
[‡]*Department of Systems Engineering and Engineering Management*
The Chinese University of Hong Kong
Shatin, New Territories, Hong Kong
E-mail: pcching@ee.cuhk.edu.hk

Cantonese is a major Chinese dialect spoken by tens of millions of people in southern China. Our research team at the Chinese University of Hong Kong (CUHK) has devoted great efforts on the research and development of Cantonese speech recognition and speech synthesis. This chapter gives an overview of our work. The linguistic and acoustic properties of spoken Cantonese are discussed. A set of large-scale Cantonese speech corpora are described as an indispensable infrastructural component for research and development. The development of Cantonese large-vocabulary continuous speech recognition (LVCSR) and text-to-speech (TTS) systems is presented in detail.

1. Introduction

Automatic speech recognition (ASR) and speech generation are the key component technologies required for voice-enabled human-computer interaction. An ASR system converts an acoustic speech signal into a sequence of words, while a speech generation system produces natural-sounding speech signals to deliver or express messages. With the advent of high-performance computers and sophisticated digital signal processing techniques, large-vocabulary continuous speech recognition (LVCSR) and text-to-speech (TTS) conversion have become viable in practical applications.

One of the challenges in ASR and TTS research is due to the great variety of languages. Language-specific considerations are most critical to the success of a spoken language processing system. These considerations are across all levels of system design and implementation, including acoustic modeling, language modeling, discourse modeling and prosody modeling. For example, spoken Chinese is considered to be a sequence of monosyllabic sounds and each syllable is divided into an initial part and a final part. Initials and finals have been found most appropriate for acoustic modeling in Chinese LVCSR, though phone-like units are commonly used for many western languages. Tones in Chinese determine the meaning of a word. Tone modeling therefore appears to be an important component in a Chinese ASR system.

There are many different Chinese dialects.[1,2] Among them, Mandarin (or *Putonghua*) is regarded as the official spoken language in both mainland China and Taiwan. Another prominent Chinese dialect is Cantonese. It is the mother tongue of people in southern China, including Hong Kong and Macau. Although Cantonese and Mandarin are both monosyllabic and tonal, there are significant differences between them at various linguistic levels.[3] Monolingual Cantonese speakers and monolingual Mandarin speakers generally cannot communicate with each other using their respective dialects. It is therefore necessary to develop spoken language technologies tailored for the Cantonese dialect.

Hong Kong is an international city where most people speak Cantonese and English in their daily life. Mandarin is also becoming more and more popular in recent years. The Chinese University of Hong Kong (CUHK) has pioneered in the research and development of Cantonese speech technologies since the early 1990's. Our work started from an acoustic-phonetic study on spoken Cantonese from an engineering point of view.[4] This study provided a solid basis for our research. We have devoted much effort to establish the infrastructure that facilitates short-term as well as long-term research in various challenging areas, not only in ASR and TTS, but also in speaker recognition, audio search and document retrieval. Several large-scale Cantonese speech corpora, text corpora and pronunciation dictionary were created.[5,6] We have developed a state-of-the-art Cantonese LVCSR system that makes use of tone information and models common pronunciation variation.[7,8] Our TTS technology has improved from simple, syllable-based concatenation to sub-syllable unit selection with prosody modeling at word and utterance levels. This chapter gives an introductory summary and overview of our work on Cantonese ASR, TTS and related topics. We try to highlight the language-specific considerations in the development of Cantonese speech technologies.

2. Linguistic and Acoustic Properties of Spoken Cantonese

2.1. *The Cantonese Dialect*

Yue dialects (粤语) refer to one of the major groups of Chinese dialects that are spoken in southern China.[1] Cantonese, also known as Guangzhouhua (广州话), is regarded as the norm of the Yue dialects.[9,10] It is spoken by tens of millions of people in the provinces of Guangdong (广东) and Guangxi (广西), the neighboring regions of Hong Kong and Macau, and many overseas Chinese communities.[11] Our research focuses on Cantonese as it is spoken in Hong Kong. All speech materials used for acoustic analysis, speech recognition and speech synthesis are collected from native Cantonese speakers in Hong Kong.

Romanization refers to the use of the Roman alphabet to transcribe a language that uses a different writing system. For computer processing of a spoken language, a Romanization system is needed to accurately and consistently represent the pronunciations. A number of different Romanization systems have been devised for Cantonese.[3,11] There is no standard system comparable to the Hanyu Pinyin (汉语拼音) which is used for Mandarin. In our studies, the Jyut Ping (粤拼) system designed by the Linguistic Society of Hong Kong has been used.[12] Jyut Ping is designed to be multi-functional, systematic, rather easy to use for general users, and compatible with all possible modern Cantonese sounds. Because it is solely based on alphanumeric characters, Jyut Ping has been widely adopted in the computer processing of Cantonese.

2.2. *Cantonese Phonology and Phonetics*

The basic unit of written Chinese is the character. In both Cantonese and Mandarin, each character is pronounced as a single syllable carrying a specific lexical tone, and is the smallest meaningful unit (morpheme) of the language. A character may have multiple alternative pronunciations, for example, "行" may be pronounced as /haang/, /hang/ or /hong/, among which /hang/ and /hong/ can carry two different tones. A syllable may also correspond to multiple characters. For example, the characters "司,私,施,思,师,斯,丝,诗" all share the same pronunciation /si/. A spoken word is composed of one or more syllables and a spoken sentence is a sequence of continuously uttered syllables.

Table 1 displays the statistics of Cantonese syllables, in comparison to Mandarin.[12,13] While the term "base syllable" refers to the tone-independent, monosyllabic units, "tonal syllable" refers to the syllable sounds that are acoustically and tonally distinct. Cantonese has a richer inventory of syllable sounds than Mandarin. There are approximately 50% more base syllables in Cantonese than in Mandarin.

Table 1. Comparison between the syllable inventories of Cantonese and Mandarin.

	Cantonese	Mandarin
Total number of base syllables	625	420
Total number of tonal syllables	1,761	1,471
Average number of tones per base syllable	2.8	3.5
Average number of base syllable pronunciations per character	1.1	1.6
Average number of tonal syllable pronunciations per character	1.2	2
Average number of homophonous characters per base syllable	17	31
Average no. of homophonous characters per tonal syllable	6	8

Tone (supra-segmental)		
Initial	*Final*	
[Onset]	Nucleus	[Coda]

Fig. 1. General structure of Cantonese syllable. [ ] means optional component.

Traditional Chinese phonology divides a syllable into two parts: the initial (声母) or onset, and the final (韵母) or rime (also, *rhyme*), as shown in Figure 1.[11] The initial is a consonant, whereas the final typically consists of a vowel nucleus and a consonant coda. The initial and the coda are optional. The simplest syllable consists of a single vowel or a syllabic nasal, and the most complex syllable takes the form "consonant+vowel+consonant." Tone is a supra-segmental component that spans the entire syllable. According to Yuan[1] and Hashimoto,[9] there are 19 initials and 53 finals in Cantonese, which are listed in Figure 2. They are labelled with both Jyut Ping and IPA (International Phonetic Alphabet) symbols for ease of comparison.

In terms of the manner of articulation, the 19 initials can be categorized into five classes: plosives, affricates, fricatives, approximants, and nasals. The first three classes are voiceless and the other two are voiced. The 53 finals can be divided into five categories: vowels (long), diphthongs, vowels with a nasal coda, vowels with a stop coda, and syllabic nasals. Except for the syllabic nasals, each final contains at least one vowel element. Six different final consonants are found in Cantonese. The three nasal codas /m/, /n/ and /ng/ are identical to those found in the English words "some", "son" and "sing" respectively. The three stop codas /p/, /t/ and /k/ are special in that they are unreleased.[11] There are eleven vowels in Cantonese. Seven of them are long vowels and can appear independently while the four short vowels are always followed by consonant codas or found in diphthongs. Cantonese has ten different diphthongs. Almost all of them end with either /u/ or /i/.

Traditionally, Cantonese is said to have nine tones.[9] They are described by their distinctive pitch contours, as shown in Figure 3. Cantonese tones are distributed across three pitch levels: high, mid, and low. At each level, the tones are further classified according to the shape of the pitch contour. "Entering tone" is a historically defined category that generally refers to abrupt and short tones. Cantonese is one of the existing Chinese dialects that preserve entering tones.[1] In Cantonese, entering tones occur exclusively with "checked" syllables, i.e., syllables ending in an occlusive coda /p/, /t/ or /k/. [14] They are contrastively shorter than non-entering tones. In terms of pitch level, each entering tone coincides roughly with one of the non-entering tones. Many linguistic researchers have suggested treating the three entering tones as abbreviated versions of their non-entering counterparts.[11] Jyut Ping defines only six distinctive tones, labelled from 1 to 6 as in Figure 3.

Initials	
Plosive	
b	p
d	t
g	k
gw	k^w
p	p^h
t	t^h
k	k^h
kw	k^{wh}
Approximant	
l	l
w	w
j	j
Nasal	
m	m
n	n
ng	ŋ
Fricative	
s	s, ʃ
f	f
h	h
Affricate	
z	ts, tʃ
c	ts^h, $tʃ^h$

Finals			
Vowel		**Diphthong**	
i	i	ui	ui
yu	y	ei	ei
u	u	eoi	ɵy
e	ɛ	oi	ɔi
oe	œ	ai	ɐi
o	ɔ	aai	ai
aa	a	iu	iu
		ou	ɔu
Vowel-Nasal		au	ɐu
im	im	aau	au
in	in		
ing	ɪŋ	**Vowel-Stop**	
yun	yn	ip	ip
un	un	it	it
ung	ʊŋ	ik	ɪk
eng	ɛŋ	yut	yt
eon	ɵn	ut	ut
oeng	œŋ	uk	ʊk
on	ɔn	ek	ɛk
ong	ɔŋ	eot	ɵt
am	ɐm	oek	œk
an	ɐn	ot	ɔt
ang	ɐŋ	ok	ɔk
aam	am	ap	ɐp
aan	an	at	ɐt
aang	aŋ	ak	ɐk
		aap	ap
Syllabic Nasal		aat	at
m	m	aak	ak
ng	ŋ		

Fig. 2. List of Cantonese initials and finals. Jyut Ping symbols are listed on the left of their IPA counterparts.

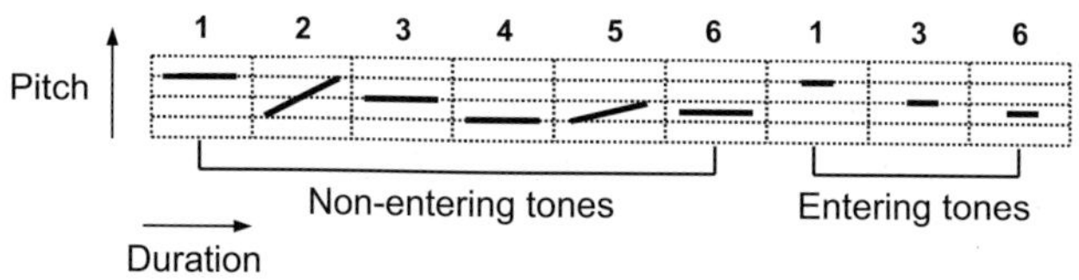

Fig. 3. Pitch contours of Cantonese tones. Each tone contour is a two-dimensional sketch of pitch movement in which the vertical dimension shows the pitch height and the horizontal dimension indicates the length of the tone.

2.3. *Acoustic Properties of Cantonese Speech*

Formant structure is an important indicator to describe vowel-like sounds in acoustic terms. It refers to the resonant frequencies of the vocal tract that have the highest energy concentration. Figure 4 plots the distribution of the first and the second formants (F_1 and F_2) of different Cantonese vowels in the "consonant+vowel+consonant" context.[15] It is noted that long and short vowel counterparts are different not only by their duration but also in terms of vowel quality. As far as F_1 and F_2 are concerned, the following pairs of vowels are found to be most easily confused: (1) long /i/ and /yu/; (2) short /i/ and /e/; (3) /eo/ and /oe/; and (iv) short /u/ and /o/. [16]

By inspecting their spectrograms, we observe that the nasal initials /n/ and /ng/ are very similar in the frequency domain. Among the fricatives and affricates, /f/, /s/, and /c/ are most difficult to be distinguished from each other.[16] Stop consonants are transient phonemes whose acoustic features depend largely on the co-articulated vowels. When occurring at the end of a Cantonese syllable, the stop consonant is unreleased and accompanied by the presence of a closure period. Its distinctive articulatory characteristics are mainly reflected in the preceding vowel.[16]

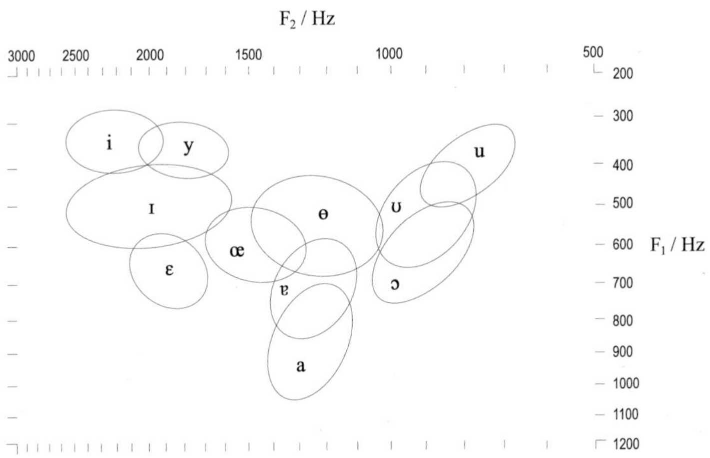

Fig. 4. $F_2 - F_1$ plots for different Cantonese vowels in the "consonant+vowel+consonant" context.

Pitch can be measured acoustically in terms of the fundamental frequency (henceforth abbreviated as F0), which quantifies the periodicity of a speech signal. Syllable-wide F0 contours have been widely used as the basis of acoustic analysis of tones in Chinese languages. For syllables uttered in isolation, their tone contours reflect the schematic patterns as in Figure 3 very well, except that the level tones (tones 1, 3, and 6) often exhibit a certain degree of falling, probably due to physiological constraints.[17] F0 is determined by both the physical and the linguistic aspects of speech production. Obviously each speaker has a specific pitch range. Even for the same speaker, the instantaneous pitch range may change from time to time because of a variety of physical, emotional, semantic and stylistic factors. In natural speech, intonation and co-articulation are the major factors that cause the tone contours to deviate from their canonical patterns. Figure 5 shows the statistical variation of the six tones of Cantonese as observed from a large amount of speech data. About 10,000 utterances from 34 male speakers are used for the analysis.[5] Each utterance contains a complete sentence of 6 to 20 syllables. The F0 contour of each syllable is divided into three even sections. The average logarithmic F0 value of each section is computed. It can be seen that the F0 levels of different tones overlap largely with each other. The confusion is particularly severe between tone 3 and tone 6, and between tone 6 and tone 4.

In Cantonese speech, duration of the voiced portion is a vital cue in discriminating entering and non-entering tones. Syllables that end with stop consonants are usually much shorter than the others. It has also been demonstrated that voice-onset-time (VOT) can be used to distinguish voiced plosives /b/, /d/ and /g/ from unvoiced ones /p/, /t/ and /k/. VOT in /k/ is found to be much longer than that in /p/ and /t/. [18] On the other hand, the duration of a vowel often varies in a consistent manner in different syllabic structures.[15]

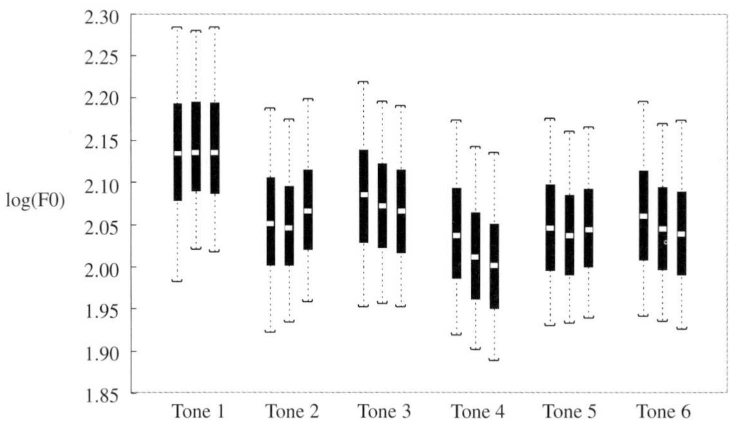

Fig. 5. Statistical variation of the F0 contours of the six Cantonese tones uttered by 34 male speakers. The thick solid bar extends from the 25th to the 75th percentile. The white strip indicates the median. The thin dashed line extends from the 5th to the 95th percentile.

3. Cantonese Speech Corpora

Speech corpora are the most important infrastructural component for the advancement of state-of-the-art spoken language technologies. Properly recorded and annotated speech data are indispensable for the analysis and modeling of different sources of variability in human speech. ASR systems require large amounts of training data recorded from speakers with different genders, voice characteristics, regional accents, educational backgrounds, etc. Most speech synthesis techniques are also based on pre-recorded speech segments, both in isolated words as well as in continuous sentences, to facilitate acoustic analysis, to derive waveform concatenation strategies and to extract prosodic features.

There have been tremendous efforts in creating large-scale speech corpora for English and other major western languages. Many of them were made publicly available as common platforms for systems development and evaluation. There are also many Mandarin speech databases developed for research purposes, for example, USTC95,[19] HKU96,[20] HKU99,[21] and MAT.[22] Since 1996, our research team at CUHK has developed a wide spectrum of speech corpora to support the development of different spoken language applications. Two major sets of corpora, named CUCorpora and CUCall respectively, have been completed since 1997. They are available both for academic research and for commercial use. Table 2 gives a summary of these corpora.[5,6] More detailed information can be found at http://dsp.ee.cuhk.edu.hk/speech/.

Table 2. A summary of Cantonese speech corpora developed by CUHK.

Corpus & Content			Speakers	Total duration	Intended Applications
CUCorpora *microphone speech*	CUSYL	Isolated syllables	4	~1 hour	Text-to-speech
	CUWORD	Polysyllabic words	28	~32 hours	Connected speech recognition
	CUDIGIT	Digit strings	50	~15 hours	Digits recognition
	CUCMD	Control commands	50	~2 hours	Voice command & control
	CUSENT	Continuous sentences	80	~20 hours	LVCSR
CUCall *telephone speech*	Domain-specific terms		~500	~25 hours	Domain-specific inquiry system
	Connected-digit strings		~1,000	~55 hours	Digits recognition
	Continuous sentences		~1,000	~61 hours	LVCSR
	Short paragraphs		~1,000	~27 hours	LVCSR
	Spontaneous conversations		~1,000	~18 hours	Spontaneous speech recognition

3.1. *CUCorpora*

CUCorpora are a series of read speech databases collected using high-quality microphone in a quiet environment. They are divided into two parts: application-specific and linguistics-oriented. The application-specific corpora, including CUDIGIT and CUCMD, were created to facilitate the development of small-scale applications of common interest. The linguistics-oriented corpora, including CUSYL, CUWORD and CUSENT, contain a large amount of speech data at various linguistic levels: isolated syllables, polysyllabic words and continuous sentences. They are intended to support general-purpose applications like speaker-independent LVCSR and TTS.

Speech from a total of 50 speakers were recorded in CUDIGIT and CUCMD. CUDIGIT consists of Cantonese connected-digit utterances. Each speaker has 570 utterances that range from 1 to 14 digits in length. CUCMD is a task-specific word corpus for command/control tasks. Each speaker read 107 commonly-used commands in Cantonese, e.g., "向前 (move forward)". CUSYL is a syllable corpus with an extended coverage of 1,801 tonal syllables. While about 1,600 of the syllables can be found in a standard Cantonese dictionary, the remaining 200 are common alternative pronunciations or colloquial sounds. CUSYL is intended for syllable-based text-to-speech synthesis. Two female and two male speakers were asked to read the entire corpus once. CUWORD is a read speech corpus of polysyllabic words. It is aimed at the training and performance evaluation of syllable and sub-syllable based speech recognition algorithms. The corpus contains 2,527 different words, with the average word length of 2.8 syllables. These words cover 1,388 tonal syllables and 559 base syllables, which correspond to 80% and 90% of the respective full sets. There were 13 male and 15 female speakers recorded. Each of them read the entire corpus once.

CUSENT is a read speech corpus of continuous Cantonese sentences. It was designed to be phonetically rich. All Cantonese syllables, initials, finals and tones were covered. Much attention was paid to the coverage of different intra-syllable and inter-syllable contexts. This ensures an adequate amount of materials for context-dependent acoustic modeling. A base corpus of 5,100 training sentences was created. Another 600 test sentences were selected separately for evaluation purposes. The training sentences were evenly divided into 17 groups, each containing 300 unique sentences. Each group of sentences were read by 2 male and 2 female speakers. Thus, a total of 20,400 training utterances were obtained from 68 speakers. The 600 test sentences were divided into 6 groups. Each group of 100 sentences were recorded from 1 male and 1 female speakers (different from those of the training data).

Most of the speakers were students at secondary or tertiary level. Their ages ranged from 14 to 30. The speech signals were sampled at 16 kHz and encoded with 16-bit linear PCM. Since the CUCorpora were meant to be the first large-scale and general-purpose resources for Cantonese speech technology, they were designed to be as versatile as possible. This can benefit many parties with diverse demands. Phonemic transcriptions of all utterances in the CUCorpora were manually verified. Each legitimate utterance is accompanied by a Chinese orthographic transcription and a verified phonemic transcription in Jyut Ping. For CUSYL in particular, attentive verification was carried out to check if the speakers had uttered the syllables correctly and accurately. By "accurately" we mean that the initial, the final and the tone were all pronounced exactly as required.

3.2. *CUCall*

CUCall is a Cantonese speech database collected over both fixed telephone network as well as mobile phone networks in Hong Kong. Figure 6 gives an overview of CUCall.[6]

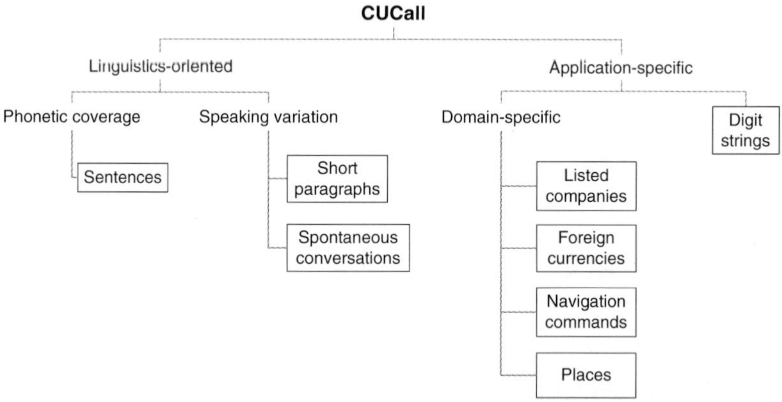

Fig. 6. Organization and composition of the CUCall Cantonese telephone speech corpora.

The corpus design was largely based on that of CUCorpora. In addition to continuous sentences, we moved one step further to record short paragraphs and spontaneous conversations. Each short paragraph typically contains multiple sentences. The inclusion of short paragraphs enriches the sentence corpus and covers different speaking behaviors and styles. For the collection of spontaneous speech, speakers were asked to answer some simple questions in an unprepared manner. The speakers were free to speak anything in response to the prompts. CUCall also contains digit strings as well as application-specific short phrases in some specific domains. The design of the digit corpus was similar to that of CUDIGIT. Phrases were chosen from various reading materials including names of listed companies and their abbreviations, names of foreign currencies, names of geographic districts and major housing estates in Hong Kong, as well as navigation commands adopted from CUCMD.

Telephone data collection was done with an automatic call-center type telephone server system. The system allowed a speaker to call in, read prescribed materials and answer prompted questions. All recorded utterances were carefully validated and transcribed. We have collected over 1,000 successful calls, which produced nearly 200 hours of speech data.[6]

4. Cantonese Speech Recognition

4.1. *Recognition of Isolated Syllables*

A neural network based speech recognition system for isolated Cantonese syllables was developed by Lee and Ching.[23] The system is made up of a tone recognizer and a base syllable recognizer. The tone recognizer adopts the architecture of multi-layer perceptron (MLP) in which each output neuron represents one of the nine tones in Cantonese. The MLP takes five input feature parameters that are extracted from the time-normalized F0 contour of a syllable. F0 normalization was done for individual speakers, based on the initial pitch values of tones 2, 4, 5 and 6, which were found to be relatively stable. The base syllable recognizer consists of a large number of recurrent neural networks (RNN), each representing a Cantonese syllable. The feedback connections in the RNNs are used to capture the temporal dependency of acoustic features.[24] The training of an RNN speech model was done in two steps: 1) iterative re-segmentation; and 2) discriminative training based on minimum classification error (MCE) criterion. An integrated recognition algorithm was developed to give the ultimate recognition results based on N-best outputs of the two recognizers. For a vocabulary of 200 commonly used Cantonese tonal syllables, the top-1 and top-3 recognition accuracies were 81.8% and 95.2% respectively.

4.2. *Large-Vocabulary Continuous Speech Recognition (LVCSR)*

An LVCSR system deals with fluently spoken speech with a vocabulary size of several thousands of words or more.[25] As shown in Figure 7, the key components of a state-of-the-art LVCSR system are acoustic models, a pronunciation lexicon, and language models. The acoustic models are a set of hidden Markov models (HMMs) that characterize the statistical variation of the input speech features. Each HMM represents a specific sub-word unit such as a phoneme. The pronunciation lexicon and language models are used to define and constrain the way in which the sub-word units can be concatenated to form words and sentences. Given an input speech signal, a sequence of acoustic feature vectors $\mathbf{O}$ are computed by the acoustic front-end. With the statistical pattern recognition approach, the most probable word sequence is determined by the maximum *a posteriori* (MAP) criterion and the Bayes' rule, i.e.,

$$\mathbf{W}^* = \arg\max_{\mathbf{W}} P(\mathbf{W}|\mathbf{O}) = \arg\max_{\mathbf{W}} P(\mathbf{O}|\mathbf{B})P(\mathbf{B}|\mathbf{W})P(\mathbf{W}) \quad (1)$$

where $\mathbf{B}$ denotes the sub-word transcription of $\mathbf{W}$, $P(\mathbf{O}|\mathbf{B})$ denotes the acoustic models and $P(\mathbf{W})$ denotes the language models. In the case that $\mathbf{W}$ has multiple pronunciations, $P(\mathbf{B}|\mathbf{W})$ implements a probabilistic pronunciation model.[26]

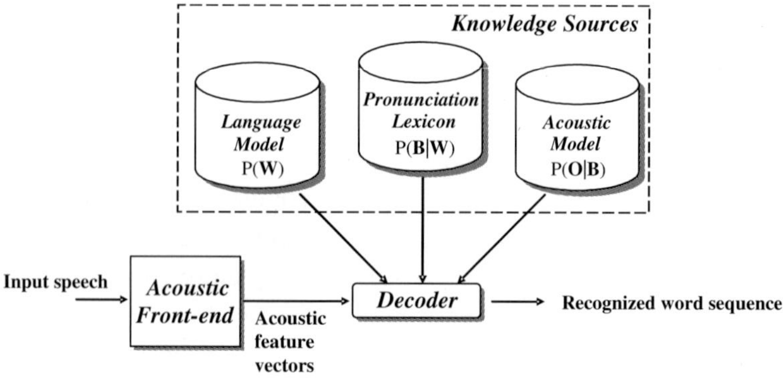

Fig. 7. Block diagram of a typical LVCSR system.

4.2.1. *Acoustic Modeling*

Currently, short-time spectral features are predominantly used for acoustic modeling in LVCSR.[27] In our studies, acoustic feature vectors are computed every 10 ms. with a 25-ms. Hamming window. Each feature vector consists of the time-domain energy, the first 12 Mel-frequency cepstral coefficients (MFCCs), as well as their first and second-order time derivatives.

The syllable appears to be a very intuitive unit choice for acoustic modeling of Cantonese speech. However, the success of this approach depends greatly on whether sufficient training data are available for each and every single syllable. Given limited training data, sub-syllable modeling is often preferred. Phonologically speaking, there are 19 initials and 53 finals in Cantonese as listed in Figure 2. Each of these initials and finals is modeled by a left-to-right HMM without skip-state transition. Each HMM state is represented by a finite mixture of Gaussian density functions. The number of states in each model corresponds roughly to the number of phonemes within the unit. An initial model has 3 states and a final model has either 3 or 6 states.

In continuous speech, co-articulation between neighboring phonemes introduces significant acoustic variation and thus context-dependent modeling has become a common practice in LVCSR. That is, the same phoneme with different left and right contexts are treated as different units and modeled separately. This results in a huge number of so-called triphone units, for which the problem of inadequate training data needs to be addressed. The technique of decision tree based clustering of context-dependent models has been widely adopted in LVCSR research. It has the advantage of flexibly integrating phonological knowledge into the process of phonetic context classification. Each basic phoneme is represented by a decision tree, in which each node corresponds to a category of left/right phonetic contexts.

The "root" node essentially refers to the context-independent base phone. At each intermediate parent node on the tree, a "yes/no" question is asked about the left and/or right context. The node can then be split into 2 child nodes, corresponding to the answers "yes" and "no" respectively, provided that there are sufficient training data available for the child nodes. In general, there are a number of phonetic questions that could be asked at each parent node. A proper evaluation function is used to determine the "best" question for node splitting. A node that cannot be split further represents a class of triphone models that share the same basic phoneme and have similar left/right contexts. Subsequently, class-triphone models are built by re-estimating the HMM state distribution from all the training data at the respective nodes.

For Cantonese, the basic phonemes are initials and finals, and the resulted context-dependent models are named tri-IF models. We use a large, collective set of questions based on the acoustic-phonetic properties of Cantonese speech. There are four types of questions included: 1) manner of articulation of the neighboring consonant onset or coda; 2) place of articulation of the neighboring consonant onset or coda; 3) the vowel identity of the neighboring nucleus or coda; and 4) exact identity of the neighboring initial or final. As a result, the number of questions concerning left and right contexts are 106 and 105 respectively.[28] The performance of tri-IF models was evaluated in the task of base syllable recognition on the CUSENT database. Phonological constraints on initial-final combinations were imposed, but there was neither lexical constraint nor language model. Figure 8 shows how the syllable recognition accuracy depends on the model complexity. The number of states in tri-IF models can be controlled by adjusting the termination criteria in decision tree construction. The best recognition accuracy is about 75.7%.[28]

The same method of context-dependent modeling was applied to Mandarin. We used the well-known speech database of the China National Hi-Tech Project 863 on Mandarin LVCSR systems development and attained a syllable recognition accuracy of 81.7%, i.e., 6% higher than for Cantonese.[29] Table 3 lists the most easily confused initials and finals found in our experiments on Cantonese and Mandarin.[29] For Cantonese, there are several pairs of "totally confused" phonemes. They are found to be alternative pronunciations or common mispronunciations that we failed to distinguish when transcribing CUSENT. Many people, especially teenagers, tend to use them interchangeably without causing much ambiguity in communication. The cases of "severe confusion" include long /aa/ versus short /a/, and among the unreleased (sometimes reduced) stop codas. For Mandarin, no case of "totally confused" was identified. The most substantial confusions were found between finals with and without the short transition vowel /u/.

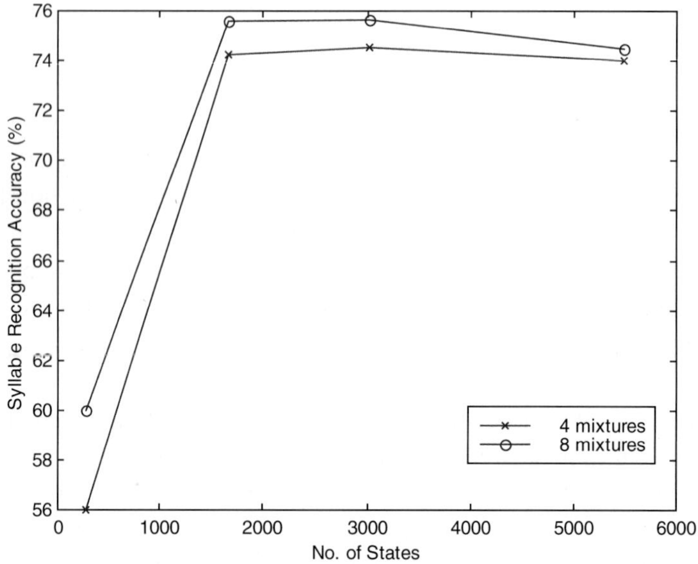

Fig. 8. Syllable recognition accuracy attained with decision-tree clustered tri-IF models.

Table 3. The most easily confused initials and finals for Mandarin and Cantonese.

	Mandarin		Cantonese	
	initials	finals	initials	finals
Totally Confused	Nil	Nil	{n, l} {ng, null}	{on, ong} {ot, ok} {ng, m}
Severely Confused	{r, y} {b, d} {p, t} {w, m}	{ing, in} {uen, en} {o, uo} {uai, ai} {uei,ei}	{gw, g} {p, t} {b, d}	{aau, au} {aak, aat} {ang, an} {ok, o} {at, ak} {eng, ing}

4.2.2. *Language Modeling*

Statistical language models attempt to encode multiple levels of linguistic knowledge: syntax, semantics, and pragmatics of a language. The *prior* probability of a word sequence $\mathbf{W} = w_1, w_2, ...w_M$ can be computed as

$$P(\mathbf{W}) = P(w_1, w_2, ..., w_M) = \prod_{i=1}^{M} P(w_i | w_1, w_2, ..., w_{i-1}) \tag{2}$$

where $P(w_i|w_1, w_2, ..., w_{i-1})$ is the conditional probability of w_i given all preceding words $w_1, w_2, ..., w_{i-1}$. Practically, only $N-1$ preceding words are considered and this gives the so-called N-gram language model. The language model probabilities can be estimated by a simple frequency count. For a vocabulary of V words, there are V^3 trigram probabilities to be estimated. When V is large, many word sequences may not appear in the training data. Various smoothing approaches were proposed to address the data sparseness problem.

Cantonese is a spoken dialect. It does not have a standard written form that is on par with standard written Chinese.[3] Written Cantonese is neither taught in schools nor used for official communication. When reciting Chinese text (e.g. a newspaper article), native Cantonese speakers seldom follow the original text content but usually substitute some of the words with typical colloquial expressions. This presents great challenges to language modeling for LVCSR. In our research, text materials from Hong Kong newspapers were used for language model training. Since there is no explicit word boundary in written Chinese, a word segmentation algorithm is needed to parse the sentence into a sequence of separate words. This was done using the forward-backward maximum matching algorithm with CULEX, which is a pronunciation lexicon of over 40,000 words.

Our Cantonese LVCSR system deals with a vocabulary of about 6,400 words. They include 3,700 polysyllabic (multi-character) words and 2,700 monosyllabic (single-character) words. With this vocabulary, the out-of-vocabulary (OOV) rate for the CUSENT utterances is around 1%. Bigram and trigram language models are trained on a text corpus of 98 million Chinese characters from five Hong Kong newspapers over a one year period. Character perplexity is used to measure the performance of the language models. It gives the average number of possible characters that can follow a given character string. The character-based perplexities of the 6,400-word Cantonese bigrams and trigrams are 58.2 and 44.3, respectively.

4.2.3. *Search Algorithm*

As described by Equation 1, the search algorithm, also known as the decoder, is to determine the most probable word sequence, given a sequence of observed acoustic feature vectors. It is a computationally complicated and demanding procedure. In an LVCSR system, words are decomposed into context-dependent phonemes and the phoneme models are described by a large number of HMM states. The search algorithm thus needs to deal with a huge network of connected states, referred to as the search space, which is formed under the constraints imposed by the pronunciation lexicon and the language models.

Both one-pass and multi-pass approaches have been applied to Cantonese LVCSR in our previous work.[28,30] Recently, we developed an improved two-pass search strategy as depicted in Figure 9. The first pass is a time-synchronous, beam-pruned Viterbi token-passing search with cross-word tri-IF models, a word-conditioned prefix lexical tree and word bigrams.[31] It generates a word graph as a compact summary of the reduced search space. A word graph is an acyclic, directed graph connected by word arcs. Each arc is labeled with the word identity, the starting and ending times, and a likelihood score contributed by various knowledge sources. A large number of possible alternative hypotheses are structurally represented in the word graph. The second pass of search is an A* stack decoder. It performs re-scoring in the word graph with word trigrams to generate recognition output in the form of either the best word sequence or a list of *N* most probable hypotheses.[31]

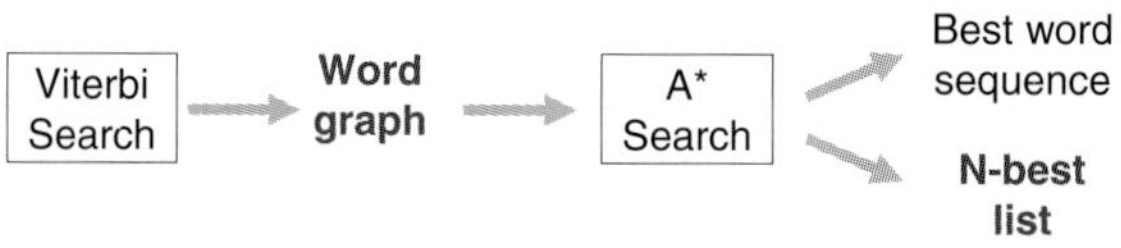

Fig. 9. Two-pass search strategy in our Cantonese LVCSR system.

Qian *et al.*[7] describes an approach of minimum character error rate (MCER) decoding for Cantonese LVCSR. It addresses the limitation of conventional MAP decoding, which aims to minimize sentence error rate. The word graph is first converted into a character graph from which the generalized character posterior probabilities (GCPP) can be computed.[32] The character graph is further converted into a character confusion network (CCN), which is a concatenation of time-aligned character confusion sets.[33] MCER decoding can be done straightforwardly on the CCN by simply collecting the character with the highest GCPP in each confusion set.[31] The use of GCPP and CCN also provides the flexibility of incorporating high-level knowledge sources that require a long time span.

4.2.4. *System Performance*

Our Cantonese LVCSR system, named CURec, has undergone several generations of development and the recognition performance has improved continually. Table 4 summarizes the performances of the various versions of CURec, in terms of character recognition accuracy. In all cases, the 6,400-word vocabulary as described in Section 4.2.2 is used. It must be noted that the performance of an LVCSR system depends not only on the advancement of acoustic and language modeling methods, but also on the improvement of engineering and computer programming techniques for algorithm implementation.

Table 4. Performance of CURec at different development stages.

	System descriptions	References	Character accuracy
(1)	First pass: syllable lattice generation by forward Viterbi search using tri-IF acoustic models Second pass: backward Viterbi search using word bigrams	Wong's MPhil Thesis[28]	75.4%
(2)	Same search algorithm as (1) Tone information integrated by syllable lattice expansion	Lau's MPhil Thesis[34]	76.6%
(3)	One-pass search with tree-structured lexicon and tri-IF acoustic models	Choi's MPhil Thesis[30]	80.3%
(4)	First pass: Viterbi beam search to generate word graph, using tri-IF acoustic models, tree-structured lexicon and word bigrams Second pass: A* stack decoder to re-score the word graph	Qian's PhD Thesis[31]	82.3%
(5)	First pass: same as (4) Second pass: minimum character error rate decoding based on restructured word graph and tone-enhanced GCPP	Qian's PhD Thesis[31]	87.6%

5. Cantonese Text-to-Speech Synthesis

5.1. *Overview*

A text-to-speech (TTS) system automatically converts given orthographic text into acoustic speech signals that sound like human speech. A typical TTS system consists of three modules as shown in Figure 10. The primary function of the text processing module is to derive a sequence of pronunciation symbols that can be spoken (or *synthesized*). The sequence of pronunciation symbols is passed to the acoustic synthesis module to generate synthetic speech. Concatenation of pre-recorded speech units has become a widely accepted approach in TTS synthesis for various languages. Prosody refers to the properties of continuous speech such as pitch, loudness, rhythm and tempo. The speech produced by the acoustic synthesis module may not carry the desired prosody. There is a need for prosody modification in which the prosody-related acoustic properties are changed with respect to certain specified targets.

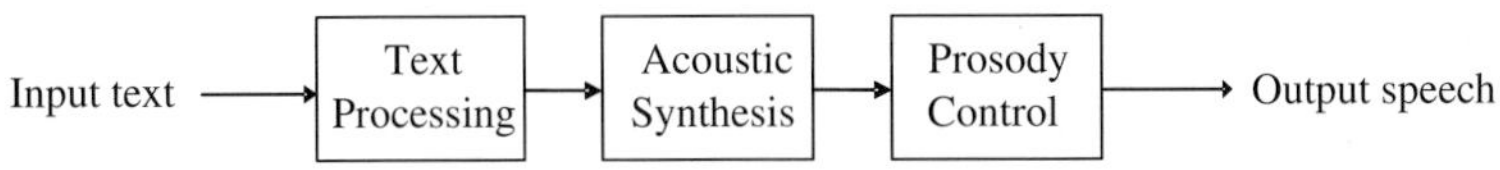

Fig. 10. Block diagram of a typical TTS system.

We have developed a few Cantonese TTS systems that can accept unrestricted Chinese text input and produce speech with a fairly high quality. Details of these systems are given in the following sections. A demonstration (with audio) is available at http://dsp.ee.cuhk.edu.hk/speech/cutalk/.

5.2. *CUTalk 2.0: Monosyllable Based Cantonese TTS*

CUTalk 2.0 was developed based on the pioneering work by Chu and Ching.[35] Its text processing module involves two steps:

- **Word segmentation** - To split a sentence into a sequence of words that can be found in the pronunciation lexicon CULEX.
- **Pronunciation assignment** - Assign pronunciations to individual words.

The text processing module can also handle special non-Chinese contents like English acronyms, alpha-numeric symbols, date and time, and punctuation marks.

CUTalk 2.0 uses the CUSYL database, which contains about 1,800 isolated syllables. Synthetic speech is produced by simple concatenation of these syllables. The time-domain pitch-synchronous-overlap-add (TD-PSOLA) technique is used to modify the F0 contours and segmental duration to match prescribed targets. Only the voiced segment of a syllable is subject to the prosodic modification and the voiceless segment is concatenated as it is. The prosody control module of CUTalk 2.0 is fundamental and minimal. It specifies the duration of the initial and the final segment, and the F0 contour for each syllable. For each base syllable, we use fixed duration values regardless of its phonetic context and the tone identity. These duration values are derived from a large amount of continuous speech data.[36] As for the tone contour, a single template is used to represent each of the nine tones. Cross-syllable tone co-articulation and phrasal movement are not considered.

CUTalk 2.0 has been engineered into an application software. The system accepts unrestricted Chinese text (Big5 or GB encoded) and generates continuous Cantonese speech. It allows free switch between a couple of male and female voices. The speaking rate is also adjustable. The software includes a set of Application Programming Interfaces (API) that can be used in MS Windows or Linux based computers. It has been deployed in a number of commercial IVRS (Interactive Voice Response System) applications.

5.3. *CUTalk 3.0: Sub-syllable Based TTS*

CUTalk 2.0 can produce highly intelligible Cantonese speech, in which individual syllables are clearly and accurately uttered. However, the synthetic speech is considered unnatural in that there is an obvious lack of perceptual continuity. To address this problem, a sub-syllable based Cantonese TTS system, named CUTalk

3.0, was developed.[37] A sub-syllable unit is defined to contain two parts. Each part is either an initial segment or a final segment. There are two different types of sub-syllable units: initial-final (I-F) and final-initial (F-I) units. An I-F unit is essentially a monosyllable. An F-I unit is an inter-syllable unit, with the final and the initial coming from a pair of adjacent syllables. Since the initial is optional, an inter-syllable unit may also be in the form of final-final (F-F). In addition, initials and finals at the beginning and the ending of a sentence are treated separately. If tonal difference is considered, the total number of distinctive sub-syllable units is about 16,000. Since post-synthesis F0 modification is applied, it becomes less critical to store all tonal variants of the finals. We tried to reduce the size of the acoustic inventory by forming two broad classes of tones: the level-tone group (tones 1, 3, 4 and 6) and the rising-tone group (tones 2 and 5). For each final, only one representative tone from each group needs to be included in the inventory. As a result, the total number of sub-syllable units reduces to about 5,750. Each required sub-syllable unit was recorded as part of a carrier word, so that it is naturally spoken as far as possible.

Waveform concatenation between a pair of sub-syllable units is done in either an initial or a final segment. In general, the concatenation point lies in the middle of a segment. The speech samples in the neighborhood of the concatenation points need to be manipulated so as to minimize undesirable discontinuities and artifacts. Based on their acoustic properties, the Cantonese initials and finals are classified into three categories: (1) transient voiced consonants (plosives and affricates); (2) stationary voiceless consonants (fricatives); and (3) voiced initials and finals. The concatenation strategy for each category is designed carefully to attain spectral continuity. Subjective listening tests show that the sub-syllable based system produces more natural and continuous speech than the monosyllable based one.

5.4. *F0 Analysis and Modeling*

CUProsody, a single-speaker continuous speech database, was developed to facilitate systematic analysis and modeling of Cantonese speech prosody.[38] It contains 1,200 long utterances and covers the major prosodic phenomena and their variations. An extensive acoustic analysis was carried out on CUProsody to investigate the variation of F0 in continuous Cantonese speech. The surface F0 contour of a continuous Cantonese utterance is considered the combination of a global component (phrase-level intonation curve) and local components (syllable-level tone contours). Taking into account the special properties of the Cantonese tone system, we developed a novel method of F0 normalization to separate the local components from the global one. Our analysis was focused specifically on co-articulated tone contours for di-syllabic words, cross-word contours, and phrase-initial tone contours. Based on the results of the analysis, a template-based model for F0 generation was established and integrated into CUTalk 3.0. Subjective listening tests showed that the proposed model significantly improves the naturalness of the output speech.

6. Conclusion

The development of spoken language systems requires a non-trivial understanding of the target language and in-depth linguistic and acoustic analysis of the language. Speech corpora and pronunciation dictionaries are indispensable resources that have to be developed with a forward-looking plan. Although the fundamental principles and methodologies for Cantonese LVCSR and TTS are similar to those for Mandarin, there are important language-specific considerations on, e.g., use of tone information, pronunciation variation, acoustic confusion between some specific phonemes. Our existing LVCSR and TTS systems have reached a fairly high performance level in terms of both accuracy/intelligibility and practicality. Nevertheless, much work remains to be done especially in dealing with the multifarious speaking behaviors which cause acoustic variation in spontaneous speech.

Acknowledgements

Our research on Cantonese speech recognition and synthesis has been supported by a number of Earmarked Grants from the Hong Kong Research Grants Council and the Innovation and Technology Funds from the Hong Kong Government.

References

1. J. Yuan, *Hanyu Fangyan Gaiyao [An Introduction to Chinese Dialectology].* (Wenzi Gaige Chubanshe, Beijing, 1960).
2. Ethnologue: Languages of the world, 15th edition. [Online]. Available: http://www.ethnologue.com/
3. S. Matthews and V. Yip, *Cantonese: A Comprehensive Grammar.* (London, Routledge, 1994).
4. P. C. Ching, T. Lee, and E. Zee, "From Phonology and Acoustic Properties to Automatic Recognition of Cantonese," in *Proc. ISSIPNN*, vol. 1, (1994), pp. 127–132.
5. T. Lee, W. K. Lo, P. C. Ching, and H. Meng, "Spoken Language Resources for Cantonese Speech Processing," *Speech Communication*, vol. 36, pp. 327–342, (2002).
6. W. K. Lo, P. C. Ching, T. Lee, and H. Meng, "Design, Compilation and Processing of CUCall: a Set of Cantonese Spoken Language Corpora Collected over Telephone Networks," in *Proc. ROCLING XIV*, (2001), pp. 193–212.
7. Y. Qian, F. K. Soong, and T. Lee, "Tone-enhanced Generalized Character Posterior Probability (GCPP) for Cantonese LVCSR," in *Proc. ICASSP*, vol. 1, (2006), pp. 133–136.
8. T. Lee, P. Kam, and F. K. Soong, "Modeling Cantonese Pronunciation Variation for Large-vocabulary Continuous Speech Recognition," *International Journal of Computational Linguistics & Chinese Language Processing*, vol. 11, pp. 17–36, (2006).

9. O.-K. Y. Hashimoto, *Studies in Yue Dialects 1: Phonology of Cantonese.* (Cambridge University Press, 1972).
10. S. R. Ramsey, *The Languages of China.* (Princeton University Press, 1987).
11. R. S. Bauer and P. K. Benedict, *Modern Cantonese Phonology (Trends in Linguistics: Studies and Monographs; 102).* (Mouton de Gruyer, 1997).
12. Linguistic Society of Hong Kong, *Hong Kong Jyut Ping Characters Table.* (Linguistic Society of Hong Kong Press, 1997).
13. ((2000)) CCDICT: Dictionary of Chinese Characters, version 3.0. [Online]. Available: http://www.chinalanguage.com/CCDICT/
14. M. Y. Chen, *Tone Sandhi: Patterns across Chinese Dialects.* (Cambridge University Press, 2000).
15. E. Zee, "A Phonetic Study of Cantonese Vowels and Diphthongs," in *Proc. 4th Int. Conf. Cantonese & Other Yue Dialects*, (1993).
16. T. Lee, *Automatic Recognition of Isolated Cantonese Syllables Using Neural Networks.* PhD Thesis, (The Chinese University of Hong Kong, 1996).
17. T. Lee, W. Lau, Y. W. Wong, and P. C. Ching, "Using Tone Information in Cantonese Continuous Speech Recognition," *ACM Trans. on Asian Language Information Processing*, vol. 1 (1), pp. 83–102, (2002).
18. Y. Y. Kong, "VOT in Cantonese: Acoustical Measurements," in *Proc. 4th Int. Conf. Cantonese & Other Yue Dialects*, (1993).
19. R. Wang, D. Xia, J. Ni, and B. Liu, "USTC95 - a Putonghua Corpus," in *Proc. ICSLP*, vol. 3, (1996), pp. 1894–1897.
20. C. Chan, "Design Considerations of a Putonghua Database for Speech Recognition," in *Proceedings of the Conference on Phonetics of the Language in China*, (1998), pp. 13–16.
21. Q. Huo and B. Ma, "Training Material Considerations for Task-independent Subword Modeling: Design and other Possibilities," in *Proc. Oriental COCOSDA*, (1999), pp. 85–88.
22. H.-C. Wang, "Speech Research Infra-structure in Taiwan - from Database Design to Performance Assessment," in *Proc. Oriental COCOSDA*, (1999), pp. 53–56.
23. T. Lee and P. C. Ching, "Cantonese Syllable Recognition using Neural Networks," *IEEE Trans. SAP*, vol. 7 (4), pp. 466–472, (1999).
24. T. Lee, P. C. Ching, and L. W. Chan, "Isolated Word Recognition using Modular Recurrent Neural Networks," *Pattern Recognition*, vol. 31 (6), pp. 751–760, (1998).
25. J. L. Gauvain and L. Lamel, "Large-vocabulary Continuous Speech Recognition: Advances and Applications," *Proc. IEEE*, vol. 88, pp. 1181–1200, (2000).
26. P. Kam, *Pronunciation Modeling for Cantonese Speech Recognition.* MPhil Thesis, (The Chinese University of Hong Kong, 2003).
27. X.-D. Huang, A. Acero, and H.-W. Hon, *Spoken Language Processing – A Guide to Theory, Algorithm, and System Development.* (Prentice-Hall, 2001).
28. Y. W. Wong, *Large Vocabulary Continuous Speech Recognition for Cantonese.* MPhil Thesis, (The Chinese University of Hong Kong, 2000).
29. S. Gao, T. Lee, Y. W. Wong, B. Xu, P. C. Ching, and T. Huang, "Acoustic Modeling for Chinese Speech Recognition: a Comparative Study of Mandarin and Cantonese," in *Proc. ICASSP*, vol. 3, (2000), pp. 1261–1264.
30. W. N. Choi, *An Efficient Decoding Method for Continuous Speech Recognition Based on a Tree-Structured Lexicon.* MPhil Thesis, (The Chinese University of Hong Kong, 2001).
31. Y. Qian, *Use of Tone Information in Cantonese LVCSR Based on Generalized Character Posterior Probability Decoding.* PhD Thesis, (The Chinese University of Hong Kong, 2005).
32. F. K. Soong, W. K. Lo, and S. Nakamura, "Generalized Word Posterior Probability (GWPP) for Measuring Reliability of Recognized Words," in *Proc. SWIM*, (2004).

33. L. Mangu, E. Brill, and A. Stolcke, "Finding Consensus in Speech Recognition: Word Error Minimization and other Applications of Confusion Networks," *Computer Speech and Language*, vol. 14, no. 4, pp. 373–400, (2000).
34. W. Lau, *Attributes and Extraction of Tone Information for Continuous Cantonese Speech Recognition*. MPhil Thesis, (The Chinese University of Hong Kong, 2000).
35. M. Chu and P. C. Ching, "A Cantonese Synthesizer Based on TD-PSOLA Method," in *Proc. ISMIP*, (1997), pp. 262–267.
36. T. Lee, H. Meng, W. Lau, W. K. Lo, and P. C. Ching, "Micro-prosodic Control in Cantonese Text-to-Speech Synthesis," in *Proc. EUROSPEECH*, vol. 4, (1999), pp. 1855–1858.
37. K. M. Law and T. Lee, "Cantonese Text-to-Speech Synthesis using Sub-syllable Units," in *Proc. EUROSPEECH*, vol. 2, (2001), pp. 991–994.
38. Y. Li, T. Lee, and Y. Qian, "Analysis and Modeling of F0 Contours for Cantonese Text-to-Speech," *ACM Trans. on Asian Language Information Processing*, vol. 3, pp. 169–180, (2004).

CHAPTER 17

TAIWANESE MIN-NAN SPEECH RECOGNITION AND SYNTHESIS

Ren-yuan Lyu[†], Min-siong Liang[‡], Dau-cheng Lyu[‡], and Yuan-chin Chiang[§]

[†]*Department of Computer Science & Information Engineering,*
[‡]*Department of Electrical Engineering, Chang Gung University, Taoyuan,*
[§]*Institute of Statistics, National Tsing-hua University, Hsinchu*
Email: {renyuan.lyu@gmail.com, minsiong@gmail.com}

In this chapter, we review research efforts in automatic speech recognition (ASR), text-to-speech (TTS) and speech corpus design for Taiwanese, or Min-nan – a major native language spoken in Taiwan. Following an introduction of the orthography and phonetic structure of Taiwanese, we describe the various databases used for these tasks, including the Formosa Lexicon (ForLex) – a phonetically transcribed database using Formosa Alphabet (ForPA), an alphabet system designed with Taiwan's multi-lingual applications in mind – and the Formosa Speech Database (ForSDat) – a speech corpus made up of microphone and telephone speech. For ASR, we propose a unified scheme that includes Mandarin/Taiwanese bilingual acoustic models, incorporate variations in pronunciation into pronunciation modeling, and create a character-based tree-structured searching network. This scheme is especially suitable for handling multiple character-based languages, such as members of the CJKV (Chinese, Japanese, Korean, and Vietnam) family. For speech synthesis, through the use of the bilingual lexicon information, the Taiwanese TTS system is made up of three functional modules: a text analysis module, a prosody module, and a waveform synthesis module. An experiment conducted to evaluate the text analysis and tone sandhi modules reveals about 90% labeling and 65% tone sandhi accuracies. Multiple-level unit selection for a limited domain application of TTS is also proposed to improve the naturalness of synthesized speech.

1. Introduction: The Languages and People of Taiwan

Taiwan's inhabitants are multi-lingual, while Taiwanese (also called *Min-nan* or Hokkienese) is the mother tongue of more than 70% of the island's population.[1] Although a majority of the people in Taiwan use Taiwanese as a native language, this language has been very much marginalized in the period after World War II.

Along with the democratic and economic achievements in Taiwan in recent years, there is a renewed confidence and interest to use Taiwanese as the main language of communication.

Linguistically, Taiwanese is a branch of the *Han* (Chinese) language family possessing many Chinese characteristics such as being a syllabic and tonal language, using *hànzì* (Chinese characters) as the major orthography in its writing system, and having a unique and systematic way to pronounce these Chinese characters. However, Taiwanese does not have a strong written tradition. Up to the 19th century, Taiwanese speakers wrote using a form of literary Chinese (文言文), which would be mostly unintelligible nowadays. A writing system made up of entirely roman characters was developed for colloquial Taiwanese in the 19th century by Western missionaries to facilitate translations of the Bible. This system is commonly called Church Romanization, or “peh-oe-ji” (POJ) in Taiwanese. A new orthographic system called *Hanlor*, proposed by Dr. IokDik Ong in the 1960’s that uses both *hànzì* and roman characters, started to gain popularity. Since the 1990’s, *Hanlor* has become the main mode of writing for Taiwanese and has been frequently used by major newspapers. Just like the increasing usage of vernacular Chinese (白話文) in Mandarin, the use of the more literary writing form becomes increasingly rare in Taiwanese.

Looking at Taiwanese phonetically, a majority of the Chinese characters used have multiple pronunciations. A character can be pronounced in the classic, literary way (文讀音, *Wen-du-in*) or in the “everyday” way (白讀音, *Bai-du-in*). It has been observed that if a word comes from classical literature, then *Wen-du-in* is used to pronounce that word. But if the origin of the word is vague, the pronunciation of the word tends to vary.

Taiwanese is a member of the Han language family, and not a dialect of Mandarin. Taiwanese, however, does have its own dialects. These varieties of Taiwanese can be classified as northern Taiwanese and southern Taiwanese, roughly corresponding to their origins from mainland China. The dialectal differences between them appear small and often insignificant to native speakers. As a result of well-developed transportation and communication systems, few pure dialectal tongues exist.

1.1. *Phonetic Structure of Taiwanese Syllables*

Phonetically, Taiwanese is a syllabic and tonal language with extensive tone sandhi rules. Similar to Mandarin, a syllable in Taiwanese can be defined by its three components: *initial* consonant, rhyme and tone; rhyme is also called *final* in speech community. There are 18 initials, and 47 finals[2] which are made up of the

28 phonemes listed in Tables 1 and 2. In the table, phonemes are expressed in the International Phonetic Alphabet (IPA) as well as in *TongYong Pinin*, a phonetic spelling system used in Taiwan since 2000. Two features are worth noting. (1) Nasalized vowels:. In Mandarin, a vowel is actually nasalized if preceded with nasal consonants /m/ and /n/ such as the /a/ vowel in "ma" and /au/ in "nau". This applies to Taiwanese as well, but Taiwanese has a rich set of nasalized vowels/rhymes even without preceding nasal consonants. Note that Taiwanese also has a third initial nasal consonant /ng/ not found in Mandarin. (2) Rhymed consonants: Among the 47 rhymes, two of them are consonants, namely /m/ and /ng/. That is, these two consonants can be rhymes and preceded by other consonants.

Table 1. The 17 Taiwanese consonants in IPA and in TongYong Pinin (in parentheses).

	Voiced	Unvoiced Unaspirated	Unvoiced Aspirated	Nasal
Alveolar		[s] (s)		
Palatoalveolar	[ʤ] (r)	[ʦ] (z)	[ʦʰ] (c)	
Bilabial	[b] (bh)	[p] (b)	[pʰ] (p)	[m] (m)
Dental	[l] (l)	[t] (d)	[tʰ] (t)	[n] (n)
Velar	[g] (gh)	[k] (g)	[kʰ] (k)	[ŋ] (ng)
Glottal			[h] (h)	

Table 2. The 11 Taiwanese vowel phonemes in IPA and in TongYong Pinin (in parentheses).

vowel phoneme	a (a)	ɛ (e)	i (i)	o (o)	ɤ (or)	u (u)
nasalized vowel	ã (a^n)	ɛ̃ (e^n)	ĩ (i^n)	õ (o^n)		ũ (u^n)

Traditional tone studies specify that there are seven tone classes in Taiwanese when a syllable is pronounced individually. However, if syllables are articulated consecutively in connected speech, a tone sandhi (or tone change) usually sets in, requiring at least two more tone classes for speech synthesis purposes. These nine tones are listed in Table 3. In contrast to the traditional order of tones, the order of tone classes in Table 3 is adopted from the *TongYong Pinin* system, mainly because of its ease in teaching as well as its simplicity in specifying tone sandhi rules.

Note that tone 6 and 7 (tone 4 and tone 8 in traditional tonal numbering) are the so-called *entering* tones and their phonetic transcriptions differ from other tones. Syllables with these tones are shorter in duration, and are traditionally treated as tonal variations. However, in speech recognition, they are handled as different syllables.

Taiwanese is known to be rich in tone sandhi, and in our on-going T3 Taiwanese treebank – a bracketed corpus of more than 180,000 words[3] – creation, we recently started to annotate the corpus with tone sandhi marks. Based on about 7,000 phrases/sentences, the tone sandhi rate is more than 80% in syllable count.

There are two questions relevant to tone sandhi: when does the tone of a syllable change, and where does it change to. At the word level, in multi-syllabic words, most syllables would undergo tone changes except the final one. However, at the sentence level, the tone sandhi may appear even at the word boundary. This phenomenon seems closely related to the syntactic roles of words in a sentence, and is being studied in an on-going research.

As for the where-to problem of the Taiwanese tone sandhi rules, the "Taiwanese boat"[2] in Figure 1 illustrates the simplest way to recap the rules. Figure 1 also shows the tone sandhi rules of entering tones.

Table 3. Tones in Taiwanese. Note that tone 8 and 9 exist only in tone sandhi.

Tone	1	2	3	4	5	6	7	8	9
Example	東 dong^1	洞 dōng^2	擋 dọng^3	黨 dòng^4	同 dǒng^5	獨 dok^6	督 dōk^7	(獨) dọk^8	(黨) dóng^9
Descrip-tion	high-level	mid-level	low-falling	high-falling	falling-rising	high-short	mid-short	low-short	rising
Traditional classes	1(陰平) InPing	7(陽去) IangChyu	3(陰去) InChyu	2(陰上) InSang	5(陽平) IangPing	8(陰入) InRu	4(陽入) IangRu		

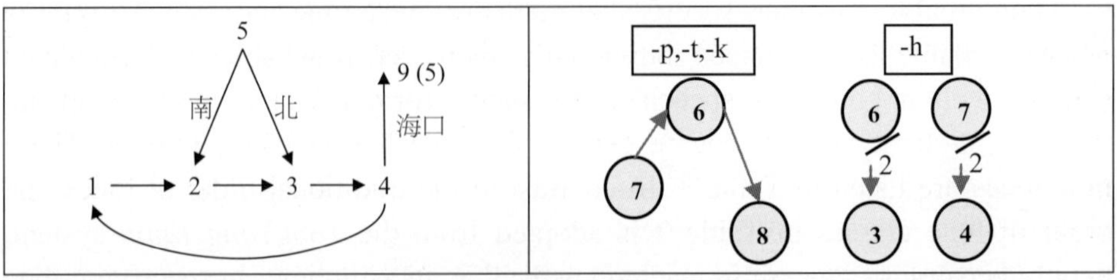

Fig. 1. The major tone sandhi rules of Taiwanese. On the left is the *Tone sandhi Boat* which captures the rules neatly. On the right are the rules for *entering* tones: syllables ending with –p, –t, –k, or –h.

1.2. *ForPA: Formosa Phonetic Alphabet*

With multi-lingual applications in mind, we design a Formosa Phonetic Alphabet (ForPA) for the three major languages in Taiwan: Taiwanese, Hakka, and Mandarin. Other systems, such as SAMPA[4] and WorldBet,[5] have been developed, but have not been adopted here for reasons of simplicity. For the phonetic transcription of Taiwanese, the symbols in ForPA are very similar to those in TongYong Pinin. It is known that phonemes can be defined in several different ways, depending on the level of detail desired. The philosophy driving the labeling process in ForPA is that when faced with choices, we prefer not to divide a phoneme into distinct allophones, except in cases where their sounds are clearly distinct (to the ear), or when their spectrograms look clearly different (to the eye). Since labeling is often performed by engineering students and researchers (as opposed to professional phoneticians), it is generally safer to keep the number of units as small as possible, assuming that the recognizer will be able to learn the finer distinctions that might exist within any context. Generally speaking, ForPA can be considered a subset of IPA, but it has been suited for applications relating to languages in Taiwan.[6]

13. *Multi-lingual ForLex: Formosa Pronunciation Lexicon*

Three lexicons have been collected to be used for corpus collection, speech recognition and speech synthesis. The first is the Formosa Lexicon, which contains about 123,000 words in Taiwanese Chinese text with their Taiwanese Mandarin pronunciations. It is a combination of two lexicons: Formosa Mandarin-Taiwanese Bilingual lexicon and Gang's Taiwanese lexicon.[7] The former is derived from a Mandarin lexicon, and thus many commonly used Taiwanese terms are missing due to the fundamental difference between these two languages. The latter lexicon contains more widely-used Taiwanese expressions from samples of radio talk shows. Some statistics of the Formosa Lexicon are summarized in Table 4, where out of a total of 123,438 pronunciation entries, 65,007 entries are with Wen-du-in pronunciations, while 58,431 entries are with Bai-du-in pronunciations. For all entries with Wen-du-in pronunciations, there are 6,890 mono-syllabic word entries, 39,840 entries of words with two syllables, and so on.

For the other two lexicons, the CKIP Mandarin lexicon and Syu's Hakka lexicon, the distribution of words according to the number of syllables are listed in Table 5.

Table 4. The number of pronunciation of Formosa bilingual Lexicons, including classic literary pronunciation (Wen-du-in) and everyday pronunciation (Bai-du-in).

	Taiwanese Wen-du-in pronunciation	Taiwanese Bai-du-in pronunciation	Total
1-Syllable	6890	2377	9267
2-Syllable	39840	36176	76016
3-Syllable	8308	15214	23522
4-Syllable	9119	4117	13236
5-Syllable	438	399	837
6-Syllable	225	94	319
7-Syllable	125	28	153
8-Syllable	52	22	74
9-Syllable	2	2	4
10-Syllable	8	2	10
Total	65007	58431	123438

Table 5. The distribution of words in two lexicons: Syu's Hakka lexicon, and the CKIP.

	1-Syl	*2-Syl*	*3-Syl*	*4-Syl*	*5-Syl*	
Syu	7322	9161	4948	2382	21	
CKIP	6863	39733	8277	9074	435	
	6-Syl	*7-Syl*	*8-Syl*	*9-Syl*	*10-Syl*	Total
Syu	3	0	0	0	0	23837
CKIP	223	125	52	2	8	64792

2. Speech Corpus

To implement a speaker-independent automatic speech recognition system, it is essential to collect a large-scale speech database. However, the years of marginalization of Taiwanese makes this task difficult in at least in two ways. Firstly, such a mammoth undertaking requires a huge amount of funding, which is difficult to obtain as funding is typically limited. Secondly, due to the limited level of education, only a small number of speakers have the capability to write Taiwanese. This low literacy level makes Taiwanese text collection difficult, which in turn makes the collection of speech data difficult – be it collecting read speech from existing texts, or phonetically transcribing existing speech data.

To overcome this problem, a moderate-sized speech database using only the lexicon is developed. In brief, we: (1) design sheets of phonetically-balanced words from the lexicon; (2) record the microphone and telephone speech of those words; and then (3) validate this speech database. The result is the ForSDat speech corpus which is detailed in the following subsections.

2.1. *Producing Phonetically-Balanced Word Sheets*

Given a lexicon, we can extract phonetically-abundant word sets such that the chosen phonetic units are not only base-syllables, phones, and right context dependent (RCD) phones, but also initial-finals, RCD initial-finals and inter-syllabic RCD phones. The process of selecting such a word set is actually a set-covering optimization problem, which is NP-hard. Here, we adopt a simple greedy heuristic approximate algorithm.[8]

First, some notation definitions. Let $W=\{w_i : 1 \le i \le N\}$ be the set of all words in the lexicon, where N is the number of words, w_i is the i-th word. $S(w_i)$ are the sets of all distinct syllables and $U(w_i)$ are denoted as cross-syllable bi-phones or cross-syllable tri-phones in the word w_i respectively. C_t^* is selected word in time t, $W(t)=\{C_1^*,\cdots,C_t^*\}$ is selected word set, and $S(t)=\{S(C_1^*),\cdots,S(C_t^*)\}$ is selected distinct syllables set and $U(t)=\{U(C_1^*),\cdots,U(C_t^*)\}$ is selected distinct bi-phones set till time t. $W^c(t)=W-W(t)$ is a non-chosen word set, $S^c(t)=S(W)-S(t)$ is a non-chosen distinct syllable set and $U^c(t)=U(W)-U(t)$ is non-chosen distinct bi-phones set or tri-phones set till time t. The algorithm of extracting phonetically-abundant word sets can then be described in the following steps:

Step 1: Initially t=0 and we have $W(0)=W$, $S(0)=S(W)$, $P(0)=P(W)$

Step 2: Choose the word w_{i^*} as C_t^* such that the union of $S^c(t-1)$ and $S(w_i)$ is maximized, i.e. $w_i = \arg\max_{w_i \in W^c(t-1)} \#(S^c(t-1) \cap S(w_i))$ -- (1) then $C_t^* = w_i$; if w_{i^*} is not unique in (1), choose $w_i = \arg\max_{w_i \in W^c(t-1)} \#S(w_i)$ -- (2) as C_t^*; if w_{i^*} is not unique in (1) and (2), choose the preceding index word as C_t^*, $S^c(t)=S^c(t-1)-S(C_t^*)$, $W^c(t)=W^c(t-1)-C_t^*$, $t=t+1$

Step 3: If $S^c(t) \ne \phi$ and $W^c(t) \ne \phi$, repeat Step 2
else if $W^c(t)=\phi$, exit the algorithm.
else if $S^c(t)=\phi$, proceed to the next step

Step 4: Choose the word w_{i^*} as C_t^* that maximizes the union of $U^c(t-1)$ and $U(w_i)$, i.e. $w_i = \arg\max_{w_i \in W^c(t-1)} \#(U^c(t-1) \cap U(w_i))$ -- (3) then $C_t^* = w_i$; if w_{i^*} is not unique in (3), choose $w_i = \arg\max_{w_i \in W^c(t-1)} \#S(w_i)$ -- (2) as C_t^*; if w_{i^*} is not unique in (3) and (2), choose the preceding index word as C_t^*, then $U^c(t)=U^c(t-1)-U(C_t^*)$, $W^c(t)=W^c(t-1)-C_t^*$ and $t=t+1$.

Step 5: If $B^c(t) \ne \phi$ and $W^c(t) \ne \phi$, repeat Step 4
else if $B^c(t)=\phi$ or $W^c(t)=\phi$, exit the algorithm.

Applying the algorithm to the three lexicons mentioned above, we identified a number of balanced-word sets. For Taiwanese, 446 balanced-word sets were generated, each sheet containing 200 syllables making up a total of 37,275 words.

2.2. *Speaker Recruitment and Recording System for Corpus Collection*

Several part-time assistants were employed to recruit speakers from around Taiwan. Each speaker was asked to record readings from one sheet, and the speaker, along with the assistant, received remuneration. We also noted the following information relating to the speaker:

(i) the name and gender of the speaker;
(ii) the age and birthplace of the speaker;
(iii) the location and time of the recording;
(iv) the number of years of education the speaker has completed.

This speaker profile information would be useful later on for organizing the collected speech data. The user can also design experiments according to these profiles.

Two systems were designed for collecting microphone and telephone speech for the ForSDat database. For the telephone system, the speakers dialed into the laboratory using a handset telephone. The input signal is in the format of 8K sampling rate with 8-bits μ-law compression. A speaker was given a prompt sheet before recording, and every word on the sheet was first played to the speaker before he/she recorded that word. The data gathered from different speakers were saved in different directories.

Table 6. The statistics of utterances, speakers and data length for speech collected over microphone and telephone channels in Taiwanese and Mandarin. (*MIC*: microphone; *TEL*: telephone; also denoted in Name by sub-tag after dash).

	Name	Channel	Gender	Quantity	Train(hr)	Test (hr)
ForSDAT	TW01-M0	*MIC*	Female	50	5.92	0.29
	TW01-M1		Male	50	5.44	
	MD01-M0		Female	50	5.65	0.27
	MD01-M1		Male	50	5.42	
	TW02-M0		Female	233	10.10	0.70
	TW02-M1		Male	277	11.66	
	TW02-T0	*TEL*	Female	580	29.21	0.95
	TW02-T1		Male	412	19.37	

For the microphone system, we used a speech recording tool that simplifies the processes of text prompting, speech prompting and saving the recorded speech and its associated phonetic label file in ForPA. This system was simply set up on a notebook computer and taken to wherever the recording needed to be done. Table 6 shows some statistics of the ForSDat speech database.

2.3. *Speech Data Verification*

To verify the consistency of the speech data and its corresponding transcriptions, an automatic as well as a manual checking are carried out after the recordings. Automatic verification involves superficially checking if the speech file is empty, or if the speech is too short, and so on. If more than 10% of such errors are found in one set, the whole dataset is considered unusable.

Manual checking is done by employing a simple concatenated TTS system to read out the prompt word, and that word's corresponding recorded speech is also played out. If the pair does not sound alright, the utterance is potentially in error, and further attention is given to it. In cases where a recorded speech does not correspond to its prompt, the prompt is changed, particularly its phonetic transcription, to match the speech. This approach seems quite effective since verification is such a tedious process, and it seems easier to detect errors by listening out for unnaturalness, compared to looking out for them visually.

Finally, a relational database using ACCESS is created to record the profiles of all speakers and their recorded items. This relational database can be queried using the SQL language to locate the waveforms transcribed using the specific phones or syllables, or even to locate the speaker who recorded the specific-phone waveforms.

3. Recognition

3.1. *Large Vocabulary Word Recognizer*

Figure 2 illustrates a series of four components, including a feature extractor, a unified acoustic model, a bilingual pronunciation dictionary and a language model. The feature extractor receives the waveform as its input and transforms it into the frame-based feature vectors O. The final outputs, the Chinese characters C, are closely dependent on the other pre-processors, and each of these pre-processors influences the results of our proposed bilingual speech recognizer.

Given the acoustic information O and the tonal syllable-based pronunciation S, the most likely Chinese character sequences C are found using the following expression:

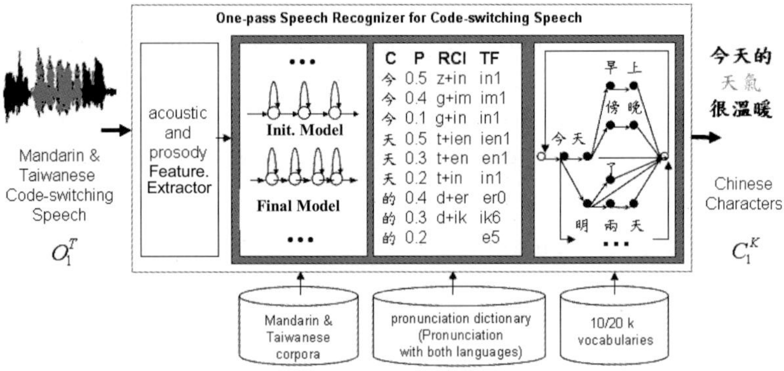

Fig. 2. The diagram of the one-pass speech recognizer.

$$\arg\max P(C \mid O, S) \quad (1)$$

Using standard probability theory, this expression can be equivalently written as

$$\arg\max P(O \mid S, C) P(S \mid C) P(C) \quad (2)$$

The three probability expressions in (2) are organized in such a way that acoustics of pronunciation and language information are contained in separate terms. In modeling, these terms are known as

1. $P(O \mid S, C)$ Tonal syllable acoustic model
2. $P(S \mid C)$ Pronunciation model
3. $P(C)$ The language model

In this framework,[9] Chinese character based decoding can be implemented by searching in a three-layer network composed of an acoustic model layer, a lexical layer, and a grammar layer. There are at least 2 critical differences between our framework and the conventional one. 1) In the lexicon layer, character-to-pronunciation mapping can easily incorporate multiple pronunciations in multiple languages, including Japanese, Korean, and even Vietnamese which also use Chinese characters. 2) In the grammar layer, characters instead of syllables are used as nodes in the searching network. Under this ASR structure, it does not matter which language the user speaks. Whether it is Taiwanese, Mandarin or a mixture of them even in one sentence, the ASR outputs only the Chinese characters, making the framework language/dialect independent. In another work,[10] we also used the framework to recognize Taiwanese-Mandarin code-switching speech.

3.2. *Feature Extraction with Tone Information*

Many researchers have included tone features in their tonal language recognizers, such as for Mandarin, Cantonese[11] and Taiwanese. They report that recognition accuracy rates increase as tonal features are incorporated into their recognizers. Our prior work[12] also confirms this point. Features carrying only acoustic information in one-pass recognizers will result in confusion and increase the number of searching nodes during the decoding process. Thus, tonal feature is necessary.

In this system, we adopted an algorithm based on auto-correlation and harmonic-to-noise ratio to estimate pitch. Pitch can only be correctly estimated in the voiced region of a waveform. In unvoiced portions, pitch is usually assigned zero in traditional pitch analysis programs. However, for speech recognition purposes, this zero padding strategy may not be appropriate because it will lead to problems of zero variances and undefined derivatives at voiced/unvoiced transitions. We fill the pitch gap with exponential decay/grow functions to connect the pitch contours of two voiced regions, and we call this *pitch smoothing by exponential functions*.

3.3. *Bilingual Acoustic Model*

For acoustic modeling, a unified approach for a hidden Markov model (HMM) based multi-lingual acoustic model is adopted. In this approach, a knowledge-based phone mapping method is applied to map phones across languages and reduce the effective number of phones in the multi-lingual acoustic model. When combining acoustic models of two different languages, we need to identify which phones are acoustically similar between the 2 languages, while knowing that other phones still need the use of language-dependent models. It is well known that language-dependent systems perform better than language-independent ones. Driven by this, using ForPA, we group all the phones in the different languages into phonetically and acoustically similar clusters.

Furthermore, in order to more efficiently merge the similar parts of the sounds from both languages, we use a tying algorithm based on a decision tree to cluster the HMM models by using the maximum likelihood criterion.[13] This approach has the advantage that every possible context acoustic model state can be classified by the tree, so that any back-off models can be avoided. In practice, this approach significantly reduced the syllable recognition error rate and the overall system parameters for unseen context acoustic model in previous LVCSR experiments.

3.4. *Tree-structured Language Searching Net*

A tree structure is a natural choice of representation for a large vocabulary lexicon, as many phonemes can be shared eliminating redundant acoustic evaluations. The advantage of using a lexicon tree representation is obvious: It can effectively reduce the state-search space of the trellis. Ney *et al.*[14] reported that a lexical tree has a saving factor of 2.5 over the linear lexicon. Besides, the efficiency of using a lexical tree is substantial, not only because it results in considerable saving of memory for representing state-search space, but it also saves a significant amount of time by searching in far fewer potential paths.

Figure 3 shows examples of a linear searching net and a tree-structured searching net. The perplexity of the linear searching net was found to be 5 while the tree-based one has a smaller perplexity of 4.89.

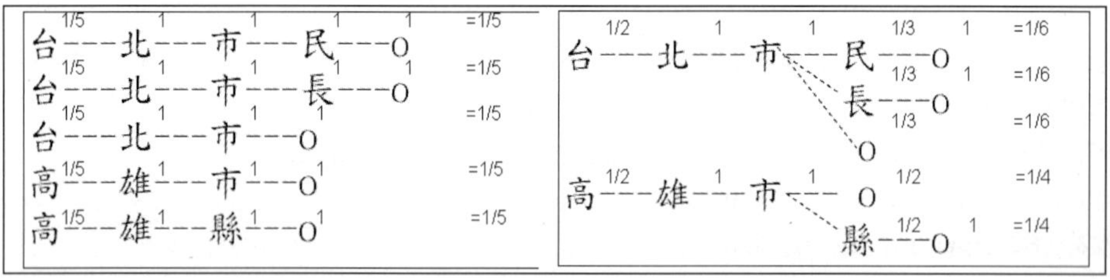

Fig. 3. The examples of isolated linear (left) and tree-structured (right) searching net with their probability values.

3.5. *Pronunciation Modeling Using Pronunciation Variation*

The pronunciation model plays an important role in our proposed one-pass Chinese character based ASR engine.[15] It not only provides more choices during decoding when the speaker exhibits variations in pronunciation, but also handles various speaking styles in different languages. As mentioned above, one Chinese character has more than two pronunciations in the combined phonetic inventory of Mandarin and Taiwanese. Accent and regional migration are also factors that influence the pronunciation or speaking style of speakers. In the following sub-sections, we propose two different methods, knowledge-based and data-driven methods, for obtaining rules of pronunciation variation.

3.5.1. *Knowledge-Based Method*

As shown by Strik,[16] information about pronunciation can be derived from knowledge sources, such as pronunciation dictionaries handcrafted by linguistic experts, or from pronunciation descriptions and rules extracted from the literature. In this approach, a pronunciation variation rule is simply the multiple pronunciations that appear in the lexicon for the same character. Associated probabilities can be calculated as follows. 1) The character-pronunciation pairs are derived; 2) the frequencies of the pairs are counted, and the relative frequency with respect to the total frequency of the same Chinese character is calculated, and; 3) the pairs with high relative frequencies are kept as multiple pronunciation rules.

3.5.2. *Data-Driven Approach*

Although regular pronunciation variations can be obtained from existing linguistic and phonological information, such as from a dictionary, this knowledge base is not exhaustive. Many language variation phenomena in real speech have not yet been described or captured. Therefore, another way to derive pronunciation variations from acoustic clues is the data-driven method.[17] The algorithms from this method can then be used to derive formalizations. The information about pronunciation variation can be represented in terms of rewrite rules,[18] decision trees,[19] or neural networks.[17] Several other measures, for example confusability measures,[20] have been used to select rules or variants. In this section, we used a forced recognition approach to align the variation between transcripts of acoustic signals and the transcriptions of single tonal syllables in the lexicon. These variations then become the pronunciation rules added to the dictionary if the frequency measure of a particular variation falls within the selection criteria.

In practice, we combine both the knowledge-based and data-driven approaches for our pronunciation model. The reasons are twofold: 1) to be able to handle multiple pronunciations for one Chinese character in both languages by using knowledge-based extraction of pronunciation rules, and 2) to be able to handle pronunciation variations resulting from the speaker's speaking style or personal articulation by using the data-driven method of obtaining rules from acoustic signals. It is difficult to select an "optimum" number of pronunciations to be represented in the pronunciation model. Therefore, the weighting in these approaches are the same, and the determining of the final number of pronunciations is done by a different task.

4. Taiwanese Text-to-Speech

The TTS system proposed is composed of 3 major functional modules, namely a text analysis module, a prosody module, and a waveform synthesis module. The system architecture is shown in Figure 4. Since Taiwanese is a tonal language, we will describe the process of the tone sandhi rules for text analysis module. In the waveform synthesis module, the system adopts TD-PSOLA to modify waveforms by adjusting the prosody parameters of selected units so that the synthesized speech sounds more natural. Finally, the new TTS architecture is implemented in a multiple-level unit selection for a limited domain application.

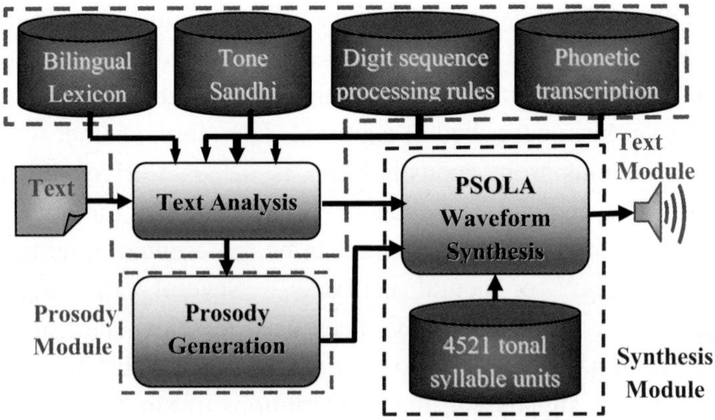

Fig. 4. The TTS system architecture is composed of 3 major functional modules: a text analysis module, a prosody module, and a waveform synthesis module.

4.1. *Word Segmentation and Mandarin-Taiwanese Translation (Sentence-to- Morpheme)*

Although the Hanlor orthography is the most common writing style of Taiwanese in contemporary Taiwan, all three types of written texts (see Section 1) can be analyzed by our text analysis module. Since there are no natural boundaries between two successive words, we must segment a Mandarin text into its word sequence first. The bilingual pronunciation dictionary is used as a basis for our word segmentation algorithm based on the sequentially maximal-length matching, which segments Mandarin sentences into maximal-length word combinations.[21]

Finally, we directly translate Mandarin into Taiwanese word-for-word, and transcribe the Taiwanese words phonetically into ForPA. This segmentation, translation and transcription process is exemplified in Figure 5, where the input Mandarin sentence is "他今天心情很好" ("he is very happy today").

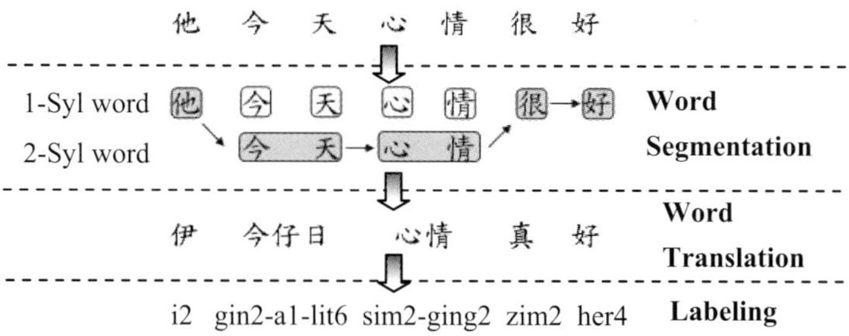

Fig. 5. The text analysis process, which combines word segmentation, translation and labeling (see next section), where the input Mandarin sentence is "他今天心情很好", "1-Syl Word" denotes one-syllable words, and so on.

4.2. *Labeling (Morpheme-to-Phoneme) and Normalization of Digit Sequences*

For each segmented word, there are more than one Taiwanese pronunciation. This multiple-pronunciation problem is tackled by a two-stage strategy. The first stage: Choose the everyday, or Bai-du-in, pronunciation first for initial phonetic labeling. If the everyday pronunciation does not exist, the classic literary pronunciation is considered. The second stage: Build a searching network with pronunciation frequencies as node information and pronunciation transitional frequencies as arc information for each sentence. Best pronunciation selection is then conducted by a Viterbi search.

Another important issue for text analysis is the normalization of digit sequences. However, for digits, the 2 manners of pronunciation are commonly heard. The choice of pronunciation depends on the position of the digit in a sequence. Another regularity is, if a digit sequence does not represent a quantity, it is pronounced in the classic literary way. These digit pronunciation rules are summarized in Table 7.

4.3. *Application of Tone Sandhi Rules*

One of the most frequently referred to sandhi rules states that, for most cases, if a syllable appears at the end of a sentence, or at the end of a word, then it is pronounced with its lexical tone. Otherwise, it is pronounced with its sandhi tone. The Taiwanese sandhi rules for each lexical tone have been shown in Figure 1.

To produce more natural synthesis, finer aspects like the triple adjectives – where the first character of 3 duplicated adjectives will carry a very different tone

Table 7. The rules for normalization of digit sequences.

Position	Pronunciation
Ten Million	Read 0-9 as EP
Million	Read 0-9 as EP
Hundred Thousand	No sound for 1, 2 as LP and others as EP.
Ten Thousand	If the digit is 0 in hundred thousand position, read 0-9 as EP. If the digit is not 0 in hundred thousand position, 1, 2 read as LP, and others as EP.
Thousand	Read 0-9 as EP
Hundred	Read 0-9 as EP
Ten	No sound for 1, 2 as LP, and others as EP.
Unit digit	If the digit is 0 in hundred thousand position, read 0-9 as EP. If the digit is not 0 in hundred thousand position, 1,2 read as LP, and others as EP.

LP: classic, literary pronunciation, EP: everyday pronunciation.

Table. 8. Tone sandhi rules for triple adjectives.

lexical	1	2	3	4	5	6	7
sandhi-tone	9	9	4	1	9	9	6

other than the traditional 7 lexical tones mentioned previously – are handled. We map this "High-Rising" tone to digit 9, and call it tone 9. The tone sandhi rules for triple adjectives are summarized in Table 8.

4.4. *Evaluation of Text Analysis and Prosody Modules*

Following text analysis and prosody generation, an evaluative experiment is conducted. Its main target is to assess the accuracy rate of automatic transcription, which is produced by the text analysis and prosody modules, in comparison with manual transcription. A large amount of news reports are collected from the internet. The selection of these is random, without emphasis on any particular news category. Of these, a set of 200 sentences to cover all distinct Chinese characters are chosen. The comparative performance of manual and automatic transcription is shown in Table 9, with three sets of results: word segmentation, labeling and tone sandhi accuracy rates.[22]

From Table 9, we infer that the system can segment and translate most articles accurately into Taiwanese words with over 97% accuracy. If we do not consider tone sandhi, the system can translate an article into its correct pronunciation close to the 88% rate, and most errors apply to names and out-of-vocabulary words. Because Taiwanese does not have uniform tone sandhi rules, it is acceptable that the accuracy rate of tone sandhi is lower.

Table 9. The statistics of performance in parts of word segmentation and transfer, labeling and tone sandhi.

	Expert1 (automatic)	Expert2 (manual)
Word Segmentation & Transfer	97.80%	98.76%
Labeling	89.96%	88.27%
Tone sandhi	65.43%	62.43%

4.5. *Waveform Synthesis Module*

There is a variety of synthesis methods, the most popular being the TD-PSOLA. We adopted this to modify the prosodic features of selected units. Synthesis components are used to not only raise or lower pitch, but also to extend or reduce duration. After the analysis of tonal syllables, we can gather duration and short pause information for each syllable. Based on the above information, the following instances were applied to the speech synthesis process:

Case 1: If the syllable consists of an unvoiced consonant (/p/-, /t/-, /g/-, /k/-, /z/-, /s/-, /c/-, /h/-), the system modifies the duration of the unvoiced initial, and modifies the duration and pitch of final.

Case 2: The system modifies duration and pitch both on the initial and final if an unvoiced initial is not present.

Case 3: The system replaces the short pause with a zero-value section.

4.6. *Multiple-Level Unit Selection for a Limited-Domain Application*

In the past, the production of audio books is a demanding process, effort-wise and time-wise. The application of TTS to a limited-domain audio book can save a considerably large amount of time, and the synthesized sentences are likely to turn out comparable to sentences recorded in natural speech.

The Taiwanese Bible seems to be a good example to prove this, being a high-quality, reliably translated document which has been validated by many high-ranking church officials and Christian devotees in general (domain experts). An audio book for this Bible would be a great help for speakers unable to read, making the Bible more accessible to the masses.[23]

Table 10. The textual statistics of the Taiwanese New Testament Bible.

Number of Chinese characters	278,633
Number of chapters	27
Number of sentences	39,171
Number of distinct words	7,189

From the statistics in Table 10, we find that the usage of duplicate words is highly frequent. If these much-duplicated syllables, words or sentences could serve as a gauge, the production cost of an audio book could be greatly reduced. But sounding natural is proportionally related to the number of synthesis units. Synthesis systems with fewer units tend to generate less natural-sounding speech. For instance, logically, any arbitrary sentence can be synthesized by all 4,609 tonal syllables in Taiwanese, but the prosody in this synthesized sentence would rank low in naturalness. When words are used as synthesized units, a total of 7,189 distinct words are required. However, the result of this would only be a slight improvement from the syllable-synthesis method. This is because, most Taiwanese words are monosyllabic anyway. Therefore, finding compromise units between the word and the sentence becomes a very important issue.

From our observation, poor quality (least natural sounding) synthesis occurs often in the concatenation of monosyllabic words. In fact, the naturalness of multi-words (or multiple words) unit combined by multi-syllabic words could result in only a slight improvement. It is therefore necessary to divide the multi-words units into two categories: concatenation of monosyllabic words and multi-syllabic words. Preference is given to concatenating monosyllabic rather than multi-syllabic words as synthesis units. To find high-frequency and longer-length synthesis units, we adopted an evolution method of maximum maximal-length words matching, called *maximal-multi-words matching*, which is described as follows:

Step 1. Let W_i be the i-th input sentence in the text corpus, where W_i is composed of N_i words and each word is separated by the equal sign denoted as $W_i = \left\{w_i^1 = w_i^2 = w_i^3 = ... = w_i^{N_i}\right\}$. The length of the matching pattern is set to n, i.e. the pattern is $W_i^n = \left\{w_i^1 = w_i^2 = w_i^3 = ... = w_i^n\right\}$, where n is smaller than or equal to N_i.

Step 2. Initially, let $n = N_i$, i.e. the matching pattern is W_i. Let $N(w_i^n)$ denote the count of the pattern of the multi-words W_i^n of the text corpus.

Step 3. If $N(w_i^n) \neq 0$ and $n = N_i$, repeat Step 1 with the next sentence. Else, if $N(w_i^n) = 0$, repeat Step 2 with $n = N_i$-1.

Finally, the number of multi-words synthesis units is 9,992, extracted from the 280,000-syllable Taiwanese New Testament Bible. There are 22,949 Chinese characters in the set, including 7,189 distinct words in this Bible. The total amount of recording counted in syllables is one of tenth of the whole Bible.

5. Conclusion

To collect a Taiwanese speech corpus, we designed a new phonetic alphabet, called the ForPA, to transcribe recorded speech read out from the phonetically-abundant word sheets. These sheets were generated by the application of a greedy heuristic algorithm and contained several kinds of context-dependent phone units. To date, the validated multi-lingual speech database has reached 92.77 hours of validated speech from 1,700 speakers.

For Taiwanese speech recognition, a new framework based on a unified approach with a one-stage searching strategy was implemented using a multiple pronunciation lexicon and a large vocabulary searching network with Chinese characters as its nodes. The lexicon was generated by both data-driven and knowledge-based statistical approaches. This framework shows its validity and efficiency to deal with the Mandarin/Taiwanese bilingual speech recognition issue from a unified angle.

For the TTS system, we significantly exploited knowledge on Taiwanese phonetics/linguistics to improve the natural quality of the synthesized speech. In addition, the Mandarin-to-Taiwanese bilingual TTS system has been successfully constructed based on the information from our bilingual lexicon. Most Mandarin articles can thus be translated into Taiwanese and automatically converted to a speech signal in Taiwanese. In a limited-domain application, a new multi-level unit selection algorithm was used to produce an audio book of the Taiwanese Bible. This technology has good potential to be used in language-learning tools and applications.

The collected Taiwanese corpus (in ForPA) is significant and can be used for further research of Taiwanese ASR and TTS. In future, a similar corpus will be created for yet another language in Taiwan, namely Hakka. It must be noted that the prediction of tone sandhi should be improved to achieve more accurate/natural synthesis. The use of signal processing techniques is also imperative to smoothen out waveforms and reduce discontinuity in most TTS systems, including ours. Finally, there is indeed a big need to propose more novel frameworks and approaches in speech recognition to significantly improve its performance for character-based languages.

References

1. Wikipedia. Available from http://en.wikipedia.org/wiki/Demographics_of_Taiwan (2006).
2. YuangChin Chiang, *A Course in Taiwanese Pinim*, (in Taiwanese) AnKor Publishing, PingTong (2005).
3. S.-Y. Zhou, *T3 Taiwanese Treebank and Brill Part-of-Speech Tagger*, (in Chinese), Master thesis of National TsingHua University, HsinChu, Taiwan (2006).
4. J. Wells, SAMPA (Speech Assessment Methods Phonetic Alphabet), http://www.phon.ucl.ac.uk/home/sampa/home.htm, April, (2003).
5. J. L. Hieronymus, "ASCII Phonetic Symbols for the World's Languages: Worldbet," *Technical Report AT&T Bell Labs*, (1994).
6. R.-Y. Lyu et al. "Toward Constructing A Multilingual Speech Corpus for Taiwanese (Min-nan), Hakka, and Mandarin," *ICLCLP Vol. 9, No. 2*, (August 2004), pp. 1-12
7. YuangChin Chiang, *An input method editor (IME) in Taiwanese Pinim*, (2005).
8. M.-S. Liang et al. "An Efficient Algorithm to Select Phonetically Balanced Scripts for Constructing Corpus," *NLP-KE*, (2003).
9. R.-Y. Lyu et al. "A Unified Framework for Large Vocabulary Speech Recognition of Mutually Unintelligible Chinese *Regionalects*," *In Proc. of ICSLP 2004*, (2004).
10. D.-C. Lyu et al.. "Speech Recognition on Code-Switching Among the Chinese Dialects," *In Proceedings of IEEE ICASSP'06*, (2006).
11. P. F. Wong and M. H. Siu, "Integration of Tone-related Feature for Chinese Speech Recognition," *in Proceedings on ICMI*, (2002) pp. 476-479.
12. D.-C. Lyu et al. "Large Vocabulary Taiwanese (Min-nan) Speech Recognition Using Tone Features and Statistical Pronunciation Modeling," *In Proc. of Eurospeech*, (2003).
13. D.-C. Lyu et al. "Speaker Independent Acoustic Modeling for Large Vocabulary Bi-lingual Taiwanese/Mandarin Continuous Speech Recognition," *In Proceedings of the 9th SST*, Melbourne (2002).
14. H. Ney et al. "Improvements in Beam Speech for 1000-Word Continuous Speech Recognition," *In Proc. of the ICASSP'92*, California, (1992), pp. 9-12.
15. D.-C. Lyu et al.. "Modeling Pronunciation Variation for Bi-Lingual Mandarin/Taiwanese Speech Recognition" *IJCLCLP, Vol. 10. no. 3*. (2005), pp. 363-380.
16. H. Strik and C. Cucchiarini, "Modeling Pronunciation Variation for ASR: Overview and Comparison of Method," *Speech Communication, Vol. 29*, (1999) pp. 225-246.
17. T. Fukada, et al. "Automatic Generation of Multiple Pronunciations Based on Neural Networks and Language Statistics," *In Proceedings of ESCA*, (1998), pp. 103-108.
18. N. Cremelie, and J. P. Martens, "In Search of Better Pronunciation Models for Speech Recognition," *Speech Communication 29*, Vol. 4 (2), (1999), pp. 115-136,
19. J. J Humphries et al. "Using Accent-Specific Pronunciation Modelling for Robust Speech Recognition," *In Proc. ICSLP-96*, (1996), pp. 2324-2327.
20. M. Wester and E. Fosler-Lussier, "A Comparison of Data-Derived and Knowledge-Based Modeling of Pronunciation Variation," *In: Proc. ICSLP 2000, Vol. 4,* (2000), pp. 270-273.
21. M.-S. Liang et al. "A Bi-lingual Mandarin-To-Taiwanese Text-to-Speech System," In *Proceedings Int. Conf. on Spoken Language Processing (ICSLP)*, (2005).
22. M.-S. Liang et al. "A Taiwanese Text-to-Speech System with Applications to Language Learning," *In Proc. ICALT 2004*, Joensuu, Finland, (2004).
23. K.-C. Chuang, *Phrase-based Synthesis Units and Study of Phrase Tone-Sandhi for Taiwanese Text-To-Speech and Application*, Master Thesis, University of Chang Gung, Taiwan, (2005).
24. S. C. Kumar et al. "Multilingual Speech Recognition: A Unified Approach," *In Proc. of Eurospeech*, Portugal, (2005).

CHAPTER 18

PUTONGHUA PROFICIENCY TEST AND EVALUATION

Ren-Hua Wang, Qingfeng Liu and Si Wei
USTC iFlytek Speech Laboratory,
University of Science and Technology of China
P.O. Box 4, Hefei
E-mail: {rhw@ustc.edu.cn, qfliu@iflytek.com}

Putonghua Shuiping Ceshi (PSC) is the official Standard Mandarin proficiency test in China. Currently evaluation of the PSC test is conducted entirely by human testers, which leads to some kind of variance between evaluators as a result of subjectivity. Furthermore, large-scale testing is practically impossible due to the low efficiency and high expenses it would incur. So there is an urgent need to implement the PSC test with the aid of a computer. This chapter introduces a computer-aided evaluation system for the PSC test. In the system, several optimized algorithms are advanced to evaluate a speaker's proficiency, such as using typical dialect error patterns to restrict recognition grammar, adjusting posterior probability by duration ratio of initials and finals, selective adaptation, F0 normalization using CDF-matching, etc. The evaluation problem is also tested as a classification problem by defining different types of pronunciation according to the speaker's proficiency. Experiments based on 1,662 persons' PSC test database indicate that these methods can efficiently improve the performance of evaluation, and that the computer-aided PSC test is indeed feasible.

1. Introduction

Standard Mandarin is the official Chinese spoken language, which is also officially known as Putonghua (普通话) in mainland China. In order to popularize the usage of Putonghua, the Chinese government conducts a national Putonghua proficiency test known as the PSC (Putonghua Shuiping Ceshi, 普通话水平测试). At the same time, the government takes a series of appropriate implementation measures, for example, requiring all government officials and teachers to get PSC certification of at least a certain level. The entire content of the PSC test is based on spoken Mandarin. There are four parts to the test. The first and second parts involve the reading of 100 mono-syllabic words and 50 di-syllabic words, respectively. The third part involves the reading of a given document which contains 400 Chinese characters. The last part of the test is an open section, where candidates are to speak freely on a given topic. As for the scoring in the PSC test, there are 3 classes or levels, and each class contains two grades, A and B. The PSC is not an evaluation of a speaker's eloquence, but rather his/her proficiency of using Putonghua. Currently, the evaluation process of the PSC test is carried out entirely by human effort, which inevitably involves some subjective differences between the evaluators. In addition, human evaluation also has the disadvantages of being low in efficiency and high in expenses. There is therefore an urgent need to implement the PSC test with the aid of a computer integrated with spoken language processing technology.

The main characteristic of the PSC test is to evaluate the speaker's proficiency in pronunciation, which is very similar to the pronunciation evaluation done through the Computer Assisted Language Learning (CALL) system. Many researchers have studied the CALL system's pronunciation evaluation, including members of the SRI speech group,[1–4] who mainly focused on evaluating the overall pronunciation quality of learners. They take word posterior probability, timing and duration scores as methods of evaluation and measure performance of evaluation by calculating the correlation between machine scores and human scores. The joint research by the speech group of Cambridge University and the AI lab of MIT[5,6] mainly focused on pronunciation error detection and phone-level pronunciation evaluation. They also investigated ways to measure performance of pronunciation error detection. The VICK system developed by the University of Nijmegen[7,8] investigates the reasonability of human scoring and the effect of prosody, fluency and segmental quality on human scoring. The system from Tokyo University and Kyoto University[9,10] considers the importance of different phonemes in language learning and the effect of different types of errors on pronunciation proficiency. Recently, structural representation has been used to assess pronunciation in order to capture the structure, or higher-level aspects of the language, when spoken by non-native speakers.[11,12]

The above systems brought about various pronunciation scoring methods, but these are not suitable for the PSC test. The reasons for this are twofold. The first is that the speakers taking the PSC test are different. Users of the CALL system are mainly foreign, non-native users of the language, while the PSC test aims to evaluate the proficiency of native speakers using their mother tongue. The second reason is that the CALL system only needs an approximate evaluation of the learner with rough scores, while the PSC test system needs to evaluate the speaker precisely. These differences indicate that the PSC test should be much more precise, and that the difference between PSC-speakers is likely to be much closer, than between those evaluated by the CALL system. This paper presents an automatic PSC test system which can precisely evaluate the speaker's proficiency.

Knowledge of typical error patterns of dialect accents is utilized to restrict the recognition grammar, and the characteristics of Mandarin are used to enhance the syllable initial's weight for optimizing the traditional posterior probability evaluation method. At the same time, a selective adaptation method is developed by selecting appropriate adaptive data according to the proficiency of the speaker, which adapts the recognition model to the speaker without decreasing distinguishability of the dialect accent. Vocal tract length normalization is done to normalize the vocal tract length of different persons, which can increase the distinguishability of the recognition model. In order to efficiently evaluate tone quality, CDF-matching is applied to normalize the F0-distribution. We use an LVCSR system to generate text for the free speech part of the PSC test and then the same evaluation method is used for the first three parts. Meanwhile the evaluation problem is also tested as a classification problem, and a relevant evaluation method via classification is presented. To date, the evaluation on the fourth part of the test is not as good as the first three parts, so linear regression is used to map the average posterior probability of the first three machine-scored parts into a score comparable to the human-evaluator's scoring convention, and these scores are then combined. Experiments based on the PSC test database indicate that the average score difference between a combination of machine and human scoring (2.44) is close to the scoring done entirely by human effort (2.30), which means that the computer-aided PSC test is indeed feasible.

This chapter is organized as follows. Sections 2 and 3 introduce the system structure and the database used, while Section 4 introduces a traditional pronunciation evaluation algorithm and an optimized algorithm for the PSC test. Experiments and their results are described in Section 5, and a mapping strategy for the system in order to get a score comparable to the human-evaluator score is introduced in Section 6. Section 7 describes the system application, and we conclude in the last section, along with some directions for future work in this area.

2. System Structure

The automatic PSC test system is made up of 3 main modules, which are the pre-processing module, the evaluation module and the mapping module. The overall structure is represented by Figure 1. The pre-processing module is used to process the input WAV file and text file in order to get the feature and label files for the evaluation module. The evaluation module completes the machine evaluation and generates the machine scores. The mapping module maps the various machine scores into a comparable human score, and integrates the human score (from part four of the test) with the mapped score to obtain the ultimate evaluation score. The model database includes a set of 4-Gaussian mono-phoneme HMM models, which are used to generate coarse segmentation and select adaptation data for the

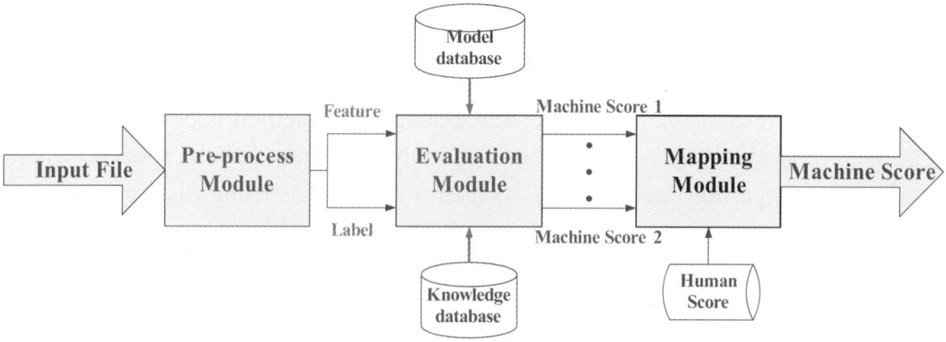

Fig. 1. Structure of the system.

evaluation module. The model database also includes a set of 16-Gaussian monophoneme HMM models which are used to carry out the evaluation after adaptation. The knowledge database includes typical error patterns of the different dialect accents of Mandarin. The outputs of the evaluation module are the various machine scores, which are used as inputs to the mapping module.

3. Database Instruction

3.1. *Standard Putonghua Database*

State-of-the-art pronunciation evaluation methods mainly rely on ASR. The ASR system to be used here, in order to build a robust one, cannot be constructed based on a universal recognition database which will always contain dialect accents. Instead, the ASR system for pronunciation should be constructed upon a standard Putonghua database. The speech recognizer portion of our work is based on a database designed for the PSC test recorded by 30 persons who have the most standard pronunciation (type A of class 1), authenticated by the national PSC test bureau. This database is recorded via close-talking microphones with a sampling rate of 16 kHz and quantized with 16 bits. The structure of the standard Putonghua database is shown in Table 1.

Table 1. Information of the standard Putonghua database.

Number of Persons	30		
Gender	15 males		15 females
Age	25 persons (between 20-30 years)		5 persons (above 30 years)
Text info	*Mono-syllabic word*	*Di-syllabic word*	*Essay*
	3,000/person	4,500/person	60/person (400 words per essay)
Duration of recording	Totally > 100 hours, 3 hours/person		

The standard Putonghua database has three parts corresponding to the first three parts of PSC test. The recognizer constructed on such a database is most pertinent to the PSC-specific task.

3.2. *PSC Test Database*

The PSC test database is used to validate the performance of an evaluation algorithm. Actual PSC test examples are collected to form this database, which is recorded in the same way as the standard Putonghua database. Table 2 shows the organization of this database.

Table 2. Dialectal breakdown of the PSC test database.

District	AnHui	WuHan	ChongQing
Number	1,659	236	290
District	Shanghai	XiaMen	ZhengZhou
Number	251	120	259

From this table, we can find that the PSC test database includes speakers from the main dialect regions of Mandarin. Human evaluation of the AnHui set of the database is carried out and the gender and proficiency distributions are shown in Table 3.

Table 3. Information of AnHui PSC test database.

Gender	*Male*	Female	
	787	872	
Proficiency	*Class 1*	*Class 2*	*Class 3*
	6%	71%	23%

3.3. *Human Scoring Database*

The human scoring database is the basis for validating the performance of the evaluation algorithm. This database is made up of three authorized national PSC human evaluator's scoring, and the score is on a 100-point scale. Without loss of universality, our experiments are all based on the AnHui database. The results can be easily extended to other dialect groups by changing the typical error pattern. We split this database into two subsets: the training and testing sets. Table 4 shows the correlation between 3 human evaluators' scores on the AnHui database. Correlation

Table 4. Performance of human evaluation on PSC test database.

(*Correlation, Average score difference*) Training/Testing set	Expert 1	Expert 2	Expert 3
Expert 1	(1.0,0.0)/ (1.0,0.0)	(0.91,1.88)/ (0.90,1.97)	(0.88,2.54)/ (0.89,2.47)
Expert 2	(0.91,1.88)/ (0.90,1.97)	(1.0,0.0)/ (1.0,0.0)	(0.91,2.19)/ (0.89,2.47)
Expert 3	(0.88,2.54)/ (0.89,2.47)	(0.91,2.19)/ (0.89,2.47)	(1.0,0.0)/ (1.0,0.0)
Average	(0.90,2.20)/(0.89,2.30)		

between two scoring is defined as Equation 1.

$$\frac{\sum_{i=1}^{N}\left[\left(S_{Ai}-\overline{S_A}\right)\times\left(S_{Bi}-\overline{S_B}\right)\right]}{\sqrt{\sum_{i=1}^{N}\left(S_{Ai}-\overline{S_A}\right)^2\times\sum_{i=1}^{N}\left(S_{Bi}-\overline{S_B}\right)^2}} \tag{1}$$

S_{Ai} and S_{Bi} denote the scores given to the i-th examinee by evaluator A and B; $\overline{S_A}$ and $\overline{S_B}$ denote the average scores given to all N examinees by A and B.

The correlation between two scorings describes the consistency between the scoring done by two evaluators on a set of examinees.

From Table 4 we can infer that correlations between human evaluators are all higher than 0.8 and the average score difference between human evaluators are all less than 3 points, which means that these human evaluators' scoring is steady and reliable. The experiments below use this correlation and average score difference between human and machine scores to measure the performance of the evaluation algorithm.

4. Pronunciation Evaluation Algorithm

This section introduces the normal pronunciation evaluation algorithm in CALL systems and the revised algorithm for the PSC test.

4.1. *Universal Evaluation Algorithm in CALL System*

The universal, language-independent evaluation algorithm is based on ASR. The features of the HMM-based ASR used here are 13-dimensional MFCCs and their first and second order derivatives. We can calculate the output probability $P(O|T)$ of given text T to the observation vector O. In other words, $P(O|T)$ is the likelihood of given HMM model T to given observation vector O. The most useful evaluation algorithm used in the CALL system is posterior probability,[1,2,3,5,7,8] which is $P(T|O)$. Using Bayes' rule, $P(T|O)$ can be calculated as Equation 2.[5]

$$\begin{aligned} P(T|O) &= \sum_{i=1}^{N} \left(\left| \log \left(P \left(T_i | O^{(T_i)} \right) \right) \right| / NF(T_i) \right) \Big/ N \\ &= \sum_{i=1}^{N} \left(\left| \log \left(\frac{P\left(O^{(T_i)}|T_i\right) P(T_i)}{\sum_{q \in Q} P\left(O^{(T_i)}|q\right) P(q)} \right) \right| / NF(T_i) \right) \Big/ N \\ &\approx \sum_{i=1}^{N} \left(\left| \log \left(\frac{P\left(O^{(T_i)}|T_i\right)}{\max_{q \in Q} P\left(O^{(T_i)}|q\right)} \right) \right| / NF(T_i) \right) \Big/ N \qquad (2) \end{aligned}$$

Q is the model set, q is the phoneme that T_i could be misread as. $NF(T_i)$ is the total frame of phoneme T_i. $P\left(O^{(T_i)}|T_i\right)$ is the likelihood of given HMM model T_i to the observation vector $O^{(T_i)}$.

Performance of posterior probability published by the other system is as follows: correlation is 0.58 at the sentence level, and 0.88 at the speaker level.[1]

4.2. *Optimized Algorithm for Mandarin Evaluation*

4.2.1. *Using Typical Dialect Error Pattern to Optimize Evaluation Algorithm*

We find that the denominator of posterior probability calculated as Equation 2 is obtained from the entire phoneme loop network. It is suitable for assessing second language learning because there may be a range of various errors made by the learner and the entire phoneme network can capture as many errors as possible. This is however not suitable for the PSC test because its examinees are native-speakers and their errors are much more compact and fewer. If we use the whole phoneme loop network as used in the CALL system, we risk a reduction in performance because of the recognition error introduced by an overly large network. We thus revise the posterior probability calculating algorithm from Equation 2 to Equation 3 as follows.

$$\begin{aligned} P(T|O) &= \sum_{i=1}^{N} \left(\left| \log \left(P \left(T_i | O^{(T_i)} \right) \right) \right| / NF(T_i) \right) \Big/ N \\ &= \sum_{i=1}^{N} \left(\left| \log \left(\frac{P\left(O^{(T_i)}|T_i\right) P(T_i)}{\sum_{q \in Q_{error}^{T_i}} P\left(O^{(T_i)}|q\right) P(q)} \right) \right| / NF(T_i) \right) \Big/ N \\ &\approx \sum_{i=1}^{N} \left(\left| \log \left(\frac{P\left(O^{(T_i)}|T_i\right)}{\max_{q \in Q_{error}^{T_i}} P\left(O^{(T_i)}|q\right)} \right) \right| / NF(T_i) \right) \Big/ N \qquad (3) \end{aligned}$$

The difference between Equation 3 and Equation 2 is the calculation of the denominator. Equation 2 uses the entire phoneme loop network to get the best path while

Equation 3 utilizes a compact network obtained from dialect analysis,[13] which can diminish the influence of recognition errors.

4.2.2. *Adjusting Posterior Probability by Duration Ratio of Initial and Final*

Posterior probability as an evaluation algorithm produces good evaluation performance for second language learning.[1,2] This performance, however, degrades when applied to the PSC test because the examinees' proficiencies are close and rather good to a certain extent. Since initials are much shorter and much more frequently misread than finals, Wei *et al.*[14] has pointed out that adjusting posterior probability by weighting initials by duration ratio of initial and final, can improve the performance of the evaluation algorithm. The adjusted posterior probability is as Equation 4.

$$G'_{Sent} = \sum_{i=1}^{N} G'_i / N$$
$$G'_i = G^i_{initial} \times \left(1 + \frac{Dur^i_{final}}{Dur^i_{initial}} \times COEF\right) + G^i_{final} \tag{4}$$

G'_{Sent} is the adjusted posterior probability of one sentence. G'_i is the adjusted posterior probability of the i-th syllable. Dur^i_{final} is the duration of i-th syllable's final. $Dur^i_{initial}$ is the duration of i-th syllable's initial. $COEF$ an adjustable factor which is used to control the weight of the initial.

4.2.3. *Speaker Normalization*

In relation to speaker normalization in ASR, the MLLR (maximum likelihood linear regression) and VTLN (vocal tract length normalization) are used here for performance improvement. MLLR[15] is a kind of model transform adaptation method. It can efficiently adjust the original model to an appointed speaker using the limited adaptation data. The adaptation of pronunciation evaluation in the CALL system is always a universal adaptation from the native model to the foreign accent model, and not an adaptation to a specific learner. The reason is that the adaptation data is often too little and the pronunciation errors are too much, such that adaptation will adjust the model into a problematic model with diminishing ability to detect pronunciation errors. However the adaptation data in the PSC test is sufficient (roughly 600 syllables per person) and the proficiency of the speakers is not as bad as having a foreign accent. If we can appropriately select the adaptation data, it is possible to prevent that adaptation from diminishing the distinguishing ability of the recognition model. The proposed method is summed up as follows:

(1) Calculate each syllable's posterior probability, as in Equation 4, and mark it as T_i .
(2) Set the threshold for each person according to his/her proficiency.
(3) Select the adaptation data according to Equation 5
(4) Carry out the adaptation using the MLLR with selected adaptation data obtained from Step 3.

The threshold in Step 2 can be determined from experience to ensure sufficient adaptation data.

$$\begin{cases} T_i \geq THRESH & \text{Keep } i\text{-th syllable} \\ T_i < THRESH & \text{Discard } i\text{-th syllable} \end{cases} \quad (5)$$

The other method for speaker normalization is by normalizing the length of the vocal tract[16,17]. Vocal tract length can be normalized via spectrum adjustment as in Equation 6.[18]

$$f' = \alpha f \quad (6)$$

An adjusted band-keeping sub-linear transform[19] is shown by Equation 7

$$f' = \begin{cases} \alpha f & 0 \leq f \leq Thresh_f \\ Af + B & Thresh_f \leq f \leq Nquist \end{cases} \quad (7)$$

The parameters in Equation 7 satisfy the continuity restriction. If α and $Thresh_f$ are defined, we can get a unique transform.

4.2.4. *Tone Evaluation*

4.2.4.1. Representation of Chinese Tones

Mandarin is a tonal language, and tones are thus very important in distinguishing Mandarin syllables. Tone evaluation is a critical part of the PSC test, and the Putonghua evaluation system also evaluates tone quality.

The tones in Mandarin can be represented by F0 contour.[20,21] The distinguishability of the F0 contours is dramatically damaged by variations across speakers and manners of pronunciation. Normalization is thus necessary for compensating these variations.

4.2.4.2. F0 Distribution of Different Persons

Recognizing tone via F0 contour is based on the assumption that a tone can be represented by its F0 contour consistently, which in turn means that different speaker's F0 distribution should be somewhat similar. Figure 2 shows two F0 distributions of two different persons.

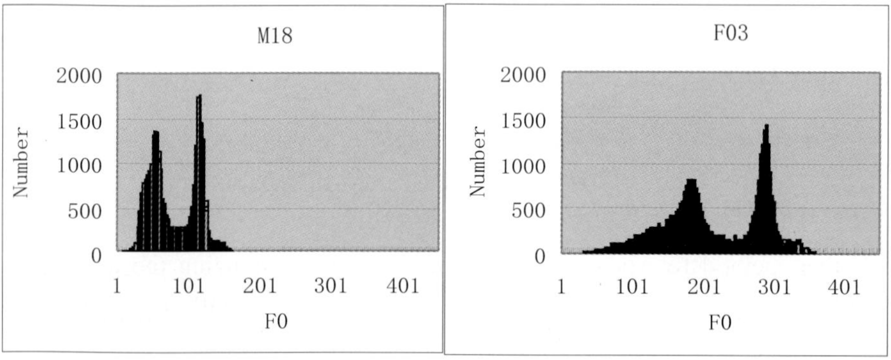

Fig. 2. F0 distribution of different speakers, F03 and M18 (Note: The F0 data is extracted from the isolated syllable part of the Standard Mandarin database. *Left*: Speaker M18. *Right*: Speaker F03.)

From Figure 2 we find that the difference between the two sets of F0 distributions is so large that the models' confusion will be very significant if F0 is directly used as a tone classification feature without any normalization.

4.2.4.3. F0 Normalization using CDF-Matching

Suppose the parameter transform to be $x = T[y]$. y is the parameter before normalization, and x is the parameter after normalization. $C_X(x)$ is the cumulative distribution function (CDF) of x and the CDF of y is $C_Y(y)$. $x = T[y]$ should satisfy $C_Y(y) = C_X(x)$. Then we can get $C_X^{-1}(C_Y(y))$. This means that CDF-matching can be implemented by Equation 8.[22]

$$x = T[y] = C_X^{-1}(C_Y(y)) \tag{8}$$

One standard person's (F03) F0 distribution is selected as the objective CDF function, and all other persons' F0 distributions are mapped to speaker F03's F0 distribution via CDF-matching. The CDF-matching is implemented using histogram equalization.

Figure 3 displays the normalization result of CDF-matching. In contrast to Figure 2, we can see that the F0 distributions of different speakers become more similar after CDF-matching.

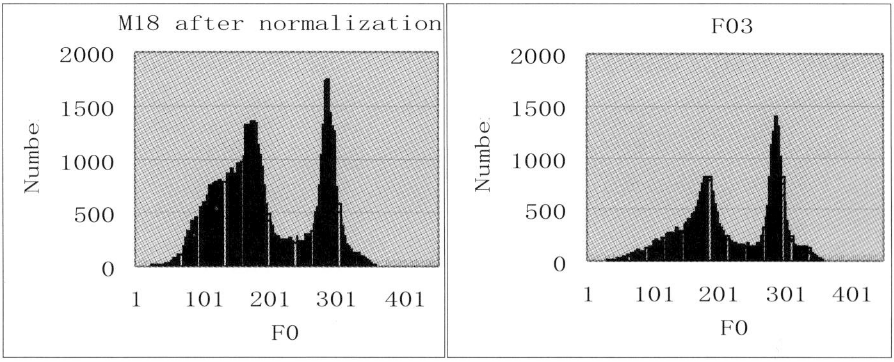

Fig. 3. Comparison between F0 distribution of speaker M18 after normalization, and standard F0 distribution of speaker F03.

4.2.4.4. Tone Evaluation Method

Posterior probability is used in this system for tone evaluation as well. The posterior probability of tone is calculated as Equation 9.

$$P(T|O) = \frac{P(O|T)P(T)}{\sum_{T' \in T_{set}} P(O|T')P(T')} \tag{9}$$

O is the F0 contour of one syllable. T is the tone label of the text. T_{set} is the set of tone models.

The posterior probability calculated by Equation 9 is for isolated tones. For continuous tone evaluation, segmentation is first obtained from alignment with the text, and then the segmentation is used to calculate tone posterior probability. The tone model is required to calculate the likelihood $P(O|T)$. With regards to tone recognition,[23,24] F0 contour serves as the feature for the tone model. Here F0 is calculated from the ETSI front-end.[25] After half-frequency and double-frequency points are removed, the F0 contour is smoothed by a 3-point mean filter. 4-tone models are used for isolated words and context-dependent tri-tone models for continuous speech. All the models are built with HTK.[26]

Next we use calculated tone posterior probability to evaluate tone. After posterior probability is derived, tone error detection is done as in Equation 10,

$$\begin{cases} Right & \text{if } P(T|O) \geq Thresh_T \\ Error & \text{if } P(T|O) < Thresh_T \end{cases} \tag{10}$$

where $Thresh_T$ is the tone error detection threshold for tone T. Equation 10 indicates that the pronounced tone T is an error if its posterior probability is less than the threshold. T is judged as accurate, if it matches or exceeds the threshold.

4.2.5. *Pronunciation Error Detection Method*

Pronunciation error detection is essential for pronunciation evaluation systems because it can give users information about the kinds of errors made as well as give them the corrective advice.

4.2.5.1. Basic Error Detection Method in CALL System

Error detection is also based on posterior probability. A segment is marked as an error if its posterior probability is below a predefined threshold. The process is shown in Figure 4.[5]

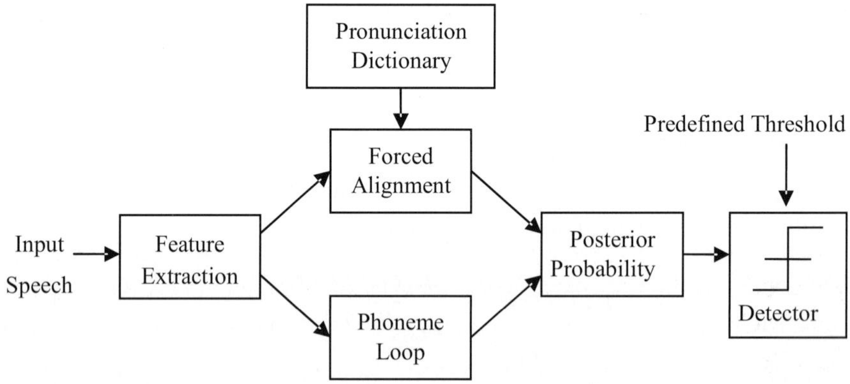

Fig. 4. Pronunciation error detection process.

Because the posterior probability varies from phone to phone, the threshold should be phone-specific. This is implemented via Equation 11,[5]

$$T_p = \mu_p + \alpha\sigma_p + \beta \tag{11}$$

where T_p is a phone-specific threshold, μ_p and σ_p are the mean and variance of the posterior probability for phone p in the standard training database, and α and β are empirically-determined scaling constants.

4.2.5.2. Differences Between Error Detection and ASR

The error detection method in Figure 4 is based on ASR. In general, ASR aims to distinguish which phone a segment belongs to, while error detection involves finding out whether the pronounced segment is good or bad. Here, we list the differences between ASR and pronunciation error detection:

- The training database for ASR should cover all kinds of speakers with different pronunciation proficiency levels so as to lighten the effect of accent. On the contrary, the training database for error detection should consist entirely of standard pronunciation in order to distinguish right pronunciation from the wrong ones.

- Speaker normalization and adaptation (e.g. VTLN and MLLR) could enhance the performance of both error detection and ASR. But, for error detection, these should not be carried out to diminish the effect of accent as presented in Section 4.2.3.
- Most pronunciation errors occur along with the influence of accent. This kind of error is typically a phoneme-to-phoneme replacement error, which means that we can use discriminative training to build an acoustic model with the best phoneme pair distinguishability. This is implemented via the minimum classification error (MCE) training on the standard Mandarin database as Equation 12,[27,28]

$$l_i(O) = \frac{1}{1+\exp(-\gamma d_i(O))} \tag{12}$$

where $d_i(O) = -g_i(O;\lambda) + g_j(O;\lambda)$ and $g_i(O;\lambda) = \log p(O|M_i,\lambda)$ and phoneme j is the phoneme replacement error of phoneme i. Referring to standard MCE training in ASR, this kind of MCE training only takes into account the effect of the phoneme replacement error.

4.2.6. *Free Speech Evaluation*

The free speech section is the most difficult yet most important part of the PSC test. It requires the examinee to talk on a specific topic for no less than three minutes. Performance in free speech is most representative of a speaker's degree of proficiency. It takes up 40 percent of the test. As the name suggests, there is no textual reference information in the free speech section, making it hard to use the computer for scoring. Here, we introduce two kinds of methods to evaluate free speech without text information.

4.2.6.1. Text-Independent Evaluation based on LVCSR

The correlation between machine evaluation and human evaluation is considerable in a text-dependent environment, but not as good in a text-independent context due to higher recognition errors in the latter situation. By building a high-performance domain-specific recognizer for transcription, free speech can be evaluated just like what has been done for the text-dependent task. This is the basic idea behind the LVCSR-based free speech evaluation.

Spontaneous speech is different from reading speech.[29,30] In order to build such a recognizer, free speech from 1,600 speakers (about 100 hours) were transcribed to obtain the training database. Using the transcribed text and speech data, an acoustic model (AM) has been constructed for building the speech recognizer with a language model (LM).

In order to increase the distinguishability of acoustic features, the VTLN and HLDA (heteroscedastic linear discriminant analysis)[31] are also integrated. At the same time, supervised adaptation is introduced to the acoustic model by MLLR using the first three test parts of read speech data, and unsupervised adaptation is done using free speech data.

The text information derived from such a recognizer serves as the supervised text and following that evaluation is implemented on a text-dependent environment.

4.2.6.2. Text-Independent Evaluation based on Classification

The evaluation method based on posterior probability is built upon the assumption that the posterior probability obtained from the speech recognizer can represent the proficiency of the speaker. This assumption is problematic in two ways. The first is that posterior probability could be affected by many factors, such as inter-speaker and intra-speaker variations. Secondly, posterior probability is calculated from the speech recognizer, which is not built to distinguish degree of proficiency but rather to distinguish between different phonemes. The posterior probability represents the competition between phonemes while evaluation is to distinguish proficiency in the production of the *same* phoneme. If we divide the same phonemes pronounced by different persons into a set of phonemes which represent the degrees of proficiencies, we can turn the evaluation problem into a classification problem. Accent recognition and identification uses a similar method.[32,33] By defining a set of pronunciation types as in Equation 13, and assigning each phoneme a pronunciation type for each person, the evaluation problem changes into a decision problem, which can be represented by Equation 14.

$$\{Type_i \quad i = 1,2,\ldots n, \ \ n \text{ is the number of pronunciation types}\} \tag{13}$$

$$\begin{aligned} Class &= \arg\max_i \left(P\left(Type_i|O\right)\right) \\ &= \arg\max_i \left(\frac{P\left(O|Type_i\right)P\left(Type_i\right)}{\sum\limits_{j=1}^{n} P\left(O|Type_j\right)P\left(Type_j\right)} \right) \end{aligned} \tag{14}$$

Equation 14 shows that transcription is not necessary. It means that we can evaluate the pronunciations without text information. We can use GMMs to model the different classes and assign each person a pronunciation type corresponding to his/her level defined in the PSC test.

Using GMMs to model a unified pronunciation type would be too coarse. A phone-specific error model can also be used to better distinguish the different pronunciation types of different phones. This is implemented by Equation 15 and 16.

$$\left\{ Type_{ij} \quad \begin{matrix} i = 1,2,\ldots n, & n \text{ is the number of pronunciation types} \\ j = 1,2,\ldots m, & m \text{ is the number of phonemes} \end{matrix} \right\} \tag{15}$$

$$\begin{aligned} Class &= \arg\max_i \left(P\left(Type_{ij}|O\right)\right) \\ &= \arg\max_i \left(\frac{P\left(O|Type_{ij}\right)P\left(Type_{ij}\right)}{\sum_{j=1}^{n} P\left(O|Type_{ij}\right)P\left(Type_{ij}\right)} \right) \end{aligned} \tag{16}$$

A phone-specific pronunciation-type model is like a phoneme HMM with different pronunciation types. This model has the ability to distinguish both phoneme and its pronunciation type. The problem is that we have to transcribe training data with not only text information but annotate their pronunciation type information. It is too difficult to give each unique phoneme a precise pronunciation type. Here we assume that each phoneme from one person has the same pronunciation type *i*, if his level of PSC is *i*. In this way, it becomes very easy to get the training label with the overall guide of each person's proficiency. This is based on the assumption that each segment from a speaker of certain (pronunciation) proficiency would have the same level. This is not always the case because many segments from different persons with different proficiency levels are correct, which means they should not be assigned with different levels. In view of this fact, we define 3 pronunciation types, which are "right", "wrong" and "defect". We collect the "right" segments to train a "right model", and the "wrong" and "defect" segments labeled by human evaluators to train the "wrong model" and the "defect model".

This phone-specific pronunciation-type modeling also requires text information for classification. That is, we still need to get text information via a speech recognizer.

5. Experiments and Results

Section 4 introduced the pronunciation evaluation algorithm and the optimized algorithm for Mandarin. In this section, we use the optimized algorithm to evaluate the PSC test database so as to validate the performance of the optimized algorithm. All experiments are carried out on the AnHui database because this set of data is sufficient. We use the correlation between human scores and machine scores to represent the performance of evaluation.

5.1. *Performance of Typical Error Pattern Knowledge*

We set the error list for each phoneme by error analysis and then calculate the posterior probability using Equation 3. Table 5 displays the performance results before and after using error pattern knowledge.

Table 5. Performance of entire phoneme loop network and error list network on PSC test database.

Training/Testing Set	**Entire phoneme loop network**	**Error-list network**
Correlation	0.65/0.61	0.77/0.73

Linguistic knowledge about typical pronunciation error patterns of a Mandarin dialect accent can effectively improve the performance of the evaluation algorithm. The reason is that the compact recognition network efficiently reduces recognition errors without losing the distinguishability across the degrees of proficiency.

5.2. *Performance of Adjustment via Initial Final Duration Ratio*

Wei *et al.*[14] has already demonstrated the performance of using initial-final duration ratio to adjust the weight of the initial. Table 6 lists the results conducted on the PSC test database. The evaluation algorithm also utilizes the knowledge of typical error patterns.

Table 6. Performance with and without duration ratio on PSC test database.

Training/Testing Set	**Without duration ratio**	**With duration ratio**
Correlation	0.77/0.73	0.81/0.77

From Table 6 we can see that the initial-final duration ratio is efficient, as has been shown by Wei *et al.*[14]

5.3. *Performance of Speaker Adaptation*

The performance of using selective adaptation method as described in Section 4.2.3 is listed in Table 7.

Table 7. Performance of universal and selective adaptation on PSC test database.

Training/Testing Set	**Without adaptation**	**Universal adaptation**	**Selective adaptation**
Correlation	0.77/0.73	0.78/0.73	0.82/0.79

From the above, we can see that the universal MLLR can only slightly improve the performance of the evaluation algorithm while selective adaptation can do much more.

5.4. *Performance of Evaluation System*

The performance of optimized methods has been discussed in the preceding sections. Table 8 shows the overall performance of the evaluation system which combines the different kinds of optimized methods.

Table 8. Performance of evaluation system on PSC test database.

Correlation (Training/Testing Set)	Baseline	Error list network + Duration ratio + Selective adaptation
Machine vs. Human	0.65/0.61	0.83/0.81
Human vs. Human	0.90/0.89	

Table 8 shows that the combination of different kinds of optimizing methods significantly improves the performance of the system. The performance of machine evaluation is close to human evaluation.

5.5. *Performance of Error Detection*

Performance of error detection is measured by the cross-correlation (CC) between two detection results.[5] CC takes into account only those syllables where a rejection in either of the two judgments exists. CC is calculated as Equation 17.

$$CC_{d1,d2} = \frac{x_{d1}^T x_{d2}}{\|x_{d1}\|_E \|x_{d2}\|_E} \tag{17}$$

Here, x_{d1} is the judgment vector for a user's pronunciation from evaluator $d1$, while x_{d2} is from evaluator $d2$. The elements of the judgment vector are 0 or 1, where 0 means the pronunciation is correct, and 1 for when it is wrong. If both judgments on a segment are correct, we discard it from the judgment vector in order to focus on error pronunciations. $\|x\|_E$ is the norm of vector x. CC measures the similarity between all segments which contain rejections in either of the two judgments. Table 9 shows the experimental result.

Table 9. Performance of error detection on PSC test database.

Cross-Correlation (Training/Testing Set)	**Mono-syllabic word**	**Di-syllabic word**	**Essay**
Machine vs. Human	0.593/0.606	0.554/0.556	0.547/0.546
Human vs. Human	0.629/0.633	0.604/0.617	0.576/0.573

5.6. *Performance of Free Speech*

Work on the evaluation of free speech is still in progress. The performance in this section is not as good as in the first three parts. The evaluation system currently in use does not contain free speech evaluation. The performance of free speech evaluation presented here is based on a different database. We split the AnHui database into two sets. Set A contains 1,600 persons and set B contains 50 persons. We use set A to train the ASR acoustic and language models and then test the performance of the evaluation algorithm on set B. The performance of traditional word posterior probability (WPP) and the performance of the classification algorithm is shown in Table 10.

Table 10. Performance of free speech evaluation algorithm.

Set B	*Correlation*	
	Male	Female
WPP vs. Human	0.58	0.70
Classification vs. Human	0.70	0.74
Human vs. Human	0.89	

The model used in the classification method is gender-dependent so as to diminish the effect of error-independent information such as gender. From Table 10, we can see that the classification method has a better correlation with human evaluation compared to that between the WPP method and human evaluation.

6. Linear Regression for Evaluation Score

The algorithm mentioned above will generate a revised average posterior probability as a machine score, which may not make sense to the examinee. The machine score should be converted to a score which is comparable to human scoring conventions. A mapping algorithm is needed to map the posterior probability into a more reasonable, genuine machine score, comparable to human scoring. Linear regression is used as the mapping method.

The PSC test is made up of four parts among which only the first three parts can be precisely evaluated. The fourth part, that is the free speech section, is still evaluated by human evaluators. The input parameters of linear regression are the revised average posterior probabilities of part one, part two and part three. The mapping algorithm is show in Equation 18.

$$\begin{cases} Score_{machine} = \sum_{i=1}^{3} \alpha_{1i} P(No_i) + Score_4 & C = Class\ 1 \\ Score_{machine} = \sum_{i=1}^{3} \alpha_{2i} P(No_i) + Score_4 & C = Class\ 2 \\ Score_{machine} = \sum_{i=1}^{3} \alpha_{3i} P(No_i) + Score_4 & C \leq Class\ 3 \end{cases} \tag{18}$$

$P(No_i)$ is the revised average posterior probability of i-th part. α_{ji} is the regression coefficient. $Score_4$ is human score of part four. C is the predicted class of the PSC test by an automatic class predictor. $Score_{machine}$ is the ultimate machine score which is comparable to the human score. The results are shown in Table 11.

Table 11. Performance of linear regression on training and testing set.

(*Correlation, Average score difference*) Training/Testing Set	Error list network + Duration ratio+ Selective adaptation	Sub-linear regression
Machine vs. Human	(0.83,-)/(0.81,-)	(0.95,1.28)/(0.84,2.44)
Human vs. Human	(0.90,2.20)/(0.89,2.30)	

From this table, we find that the correlation of the system increases with the use of linear regression. At the same time, linear regression provides a score comparable to the human score. The machine's average score difference on the test set (2.44) is close to the human evaluator's average score difference (2.30).

7. Application of the System

To date, the Putonghua evaluation system has been used in the PSC test for examinees in AnHui, and thousands of them have been tested by this system. Meanwhile, the system has also been tested in ShangHai and TianJin. The results are encouraging. Here is a description of how the evaluation system is used.

First the examinee logs into the system and check whether his personal information is right. Then the examinee adjusts the volume of his/her microphone with guidance from the system. After the adjustment, the exam begins upon the command of the examiner, as shown in Figure 5. The recorded data of the examinee will be sent to the server after all 4 parts have been completed. Human evaluators can download data from the server and evaluate part 4 of the PSC test and upload his part 4 scores for that examinee. At the same time, the computer evaluates the first 3 parts. As soon as the evaluation system gets the human scores, it will calculate the PSC test score for each examinee, as shown in Figure 6.

8. Conclusion

This paper presents a Mandarin evaluation system aiming at efficiently evaluating speaker proficiency for the PSC test. The proposed system utilizes knowledge of typical error patterns of dialect accents to restrict the recognition grammar and the characteristics of Mandarin to enhance the syllable initial's weight, thereby optimizing the traditional posterior probability evaluation method. At the same time, we introduced a selective adaptation method by selecting appropriate adaptation

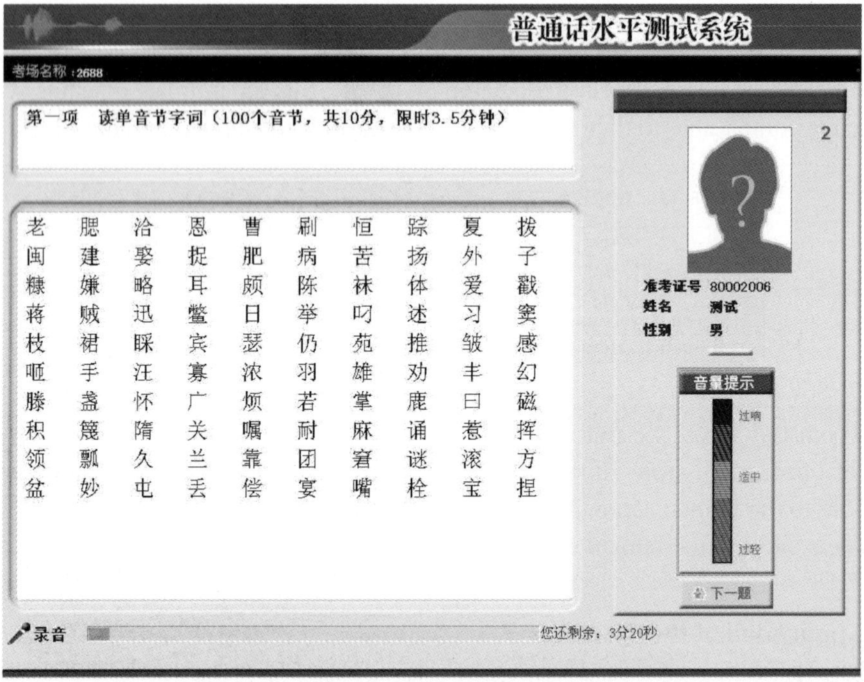

Fig. 5. Putonghua Evaluation System (Exam Screen).

data according to the proficiency of the speaker, which adapts the recognition model to the speaker without decreasing distinguishability of the dialect accent. We also utilized vocal tract length normalization to normalize the vocal tract length of different persons, which can increase the distinguishability of the recognition model. In order to efficiently evaluate tone quality, we applied CDF-matching to normalize F0-distribution. Finally, we use linear regression to map the average posterior probability into the human-evaluator scoring scheme so as to get a comparable machine score. Experiments indicate that the correlation increases from 0.65/0.61 to 0.83/0.81 on the training and testing sets. Compared to the correlation of human evaluation (0.90/0.89) and average score difference (2.20/2.30), the machine score's correlation and average score difference are 0.83/0.81 and 1.28/2.44 on the training and testing sets. To date, the automatic evaluation of free speech is not good enough to replace human evaluators. Thus, human evaluators are still used to assign scores for the free speech section, which means that this evaluation system requires human participation. Experiments showed in this paper are all conducted on the AnHui database. However, good results have also been achieved on the ShangHai, WuHan, TianJin and HuBei databases. Experimental results on the ShanDong and Shanxi databases are not as good as the others. Here are some reasons. First, the

Fig. 6. Putonghua Evaluation System (Scoring Screen).

mapping algorithm is based on the AnHui database of the PSC test, while evaluators from a different area may have a different scoring style. In addition, tone evaluation for continuous speech is not as good as segmental evaluation, and speakers of the above areas make more tonal errors than in other areas. These areas deserve more attention in future work. At the same time, evaluation for the free speech section is still an unsolved problem, although our preliminary results have given us some confidence to solve it in the near future. Finally, investigating the other training algorithms designed for pronunciation evaluation, such as the discriminative training method based on speaker's proficiency is also a worthwhile research direction.

Acknowledgements

The authors would like to thank Dr. Xiaoru Wu, Dr. Qingsheng Liu, and Mr. Zhonghua Yi from USTC iFlytek Co., Ltd. for their contributions to this work.

References

1. H. L. Franco, L. Neumeyer, Y. Kim, and O. Ronen, "Automatic Pronunciation Scoring for Language Instruction," in *Proc. ICASSP*, (1997), p. 1465.

2. L. Neumeyer, H. Franco, V. Digalakis, and M. Weintraub, "Automatic Scoring of Pronunciation Quality," *Speech Communication*, p. 83, (2000).
3. H. L. Franco, L. Neumeyer, V. Digalakis, and O. Ronen, "Combination of Machine Scores for Automatic Grading of Pronunciation Quality," *Speech Communication*, p. 121, (2000).
4. L. Neumeyer, H. Franco, M. Weintraub, and P. Price, "Automatic Text-Independent Pronunciation Scoring of Foreign Language Student Speech," in *Proc. ICSLP*, (1996), p. 217.
5. S. M. Witt and S. J. Young, "Phone-level Pronunciation Scoring and Assessment for Interactive Language Learning," *Speech Communication*, p. 95, (2000).
6. S. M. Witt, *Use of Speech Recognition in Computer-assisted Language Learning*. PhD Dissertation, (1999).
7. C. Cucchiarini, F. D. Wet, H. Strik, and L. Boves, "Assessment of Dutch Pronunciation by means of Automatic Speech Recognition Technology," in *Proc. ICSLP*, (1998), p. 1739.
8. C. Cucchiarini, H. Strik, and L. Boves, "Automatic Evaluation of Dutch Pronunciation by using Speech Recognition Technology," in *Proc. IEEE Workshop ASRU*, (Santa Barbara, 1997), p. 622.
9. A. Raux and T. Kawahara, "Automatic Intelligibility Assessment and Diagnosis of Critical Pronunciation Errors for Computer-assisted Pronunciation Learning," in *Proc. ICSLP*, (2002), p. 737.
10. Y. Tsubota, T. Kawahara, and M. Dantsuj, "Practical Use of English Pronunciation System for Japanese Students in the CALL Classroom," in *Proc. ICSLP*, (2004), p. 849.
11. N. Minematsu, "Pronunciation Assessment based upon the Compatibility between a Learner's Pronunciation Structure and the Target Language's Lexical Structure," in *Proc. ICSLP*, (2004), p. 1317.
12. S. Asakawa, N. Minematsu, T. Isei-Jaakkola, and K. Hirose, "Structural Representation of the Non-native Pronunciation," in *Proc. EuroSpeech*, (2005), p. 165.
13. A. Li and X. Wang, "A Contrastive Investigation of Standard Mandarin and Accented," in *Proc. EuroSpeech*, (2003), p. 1139.
14. S. W. L. Qingsheng, H. Yu, and W. Renhua, "Automatic Mandarin Pronunciation Scoring for Native Learners with Dialect Accent," in *Proc. 8th Conference of Man-Machine Communication of China*, (2005), p. 22.
15. C. J. Leggetter and P. C. Woodland, "Maximum Likelihood Linear Regression for Speaker Adaptation of Continuous Density Hidden Markov Models," *Computer Speech and Language*, p. 171, (1995).
16. Y. Ono, H. Wakita, and Y. Zhao, "Speaker Normalization using Constrained Spectra Shifts in Auditory Filter Domain," in *Proc. Eurospeech*, (1993), p. 355.
17. H. Wakita, "Normalization of Vowels by Vocal-Tract Length and its Application to Vowel Identification," *IEEE Trans. ASSP*, p. 183, (1977).
18. E. Eide and H. Gish, "A Parametric Approach to Vocal Tract Length Normalization," in *Proc. ICASSP*, (1996), p. 346.
19. E. B. Gouvea, *Acoustic Feature Based Frequency Warping for Speaker Normalization*. PhD Dissertation, (CMU, 1998).
20. W. S. Y. Wan, "Phonological Features of Tone," *International Journal of American Lingustics*, p. 93, (1967).
21. J. lai Zhou, Y. Tian, Y. Shi, C. Huang, and E. Chang, "Tone Articulation Modeling for Mandarin Spontaneous Speech Recognition," in *Proc. ICASSP*, (2004), p. 997.
22. J. C. Segura, *CDF-matching based Nonlinear Feature Transformations for Robust Speech Recognition*. Presentation at Edimburgo, (2002).
23. J. Zhang and K. Hirose, "Tone Nucleus Modeling for Chinese Lexical Tone Recognition," *Speech Communication*, p. 447, (2004).

24. W. Lin and L. Lee, "Improved Tone Recognition for Fluent Mandarin Speech Based on New Inter-Syllabic Features and Robust Pitch Extraction," in *ASRU Workshop*, (2003), p. 237.
25. ETSI, *ETSI Standard Doc, Extended Advanced Front-end Feature Extraction Algorithm.* ETSI ES 202 050 Ver.1.1.2, (2005).
26. S. Young, D. Kershaw, J. Odell, D. Ollason, and V. Valthev, *The HTK Book (for HTK Version 3.0).* Microsoft Corporation, (2000).
27. B. H. Juang and S. Katagiri, "Discriminative Learning for Minimum Error Classification," *IEEE Transactions on Signal Processing*, p. 3043, (1992).
28. B. H. Juang, W. Chou, and C. H. Lee, "Minimum Classification Error Rate Methods for Speech Recognition," *IEEE Transactions on Speech and Audio Processing*, p. 266, (1997).
29. M. Nakamura, K. Iwano, and S. Furui, "Analysis of Spectral Space Reduction in Spontaneous Speech and its Effects on Speech Recognition Performances," in *EuroSpeech*, (2005), p. 3381.
30. S. Furui, "Recent Progress in Corpus-Based Spontaneous Speech Recognition," *IEICE Transactions on Information and System*, p. 366, (2005).
31. N. Kumar and A. G. Andreou, "Heteroscedastic Discriminant Analysis and Reduced Rank HMMs for Improved Speech Recognition," *Speech Communication*, p. 283, (1998).
32. C. Huang, T. Chen, and E. Chang, "Accent Issues in Large Vocabulary Continuous Speech Recognition," *International Journal of Speech Technology*, p. 141, (2005).
33. Y. Zheng, R. Sproat, L. Gu, I. Shafran, H. Zhou, D. Jurafsky, R. Starr, and S. Yoon, "Accent Detection and Speech Recognition for Shanghai-Accented Mandarin," in *EuroSpeech*, (2005), p. 217.

Advances in Chinese Spoken Language Processing **Part III**

Systems, Applications and Resources

CHAPTER 19

AUDIO-BASED DIGITAL CONTENT MANAGEMENT AND RETRIEVAL

Bo Xu, Shuwu Zhang and Taiyi Huang
Institute of Automation, Chinese Academy of Sciences
No. 95 Zhongguancun East Road, Beijing
E-mail :{xubo, swzhang, huang}@nlpr.ia.ac.cn

In this digital era, digital media data is available everywhere, such as internet online audio/video (AV) broadcasting, digital TV news, music, telephone conversations, etc., and this volume is ever-increasing. Digital content management and retrieval (DCMR) technology is thus expected to be helpful for the management and access of this huge amount of digital media data. Since the audio channel is an important component in digital media which contains rich information or features describing the digital media content, our studies are mainly focused on the techniques of audio-based digital content management and retrieval (AD-CMR), in which textual audio information retrieval (TAIR) and content-based audio retrieval (CBAR) are its two important research directions. This chapter introduces our recent studies on TAIR and CBAR, as well as their potential applications.

1. Introduction

In this digital age, various digital media materials are easily available in ever-increasing volumes, especially on the internet. Besides the internet, television and other news broadcast stations have immense historical archives, which are practically worthless resources until the right tools are available for efficient browsing and searching. The challenge of digital content management and retrieval (DCMR) is to find an efficient way to manage these large-scale digital media databases, to provide a tool to browse and access the information contained in the databases, and to allow users to retrieve the relevant content and information with their queries. Currently, the web search engines, such as Google and Yahoo, have been successful in text document retrieval. For digital media databases, however, a content-based search engine is not fully ready for commercial application. Digital media content, which contains visual, textual and audio features and information, is much more complex than textual content. Unlike text, digital media data is unstructured. A lot of work must be carried out in order to structure it such that efficient indexing and management can be done. The audio channel is an important component of the digital media signal as it provides rich information relating to the digital content. In this regard, we will mainly focus on the techniques of audio-based digital content management and retrieval (ADCMR).

In digital media data, especially television programs and news broadcasts, the audio signal has sufficient features or information to describe the digital content. For example, we may ask: when and where does an anchor person appear in the news program? Who is speaking (using speaker identification technique)? What are the speakers talking about (using automatic speech recognition and natural language understanding)? Is the audio clip a piece of music, speech or applause (using pattern classification)? Is it a specific advertisement, music or other scenes (using detection techniques)? Effective audio signal analysis, integrated with the various technologies, is able to supply the answers for all these questions, and even more.

As for the meaning of audio-based digital media content, generally, there are two kinds of expressions. One is textual audio information such as textual transcription, textual keywords, speakers or languages of the speech clip, as well as some metadata tags. Correspondingly, textual audio information retrieval (TAIR) is to extract this kind of audio content by a series of recognition-based audio processing and retrieval techniques that may quickly transcribe spoken audio documents and essentially reduce the audio retrieval problem to the more straightforward problem of text retrieval. The second expression refers to some kinds of audio signal features which are sound objects quickly detectable and located in a stream of audio data in content-based audio retrieval (CBAR) systems. This latter type of audio features is the concern in content-based video retrieval (CBVR). ADCMR is thus to provide the functions for detecting and browsing these two types of digital content from the massive amount of digital media material.

ADCMR integrates the techniques developed in speech and audio signal processing, pattern classification, machine learning, database management, information retrieval and distributed computing. Among them, TAIR and CBAR are two of the most important supporting components. In the rest of this chapter, we discuss ADCMR in light of these two techniques and introduce our works that address the relevant problems.

In Section 2, we will first discuss textual audio information retrieval (TAIR) techniques in ADCMR, including audio signal pre-processing, textual audio information recognition and retrieval. Content-based audio retrieval (CBAR) is introduced in Section 3, and finally, a summary of our findings is presented in Section 4.

2. Textual Audio Information Retrieval (TAIR)

With the advent of unlimited storage capabilities and the proliferation of the use of the internet, it has become necessary to retrieve information inherent in digital media. Significant portions of these media data are in the form of audio, and an audio channel does contain rich textual information that describes the digital content, such as textual transcription, textual keywords, speaker and language information, and so on. It thus makes sense to tap on this audio resource and develop textual audio information analysis, recognition and retrieval techniques for the purpose of digital content management and retrieval.

TAIR is currently an important research topic in the area of spoken language recognition and understanding. The approach and system described here is related to several typical systems. Pioneering systems include the Informedia system developed by the Carnegie-Mellon University,[1] the Rough'n'Ready system developed by BBN,[2] and the Broadcast News Navigator by the MITRE Corporation[3] and LIMSI.[4] All these aim to automatically transcribe and time-align the audio signal in broadcast news recordings, such that the data is ready for users to search for their desired digital information using specific phrases or keywords in the transcript, and to retrieve the audio as a practical means to access information in spoken language audio and video sources. More recently, some of the systems have been applied to commercial applications, such as Pod Zinger.[5] A recent research trend is to move away from audio indexing, and towards the more comprehensive goals of understanding and organization.[6]

In general, a textual audio information retrieval (TAIR) system mainly consists of three parts: audio signal pre-processing, textual audio information extraction and recognition, and textual audio information management and retrieval. In the rest of this section, we will discuss these technologies in detail.

2.1. *Audio Pre-Processing for TAIR*

In a digital media database, audio signal may be acoustic speech, music, environmental sounds or a mixture of these. Each of them has distinct characteristics. Some audio signal processing techniques, such as acoustic boundary detection and audio scene classification, are useful pre-processing steps that further assist textual audio information extraction and recognition. For example, identifying non-speech segments in the audio stream and preventing them from recognition would save computation time in automatic speech recognition as well as result in more meaningful transcriptions. Here, we focus on two main audio pre-processing topics - acoustic boundary detection and audio scene classification - while introducing our recent work.

2.1.1. *Acoustic Boundary Detection*

Acoustic boundary detection is a task to automatically detect the salient changing point of an audio signal along a given time interval so that the audio stream can be divided into homogeneous segments. The degree of salience is measured by a predefined distance function. Acoustic change point detection is an important component in TAIR. Firstly, the audio segment has some semantic meaning, compared to the frame. Thus indexing at the segment is more efficient and robust than at the frame. Secondly, different operations will be done for different types of audio segments, which is another reason for segmentation.

In speaker-based acoustic change point segmentation, each segment is assumed to belong to one speaker. It is a critical module in the TAIR system because speech recognition and adaptation is often used to improve the performance of transcribing the speech signal. The proposed segmentation algorithms can be categorized into four methods, and they are the decoder-guided, model-based, metric-based, and model-selection-based approaches. Each of these methods has its advantages as well as limitations. It would be expected that combining the different methods will produce better results. Recent experimental results prove that a hybrid algorithm performs better than any one method alone.[7–12] The hybrid approaches often detect the potential candidates of speaker changing points using the distance-based method. They are sensitive to the size of the detection window. Here, we will introduce the unsupervised speaker-based audio segmentation using the two-level method.[13] In the first level, the potential changing regions, which contain the potential speaker changing points, are initially detected using the metric-based method. Then in the second level, the true changing points are searched for and confirmed within these candidates of changing regions. The two-level segmentation framework introduced here is not only for speaker-based audio segmentation, but also suitable for generic audio segmentation. Its disadvantage is that the computation cost may be high, although it can achieve high performance in speaker-based indexing.

1) Two-level speaker change point segmentation scheme

The flowchart of the two-level segmentation algorithm is depicted in Figure 1. Silence is first detected using a simple energy-based algorithm and removed because it will result in many false alarms for speaker change detection. Then the two-level approach, i.e. region level and boundary level, is performed for audio segmentation. The silence smoothing module is to align the changing points with the original audio signal. Thus, the audio stream is broken down into segments with each smaller duration segment assumed to contain the speech of a single speaker.

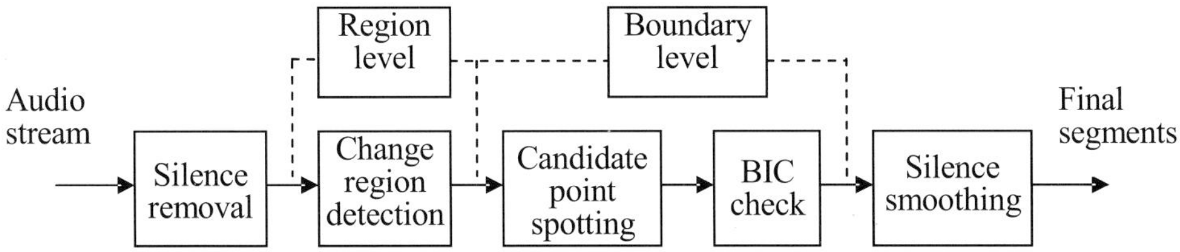

Fig. 1. The two-level framework for speaker change detection.

2) Detecting potential changing regions

This step is to decide whether or not there is a speaker changing point in the detection window. It is not necessary to find its exact position, although we hope to get a high recall in this step. The modified generalized likelihood ratio (MGLR)[14] is chosen to be the distance measure. A sliding window is applied to ensure that potential changing points are detected. We use the Gaussian mixture distribution to model the features in the detection window. For two contiguous windows, D_a and D_b, being modeled with the parameters, θ_a and θ_b respectively, the detection window is $D = D_a \cup D_b$ modeled by θ, the sum of Gaussian components in θ_a and θ_b. Then the detection window is a potential changing region if the MGLR similarity measure is more than a threshold; here it is set to zero:

$$d_{MGLR} = \log \frac{p(D_a|\theta_a)}{p(D_a|\theta)} + \log \frac{p(D_b|\theta_b)}{p(D_b|\theta)} \geq 0 \qquad (1)$$

The MGLR shows high peaks at the change regions and gives the best results, as reported in previous works.[13,14] To speed up the detection process, the single Gaussian distribution is used for modeling the features in two contiguous windows and the relatively large shift step is used for detecting the potential changing regions.

3) Detecting speaker change boundary

The speaker change boundary is detected in the candidate regions obtained from the above. The T^2-statistic metric and the BIC criterion are applied in this step.

Fast search using T^2-statistic metric
Hotelling's T^2-statistic value is used as the similarity function.[7] It is assumed that two neighboring windows have Gaussian distributions with the same, but unknown, covariance. Then we will test the hypothesis, $H_0 : \mu_1 = \mu_2$. μ_1 and μ_2 are the means for the samples in two windows, respectively. Let n_1 and n_2 be the frame number in two windows. Thus, the likelihood ratio test can be determined using the T^2-

statistic value calculated as,

$$T^2 = (\mu_1 - \mu_2)\left(\sum\left(\frac{1}{n_1}+\frac{1}{n_2}\right)\right)^{-1}(\mu_1 - \mu_2) \quad (2)$$

where $\sum$ is the common covariance. Within the detection window, the T^2-statistic is calculated at uniform interval points and the local peak point is selected as the potential speaker changing point.

Checking speaker changing points using BIC metric

The potential changing points, located using the above T^2-statistic value, are further confirmed by the BIC metric. The BIC check is also a hypothesis test.[15] For a changing point candidate t, within a detection window, the distribution of N samples $(x_1,\cdots,x_N)$ in the window is modeled by one single Gaussian distribution $N(\mu,\Sigma)$. We assume that it can be modeled by two neighboring Gaussian distributions, $(x_1,\cdots,x_t)\sim N(\mu_1,\Sigma_1)$ having N_1 samples and $(x_{t+1},\cdots,x_N)\sim N(\mu_2,\Sigma_2)$ having N_2 samples $(N_1+N_2=N)$. The BIC metric is thus to calculate the value as,

$$\triangle BIC = N\log\left|\sum\right| - N_1\log\left|\sum\nolimits_1\right| - N_2\log\left|\sum\nolimits_2\right| - \lambda p \quad (3)$$

where $\lambda = 1, p = 0.5(d+0.5d(d+1))\log N$, and d is the feature dimension. A positive value means the index t is a true boundary of the segmentation. As the potential speaker changing point is confirmed by the BIC check, the new detection window will start from this point to search for the next boundary.

4) Experimental evaluation

The above algorithm is evaluated on the 1997 NIST Hub4-NE Mandarin evaluation data. It contains a one-hour broadcast news data which has 136 changing points including 91 speaker changing points and 45 other acoustic changing points. The features are a 12-dimensional MFCC, a one-dimensional normalized energy in the log-domain, and their first order derivatives.

The evaluation metrics are the recall, precision, and F-measure, which are widely used in information retrieval.[16] The two-level algorithm is compared with the BIC metric based algorithm (row *BIC* in Table 1) and the hybrid-based algorithm (row *GLR-BIC* in Table 1). The latter uses generalized likelihood ratio (GLR) as the distance measure to detect potential speaker changing points, while the BIC is used for refining the boundaries. We assume the detecting point is correct if its bias from the hand-labeled point is less than one second. The results for the three algorithms are shown in Table 1. It is observed that the two-level method performs significantly better than the benchmarks.

Table 1. Performance comparison with BIC and GLR-BIC.

Algorithm	Recall	Precision	F-measure
BIC	76.47	74.78	75.62
GLR-BIC	77.21	80.15	78.65
Two-level method	85.29	81.12	83.15

The effects on the performance of the window size of fixed detection and shift window are studied and shown in Figure 2. We can see that when the window size is within a reasonable range, it has no obvious effect on the performance.

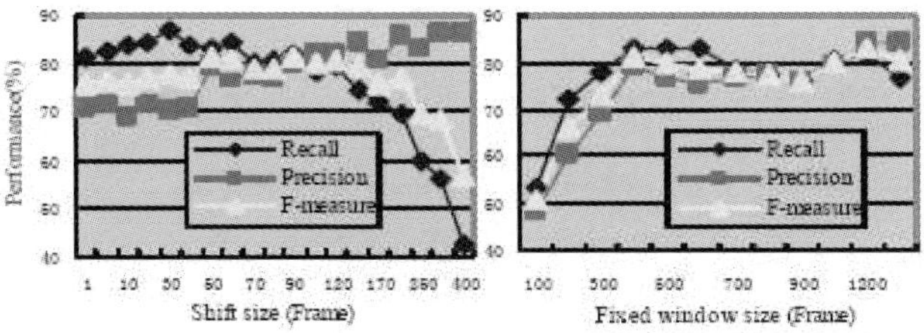

(a) fixed window size = 400 (b) shift size = 50

Fig. 2. Segmentation performance versus different sizes of shift window and fixed window.

2.1.2. *Audio Scene Classification*

In audio pre-processing, another important cue for textual audio recognition is audio scene classification. We often need to know of which type or class an audio segment is in order to prevent non-speech clips from successive content recognition modules. In audio-based digital media information retrieval, we usually classify the audio segment or clip into the predefined audio scene classes such as music, speech, environment sound, silence, etc.

Many works on audio scene classification have been reported. Scheirer and Slaney used 13 features and a classifier (e.g. such as GMM, KNN, etc.) to discriminate speech and music and achieved more than 90% accuracy rate.[17] Kimber and Wilcox segmented and classified audio recordings into speech, silence, laughter and non-speech sound using MFCC and HMM.[18] A fixed threshold scheme was applied to discriminate 8 audio classes,[19] i.e., silence, speech, music, song, environment sound and their various combinations. They reported an accuracy rate of more than 90%. The audio signals of TV programs were classified into the different categories using cepstral coefficients as the features and artificial neural network as the classifier.[20] Lu *et al.* adopted the hierarchical approach to classify five audio classes using a support vector machine (SVM) classifier and various audio features such as MFCC, zero-crossing rate (ZCR), spectral centroid (SC), spectrum flux (SF), etc.[21]

In our work, we use an SVM-based audio classification scheme with 16 kinds of audio features to classify audio streams into five classes of audio scenes. They are pure speech, non-pure speech, music, environment sound, and silence.[22]

SVM is widely and successfully applied in many classification tasks such as text categorization, natural language processing, speech recognition, and speaker identification. SVM is trained by maximizing the margin between the positive and negative classes. By adjusting the kernel function, the original feature will be implicitly mapped onto a high-dimensional space. An SVM classifier for multi-class audio scene classification is designed, as shown in Figure 3.

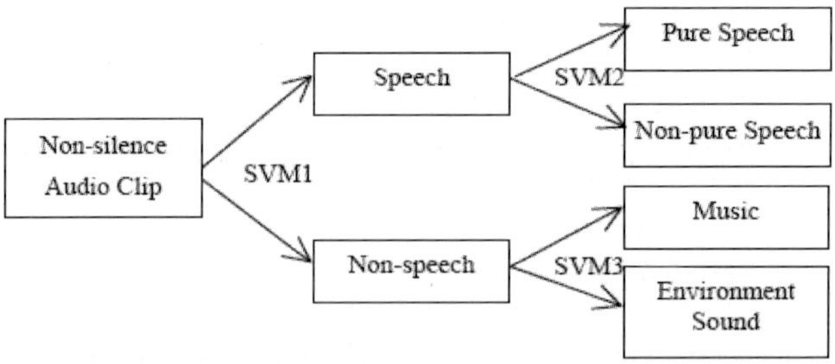

Fig. 3. The framework of SVM-based audio scene classifier.

Prior to the SVM classifier, we first filtered out silence segments from the audio stream using the silence frame ratio (SFR). The SVM audio scene classifier is a two-level framework. In the first level, the non-silence clips are determined as speech or non-speech using the SVM1 classifier. Then, the speech portions are classified as pure speech or non-pure speech using the SVM2 classifier, while the non-speech parts are further classified as music or environment sounds using the second-level classifier SVM3.

Feature selection is an important factor for SVM modeling. We found that 16 kinds of temporal and spectral features can be utilized in audio scene classification. They are zero-crossing rate (ZCR), high ZCR ratio (HZCRR), short-time energy (STE), low STE ratio (LSTER), root mean square (RMS), silence frame ratio (SFR), sub-band energy distribution (SED), spectrum flux (SF), spectral centroid (SC), spectral spread (SS), spectral rolloff frequency (SRF), sub-band periodicity (BP), noise frame ratio (NFR), linear spectrum pair (LSP), linear predictive cepstral co-efficients (LPCC) and Mel-frequency cepstral co-efficients (MFCC). The detailed descriptions of these features can be found in their respective references.[19–25] In our SVM audio scene classifier, we use different feature sets for training the 3 different SVM models (*SVM1*, *SVM2*, and *SVM3*). The feature set for a binary SVM classifier is determined by the similarity comparison of the probability distributed curves of the feature value between two kinds of audio classes.[22] Table 2 lists a final selection of feature sets with regard to the respective SVM models.

Table 2. Feature set selection for different SVM classifiers.

SVMs	Class Pairs	Feature Sets
SVM1	Speech/Non-speech	BP, HZCRR, LPCC, LSP, LSTER, MFCC, RMS, SBE, SC, SS, ZCR
SVM2	Pure speech/Non-pure speech	BP, LPCC, LSP, MFCC, RMS, SC, SF, SFR, SS, ZCR
SVM3	Music/Environment sound	BP, NFR, RMS, SBE, SF, STE

We evaluate the framework for audio scene classification on a dataset collected from actual TV programs. This dataset has about 343 minutes, of which 94 minutes of the data are used for training and the rest for testing. The training set has 25 minutes of pure speech, 25 minutes of non-pure speech, 25 minutes of music, and 19 minutes of environment sound. The test set has 109 minutes of pure speech, 103 minutes of music, 25 minutes of non-pure speech, and 12 minutes of environment sound. Most of the pure speech are from news reports, movies or sitcoms, and talk shows. Non-pure speech includes mainly speech with music, speech with noise, and advertisement speech with rather strong background music. Music consists of pure instrumental music produced by different musical instruments, songs sung by male, female, or children, and operas. Environment sounds include sounds produced by applause, animals, footsteps, explosions, vehicles, laughs, crowds, and so on. Pure speech and non-pure speech are then merged into the speech class, while music and environment sound are merged into the non-speech class.

We use a one-second audio clip as the segment unit to calculate the classification accuracy. That is, we cut the audio stream for each scene into a set of one-second audio clips and assume that each one-second clip belongs to only one scene. The classification accuracies and the confusion matrix are shown in Table 3.

Table 3. SVM-based audio scene classification results.

	Pure Speech	Non-pure Speech	Music	Environment Sound
Pure speech	6061	16	10	0
Non-pure speech	61	1383	212	0
Music	9	65	5924	9
Environment sound	11	9	55	689
Silence	440	0	3	2
Recall(%)	98.68	93.89	95.53	98.71
Precision(%)	99.57	83.51	98.62	90.18
F-measure(%)	99.13	88.40	97.05	94.25

The average accuracy is about 96.85%. From the confusion matrix, it is easy to see that pure speech holds the highest accuracy and the scene with the lowest accuracy is non-pure speech. It is hard to discriminate the non-pure speech and music due to two factors: 1) advertisement speech in non-pure speech is easily misclassified into music because of the co-presence of strong background music, and 2) some songs in the music scene having weaker background music are falsely classified into non-pure speech.

2.2. *Textual Audio Information Recognition*

As mentioned in the introduction, audio content includes rich textual information, such as textual transcriptions, textual keywords, speaker and language information, even topic information, as well as some kinds of metadata tags. These information need to be extracted by a set of recognition-based speech processing and understanding techniques. Among them, automatic speech recognition, speaker recognition, and language identification are three core components. Due to the limitations of this chapter, we briefly introduce our work on ASR, speaker recognition and language identification.

2.2.1. *Automatic Speech Recognition*

Automatic Speech Recognition (ASR) is a technology rapidly coming out of research laboratories into everyday use. Recent advances in search algorithms and more easily available high-performance computing are making ASR systems increasingly practical. A perfect system that could quickly transcribe spoken audio documents would be an ideal solution to most audio indexing and retrieval tasks (at least for speech). Such a system would essentially reduce the audio retrieval problem to the more straightforward problem of text retrieval.

Practically all ASR systems in use today are based on hidden Markov models (HMMs). A HMM is a statistical representation of a speech event, like a word, and its model parameters are typically trained on a large corpus of labeled speech data. This approach has proved successful for large-vocabulary recognition systems. In addition, a large-vocabulary system requires a statistical language model that defines likely word combinations.

In our system, a state-tied tri-phone model is used as the acoustic model, which has about 4,000 states with 32 GMMs for each one of them. The language model is a tri-gram trained on a Chinese newspaper corpus. The lexicon includes about 64,000 Chinese words and is organized in a prefix tree format. The decoder, which finds the most probable word hypothesis, is a time-synchronous one-pass decoder.[26] Hence, the development of an ASR system is rather complex and requires careful analysis, design and implementation of its individual parts. On a test set of news broadcasts, the word error rate (WER) of the system can be less than 10%, and the real-time factor of the system is less than 1.2 times.

Key word spotting (KWS) is also a kind of ASR technology for extracting only key textual segment distinguished from full textual transcription in large-vocabulary continuous speech recognition (LVCSR). Our KWS system architecture is shown in Figure 4, where the feature extraction, lexical tree and acoustic model training methods are the same as in our ASR system. The filler network consists of 1,460 Mandarin tonal syllables, while the keyword network consists of about 100 words. The filler network serves two functions: first, as garbage models to filter out non-keyword speech intervals, and second, as background models (or *anti-models*) to calculate the confidence measures for putative keywords. By using a Viterbi search algorithm and "online-garbage model"-based confidence measure,[27] the equal error rate (EER) of our KWS system can reach up to 15% for a news broadcast corpus, and the real-time factor of the system is less than 0.8.

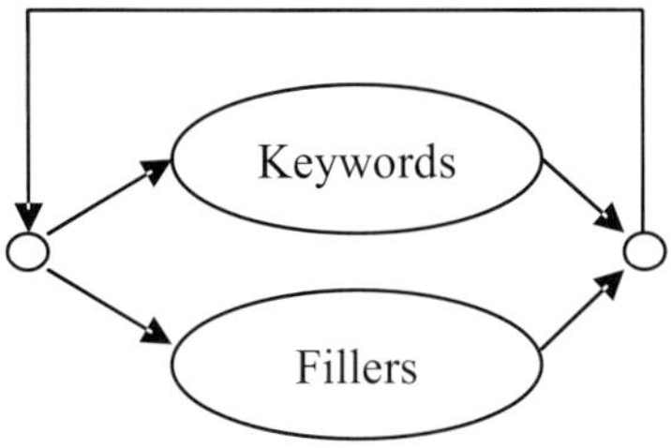

Fig. 4. KWS network Architecture.

2.2.2. *Speaker Recognition*

Over the past ten years, Gaussian mixture models (GMMs) have become the dominant approach to text-independent speaker recognition systems, especially with the use of the maximum *a posteriori* (MAP) adaptation algorithm. The Gaussian mixture model-universal background model (GMM-UBM) method has reported high performance in several NIST evaluations. It is also adopted in our system for speaker identification.

In the study of speaker recognition, some robust feature normalization methods for reducing noise and/or channel effects have been proposed, such as CMN, cepstral mean and variance normalization (CMVN), RASTA, and feature warping. In our experiments,[28] we evaluated two types of additional derivation of delta co-efficients compared to the original CMVN method. In the output score domain, score normalization has been introduced to deal with score variability and to make the speaker-independent threshold more robust and effective. In previous works, the use of score normalization significantly improved the performance of speaker recognition systems, such as cohort normalization, *Znorm* (zero normalization), *Hnorm* (handset normalization), and *Tnorm* (test normalization). Due to score variability between verification trials, test-dependent zero-score normalization (*TZnorm*) and zero-dependent test-score normalization (*ZTnorm*), are comparatively presented to transform the output scores entirely. Table 4 and Table 5 list our experimental results with different types of feature normalization and score normalization on the NIST 2002 corpus using GMM-UBM.

Table 4. Equal Error Rate (EER) and minimal Detection Cost Function (DCF)[29] for different types of feature normalization on the NIST 2002 corpus using GMM-UBM.

Feature normalization	**EER(%)**	**DCF**
CMN + Znorm (Baseline)	10.8	0.0457
Feature Warping + Znorm	9.7	0.0472
CMVN + Znorm	9.4	0.0436

Table 5. EER and minimal DCF for different types of score normalization on the NIST 2002 corpus using GMM-UBM.

Score normalization	**EER(%)**	**DCF**
CMVN + Znorm	9.4	0.0436
CMVN + Tnorm	12.0	0.0410
CMVN + TZnorm	9.4	0.0391
CMVN + ZTnorm	8.6	0.0374

Meanwhile, support vector machines (SVMs)[30] are now often used in machine-learning applications. Several recent studies consider the application of SVMs to speaker recognition. A sequence kernel-based learning algorithm, known as generalized linear discriminant sequence (GLDS), is proven to be the one of the most powerful approaches. Table 6 lists our experimental results on the NIST 2002 corpus using SVM.

Table 6. EER and minimal DCF comparisons for male and female partitions on the NIST2002 corpus using SVM.

Partition	**EER(%)**	**DCF**
Male	8.85	0.0319
Female	8.63	0.0363

2.2.3. *Language Identification (LID)*

Language identification (LID) is the process by which the language (type) spoken from a sample of speech by an unknown speaker is recognized. With increasing interest in multi-lingual machine translation systems and speech recognition systems, there has been a great deal of research in LID techniques over the past three decades.

The years of formal evaluation of systems by NIST have indicated that the most successful approach to LID is based on the phonotactic characteristics of the different languages. For example, the parallel phone recognition and language modeling (PPR-LM) system typically employs a group of phone recognizers to generate a parallel stream of phone sequences and a band of n-gram language models to capture these phonotactics. Although phone recognition based systems provide the best LID performance, their training and testing speed is so slow that they cannot be extensively used in low-cost, real-time applications.

Oriented to language detection of broadcast audio streams, we develop two alternative approaches to LID which are called the GMM-UBM system and the SVM system. Based on the acoustic content described by the features extracted from the speech signal, the GMM-UBM system incorporates the adapted universal background model (UBM) technique to greatly reduce the computation in both training and testing, while demonstrating robust performance. Designed to operate on sequence data, the SVM system uses a GLDS kernel and a simpler minimum mean squared error (MSE) estimator to build SVM classifiers of each language. Its superior performance is comparable to performances of the PPR-LM approaches, although at a much slower speed. Table 7 lists our experimental results on the OGI-TS corpus in comparison with the GMM-UBM and SVM approaches.

Table 7. LID performance comparison between GMM-UBM and SVM on 11 languages of OGI-TS corpus.

LID Approaches	**10-second**	**30-second**	**45-second**
GMM-UBM	73.28%	82.62%	85.23%
SVM	78.72%	90.15%	92.99%

2.3. *Textual Audio Information Retrieval*

Based on the above textual audio information extraction and recognition techniques, the speech signal in the audio stream is transcribed into textual information. The user is thus able to access and browse the textual audio information in the same manner as text retrieval.

Audio keyword is the most important information in TAIR. One important factor affecting retrieval precision of audio keywords is the language model in ASR. Therefore, we studied the relationship between retrieval performance and speech recognition accuracy.[31]

The experimental data is the 2004 CCTV news collected from the CCTV website, including 4,917 MPEG files and their corresponding reference text files. We trained three sets of language models corresponding to three different speech recognition accuracies, i.e. 73% (LM1), 64% (LM2) and 56% (LM3). Because name entities, which contain rather rich information, are often used as users' query words, we extracted 3,000 name entities (i.e., organization, person, and location names) from the reference text files as the first set of query words in the experiment. As a comparison set, we also extracted 3,000 common names for a second set of query words. The retrieval performance is reported as the average precision and average recall over all query words. For more detailed analysis, we also constructed 3 other query sub-sets according to the occurrence frequency of query words sorted from the highest to the lowest; that is, a query set having 250 words, one having 500 words, and one with 1,000 words.

Table 8. Retrieval performances vs. ASR accuracies and query frequencies (name entity).

Name Entity	LM1			LM2			LM3		
	P	*R*	*F*	*P*	*R*	*F*	*P*	*R*	*F*
250	0.7244	0.7415	0.7326	0.6728	0.7056	0.6888	0.6327	0.6696	0.6506
500	0.7436	0.7139	0.7285	0.6902	0.6653	0.6775	0.6468	0.6107	0.6282
1000	0.7523	0.6743	0.7112	0.7008	0.6209	0.6584	0.6514	0.5469	0.5946
3000	0.7473	0.5966	0.6635	0.6862	0.5026	0.5802	0.7260	0.3420	0.4650

(Note: *P*: average precision, *R*: average recall, *F*: F1-measure)

Table 9. Retrieval performances vs. ASR accuracies and query frequencies (common name).

Common Name	LM1			LM2			LM3		
	P	*R*	*F*	*P*	*R*	*F*	*P*	*R*	*F*
250	0.7514	0.7515	0.7515	0.6755	0.7003	0.6877	0.6254	0.6541	0.6394
500	0.7334	0.7353	0.7343	0.6486	0.6677	0.6580	0.5927	0.6092	0.6008
1000	0.7125	0.7107	0.7116	0.6175	0.6200	0.6188	0.5515	0.5494	0.5504
3000	0.7045	0.6579	0.6804	0.5868	0.5212	0.5521	0.5013	0.4206	0.4574

(Note: *P*: average precision, *R*: average recall, *F*: F1-measure)

Tables 8 and 9 list the retrieval performances on the different query frequency sets according to the different language models in ASR. The retrieval is carried out using exact matching, where the audio document is assumed relevant if its ASR text contains the exact query word. First, we analyze how the classification accuracy of ASR affects the retrieval performance. From Table 8 we can see that compared to LM1, the relative reduction of F value on the set of 250 high frequency query words is 6.0% for LM2 and 11.2% for LM3, while the relative reduction of F value on the set of the overall 3,000 query words reaches 12.6% for LM2 and 30% for LM3. This shows that lower frequency query words are affected by language model much more than higher frequency query words. A similar conclusion is also derived from the statistics of the common name set in Table 9.

2.4. *Application System*

In the above section, we have introduced the critical components for building a TAIR system. Based on these techniques, we developed a large-scale textual audio information management and retrieval system (CASIA-TAIMR). The system framework and a screen shot of its application are shown in Figures 5 and 6.[31]

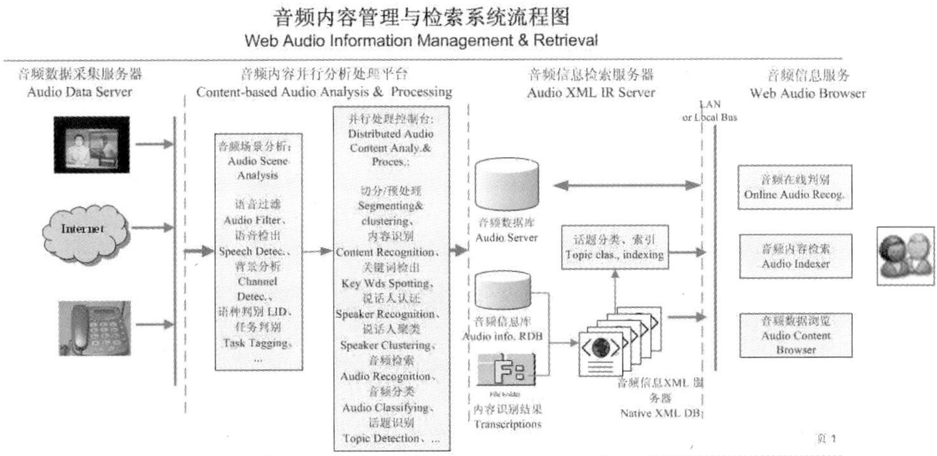

Fig. 5. The Structure of Audio Textual Information Management and Retrieval System.

This system can capture audio streams from TV programs, the telephone network or the internet. For each signal source, we built a specific module to capture and process the source data for further processing. Then, the captured audio data is further analyzed to understand its content using techniques such as speaker change point detection, audio scene classification, language identification, speech recognition, speaker identification and verification. Finally the analyzed data is pushed into the data management and delivery module, ready for a user's query. The user can access and browse the textual audio information through the website's browser or a private client browser. Just like in text search engines such as Google and Yahoo, the user can browse and retrieve the desired audio content using keywords.

Fig. 6. A page of CASIA-TAIMR.

3. Content-Based Audio Retrieval (CBAR)

In contrast with TAIR, content based audio retrieval (CBAR) is to detect and locate a piece of sound object from a long audio stream directly by content matching on the level of audio signal or features. It has good potential for applications in the fields of TV and other broadcasting media asset management, web multimedia search and music retrieval.

In recent years, there is an increasing interest on the study of CBAR compared to content-based video retrieval (CBVR) in multimedia retrieval. As a result, some new audio features were experimented for CBAR. For example, Wold *et al.* employed loudness, brightness, pitch, and timbre as audio perceptual features for audio retrieval.[32] Foote proposed a content-based retrieval of music and audio using a 12-dimension MFCC and Energy features.[33] Kashino and Smith proposed a histogram search method based on zero crossing rate (ZCR) for quick audio retrieval.[34] Spevak developed an audio retrieval system based on MFCC.[35] and Gao *et al.* proposed an unsupervised learning approach to music event detection.[36] Meanwhile, audio modeling approaches for CBAR are still the GMM, HMM, SVM, and the histogram.

3.1. *Robust Audio Retrieval Based on Dominant Spectral Components (DSC)*

Most of the above CBAR approaches have been well-studied under lower-noise and less-distorted conditions. However, the multimedia signal could often be a mixed channel of different sources and be under various distorted environments. Thus, it is necessary to design a group of features, that would be beneficial for both noise resistance and computing cost to obtain a more robust audio content matching. Here, we propose a more robust audio search algorithm based on dominant spectral components (DSC) features. The algorithm consists of three steps: (1) Feature extraction of dominant spectral components; (2) histogram modeling for target audio object detecting; and (3) verification of detected object. In the following subsections, we will introduce this algorithm in detail.

3.1.1. *Feature Extraction of Dominant Spectral Component (DSC)*

Based on the human psycho-acoustic model, the hearing system carries two main identities: (1) finite frequency precision, and (2) hearing masking. It has been proven that audible frequency range of the human hearing is between 20 Hz and 20 kHz. However, the dominant frequency range for audio retrieval is generally concentrated between 100 Hz and 4 kHz. The frequency range can be non-linearly divided into a series of critical bands. Meanwhile, there may be multiple components in a band. Generally, when multiple components occur simultaneously in the same band, only the strongest component is audible to humans.

Thus, we have to define a set of mask and silence thresholds for masking those inaudible components in a band. Before computing the thresholds, the frequency domain (f) is firstly converted to critical band domain (z):

$$z = \frac{26.81 f}{(1960 + f)} - 0.53 \tag{4}$$

Based on the convolution of critical spectral and membrane spread function, Figure 7 displays the mask threshold curve.

$$\Lambda(z) = 15.8114 + 7.5(z + 0.474) - 17.5\left(1 + (z + 0.474)^2\right)^{1/2} \tag{5}$$

Through this masking process, inaudible components in a band are filtered out. Meanwhile, the energy of the components between multiple bands is a Gaussian distribution. We apply a second masking procedure among the bands for filtering out some non-dominant components whose energy is lower than a certain threshold. Thus, a set of dominant spectral components (DSC) can be obtained from a frame of audio signals. Based on the DSC, we then extract its energy relative ratio of multiple bands as the basic audio feature.[37]

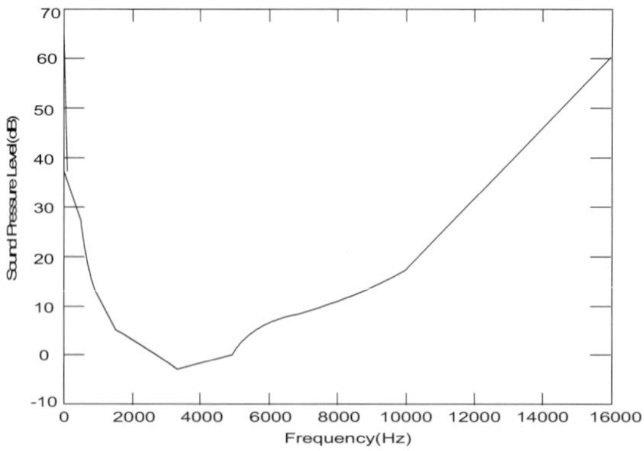

Fig. 7. Hearing mask threshold curve.

3.1.2. *Histogram Modeling for Target Audio Object Detecting*

After feature extraction, we need to train the model for each audio clip. Some modeling approaches, such as GMM, HMM, and SVM, have already been employed for audio modeling. However, because of computationally expensive processing, it is hard to meet the demands of a quick audio search and retrieval system. Histograms can be used as a type of non-parametric signal model for both the reference and input signals over a shifted window. These do not need computationally expensive processing as they are relatively stable even under adverse environments. Thus, we adopt a histogram modeling approach for specific audio detection. Figure 8 shows the framework of this histogram-based audio object detecting.

For the sake of removing the influence of noises, the feature vector needs to be first quantized (VQ) before histogram modeling. We use the codebook of VQ to build the histogram. The similarity distance between the histogram of reference and input feature vector can be measured by a histogram intersection. The histogram intersection for a window is defined as:

$$S_n\left(h^R, h^T(n)\right) = \frac{1}{L}\sum_{j=1}^{L}\min\left(h_j^R, h_j^T(n)\right) \tag{6}$$

where h^R is the histogram for the reference; $h_j^T(n)$ is the histogram started from the i-th frame; and L denotes the number of bins.

As the window for input signal shifts forward in time, the similarity based on reference and input feature vector histograms changes with regard to the correlated overlapping between the reference and an object segment in the input stream. Thus, we may predict the next upper bound of the similarity in terms of the current value.

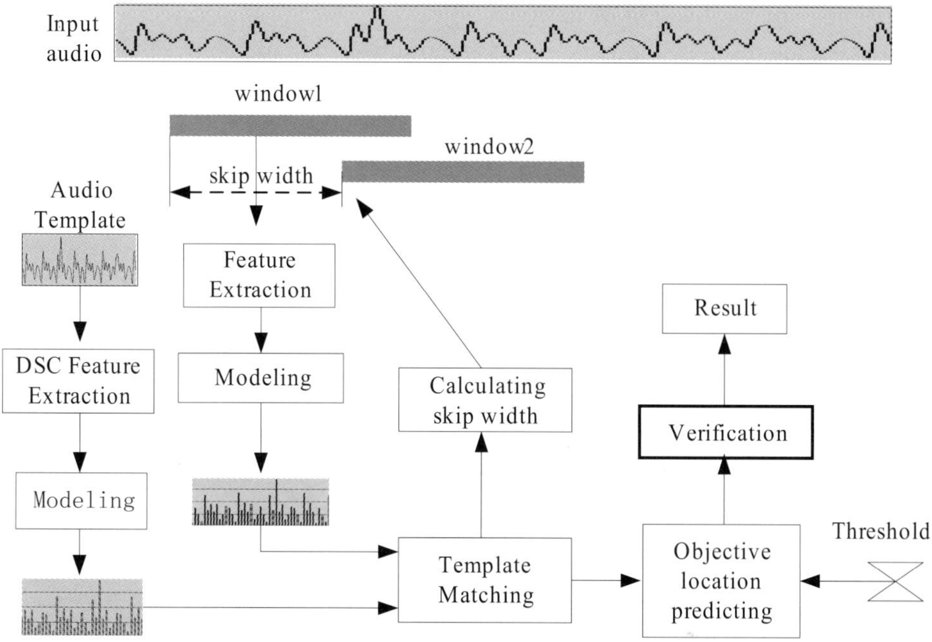

Fig. 8. Framework of Audio Object Detecting.

The upper bound on $S_n\left(h_i^R, h_i^T\right)$ can be defined as:

$$S_{ub}\left(h_i^R, h_i^T(n2)\right) = S\left(h_i^R, h_i^T(n1)\right) + \frac{n2 - n1}{p_i} \tag{7}$$

where $h_i^T(n1)$ and $h_i^T(n2)$ are the histograms for windows started from $n1$ and $n2$ frame respectively, $n1 < n2$; p_i denotes the total number of frames in each histogram. When the window is shifted to the $n2$-th frame, the similarity should be no larger than $S_{ub}\left(h_i^R, h_i^T(n2)\right)$. We may set the threshold to skip the durations where the similarity is lower than the threshold. Using Equation 7, the skip width can be calculated as:

$$w = \begin{cases} floor(p_i(\theta - S)) + 1 & \text{if } (S < \theta) \\ 1 & \text{otherwise} \end{cases} \tag{8}$$

Where $floor(x)$ means the greatest integral value less than x; θ is the threshold; and S denotes the value of the current similarity.

3.1.3. *Verification of Detected Object*

Sometimes, the result of histogram-based audio detecting may have errors caused by some disturbing factors such as channel noises, similar clips with audio object, and so on. The verification of detected object is to ensure the correctness and robustness of the result by template-based audio sub-section matching. The procedure of result verification is made up of two steps: 1) template extraction and 2) template matching.

1) Template extraction

The length of the referenced template is subject to the object audio clip. The algorithm of the template extraction is as follows:

(i) Extract the spectral of objective audio;
(ii) Compute the sub-band energy $E(n,m)$ by

$$E(n,m) = \frac{1}{(F_H(m) - F_L(m) + 1)} \sum_{k=F_L(m)}^{F_H(m)} |P(n,k)|^2 \qquad (9)$$

where $F_H(m)$ and $F_L(m)$ represent the upper and lower limits of the m-th sub-band, respectively;
(iii) Compute the difference of sub-band energy as such:

$$ED(n,m) = E(n,m) - E(n,m+1) - (E(n-1,m) - E(n-1,m+1)) \qquad (10)$$

(iv) Compute the bit flag of the template by

$$F(n,m) = \begin{cases} 1 & ED(n,m) > 0 \\ 0 & ED(n,m) \le 0 \end{cases} \qquad (11)$$

where, $F(n,m)$ denotes the bit flag of the n-th frame and m-th frequency bin. Thus, a set of sub-band energy vectors can be created as the template of an audio object.

2) Verification by template matching

We adopt a template subsection matching for result verification. The matching between a referenced template and an object template is conducted by each frame and frequency bin.

The distance of the i-th frame is defined as

$$dist(i) = \sum_{n=0}^{N-1} \sum_{m=0}^{M-1} R(n,m) \oplus T(i+n,m) \qquad (12)$$

where, $dist(i)$ denotes the distance of the i-th frame between the referenced template and the object template, $R(n,m)$ denotes the bit flag of the object template in the n-th frame and m-th frequency bin, and $T(n,m)$ is the bit flag of the referenced template in the n-th frame and m-th frequency bin.

Thus, the similarity between the referenced template and object template can be computed as

$$S(i) = 1 - dist(i) / (N * M) \tag{13}$$

3.1.4. *Experiment and Analysis*

The experiments on the DSC-based quick audio search algorithm have been conducted based on the recordings of actual TV programs. We picked out 211 different commercial advertisement templates with different durations from actual TV broadcasts and edited a 15.3-hour test set of TV programs in which each advertisement template may randomly occur several times. In the audio feature extraction process, the audio of the recording was first digitized at 8 kHz sampling frequency and 16 bit quantization accuracy.

The experiments were conducted on a Pentium 4, 2.4GHz CPU, 256MB RAM workstation. The performance was evaluated in terms of average search accuracy (F1-measure) and search speed under different levels of distortion and different durations of audio clips. In order to generate the test set with various distortions, we used the CoolEdit tool to produce different levels of distortion. Table 10 lists the attributes of the basic test data, and Figure 9 shows the different levels of distortion:

Table 10. Test set setup.

TV	Test length (hour)	No. of advertisement templates	Duration of advertisement (seconds)		
			t<5s	5s≤t≤10s	t>10s
CETV	15.3	211	4	6	201

A comparison between the quick audio search algorithm with second verification (QAS&V) and the same search algorithm without second verification (QAS) was made. In order to test their robustness, we conducted the experiments under different distortion levels. Table 11 displays these results. We can see that the QAS&V approach is more robust than QAS with strong audio distortion.

Meanwhile, the search costs (in hours) of 211 target audio templates within a 15.3-hour test stream are shown in Table 12. It can be inferred that no significant

Table 11. The average accuracy (F1-measure) comparison with different distortions.

Method	**0db**	**-1db**	**-2db**	**-3db**	**-4db**	**-5db**
QAS	89.24%	75.57%	78.85%	70.1%	73.84%	71.18%
QAS&V	98.52%	97.53%	97.53%	96.51%	94.99%	92.3%

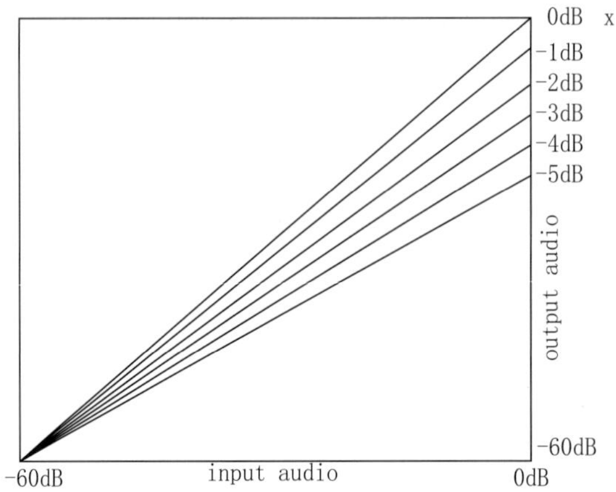

Fig. 9. Distortion of different levels.

Table 12. The search cost (in hours) of 211 advertisement templates in a 15.3-hour test stream.

Method	**0dB**	**-1dB**	**-2dB**	**-3dB**	**-4dB**	**-5dB**	**Ave**
QAS	0.67	0.67	0.46	0.56	0.43	0.50	0.54
QAS&V	0.69	0.71	0.66	0.67	0.61	0.64	0.66

additional time is taken by conducting a second verification, and that our quick audio search algorithm can indeed carry out a fast search for a target audio clip.

3.2. *Application Systems*

Based on the above quick audio search technique, we have developed two CBAR systems: the TV/Broadcasting Advertisement Monitoring (CASIA-AdM) system, and the Digital Content Management and Retrieval (CASIA-DCMR) platform. Figures 10 and 11 display the screenshots of these systems respectively.

The CASIA-AdM system can monitor multiple channels of TV programs online. The accuracy achieved is above 98%. This system has been practically and successfully applied by tens of departments of industry and business administration in China.

The CASIA-DCMR system is a digital media management platform supporting various digital media content tagging, editing and retrieval, including audio, music, video, image, and textual information. It is based on a distributed client-server architecture. The system also supports more interactive functions such as digital media information browsing, AV playback, content summary, information customizing, and so on.

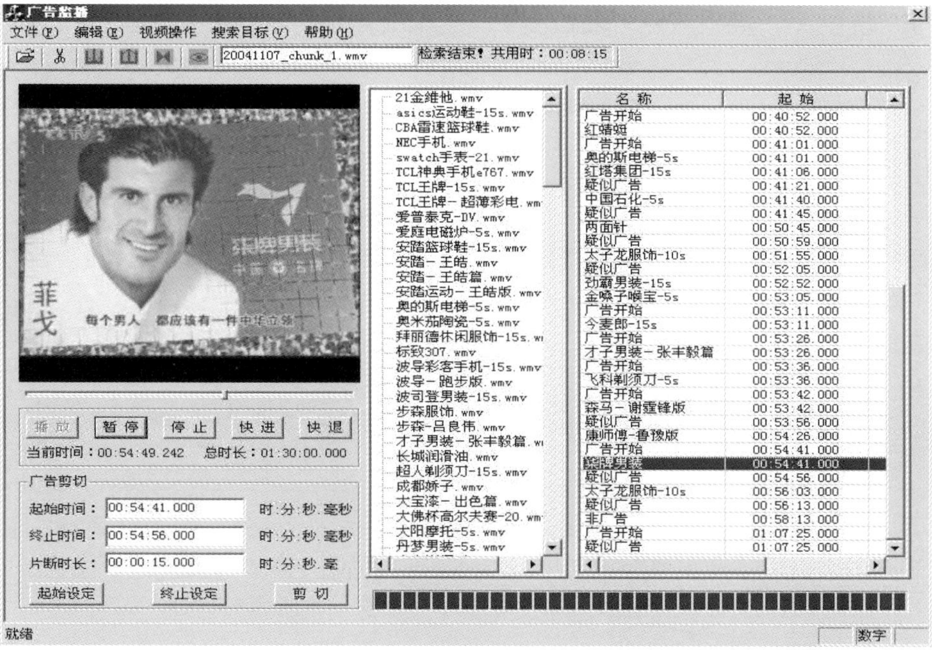

Fig. 10. CASIA TV/broadcasting Ad. Monitoring system.

4. Conclusion

Audio signals contain rich and important information that describe the digital media content at the semantic level. Thus, interests and activities in audio-based digital media content management and retrieval has been growing in recent years. ADCMR integrates techniques developed in speech and audio signal processing, pattern classification, machine learning, database management, information retrieval, and distributed computing, among others. It therefore creates many new research directions. In this chapter, we introduced our recent work in TAIR and CBAR, which are the two important branches of ADCMR, and some of their potential applications. Beyond this chapter, there are many more interesting topics relating to ADCMR, like audio fingerprint or identification, musical information retrieval, and music genre classification.

5. Acknowledgements

We would like to thank Dr. Sheng Gao of the Institute for Infocomm Research, Singapore, Mr. Shilei Zhang, Mr. Hongchen Jiang, Dr. Wei Liang, Dr. Jiaen Liang, Dr. Peng Ding, and Mr. Rong Zheng from the NLPR lab of CASIA for their contributions to the work.

Fig. 11. A page of digital content management and retrieval (CASIA-DCMR) platform.

References

1. M. Christel, T. Kanade, M. Mauldin, R. Reddy, M. Sirbu, S. Stevens, and H. Wactlar, "Informedia Digital Video Library," *Commun. ACM*, vol. 38, pp. 57–58, (1995).
2. J. Makhoul, F. Kubala, T. Leek, D. Liu, L. Nguyen, R. Schwartz, and A. Srivastava, "Speech and Language Technologies for Audio Indexing and Retrieval," in *Proc. IEEE*, vol. 88, (2000), pp. 1338–1353.
3. M. Maybury, "Intelligent Multimedia for the New Millennium," in *Proc. Eurospeech99*, vol. 1, (Budapest, Hungary, 1999), pp. 1–15.
4. J.-L. Gauvain, L. Lamel, and G. Adda, "Transcribing Broadcast News for Audio and Video Indexing," *Communications of the ACM*, vol. 43, (2000).
5. [Online]. Available: http://www.podzinger.com/
6. L.-S. Lee and B. Chen, "Spoken Document Understanding and Organization," *IEEE Signal Processing Magazine*, vol. 22, pp. 42–60, (2005).
7. B. Zhou and J. Hansen, "Efficient Audio Stream Segmentation via T2 Statistic Based Bayesian Information Criterion," *IEEE Trans. on Speech Audio Processing*, vol. 13, (2005).
8. ——, "Unsupervised Audio Stream Segmentation and Clustering via the Bayesian Information Criterion," in *Proc. ICSLP00*, (2000), pp. 714–717.
9. L. Lu and H. Zhang, "Real-Time Unsupervised Speaker Change Detection," in *Proc. ICPR*, (2002), pp. 358–361.
10. P. Delacourt and C.-J. Wellekens, "DISTBIC: A Speaker Based Segmentation for Audio Data Indexing," *Speech Communication*, vol. 32, pp. 111–126, (2000).
11. S. Cheng and H. Wang, "A Sequential Metric-Based Audio Segmentation Method via the Bayesian Information Criterion," in *Proc. Eurospeech'03*, (2003).
12. ——, "METRIC-SEQDAC: A Hybrid Approach for Audio Segmentation," in *Proc. ICSLP'04*, (2004).

13. S. Zhang, S. Zhang, and B. Xu, "A Two-Level Method for Unsupervised Speaker-Based Audio Segmentation," in *Proc. ICPR'06*, (2006).
14. J. Ajmera, *Robust Audio Segmentation*. PhD Thesis, (2004).
15. S. Chen and P. Gopalakrishnan, "Speaker, Environment and Channel Change Detection and Clustering via the Bayesian Information Criterion," *DARPA Broadcast News Trans. and Under. Workshop*, (1998).
16. B.-Y. Ricardo and R.-N. Berthier, *Modern information retrieval*. Addison-Wesley, (1999).
17. S. Srinivasan, D. Petkovic, and D. Ponceleon, "Towards Robust Features for Classifying Audio in the Cue Video System," in *Proc. ACM Multimedia*, (1999).
18. Kimber and L. Wilcox, "Acoustic Segmentation for Audio Browsers," in *Computing Science and Statistics: Graph-Image-Vision: Proc. 28th Symposium on the Interface*, vol. 28, (1997), pp. 295–304.
19. T. Zhang and C.-C.-J. Kuo, "Audio Content Analysis for Online Audiovisual Data Segmentation and Classification," *IEEE Trans. on Speech and Audio Processing*, vol. 3, (2001).
20. J. H. Z. Liu, Y. Wang, and T. Chen, "Audio Feature Extraction and Analysis for Scene Classification," *IEEE Signal Processing Society Workshop on Multimedia Signal Processing*, (1997).
21. L. Lu, H.-J. Zhang, and S. Li, "Content-Based Audio Classification and Segmentation by Using Support Vector machines," *ACM Multimedia Systems Journal*, vol. 8, pp. 482–492, (2003).
22. H. Jiang, J. Bai, S. Zhang, and B. Xu, "SVM-Based Audio Scene Classification," in *Proc. IEEE NLP-KE'05*, (Wuhan, 2005), pp. 131–137.
23. Gouyon, F. Pachet, and F. Delerue, "On the Use of Zero-Crossing Rate for an Application of Classification of Percussive Sounds," in *Proc. COST G-6 Conference on Digital Audio Effects (DAFX-00)*, (2000).
24. G. Williams and D. Ellis, "Speech/Music Discrimination Based on Posterior Probability Features," in *Proc. Eurospeech '99*, (1999).
25. Scheirer and M. Slaney, "Construction and Evaluation of a Robust Multifeature Music/Speech Discriminator," in *Proc. ICASSP'97*, (1997).
26. 高升, 徐波, and 黄泰翼, "基于决策树的汉语三音子模型," 声学学报, vol. 25, pp. 504–509, (2000).
27. J. Liang, M. Meng, X. Wang, P. Ding, and B. Xu, "An Improved Mandarin Keyword Spotting System Using mce Training and Context-Enhanced Verification," in *Proc. ICASSP*, (2006), pp. 1145–1148.
28. R. Zheng, S. Zhang, and B. Xu, "A Comparative Study of Feature and Score Normalization for Speaker Verification," in *Lecture Notes in Computer Science*, vol. 3832, pp. 531–538.
29. Nist speaker recognition evaluation plans. [Online]. Available: http://www.nist.gov/speech/tests/spk/index.htm
30. V. N. Vapnik, *The Nature of Statistical Learning Theory*. Springer, Second Edition, (1995).
31. 周梁, 高鹏, 丁鹏, and 徐波, "语音识别准确率与检索性能的关联性研究," in *Proc.* 第二届全国信息检索与内容安全学术会议*(NCIRCS'05)*, (2005).
32. E.-B. Wold, T. Keislar, and J. Wheaton, "Content-Based Classification, Search and Retrieval of Audio," *IEEE Multimedia Magazine*, vol. 3, pp. 27–36, (1996).
33. J. Foote, "Content-Based Retrieval of Music and Audio," in *Proc. SPIE Multimedia Storage Archiving Systems II*, vol. C.-C.-J. Kuo et al., Eds., (1997), pp. 138–147.
34. G. Smith, H. Murase, and K. Kashino, "Quick Audio Retrieval Using Active Rearch," in *Proc. IEEE International Conference on Acoustics, Speech and Signal Processing (ICASSP'98)*, vol. 6, (1998), pp. 3777–3780.
35. C. Spevak and E. Favreau, "Soundspotter - A Prototype System for Content-Based Audio

Retrieval," in *Proc. 5th International Conference on Digital Audio Effects (DAFx-02)*, (Hamburg, 2002).
36. S. Gao, C.-H. Lee, and Y.-W. Zhu, "An Unsupervised Learning Approach to Music Event Detection," in *Proc. IEEE International Conference on Multimedia and Expo (ICME)*, (2004), pp. 1307–1310.
37. W. Liang, S. Zhang, and B. Xu, "A Histogram Algorithm for Fast Audio Retrieval," in *Proc. ISMIR'05*, (London, 2005), pp. 586–589.

CHAPTER 20

MULTILINGUAL DIALOG SYSTEMS

Helen M. Meng
Department of Systems Engineering & Engineering Management
The Chinese University of Hong Kong, Shatin, N.T., Hong Kong
E-mail:hmmeng@se.cuhk.edu.hk

Spoken dialog systems demonstrate a high degree of usability in many restricted domains, and these range from air travel, train schedules, restaurant guides, ferry timetables, electronic automobile classifieds, weather information and email access. A user typically interacts with these systems to retrieve certain information for example a train schedule; or to complete a task, such as booking a flight, reserving a restaurant table, or finding an apartment. Dialog modeling in these systems plays an important role in assisting users to achieve their goals effectively. This chapter presents an introduction to multilingual dialog systems in two parts: the first part describes the key components of a multilingual dialog system, using an illustrative example based on the CU FOREX system. The second part introduces the various kinds of dialog models, highlights the advantages of the mixed-initiative dialog model, and presents a possible data-driven approach for its implementation.

1. Introduction

Spoken dialog systems demonstrate a high degree of usability in many restricted domains and these range from air travel,[1] railway information,[2] restaurant guides,[3] ferry timetables,[4] weather information,[5] electronic automobile classifieds,[6] electronic assistants[7] and tourist information.[8] The user typically interacts with these systems to retrieve certain domain-specific information. The system attempts to "understand" the user's informational goal, retrieve the relevant information from a database and generates a verbal response of the information in order to reply to the user's request. The main languages concerned include English as well as a number of European languages. A few systems have also been developed for Mandarin Chinese.[9] A typical spoken dialog system includes these key components:

- *Automatic speech recognition*: This component recognizes the user's input speech and transcribes it into text. Multilingual speech recognizers are used to support multilingual spoken input.
- *Natural language understanding*: This component analyzes the textual transcription to generate a meaning representation for the user's input. Multilingual grammars are used to support the "understanding" of multilingual speech input. The semantic (i.e. meaning) representation generated, however, is largely independent of the languages that are used.
- *Application manager*: This component may incorporate necessary elements from the discourse history and also perform database retrieval based on the user's request.
- *Dialog modeling*: Based on the user's request, the dialog history and the retrieved information (possibly raw data), this component plans out an appropriate response in correspondence to the user's request and thus controls how the dialog progresses.
- *Natural language generation*: Based on the output of the dialog model, this component generates a verbalized form of the response message.
- *Text-to-speech synthesis*: this component generates synthetic speech based on the input text from the natural language generation component to form the spoken response to the user.

This chapter offers an introduction to multilingual dialog systems and is divided into two parts. The first part presents a detailed description of the key components of a multilingual dialog system (listed above), drawing upon an illustrative example for the sake of clarity. The second part introduces the main types of dialog models and describes the advantages of the mixed-initiative dialog model as well as a possible data-driven approach for its implementation.

PART I — OVERVIEW WITH AN ILLUSTRATIVE EXAMPLE

2. The CU FOREX System

In this section, we will illustrate the key components of a spoken dialog system in the context of CU FOREX – a telephone inquiry system for real-time foreign exchange (FOREX) information. This domain is well-suited for Hong Kong, as the region has one of the largest foreign exchange trading centers in the world. The scope of our initial system covers the globally-traded currencies included in the Reuters data feed. The global nature of this application is appropriate for the development of a multilingual application. As mentioned earlier, we have also chosen to support telephone access via fixed-line and cellular phones. Special considerations have also been devoted to the following aspects in CU FOREX:

- Multilingualism – we cover English and two major dialects of Chinese, namely Cantonese and Putonghua.
- Affordance in dialog design – we aim to support effective interaction for novice users by using directed dialogs and for expert users by using natural language shortcuts.

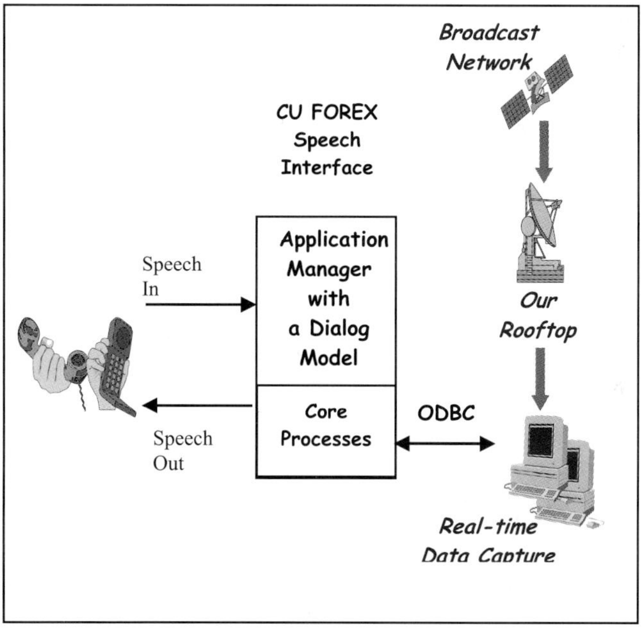

Fig. 1. Overall architecture of CU FOREX system.

CU FOREX supports inquiries on foreign exchange, including the bid/ask exchange rates between two currencies, and deposit interest rates for a particular currency at various time durations (twenty four hours, one week, one month, two months, up to one year). Figure 1 presents a conceptual illustration of the system.

The system receives a dedicated real-time data feed from Reuters through a satellite dish mounted on the rooftop of our building. We have developed a software data capture component that continuously updates a relational database (SQL server) with the real-time data. The CU FOREX system communicates with this database via ODBC. Users can call up via a fixed-line phone or a cellular phone, and converse with the system to inquire about foreign currency rates. In order to support such an interaction, these core technologies are included:

- *Multilingual speech recognition* for Cantonese, Putonghua and English (the common languages used in Hong Kong);
- *Natural language understanding* to derive semantic meaning based on the user's spoken language input;
- *A dialog model* that determines a planned response in guiding the progress of the dialog;
- *A natural language generation* module that verbalizes the response message and relevant data in textual form (Chinese or English); and
- *A concatenative text-to-speech synthesizer* to synthesize multilingual speech (Cantonese, Putonghua or English) based on the response messages mentioned above.

The following subsections present an elaboration of these components.

2.1. *Speech Recognition*

The speech recognition component can handle utterances of keywords as well as a full sentence or phrase, in any of the three languages. The Cantonese transcription is based on the LSHK standard[10] and contains tonal information, for example, "美金" (US dollar) is pronounced as the two-syllable word /mei3_gam1/ in Cantonese, where the numbers refer to tones.[a] The Putonghua transcription is based on Pinyin and also contains tonal information, for example, "美金", is pronounced as the two-syllable word /mei3_jin1/ in Putonghua, where the numbers also refer to the tones of the syllables.[b] The English transcription adopts the ARPABET phonetic labels. The vocabulary has approximately 500 entries, covering country and currency names in the foreign exchange domain, as well as their (colloquial) variations, e.g. the "greenback" for "US Dollar". The CU FOREX speech recognizer contains a single set of acoustic models that is trained on a corpus of mixed fixed-line and cellular phone speech data.

2.2. *Natural Language Understanding*

We have developed parallel context-free grammars for natural language understanding, one for English and the other for Chinese. This is necessary as

---

[a] There are six lexical tones in Cantonese.

[b] There are four lexical tones in Putonghua, as well as a light tone.

English and Chinese have rather different word orders. As an illustration, consider the following query pairs:

English:What is the exchange rate between the US dollar and the Hong Kong dollar?
Chinese: 我想問美金兌港幣的匯率係幾多
Approximate Translation for the Chinese query:
<US dollar><versus><HK dollar><exchange rate>

The grammar rules specify the semantics and syntax that can be understood by the CU FOREX system. The grammar can accommodate minor disfluencies in the input, like "um", "ah"; by virtue of robust parsing.[11] Natural language understanding is bypassed should the user select a directed dialog interaction. In a directed dialog interaction, the user inputs only one informational attribute per dialog turn.

2.3. *Dialog Modeling*

The system provides a directed dialog (DD) interaction for novice users, and a shortcut natural language (NL) interaction for expert users. The dialog structure is consistent across the two languages. Some example dialogs are shown in Tables 1 and 2. The DD guides the user through a session, and elucidates what may be said at various stages of the interaction. System feedback to the user is enriched by the use of *audio icons* to help distinguish the various menu choices. Novice users may also take control and self-navigate around the dialog tree by the use of meta-commands, which include:

- HELP 求助: context-sensitive help instructions
- REPEAT 重覆: repeat the last generated response
- START AGAIN 重新開始: return to the main menu
- CHANGE LANGUAGE 轉換語言: switch to the other language and start again from the main menu
- GOODBYE 拜拜: end the session

More details will be provided for dialog modeling in later sessions of this chapter. The NL interaction is tailored for expert users who wish to expedite the inquiry session by uttering a full query, and traverse the entire session within one interaction. Hence the query may carry multiple attributes for database retrieval, as opposed to a single attribute per utterance in the directed dialog case.

Table 1. Example of a directed dialog (DD) interaction.

System	Welcome to CU FOREX Hotline. Which language would you prefer, "Cantonese", "Putonghua", or "English"? 歡迎致電寰宇之聲.請講出你想用的語言廣東話', '普通話', 定係 '英文'?
Caller	English
System	This system will guide you through a directed dialog to accomplish your inquiry. Main Menu. Would you like "exchange rates" or "interest rates"?
Caller	Interest rate.
System	Interest rate menu. Which currency are you interested in?
Caller	<unrecognized>
System	Sorry, I didn't understand you. Please say the currency name or the country name again.
Caller	Australian Dollar.
System	I think you said Australian Dollar. Is that correct? Please say "yes" or "no".
Caller	Yes.
System	Would you like deposit durations for twenty four hours, one month.... or one year? Or, you can say "all of them" to hear all the interest rate quotes.
Caller	One month.
System	The quotes we provide are for reference only. Interest rates, Australian dollar for one month is four point nine. Main menu. Please select "exchange rates" or "interest rates".
Caller	Change language.
System	請問你想查詢邊種服務,'外幣匯率'定係 '存款利率' (English Translation: Would you like "exchange rates" or "interest rates"?)
Caller	外幣滙率 (English Translation: Exchange rates)
System	請問你想查的匯率是兌港幣還是兌其他外幣? (English Translation: Would you like exchange rate against the HK dollars or other currencies?)
Caller	兌港幣 (English Translation: Against the HK dollar)
System	請問你想查詢邊種貨幣的匯率? (English Translation: Which currency are you interested in?)
Caller	星加坡元 (English Translation: Singapore Dollar)
System	以下資料只供參考. 星加坡元兌港幣,買入價係 1.087,賣出價係 1.086. (English Translation: The quotes we provide are for reference only. Exchanges rates, Singapore dollar to Hong Kong dollar, the buying rate is 1.087, the selling rate is 1.086)

Table 2. Example of Natural Language (NL) interaction.

System	Welcome to CU FOREX Hotline. Which language would you prefer, "Cantonese", "Putonghua", or "English"? 歡迎致電寰宇之聲.請講出你想用的語言: 廣東話', '普通話', 定係 '英文'?
Caller	English
System	This system can handle a full question for your inquiry. Main Menu. What kind of currency information are you interested in?
Caller	I'd like to know the exchange rate between the Greenback and the New Zealand dollar please.
System	The quotes we provide are for reference only. Exchange rate. US Dollar to Deutsche Mark. The buying rate is one point six four. The selling rate is one point six three. What kind of currency information are you interested in?
Caller	Change language.
System	請講出你想查詢的外滙資料. (English Translation: Which kind of currency information are you interested in?)
Caller	澳幣 一星期的存款利率 (English Translation: Interest rate of the Australian dollar for one week.)
System	以下資料只供參考 澳幣一星期存款利率係 4.82 (English Translation: The quotes we provide are for reference only. Interest rate, Australian dollar for one week is four point eight two.)

2.4. *Response Generation*

Both the DD and NL interactions produce a semantic frame to invoke database access. Generation of the response message that carries the retrieved data is achieved by a template-based approach. The response message is then synthesized into speech using off-the-shelf English and Putonghua synthesizers, as well as a home-grown concatenative Cantonese speech synthesizer.[c]

3. Evaluation

CU FOREX was made available to the public for experimentation. We ran two phone lines constantly throughout the day – one for the directed dialog interaction and the other for the shortcut, natural language interaction. Calls were recorded at certain times and the data acquired were then used for usability studies. We recruited 89 subjects[d] over a three-week period to conduct system evaluation. All our subjects were interacting with a spoken language system for the first time. They were asked to refer to the system's webpage[e] to obtain some brief information about the system. Each subject was asked to formulate several

[c] www.se.cuhk.edu.hk/hccl/cuforex/
[d] Our evaluators are students from The Chinese University of Hong Kong.
[e] http://www.se.cuhk.edu.hk/hccl/demos/cu_forex

foreign exchange queries prior to calling the system. They were also asked to speak naturally to the system without reading, to record occurrences of system errors, and to note whether the system was able to recover from these errors. In addition, we encouraged the subjects to offer suggestions for possible usability improvements. All calls from the subjects were recorded and logged. Our analysis is based on system logs, as well as questionnaires returned to us by these subjects. Since only a small number of the call-in subjects spoke Putonghua, we conducted the analysis mainly for Cantonese and English. We received a total of 423 foreign exchange queries in all, with a breakdown tabulated in Table 3.

Table 3. Breakdown of queries from our evaluators. *Ex.* and *Int.* stand for Exchange Rate and Interest Rate queries respectively.

Directed Dialog Queries: 277				**Natural Language Queries**: 146			
Cantonese: 112		*English*: 165		*Cantonese*: 56		*English*: 90	
Ex.	Int.	Ex.	Int.	Ex.	Int.	Ex.	Int.
76	36	88	77	33	23	53	37

3.1. *The KAPPA Statistic*

We adopted the kappa statistic (κ) to evaluate system performance in task completion. The use of kappa for task evaluation was proposed in the PARADISE framework,[12] which pointed out that kappa includes considerations in task complexity. As an illustration, consider one of the subtasks in the CU FOREX domain – identification of the desired deposit duration. Possible values to this attribute include 24 hours, 1 month, 2 months, 3 months, 6 months, 9 months and 1 year. The system is successful in this subtask if the duration it identifies matches the duration uttered by the user. This information can be represented in an attribute value matrix (AVM) – the rows in the matrix represent the actual deposit duration uttered by the user, and the columns represent the deposit duration elicited from the system. If our system receives a total number of T calls with inquiries on deposit interest rates and if our system correctly identifies all the deposit durations, then all the non-zero counts will lie along the matrix diagonal, i.e. $n_{11} + n_{22} \ldots + n_{77} = T$.

If our system simply performs random selection of deposit durations, regardless of the actual spoken input from the user, then we may still be able to observe chance agreements in our AVM. The expected proportion of random agreement across the set of attributes should be $P(E)$:

$$P(E) = \sum_{i=1}^{n} \left(\frac{C_i}{T}\right)^2 \quad (1)$$

where C_i is the total count.

The kappa statistic (κ) evaluates task success by computing the proportion of counts on the diagonal of the AVM, i.e. $P(A)$, and corrects for chance agreement,

$$P(A) = \frac{\sum_{i=1}^{n} AVM(i,i)}{T} \tag{2}$$

$$K = \frac{P(A) - P(E)}{1 - P(E)} \tag{3}$$

as shown in Equations (2) and (3).

The full set of attributes in the CU FOREX task includes LANGUAGE, EXCHANGE_RATE, INTEREST_RATE, CURRENCY_TO_BUY, CURRENCY_TO_SELL, CURRENCY_FOR_DEPOSIT and TIME_DURATION. The attribute values include bilingual lexical items. The AVM should be expanded to encompass all these attributes for evaluating the full task. Kappa values may be computed based only on the DD interactions (i.e. the AVM only stores the counts from the DD interactions), or only on the NL interactions. Alternatively, kappa values may be computed separately based on the exchange rate inquiries or interest rate inquiries.

3.2. *Comparison between Interaction Styles*

A comparison was made between the DD interaction style and the NL interaction style. We expected the recognition task through the DD style to be easier and the recognition performance more accurate, leading to a better task completion performance and larger kappa value. We have also measured the average transaction time per interaction session. Results are shown in Table 4.

Table 4. Comparison between two interaction styles in terms of success rate and transaction times for task completion.

Task Completion	Directed Dialog Interaction	Natural Language Interaction
Kappa statistic (κ)	0.938	0.876
Average Transaction Time	2 min 9 sec	1 min 57 sec

From Table 4 we see that the kappa value for DD is larger than NL by approximately 7%. Analysis shows that the inferior performance of NL is due to (i) the greater difficulty in recognizing full queries versus keyword-based utterances; (ii) the absence of re-confirmation in the NL interaction and (iii) parse failures on the recognized query.

Task failures were mostly caused by recognition errors, out-of-domain queries (e.g. the "Finland Markka"), and parse failures from the NL interaction. Spoken disfluencies (e.g. false starts, filled pauses, repairs, etc.) may have caused spurious or incorrect vocabulary items to be inserted by the recognizer, in such a way that it outputs a sentence that cannot be parsed. Spoken disfluencies are frequently observed in our recordings. Some examples include:

- "um…What can I say…what is the interest rate of Yen?"
- "Tell me … ah… what is the exchange rate of Yen against Hong Kong Dollar?"
- "What is the exchange rate of um…US Dollar?"

The first two examples were correctly handled by our system. The third example was recognized incorrectly as requesting the exchange rate between a currency and the US Dollar – the NL interaction style was able to parse the misrecognized output and the system gave the corresponding (incorrect) response.

Average transaction time for the DD interaction is 12 seconds longer than for the NL interaction, which implies that NL expedites the transaction to some extent. The perceived speed-up due to NL is reduced by the longer latency in recognizing a full query over a short keyword. Our system takes an average of seven seconds to recognize a full query, and three seconds to recognize a keyword.

The above is an overview of a spoken dialog system in the context of a case study, the CU FOREX system. In the next part of this chapter, we will address in detail the design and implementation of a dialog model.

PART II — DIALOG MODELING

In the second half of the chapter, we delve deeper into the details of dialog model design and implementation. Dialog modeling plays an important role in assisting users to achieve their goals effectively. The system-initiative dialog model assumes complete control in providing step-wise guidance for the user through an interaction. At each step, the model elucidates what the user may say or input into the system. The system-initiative model does not permit deviations from the pre-set course of interaction, but such restrictions also help attain high rates of task completion. Conversely, the user-initiative model offers maximum flexibility for the user to determine his preferred course of interaction. With this type of interaction, it may be difficult to elucidate the system's scope of competence to the user. Should the user's request fall outside of this scope, the system may fail to help the user fulfill his goal. To strike a balance between the system-initiative and user-initiative models, the mixed-initiative dialog model allows both the user and the system to influence the course of interaction. It is possible to handcraft a sophisticated mixed-initiative dialog flow, but the task is expensive, and may become intractable for complex application domains.

4. Recent Approaches in Dialog Modeling

Recent research efforts in dialog modeling attempt to reduce manual handcrafting by adopting data-driven approaches. Dialog design is formulated as a stochastic optimization problem, where machine learning techniques are applied to learn the "optimal" dialog strategy from training data. For example, ergodic hidden Markov models have been applied,[13] and reinforcement learning based on a Markov decision process[14,15] was used to learn the dialog process with states, actions and sequential decisions that is optimal from the perspective of a reward/cost function.[12] This function is dependent on factors such as user satisfaction, task completion rate, user effort, etc.

An alternative approach involves the use of belief networks (BNs) for modeling dialog interactions. Pulman[16] proposed to use the BN framework to model the mental states of dialog participants and changes in the mental states along with incoming evidence connected to utterances in a conversation. He argued that the BNs provide a probabilistic and decision-theoretic framework for modeling dialog, and the framework is plausible for computational implementation. Horvitz[17] applied BNs to infer the user's intention and attention in a mixed-initiative interaction, combined with the maximization of expected user utility when the computer selects the "best" response or action. This framework has been demonstrated in the implementation of a virtual front desk receptionist and also an appointment scheduling agent.[18,19]

5. Use of Belief Networks for Dialog Modeling

We propose to utilize BN in mixed-initiative interactions. As can be seen in the case study, there is a multitude of ways in which the user can express his domain-specific informational goal(s) in natural (spoken) language. Furthermore, the expression may span multiple utterances in the dialog interaction. BNs are used to infer the user's informational goal based on the semantics of a query expression that is either self-contained or dependent on the discourse context. In addition, effective database retrieval for a given informational goal may require a set of necessary attributes. If this set of attributes is fully specified in the user's query, the interaction should conclude with successful task completion. However, if there are attributes missing from the query expression, the application manager may search for values for such attributes in previous dialog turns, which constitutes the process of discourse inheritance.[f] If the discourse history yields no information, the mixed-initiative dialog model should automatically prompt the user for the attribute value. Alternatively, there may be spurious attributes in the query expression – these may be optional attributes specified by the user or attributes resulting from speech recognition errors. The mixed-initiative dialog model should automatically clarify such spurious attributes with the user. Hence prompting and clarification are the dialog acts[20] of focus in this work. We believe that BNs offer several advantages to the dialog modeling problem:

(i) BN probabilities can be automatically trained from available data. Automation eases portability across domains and scalability to more complex domains. The user's informational goal can be identified by probabilistic inference in the BNs.
(ii) The BN topology can also be automatically learned from training data. The topology can capture the inter-node dependencies in the BN, where each node represents a semantic concept characterizing the knowledge domain.
(iii) Belief propagation within a BN corresponds to computing the probability of events that can be used for reasoning. This procedure enables automatic detection of missing and spurious concepts which can drive the mixed-initiative dialog model. The procedure is also suitable for belief revision as the discourse evolves in the course of the dialog interaction.
(iv) The BN framework is amenable to the optional incorporation of human knowledge should training data be sparse. For example, the BN topology may be handcrafted, learned from training data, or both. Similarly, BN probabilities may be trained or assigned/refined by hand, according to the developer's "degree of belief" in inter-node dependencies.

5.1. *Inference of Informational Goals*

An incoming user's request is processed by the speech recognition and natural language understanding (NLU) modules prior to reaching the dialog model. NLU involves the interpretation of the user's input query into a series of domain-specific *semantic concepts*, and from these we infer the *informational goal* of the user's query. Semantic concepts correspond to the pieces of information that are

[f] Discourse inheritance is a research problem in and of itself. As an initial step, our system inherits all attributes from the previous dialog turn and records the latest value for each attribute over the course of the dialog. This is done unless the user explicitly request disinheritance by commands such as "clear history" or "start over".

relevant to the application (as described in Section 2.2). An information goal is the service or the information requested by the user. It is assumed that within a restricted application domain, there is a finite set of (M) semantic concepts as well as a finite set of (N) informational goals. The goals G_i and concepts C_j are all binary, and the concept C_j is true if it appears in the utterance. Hence, we can formulate the NLU problem as making N binary decisions with N BNs, one for each informational goal. The BN for goal G_i takes as input a set of semantic concepts $\overline{C}$ [g] extracted from the user's query. The BN gives the *a posteriori* probability $P(G|\overline{C})$ and from this, the binary decision is made by thresholding. The topology of the BN may assume conditional independence among the concepts in $\overline{C}$ i.e., there are direct links between the goal and the concept nodes, but no linkages among the concepts nodes. This is equivalent to a naïve Bayes formulation, and is illustrated in Figure 2.

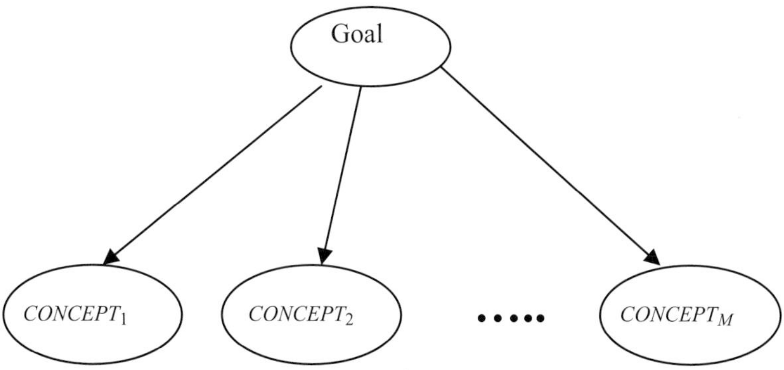

Fig. 2. The basic topology for our belief networks (BNs). This topology assumes conditional independence among concepts. The arrows of the acyclic graph are drawn from cause to effect. This topology is equivalent to the naïve Bayes formulation.[21]

Goal inference based on $P(G|\overline{C})$ may be computed as shown in Equation (4) with the conditional independence assumption. As mentioned, this is equivalent to the naïve Bayes formulation and Equation (4) simply applies Bayes' rule. We assume that the goal G_i is present if $P(G_i|\overline{C})$ is greater than a threshold θ; and that the goal G_i is absent otherwise. θ may be set to 0.5 for simplicity since $P(G_i=0|\overline{C})+P(G_i=1|\overline{C})=1$. This formulation provides us with a means of rejecting out-of-domain (OOD) queries – a query is classified as OOD when all BNs vote negative for their corresponding goals. In addition, the formulation also

---

[g] $\overline{C}$ represents a concept vector.

accommodates queries with multiple goals, i.e. when multiple BNs vote positive. We may also force the selection of a single goal (even when multiple BNs vote positive) by applying the maximum *a posteriori* rule.

$$P(G_i = 1 | \overline{C} = \frac{P(\overline{C} | G_i = 1) P(G_i = 1)}{P(\overline{C})}$$

$$= \frac{\prod_{k=1}^{M} P(C_k | G_i = 1) P(G_i = 1)}{\prod_{k=1}^{M} P(C_k | G_i = 0) P(G_i = 0) + \prod_{k=1}^{M} P(C_k | G_i = 1) P(G_i = 1)} \quad (4)$$

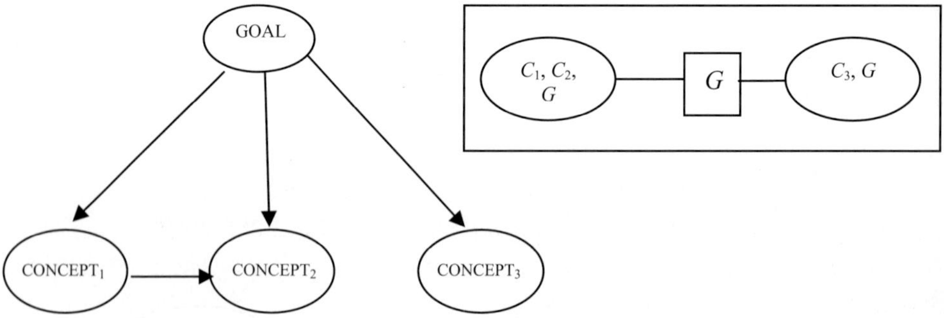

Fig. 3. The trained topology for our belief networks (BNs). This topology captures the casual dependencies between the goal and a concept as well as between two concepts. The arrows of the acyclic graph are drawn from cause to effect. Dependencies among concepts are automatically learned from training data according to the minimum description length (MDL) principle. The inset shows the cliques of the network. The two cliques are (C_1, C_2, G) and (C_3, G). G is the separator node between the two cliques.

For trained BN topologies similar to that shown in Figure 3, probability propagation for goal inference is more complex than shown in Equation (4). We provide a brief explanation here. Take the BN in Figure 3 as an example, there are two *cliques* (i.e. maximal sets of nodes that are all linked pairwise) –(G, C_1, C_2) and (G, C_3). This is illustrated in the inset of the figure, which also shows that the cliques can communicate through the separator node G. Each clique relates to a joint probability $P(G | \overline{C})$. For example, in Figure 3 the clique (G, C_1, C_2) relates to the joint probability $P(G, C_1, C_2)$ and the clique (G, C_3) relates to the joint probability $P(G, C_3)$. Given a user's query, we derive the presence and absence of the various concepts $\overline{C}$, and update the joint probability according to

Equation (5). The updated joint probability is eventually marginalized to produce a probability for goal identification $(P^*(G))$.

$$P^*(G_i,\overline{C}) = P(G_i \mid \overline{C})P^*(\overline{C}) = P(G_i,\overline{C})\frac{P^*(\overline{C})}{P(\overline{C})} \tag{5}$$

where $P^*(\overline{C})$ is instantiated according to the presence or absence of the concepts in the user's query, $P(G_i,\overline{C})$ is the joint probability obtained from the training set, and $P^*(G_i,\overline{C})$ is the updated joint probability. The asterisk denotes an updated probability with knowledge about the presence/absence of the various concepts in the user's query.

Figure 4 illustrates the process of computing the updated probability $P^*(G)$ for goal identification, using the BN in Figure 4 as an example. Detailed calculations may be found in another work.[22]

5.2. *Backward Inference*

We extend the above framework to enable the BNs to automatically detect missing or spurious concepts according to domain-specific constraints captured by their probabilities. Should a missing concept be detected, the BN will drive the dialog model to prompt the user for the necessary information. Should a spurious concept be detected the BN will drive the dialog model to clarify with the user regarding the unnecessary information. Automatic detection of missing and spurious concepts is achieved by the technique of *backward inference*.

Backward inference involves probability propagation within the BN. Having inferred the informational goal (G_i) for a given user's query, the goal node of the corresponding BN is instantiated (to either 1 or 0) to test the network's confidence in each of the input concepts. If the BN topology assumes conditional independence among the concepts, the updated probability of the concepts will simply be $P(C_j, G)$. However, in our BN in which the concepts depend on each other, the updated goal probability $P^*(G_i)$ will propagate to update the joint probabilities of each clique $P^*(\overline{C}, G_i)$. Thereafter we may obtain each $P^*(C_j)$ by marginalization. This procedure is described by Equation (6), and it is similar to the procedure described by Equation (5) for updating concept probabilities.

$$P^*(\overline{C},G_i) = P(\overline{C} \mid G_i)P^*(G_i) = P(\overline{C},G_i)\frac{P^*(G_i)}{P(G_i)} \tag{6}$$

Assume we know $C_1 = 1, C_2 = 1, C_3 = 0$ from the user's query, we would like to find the probability of G=1 for the query as follows:

Update the joint probability in the first clique. Since C_1 is present,

$$P^*(C_1 = 1) = 1$$

$$P^*(C_1 = 1, C_2 = 1, G = 1) = P(C_1 = 1, C_2 = 1, G = 1)\frac{P^*(C_1 = 1)}{P(C_1 = 1)}$$

↓

Since C_1 is known, we obtain $P^*(C_2 = 1, G = 1)$ from $P^*(C_2 = 1, G = 1, C_1)$

Marginalize $P^*(C_2 = 1, G)$ to obtain $P^*(C_2 = 1)$

↓

Update the joint probability in the first cliq ue, since C_2 is present,

$$P^{**}(C_2 = 1)$$

$$P^{**}(C_2 = 1, G = 1) = P^*(C_2 = 1, G = 1)\frac{P^{**}(C_2 = 1)}{P^*(C_2 = 1)}$$

↓

Marginalize $P^{**}(G = 1, C_2)$ to obtain $P^*(G = 1)$

↓

Propagate $P^*(G = 1)$ through the connecting node G to the second clique

↓

Update the joint probability in the second clique with $P^*(G = 1)$

$$P^*(C_3 = 0, G = 1) = P(C_3 = 0, G = 1)\frac{P^*(G = 1)}{P(G = 1)}$$

↓

Marginalize $P^*(C_3 = 0, G)$ to obtain $P^*(C_3 = 0,)$

↓

Update the joint probability in the second clique with $P^{**}(C_3 = 0,)$ because C_3 is absent

$$P^{**}(C_3 = 0, G = 1) = P^*(C_3 = 0, G = 1)\frac{P^{**}(C_3 = 0)}{P^*(C_3 = 0)}$$

↓

Marginalize $P^{**}(G = 1, C_3)$ to obtain $P^{**}(G = 1)$

Fig. 4. Probability propagation through the trained belief network topology as Figure 3, for inferring the informational goal G based on the input concepts C_1, C_2, and C_3.

where $P^*(G_i)$ is updated from instantiating the goal node, $P(\overline{C}, G_i)$ is the joint probability of the clique obtained from the training set, and $P^*(\overline{C}, G_i)$ is the updated joint probability of the clique.

Based on the value of $P^*(C_j)$, we make a binary decision (by thresholding) regarding whether C_j should be present or absent. This decision is compared to the actual occurrence of C_j in the user's query. If the binary decision indicates that C_j should be absent but it is actually present in the input query, the concept is labeled spurious and the dialog model will invoke a clarification act. If the binary decision indicates that C_j should be present but it is absent from the query, the concept is labeled missing and the dialog model will invoke a prompting act. In the following section, we demonstrate the applicability of this BN-based dialog model to a spoken language system in the foreign exchange domain.

6. Applicability to the CU FOREX System

We incorporated this BN-based dialog model into the CU FOREX System. Two BNs were developed one for each informational goal – exchange rate and interest rate. Each BN supports five domain-specific concepts as input – two currency concepts, time duration, exchange_rate and interest_rate. For database access, there are two domain-specific constraints:

- An exchange rate inquiry requires that the currencies to be bought and sold be specified.
- An interest rate inquiry requires that a currency and a time duration be specified.

We have also used the trained topology automatically learned according to the MDL principle.[23] The training data used here consists of a new set of 523 transcribed utterances collected from the NLS hotline, equally distributed between the exchange rate and interest rate inquiries. The resulting topology is illustrated in Figure 5. The dotted arrow shows the causal dependency between the concepts CURRENCY_1 and CURRENCY_2 learned from data. This network contains the cliques (GOAL, CURRENCY_1, CURRENCY_2), (GOAL, DURATION), (GOAL, EX_RATE) and (GOAL, INT_RATE).

Goal inference proceeds as described in the previous section. The decisions across the two BNs are combined to identify the output goal of the input query. Typical values of *a posteriori* probabilities obtained from goal inference are shown in Table 5. These values are compared with the threshold $\theta = 0.5$ for making binary decisions.

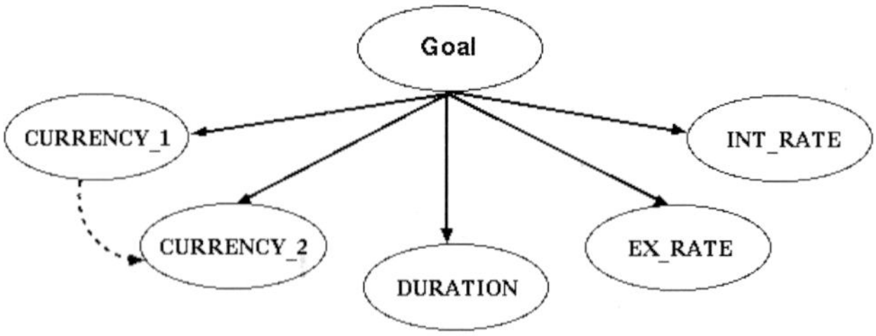

Fig. 5. The trained topology of our BNs in the CU FOREX domain. The EXCHANGE_RATE and INTEREST_RATE BNs have the same topology.

Table 5. Typical values of updated probabilities obtained from goal inference using BNs in the CU FOREX domain.

User: ***Can I have the exchange rate of the yen please?*** • Inference by the BN for Exchange Rates: *P*(Goal =*Exchange Rates*)* = 0.823 ➔ goal *present* • Inference by the BN for Interest Rates: *P*(Goal =*Interest Rates*)* = 0.256 ➔ goal *absent* Hence, the inferred goal is Exchange Rates.
User: ***Tell me about stock quotes*** • Inference by the BN for Exchange Rates: *P**(*Goal* =Exchange Rates) = 0.14 ➔ goal *absent* • Inference by the BN for Interest Rates: *P**(*Goal* =Interest Rates) = 0.13 ➔ goal absent Hence, the user's query is considered out-of-domain (OOD).

The single asterisk in $P^*(G)$ indicates that the probability of goal G has been updated during probability propagation in the BN. In reality, the $P^*(G)$ for this example has been updated four times (once for each clique). For the sake of simplicity, we use a single asterisk to indicate that a probability has been updated, regardless of the number of updates. Detailed calculations may be found in another work.[22] Having instantiated the inferred goal, backward inference verifies the validity of the input query against domain-specific constraints. In this way we can test for cases of missing or spurious concepts,[h] and generate an appropriate system response. Consider the example of an interest rate inquiry, "*Can I have the interest rates of the yen for one month please?*" We instantiated the goal node of the BN (for Interest Rates) to 1, and performed backward inference for each input concept C_j to obtain $P^*(C_j)$. This probability is compared with the threshold $\theta = 0.5$ to determine whether the concept should be present or absent.

[h] These may be due to speech recognition errors in an integrated spoken dialog system.

$$P^*(C_i) = \begin{bmatrix} \geq \theta \rightarrow C_i \text{ should be present in the given query with goal } G_i \\ < \theta \rightarrow C_i \text{ should be absent in the given query with goal } G_i \end{bmatrix}$$

The probabilities and binary decisions obtained in this example are shown in Table 6. The binary decision for each concept *agrees* with their actual occurrence in the input query. Thus we can use the concept-value pairs to form a semantic frame (see Figure 6), which can be further processed for database retrieval.

Table 6. The input query is "*Can I have the interest rates of the yen for one month please?*" Goal inference identifies that the underlying goal is Interest Rates. The goal node of the corresponding BN is instantiated, and backward inference produces $P^*(C_j)$ for each concept. These probabilities are compared with the threshold $\theta = 0.5$ to make a binary decision regarding the presence/absence for each concept. The binary decisions agree with the actual occurrences of the concepts.

Concept C_j	**$P^*(C_j)$**	**Binary Decision for C_j**	**Actual Occurrence for C_j**
currency_1	0.910	present	present
currency_2	0.006	absent	absent
duration	0.770	present	present
ex_rate	0.011	absent	absent
int_rate	0.867	present	present

GOAL: Interest_Rate
CURRENCY: yen
DURATION: one month

Fig. 6. Illustration of the semantic frame corresponding to the query "*Can I have the interest rates of the yen for one month please?*".

However, if the binary decision for a concept disagrees with its actual occurrence, a prompt will be invoked to request the missing concept or to clarify spurious concepts. We illustrate these two cases by the following examples.

Case 1. Prompt for a Missing Concept

Consider the interest rate query "*Can I have the interest rate of the yen?*". Backward inference gives $P^*(C_j)$ for the concept <DURATION> which equals 0.770. This is greater than the threshold $\theta = 0.5$, which suggests that the concept <DURATION> should be present but is missing. Hence the system prompts the user with "*Please specify the deposit duration*".

Case 2. Clarify for a Spurious Concept

Consider the query "*Can I have the interest rate of the lira against the yen.*" The inferred goal is Exchange Rates and results from backward inference are shown in Table 7. Comparison between the binary decisions for each concept with its actual occurrence in the query results in the automatic detection that the concept <INT_RATE> is spurious. This invokes the dialog model to generate the clarification response: "*Are you referring to the exchange rate between the lira and the yen?*"

Table 7. The input query is "*Can I have the interest rate of the lira against the yen?*" Goal inference identifies that the underlying goal is Exchange Rates. The goal node of the corresponding BN is instantiated, and backward inference produces $P^*(C_j)$ for each concept. These probabilities are compared with the threshold θ=0.5 to make a binary decision regarding the presence/absence for each concept. The binary decision of the concept <INT_RATE> from backward inference (BN of Interest Rates) does not agree with its actual occurrence (shaded). Hence <INT_RATE> is deemed spurious and the dialog model issues a clarification response.

Concept C_j	**$P^*(C_j)$**	**Binary Decision for C_j**	**Actual Occurrence for C_j**
currency_1	0.910	present	present
currency_2	0.920	present	present
duration	0.017	absent	absent
ex_rate	0.840	present	absent
int_rate	0.023	absent	present

7. Evaluation of the BN-based Dialog Model

Evaluation of the BN-based dialog model is based on a new set of 550 dialog sessions collected using the CU FOREX system. Recorded dialogs come from two hotlines – one with a directed dialog (DD) mode of interaction and the other with natural language shortcuts (NLS). Approximately 17% were rejected manually as the users were clearly attempting to break the system. Of the remaining queries, 285 calls were obtained from the DD hotline while 170 calls were obtained from the NLS hotline. The task completion rates of the original DD and NLS models are 85% and 63% respectively.

Recall that our original DD model only accepts one attribute for each dialog turn, hence failures in the DD model are mainly caused by queries with multiple information attributes or OOD input. Failures in the NLS model are due to missing concepts, spurious concepts or OOD queries.[i] We input these failed

[i] Note that we could have handcrafted some heuristics in a dialog manager to catch these errors in the original system but instead we have chosen to use the BN to work out the answer.

queries into our BN-based mixed-initiative dialog model to simulate online processing by this new model, and observed that the BN-based dialog model can automatically reject OOD input, and offered a continuation option at the failure points of *all* the dialogs. As a result, the BN-based dialog model achieves over 96% task completion rate overall. The remaining errors were due to OOD rejection. Table 8 shows typical examples of failure in the DD and NLS models, and how these are handled by the BN-based dialog model.

Table 8. Example dialogs illustrating the causes of failure in the original CU FOREX systems with DD and NLS interactions, and how these can be handled appropriately by the new BN-based dialog model.

Dialog 1: Directed Dialog (DD) Interaction		
System	:	Would you like exchange rates or interest rates?
User	:	Exchange rates
System	:	Which currency you would like to sell?
User	:	Yen to Hong Kong please.
System (Original CU FOREX)	:	Failed (Reason: Multiple information attributes in a DD interaction)
System (New BN-based Dialog Model)	:	The exchange rate between the Yen and the Hong Kong dollar is XXX. (Concepts pass the domain constraints)
Dialog 2: Natural Language Shortcut (NLS) Interaction		
System	:	What kind of currency information are you interested in?
User	:	Tell me about interest rates.
System (Original CU FOREX)	:	Failed (Reason: Missing the concepts <currency_1> and <duration>)
System (New BN-Based Dialog System)	:	Please tell me the currency you are interested in (Prompt for the missing concepts.)

8. Summary and Conclusion

In this chapter, we have discussed the design, development and evaluation of a multilingual dialog system and offered illustrations of these aspects in the context of the CU FOREX system. Multilingual dialog systems strive towards universal usability in developing speech and language technologies by targeting user language diversity, device variety and by avoiding user knowledge gaps.[24] We have also discussed the flexibility of the mixed-initiative dialog model, which can allow either the user or system to assume control in guiding the dialog interactions. There are a number of ways for realizing the mixed-initiative dialog model and data-driven approaches are preferred. We have presented one instance of a data-driven approach that uses belief networks (BN).[25] The BN topology may be used to model the semantic constraints in the dialog interaction and BN inference may be used to validate the relevance of a concept automatically. This, in turn, can be used to drive the mixed-initiative dialog model, through acts of prompting for missing concepts and clarifying of spurious concepts.

Acknowledgements

This work was partially supported by the Hong Kong Government Research Grants Council Earmarked Research Grant and a grant from SpeechWorks International Ltd. We thank Carman Wai, Steve Lee, and Brian Lawrence for their contributions to this work.

References

1. P. Price "Evaluation of Spoken Language Systems: the ATIS Domain," *Proceedings of the DARPA Speech and Natural Language Workshop*; Morgan Kaufman (1990), pp.91-95.
2. E. den Os, L. Boves, L. Lamel, P. Baggia, "Overview of the Arise Project," *Proceedings of 6th European Conference on Speech Communication and Technology* (cd-rom) (1999).
3. D. Jurafsky, C. Wooters, G. Tajchman, U. Segal, A. Stolcke, E. Fosler, and N. Morgan, "The Berkeley Restaurant Project," *Proceedings of the International Conference on Spoken Language Processing* http://www.icsi.berkeley.edu/real/berp.html (1994).
4. R. Carlson, "Recent Developments in the Experimental WAXHOLM Dialog System," *Proceedings of the ARPA Human Language Technology Workshop, Morgan Kaufman* (1994), pp.207-212.
5. V. Zue, S. Seneff, J. Glass, L. Hetherington, E. Hurley, H. Meng, C. Pao, J. Polifroni, R. Schloming, P. Schmid, "From Interface to Content: Translingual Access and Delivery of On-Line Information," *Proceedings of the 5th European Conference on Speech Communication and Technology*; ESCA (1995), pp. 2227-2230.
6. H. Meng, S. Busayapongchai, J. Glass, D. Goddeau, L. Hetherington, E. Hurley, C. Pao, J. Polifroni, S. Seneff and V. Zue, "WHEELS: A Conversational System in the Automobile Classifieds Domain," In *Proceedings of the 4th International Conference on Spoken Language Processing*, (1998).
7. P. Jeanrenaud, G. Cockroft, A. VanderHeidjen, "A Multimodal, Multilingual Telephone Application: The Wildfire Electronic Assistant," *Proceedings of 6th European Conference on Speech Communication and Technology* (cd-rom) (1999).
8. L. Deviller, and H. Bonneau-Maynard, "Evaluation of Dialog Strategies for a Tourist Information Retrieval System," *Proceedings of 6th European Conference on Speech Communication and Technology* (cd-rom) (1999).
9. Y. Yang and L.S. Lee, "A Syllable-based Chinese Spoken Dialogue System for Telephone Directory Services Primarily Trained with a Corpus," *Proceedings of the International Conference on Spoken Language Processing* (cd-rom) (1998).
10. *Linguistic society of Hong Kong* www.lshk.org

11. C. Wang, J. Glass, H. Meng, J. Polifroni, S. Seneff and V. Zue, "Yinhe: A Mandarin Chinese version of the Galaxy System," *Proceedings of Eurospeech*, (1997).
12. M. Walker, D. Litman, C. Kamm and A. Abella, "PARADISE: A Framework for Evaluating Spoken Dialogue Agents," *Proceedings of the 35th Annual Meeting of the Association of Computational Linguistics* (1997).
13. K. Kita, Y. Fukui, M. Nagata and T. Morimoto, "Automatic Acquisition of Probabilistic Dialogue Models," In *Proceedings of the 4th International Conference on Spoken Language Processing* (1998).
14. E. Levin, R. Pieraccini and W. Eckert, "A Stochastic Model of Human-Machine Interaction for Learning Dialogue Strategies", *Speech and Audio Processing, IEEE Transactions*, Vol 8, Jan. (2000), pp. 11-23.
15. M. Walker, J. Aberdeen, J. Boland, E. Bratt, J. Garofolo, L. Hirschman, A. Le, S. Lee, S. Narayanan, K. Papineni, B. Pellom, J. Polifroni, A. Potamianos, P. Prabhu, A. Rudnicky, G. Sanders, S. Seneff, D. Stallard and S. Whittaker, "DARPA Communicator Dialog Travel Planning Systems: The June 2000 Data Collection," *Proceedings of the Eurospeech, Aalborg* (2001).
16. S. Pulman, "Conversational Games, Belief Revision and Bayesian Networks," *Proceedings of the 7th Computerational Linguistics in the Netherlands Meeting* (1996).
17. E. Horvitz, "Principles of Mixed-Initiative User Interfaces," *Proc. of the ACM SIGCHI Conference* (1999).
18. E. Horvitz, and T. Paek, "A Computational Architecture for Conversation," *Proceedings of the 7th User Modeling Conference* (1999).
19. T. Paek, and E. Horvitz, "Conversation as Action Under Uncertainty," *Proceedings of Uncertainty in Artificial Intelligence Conference* (2000).
20. J. Alexandersson, B. Buschbeck-Wolf, M. K. Fujinami, E. M. Koch, B. S. Reithinger, *Acts in VERBMOBIL-2 Second Edition: Verbmobil Report* 226, Universitat Hamburg, DFKI Saarbrucken, Universitat Erlangen, TU Berlin (1998).
21. S.M. Weiss and C. A Kulikowski, *Computer Systems that Learn: Classification and Prediction Methods from Statistics, Neural Nets, Machine Learning and Expert Systems*, M. Kaufman (1991).
22. H. Meng, C. Wai and R. Pieraccini, "The Use of Belief Networks for Mixed-Initiative Dialog Modeling," *IEEE Transactions on Speech and Audio Processing*, Vol. 11, No. 6, November 2003 (2003).
23. B. Shneiderman, "Universal Usability," *Communications of the ACM*, May 2000, Vol. 43, No. 5, (2000), pp. 84-91.
24. H. Meng, W. Lam and K. F. Low, "Learning Belief Networks for Language Understanding," *Proceedings of the International Workshop on Automatic Speech Recognition and Understanding* (ASRU), Keystone, Colorado, USA, December (1999).
25. H. Meng, S. Lee, and C. Wai, "CU FOREX: A Bilingual Spoken Dialog System for Foreign Exchange Inquiries," *Proceedings of IEEE International Conference on Acoustics, Speech and Signal Processing* (2000), (cdrom).

CHAPTER 21

DIRECTORY ASSISTANCE SYSTEM

Jung-Kuei Chen, Chung-Chieh Yang and Jin-Shea Kuo

Chunghwa Telecommunication Laboratories, Taoyuan
E-mail: {jkchen, owenyang, jskuo}@cht.com.tw

Among all of the services provided by telecom companies, directory assistance (DA) is undoubtedly the most likely one to be automated. With increasing competition and revenue decline, directory assistance providers are seeking more cost-effective operational models. Speech technology is definitely a key solution to automation. Providing automated DA concerns most of the speech recognition technologies such as model training, large vocabulary continuous speech recognition, confidence measure, noise/channel robustness, etc. The more specific challenge is that this speech recognition application needs to handle very large vocabulary which includes homonyms, abbreviations and variations of speaker expressions. Although there is much literature and many system deployments regarding automated DA in Western languages, only a few deal with Chinese languages. A trial system has been developed in Chunghwa Telecom since April 2004 and significantly benefits the telecom company. The speech technologies and business concerns in the system development of this application will be discussed in detail.

1. Introduction

Among all of the services provided by telecom companies, directory assistance (DA) is undoubtedly the one most expected to be automated by digital speech processing technologies. From the economic viewpoint, the DA service experiences heavy-volume traffic and is labor-intensive, such that even partial automation of this service would imply significant cost savings. Most important of all, DA callers have definite objectives and obviously know the names of enquired targets. This clear and predictable user behavior makes DA automation even more tangible and realizable. However, this application has its specific challenges brought about by other telephone value-added services such as those provided by voice portals.

Tracing the history of speech-technology-enabled DA automation, ADAS Plus, developed by Nortel, is one of the pioneer trial systems applied to service a large geographical area.[1] The system achieved partial automation and was deployed across Quebec in Canada, in the western US, and by BellSouth in 1998. It primarily automated the locality input by asking callers "for what city?" Then the call was transferred to a live agent with the locality result of speech recognition shown on the agent's screen.

In Europe, a three-year project called SMADA, Speech-driven Multimodal Automated Directory Assistance, started in January 2000.[2,3] The project was an initiative of several European telecom operators and universities, and it involved the development of some key automated DA technologies, including robust acoustic features, confidence measures, and techniques for deriving acoustic and linguistic models from application-specific data. The project has even established multi-country databases and evaluation procedures.

As a result of significant technology improvements and field trial experiences, some automated Directory Assistance (ADA) systems have been successfully deployed in the past few years. For example, Telecom Italia launched their ADA in 2001 nationwide after a field trial from 1998;[4,5] Belgacom, a major DA provider in Belgium, started their fully-automated directory services in January 2001. Today, many speech solution providers and call center vendors have been providing commercial ADA solutions.[6-10]

Generally speaking, the scenario of a non-automated DA service is quite straightforward. A caller inquires about the telephone number of a person, a company or a government department by saying out the person's or organization's name. The operator keys in the query to search in the directory database. The results, usually multiple candidates, are shown on the operator's screen. Then, if needed, the operator asks for other cues such as address for further identification. The call completes after the desired telephone number is given to the caller. An automated DA service is trying to achieve the described goal by using voice interaction technologies, including dialogue, speech recognition and text-to-speech.

Basically, an automated DA is concerned with most of the speech recognition technologies, such as model training, Large Vocabulary Continuous Speech Recognition (LVCSR), confidence measure and robustness, etc. In which the specific challenge is the very large vocabulary speech recognition accompanied with grammar issues. There are two categories of DA, residential and business listings each of which having different problems. For residential listings, recognition errors originate from homonyms and pronunciation variations.[11,12] Homonymy errors are caused by the same first and last names, and this problem gets worse with increasing vocabulary size. The common strategy used is a system-driven approach which includes the last name, first name, and, if necessary, the address of the requested listing, in that order. Callers could further be asked to spell out the queried name for a joint decision.[13-15] The pronunciation variation issue arises when callers are not familiar with the queried names, such as foreign names. These unfamiliar names might also contain imprecise phone sequences in the lexicon. To overcome this problem, some rescoring methods are proposed to rescore the N-best hypotheses.[16]

On the other hand, the main challenge for business listings DA is to formulate the variances of user expressions. There are different ways that callers can query a listing. A rule-based approach has been proposed to derive grammar rules from users' spoken expressions.[17] An unsupervised solution is applied to decode the phonetic transcriptions of field data in order to generate new formulations.[18] A different approach using a statistical n-gram recognizer and retrieval engine allow for inexact matching between the spoken query and the directory listing.[19] In general, there are no *a priori* and complete knowledge that can be used to automatically generate the query grammar from the directory database very well. The early prototypes focused on the most frequently requested listings (FRL) as a trade-off between recognition success rate and directory coverage. Although recently-deployed systems have full coverage capability, the queries for FRLs still account for much of the call traffic.

Dialogue management, text-to-speech, directory database normalization, operator fallback and network integration are all as important as speech recognition in ADA design. Furthermore, business considerations and motivations as well as user needs should be carefully considered before seeking an automated DA solution.[20] In this chapter, the more common ASR issues will not be discussed, although they are all important to ADA. Instead, a real case of ADA development and field trial experience is presented.

The chapter is organized as the following: In Section 2, the ecosystem of directory assistance market and the impact of technology are briefly overviewed. In Section 3, the specific technical issues for residential and business listings ADA are discussed. The automated DA system built in Chunghwa Telecom together with its engineering and business issues are introduced in Section 4. Finally, experiences from the field trial, system performance and future plans are presented in Section 5.

2. Ecosystem of Directory Assistance Services

The traditional business model of DA service providers is providing operator-assisted and printed DA services to customers, including white pages and yellow pages. In the past few years, the ecosystem of DA service has somewhat changed due to several factors, including the advent and proliferation of the Internet, wireless, and speech technologies, as well as telecom deregulation. Some factors result in increasing competition, while others bring in more opportunities.

The Internet provides alternative ways of directory assistance, through web-based yellow pages or search portals like Google. In addition to querying for telephone numbers, people can and do search for more detailed information about the inquired individual or organization, such as location and business hour. These Internet-based competition are either local or foreign web portals and are always free of charge, making a negative impact on traditional DA businesses. Traditional DA providers have thus been facing declining traffic and revenue in their operator-assisted and printed DA business.

Telecom deregulation, a trend of globalization, in some countries and regions like the European Union, for example, is another source that brings about more competition to traditional DA providers. Local telecom carriers used to be the traditional DA providers in the past. Because of deregulation, new competitors – Internet service providers and overseas call centers – can enter the market. This forces the traditional DA providers to extend their services from local to national listings, and from fixed-line to mobile DA.

On the other hand, the rapid increase of wireless users opens up new opportunities to enhance DA services, such as providing location-based services, short message services and multimedia message services. These enhanced services could extend callers' connection time and also bring in more advertising revenue. However, with the growth of GPRS, 3G and all-IP networking in the near future, querying business information through handheld devices in package mode would have yet another big impact on the DA business.

Facing various competition and revenue decline, DA providers have been seeking more cost-effective models. The automation of directory services by speech recognition, with the potential to reduce or even eliminate human effort, is definitely a key to cost reduction and profit increase. However, the introduction of automated DA should be carefully done to ensure the balance between the percentage of automation and customer acceptance. In order to increase automation rate, more dialogue and back-end processing will be required, and their results usually leave customers dissatisfied. The strategy usually depends on the provider's business goal. For directory assistance service which is provided free by regulation, the system could be designed to increase automation to the highest, even to a fully automatic level without human operator backup.

3. Key Technology Issues for Automated Directory Assistance

Basically, automated DA involves most of the speech recognition technologies: model training, LVCSR, confidence measure, noise/channel robustness, etc. In this section, only those key technologies related to ADA in particular are discussed.

3.1. *Residential listings*

The main problem of residential DA lies in the very large and extensive name listings. The name listings for a big city DA alone could be more than one million, not to mention a DA for the whole country. Generally, the ADA dialogue is designed with a high structure that leads callers to respond in shorter, simpler ways, like with single-word answers. However, name recognition based on million-sized vocabulary does not perform acceptably.[11] Since every listing is almost equally requested, the perplexity is proportional to the vocabulary size.

The vocabulary size can be reduced by asking callers to state the locality in the first prompt. The (speech) recognition of city names is not difficult and the size of residential listings in a town or a small city is usually manageable. The ADA system will then ask callers to say out the queried last name, first name and street name, if necessary. For names that can be confusing, making callers spell them out can help in further discrimination. Basically, the name listing DA adopts a form-filling approach. Callers are guided to "fill in" (by speaking out) the field that is the most needed in every step by dialogue manager. The call ends when a unique listing is identified.

However, some residential directory databases do not contain a first name field. In fact, callers might not know the first name or street name exactly. The spelling of names in some countries can be unusual.[3] These issues make ADA systems for residential listings require different specifications across different countries.

As compared to Western-language names, Chinese names are much shorter. Most Chinese names consist of two to four characters, which correspond to Mandarin syllables of the same number. The short name length seriously affects the homonym problem in name listings, not to mention the highly confusing phenomenon that occurs between Mandarin syllables.

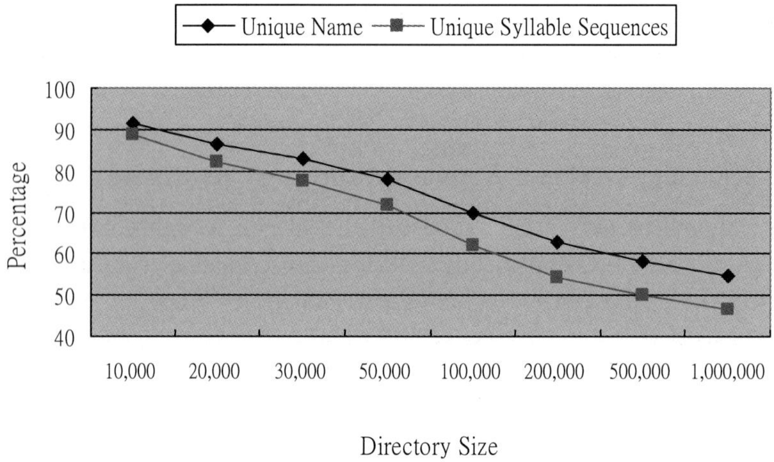

Fig. 1. Percentage of unique name and unique syllable sequence as a function of directory size in Taipei.

According to a distribution analysis of one million names in Taipei, the ratio of unique names and unique syllable-sequences to directory size is shown in Figure 1. The ratio for unique names continually decreases from 92% to 55% in a directory size of tens of thousands to one million; while the ratio for syllable sequences decreases from 89% to 46%. The highest frequency name occurs 260 times. There are 10,382 names occurring more than 10 times. This analysis shows that the problem of homonyms gets worse as the directory size grows. There are 885 monosyllabic last names, in which the top 10 names account for 50% of the population and top 100 names account for 90%. An interesting finding shows that there are 8,534 bi-syllabic last names, the most belonging to wives who also adopt their husbands' last name.

The recognition accuracy of Mandarin last names is worse than that of Western-language names due to the monosyllabic property of Chinese characters. As for full name recognition, recognition error rate could be about 28% for a lexicon of about 50,000.[21] However, for a big city like Taipei with more than 3 million residential listings, an adequate dialogue strategy combining locality query is definitely necessary.

To solve the homonym problem, Tsai *et al.*[22] proposed a spelling recognition approach which elicits callers to describe the Chinese characters. For example, people use "three horizontal bars and one vertical bar" (三橫一豎) to describe the character "Wang" (王). This method is trying to identify a monosyllabic character with a multi-syllabic phrase, much like the way to identify "A" with

"Alpha" in English. Experimental results show that positive performance can be obtained for cooperative speakers. However, not all callers share the same describing rules, and a longer interactive dialogue period is also needed.

3.2. *Business listings*

In addition to the very large vocabulary issue, the major problem of automating directory assistance for business listings is that callers express their requests for the same listing with much variability. The first kind of expression or language variation exists in the expressions of business categories. For example, "café", "snack bar" and "cafeteria" may be referred to the same category of restaurants. In Chinese, "蔘藥行" and "中藥房" could be registered as Chinese herbal medicine shops in the directory database. These terms are considered as some form of synonyms. The second source of utterance variation comes from abbreviations. "/tai2 da4/"(台大), for example, is the nickname of "/tai2 wan da4 xue2/" (Taiwan University, 台灣大學). Finally the third variance type is the ordering of compound words, especially for a company with branch offices or departments. For example, users may call "Taiwan Bank, PeiTou" in Chinese as "台灣銀行北投分行", "北投台灣銀行", or "台灣銀行" directly if they live in PeiTou district.

In brief, the main sources of variations in user expressions are abbreviation of proper nouns, category synonyms and keyword sequences. Therefore the main challenge for business listings DA is how to generate ASR grammars as automatically as possible. The intuitive method is to collect actual utterances of callers' requests, transcribe these manually, and train statistical grammars or construct finite state grammar for each listing. However, it is hard to collect sufficient data, not to mention the enormous task of manual transcription. In practice, initial grammar rules can be designed by domain experts, like senior DA operators. These rules depend heavily on the attributes of the business listings in the DA database. In general, a business listing consists of a company name, business category, department, sub-department, address, phone number, etc. These fields are used to design grammar rules which can generate consequent sentences to hopefully cover all user expressions.

Based on the initial grammar, collecting new expressions from field data with automatic procedures can further improve system performance. Suitable utterances are those unsuccessfully recognized by the system but related to a listing which is confirmed by operators. The decoding of such utterances containing the vocabulary of the known listing can help to obtain good candidates for new expression variants.[18]

3.3. *Pre-processing of the Database*

In general, the original registered information of subscribers is full of abnormalities and typographical errors. Some rules for data cleaning are designed for processing the DA database automatically. However, the directory database is organized according to the search strategy of operator-assisted DA systems, not according to the ADA's purpose. The ADA database could be the same as the DA database, or a separate copy of it consisting only of the most frequently requested listings.

4. Development of the CHT ADA Trial System

In this section, a real case of ADA implementation in Chunghwa Telecom (CHT) will be addressed. CHT is the largest integrated telecommunication operator in Taiwan, whose service range covers fixed, mobile and data networks. It has more than 90% fixed-line subscribers and is also the major DA service provider in Taiwan. Even by out-sourcing DA operators, the operational cost is still far greater than the revenue it brings in, since the DA fee, by government regulation, is only about ten US cents per call.

There are two DA service codes in Taiwan: 104 and 105. 104 is for calls from fixed network and for local directory query only. 105 is for all other DA queries, including calls from mobile and pay phones, and for nationwide directory queries. To design the CHT ADA system, some technical and business constraints, and requirements were taken into account:

(1) *Listing type: business vs. residential.* Business enquiries account for 80% of all DA calls, while business listing size is about 20% of the database. The high occurrence of homonym cases in Chinese names which requires user verification, results in longer interactive dialogues. These would annoy customers in the preliminary phase of the service. Applying the 80/20 principle, only business listings are included at the initial phase of development.

(2) *DA scope: local vs. nationwide.* For nationwide ADA deployments, it is necessary to ask for locality information in order to reduce vocabulary complexities. The city of Taipei, being the biggest in Taiwan, was chosen for pilot trial because if deployment works well here, it will guarantee successful deployment in other cities of Taiwan.

(3) *Listing coverage: all listings vs. frequently requested listings* (FRL). There is a trade-off between listing size and recognition rate. Although in the literature, performance of FRL approaches are shown to be only limited,[18]

we believe that given the limitation of current ASR technologies as well as the deficiency of automatic grammar generation, FRL is still an adequate approach if its coverage of incoming calls is high enough.

(4) *Service code: new code vs. existing code.* A new service code is suitable for a new player in the DA market. For CHT, as the pioneer and major DA provider in Taiwan, a new service code will be taken into account only for the purpose of market separation, e.g. to launch a new DA service at lower price. However, there is little, if any, attraction for people to use this service since operator-assisted DA call rates are currently very low. Besides, additional promotion effort for a new service code is not reasonable in the trial phase.

Based on the above considerations, an ADA system was developed for Taipei, whose area code is 02 in Taiwan, and integrated with the existing DA system. Only part of the 104 DA traffic were routed to the ADA system to avoid affecting customer satisfaction of existing DA services. Since the 104 code is only for fixed-line and excludes pay telephone calls, a better user environment will boost the level of customer acceptance and automatic completion rate.

4.1. *System Architecture*

The system architecture of CHT ADA is shown in Figure 2. The ADA system is connected with the existing operator-assisted DA system. The ACD (automatic

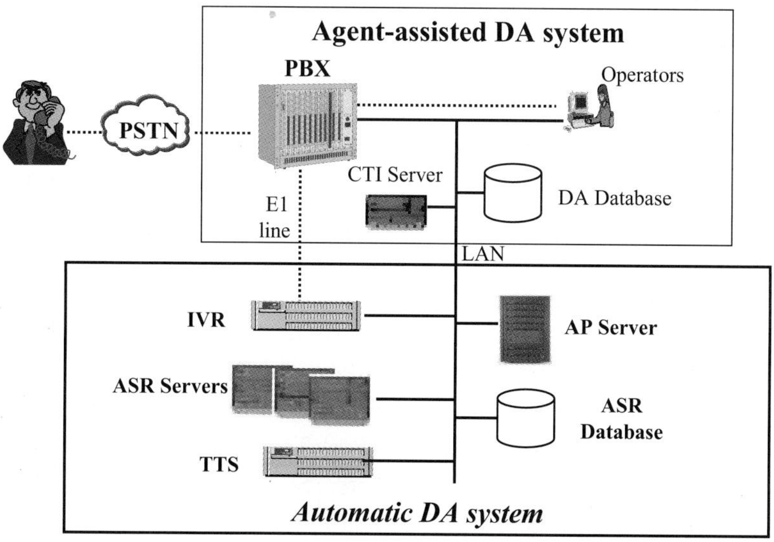

Fig. 2. System architecture of CHT automated DA system.

call distribution) of PBX (Private Branch Exchange) is set adequately to select part of the incoming calls to be routed to the ADA. The selection criteria include concurrent usage, agent status, and the location where the calls are made.

The ADA system consists of a database, an IVR (Interactive Voice Response) and TTS server, an application server and ten ASR servers. All components are modularized for scalability and future extension. The IVR includes the telephone interface board, handles call interface and manages the dialogue. The TTS is based on a plain concatenative approach which makes use of larger phrasal units of high frequency, in addition to basic syllable units. The ADA database is separated from the DA database to avoid influencing existing DA operations. All the speech software are developed by the speech group of Chunghwa Telecom laboratories.

4.2. *Dialogue Design*

When people ask for directory assistance as a public service, they expect quality service all the time: fast, accurate and polite responses. Since voice-enabled services are not popular in Taiwan, callers tend to feel uneasy talking to a machine. Therefore, the call flow is designed as simply as possible avoiding complicated dialogues. For any kind of failure, such as caller silence, hesitation, non-complete utterance or low ASR confidence score, the call is routed to a live agent immediately to ensure an acceptable quality of service, even though the call might successfully proceed in the next step.

The CHT ADA is designed in a system-driven style. Figure 3 shows a typical dialogue example. The initial prompt guides the caller to press 9 for residential queries or to directly say out the company name to be queried. After receiving the caller's utterance, the recognizer generates an *N*-best list of hypotheses accompanied with their confidence scores. The candidates above a specified confidence threshold, three at most, are read out to the caller by the TTS. After that the caller is asked to select the correct candidate or to commence another attempt. Once the caller selects a candidate, the system reads out the related phone number and invites the caller to a direct connection service. Throughout the dialogue, the caller can always choose to be routed to a live agent by pressing 9.

As a new service introduced to customers, a fully voice-enabled DA system would surely involve considerable mistakes. Too many confirmations will also lengthen call durations and annoy users. So instead of using full speech recognition through dialogue, only the name query portion requires voice input and other tasks are performed by DTMF input.

System:	This is CHT automated directory assistance. For residential query, please press 9; otherwise, say out the company name directly.
User:	Taiwan Bank, DuenNan branch office.
System:	Taiwan Bank, DuenNan branch office; press 1. Taiwan Bank, DuenBei branch office; press 2. Taiwan Bank, FuXin branch office; press 3. For querying again, press 4. To transfer to an agent, press 9.
User:	(press 1)
System:	The phone number of Taiwan Bank, DuenNan branch office is xxxx-xxxx. For connecting to the company, press 2. For playing again, press 3. For querying again, press 4. To transfer to an agent, press 9.
User:	…..

Fig. 3. A dialogue example of CHT ADA.

4.2. *Grammar Design*

Based on interviews with senior DA agents, we generalize four descriptive rules for business listings as follows:

Type #1: [filler] <company name> <business category> [filler]
Type #2: [filler] < headquarters > [filler] < pos-branch-identifier > [filler]
Type #3: [filler] < pre-branch-identifier > [filler] < headquarters > [filler]
Type #4: [filler] <company name> [filler]

Words between angled brackets are variables. Any variable is expressed as a combination of keywords with option notation "[ ]" and selection notation "{ | }". Optional fillers are inserted at the beginning and ending of sentence, and between keyword variables, since the callers' responses to ADA may still contain many variations of unexpected expressions despite careful guidance by the system. For each directory listing, more than one grammar rule could be written.

Type #1 is for companies whose names contain keywords that clearly match business categories, like bank, hospital, school, etc. For example, the grammar for "中山國小"(JhongShan elementary school) is "[filler] 中山{國小|國民小學} [filler]", in which "{國小|國民小學}" is the grammar for the business category of elementary school. Currently the CHT ADA contains more than 300 business categories.

Type #2 is for companies that have many branch offices or departments, especially in the banking and government sectors. The branch-identifier is usually the street or region name which is used to distinguish it from other branches. For example, the grammar of "台灣銀行敦南分行" (Taiwan Bank, DuenNan branch office) is "[filler] {台灣銀行|台銀} [filler]敦南分行[filler]", in which "{台灣銀行|台銀}" is the grammar for Taiwan Bank, headquarters, and "敦南分行" is the phrase for DuenNan branch office. There are more than 500 company groups in the system.

Type #3 is an alternative of Type #2. People do usually say out the street name first before the branch office name, that is, in a reverse sequence. "[filler] {敦化南路}[filler] {台灣銀行|台銀} [filler]" is an alternative expression of the example in Type #2.

Type #4 is for companies whose business category keyword is made up of only one character and for those without a category keyword. For example, "[filler]龍山寺[filler]" is the grammar for the LongShan Temple, a famous temple in Taipei.

In the beginning, these grammar lists were edited manually by experienced DA agents. This approach is fairly simple and efficient for listings in sizes of tens of thousands, compared to the efforts of establishing a data gathering environment, recording DA transactions and transcribing a huge amount of utterances. However, this grammar-writing approach is only suitable for a quick development in a trial system and cannot be extended to a nationwide DA system. Besides the inconsistency of rules between grammar editors is also a real problem yet to be solved.

A learning approach exploiting contextual information to generate synonyms, which are terms referring to concepts that are similar, is proposed. Two terms are considered as near synonyms under the assumption that if the two terms collocate in the brackets "{}" of the existing grammar. Mutual information is applied to estimate their similarity. The manual-edited grammars for the top 35,000 directory listings are used as a training corpus and a set of near synonyms are derived automatically by the learning approach.

For a new business listing, the input string, consisting of a listing name with other directory information, is decomposed into word entities iteratively. Then its grammar expressions are generated in the following sequence.

(1) Type #2 and Type #3 grammars are produced if the expression conforms to the headquarter-branch format.
(2) Type #1 grammar is produced if it contains any keyword within the business categories.
(3) Type #4 grammar, as a backup, is a free-form concatenation of word entities.

(4) Recognize common terms even if they are prefixes or suffixes, such as "Taipei" (台北) and "company" (公司).
(5) Extend those entities with near synonyms, which are learned from the training corpus.

The automatic generation approach is used in daily grammar updates. Manual checking is also performed to ensure 100% accuracy.

4.3. *Search Strategy and Confidence Measurement*

Instead of directly searching in the entire grammar network, a two-stage search is used in the CHT ADA system to reduce computational time. In the first stage, keyword spotting is applied to a grammar consisting of all <business category> and <headquarters> to produce *N*-best candidates of business categories and major companies. Detailed searches are then applied to those lists containing the candidate keywords in the second stage. The grammar of Type #4 is also searched in this stage.

A multilevel confidence measure combining syllable confidence and keyword confidence is applied to reject utterances with low confidence and reorder the rest according to their confidence scores. The confidence score can then be used to determine the next move in a dialog, for example to apply implicit or explicit confirmation depending on the score, or to skip confirmation when the score is very high. However, based on the experiments on the field data, we find it very difficult to set adequate thresholds. Eventually, we decide to apply a loose strategy where confidence scores are used only to reduce the number of candidates. Whenever there are no candidates above the threshold, the caller is immediately forwarded to a live agent.

5. Field Trial Experience

The CHT ADA project was initiated in 2002 for three years, the first two years for technology investigation and system development, and the third year for field trial and system tuning. The baseline HMM model was trained with a CHT speech corpus which contains a general telephone corpus and a directory query corpus, which was recorded in a reading style in an office environment.

The size of the frequently requested listings was about 35,000, around 12% of the total business listings in Taipei. In an analysis of 630,000 DA calls, the ADA listings covered about 90%. It means that in-listing and out-of-listing calls account for 90% and 10%, respectively. For higher coverage, however, the listing size would need to grow rapidly but this is at the expense of lower recognition rate.

We started Phase I of the field trial in April 2004. One year later, another routing mode, Phase II, was applied. The details are described as follows.

Phase I (random mode)**:** A small amount of DA calls were routed to an initial system in the size of five lines from 9:00 a.m. to 5:00 p.m. every weekday. The incoming calls were randomly selected from a specific district of Taipei city and routed to the ADA system. A typical call flow of this phase is shown in Figure 3. Since the callers were randomly chosen among callers to an ordinary DA, they were not previously informed of the existence of an automated DA system. The utterances obtained from the first ten weeks were collected and transcribed manually in order to retrain the acoustic models of the ADA system. The dialogue flow was also slightly modified according to callers' responses. Four months later, the system was scaled up to ten lines. A customer satisfaction evaluation was also conducted in the last three months of 2004.

Phase II (busy mode)**:** A different mode of call selection was implemented in two other districts in Taipei from July 2005. DA callers were invited to choose the automatic service when all the human agents were busy. The call flow of this phase is shown in Figure 4. Only the callers who choose automatic service by pressing the assigned phone button were routed to the ADA system; the others were routed to live agents directly.

System:	This is CHT automated directory assistance. All operators are busy now. For business query with speech recognition system, please press 1; otherwise, wait a moment for operators' service.
User:	(press 1)
System:	Say the company name directly please.
(the rest of the steps that follow are the same as the second step onwards in Figure 3)	

Fig. 4. A dialogue example of *busy* mode.

5.1. *Call Distribution*

The distribution of completion type of all received calls in March 2006 is summarized in Table 1. The hang-up rate at the first system prompting (row 1) is 13.7% and 7.3% for random and busy modes respectively. The random mode, in which callers were not informed of the existence of the ADA in advance, has a higher hang-up rate as predicted. However the hang-up rate still accounts for a significant portion in busy mode, which means that people are still not comfortable to use an automatic speech system even when they have the option of using the ADA service themselves. The overall automatic call completion rate is 43.3% and 52.7% for random and busy modes respectively.

The threshold of confidence score is set at an operation point of 7.5% false rejection rate. The ASR-rejected calls (row 2 in Table 1) contains caller silence or hesitation, non-complete utterances detected by end-pointers, false rejection and correct rejection. It is difficult to distinguish between false rejection and correct rejection in these calls unless the utterances are verified manually. Besides, the hung-up calls in row 1 are not relevant to the recognition rate. Thus we exclude the first two rows and sum up rows 3 and 4 as recognition failures, which may include out-of-listing, out-of-expression and speech recognition errors. This recount resulted in recognition accuracies of the top 3 candidates to be 66.9% and 73.1% for random and busy modes respectively.

The duration of automatic completed calls is about 40 seconds on average, including the time taken for the system to read out the retrieved phone number, but not including the first prompt that invites callers to select the ADA service. It is acceptable compared to the service time of a human agent which is 30 seconds on average.

Table 1. The distribution of completion types for different incoming calls.

Completion type	Random Mode	Busy Mode
Hang up before ASR session	13.7%	7.3%
Transfer to agent by ASR rejection	21.7%	20.7%
Hang up in playing candidates	3.1%	4.2%
Transfer to agent since ASR failure	18.3%	15.2%
Complete query automatically	43.3%	52.7%

5.2. *Performance of the Speech Recognizer*

Standard MFCC features with their first derivatives, 26 dimensions in total, are used in the CHT ADA system. Three HMM models, described below, have been used through the two trial phases.

Baseline model: Right-context-dependent initial and context-independent final models, 440 states in total, trained with original corpus.
Retrained model: the same structure as the baseline model, retrained from the baseline model with 13 weeks' field data.
Hybrid model: 134 syllable models of high frequency syllables trained in addition to the retrained model, 1,512 states in total.

A testing corpus, 7,873 utterances in total, was collected for evaluation. Each utterance was verified as existing in the list and corresponding to a unique listing. Among these, 6,834 utterances, or about 87%, are in-grammar; the others are out-of-grammar. In-grammar means that the transcribed character sequence of an utterance is included in the set generated by the grammar of that listing. It also implies that around 13% of user expressions of business listings could not be generated.

The in-listing recognition rates of different models with 7.5% false rejection rate are shown in Table 2. The test results show that the model retrained with field data can improve performance significantly, from 67.1% to 77.3% for the top 3 candidates' recognition rate. The hybrid model, with detailed modeling for high frequency syllables, can further boost performance to 80.5%. The in-listing recognition rate multiplied by the in-listing percentage (90%) is 72.5%, which approximates to the recognition rate 73.1% discussed in Section 5.1.

The recognition rate of the top 1 candidate is relatively 16% worse off than that of the top 3. Therefore the CHT ADA is designed in a way that 3 candidates, at most, are being read out to callers for their further selection and confirmation. Obviously the recognition rate of in-grammar utterances is far better than that of out-of-grammar utterances. It is believed that the performance can be further improved if the in-grammar percentage is increased.

Table 2. In-listing recognition rate analyses.

	Original model		Retrained model		Hybrid model	
	Top 1	Top 3	Top 1	Top 3	Top1	Top 3
In-Grammar utterances	59.4%	74.0%	71.0%	84.7%	73.5%	87.3%
Out-of-Grammar utterances	10.1%	12.6%	12.2%	18.3%	14.3%	21.3%
Average	53.8%	67.1%	64.5%	77.3%	67.3%	80.5%

5.3. *Customer Satisfaction*

Customer satisfaction was also assessed in the period of September to December in 2004. 1,040 customers, 571 with successful DA experience and 469 with failed experience, were interviewed within one hour after his/her calling. The interview questions include acceptance of dialogue flow, TTS quality, ASR performance and global acceptance. The opinion scores for each question, ranging from 5 to 1 points for 'Excellent', 'Good', 'Fair', 'Poor' and 'Unsatisfactory' respectively, were also collected. The mean opinion score rating results are shown in Figure 5. The average mean opinion score ratings are 3.24 and 2.45 for success and failure cases respectively. Since this assessment was performed on callers in random mode (Phase I), we believe that customer acceptance level would be better for callers in busy mode (Phase II).

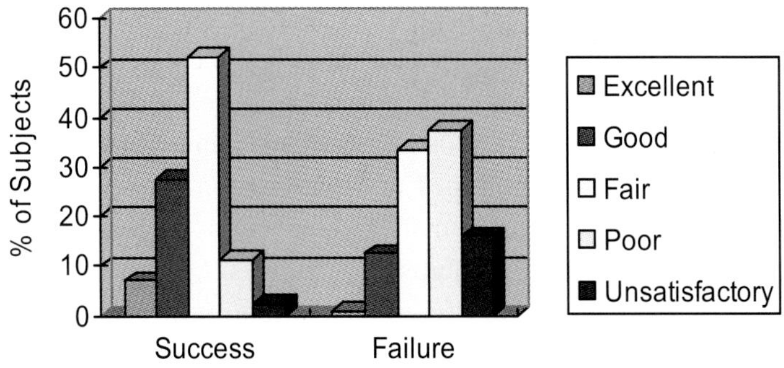

Fig. 5. The mean opinion score rating results for success and failure cases respectively.

5.4. *Future Works*

The CHT ADA system is still in operation today and has been extended to serve DA callers from all Taipei districts. Although it provides only an alternative for DA customers when all the agents are busy, the significant benefit has convinced business managers to consider its further deployment. The plan to deploy this system in Central and Southern Taiwan is currently underway.

Increasing in-grammar coverage is believed to improve recognition rate further. Using field utterances to explore more expressions from callers automatically is an achievable approach. It will also be beneficial if some extra resources are available in addition to the directory service. The Web is growing at a fast pace, providing rich and even live information. Exploiting Web corpora has been reported to have promising results in extracting translation/ transliteration pairs.[23,24]

6. Conclusion

Beyond general ASR issues, very large vocabulary with high perplexity and variance of user expressions are the main specific challenges for automated DA applications. Basically, Chinese ADA has similar issues, with slight differences originating from its linguistic characteristics. For business listings, the more accurately the grammars are automatically generated from the DA database or from speech utterances, the better is recognition performance. Besides ASR issues, engineering tasks like database normalization and dialogue management should also be carefully dealt with for further system development. In this chapter, we have presented our development and trial experience of the CHT ADA system.

Automated DA is one of the most beneficial services that speech recognition technology brings to telecom operators. Facing competition from the Internet, automation by speech technology is a key solution to cost-cutting. Although there have been several deployments in various countries today, those experiences cannot guarantee successful application in other countries. An ADA solution is not only about speech technologies and automation rates, as it also concerns system integration as well as human and business processes. Besides speech technologies being different across languages, cultural differences also significantly influence the level of acceptance to a new technology, especially a voice-enabled service. The worldwide deployment of automated DA system today is just a beginning. On one hand, the ASR technologies should be further improved, and on the other hand, people need time to be more accustomed to the voice automation interface.

Acknowledgements

The work reported in this chapter is based on the contributions made by various members of the speech group of Chunghwa Telecom Laboratories. Special credits are due to the designers of the CHT ADA system, including Eng-Fong Huang and Jen-Yu Lin. The authors would also like to thank Dr. Bor-Shenn Jeng, Dr. Lung-Sing Liang and Dr. John Hsueh for their encouragement and support of the ADA project over the years.

References

1. V. Gupta, S. Robilllard, C. Pelletier, "Automation of Locality Recognition in ADAS Plus," *Proc. IVTTA-98*, Turing, (1998), pp. 1-4.
2. L. Boves, D. Jouvet, J. Sienel, R. de Mori, F. Béchet, L. Fis-sore, and P. Laface, "ASR for automatic directory assistance: the SMADA project", *Proc. ASR2000*, Paris, (2000), pp. 249-254.
3. F. Béchet, E. den Os, L. Boves, and J. Sienel, "Introduction to The IST-HLT Project Speech-driven Multimodal Automatic directory assistance (SMADA)", *Proc. ICSLP-2000*, Beijing, vol.2, (2000), pp. 731-734.
4. R. Billi, F. Canavesio, and C. Rullent, "Automation of Telecom Italia directory Assistance Service: Field Trial Results," *Proc. IVTTA-98*, Turing, (1998), pp. 11-16.
5. C. Popovici, M. Andorno, L. Fissore, M. Nigra, and C. Vair, "Learning New User Formulations in Automatic Directory Assistance," *Proc. ICASSP-02*, Orlando, (2002), pp. I-17-20.
6. http://www.belgacom.be/
7. http://www.varetis.de/
8. http://www.nuance.com/
9. http://www.btslogic.com/

10. http://www.voltdelta.com/
11. C.A. Kamm, K.-M. Yang, C.R. Shamieh, and S. Singhal, "Speech Recognition Issues for Directory Assistance applications," *Proc. IVTTA-94*, Kyoto, (1994), pp 15-19.
12. Y. Gao, B. Ramabhadran, J. Chen, H, Erdogan and M. Picheny, "Innovative Approaches for Large Vocabulary Name Recognition," *Proc. ICASSP-01*, Salt Lake City, (2001), pp. 53-56.
13. M. Meyer, and H. Hild, "Recognition of Spoken and Spelled Proper Names," *Proc. EUROSPEECH-97*, Rhodes, vol. 3, (1997), pp. 1579-1582.
14. D. Jouvet and J. Monné, "Recognition of Spelled Names over the Telephone and Rejection of Data out of the Spelling Lexicon," *Proc. EUROSPEECH-99*, Budapest, (1999), pp. 283-286.
15. H. Schramn, B. Rueber, and A. Kellner, "Strategies for Name Recognition in Automatic Directory Assistance Systems," *Speech Communication*, vol. 31, (2000), pp. 329-338.
16. F. Béchet, R. de Mori, and G. Subsol, "Dynamic Generation of Proper Name pronunciations for Directory Assistance," *Proc. ICASSP-02*, Orlando, (2002), pp. I-745-748.
17. Scharenborg, J. Sturm, and Lou Boves, Business Listings in Automatic Directory Assistance, *Proc. EUROSPEECH-01*, Aalborg, (2001), pp. 2381-2384.
18. M. Andorno, L. Fissore, P. Laface, M. Nigra, C. Popovici, F. Ravera, and C. Vair, "Incremental Learning of New User Formulations in Automatic Directory Assistance", *Proc. EUROSPEECH-2003*, Geneva, (2003), pp. 1925-1928.
19. P. Natarajan, R. Prasad, R. Schwartz, and J. Makhoul, "A scalable architecture for directory assistance automation", *Proc. ICASSP-2002*, Orlando, Florida, (2002), pp. I21-42.
20. E. Levin and A. M. Mane, "Voice User Interface Design for Automated Directory Assistance", *Proc. INTERPEECH-2005*, Lisbon, (2005), pp. 2509-2512.
21. Y.F. Liao and George Rose, "Recognition of Chinese Names In Continuous Speech for Directory Assistance Applications," *Proc. ICASSP-2002*, Orlando, (2002), pp. I-741-744.
22. C.H. Tsai, N. Wang, P. Huang and J.L. Chen, "Open Vocabulary Chinese Name Recognition with the Help of Character Description and Syllable Spelling recognition," *Proc. ICASSP-2005*, Philadelphia, (2005), pp. I-1037-1040.
23. J. S. Kuo and Y. K. Yang, "Incorporating Pronunciation Variation into Extraction of Transliterated-term Pairs from Web Corpora," *Proc. International Conference on Chinese Computing (ICCC)*, (2005), pp. 131-138.
24. W. H. Lu, L. F. Chien and H. J Lee, "Translation of Web Queries Using Anchor Text Mining," *ACM Transactions on Asian Language and Information Processing (TALIP)*, Vol. 1, Issue 2, (2002), pp. 159- 172.

CHAPTER 22

ROBUST CAR NAVIGATION SYSTEM

Jhing-Fa Wang†, Hsien-Chang Wang‡ and Jia-Ching Wang†

†*Department of Electrical Engineering, National Cheng Kung University, Tainan City*
‡*Department of Information Management, Chang Jung University, Tainan County*
E-mail: {wangjf@csie.ncku.edu.tw, wangbb@mail.cju.edu.tw, wjc@icwang.ee.ncku.edu.tw}

For a safer and more convenient operation, a car navigation and assistance system with speech-enabled functions is essential. This chapter addresses two challenges for this purpose. The first is that the speech signal is inevitably corrupted by the ambient noise coming from the car. The distance between a hands-free car microphone and the speaker makes this problem even more serious. In this chapter, an integration of a perceptual filterbank and subspace-based speech enhancement are presented to reduce the effects of the first problem. The next challenge is that traditional spoken dialogue systems (SDS) merely concentrate on the interaction between the system and a single speaker. For this reason we are motivated to conduct a further study on multi-speaker dialogue systems. Here, the interactions between multiple speakers and the system are classified into three types: independent, cooperative, and conflicting interactions. An algorithm for the multi-speaker dialogue management is proposed to determine the interaction type, and to keep the interaction running smoothly.

1. Introduction

In the past decade, there has been much investigation on car navigation systems. In the early days of these systems, only textual information indicating car position were given. Recently-developed systems display the shortest route possible along with car position onto an LCD screen. A car navigation and assistance system with speech-enabled functions allows users to listen, rather than read/view these information, facilitating the safety and making its operation a convenience. To realize this, two challenges are dealt with here: speech enhancement with in-car noise, and multi-speaker dialogue systems (MSDS).

A common problem for car navigation and assistance systems is that the speech signal is corrupted by the ambient noise coming from the car. It is quite important to enhance speech from a noisy environment to create a robust human-computer speech interaction in such environments. In speech enhancement, the spectral subtraction approach[1-3] has gained much popularity in recent years. However, this approach has a musical noise drawback, which means it results in residual noise with noticeable tonal characteristics which can be annoying. Ephraim and Van Trees[4] proposed a subspace-based speech enhancement method which seeks for an optimal estimator that would minimize the signal distortion subject to the constraint that the residual noise falls below a preset threshold. Using the eigenvalue decomposition of the covariance matrix, it is shown that the decomposition of the vector space of the noisy speech into a signal and noise subspace can be obtained by applying the Karhunen-Loeve transform (KLT) to the noisy speech. The KLT components representing the signal subspace are modified by a gain function determined by the estimator, while the remaining KLT components representing the noise subspace are nulled. The enhanced speech is obtained from the inverse KLT of the modified components.

In the work done by Ephraim and Van Trees,[4] the additive noise was assumed to be white. Good performance was demonstrated in simulations when the computer-generated white Gaussian had been introduced. For enhancing speech degraded by colored noise, Mittal *et al.*[5] presented a signal/noise KLT based approach. They classified the noisy speech frames into speech-dominated frames and noise-dominated frames. The signal KLT matrix and noise KLT matrix were used in speech-dominated and noise dominated frames, respectively. Rezayee *et al.*[4] assumed the covariance matrix of the KLT-transformed noise to be diagonal. In practical situations, the assumed model is more accurate and matches noise behaviors better than the white noise model. Hu *et al.*[6] proposed a generalized subspace approach to deal with colored noise. A nonunitary transform derived from the simultaneous diagonalization of the clean speech and noise covariance matrices was used to replace the KLT. This transform has built-in prewhitening and could be used in general for colored noise.

In this chapter, a new speech enhancement technique based on a perceptual filterbank and a subspace-based method is proposed. The perceptual filterbank is obtained by adjusting the decomposition tree structure of the conventional wavelet packet transform in order to approximate the critical bands of the psycho-acoustic model as close as possible. The prior signal-to-noise ratio (SNR) of each critical band is then used to provide a suitable gain adaptation of the estimator.

The second challenge in creating an efficient car navigation and assistance system is that traditional spoken dialogue system (SDS) merely concentrate on the interaction between the system and a single speaker. In some situations, it is natural and necessary to be able to handle the interaction between multiple speakers and the system. For example, if several passengers in a car are deciding where to go for lunch, the traditional SDS would need to be improved in order to deal with the multiple speaker interaction. This motivates the present investigation into the study of multi-speaker dialogue systems (MSDS).

There are many factors to be considered when multiple parties are engaged in an HCI system. Studies of HCI systems that involve multiple users are in their initial stages, and thus publications, lectures and studies on this subject are very limited. Among the reported studies, Young developed a discourse structure for multi-speaker spoken dialogues based on a stochastic model.[7] Bull and Aylett[8] analyzed the timing of turn-taking in dialogues, while cross-speaker anaphora was reported by Poesio.[9] These research efforts were based on theoretical studies or the analyses of tagged text-based multi-speaker interactions. Similar papers[10-13] can be found. Besides these theoretical studies, Matsusaka *et al.*[14] built a robot that can communicate with multiple users using a multi-modal interface. The robot is equipped with several workstations and cameras to track and process the speaker input. So, in all, previous multi-speaker research either focused on the theoretical discussion of dialogues,[7-13] or required additional expensive, heterogeneous hardware for multi-modal input.[14-18] The issue that previous research has failed to analyze is the interaction between a dialogue system and its speakers. This chapter focuses on the analysis of such interactions and proposes an algorithm for the dialogue manager to handle these various interactions that take place in an MSDS. Note that two kinds of interaction may occur in a multi-speaker dialogue, as classified as follows. One is the interaction between speaker(s) and the system (referred to as “inter-action”), and the other is the interaction between the speakers themselves (“intra-action”). This chapter discusses only the former.

In various multi-speaker interactions, it is observed that during a dialogue, one speaker may either interrupt the utterance of another speaker or he may wait until the other speaker completes his utterance. That is, the speakers are either making simultaneous inputs or they utter the input in turns. If an MSDS can handle simultaneous speech inputs, we call it a simultaneous MSDS (Sim_MSDS); otherwise, it is called a sequential MSDS (Seq_MSDS). In a Seq_MSDS, utterances of speakers are first buffered, and then they are processed together. In this chapter we only consider Seq_MSDS.

In multi-speaker dialogues, speakers may cooperate to accomplish a common goal or negotiate to solve conflicting opinions to achieve the same goal. We define two types of goals in MSDS (i.e., the individual goal and the global goal). The individual goal is the answer that one speaker wants to obtain from the inquiry. Since individual goals may conflict with each other, the system should maintain a global goal in which it can integrate the individual goals. The following examples will demonstrate different cases in which individual goals do or do not conflict with each other. Depending on the relationship between two individual goals, the interactions between speakers and the system are classified as one of three types: independent, cooperative, and conflicting. Examples are shown below, where S_1 and S_2 are different speakers:

(i) Independent interaction*: speakers S_1 and S_2 have independent goals*

S_1: `What's the weather in Taipei?`
S_2: `Where is the Tainan train station?`

In the first example, the individual goal of each speaker is different and independent.

(ii) Cooperative interaction: *speakers have a common goal*

S_1: `Please find a place to eat.`
S_2: `I want to eat Japanese noodles.`

In the second example, the individual goal of S_1 is to find a restaurant, and the goal of S_2 is to eat Japanese noodles. The dialogue manager should detect and integrate these individual goals to form the global goal, i.e., a place where Japanese noodles are available.

(iii) Conflicting interaction: *speakers have conflicting goals*

S_1: `Tell me a Chinese restaurant.`
S_2: `I think we should go to an Italian restaurant.`

In the third example, S_1 wants to go to a restaurant which supplies Chinese food while; in contrast, S_2 wants to go to an Italian restaurant. Their intentions are similar, but the destinations conflict. The global goal should be adjusted when speaker S_2 has an individual goal different from that of S_1.

In an MSDS, the interactions between the speakers and the system should be handled carefully to keep the dialogue going smoothly. This task is often accomplished by the dialogue manager and is the major issue discussed in this chapter.

This chapter is organized as follows. Section 2 details the in-car noise reduction process; Section 3 shows the major components of an MSDS; Section 4 illustrates the algorithm of a multi-speaker dialogue manager, along with several examples; and finally, the concluding remarks are given in Section 5.

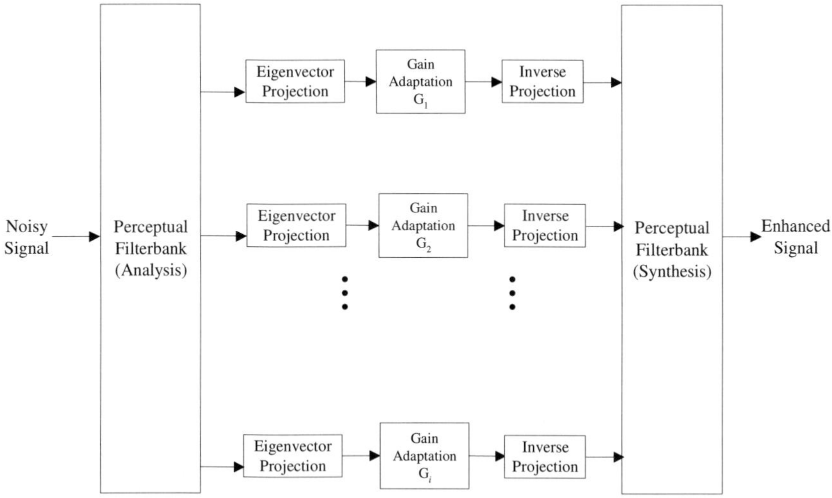

Fig. 1. Block diagram of proposed speech enhancement system.

2. In-Car Noise Reduction

A block diagram of the proposed speech enhancement system is depicted in Figure 1. The input noisy signal is first divided into critical band time series by the wavelet analysis filterbank. The subspace-based enhancement is performed in each critical band. The gain adaptation for estimating the clean signal is based on the prior SNR in each critical band. The wavelet synthesis filterbank is applied to the gain-modified vector of critical band signal to reconstruct the enhanced full-band signal.

2.1. *Subspace-Based Speech Enhancement*

The speech enhancement problem can be described as a clean signal $\bar{x}$ being corrupted by additive noise $\bar{n}$. The resulting noisy signal $\bar{y}$ can be expressed as

$$\bar{y} = \bar{x} + \bar{n}, \tag{1}$$

where $\bar{x} = [x_1, x_2, \ldots, x_M]^H$, $\bar{n} = [n_1, n_2, \ldots, n_M]^H$, and $\bar{y} = [y_1, y_2, \ldots, y_M]^H$. The observation period has been denoted as M. Henceforth, the vectors $\bar{x}$, $\bar{n}$, $\bar{y}$ will be considered as part of complex space C^M.

If it is assumed that clean signal is confined to a subspace of dimensionality K, where $K < M$, then C^M can be decomposed into two subspaces: a signal subspace and a noise subspace. Ephraim and Van Trees realize this partitioning by postulating a linear model for the signal frame under analysis. The range and the null space are characterized as the signal and noise subspaces, respectively. The linear model for the clean signal assumes that every M-sample frame can be represented using the model:

$$\bar{x} = \boldsymbol{V}\bar{s} = \sum_{i=1}^{K} s_i v_i \,, \quad K \le M, \tag{2}$$

where $\bar{s} = [s_1, s_2, \ldots, s_K]^H$ is a sequence of zero mean complex random variables. $\boldsymbol{V} \in R^{MxK}$ is known as the model matrix. Assuming that the columns of $\boldsymbol{V}$ are linearly independent, and the rank of $\boldsymbol{V}$ is K. The range of $\boldsymbol{V}$ defines the signal subspace. The noise subspace is the null space of the model matrix. This subspace has rank M–K and contains only vectors resulting from the noise process.

The subspace decomposition can be achieved using the KLT, i.e. eigenvector matrix. Let $\boldsymbol{R}_x$ and $\boldsymbol{R}_y$ denote the covariance matrix of the $\bar{x}$ and $\bar{y}$, respectively. The eigen-decomposition is performed on the covariance matrix $\boldsymbol{R}_x$ and the following form is obtained

$$\boldsymbol{R}_x = [\boldsymbol{U}_1 \boldsymbol{U}_2] \begin{bmatrix} \boldsymbol{\Lambda}_{x1} & \boldsymbol{0} \\ \boldsymbol{0} & \boldsymbol{0} \end{bmatrix} \begin{bmatrix} \boldsymbol{U}_1^H \\ \boldsymbol{U}_2^H \end{bmatrix}, \tag{3}$$

where $\boldsymbol{\Lambda}_{x1}$ is a $K \times K$ diagonal matrix with eigenvalues $\lambda_x(1), \lambda_x(2), \ldots, \lambda_x(K)$, as diagonal elements, i.e., $\mathrm{diag}(\lambda_x(1), \lambda_x(2), \ldots, \lambda_x(K))$. The eigenvector matrix $\boldsymbol{U}$ has been partitioned into two sub-matrices, $\boldsymbol{U}_1$ and $\boldsymbol{U}_2$. The matrix $\boldsymbol{U}_1$ contains eigenvectors corresponding to non-zero eigenvalues. These eigenvectors form a basis for the signal subspace. Meanwhile, $\boldsymbol{U}_2$ contains the eigenvectors which span the noise subspace.

Let $\boldsymbol{\Lambda}_{y1}$ denote $\mathrm{diag}(\lambda_y(1), \lambda_y(2), \ldots, \lambda_y(K))$. and $\boldsymbol{\Lambda}_{y2}$ represent $\mathrm{diag}(\lambda_y(K+1), \lambda_y(K+2), \ldots, \lambda_y(M))$. The notations $\boldsymbol{\Lambda}_{n1}$ and $\boldsymbol{\Lambda}_{n2}$ are in the same fashion. Similar to (3), the eigen-decomposition of $\boldsymbol{R}_y$ is given by

$$\boldsymbol{R}_y = [\boldsymbol{U}_1 \boldsymbol{U}_2] \begin{bmatrix} \boldsymbol{\Lambda}_{y1} & \boldsymbol{0} \\ \boldsymbol{0} & \boldsymbol{\Lambda}_{y2} \end{bmatrix} \begin{bmatrix} \boldsymbol{U}_1^H \\ \boldsymbol{U}_2^H \end{bmatrix} = [\boldsymbol{U}_1 \boldsymbol{U}_2] \begin{bmatrix} \boldsymbol{\Lambda}_{x1} + \boldsymbol{\Lambda}_{n1} & \boldsymbol{0} \\ \boldsymbol{0} & \boldsymbol{\Lambda}_{n2} \end{bmatrix} \begin{bmatrix} \boldsymbol{U}_1^H \\ \boldsymbol{U}_2^H \end{bmatrix}. \tag{4}$$

As indicated by (4), the clean signal lies only within the signal subspace while the noise spans the entire space. Therefore, only the contents of the signal subspace are used to estimate the clean signal.

The clean signal can be estimated using a linear estimator

$$\hat{x} = \boldsymbol{H}\overline{y}\,, \tag{5}$$

which $\boldsymbol{H}$ is a $K \times K$ matrix. The residual signal, $\overline{e}$, can then be represented as

$$\overline{e} = \hat{x} - \overline{x} = (\boldsymbol{H} - \boldsymbol{I})\overline{x} + \boldsymbol{H}\overline{n} = \overline{e}_x + \overline{e}_n \tag{6}$$

where $\overline{e}_x$ refers to the signal distortion while $\overline{e}_n$ denotes the residual noise. The energy of the signal distortion can be calculated from (6)

$$\varepsilon_x^2 = \mathrm{tr}E\{\overline{e}_x\overline{e}_x^H\} = \mathrm{tr}\{(\boldsymbol{H} - \boldsymbol{I})\boldsymbol{R}_x(\boldsymbol{H} - \boldsymbol{I})^H\}\,. \tag{7}$$

Similarly, the energy of the residual noise can be derived from (7)

$$\varepsilon_n^2 = \mathrm{tr}E\{\overline{e}_n\overline{e}_n^H\} = \mathrm{tr}\{\boldsymbol{H}\boldsymbol{R}_n\boldsymbol{H}^H\}\,. \tag{8}$$

The energy of the total error, ε thus can be calculated as

$$\varepsilon^2 = \varepsilon_x^2 + \varepsilon_n^2\,. \tag{9}$$

The time domain constrained estimator minimizes signal distortion while constraining the average residual noise power to be less than a positive constant α. Thus

$$\boldsymbol{H}_{opt} = \arg\min_{\boldsymbol{H}} \varepsilon_x^2\,,$$

$$\text{subject to: } \varepsilon_n^2 \le \alpha\,. \tag{10}$$

The resulting optimal linear estimator from the time domain constraints has the form

$$\boldsymbol{H}_{opt} = \boldsymbol{R}_x(\boldsymbol{R}_x + \gamma\boldsymbol{R}_n)^{-1}, \tag{11}$$

where γ is the Lagrange multiplier.

Based on the eigen-decomposition of $\boldsymbol{R}_x$, (11) is rewritten as

$$\boldsymbol{H}_{opt} = \boldsymbol{U}\boldsymbol{\Lambda}_x(\boldsymbol{\Lambda}_x + \gamma\boldsymbol{U}^H\boldsymbol{R}_n\boldsymbol{U})^{-1}\boldsymbol{U}^H\,. \tag{12}$$

The $\boldsymbol{U}^H\boldsymbol{R}_n\boldsymbol{U}$ can be approximated by a diagonal matrix $\boldsymbol{\Lambda}_n$, we thus have an approximated linear estimator

$$\tilde{\boldsymbol{H}}_{opt} = \boldsymbol{U}\boldsymbol{\Lambda}_x(\boldsymbol{\Lambda}_x + \gamma\boldsymbol{\Lambda}_{\mathrm{n}})^{-1}\boldsymbol{U}^H\,. \tag{13}$$

Remove the noise subspace, we can rewrite the estimator as

$$\tilde{\boldsymbol{H}}_{opt} = \boldsymbol{U}\begin{bmatrix}\boldsymbol{G} & \boldsymbol{0}\\ \boldsymbol{0} & \boldsymbol{0}\end{bmatrix}\boldsymbol{U}^H\,, \tag{14}$$

where

$$G = \Lambda_{x1}(\Lambda_{x1} + \gamma \Lambda_{n1})^{-1}. \tag{15}$$

Hence, the signal estimate $\hat{x} = \tilde{\boldsymbol{H}}_{opt}\,\bar{y}$ is obtained by applying the KLT to the noisy signal, appropriately modifying the components of the KLT $\boldsymbol{U}^{H}\,\bar{y}$ by a gain function, and by inverse KLT of the modified components.

2.2. *Perceptual Filterbank*

The perceptual filterbank is obtained by adjusting the decomposition tree structure of the conventional wavelet packet transform to approximate the critical bands of the psycho-acoustic model. One class of critical band scales is called the Bark scale. The Bark scale z can be approximately expressed in terms of the linear frequency by

$$z(f) = 13\arctan(7.6\times10^{-4} f) + 3.5\arctan(1.33\times10^{-4} f)^2, \tag{16}$$

where f is the linear frequency in Hertz. The corresponding critical bandwidth (CBW) of the center frequencies can be expressed by

$$\mathrm{CBW}(f_c) = 25 + 75(1 + 1.4\times10^{-6} f_c^{\,2})^{0.69}, \tag{17}$$

where f_c is the center frequency (unit: Hertz). In this study, the underlying sampling rate was chosen to be 8 kHz, yielding a bandwidth of 4 kHz. Within this bandwidth, there are approximately 17 critical bands as listed in Table 1.

Table 1. Characteristics of the Critical Bands.

Critical Band Number	Center Frequency (Hz)	CBW	Lower Cutoff frequency (Hz)	Upper Cutoff Frequency (Hz)
1	50	-	-	100
2	150	100	100	200
3	250	100	200	300
4	350	100	300	400
5	450	110	400	510
6	570	120	510	630
7	700	140	630	770
8	840	150	770	920
9	1000	160	920	1080
10	1170	190	1080	1270
11	1370	210	1270	1480
12	1600	240	1480	1720
13	1850	280	1720	2000
14	2150	320	2000	2320
15	2500	380	2320	2700
16	2900	450	2700	3150
17	3400	550	3150	3700

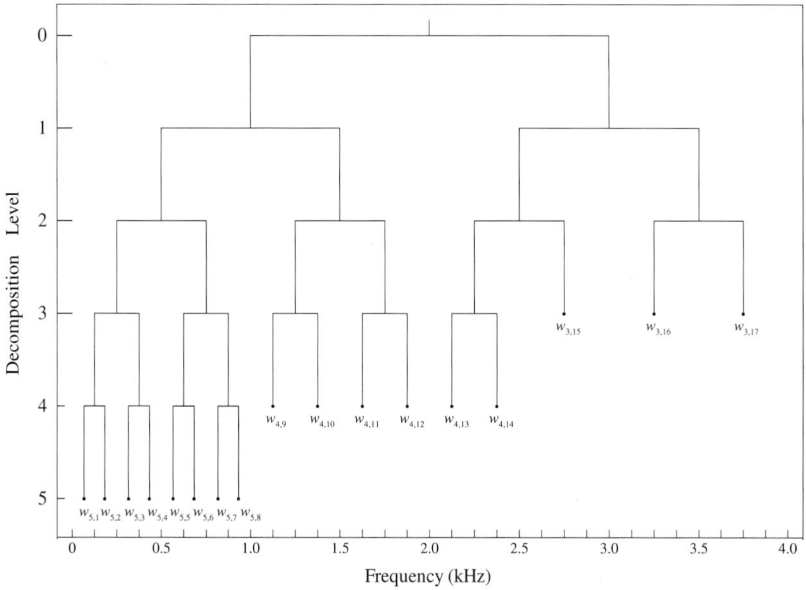

Fig. 2. Tree structure of the perceptual filterbank.

According to the specifications of center frequencies, CBW, lower and upper cut-off frequencies given in Table 1, the tree structure of the perceptual wavelet packet transform can be constructed as shown in Figure 2. It contains 16 bands which are corresponding to wavelet packet coefficient sets $w_{j,m}$, where j = 3, 4, 5, m = 1, …, 17. The resulting 17-band perceptual wavelet packet transform of the Bark scale and the CBW are also plotted in Figures 3 and 4, respectively.

2.3. *SNR-Aware Gain Estimation*

The perceptual filterbank is integrated with the subspace-based enhancement technique. For each critical band within the perceptual filterbank, individual subspace analysis is applied. Therefore, the optimal linear estimator for i-th critical band has the following form

$$\tilde{\boldsymbol{H}}_{opt}^{i} = \boldsymbol{U}^{i} \begin{bmatrix} \boldsymbol{G}^{i} & \boldsymbol{0} \\ \boldsymbol{0} & \boldsymbol{0} \end{bmatrix} (\boldsymbol{U}^{H})^{i}, \tag{18}$$

where

$$\boldsymbol{G}^{i} = \boldsymbol{\Lambda}_{x1}^{i} (\boldsymbol{\Lambda}_{x1}^{i} + \gamma^{i} \boldsymbol{\Lambda}_{n1}^{i})^{-1}. \tag{19}$$

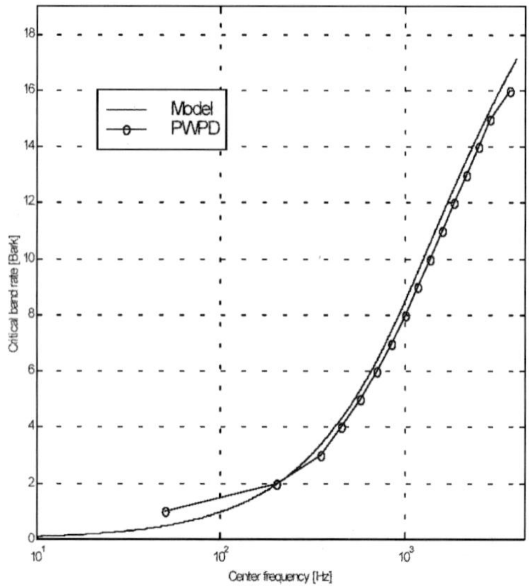

Fig. 3. Bark scale as a function of center frequency.

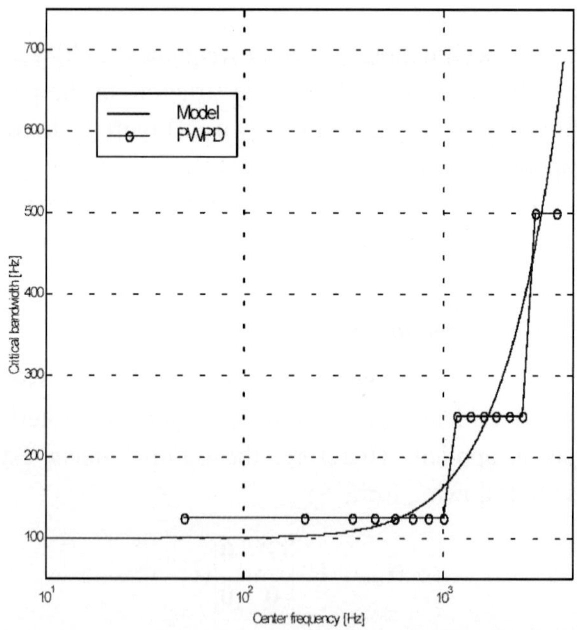

Fig. 4. Critical bandwidth as a function of center frequency.

The $\boldsymbol{G}^i$ is a diagonal gain matrix for *i*-th critical band. The gains within the same critical band are assumed to be equal and all the elements of $\boldsymbol{\Lambda}_{x1}^i$ and $\boldsymbol{\Lambda}_{n1}^i$ are respectively summed to have the signal power P_x^i and noise power P_n^i of *i*-th critical band. Accordingly, the gain for *i*-th critical band can be expressed by

$$G^i = \frac{P_x^i}{P_x^i + \gamma^i P_n^i} = \frac{P_x^i (P_n^i)^{-1}}{P_x^i (P_n^i)^{-1} + \gamma^i}, \tag{20}$$

where γ^i is the attenuation factor for *i*-th critical band.

The attenuation factor controls the trade-off between signal distortion and residual noise in *i*-th critical band. A larger value of the attenuation factor will yield more signal distortion and less residual noise, and vice versa. How to determine the attenuation factor thus plays an essential role for the enhancement process.

Instead of applying the same attenuation value to the whole frequency span, determining the attenuation degree of each critical band within the perceptual filterbank respectively is a better solution. In (20), $P_x^i (P_n^i)^{-1}$ can be considered as the prior SNR of the *i*-th critical band. The prior SNR is calculated in accordance to the noise power spectrum estimated by a pre-obtained noise segment and the signal power spectrum derived by subtracting noise power spectrum from noisy signal power spectrum. The attenuation factor in each critical band is determined according to the prior SNR of the corresponding one. Assume the maximum attenuation value is κ. The attenuation factor of *i*-th critical band is decided by a monotonic decreasing function

$$\gamma^i = \frac{\kappa e^{-\chi^i}}{1 + e^{-S\chi^i}}, \tag{21}$$

where χ^i is the prior SNR of *i*-th critical band.

3. Fundamentals of MSDS

According to the model provided by Huang *et al.*[19], a traditional single-speaker SDS can be modeled as a pattern recognition problem. Given a speech input *X*, the objective of the system is to arrive at actions *A* (including a response message and necessary operations) so that the probability of choosing *A* is maximized. The optimal solution, i.e., the maximum *a posterior* (MAP) estimation, can be expressed as the following equation:

$$A^* = \arg\max_A P(A \mid X, S_{n-1}) \approx \arg\max_{A,S_n} P(A \mid S_n) \sum_F P(S_n \mid F, S_{n-1}) P(F \mid X, S_{n-1}), \quad (22)$$

where F denotes the semantic interpretation of X and S_n, the discourse semantics for the n-th dialogue turn. Note that (22) shows the model-based decomposition of an SDS. The probabilistic model of an SDS can be found in the work of Young.[20, 21]

For the case of multi-speaker dialogue system, assuming that only single-thread speech input is allowed, and speech is input from multiple microphone channels, Equation (22) can be extended to the formulation below.

$$A^* \approx \arg\max_A P(A \mid G_n) P(G_n \mid S_n^{1^*}, ..., S_n^{m^*}, G_{n-1}), \quad (23)$$

where G_n denotes the integration of m discourse semantics for the n-th dialogue turn, it contains all the information in S^i_n. And, m is the number of speakers. The discourse semantics S^i_n can be derived using (24) shown below:

$$S_n^{i^*} = \arg\max_{S_n^i} \sum_{F^i} P(S_n^i \mid F^i, S_{n-1}^i) P(F^i \mid X^i, S_{n-1}^i) P(X^i \mid U), \quad (24)$$

where U denotes the multiple input from the multiple microphones and i is the speaker index. Based on (24), an MSDS can be decomposed into five components as described below:

1. *Active speaker determination:* deciding the active speaker i and their speech input X^i, using model $P(X^i|U)$. In order to assist in the determination of the active speaker along with multiple microphone input, the matched filter can be a useful technique. The output of the matched filter from each microphone is compared with a predetermined threshold to determine the primary channel, i.e., the active speaker.
2. *Individual semantic parser*: performing the same parsing process, as in the case of traditional SDS, for each speaker. The semantic model $P(F^i|X^i, S^i_{n-1})$ to parse sentence X^i into semantic objects F^i. This component is often divided into individual target speech recognition and sentence parsing. The speech recognizer translates each speaker's utterance into a word/keyword lattice. Current development of keyword spotters allows them the ability to detect thousands of keywords and yields acceptable results for the applications of SDS. It would be suitable to make use of a keyword spotter in an MSDS in order to detect the meaningful part of a speaker utterance. Our proposed MSDS uses the technique developed by Wu and Chen.[22]

Furthermore, we adopt the partial parser which concentrates on describing the structure of the meaningful clauses and sentences that are embedded in the spoken utterance.

3. *Individual discourse analysis:* the discourse model $P(S^i_n|F^i, S^i_{n-1})$ is used to derive new dialogue context S^i_n. This process is also performed for each speaker.
4. *Multiple discourse integration:* the discourse semantics of all speakers are integrated using model $P(G_n|S^1_n, \ldots, S^m_n, G_{n-1})$. The discourse integration model together with the individual discourse analysis model combine and integrate each speaker's dialogue semantics. The result of discourse integration is sent to the multi-speaker dialogue manager.
5. *Multi-speaker dialogue manager*: to determine the most suitable action by the model $P(A|G_n)$. After multi-speaker speech input is handled properly by these modules, the dialogue manager is responsible for maintaining the dialogue and keeping it running smoothly. It plays an important role in an MSDS that is described in the next section.

4. Dialogue Management for MSDS

Once the active speaker is determined, the target speech is sent to the speech recognition and natural language processing components. The keyword spotting and partial parsing techniques that are popular in the field of spoken language processing can be adopted into an MSDS. The parsed result will be the most likely sequence of words with their part-of-speech tags. The sequence is then fed to the dialogue manager. The dialogue manager maintains the interaction among the system and the multiple speakers, and keeps it running smoothly. In an MSDS, each speaker may have his own individual goal for information retrieval. In contrast to the individual goal, the global goal is the integration of each individual goal. The management of the multi-speaker dialogue has several functions: 1) to interpret the intentions and semantics of each individual speaker in order to detect if there is a conflict between speakers; 2) to integrate individual goals into global goals; 3) to determine whether a specific goal is achieved; and 4) to generate the appropriate response. In this section, we illustrate how the management of MSDS works by providing an algorithm and some examples.

4.1. *Algorithm for Multi-Speaker Dialogue Manager*

Figure 5 shows the block diagram of the MSDS system. The detailed algorithm of the multi-speaker dialogue management is shown in Figure 6. Each time the

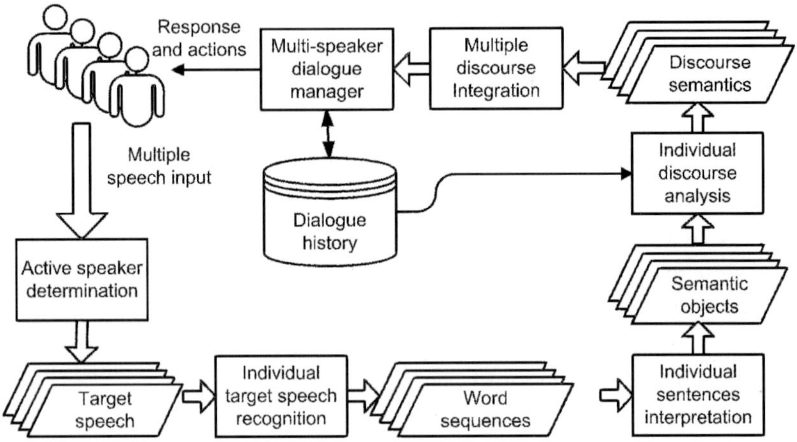

Fig. 5. Basic components of a multi-speaker dialogue system. The rectangular blocks are the processing units; the parallelograms are multiple outputs derived from the processing units.

system receives input from a speaker, the natural language processing technique (as introduced in Section 2) is applied to understand the intention and semantics of this speaker. We used a data structure, the *semantic frame*, to record this information. The semantic frame *SF* is defined below (assuming there are *m* speakers): $SF_i = (V_D^i, V_{PA}^i, V_{SA_1}^i, V_{SA_2}^i, ...)$, $i = 1 \sim m$.

For speaker *i*, V_D^i represents the domain that this speaker mentioned; V_{PA}^i is the primary attribute for this domain, i.e., the purpose of the query; and $V_{SA_j}^i$ are secondary attributes that specify additional information needed for this query. Note that the number of secondary attributes varies with the domain. For the inquiry, "please show me the route to the train station", for example, the semantic frame will be: *SF* = (*"NAVIGATION"*, *"DESTINATION"*, *"train station"*, *Null...*).

The *SF* of the current dialogue turn are combined with those of previous turns. The interaction types between speakers are then determined based on the derived *SF*. For the case in which more than two speakers are engaged, the integration for different interaction types is described below. For each two speakers, if the interaction type is independent, the individual semantic slots are maintained and remain unmodified. If the interaction type is cooperative, the semantic slots for these two speakers are combined together. If the interaction type is conflicting, the semantic slots are unmodified but an extra message is issued to the dialogue manager indicating that a conflict has happened.

Input: Partial parsing results of speech recognition for each speaker, denoted as PP_1, PP_2, … , PP_m, where m is the number of total speakers.

Output: response to speakers.

Step 1: Initialization

- Initialize the semantic frames SF_i to be NULL.

$$SF_i = (V_D^i, V_{PA}^i, V_{SA1}^i, V_{SA2}^i, \ldots),\ i = 1 \sim m$$

For speaker i, V_D^i represents the mentioned speaker domain; V_{PA}^i is the primary domain attribute; and V_{SAj}^i are secondary attributes, where j varies with the domain.

- Initialize the dialogue history lists, Hi, for each speaker to NULL.

Step 2: Determine the semantic frame

Apply NLP techniques to PP_i to determine the corresponding semantic frame SF_i. Semantic frame SFi for this turn is copied to the history Hi.

Step 3: Determine interaction type for any speaker pair (i, j)

If $V_D^i = V_D^j$

if $V_{PA}^i \neq V_{PA}^j$ then **Cooperative interaction**

else_if $V_{PA}^i = V_{PA}^j$ then **Conflicting interaction**

else_if $V_D^i \neq V_D^j$

then **Independent interaction**

Step 4: Semantic integration

SF_i's and H_i's are integrated to determine if a goal is completed.

(Detailed method for semantic integration is listed in Section 3.1.)

Step 5: Determine the accomplished goal(s)

For each speaker, check if the necessary information slots for completing a goal are filled or not. A goal is completed ⇔ ($V_D \neq$ Null) AND ($V_{PA} \neq$ Null) AND ($V_{SA} \neq$ Null)

Step 6: Decision

If any goal is completed, go to Step 7; else go to Step 8.

Note that the conditions for a goal to be completed are definable for each domain.

Step 7: Response: Perform database query and generate response to the user according to the goal(s) found in Step 3. Go to Step 8.

Fig. 6. The algorithm for multi-speaker dialogue management.

After interaction types are determined, the dialogue manager determines if any goal has been achieved. This is based on whether all essential information needed for a specific query is available. For example, if the speaker is querying about the weather, the essential information would be the location (e.g., city name), weather type (e.g., temperature or rainfall density), and time (e.g., tomorrow or this afternoon). Once a goal has been completed, the system may perform database queries and generate a proper response to the speaker. If certain essential information is missing or the speaker interactions are in conflict, further confirmation and repair processes should be undertaken to realize the final intention of the speakers.

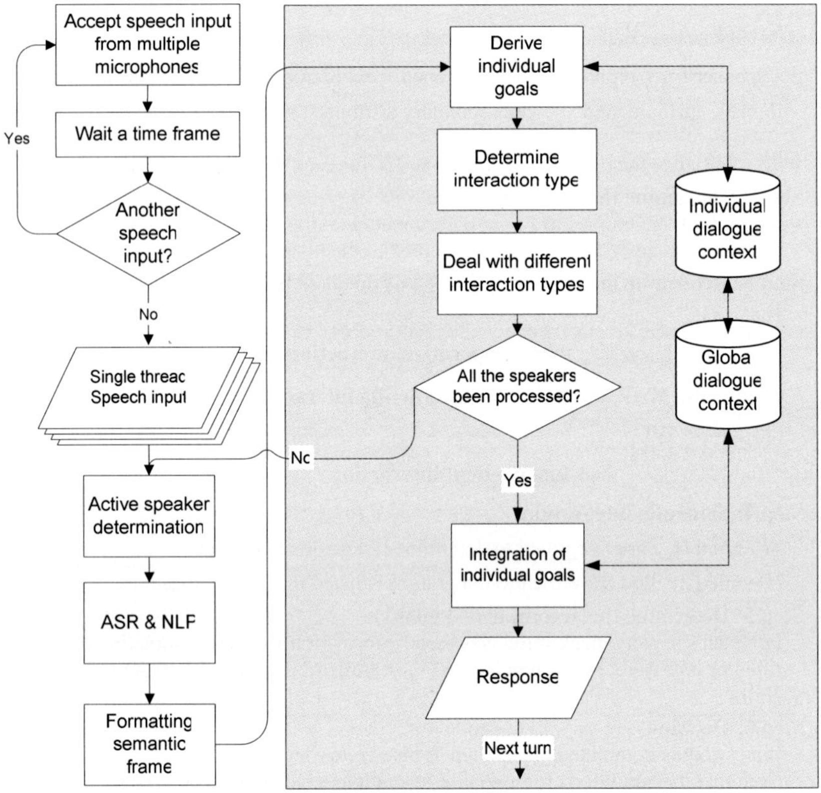

Fig. 7. Block diagram of the multi-speaker dialogue manager.

4.2. *Examples of Interactions and Dialogue Management of MSDS*

In the following examples, we illustrate the cases of 1) speakers who have independent individual goals, which can be solved easily; 2) speakers with conflicting individual goals, in which the system must resolve this before further information can be relayed to the speakers; and 3) speakers who have a common goal, where they provide the necessary information for the system in a mutually-cooperative fashion.

Example 1. Speakers have different individual goals.

Time index	Action	Content
1	($Speaker_1$) inputs	"I want to go to the city hall".
2	($Speaker_2$) inputs	"Tell me the weather in Taipei"
3	(System) derives *SFi*	SF_1 = ("NAVIGATION", "ROUTE", "city hall", Null…) SF_2 = ("WEATHER", "LOCATION", "Taipei", Null…)
4	(System) checks goal completeness	$Speaker_1$ = TRUE $Speaker_2$ = TRUE
5	(System) checks if conflict happened	NO
6	(System) generates response	"The weather in Taipei is rainy." "The city hall is about 450 meters away, please follow the instructions."

Example 2. Speakers have conflicting individual goals.

Time index	Action	Content
1	($Speaker_1$) inputs	"Find me a Chinese food restaurant".
2	($Speaker_2$) inputs	"No, I want to eat Italian food"
3	(System) derives *SFi*	SF_1 = ("NAVIGATION", "ROUTE", "destination=restaurant", "attribute=Chinese food", Null…) SF_2 = ("NAVIGATION", "ROUTE", "destination=restaurant", "attribute=Italian food", Null…)
4	(System) checks goal completeness	$Speaker_1$ = TRUE $Speaker_2$ = TRUE
5	(System) checks if conflict	YES
6	(System) resolves conflict	"Please specify again, do you want Chinese food or Italian food"

Example 3. Speakers have a common goal.

Time index	Action	Content
1	(Speaker$_1$) input	"I want to know the route to …".
2	(System) derives *SFi*	SF$_1$=("NAVIGATION", "ROUTE", Null…)
3	(System) checks goal completeness	Speaker$_1$=FALSE, (no DESTINATION)
4	(System) generate response	"Please specify the destination."
5	(Speaker$_1$) input	"To the nearest gas station"
6	(Speaker$_2$) input	"And, how far is the gas station?"
7	(System) combines new *SFi* with old ones	SF$_1$=("NAVIGATION", "ROUTE", "destination=gas station", "attribute=nearest" Null…) SF$_2$=("NAVIGATION", "DISTANCE", "destination=gas station", "attribute=nearest", Null…)
8	(System) checks goal completeness	Speaker$_1$=YES Speaker$_2$=YES
9	(System) checks if conflict	NO
10	(System) generates response	"The nearest gas station is 540 meters ahead, please continue straight ahead."

These examples demonstrate three types of interaction between two speakers. For the cases in which more than two speakers are involved, the same approach is applied to check the interaction type and goal completeness, and generate the response to the speakers.

5. Conclusion

In this chapter, we have addressed two important issues for the development of a robust car navigation and assistance system with speech-enabled functions. First, a new subspace-based speech enhancement algorithm is presented. We construct a perceptual filterbank from a psycho-acoustic model and incorporate it with the subspace-based enhancement approach. This filterbank is created through a five-level wavelet packet decomposition. The gain adaptation plays a crucial rule in the critical band signal estimation. An attenuation factor based on prior SNR of each critical band is presented to adjust the estimator's gain of the optimal linear estimator.

Second, we have presented a multi-speaker dialogue system. The interaction types between the speakers and the system are analyzed, and an algorithm of the multi-speaker dialogue management is presented. Based on the proposed techniques, an MSDS system was built to provide vehicular navigation information and assistance in the car environment where every passenger may want to interact with the system. The proposed MSDS system can interact with multiple speakers and resolve conflicting opinions. Speakers are also able to acquire multi-domain information independently or cooperatively. Since our research is in its initial stage, only interactions (as opposed to *intra*-action) between speakers and the system are studied in the present work. Modeling both inter-actions and intra-actions in an MSDS is a more difficult task that requires further study, both in the theoretical as well as practical arena. Research concerning multi-speaker spoken dialogue systems is in its initial stage and we hope that our work will help to encourage further research into the techniques of MSDS.

Acknowledgments

This work was supported by the National Science Council. We would like to thank the valuable discussions and comments from C. H. Wu, J. T. Chien and C. H. Yang.

References

1. M. Berouti, R. Schwartz, and J. Makhoul, "Enhancement of speech corrupted by acoustic noise," in *Proceedings of IEEE International Conference on Acoustics, Speech, and Signal Processing*, 1979, pp. 208-211.
2. D. O'Shaughnessy, "Enhancing speech degraded by additive noise or interfering speakers," *IEEE Communication Magazine*, pp 46-52, Feb. 1989.
3. N. Virag, "Single channel speech enhancement based on masking properties of the human auditory system," *IEEE Transactions on Speech and Audio Processing*, vol. 7, no. 2, pp. 126-137, March 1999.
4. Y. Ephraim and H. L. Van Trees, "A signal subspace approach for speech enhancement," *IEEE Transactions on Speech and Audio Processing*, vol. 3, no. 4, pp. 251-266, July 1995.
5. U. Mittal and N. Phamdo, "Signal/noise KLT based approach for enhancing speech degraded by colored noise," *IEEE Transactions on Speech and Audio Processing*, vol. 8, pp. 159-167, Mar. 2000.
6. Y. Hu and P. C. Loizou, "A generalized subspace approach for enhancing speech corrupted by colored noise; *IEEE Transactions on Speech and Audio Processing*, vol. 11, no. 4, pp. 334-341, July 2003.
7. S. J. Young, "Talking to Machines (Statistically Speaking)", in the *Proceeding of International Conference on Spoken Language Processing*, Denver, Colorado, 2002.
8. M. Bull and M. Aylett, "An Analysis of The Timing of Turn-Taking in A Corpus of Goal-Oriented Dialogue", in *Proceedings of the International Conference on Spoken Language Processing*, volume 4, pages 1175-1178, Sydney, Australia, 1998.

9. M. Poesio, "Cross-speaker Anaphora and Dialogue Acts", in Proceeding of the workshop on Mutual Knowledge, *Common Ground and Public Information* ESSLLI Summer School, 1998.
10. J. Berg and N. Francez, "A Multi-Agent Extension of DRT, .Technical report of Laboratory for Computation Linguistics", in *Proceeding of the 1st International Workshop on Computational Semantics*, pp. 81-90. University of Tilburg, 1994.
11. P. R. Cohen, R. Coulston, and K. Krout, "Multiparty Multimodal Interaction: A Preliminary Analysis", in *Proceeding of International Conference on Spoken Language Processing*, 2002.
12. E. A. Hinkelman and S. K. Spaceman, "Communication with Multiple Agents", in *Proceedings of the 15th International Conference on Computational Linguistics (COLING'94)*, vol. 2, pp. 1191-1197, Kyoto, Japan, 1994.
13. T. R. Shankar, M. VanKleek, A. Vicente and B. K. Smith, "Fugue: A Computer Mediated Conversational System that Supports Turn Negotiation", in *33rd Hawaii International Conference on System Sciences*, Los Alamitos: IEEE Press, 2002.
14. Y. Matsusaka, T. Tojo, S. Kubota, K. Furukawa, D. Tamiya, K. Hayata, Y. Nakano, and T. Kobayashi, "Multi-person Conversation via Multi-modal Interface – A Robot who Communicate with Multi-user", in *Proceeding of EuroSpeech'99*, pp.1723-1726, 1999.
15. M. Johnston, S. Bangalore, A. Stent, G. Vasireddy, and P. Ehlen, (2002). "Multimodal Language Processing for Mobile Information Access", in *Proceeding of International Conference on Spoken Language Processing*, 2002.
16. I. Marsic, "Natural Communication with Information Systems", *Proceedings of the IEEE*, Vol. 88, pp. 1354-1366, 2002.
17. H. Rössler, J. S. Wajda, J. Hoffmann, and M. Kostrzewa, "Multimodal Interaction for Mobile Environments", in *Proceeding of International Workshop on Information Presentation and Natural Multimodal Dialogue*, 2001.
18. D. Traum and J. Rickel, "Embodied Agents for Multi-party Dialogue in Immersive Virtual Worlds", in *Proceedings of the first international joint conference on Autonomous agents and multiagent systems*: part 2. pp.766-773, 2001.
19. X. Huang, A. Acero and H. W. Hon, *Spoken Language Processing,* New Jersey: Prentice Hall, 2001.
20. S. R. Young, "Discourse Structure for Multi-speaker Spontaneous Spoken Dialogs: Incorporating Heuristics into Stochastic RTNS", in *Proceeding of International Conference on Acoustic and Speech Signal Processing*, pp.177-180, 1995.
21. S. J. Young, "Probabilistic Methods in Spoken Dialogue Systems", *Philosophical Transactions of the Royal Society (Series A)* 358(1769): pp.1389-1402, 2000.
22. C. H. Wu and Y. J. Chen, "Multi-Keyword Spotting of Telephone Speech Using a Fuzzy Search Algorithm and Keyword-Driven Two-Level CBSM," *Speech Communication*, Vol.33, pp.197-212, 2001.
23. M. Danieli and E. Gerbino, "Metrics for evaluating dialogue strategies in a spoken language system". in *Proceedings of the 1995 AAAI Spring Symposium on Empirical Methods in Discourse Interpretation and Generation*, Stanford, CA, pp. 34–39, 1995.

CHAPTER 23

CSLP CORPORA AND LANGUAGE RESOURCES

Hsiao-Chuan Wang[†], Thomas Fang Zheng[‡], and Jianhua Tao[§]

[†]*National Tsing Hua University, Hsinchu*
[‡]*Research Institute of Information Technology, Tsinghua University, Beijing*
[§]*Institute of Automation, Chinese Academy of Sciences, Beijing*
E-mail:{hcwang@ee.nthu.edu.tw, fzheng@tsinghua.edu.cn, jhtao@nlpr.ia.ac.cn}

This chapter discusses the fundamental issues related to the development of language resources for Chinese spoken language processing (CSLP). Chinese dialects, transcription systems, and Chinese character sets are described. The general procedure for speech corpus production is introduced, along with the dialect-specific problems related to CSLP corpora. Some activities in the development of CSLP corpora are also presented here. Finally, available language resources for CSLP as well as their related websites are listed.

1. Introduction

Language resources usually refer to large sets of language data or descriptions which are in machine-readable form. They can be used for developing and evaluating natural language and speech processing algorithms and systems. A language resource can be in the form of a written language corpus, spoken language corpus, a lexical database, or an electronic dictionary. It may also include software tools for the use of that resource. A written language corpus is a text corpus which can be made up of whole texts or samples of texts. The development of corpus linguistics requires the use of computational tools to process large-sized text corpora.[1] A spoken language corpus refers to the speech database which is designed for the development and evaluation of speech processing systems. For example, a speech recognition system based on statistical model techniques needs to train acoustic models of speech units by using a large amount of speech data, as well as to train its language models by the use of a large text corpus.

The building of a large language corpus involves a huge effort that is required for data collection, transcription, representation, annotation, validation, documentation, and distribution. Some organizations have been established in the past decades to create and gather language resources, promote the reuse of these resources, and develop new technologies in the process of building language resources. The two most important and internationally-recognized organizations are the Linguistic Data Consortium (LDC) and the European Language Resources Association (ELRA). The LDC, founded in 1992, is an open consortium of universities, private organizations and government research laboratories. It creates, collects and distributes speech and text databases, lexicons, and other resources for research and development purposes.[2,3] ELRA was established as a non-profit organization in 1995. It is active in identification, distribution, collection, validation, standardization, improvement, and production of language resources. Its focus is on the issues of making language resources available to different sectors of the language engineering community.[4,5]

Chinese is one of the major languages of the world. However, research on Chinese spoken language processing is about one or two decades behind the level of research done on English, Japanese, and some European languages. Some research on Chinese speech synthesis and recognition started in the mid-1980s. Thereafter, much more research were reported in the 1990's.[6-12] Almost in the same period, some projects involving the creation of large scale Chinese language resources were initiated in mainland China, Taiwan and Hong Kong. In mainland China, the 863 Program had created several language corpora in various domains, such as the corpora for speech recognition, speech synthesis, parallel language processing (for Chinese, English, and Japanese), information indexing, and dialogue systems.[13-16] Some corpora were created in cooperation with private companies.[16] In Taiwan, the CKIP (Chinese Knowledge and Information Processing) group was formed in the Academia Sinica to establish a fundamental research environment for Chinese natural language processing. The goal of CKIP was to construct research infrastructures with reusable resources that could be shared by domestic and international research institutes. Their accomplished sets of resources include Chinese electronic dictionaries, Mandarin Chinese corpora, and processing technologies for Chinese texts.[17] MAT (Mandarin across Taiwan) was a speech data collection project for creating telephone speech databases of Mandarin Chinese spoken in Taiwan.[18] In Hong Kong, Cantonese corpora were created for speech recognition, translation, and language understanding by a few universities.[19] Besides these, some research institutions in the United States also collected Mandarin Chinese data, such as the

CALLHOME Mandarin Chinese speech data collected by the LDC[3] and the Chinese speech data collected by the Johns Hopkins University.[20]

2. Chinese Spoken Languages, Transcription Systems, and Character Sets

Many dialects are spoken in China. Mandarin is a category of related Chinese dialects spoken in most of the northern, central, and western parts of China. However, *Mandarin,* as it is known to the world, refers to standard Mandarin (or modern standard Chinese) which is based on the Mandarin dialect spoken in Beijing. Standard Mandarin is the official spoken language known as *Putonghua* in mainland China and as *Guoyu* in Taiwan. In Singapore, Mandarin is one of the four official languages. Standard Mandarin is also one of the five official languages of the United Nations, and is used in many international organizations.[21] Putonghua and Guoyu are quite similar except in some areas of their vocabularies. Phonological descriptions show that the structural pattern of a Mandarin syllable is an optional initial consonant followed by the vowel, and then optionally followed by a velar or alveolar nasal ending. Another component of the Mandarin syllable is the tone which mainly specifies the syllable's pitch pattern. Technically, a syllable is presented in terms of its *initial*, *final*, and *tone*.[22] Mandarin is a tonal language because the tones, just like consonants and vowels, are used to distinguish words from each other.

Chinese linguists have proposed various transcription systems for Mandarin. But the most popular ones are *Hanyu Pinyin* and *Zhuyin Fuhao*. Hanyu Pinyin was accepted as the official transcription system for the Chinese language in 1958 by the government of China. Zhuyin Fuhao (or *Bopomofo*), a set of Chinese phonemic alphabets proposed in 1930, is used in Taiwan as an educational instrument for teaching the Chinese language. Both these transcription systems are used in the input of Chinese characters in computer systems.

Today, there are two Chinese character sets used by Chinese-language users, i.e., the traditional Chinese characters and the simplified Chinese characters. The traditional Chinese characters have been used since the 5th century. This character set is still being used in Taiwan and some overseas Chinese communities today. The simplified Chinese characters originate from the official character simplification during 1950s and 1960s. Now, this set of simplified Chinese characters is the official writing system in mainland China, and is accepted by the United Nations. In computer systems, different codes are used for these two character sets. The *Guobiao* code (GB) is a national standard character encoding in mainland China. It refers to the GB 2312-80 set issued in 1981, or the GB 18030-2000 set issued in 2000. There are 6,763 Chinese characters in the GB

3212-80 code set. *Big5* code is a character encoding method used in Taiwan for traditional Chinese characters. It contains 13,053 Chinese characters in its code set.

Mandarin Chinese is referred to as monosyllabic because the majority of words are one syllable in length. This is true for classical Chinese, but no longer true for modern Chinese. A large number of polysyllabic words are used today in daily spoken Chinese. One syllable when uttered with different tones corresponds to different characters. A word in polysyllabic form is written with two or more characters. Since Chinese texts have no spacing between words, extra effort is required to segment a sentence into word-parts. Because of these particular characteristics, the design of Chinese language corpora needs extra considerations. Most of the Chinese spoken language processing systems developed recently deal with standard Mandarin. Few of them cater for other dialects, such as Cantonese, Min-nan, Hakka, Wu, etc.[23]

3. Design of Chinese Language Resources

In general, speech corpus production involves the following procedures: (1) corpus specification, (2) preparation, (3) data collection, (4) postprocessing, (5) annotation, (6) pronunciation encoding, (7) documentation, (8) validation, and (9) distribution.[24,25] A corpus is created for the study of the language or the development of speech technology. The contents of the corpus should therefore be chosen and designed to achieve its purpose.

The specifications of a spoken language corpus includes defining the speaker profiles, the number of speakers, the spoken contents, the speaking style, the recording setup, the desired annotation, the recorded format, the corpus structure, and its validation procedure. Before data collection, preparations must be done. The instructions and prompting should be provided before the recording starts. Usually, an automatic process is used to control the actions in a recording session. A pre-test is necessary to ensure that the recording setup and equipment are functioning well. The final concern before going into the data collection phase is the recruitment of speakers. Corpus builders should obtain a sufficient number of speakers for a given data collection task.

In the data collection phase, all processes of data collection must be documented. This logging can be done on paper or online. It is desirable to perform the pre-validation after a small amount of data is collected. Besides, an ongoing quality control is necessary to detect systematic errors. The recorded data must be safely stored. Then, the recorded raw signal data are post-processed typically by the steps of file transfer, file name assignment, editing, and error detection. Sometimes, resampling of the signals may be required to get desired sampling rate or to make format conversions.

The annotation of a speech corpus includes the following processes: segmentation and labeling, transcription and tagging, and internal validation. Segmentation is a process to get a combination of time information and categorical content. Segmental units can be phones, syllables, morphemes, words, prosodic categories, or dialogue acts. Manual segmentation is believed to be more accurate, but is extremely expensive, time- and effort-wise. Automatic or semi-automatic segmentation done by using a software tool is desirable to process a large database. Transcription is a process to represent speech in terms of its semantic contents. Typically, a recorded item is transcribed into a chain of words. Tagging refers to the markup of categorical classes on words. Some software tools can be used for transcription. These annotations should undergo a verification step to ensure good quality. The internal validation process is ideally performed by a single person or a well-trained group to ensure consistency. Documentation must be made to summarize all relevant information regarding the production and usage of the corpus. Finally, a validation process is further conducted to validate the documentation, signal data, annotation data, readability, and quality.

The production of language corpora for Chinese spoken language processing (CSLP) involves almost the same procedures as described above. Since there are many dialects spoken in different regions across China, accent differences do affect pronunciation when speaking in Mandarin. For example, the Mandarin spoken in Taiwan is somewhat different from the Mandarin spoken in Beijing, not only in terms of accent, but also in terms of the vocabulary used. For this reason, a Mandarin speech corpus should be a dialect-specified corpus.

In recent years, much language corpora have been designed by collecting data from radio and television broadcasts.[26] Some text data are collected from the internet. The option of obtaining spoken and textual data available in public channels and networks provides a quick way to gather large amounts of data. However, the collection of data alone does not imply the creation of a corpus, unless the contents are well defined and organized to meet a specific purpose. Further, the major effort of corpus building lies in the annotation, documentation and validation of the collected data. In addition to standard Mandarin, certain widely-spoken dialects need language corpora for developing their specific application systems. These also face annotation problems. Proper phonetic alphabet systems need to be developed as well.[27,28]

4. Activities in Developing CSLP Corpora

There are many organizations dedicated to the development of CSLP corpora. Among them, the ChineseLDC (Chinese Linguistic Data Consortium) is a nationwide, voluntary entity, legally-registered by researchers engaged in the creation and development of Chinese linguistic data. It is an academic and non-profit public association, with the aim of uniting various researchers in the CSLP area and producing Chinese linguistic databases to promote speech and language technology.[23] The ChineseLDC started with a project (Image, Speech, Natural Language Understanding and Knowledge Exploration Project) supported by the 973 Program (Program of National Key Foundation Research and Development) and the Chinese Hi-tech Research and Development Program (General Technical Research and Basic Database for the Establishment of the Chinese Platform). As a subordinate body to the Chinese Information Association, the ChineseLDC receives professional guidance and supervision from the association. Its office is located within the Institute of Automation, Chinese Academy of Sciences.

The goal of the establishment of the ChineseLDC is to set up a general linguistic database that is made up of the best quality Chinese databases that are currently available internationally. To achieve this goal, the ChineseLDC is creating and collecting open Chinese linguistic data that are highly integral, authorized, and systematic. It also targets data that cater to the requirements of various areas, such as lexicons, language corpora, data and instrumental references. This is to set a uniform series of standards and criteria for the users of these resources. While creating and collecting linguistic data, the ChineseLDC distributes existing data to various departments for educational, scientific research and governmental purposes, as well as for the development of industrial technology. The ChineseLDC also offers support to the fundamental research and application development in CSLP.

The Chinese Corpus Consortium (CCC), founded in 2004, is another organization for the distribution of Chinese language corpora.[20] The CCC has been sponsored by a group of universities, institutes, and private companies. Current sponsors include:

- Beijing d-Ear Technologies Co., Ltd. (d-Ear), China.
- Center for Speech Technology, Tsinghua University (CST), China.
- Institute of Linguistics, Chinese Academy of Social Sciences (CASS), China.
- Human Computer Interaction and Multimedia Lab, Tsinghua University, China.
- Chinese & Oriental Language Information Processing Society (COLIPS), Singapore.

- Dept. 1, ATR Spoken Language Translation Research Labs, Japan.
- Center for Language & Speech Processing, The Johns Hopkins University, USA.
- The Chinese University of Hong Kong (CUHK), Hong Kong SAR, China.

The CCC aims to provide language corpora for the areas of Chinese automatic speech recognition (ASR), text-to-speech (TTS) synthesis, natural language processing (NLP), perception analysis, phonetic analysis, linguistic analysis, and other related tasks. The functions of the CCC include:

- Collecting and integrating existing Chinese speech and linguistic corpus resources, and continuing the creation of such resources.
- Integrating existing tools for the creation, transcription, and analysis of Chinese speech and linguistic corpus resources, improving their usability, and creating new tools.
- Collecting, organizing and introducing the specifications and standards for Chinese speech and language research and development.
- Promoting the exchange of Chinese speech and linguistic corpus resources.

Headquartered in Beijing, China, the CCC is supported by the Chinese Language Resources branch of the High-tech Enterprises Association of the Beijing Experimental Zone for the Development of New Technology Industries (HTEA), and receives supervision, inspection and management from the Beijing Municipal Commission of Science and Technology and the Beijing Social Organization Managing Office. Under the guidance of the HTEA, the CCC works for the mutual promotion of the standardization and industrialization of Chinese language resources.

The Association for Computational Linguistics and Chinese Language Processing (ACLCLP), established in Taipei in 1988, is a non-profit organization. Its goals are to conduct research in computational linguistics, to promote the utilization and development of computational linguistics, to encourage research in the field of Chinese computational linguistics both domestically and internationally, and to maintain contact with international groups who have similar goals as well as to cultivate academic exchange. To promote resource sharing, the ACLCLP also releases a wide variety of Mandarin corpora including the Sinica Corpus, the CKIP lexicon, the Chinese News Corpus, the Sinica Treebank, the Chinese Information Retrieval Testing Corpus and the Mandarin Speech Databases.[29,30] After more than a decade of effort, the International Journal for Computational Linguistics and Chinese Language Processing

(IJCLCLP) published by the ACLCLP has become one of the most important journals specializing in Chinese computational linguistics.[31]

In Singapore, the Chinese and Oriental Languages Information Processing Society (COLIPS) is a non-profit professional organization formed to advance the science and technology of information processing in Chinese and other similar oriental languages. One of the objectives is to promote the free exchange of information relating to information processing of these languages in the best scientific and professional tradition. In the past, COLIPS has organized international conferences on Chinese and Oriental Languages, computer exhibitions and Chinese input competitions. It has also held short courses and talks for members and the public at large. Its society journal, the Journal of Chinese Language and Computing (JCLC), published four times a year, is circulated world-wide.[32]

The LDC, established in the University of Pennsylvania, USA, creates and distributes corpora of many languages. These do include Chinese speech and text corpora.[3] The typical ones are the CALLFRIEND and CALLHOME Mandarin Chinese corpora collected through telephone networks. There are also Mandarin Chinese (and multilingual) text, transcripts, lexicon, and broadcast news corpora.

Many universities have produced their own Chinese Language corpus for CSLP, such as the Cantonese spoken language corpus,[20,33] developed at Chinese University of Hong Kong, the Chinese Spontaneous Speech and Wu dialectal speech[20] developed at the Johns Hopkins University, and the multilingual speech corpus for Min-nan, Hakka, and Mandarin[34] developed at the Chang Gung University, Taiwan. CSLP corpora for various application domains have been produced in recent years. Typical applications include in-car conversations, mobile phone conversations, hotel reservations, spoken dialogues, and information retrieval.[20,23,26,35]

5. Available Language Resources for CSLP

Much CSLP corpora are distributed by the language resource associations, such as LDC, ChineseLDC, CCC, and ACLCLP. Some of them are categorized and listed as follows.

(1) *Telephone Speech*

- CALLFRIEND Mandarin Chinese-Mandarin Dialect (LDC)
- CALLFRIEND Mandarin Chinese-Taiwan Dialect (LDC)
- CALLHOME Mandarin Chinese Speech (LDC)
- Hub-5 Mandarin Telephone Speech (LDC)

- TSC973 – Telephone Speech Corpus (ChineseLDC)
- Telephone speech corpus for speech recognition (ChineseLDC)
- The identifiable speech database of telephone speech – the name of person, the name of place (265 people using mobile telephone) (ChineseLDC)
- The identifiable speech database of telephone speech – the name of person, the name of place (285 speakers using stable telephone) (ChineseLDC)
- The identifiable speech database of telephone speech – number strings (265 people using mobile telephone) (ChineseLDC)
- The identifiable speech database of telephone speech – number strings (285 speakers using stable telephone) (ChineseLDC)
- The identifiable speech database of telephone speech – stocks (265 people using mobile telephone) (ChineseLDC)
- The identifiable speech database of telephone speech – stocks (285 people using stable telephone) (ChineseLDC)
- The identifiable speech database of telephone speech – messages (64 people using mobile telephone) (ChineseLDC)
- The identifiable speech database of telephone speech – messages (86 people using mobile telephone) (ChineseLDC)
- CSTSC-Flight Corpus – Chinese Spontaneous Telephone Speech Corpus in the Flight Enquiry and Reservation Domain (CCC)
- TRSC – 500-people Telephone Read Speech Corpus (CCC)
- BIT-TeleSpeech – Telephone Read Speech Corpus (CCC)
- CHRD – Chinese Hotel Reservation Dialogue (CCC)
- MAT-160 – Mandarin spoken in Taiwan, 160 persons (ACLCLP)
- MAT-400 – Mandarin spoken in Taiwan, 400 persons (ACLCLP)
- MAT-2000 – Mandarin spoken in Taiwan, 2,000 persons (ACLCLP)
- MAT-2500Ext – Mandarin spoken in Taiwan, 2,500 persons (ACLCLP)

(2) *Broadcast Speech*

- 1997 Mandarin Broadcast News Speech (LDC)
- TDT2 Mandarin Audio (LDC)
- TDT3 Mandarin Audio (LDC)
- Natural Broadcasting Speech Corpus (ChineseLDC)
- CASIA – The Weather Forecast Broadcasts (ChineseLDC)

(3) *Mobile Phone Speech*

- BIT-MobileSpeech – Mobile Phone Speech Corpus for Traffic Information Query (CCC)

- BIT-MobileTalk – Mobile Phone Conversational Speech Corpus for Travel (CCC)
- BIT-TonalName – Tonally Confusing Name Speech Corpus (CCC)

(4) *Microphone Speech*

- Tsinghua- Corpus of Speech Synthesis (ChineseLDC)
- ASCCD – Annotated Speech Corpus of Chinese Discourse (ChineseLDC, CCC)
- CADCC – Chinese Annotated Dialogue and Conversation Corpus (ChineseLDC, CCC)
- SCSC – Syllable Corpus of Standard Chinese (ChineseLDC, CCC)
- WCSC – Word Corpus of Standard Chinese (ChineseLDC, CCC)
- CASIA – Chinese Question Structures Corpus (ChineseLDC)
- CASIA – Chinese Emotion Speech Corpus (ChineseLDC)
- Chinese Part-of-Speech Tagged Corpus (ChineseLDC)
- Chinese Geographic Name Corpus (ChineseLDC)
- CASIA – Single Syllable Isolated Word Speech Corpus (ChineseLDC)
- CASIA – Northern China Accent Speech Corpus (ChineseLDC)
- CASIA – Southern China Accent Speech Corpus (ChineseLDC)
- CASIA – Mandarin Continuous Digit Speech Corpus (ChineseLDC)
- CASIA – Chinese Speech Synthesis Corpus (ChineseLDC)
- RASC863-annotated 4 regional accent speech corpus (ChineseLDC)
- Chinese and English speech corpus (ChineseLDC)
- Special Scene and special domain dialogue corpus (ChineseLDC)
- The identifiable speech database of Chinese Mandarin – wide label (ChineseLDC)
- Identifiable speech database of Chinese Mandarin – extract database (ChineseLDC)
- Identifiable speech database of tabletop speech – messages (200 persons) (ChineseLDC)
- Identifiable speech database of tabletop speech – number strings (200 persons) (ChineseLDC)
- Identifiable speech database of tabletop speech – number strings (100 persons) (ChineseLDC)
- Identifiable speech database of tabletop speech – messages (120 persons) (ChineseLDC)
- Identifiable speech database of tabletop speech – number strings (120 persons) (ChineseLDC)

- Identifiable speech database of tabletop speech – people names, place names (120 persons) (ChineseLDC)
- Identifiable speech database of tabletop speech – stocks (70 persons) (ChineseLDC)
- Identifiable speech database of tabletop speech – topics (50 persons) (ChineseLDC)
- CACSC – Cantonese Accent Chinese Speech Corpus (CCC)
- CUCorpus – Cantonese Spoken Language Corpus (CCC)
- CASS – Chinese Annotated Spontaneous Speech (CCC)
- WDCS – Wu-dialectal Chinese Speech (CCC)
- BIT-MonoSyllable – Mandarin Mono-Syllable Corpus (CCC)
- CCC-VPR2C – 2-channel Corpus for Voiceprint Recognition (CCC)
- CCC-VPR3C – 3-channel Corpus for Voiceprint Recognition (CCC)
- CCC-VPR27C – 27-channel Corpus for Voiceprint Recognition (CCC)
- CCC-VPR36C – 36-channel Corpus for Voiceprint Recognition (CCC)
- TCC-300 – Mandarin Speech, 300 persons (ACLCLP)
- Sinica MCDC – Mandarin conversations (ACLCLP)

(5) *Multiple Language Speech*

- CSLU: 22 Languages Corpus (LDC)
- TDT4 Multilingual Broadcast News Speech (Arabic-Chinese-English) (LDC)
- Chinese-English Sentence aligned Bilingual Corpus (ChineseLDC)
- Parallel Language Corpus for the Olympics (Chinese-English-Japanese) (ChineseLDC)
- Parallel Language Corpora (Chinese-English, Chinese-Japanese) (ChineseLDC)

(6) *Chinese Text*

- HKUST Mandarin Telephone Transcript Data (LDC)
- TREC Mandarin (LDC)
- Mandarin Chinese News (LDC)
- Chinese Gigawords (LDC)
- Hub-5 Mandarin Transcripts (LDC)
- Chinese Treebank (LDC)
- Chinese Proposition Bank (LDC)
- Tsinghua Chinese Treebank (ChineseLDC)
- Academic Sinica Balanced Corpus (ACLCLP)
- Sinica Treebank (ACLCLP)

- Sinica BOW (ACLCLP)
- Word List with Accumulated Word Frequency in Sinica Corpus (ACLCLP)

(7) *Parallel Text*

- Chinese-English News Magazine (LDC)
- Hong Kong News Parallel Text (Chinese-English) (LDC)
- Hong Kong Laws Parallel Text (Chinese-English) (LDC)
- Hong Kong Parallel Text (LDC)
- Multiple Translation Chinese (Chinese-English) (LDC)
- TDT4 Multilingual Text and Annotations (Arabic-Chinese-English) (LDC)

(8) *Dictionary*

- Chinese-English Olympics Dictionary (ChineseLDC)
- Modern Chinese Semantic Dictionary (ChineseLDC)
- Modern Chinese Semantic Dictionary based on International Logical Model (ChineseLDC)
- Chinese Electronic Dictionary (ACLCLP)

(9) *Lexicon*

- Chinese Lexicon (ChineseLDC)
- Reference Lexicon for Segmentation Standard Dictionary (ACLCLP)
- Standard Segmentation Corpus (ACLCLP)
- CKIP Lexicon and Chinese Grammar (ACLCLP)
- The Grammatical Knowledge-base of Contemporary Chinese (High Frequency Words) (ChineseLDC)

(10) *Evaluation Data*

- 863 program in 2003 speech recognition evaluation data (ChineseLDC)
- 863 program in 2004 speech recognition evaluation data (ChineseLDC)
- 863 program in 2003 speech synthesis evaluation data (ChineseLDC)
- 863 program in 2004 speech synthesis evaluation data (ChineseLDC)
- 863 program in 2003 machine translation evaluation data (ChineseLDC)
- 863 program in 2004 machine translation evaluation data (ChineseLDC)
- 863 program in 2003 automatic index evaluation data 8 (ChineseLDC)
- 863 program in 2004 automatic index evaluation data (ChineseLDC)
- 863 program in 2003 Assessment and test data of text classification (ChineseLDC)

- 863 program in 2004 Assessment and test data of text classification (ChineseLDC)
- 863 program in 2003 Assessment and test data of chinese recognition (ChineseLDC)
- 863 program in 2004 information index evaluation data (ChineseLDC)
- 863 program in 2003 full text retrieval evaluation data (ChineseLDC)
- 863 program in 2003 name entry identification evaluation data (ChineseLDC)
- 863 program in 2003 part-of-speech evaluation data (ChineseLDC)
- 863 program in 2005 machine translation evaluation data (ChineseLDC)
- 863 program in 2005 information index evaluation data (ChineseLDC)
- 863 program in 2005 speech recognition evaluation data (ChineseLDC)
- CASIA98-99 speech testing library (ChineseLDC)

There are CSLP corpora currently being developed in various universities and research institutes. They should be available from these associations in the near future. It can be expected that more advanced technology will be applied to speed up corpus production. Language corpora will inevitably increase rapidly in size and number of types and categories due to the increasing diversity of speech processing applications.

6. Conclusion

The development of language corpora is a major part in the advancement of natural language and speech processing technologies. Building a re-usable, expandable, and consistent speech corpus for research and development purposes is a requirement for improving the research infrastructure. For CSLP, we need more good-quality language corpora to boost NLP and speech processing research and techniques. In other words, more effort should be channeled to promote the production of good language corpora in the future.

References

1. C. R. Huang, "Corpus-based studies of Chinese linguistics", *Computational Linguistics and Chinese language Processing*, vol.2, no.1. (1997)
2. M Liberman and C Cieri, "The Creation, Distribution and Use of Linguistic Data", *Proc. First International Conference on Language Resources and Evaluation*. (1998)
3. LDC – Lingustic Data Consortium. http://www.ldc.upenn.edu/
4. K. Choukri, "European language resources association: History and recent developments", *Proc. Oriental COCOSDA Workshop 1999*, (1999), pp. 15-23.
5. ELRA – European Language Resources Association. http://www.elra.info/

6. S. H. Chen, S. H. Hwang and Y. R. Wang, "An RNN-based prosodic information synthesizer for Mandarin text-to-speech", *IEEE Trans. on Speech & Audio Processing*, vol. 6, (1998), pp. 226-239.
7. K. W. Gan, K. T. Lua and M. Palmer, "A statistically emergent approach for language processing: application to modeling context effects in ambiguous Chinese word boundary perception", *Computational Linguistics,* (1996), vol.44, pp. 531-553.
8. L. S. Lee., C. Y. Tseng and M. Ouh-Young, "The synthesis rules in a Chinese text-to-speech system", *IEEE Trans. On Acoustics, Speech, & Signal Processing,* vol. 37, (1989), pp. 1309-1320.
9. L. S. Lee, "Voice dictation of Mandarin Chinese", *IEEE Signal Processing Magazine*, vol. 14, no. 4. (1997).
10. T. Lee and P. C. Ching, "Cantonese syllable recognition using neural networks", *IEEE Trans. On Speech & Audio Processing*, vol. 7, (1999), pp. 466-472.
11. T. Lee, P. C. Ching, L. W. Chan, Y. H. Cheng and B. Mak, "Tone recognition of isolated Cantonese syllables", *IEEE Trans. On Speech & Audio Processing*, vol. 3, (1995), pp. 204-209.
12. Y. R. Wang and S. H. Chen, "Tone recognition of continuous Mandarin speech assisted with prosodic information", *J. Acoustical Society of America*, vol. 96, (1994), pp. 2637-2645.
13. L. Du, "Recent activities in China: Speech corpora and assessment", *Proc. Oriental COCOSDA Workshop 2000*,. (2000)
14. A. Li, Y. Zu, Z. Li, "A national database design and prosodic labeling for speech synthesis", *Proc. Oriental COCOSDA Workshop,* (1999)
15. B. Xu, T. Y. Huang, X. Zhang and C. Huang, "A Chinese spoken dialogue database and its application for travel routine information", *Proc. Oriental COCOSDA Workshop 1999*. (1999)
16. C. Zheng, X. Liu and Z. Li, "A Chinese database for network service", *Proc. Oriental COCOSDA Workshop 1998*. (1998).
17. CKIP -- Chinese Knowledge and Information Processing Group, Academia Sinica. http://godel.iis.sinica.edu.tw/new/
18. H. C. Wang, "MAT—A project to collect Mandarin speech data through telephone networks in Taiwan", *Computational Linguistics and Chinese language Processing*, vol.2, (1997), pp. 73-90..
19. S. Li, F. Zheng, M. Xu, Z. Song and D. Fang, "A Cantonese accent Chinese speech corpus", *Proc. Oriental COCOSDA Workshop,* (1999).
20. CCC -- Chinese Corpus Consortium. http://www.CCCForum.org
21. Encyclopædia Britannica. 2006. "Chinese languages." http://www.britannica.com/eb/article?tocId=75050
22. C. N. Li and S. A. Thompson, Mandarin Chinese : A functional reference grammar, University of California Press. (1981)
23. Chinese LDC – Chinese Linguistic Data Consortium. http://www.chineseldc.org/
24. M. Wynne, Ed., *Developing Linguistic Corpora: a Guide to Good Practice*, AHDS: Arts and Humanities Data Service, (2006). http://www.ahds.ac.uk/.
25. F. Schiel and C. Draxler, The Production of Speech Corpora, Version 2.5 , *BAS- Bavarian Archive for Speech Signals*, (2004). http://www.phonetik.uni-muenchen.de/Forschung/BITS/TP1/Cookbook/node1.html
26. H. M. Wang, B. Chen, J. W. Kuo and S. S. Cheng, "MATBN – A Mandarin Chinese broadcast news corpus", *Computational Linguistics and Chinese language Processing*, vol.10, (2005), pp. 219-236.
27. C. Y. Tseng, "Machine readable phonetic transcription system for Chinese dialects spoken in Taiwan", *Proc. Oriental COCOSDA Workshop 1998*. (1998).

28. J. Zhang, "A SAMPA system for putonghua (Standard Chinese)", *Proc. Oriental COCOSDA Workshop 1999* (1999)..
29. H. C. Wang, "Speech research infra-structure in Taiwan – From database design to performance assessment", *Proc. Oriental COCOSDA Workshop 1999.* (1999)
30. H. C. Wang, F. Seide, C. Y. Tseng, and L. S. Lee, "MAT-2000 — Design, collection, and validation of a Mandarin 2000-speaker telephone speech database," *Proc. ICSLP 2000* (2000).
31. ACLCLP – The Association for Computational Linguistics and Chinese Language Processing
32. COLIPS – Chinese and Oriental Language Information Processing Society. http://www.colips.org/
33. T Lee, W. K. Lo, P. C. Ching, H. Meng, "Spoken language resources for Cantonese speech processing", *Speech Communication*, vol. 36, (2002), pp. 327-342.
34. R. Y. Lyu, M. S. Liang and Y. C. Chiang, "Toward constructing a multilingual speech corpus for Taiwanese (Min-nan), Hakka, and Mandarin Chinese", *Computational Linguistics and Chinese language Processing*, vol. 9, (2004) , pp. 1-12.
35. H. C. Wang, C. H. Yang, J. F. Wang, C. H. Wu, and J. T. Chien, "TAICAR – The collection and annotation of an in-car speech database created in Taiwan", *Computational Linguistics and Chinese language Processing*, vol.10, (2005), pp. 237-250.
36. R. H. Wang, "National performance assessment of speech recognition system for Chinese", *Proc. Oriental COCOSDA Workshop 1999.* (1999)
37. AHDS -- Arts and Humanities Data Service. http://www.ahds.ac.uk/.
38. BAS- Bavarian Archive for Speech Signals. http://www.phonetik.uni-muenchen.de/Forschung/BITS/TP1/Cookbook/node1.html
39. COCOSDA – The International Committee for the Co-ordination and Standardisation of Speech Databases and Assessment Techniques. http://www.slt.atr.co.jp/cocosda/
40. IPA – The International Phonetic Association. http://www.arts.gla.ac.uk/IPA/ipa.html
41. NIST Speech Group. http://www.nist.gov/speech/index.htm
42. O-COCOSDA – Oriental COCOSDA. http://www.slt.atr.jp/o-cocosda/org.html
43. Wikipedia, "Mandarin," http://en.wikipedia.org/wiki/MandarinChinese

INDEX